THE OXFORD HANDBOOK OF
CRIME PREVENTION

THE OXFORD HANDBOOKS IN CRIMINOLOGY AND CRIMINAL JUSTICE

General Editor: Michael Tonry, University of Minnesota

. . . .

THE OXFORD HANDBOOKS IN CRIMINOLOGY AND CRIMINAL JUSTICE offer authoritative, comprehensive, and critical overviews of the state of the art of criminology and criminal justice. Each volume focuses on a major area of each discipline, is edited by a distinguished group of specialists, and contains specially commissioned, original essays from leading international scholars in their respective fields. Guided by the general editorship of Michael Tonry, the series will provide an invaluable reference for scholars, students, and policy makers seeking to understand a wide range of research and policies in criminology and criminal justice.

OTHER TITLES IN THIS SERIES:

Criminological Theory
Francis T. Cullen and Pamela Wilcox

Sentencing and Corrections
Joan Petersilia and Kevin R. Reitz

Juvenile Crime and Juvenile Justice
Barry C. Feld and Donna M. Bishop

Crime and Criminal Justice
Michael Tonry

Crime and Public Policy
Michael Tonry

THE OXFORD HANDBOOK OF

CRIME PREVENTION

Edited by

BRANDON C. WELSH
DAVID P. FARRINGTON

OXFORD
UNIVERSITY PRESS

OXFORD
UNIVERSITY PRESS

Oxford University Press, Inc., publishes works that further
Oxford University's objective of excellence
in research, scholarship, and education.

Oxford   New York
Auckland   Cape Town   Dar es Salaam   Hong Kong   Karachi
Kuala Lumpur   Madrid   Melbourne   Mexico City   Nairobi
New Delhi   Shanghai   Taipei   Toronto

With offices in
Argentina   Austria   Brazil   Chile   Czech Republic   France   Greece
Guatemala   Hungary   Italy   Japan   Poland   Portugal   Singapore
South Korea   Switzerland   Thailand   Turkey   Ukraine   Vietnam

Published by Oxford University Press, Inc.
198 Madison Avenue, New York, New York 10016

www.oup.com

Oxford is a registered trademark of Oxford University Press

Library of Congress Cataloging-in-Publication Data
The Oxford handbook of crime prevention / edited by Brandon C. Welsh, David P. Farrington.
  p.   cm.
Includes bibliographical references and index.
ISBN 978-0-19-539882-3 (cloth : alk. paper) 1. Crime prevention—Handbooks, manuals, etc.
I. Welsh, Brandon, 1969– II. Farrington, David P. III. Title: Handbook of crime prevention.
HV7431.O94   2011
364.4—dc23   2011019884

1 3 5 7 9 8 6 4 2
Printed in the United States of America
on acid-free paper

Contents

························

PART III: SITUATIONAL CRIME PREVENTION

PART IV: ADVANCING KNOWLEDGE AND BUILDING A SAFER SOCIETY

PREFACE

....

Crime prevention, the subject of this volume, is an important component of an overall strategy to reduce crime. It can involve early interventions to improve the life chances of children and prevent them from embarking on a life of crime (developmental prevention); programs and policies designed to ameliorate the social conditions and institutions that influence offending (community prevention); or the modification or manipulation of the physical environment, products, or systems to reduce everyday opportunities for crime (situational prevention). Here, the focus is on preventing crime or criminal offending in the first instance—before the act has been committed. Also important is that each of these strategies takes place outside of the formal criminal justice system, representing an alternative, perhaps even a socially progressive, way to reduce crime.

The main goal of the volume is to provide a comprehensive, up-to-date, and authoritative review of research on crime prevention. Specifically, it includes critical reviews of the main theories that form the basis of crime prevention and key issues that confront the prevention of crime, evidence-based reviews on the effectiveness of the most important interventions to prevent crime and criminal offending, and cross-cutting essays that examine implementation, evaluation methodology, and public policy.

For all of this volume's uniqueness and contemporary nature, it has some history. In 1995, the University of Chicago Press, as part of its *Crime and Justice* series, published *Building a Safer Society: Strategic Approaches to Crime Prevention*. Michael Tonry and David Farrington were the volume's editors. It was advertised as the "most comprehensive exposition of research and experience concerning crime prevention ever published." It more than lived up to this claim. Its only drawback is that it was never updated or duplicated by any other publishing house. *The Oxford Handbook of Crime Prevention* is to some extent the sequel to this highly successful volume. The present volume builds on the earlier one's conceptual advances in the study of crime prevention, its comprehensive coverage of different types of crime-prevention research, and its rigorous scholarship and policy analysis. With our great cast of contributors, we set out to make this Handbook the most authoritative and scholarly resource on crime prevention in the United States and across the Western world.

The volume is divided into four parts. Parts I, II, and III are organized around the three major crime-prevention strategies: developmental, community, and situational. Each of these parts includes chapters on the prevention strategy's theoretical foundations, core issues, and evidence-based reviews on the effectiveness of the most important interventions. Part IV is focused on advancing knowledge and on the role of crime prevention in contributing to a safer, more sustainable society.

Many people made this book possible. First and foremost, we are grateful to the 44 contributors. We made them work—with tight deadlines, multiple drafts, and no doubt a great deal of nitpicking—and they delivered in brilliant fashion. It was an absolute pleasure to work with every one. While we are mindful that our acknowledgment of the next two people is verging on chronic flattery, they proved (once again) to be nothing short of indispensible on this project. Michael Tonry, the Oxford Handbooks series editor, and James Cook, editor at Oxford University Press, are simply topnotch and we are truly honored to work with them.

Brandon C. Welsh
David P. Farrington

CONTRIBUTORS

DORIS BENDER is a Senior Lecturer in the Institute of Psychology at the University of Erlangen-Nuremberg.

MICHAEL L. BENSON is a Professor in the School of Criminal Justice at the University of Cincinnati.

KATE J. BOWERS is a Reader in the Department of Security and Crime Science at University College London.

ANTHONY A. BRAGA is a Professor in the School of Criminal Justice at Rutgers University and a Senior Research Fellow in the Program in Criminal Justice Policy and Management at Harvard University.

JULIA BURDICK-WILL is a doctoral candidate in the Department of Sociology at the University of Chicago.

RONALD V. CLARKE is University Professor in the School of Criminal Justice at Rutgers, the State University of New Jersey.

PHILIP J. COOK is ITT/Sanford Professor of Public Policy in the Sanford School of Public Policy at Duke University.

FRANCIS T. CULLEN is Distinguished Research Professor of Criminal Justice and Sociology at the University of Cincinnati.

JOHN E. ECK is a Professor in the School of Criminal Justice at the University of Cincinnati.

PAUL EKBLOM is Professor of Design Against Crime at Central Saint Martins College of Art and Design at University of the Arts London.

ABIGAIL A. FAGAN is an Assistant Professor in the Department of Criminology and Criminal Justice at the University of South Carolina.

GRAHAM FARRELL is a Professor of Criminology at Loughborough University and a Visiting Professor in the School of Criminology at Simon Fraser University.

DAVID P. FARRINGTON is Professor of Psychological Criminology in the Institute of Criminology at Cambridge University.

DEBORAH GORMAN-SMITH is a Research Fellow at Chapin Hall at the University of Chicago.

DENISE C. GOTTFREDSON is a Professor in the Department of Criminology and Criminal Justice at the University of Maryland at College Park.

LOUISE GROVE is a Lecturer in Criminology at Loughborough University.

ROB T. GUERETTE is an Associate Professor of Criminal Justice in the School of International and Public Affairs at Florida International University.

ROSS HASTINGS is a Professor of Criminology and Director of the Institute for the Prevention of Crime at the University of Ottawa.

J. DAVID HAWKINS is an Endowed Professor of Prevention in the Social Development Research Group, School of Social Work, at the University of Washington.

JOSHUA C. HINKLE is an Assistant Professor in the Department of Criminal Justice at Georgia State University.

ROSS HOMEL is Foundation Professor of Criminology and Criminal Justice at Griffith University.

PETER HOMEL is Research Manager for Crime Reduction and Analysis for the Australian Institute of Criminology and Adjunct Professor at Griffith University.

WESLEY G. JENNINGS is an Assistant Professor in the Department of Criminology at the University of South Florida.

DARRICK JOLLIFFE is a Senior Lecturer in the Department of Criminology at the University of Leicester.

SHANE D. JOHNSON is a Reader in the Department of Security and Crime Science at University College London.

ROLF LOEBER is Distinguished Professor of Psychiatry and Professor of Psychology and Epidemiology at the University of Pittsburgh, and Professor of Juvenile Delinquency and Social Development at Free University of Amsterdam.

FRIEDRICH LÖSEL is Director of and a Professor in the Institute of Criminology at Cambridge University.

JENS LUDWIG is McCormick Foundation Professor of Social Service Administration, Law, and Public Policy at the University of Chicago.

DORIS LAYTON MACKENZIE is a Professor in the Crime, Law, and Justice Program and Director of the Justice Center for Research at Pennsylvania State University.

MATTHEW D. MAKARIOS is an Assistant Professor of Criminal Justice at the University of Wisconsin-Parkside.

STEVEN F. MESSNER is Distinguished Teaching Professor of Sociology at the University at Albany, State University of New York.

CHONGMIN NA is a doctoral candidate in the Department of Criminology and Criminal Justice at the University of Maryland at College Park.

ALEX R. PIQUERO is Ashbel Smith Professor of Criminology at the University of Texas at Dallas.

JULIAN V. ROBERTS is a Professor in the Centre for Criminology at Oxford University.

DENNIS P. ROSENBAUM is a Professor of Criminology and Psychology and Director of the Center for Research in Law and Justice at the University of Illinois at Chicago.

HOLLY S. SCHINDLER is a Project Director at Harvard University's Center on the Developing Child and a Lecturer at the Harvard Graduate School of Education.

AMIE M. SCHUCK is an Associate Professor and Head of the Department of Criminology, Law, and Justice at the University of Illinois at Chicago.

WESLEY G. SKOGAN is a Professor of Political Science and a member of the research faculty of the Institute for Policy Research at Northwestern University.

MARTHA J. SMITH is an Associate Professor in the School of Community Affairs at Wichita State University.

CHRISTOPHER J. SULLIVAN is an Assistant Professor in the School of Criminal Justice at the University of Cincinnati.

MARIA M. TTOFI is Leverhulme and Newton Trust Postdoctoral Fellow in the Institute of Criminology at Cambridge University.

ALANA M. VIVOLO is a Public Health Advisor and Project Officer in the Division of Violence Prevention at the Centers for Disease Control and Prevention.

DAVID WEISBURD is Walter E. Meyer Professor of Law and Criminal Justice at the Institute of Criminology, Faculty of Law at The Hebrew University, and a Distinguished Professor in the Department of Criminology, Law, and Society at George Mason University.

BRANDON C. WELSH is an Associate Professor in the School of Criminology and Criminal Justice at Northeastern University and Senior Research Fellow at the Netherlands Institute for the Study of Crime and Law Enforcement.

HIROKAZU YOSHIKAWA is a Professor of Education at the Harvard Graduate School of Education.

GREGORY M. ZIMMERMAN is an Assistant Professor in the School of Criminology and Criminal Justice at Northeastern University.

THE OXFORD HANDBOOK OF

CRIME PREVENTION

CHAPTER 1

....

CRIME PREVENTION AND PUBLIC POLICY

....

BRANDON C. WELSH AND DAVID P. FARRINGTON

CRIME prevention has come to mean many different things to many different people. Programs and policies designed to prevent crime can include the police making an arrest as part of an operation to deal with gang problems, a court sanction to a secure correctional facility, or, in the extreme, a death penalty sentence. These measures are more correctly referred to as crime control or repression. More often, though, crime prevention refers to efforts to prevent crime or criminal offending in the first instance—before the act has been committed. Both forms of crime prevention share a common goal of trying to prevent the occurrence of a future criminal act, but what further distinguishes crime prevention from crime control is that prevention takes place outside of the confines of the formal justice system.[1] In this respect, prevention is considered the fourth pillar of crime reduction, alongside the institutions of police, courts, and corrections (Waller 2006). This distinction draws attention to crime prevention as an alternative approach to these more traditional responses to crime.

In one of the first scholarly attempts to differentiate crime prevention from crime control, Peter Lejins (1967, p. 2) espoused the following: "If societal action is motivated by an offense that has already taken place, we are dealing with control; if the offense is only anticipated, we are dealing with prevention." What Lejins was trying to indicate was the notion of "pure" prevention, a view that had long existed in the scholarship and practice of American criminology (Welsh and Pfeffer 2011). It is this notion of crime prevention that is the chief concern of this volume.

There are many possible ways of classifying crime prevention programs.[2] An influential scheme distinguishes four major strategies (Tonry and Farrington 1995*b*). *Developmental prevention* refers to interventions designed to prevent the development of criminal potential in individuals, especially those targeting risk and protective factors discovered in studies of human development (Tremblay and Craig 1995; Farrington and Welsh 2007). *Community prevention* refers to interventions designed to change the social conditions and institutions (e.g., families, peers, social norms, clubs, organizations) that influence offending in residential communities (Hope 1995). *Situational prevention* refers to interventions designed to prevent the occurrence of crimes by reducing opportunities and increasing the risk and difficulty of offending (Clarke 1995*b*; Cornish and Clarke 2003). *Criminal justice prevention* refers to traditional deterrent, incapacitative, and rehabilitative strategies operated by law enforcement and agencies of the criminal justice system (Blumstein, Cohen, and Nagin 1978; MacKenzie 2006).

In *Building a Safer Society: Strategic Approaches to Crime Prevention*, Michael Tonry and David Farrington (1995*a*) purposely did not address criminal justice prevention in any substantial fashion. This was because this strategy had been adequately addressed in many other scholarly books and, more importantly, there was a growing consensus for the need for governments to strike a greater balance between these emerging and promising alternative forms of crime prevention and some of the more traditional responses to crime. Also important in their decision to focus exclusively on developmental, community, and situational prevention is the shared focus of the three strategies on addressing the underlying causes or motivations that lead to a criminal event or a life of crime. Crucially, each strategy operates outside of the criminal justice system, representing an alternative, perhaps even a socially progressive, way to reduce crime. For these same reasons, we have adopted a similar approach in this volume.

A chief aim of this essay is to provide some background on this view of crime prevention. It also serves as an overview of the key theories that support these three main crime-prevention strategies, important research on effectiveness, and key issues that challenge the prevention of crime. Several observations and conclusions emerge:

- Crime prevention is best viewed as an alternative approach to reducing crime, operating outside of the formal justice system. Developmental, community, and situational strategies define its scope.
- Developmental prevention has emerged as an important strategy to improve children's life chances and prevent them from embarking on a life of crime. The theoretical support for this approach is considerable and there is growing evidence based on the effectiveness of a range of intervention modalities.
- Community crime prevention benefits from a sound theoretical base. It seemingly holds much promise for preventing crime, but less is known about its effectiveness. Advancing knowledge on this front is a top priority. Nevertheless, there are a wide range of effective models in community-based substance-use prevention and school-based crime prevention.

- The theoretical origins of situational crime prevention are wide ranging and robust. The strategy boasts a growing evidence base of effective programs and many more that are promising. There is also evidence that crime displacement is a rare occurrence.
- Crime prevention is an important component of an overall strategy to reduce crime and is widely supported by the public over place and time. A special focus on implementation science and higher quality evaluation designs will further advance crime-prevention knowledge and practice. Striking a greater balance between crime prevention and crime control will go a long way toward building a safer, more sustainable society.

The organization of this essay is as follows. Section I looks at key historical events that have influenced the development of crime prevention in America. Sections II, III, and IV introduce, respectively, the major crime-prevention strategies of developmental, community, and situational prevention. Section V discusses a number of important cross-cutting issues.

I. A SHORT HISTORY OF CRIME PREVENTION IN AMERICA

The modern-day history of crime prevention in America is closely linked with a loss of faith in the criminal justice system that occurred in the wake of the dramatic increase in crime rates in the 1960s. This loss of faith was caused by a confluence of factors, including declining public support for the criminal justice system, increasing levels of fear of crime, and criminological research that demonstrated that many of the traditional modes of crime control were ineffective and inefficient in reducing crime and improving the safety of communities (Curtis 1987). For example, research studies on motorized preventive patrol, rapid response, and criminal investigations—the staples of law enforcement—showed that they had little or no effect on crime (Visher and Weisburd 1998). It was becoming readily apparent among researchers and public officials alike that a criminal justice response on its own was insufficient for the task of reducing crime. This observation applied not only to law enforcement but also to the courts and prisons (Tonry and Farrington 1995b). Interestingly, this loss of faith in the justice system was not unique to the United States. Similar developments were taking place in Canada, the United Kingdom, and other Western European countries, and for some of the same reasons (Waller 1990; Bennett 1998).

Writing in the mid-1980s, the observations of American urban affairs scholar Paul Lavrakas perhaps best captures this need to move beyond the sole reliance on the criminal justice system:

> Until we change the emphasis of our public policies away from considering the
> police, courts, and prisons to be the primary mechanisms for reducing crime, I
> believe that we will continue to experience the tragic levels of victimization with
> which our citizens now live. These criminal justice agencies are our means of
> *reacting* to crime—they should not be expected to *prevent* it by themselves. (1985,
> p. 110, emphasis in original)

These events, coupled with recommendations of presidential crime commissions
of the day—the President's Commission on Law Enforcement and Administration of Justice (1967), chaired by Nicholas Katzenbach, and the National Commission on the Causes and Prevention of Violence (1969), chaired by Milton S.
Eisenhower—ushered in an era of innovation of alternative approaches to
addressing crime. A few years later, the National Advisory Commission on Criminal Justice Standards and Goals (1973) sought to reaffirm the role of the community in preventing crime. Operating outside of the purview of the justice system,
crime prevention came to be defined as an alternative, non–criminal justice
means of reducing crime.

A focus on neighborhood, family, and employment was at the heart of this new
approach to addressing crime, with a special emphasis on the most impoverished
inner-city communities. Nonprofit organizations were the main vehicle used to deliver programs in these substantive areas. A number of situational or opportunity-
reducing measures were also implemented to ensure the immediate safety of
residents. Some of these programs included neighborhood patrols and block
watches (Curtis 1987, p. 11). By some accounts, this urban crime-prevention and
reconstruction movement produced a number of models of success and many more
promising programs (see Curtis 1985, 1987).

This mode of crime prevention also came to be known as *community-based
crime prevention*, an amalgam of social and situational measures (see Rosenbaum
1986, 1988). The approach was popularized with a number of large-scale, multisite programs referred to as *comprehensive community initiatives* (Hope 1995;
Rosenbaum, Lurigio, and Davis 1998). Examples included T-CAP (Texas City
Action Plan to Prevent Crime) and PACT (Pulling America's Communities
Together).

The roots of this comprehensive approach—on the social side, at least—go as far
back as the early 1930s, with Clifford Shaw and Henry McKay's Chicago Area Project
(CAP; Shaw and McKay 1942). The CAP was designed to produce social change in
communities that suffered from high delinquency rates and gang activity. Local civic
leaders coordinated social service centers that promoted community solidarity and
counteracted social disorganization, and they developed other programs for youths,
including school-related activities and recreation. Some evaluations indicated desirable results, but others showed that CAP efforts did little to reduce delinquency (see
Schlossman and Sedlak 1983).

The New York City–based Mobilization for Youth (MOBY) program of the
1960s is another example of this type of crime-prevention initiative. Funded by
more than $50 million, MOBY attempted an integrated approach to community

development (Short 1974). Based on Richard Cloward and Lloyd Ohlin's (1960) concept of providing opportunities for legitimate success, MOBY created employment opportunities in the community, coordinated social services, and sponsored social-action groups such as tenants' committees, legal-action services, and voter registration. But the program ended for lack of funding amid questions about its utility and use of funds.

A newer generation of these programs, which includes the well-established Communities That Care (CTC) strategy developed by David Hawkins and Richard Catalano (1992), incorporates principles of public health and prevention science— identifying key risk factors for offending and implementing evidence-based prevention methods designed to counteract them. The CTC has become the best developed and tested of these prevention systems.

By the early 1990s, crime prevention found itself in the national spotlight, although not always to the liking of its supporters. This came about during the lead up to and subsequent passage of the federal crime bill of 1994—the most expensive initiative in history (Donziger 1996). Known officially as the Violent Crime Control and Law Enforcement Act, it ultimately became famous for its authorization of funding to put 100,000 new police officers on the streets, as well as infamous for making 60 more federal crimes eligible for the death penalty and authorizing $10 billion for new prison construction. Crime-prevention programs (in the broadest sense) were allocated a sizable $7 billion, but most of this was used on existing federal programs like Head Start in order to keep them afloat (Gest 2001).

From the beginning of the bill's debate on Capitol Hill and across the country, crime prevention—especially programs for at-risk youth—was heavily criticized. The growing political thirst to get tough on juvenile and adult criminals alike, with an array of punitive measures, sought to paint prevention and its supporters as soft on crime. Midnight basketball became their scapegoat. Prevention was characterized as nothing more than pork-barreling—wasteful spending of taxpayer dollars. The end result of all of this was mixed: crime prevention had received substantial funding, but it had been relegated to the margins in the public discourse on crime (Mendel 1995).

In more recent years, crime prevention has emerged as an important component of an overall strategy to reduce crime. One reason for this is the widely held view of the need to strike a greater balance between prevention and punishment (Waller 2006). Another key reason has to do with a growing body of scientific evidence showing that many different types of crime-prevention programs are effective (Sherman et al. 1997, 2006; Welsh and Farrington 2006) and many of these programs save money (Drake, Aos, and Miller 2009). Not surprisingly, the economic argument for prevention has attracted a great deal of interest from policymakers and political leaders (Greenwood 2006; Mears 2010). The recent evidence-based movement (see Welsh and Farrington 2011) has figured prominently in these developments in raising the profile of crime prevention.

II. Developmental Crime Prevention

The developmental perspective postulates that criminal offending in adolescence and adulthood is influenced by "behavioral and attitudinal patterns that have been learned during an individual's development" (Tremblay and Craig 1995, p. 151). The early years of the life course are most influential in shaping later experiences. As Greg Duncan and Katherine Magnuson (2004, p. 101) note: "Principles of developmental science suggest that although beneficial changes are possible at any point in life, interventions early on may be more effective at promoting well-being and competencies compared with interventions undertaken later in life." They further state that: "early childhood may provide an unusual window of opportunity for interventions because young children are uniquely receptive to enriching and supportive environments. . . . As individuals age, they gain the independence and ability to shape their environments, rendering intervention efforts more complicated and costly" (pp. 102–103).

Developmental prevention is informed generally by motivational or human development and life-course theories on criminal behavior, as well as by longitudinal studies that follow samples of young persons from their early childhood experiences to the peak of their involvement with crime in their teens and twenties. Developmental prevention aims to influence the scientifically identified risk factors or "root causes" of delinquency and later criminal offending.

The theoretical foundation of developmental prevention is robust, and is the subject of the two opening essays of this volume. Frank Cullen, Michael Benson, and Matthew Makarios overview the major developmental and life-course theories of offending, with a special interest in how the theories explain why some individuals "are placed on a pathway, or trajectory, toward a life in antisocial conduct and crime." David Farrington, Rolf Loeber, and Maria Ttofi summarize the most important risk and protective factors for offending. They conclude that impulsiveness, school achievement, child-rearing methods, young mothers, child abuse, parental conflict, disrupted families, poverty, delinquent peers, and deprived neighborhoods are the most important factors that should be targeted in intervention research.

Richard Tremblay and Wendy Craig's (1995) classic, sweeping review of developmental crime prevention documented its importance as a major strategy in preventing delinquency and later offending. It also identified three key characteristics of effective developmental prevention programs: (1) they lasted for a sufficient duration—at least one year; (2) they were multimodal, meaning that multiple risk factors were targeted with different interventions; and (3) they were implemented before adolescence. Since then, many other reviews have been carried out to assess the effectiveness of developmental prevention, often focusing on a specific intervention modality. This is the approach taken in the next three essays.

Holly Schindler and Hirokazu Yoshikawa review the evidence on preschool intellectual enrichment programs. They find that preschool interventions focused specifically on child-relevant processes (i.e., cognitive skills, behavior problems, or executive functioning) have shown impressive results. Equally desirable effects on long-term behavioral outcomes, including crime, have been demonstrated by what they call "two-generation" preschool programs, which also include a focus on parenting skills or offer comprehensive family services.

A systematic review and meta-analysis of the effects of parent training for children up to age five years, by Alex Piquero and Wesley Jennings, shows that this intervention is effective in reducing antisocial behavior and delinquency. The authors also find that parent-training programs produce a wide range of other important benefits for families, including improved school readiness and school performance on the part of children and greater employment and educational opportunities for parents. Training in child social skills, also known as social competence, is the subject of another systematic review and meta-analysis by Friedrich Lösel and Doris Bender. This type of intervention generally targets the risk factors of impulsivity, low empathy, and egocentrism. The authors find that the overall effect of skills training is desirable and that the most effective programs used a cognitive-behavioral approach and were implemented with older children and higher risk groups who were already exhibiting some behavioral problems.

In the final essay in this section, Deborah Gorman-Smith and Alana Vivolo take on the much broader subject of the prevention of female offending through a developmental approach. This is important because little is known about what may work for this population. Their review of prevention programs confirms that most studies continue to focus on male offending; the mostly poor evaluation designs of existing programs for girls and adolescent females prohibit a valid assessment of effectiveness, and a gendered analysis of mixed programs is often lacking.

III. COMMUNITY CRIME PREVENTION

More often than not, community-based efforts to prevent crime are thought to be some combination of developmental and situational prevention. Unlike these two crime-prevention strategies, there is little agreement in the academic literature on the definition of community prevention and the types of programs that fall within it. This stems from its early conceptions, with one view focused on the social conditions of crime and the ability of the community to regulate them, and another that "it operates at the level of whole communities regardless of the types of mechanisms involved" (Bennett 1996, p. 169).

Tim Hope's (1995) definition that community crime prevention involves actions designed to change the social conditions and institutions that influence offending in residential communities is by far the most informative. This is not just because it distinguishes community prevention from developmental and situational prevention, but also because it highlights the strength of the community to address the sometimes intractable social problems that lead to crime and violence. This focus on the social factors leaves aside physical redesign concepts, including Oscar Newman's (1972) defensible space and C. Ray Jeffery's (1971) crime prevention through environmental design. Ron Clarke (1992, 1995b) describes how these important concepts are more correctly viewed as contributing to the early development of situational crime prevention.

Numerous theories have been advanced over the years to explain community-level influences on crime and offending and that serve as the basis of community crime-prevention programs (for excellent reviews, see Reiss and Tonry 1986; Farrington 1993; Sampson and Lauritsen 1994; Wikström 1998). Steven Messner and Gregory Zimmerman's essay makes a unique contribution to this body of knowledge. Through a macro-sociological lens, the authors elucidate the distinguishing features and evolution of the community–crime link. In a separate essay, Wesley Skogan expounds on the nature of disorderly behavior and its relevance to crime, communities, and prevention. Of particular importance is the role that disorder may play in the destabilization and decline of neighborhoods.

While there is a rich theoretical and empirical literature on communities and crime, up until recently less was known about the effectiveness of community crime-prevention programs. Review after review on this subject—going back to Rosenbaum's (1988) and Hope's (1995) classics—have consistently reported that there are no program types with proven effectiveness in preventing crime. Importantly, this was not a claim that nothing works and that community crime prevention should be abandoned (Sherman 1997; Welsh and Hoshi 2006). Some program types were judged to be promising.[3]

More recent research finds that some community-based programs can make a difference in preventing crime. Jens Ludwig and Julia Burdick-Will report on the effects of the Moving to Opportunity (MTO) program, which gave vouchers to low-socioeconomic status (often, minority) families to enable them to move to better areas. The large-scale experimental test of the program, which involved 4,600 families in five cities across the country, showed that it was particularly effective in reducing violent crime by youths. The authors also discuss another similar poverty-deconcentration experiment in Chicago that was equally effective.

Christopher Sullivan and Darrick Jolliffe review the effectiveness of two well-known community-based crime-prevention modalities: peer influence and mentoring. They find that programs designed to influence peer risk factors for delinquency are somewhat promising, while mentoring, where the evaluation research is more extensive and robust, can be effective in preventing delinquency. In one systematic review and meta-analysis it was found that mentoring was more effective in reducing offending when the average duration of each contact between mentor and mentee was greater, in smaller scale studies, and when mentoring was combined with other interventions.

Important to all forms of crime prevention, but implicit in community prevention, is the element of partnerships among stakeholder agencies and individuals. Dennis Rosenbaum and Amie Schuck review and assess the literature on comprehensive community partnerships in the context of community crime prevention. They offer several key conclusions, including that these partnerships have wide public appeal, can be difficult to implement because of their complexity, and are most effective when there is a commitment to prevention science and evidence-based practice.

The next two essays diverge slightly from our focus on communities and the prevention of crime, but their importance to the field and this volume cannot be overstated. Abigail Fagan and David Hawkins review the evidence of the effectiveness of community-based substance-use prevention initiatives, while Denise Gottfredson, Philip Cook, and Chongmin Na summarize the evidence of the effectiveness of school-based crime-prevention programs. In both cases, the authors report on a number of successful preventive interventions for youths.

IV. SITUATIONAL CRIME PREVENTION

Situational prevention stands apart from the other crime-prevention strategies by its special focus on the setting or place in which criminal acts take place, as well as its crime-specific focus. No less important is situational prevention's concern with products (e.g., installation of immobilizers on new cars in some parts of Europe, action taken to eliminate cellphone cloning in the United States) and on large-scale systems such as improvements in the banking system to reduce money laundering (Clarke 2009).

Situational crime prevention has been defined as "a preventive approach that relies, not upon improving society or its institutions, but simply upon reducing opportunities for crime" (Clarke 1992, p. 3). Reducing opportunities for crime is achieved essentially through some modification or manipulation of the physical environment, products, or systems in order to directly affect offenders' perceptions of increased risks and effort and decreased rewards, provocations, and excuses (Cornish and Clarke 2003). These different approaches serve as the basis of a highly detailed classification system of situational crime prevention, which can further be divided into 25 separate techniques, each with any number of examples of programs (Cornish and Clarke 2003). Part of Martha Smith and Ron Clarke's essay is devoted to an overview of the current classification scheme, as well as the theoretical and practical developments that led to its present form.

The theoretical origins of situational crime prevention are wide-ranging (see Newman, Clarke, and Shoham 1997; Garland 2000), but it is largely informed by opportunity theory. This theory holds that the offender is "heavily influenced by environmental inducements and opportunities and as being highly adaptable to changes in the situation" (Clarke 1995a, p. 57). Opportunity theory is made up of several more specific theories, including the rational-choice perspective, the routine-activity approach, and crime-pattern theory. According to Smith and Clarke, these three theories have had the greatest influence on the research and practice of situational crime prevention, and they are described in detail in their essay.

Also important to the theoretical basis and the practical utility of situational prevention is the widely held finding that crime is not randomly distributed across a city or community but is, instead, highly concentrated at certain places known as crime "hot spots" (Sherman, Gartin, and Buerger 1989). For example, it is estimated that across the United States, 10 percent of the places are sites for around 60 percent of the crimes (Eck 2006, p. 242). In the same way that individuals can have criminal careers, there are criminal careers for places (Sherman 1995). The essay by Anthony Braga reviews the empirical and theoretical evidence on the concentration of crime at places, times, and among offenders.

Fairly or unfairly, situational crime prevention often raises concerns over the displacement of crime. This is the notion that offenders simply move around the corner or resort to different methods to commit crimes once a crime-prevention project has been introduced.[4] Thirty years ago, Thomas Reppetto (1976) identified five different forms of displacement: temporal (change in time), tactical (change in method), target (change in victim), territorial (change in place), and functional (change in type of crime).

What Clarke (1995b) and many others (e.g., Gabor 1990; Hesseling 1995) have found and rightly note is that displacement is never 100 percent. Furthermore, a growing body of research has shown that situational measures may instead result in a diffusion of crime-prevention benefits or the "complete reverse" of displacement (Clarke and Weisburd 1994). Instead of a crime-prevention project displacing crime, the project's crime-prevention benefits are diffused to the surrounding area, for example. The essay by Shane Johnson, Rob Guerette, and Kate Bowers, which reports on a meta-analysis of displacement and diffusion, provides confirmatory evidence for these general points. They also find that a "diffusion of benefit is at least as likely as crime displacement."

Like the other crime-prevention strategies, numerous reviews have been carried out over the years to assess the effectiveness of situational crime-prevention programs. By far the most comprehensive reviews have been conducted by John Eck (1997, 2006). They focused on the full range of place-based situational measures implemented in both public and private settings. In keeping with their evidence-based approach, the reviews included only the highest quality evaluations in arriving at conclusions about what works, what does not work, and what is promising. This had the effect of excluding many situational measures with demonstrated preventive effects—including steering-column locks, redesigned credit cards, and exact-change policies (see Clarke 1997). Some of these first-generation situational prevention measures were assessed in weak evaluations that could not convincingly support the assertion that the program produced the reported effect.

John Eck and Rob Guerette's esssay presents an updated and slightly modified review of place-based crime prevention. They assess the evidence for the effectiveness of various situational measures implemented in five common types of places: residences, outside/public, retail, transportation, and recreation. They find a range of situational measures that are effective in preventing different crimes in each of these settings.

Two other essays review the effectiveness of situational measures applied in other contexts. Paul Ekblom looks at the role of the private sector in designing products that work against crime. A number of successful programs are profiled and critical issues discussed in what the author calls the "arms race" between preventers and offenders. Louise Grove and Graham Farrell review the effectiveness of situational measures designed to prevent repeat victimization of residential and commercial burglary and domestic and sexual violence. The authors find that a number of different measures are effective in preventing repeat victimization, especially of residential and commercial burglary.

V. Advancing Knowledge and Building a Safer Society

The final section of this volume looks at a number of key issues that cut across the three crime-prevention strategies. The first of these concerns implementation. Ross Homel and Peter Homel cover the complexities and challenges of implementing crime-prevention programs, as well as the process of moving from small-scale projects to large-scale dissemination and how to mitigate the attenuation of program effects. As with the science of the effectiveness of crime prevention, the authors call for a science of implementation that conforms with principles of good governance.

The second of these key issues concerns evaluation. An evaluation of a crime-prevention program is considered to be rigorous if it possesses a high degree of internal, construct, and statistical conclusion validity[5] (Cook and Campbell 1979; Shadish, Cook, and Campbell 2002). Put another way, we can have a great deal of confidence in the observed effects of an intervention if it has been evaluated using a design that controls for the major threats to these forms of validity. Experimental and quasi-experimental research methods are the types of designs that can best achieve this, and the randomized controlled experiment is the most convincing method of evaluating crime-prevention programs. This is the subject of David Weisburd and Joshua Hinkle's essay. Among the many benefits of randomized experiments, the authors note that randomization is the only method of assignment that controls for unknown and unmeasured confounders, as well as those that are known and measured. They also note that the randomized experiment is no panacea and may not be feasible in every instance, and in these cases other high-quality evaluation designs should be employed.

The next essay by Doris MacKenzie, on the effectiveness of correctional treatment, represents a departure from our focus on alternative, non–criminal justice approaches to preventing crime. Its inclusion in this volume is meant to be an important reminder of a key policy conclusion in our field: it is never too early and never too late to effectively intervene to reduce criminal offending (Loeber and Farrington 1998, forthcoming). While we maintain that it is far more socially worthwhile and just as well as sustainable to intervene before harm is inflicted on a victim and the offender is under the supervision of the justice system, it is important to recognize that this is not always possible; prevention programs are by no means foolproof.

Public opinion on crime prevention is also important to its future development and practice. Encouragingly, there appears to be a great deal of public support for the kinds of crime prevention covered here. Traditional and economic-based opinion polls consistently show that the public supports government spending on crime prevention rather than on more punitive responses, including building more prisons (Cullen et al. 2007), and that the public is willing to pay more in taxes if people know that the money will be directed toward crime prevention rather than crime control (Cohen, Rust, and Steen 2006; Nagin et al. 2006). These and other important findings are at the center of Julian Roberts and Ross Hastings's review of international trends in public opinion concerning crime prevention.

In the final essay of the volume we set out our modest proposal for a new crime-prevention policy to help build a safer, more sustainable society. Among its central features are the need to overcome the "short-termism" politics of the day; to ensure that the highest quality scientific research is at center stage in political and policy decisions; and to strike a greater balance between crime prevention and crime control.

NOTES

1. Crime-prevention programs are not designed with the intention of excluding justice personnel. Many types of prevention programs, especially those that focus on adolescents, involve justice personnel such as police or probation officers. In these cases, justice personnel work in close collaboration with those from such areas as education, health care, recreation, and social services.

2. Among the most well known classification schemes include those by Brantingham and Faust (1976), van Dijk and de Waard (1991), and Ekblom (1994).

3. Promising programs are those where the level of certainty from the available scientific evidence is too low to support generalizable conclusions, but where there is some empirical basis for predicting that further research could support such conclusions (Farrington et al. 2006).

4. See Barr and Pease (1990) for a discussion of "benign" or desirable effects of displacement.

5. *Internal validity* refers to how well the study unambiguously demonstrates that an intervention had an effect on an outcome. *Construct validity* refers to the adequacy of the operational definition and measurement of the theoretical constructs that underlie the intervention and the outcome. *Statistical conclusion validity* is concerned with whether the presumed cause (the intervention) and the presumed effect (the outcome) are related.

REFERENCES

Barr, Robert, and Ken Pease. 1990. "Crime Placement, Displacement, and Deflection." In *Crime and Justice: A Review of Research*, vol. 12, edited by Michael Tonry and Norval Morris. Chicago: University of Chicago Press.

Bennett, Trevor H. 1996. "Community Crime Prevention in Britain." In *Kommunale Kriminalprävention: Paradigmenwechsel und Wiederentdeckung alter Weisheiten*, edited by Thomas Trenczek and Hartmut Pfeiffer. Bonn, Germany: Forum Verlag Godesberg.

Bennett, Trevor H. 1998. "Crime Prevention." In *The Handbook of Crime and Punishment*, edited by Michael Tonry. New York: Oxford University Press.

Blumstein, Alfred, Jacqueline Cohen, and Daniel S. Nagin, eds. 1978. *Deterrence and Incapacitation*. Washington, DC: National Academy Press.

Brantingham, Paul J., and Frederick L. Faust. 1976. "A Conceptual Model of Crime Prevention." *Crime and Delinquency* 22:284–96.

Clarke, Ronald V. 1992. Introduction. In *Situational Crime Prevention: Successful Case Studies*, edited by Ronald V. Clarke. Albany, NY: Harrow and Heston.

Clarke, Ronald V. 1995a. "Opportunity-Reducing Crime Prevention Strategies and the Role of Motivation." In *Integrating Crime Prevention Strategies: Propensity and Opportunity*, edited by Per-Olof H. Wikström, Ronald V. Clarke, and Joan McCord. Stockholm, Sweden: National Council for Crime Prevention.

Clarke, Ronald V. 1995b. "Situational Crime Prevention." In *Building a Safer Society: Strategic Approaches to Crime Prevention*, edited by Michael Tonry and David P. Farrington. Vol. 19 of *Crime and Justice: A Review of Research*, edited by Michael Tonry. Chicago: University of Chicago Press.

Clarke, Ronald V., ed. 1997. *Situational Crime Prevention: Successful Case Studies*, 2nd ed. Guilderland, NY: Harrow and Heston.

Clarke, Ronald V. 2009. "Situational Crime Prevention: Theoretical Background and Current Practice." In *Handbook on Crime and Deviance*, edited by Marvin D. Krohn, Alan J. Lizotte, and Gina Penly Hall. New York: Springer.

Clarke, Ronald V., and David Weisburd. 1994. "Diffusion of Crime Control Benefits: Observations on the Reverse of Displacement." In *Crime Prevention Studies*, vol. 2, edited by Ronald V. Clarke. Monsey, NY: Criminal Justice Press.

Cloward, Richard, and Lloyd Ohlin. 1960. *Delinquency and Opportunity*. New York: Free Press.

Cohen, Mark A., Ronald T. Rust, and Sara Steen. 2006. "Prevention, Crime Control or Cash? Public Preferences toward Criminal Justice Spending Priorities." *Justice Quarterly* 23:317–35.

Cook, Thomas D., and Donald T. Campbell. 1979. *Quasi-Experimentation: Design and Analysis Issues for Field Settings*. Chicago: Rand-McNally.

Cornish, Derek B., and Ronald V. Clarke. 2003. "Opportunities, Precipitators and Criminal Decisions: A Reply to Wortley's Critique of Situational Crime Prevention." In *Theory for Practice in Situational Crime Prevention*, edited by Martha J. Smith and Derek B. Cornish. Vol. 16 of *Crime Prevention Studies*, edited by Ronald V. Clarke. Monsey, NY: Criminal Justice Press.

Cullen, Francis T., Brenda A. Vose, Cheryl N. L. Jonson, and James D. Unnever. 2007. "Public Support for Early Intervention: Is Child Saving a 'Habit of the Heart'?" *Victims and Offenders* 2:109–24.

Curtis, Lynn A. 1985. "Neighborhood, Family, and Employment: Toward a New Public Policy against Violence." In *American Violence and Public Policy: An Update of the National Commission on the Causes and Prevention of Violence*, edited by Lynn A. Curtis. New Haven, CT: Yale University Press.

Curtis, Lynn A. 1987. Preface. "Policies to Prevent Crime: Neighborhood, Family, and Employment Strategies." *Annals of the American Academy of Political and Social Science* 494:9–18.

Donziger, Steven R., ed. 1996. *The Real War on Crime: The Report of the National Criminal Justice Commission*. New York: HarperPerennial.

Drake, Elizabeth K., Steve Aos, and Marna G. Miller. 2009. "Evidence-Based Public Policy Options to Reduce Crime and Criminal Justice Costs: Implications in Washington State." *Victims and Offenders* 4:170–96.

Duncan, Greg J., and Katherine Magnuson. 2004. "Individual and Parent-Based Intervention Strategies for Promoting Human Capital and Positive Behavior." In *Human Development Across Lives and Generations: The Potential for Change*, edited by P. Lindsay Chase-Lansdale, Kathleen Kiernan, and Ruth J. Friedman. New York: Cambridge University Press.

Eck, John E. 1997. "Preventing Crime at Places." In *Preventing Crime: What Works, What Doesn't, What's Promising*, Lawrence W. Sherman, Denise C. Gottfredson, Doris L. MacKenzie, John E. Eck, Peter Reuter, and Shawn D. Bushway. Washington, DC: US Department of Justice, National Institute of Justice.

Eck, John E. 2006. "Preventing Crime at Places." In *Evidence-Based Crime Prevention*, rev. ed., edited by Lawrence W. Sherman, David P. Farrington, Brandon C. Welsh, and Doris L. MacKenzie. New York: Routledge.

Ekblom, Paul. 1994. "Proximal Circumstances: A Mechanism-Based Classification of Crime Prevention." In *Crime Prevention Studies*, vol. 2, edited by Ronald V. Clarke. Monsey, NY: Criminal Justice Press.

Farrington, David P. 1993. "Have Any Individual, Family or Neighbourhood Influences on Offending Been Demonstrated Conclusively?" In *Integrating Individual and Ecological Aspects of Crime*, edited by David P. Farrington, Robert J. Sampson, and Per-Olof H. Wikström. Stockholm, Sweden: National Council for Crime Prevention.

Farrington, David P., Denise C. Gottfredson, Lawrence W. Sherman, and Brandon C. Welsh. 2006. "The Maryland Scientific Methods Scale." In *Evidence-Based Crime Prevention*, rev. ed., edited by Lawrence W. Sherman, David P. Farrington, Brandon C. Welsh, and Doris L. MacKenzie. New York: Routledge.

Farrington, David P., and Brandon C. Welsh. 2007. *Saving Children from a Life of Crime: Early Risk Factors and Effective Interventions*. New York: Oxford University Press.

Gabor, Thomas. 1990. "Crime Displacement and Situational Prevention." *Canadian Journal of Criminology* 32:41–74.

Garland, David. 2000. "Ideas, Institutions and Situational Crime Prevention." In *Ethical and Social Perspectives on Situational Crime Prevention*, edited by Andrew von Hirsch, David Garland, and Alison Wakefield. Oxford, UK: Hart.

Gest, Ted. 2001. *Crime and Politics: Big Government's Erratic Campaign for Law and Order*. New York: Oxford University Press.

Greenwood, Peter W. 2006. *Changing Lives: Delinquency Prevention as Crime-Control Policy*. Chicago: University of Chicago Press.

Hawkins, J. David, and Richard F. Catalano. 1992. *Communities That Care: Action for Drug Abuse Prevention*. San Francisco, CA: Jossey-Bass.

Hesseling, René. 1995. "Theft from Cars: Reduced or Displaced?" *European Journal on Criminal Policy and Research* 3(3): 79–92.

Hope, Tim. 1995. "Community Crime Prevention." In *Building a Safer Society: Strategic Approaches to Crime Prevention*, edited by Michael Tonry and David P. Farrington. Vol. 19 of *Crime and Justice: A Review of Research*, edited by Michael Tonry. Chicago: University of Chicago Press.

Jeffrey, C. Ray. 1971. *Crime Prevention Through Environmental Design*. Beverly Hills, CA: Sage.

Lavrakas, Paul J. 1985. "Citizen Self-Help and Neighborhood Crime Prevention Policy." In *American Violence and Public Policy: An Update of the National Commission on the Causes and Prevention of Violence*, edited by Lynn A. Curtis. New Haven, CT: Yale University Press.

Lejins, Peter P. 1967. "The Field of Prevention." In *Delinquency Prevention: Theory and Practice*, edited by William E. Amos and Charles F. Wellford. Englewood Cliffs, NJ: Prentice-Hall.

Loeber, Rolf, and David P. Farrington, eds. 1998. *Serious and Violent Juvenile Offenders: Risk Factors and Successful Interventions*. Thousand Oaks, CA: Sage.

Loeber, Rolf, and David P. Farrington, eds. Forthcoming. *Transitions from Juvenile Delinquency to Adult Crime*. New York: Oxford University Press.

MacKenzie, Doris L. 2006. *What Works in Corrections: Reducing the Criminal Activities of Offenders and Delinquents*. New York: Cambridge University Press.

Mears, Daniel P. 2010. *American Criminal Justice Policy: An Evaluation Approach to Increasing Accountability and Effectiveness*. New York: Cambridge University Press.

Mendel, Richard A. 1995. *Prevention or Pork? A Hard-Headed Look at Youth-Oriented Anti-Crime Programs*. Washington, DC: American Youth Policy Forum.

Nagin, Daniel S., Alex R. Piquero, Elizabeth S. Scott, and Laurence Steinberg. 2006. "Public Preferences for Rehabilitation versus Incarceration of Juvenile Offenders: Evidence from a Contingent Valuation Survey." *Criminology and Public Policy* 5:627–52.

National Advisory Commission on Criminal Justice Standards and Goals. 1973. *Report on Community Crime Prevention*. Washington, DC: US Government Printing Office.

National Commission on the Causes and Prevention of Violence. 1969. *To Establish Justice, To Insure Domestic Tranquility, Final Report*. Washington, DC: US. Government Printing Office.

Newman, Oscar. 1972. *Defensible Space: Crime Prevention Through Urban Design*. New York: Macmillan.

Newman, Graeme, Ronald V. Clarke, and Shlomo Giora Shoham, eds. 1997. *Rational Choice and Situational Crime Prevention: Theoretical Foundations*. Aldershot, UK: Ashgate/Dartmouth.

President's Commission on Law Enforcement and Administration of Justice. 1967. *The Challenge of Crime in a Free Society*. Washington, DC: US Government Printing Office.

Reiss, Albert J., Jr., and Michael Tonry, eds. 1986. *Communities and Crime*. Vol. 8 of *Crime and Justice: A Review of Research*, edited by Michael Tonry. Chicago: University of Chicago Press.

Reppetto, Thomas A. 1976. "Crime Prevention and the Displacement Phenomenon." *Crime and Delinquency* 22:166–77.

Rosenbaum, Dennis P., ed. 1986. *Community Crime Prevention: Does It Work?* Beverly Hills, CA: Sage.

Rosenbaum, Dennis P. 1988. "Community Crime Prevention: A Review and Synthesis of the Literature." *Justice Quarterly* 5:323–95.

Rosenbaum, Dennis P., Arthur J. Lurigio, and Robert C. Davis. 1998. *The Prevention of Crime: Social and Situational Strategies*. Belmont, CA: Wadsworth.

Sampson, Robert J., and Janet Lauritsen. 1994. "Violent Victimization and Offending: Individual-, Situational-, and Community-Level Risk Factors." In *Understanding and Preventing Violence. Social Influences*, vol. 3, edited by Albert J. Reiss, Jr. and Jeffrey A. Roth. Washington, DC: National Academy Press.

Schlossman, Steven, and Michael Sedlak. 1983. "The Chicago Area Project Revisited." *Crime and Delinquency* 29:398–462.

Shadish, William R., Thomas D. Cook, and Donald T. Campbell. 2002. *Experimental and Quasi-Experimental Designs for Generalized Causal Inference*. Boston: Houghton Mifflin.

Shaw, Clifford R., and Henry D. McKay. 1942. *Juvenile Delinquency and Urban Areas: A Study of Rates of Delinquents in Relation to Differential Characteristics of Local Communities in American Cities*. Chicago: University of Chicago Press.

Sherman, Lawrence W. 1995. "Hot Spots of Crime and Criminal Careers of Places." In *Crime and Place*, edited by John E. Eck and David Weisburd. Vol. 4 of *Crime Prevention Studies*, edited by Ronald V. Clarke. Monsey, NY: Criminal Justice Press.

Sherman, Lawrence W. 1997. "Communities and Crime Prevention." In *Preventing Crime: What Works, What Doesn't, What's Promising*, Lawrence W. Sherman, Denise C. Gottfredson, Doris L. MacKenzie, John E. Eck, Peter Reuter, and Shawn D. Bushway. Washington, DC: US Department of Justice, National Institute of Justice.

Sherman, Lawrence W., David P. Farrington, Brandon C. Welsh, and Doris L. MacKenzie, eds. 2006. *Evidence-Based Crime Prevention*, rev. ed. New York: Routledge.

Sherman, Lawrence W., Patrick R. Gartin, and Michael E. Buerger. 1989. "Hot Spots of Predatory Crime: Routine Activities and the Criminology of Place." *Criminology* 27:27–55.

Sherman, Lawrence W., Denise C. Gottfredson, Doris L. MacKenzie, John E. Eck, Peter Reuter, and Shawn D. Bushway. 1997. *Preventing Crime: What Works, What Doesn't, What's Promising*. Washington, DC: US Department of Justice, National Institute of Justice.

Short, James F. 1974. "The Natural History of an Applied Theory: Differential Opportunity and 'Mobilization for Youth.'" In *Social Policy and Sociology*, edited by Nicholas J. Demerath, Otto Larsen, and Karl F. Schuessler. New York: Seminar Press.

Tonry, Michael, and David P. Farrington, eds. 1995a. *Building a Safer Society: Strategic Approaches to Crime Prevention*. Vol. 19 of *Crime and Justice: A Review of Research*, edited by Michael Tonry. Chicago: University of Chicago Press.

Tonry, Michael, and David P. Farrington. 1995b. "Strategic Approaches to Crime Prevention." In *Building a Safer Society: Strategic Approaches to Crime Prevention*, edited by Michael Tonry and David P. Farrington. Vol. 19 of *Crime and Justice: A Review of Research*, edited by Michael Tonry. Chicago: University of Chicago Press.

Tremblay, Richard E., and Wendy M. Craig. 1995. "Developmental Crime Prevention." In *Building a Safer Society: Strategic Approaches to Crime Prevention*, edited by Michael Tonry and David P. Farrington. Vol. 19 of *Crime and Justice: A Review of Research*, edited by Michael Tonry. Chicago: University of Chicago Press.

van Dijk, Jan J. M., and Jaap de Waard. 1991. "A Two-Dimensional Typology of Crime Prevention Projects; with a Bibliography." *Criminal Justice Abstracts* 23: 483–503.

Visher, Christy A., and David Weisburd. 1998. "Identifying What Works: Recent Trends in Crime Prevention Strategies." *Crime, Law and Social Change* 28: 223–42.

Waller, Irvin. 1990. "With National Leadership Canada Could Turn the Tide on Crime." *Canadian Journal of Criminology* 32:185–90.

Waller, Irvin. 2006. *Less Law, More Order: The Truth about Reducing Crime.* Westport, CT: Praeger.

Welsh, Brandon C., and David P. Farrington, eds. 2006. *Preventing Crime: What Works for Children, Offenders, Victims, and Places.* New York: Springer.

Welsh, Brandon C., and David P. Farrington. 2011. "Evidence-Based Crime Policy." In *The Oxford Handbook of Crime and Criminal Justice*, edited by Michael Tonry. New York: Oxford University Press.

Welsh, Brandon C., and Akemi Hoshi. 2006. "Communities and Crime Prevention." In *Evidence-Based Crime Prevention*, rev. ed., edited by Lawrence W. Sherman, David P. Farrington, Brandon C. Welsh, and Doris L. MacKenzie. New York: Routledge.

Welsh, Brandon C., and Rebecca D. Pfeffer. 2011. "Reclaiming Crime Prevention: A Revisionist American History." Paper, School of Criminology and Criminal Justice, Northeastern University.

Wikström, Per-Olof H. 1998. "Communities and Crime." In *The Handbook of Crime and Punishment*, edited by Michael Tonry. New York: Oxford University Press.

PART I

DEVELOPMENTAL CRIME PREVENTION

CHAPTER 2

DEVELOPMENTAL AND LIFE-COURSE THEORIES OF OFFENDING

FRANCIS T. CULLEN, MICHAEL L. BENSON, AND MATTHEW D. MAKARIOS

THEORIES perform three useful functions. First, amid the many potential risk factors for crime, they identify which ones are most salient. Second, they delineate the relationships among or sequencing of these criminogenic risk factors. And third, they propose the origins of these risk factors. If true, theories thus enrich our understanding of criminal behavior. But they also carry two limitations—one obvious and one not so obvious. On the one hand, if theories identify risk factors that are either unrelated or only weakly related to crime, they mislead scholars and misguide practitioners' intervention efforts. On the other hand, there is a less obvious difficulty: even if substantially accurate, theories restrict our vision as to the possible sources of criminal conduct. Similar to a flashlight in the night, theories shine a concentrated light on and thus allow us to see the importance of certain risk factors, but in doing so, they leave other factors in the dark and outside our consideration.

Many traditional theories of crime—those that directed our thinking about crime for the better part of the 20th century—focused their beam primarily on one stage in life: the teenage years. As a result, criminology was replete with a roster of "theories of delinquency." Scholars pointed their theoretical lights on this stage in life for criminological and practical reasons. Criminologically, adolescence appeared to be a time during which participation in illegal activities skyrocketed. The hump of the bell curve of crime was centered on the teenage years for most offenses (a bit later for serious violent offenses). This was also the point in life at which individuals joined together to form gangs, including those heavily involved in drugs and violence. Practically, youths were easily studied. It was possible to survey most teenagers in a community by distributing questionnaires in junior and senior high schools. By contrast, children were too young to fill out such questionnaires and adults rarely congregated in one place where they might be polled.

This approach—theorizing about and collecting data on teenagers—contributed many important insights to our understanding of crime causation. Even so, it was an approach that left too much about life in the dark—outside what criminologists would see and study. Although criminologists never argued that childhood was irrelevant to crime, they ignored the beginning stages of life and focused their attention on the post-childhood years. Implicitly, their theories assumed that most youngsters arrived at the teenage years as blank slates, at which time they either conformed or were driven, encouraged, or permitted to break the law. After the teenage years, it was assumed, again mostly in unspoken terms, that those in trouble as adults would be drawn from those in trouble as juveniles. Little direct investigation was undertaken of the unique aspects of adulthood that might encourage or discourage criminal involvement.

Beginning in the 1990s, however, a relatively small group of scholars questioned the implicit assumptions of mainstream criminology. They pointed out something that most parents worry about: that what happens in childhood—indeed, in the womb—may be a precursor to what comes later in life. That is, risk factors for delinquency may not be limited exclusively to the teenage years. Rather, they might well emerge early in life and, at that time, determine who will grow up to be a serious offender. An even smaller group of scholars looked at the back two-thirds of life—the adult years. They cautioned that what occurs in adulthood is affected by childhood factors and by life events that are unique to being a grown-up.

These simple insights had profound implications. First, they suggested that most existing theories were limited, if not simply incorrect (we use the term "misspecified"). They left out too many important risk factors at other stages of life to provide an accurate and complete understanding of the criminal enterprise. Second, these insights created fresh opportunities for thinking about how to prevent crime. If risk factors for crime were found across the life course, then it made sense that interventions aimed at preventing criminal behavior could be designed for distinct stages of the life course (Farrington and Welsh 2007).

Importantly, over the past two decades, theories have emerged to address these issues. These perspectives are like shining two or three flashlights, rather than a single one, so that an entire dark room can be illuminated. Thus, with these newer theories, we can see multiple dimensions of life simultaneously, allowing our criminological eyes to scan the life course from "womb to tomb." Freed from a narrow focus on the juvenile years, we are able to consider how individuals grow into and out of crime. This opportunity to see broadly, however, has not made our scholarly lives easier. With our field of vision expanded, there is now more to see and more to try to make sense of.

In this regard, the theories discussed in this essay assist in the daunting task of trying to understand crime across people's lives. Some scholars use the constructs of *developmental* and *life-course* as synonyms—that is, to refer to theories that try to explain criminal involvement across life. Other scholars, however, use the terms in a more technical way so as to show how these criminological approaches differ. Thus, in this debate, *developmental* theories assume that people grow up or "develop" as humans in predictable ways, going through standard stages in life. Most youngsters are on a prosocial or "normal" pathway, but others are not; they are headed into crime. Even here, these youngsters also grow up or develop in a predictable way—albeit one that is antisocial. By contrast, *life-course* theories portray the growth process as a messier affair. People do not flower like a plant in ways that can be neatly and confidently predicted. Rather, they head along trajectories—either conformist or criminal—until some event redirects their lives. In this view, going into and out of crime can be explained by pointing to risk and protective factors, but the precise timing of changes in life for any individual is virtually random.

In this essay, our concern is not with the technical distinctions between developmental and life-course theories. This debate is useful to keep in mind, but our assigned task lies elsewhere. Specifically, our goal is to present an overview of the major developmental *and* life-course theories. In doing so, our special interest is in explaining how different theories explain why some individuals—typically starting in childhood—are placed on a pathway or trajectory toward a life in antisocial conduct and crime. Some theories also have something to say about change—how offenders extricate themselves from a criminal pathway. Where relevant, the issue of change is highlighted.

Having a firm grasp of the prevailing developmental and life-course theories is essential because the future investigations of crime will be shaped intimately by these competing perspectives. In a real sense, today's criminology is life-course criminology. But sound theoretical knowledge also is relevant to this handbook because these perspectives identify key points in the life course where interventions might be targeted and key processes through which crime prevention might naturally occur in the social world. In the end, the apparent gulf between theory and intervention—the esoteric and the practical—is more myth than reality. To use our flashlight metaphor a final time, theories illuminate for practitioners the risk factors that should be targeted for intervention.

This essay provides a tour of developmental and life-course theories and thus is not arranged to derive empirical insights. Still, it is possible to demarcate several key lessons from the theoretical discussion that follows:

- Traits or propensities conducive to antisocial conduct and crime develop in the womb and early in childhood. The roots of crime thus extend over the life course.
- Antisocial orientations and behavior will be deepened if at-risk youngsters travel through family, peer, school, and community contexts that are troubled and criminogenic.

- Punitive, stigmatizing criminal justice sanctions, including imprisonment, likely deepen criminal propensities.
- Desistance from crime in adulthood requires not only social opportunities for change but also cognitive orientations that inspire offenders to forfeit a life in crime.
- The sources of continuity in offending are often robust—which is why criminal careers persist over a number of years—but many also are amenable to change. Theoretically informed, evidence-based, and carefully planned interventions thus are likely to save many at-risk youngsters and adults from life-course-persistent offending.

The remainder of the essay is divided into eight sections. Section I examines Gottfredson and Hirschi's claim that stable criminal behavior across life is due to low self-control, a propensity established in childhood. Section II reviews Moffitt's insight that life unfolds in two distinct developmental pathways, including one that involves life-course-persistent offending. Section III discusses Hawkins and Catalano's socio-logical theory of why youngsters develop along a delinquent as opposed to a proso-cial pathway and how this information has been used to save youngsters from a criminal future. Section IV shows how Farrington has used empirical information on risk factors to formulate an integrated developmental theory of offending. Section V focuses on a perspective, labeling theory, often not defined as a life-course or devel-opmental theory. Labeling theory is significant precisely because it cautions that at-tempts, especially by the criminal justice system, to dissuade people from offending can have the unanticipated consequence of increasing their criminality. Section VI highlights Hagan's efforts to unravel why youngsters become embedded in a criminal trajectory. His special contribution is in revealing the necessity to take into account the criminogenic community contexts in which troubled youths are so often enmeshed. Section VII presents Sampson and Laub's life-course theory that argues that the absence of social bonds explains why persistent offending occurs and the presence of social bonds explains how criminals desist from crime. They also assert that leaving crime involves something they call human agency, which roughly means that offenders exercise the will to halt their illegal conduct. Finally, building on the research of Maruna and of Giordano and colleagues, section VIII conveys another view of why offenders desist: they experience a cognitive transformation.

I. IT'S USUALLY TOO LATE: GOTTFREDSON AND HIRSCHI'S SELF-CONTROL THEORY

The developers of self-control theory, Michael Gottfredson and Travis Hirschi, assume that the precursors to crime are laid down early in the life course (Gott-fredson and Hirschi 1990). Indeed, according to this theory, by the time children reach the ages of 11 or 12, the most important developmental events have already occurred. After children have passed that age, whatever remains in the way of human developmental stages is not particularly important for criminologists. So, what are the important developmental events? They can be found in the relationships and interactions that children have with their parents in the first decade of life. Depending on how parents treat their children early in the life course, the children will develop in one of two ways. If the parents do the "right" things, their children will become normal, conforming, and prosocial individuals. However, if the parents do the "wrong" thing, their children will develop into self-centered, impulsive, and anti-social individuals.

Good parents—that is, parents who do the right things—are strongly attached to their children. They care about their children and want them to develop as positively as possible. As a result of that caring and attachment, they monitor their children for signs of misbehavior, recognize misbehavior when it occurs, and punish such behavior in a firm and consistent manner. Treated in such a way, children will gradually develop self-control. People with self-control are not impulsive; they learn from experience; they are sensitive to the rights and feelings of others; and they think about the potential long-term consequences of their actions. It is important to note that in the eyes of Gottfredson and Hirschi (1990, pp. 94–95), self-control is not something that people are born with or something that develops naturally over time. Rather, self-control results only from the positive actions of parents. It must be built into children.

Ineffective parents can fail in one or more ways. They may not be attached to their children, in which case nothing else matters. Even if they do care about their children, they may fail to monitor, recognize, or punish their deviant behavior. When parents consistently fail to perform these actions early in the life course, their children will not develop self-control. Rather, they will become people who are "impulsive, insensitive, physical (as opposed to mental), short-sighted, and non-verbal" (Gottfredson and Hirschi 1990, p. 90). That is, they will have low self-control.

People with low self-control are attracted to crime because it offers quick and relatively certain rewards. Most crimes do not require a lot of planning or effort. They are easy to carry out, potentially rewarding, fun, and exciting. People with low self-control are attracted to all of these characteristics. The fact that crimes hurt other people and do not pay off in the long run does not bother them.

Thus, in developmental terms, self-control theory is a propensity theory. It assumes that people have a more or less stable propensity to commit crime. This propensity is established early in the life course and does not change over time. That is, it is not influenced by later events that may happen in the life course. According to Gottfredson and Hirschi, then, there are only two main trajectories in crime—criminal or not—and they are established early as a result of the type of parenting the individual receives. Once a person has low self-control, it is too late to change him or her.

II. Focusing on Life-Course-Persistent Offenders: Moffitt's Taxonomy Theory

In contrast to Gottfredson and Hirschi, Terrie Moffitt (1993) does not assume that criminal propensity is gradational, with people aligning on a continuum that ranges from a lot of self-control to no self-control. Rather, she has offered a taxonomy that divides youngsters into two very distinct groups that develop in quite different ways. Most children, she claims, engage in *adolescence-limited* offending. They are prosocial during childhood, get into trouble in adolescence, and then mature and leave crime behind. A smaller group of children, however, start life on a pathway to *life-course-persistent* offending. These individuals engage in a wide variety of criminal and antisocial behaviors throughout the life course. Thus, like Gottfredson and Hirschi, Moffitt believes that antisocial behavior remains stable in some individuals from very early childhood to adulthood. Accordingly, her theory of life-course persistence focuses on factors present at the very earliest moments in the life course. But here the two theories depart in their explanation of what occurs in childhood and beyond.

Moffitt contends that the life-course-persistent pattern of antisocial behavior arises out of the combination of a "vulnerable and difficult infant with an adverse rearing context" (Moffitt 1997, p. 17). She envisions a child with a difficult temperament who is born to parents who are ill-equipped to handle the child's problems. The child's difficult temperament flows from what Moffitt calls neuropsychological deficits. These deficits may be genetically based or they may be caused by unhealthy prenatal conditions, such as poor nutrition, inadequate health care, and alcohol or drug use during pregnancy. Deficits in neuropsychological conditions and processes may affect temperament in such areas as activity level and emotional reactivity; behavioral development in speech, motor coordination, and impulse control; and cognitive abilities in attention, language, and reasoning (Moffitt 1997, p. 18).

Children who suffer from neuropsychological deficits and who are born into disadvantaged or troubled families undergo negative encounters with their parents. The parents do not recognize or know how to properly respond to the child's problems. In interactions with the child, they do the wrong thing at the wrong time. Over time, this "chain of failed parent/child encounters" aggravates the behavioral problems or tendencies that flow from the child's neuropsychological deficits. Thus, a child with a neuropsychological deficit that promotes impulsivity grows up to be very impulsive because parents have not taken steps to help the child handle or ameliorate the behavioral effects of the condition. Thus, life-course-persistent antisocial behavior begins with the interaction between problem children and problem parents.

The early pattern of antisocial behavior persists into adolescence and later into adulthood. In part, this persistence is caused by the behavioral style that the individual developed as a child and carries over into later stages in the life course. The hyperactive child with poor self-control and limited cognitive abilities becomes an overactive adult who is self-indulgent and not very smart. When the person is a child, this constellation of traits leads to trouble, and it continues to do so as the person ages, producing continuous contemporary consequences. At each stage of the life course, this person's behavioral style gets him or her into trouble with others.

Persistence in antisocial behavior, and specifically criminal behavior, also results from the cumulating effects of problems and failure over time. Beginning early in life, individuals on a life-course-persistent trajectory behave in ways that limit their future opportunities. Because they are so bothersome to be around, life-course-persistent individuals are often rejected and avoided by others. They have difficulty learning how to behave in a prosocial manner and so have few prosocial friends and little opportunity to practice conventional social skills. They do poorly in school and so never attain basic math and reading skills. Without these skills, their opportunities for legitimate employment are curtailed. Involvement in crime and delinquency leads to arrests and incarcerations, which further diminish opportunities for success in a conventional lifestyle. Cumulating consequences eventually ensnare the life-course-persistent individual in a deviant lifestyle from which escape becomes ever more difficult as time passes (Moffitt 1997, pp. 21–23).

Like Gottfredson and Hirschi, Moffitt (1997) is not hopeful about the life-course-persistent individual's chances for reform and reintegration into normal life. Her theory assumes that in regard to crime and antisocial behavior, there are a limited number of developmental paths or templates available for individuals to follow. Once a person is set upon one path early in life, there is little possibility that the person will change or develop in a different way. Her theory differs from low self-control theory in that she asserts that biological and genetic conditions play an important role in influencing developmental trajectories.

III. SOCIAL DEVELOPMENT AND CRIME: HAWKINS AND CATALANO'S THEORY

David Hawkins, Richard Catalano, and their colleagues in the School of Social Work at the University of Washington designed their social development theory specifically to guide the creation of the Seattle Social Development Project (SSDP). Reflecting their background in social work, the SSDP was an early prevention intervention, with a research component, implemented in elementary schools that served high crime areas (Hawkins et al. 2007). It sought to target a variety of social factors in the individual youths, in their homes, and in their classrooms (Hawkins et al. 2007). Social-development theory was designed by identifying protective factors that promote prosocial development and thus sought to explain both prosocial and antisocial development (for a thorough review, see Catalano and Hawkins 1996).

Social development theory specifies how protective factors and risk factors interact to encourage either prosocial or antisocial development (Hawkins et al. 2007). It suggests that as individuals socially develop from early childhood to adolescence, prosocial and antisocial influences have a cumulative effect on behavioral tendencies. As its name suggests, the theory is *developmental*, arguing that youngsters take one of two possible pathways: prosocial or antisocial. Also as its name suggests, the causal factors are seen as primarily *social*, which means that youths on the antisocial pathway can be saved if exposed to a new set of social experiences. This is unlike the more dismal views of self-control theory and Moffitt's taxonomy perspective that locate antisocial propensities in more resistant individual traits.

Social development theory is an integrated perspective, drawing ideas mainly from social bond theory and differential association/social learning theory. According to this model, individuals are presented with opportunities to engage in various activities and to interact with certain people. If individuals have the skills to participate with others, they are positively reinforced. They then form attachments or bonds to these people. These bonds are a conduit for embracing moral beliefs, which then direct behavioral choices (Catalano et al. 2005).

This sequence characterizes both the prosocial and antisocial developmental pathways. Youths on the prosocial trajectory have opportunities to develop prosocial associations. If they are skilled, they are reinforced during these interactions (e.g., praised, accepted by peers) and form bonds to prosocial others. They come to believe in the conventional moral order and thus engage in conventional conduct. By contrast, some youngsters have access to antisocial opportunities for interaction. Again, if skilled in these engagements, they are positively reinforced, develop close social bonds with deviant others, and thus internalize antisocial values. The result is antisocial behavior.

Importantly, most theories do not include the variable of "skills for interaction" (Catalano et al. 2005). This is a key insight because it means that simple exposure to prosocial influences may not ensure a healthy social development if youngsters lack the skills to interact with prosocial peers and succeed in school. Youths lacking effective social and emotional skills thus risk rejection and failure and might then seek out antisocial peers.

A critical issue is what determines why, early in life, some youngsters are presented with an abundance of prosocial opportunities whereas others have easy access to antisocial opportunities. The causal model proposed by social development theory specifies three "exogenous" factors that push children in one direction or another. The first is position in the social structure, which places youngsters in contexts that provide differential opportunity (e.g., an inner city marked by concentrated disadvantage versus an affluent neighborhood). The second factor is captured by the construct of external constraints. By this, Hawkins and colleagues mean the extent to which youths confront laws, norms, and expectations that promote prosocial conduct. Prosocial constraints might be more available in middle-class areas, but they can flourish as well within families and classrooms within at-risk communities. This is why interventions that improve parental and classroom management skills can foster prosocial behavior. The third factor is termed individual constitutional factors, such as hyperactivity and difficult temperament. Youths with these traits are, without intervention, less likely to be successful in prosocial interactions and find more reinforcement and attractive bonds from antisocial peers (Catalano et al. 2005; Hawkins et al. 2003; Hawkins et al. 2007).

Finally, social development theory is dynamic, not static. It assumes that development is ongoing and that what happens at one life stage affects what happens at later stages. In particular, the model proposes a "recursive process in which behavioral outcomes at each age affect developmental trajectories by affecting the subsequent opportunities encountered by the individual" (Hawkins et al. 2003, p. 274). In this way, antisocial behavior tends to trap youngsters on an antisocial pathway where they will stay unless an intervention is forthcoming.

In this regard, based on social development theory, SSDP was implemented to encourage the exposure of youths to protective factors and to discourage the exposure of youths to risk factors. Social development theory suggests that prosocial development is affected by individual, family, and school-based factors. As a result, the intervention provided social and emotional skill development programming for children, child behavioral management training programming for parents, and classroom instruction and management programming for teachers (Hawkins et al. 2007). The intervention's evaluation employed a longitudinal panel design, which was able to track youths on a variety of social development factors throughout the course of their lives. The evaluation research has shown that youths who received the full treatment from the intervention were more likely to score higher on measures of prosocial development and to score lower on measures of antisocial development at many stages in the study, including during the intervention (age 12) and years after the intervention ended (ages 18 and 21) (see Hawkins, Von Cleve, and Catalano 1991; Hawkins et al. 1999; Hawkins et al. 2005).

IV. Explaining Criminal Tendencies and Criminal Events: Farrington's Integrated Cognitive Antisocial Potential Theory

As the long-term director of the Cambridge Study in Delinquent Development and investigator of criminal careers, David Farrington developed a broad and deep knowledge of criminogenic risk factors and how they cause wayward behavior (Farrington 2003). With this empirical knowledge, he finally ventured forth to formulate a developmental/life-course theory, which he calls an Integrated Cognitive Antisocial Potential Theory (IACP Theory) (Farrington 2005a). The Cambridge Study allowed Farrington to examine the development of delinquency in a sample of 411 males from South London for 40 years. In the process, Farrington became interested in the identification and measurement of a variety of short- and long-term influences of delinquency (for a review, see Farrington 2003).

Farrington (1996) developed his theory in an integrative fashion in order to explain the risk factors that had been shown to have the most support in explaining crime and criminal behavior. Incorporating concepts from social learning theory, cognitive theory, strain theory, several control theories, labeling theory, and routine activity theory, Farrington (1996) sought to explain the causation of both crime and criminals. The empirically established risk factors (Farrington 2003) can be categorized into one of two types: first, long-term risk factors that encouraged the development of criminal tendencies; and, second, short-term environmental risk factors that immediately encourage criminal events.

Farrington (2005a) suggested that to adequately explain criminal behavior, it is necessary to address two different questions: (1) "Why do people become criminals?"; (2) "Why do people commit offenses?" (Farrington 2005a, p. 73). That is, the explanation of criminal behavior must be concerned with the interactions between individual long-term developmental tendencies and short-term environmental factors. Similar to other life-course research, Farrington's theory focuses on how stable characteristics between individuals and short-term characteristics within individuals interact to produce crime (see, e.g., Horney, Osgood, and Marshall 1995).

Long-term risk factors are those that are related to the development of stable, individual differences in the likelihood to offend. These factors can be categorized as energizing, modeling, and socialization. Energizing factors—such as desires for material items, status, excitement, or sexual activity—produce drives that can be satisfied in an antisocial manner. Farrington (2005a) suggested that antisocial role models also are a factor in producing antisocial tendencies because they model and reinforce the antisocial means of meeting their energizing drives. Socialization is thought to discourage antisocial behavior by producing attachments to prosocial parents and developing self-control with the consistent use of discipline (Gottfredson and Hirschi 1990; Sampson and Laub 1993). The failure to develop prosocial attachments or forming attachments to antisocial individuals thus encourages long-term antisocial development.

Criminologists have noted that although there are individual differences in long-term criminal tendencies, even the highest risk criminals are not engaging in crime all of the time (see Horney, Osgood, and Marshall 1995). Instead, each individual criminal interacts with short-term changes in their environment that provide opportunities and incentives to offend. These immediate environmental influences thus encourage the onset of a specific criminal event. Farrington's ICAP theory seeks to explain how criminal tendencies interact with these short-term environmental influences to produce crime.

Short-term energizing factors include anger, boredom, frustration, and intoxication. These factors produce immediate pressure (or strain) to engage in antisocial behavior. Being in environments that expose individuals to antisocial opportunities is considered a product of the routine activities of criminals (e.g., partying, drug use) and is viewed as encouraging criminal behavior in the short term. An individual's cognitive thought process is important because it works to moderate the impact of the environment on criminal behavior. That is, when provided with a drive and opportunity to engage in crime, individuals' cognitive ability is related to how they interpret the positive and negative consequences for their actions. Finally, if individuals are rewarded for their antisocial behavior, their attitudes regarding rewards and punishment for the act could become more favorable toward the criminal act, thus encouraging future criminal behavior (Farrington 2005a).

Notably, Farrington has written a fair amount regarding how his theory can be used to prevent criminals and crime (for a review, see Farrington 1996). Not surprisingly, the interventions he suggests can be divided into two categories: first, early interventions that work to discourage the development of criminal tendencies; and, second, interventions that target individuals who have developed criminal tendencies and attempts to discourage them from engaging in criminal acts in the short term. Early interventions, such as prenatal nursing care, parental management classes, and early intellectual enrichment, target at-risk youth and seek to discourage the development of an individual who is predisposed to engage in antisocial behavior (Farrington and Welsh 2007). In the short term, situational crime prevention strategies and community mobilization seek to increase guardians and reduce the opportunities that provide incentives to engage in criminal behavior.

In sum, by focusing on both long-term and short-term causes of criminal behavior, Farrington's (2005a) ICAP theory seeks to explain the development of both criminal individuals and criminal events. He proposes that an individual's criminal tendencies are developed over time and interact with short-term environmental factors to produce criminal behavior. His theory suggests that crime can be prevented by discouraging the development of criminal tendencies and by using situational crime-prevention approaches to reduce the likelihood that criminal individuals will engage in crime.

V. Making Matters Worse: Labeling Theory

In the 1970s, labeling theory emerged as a leading explanation for criminal behavior. When people break the law, it seems logical to arrest them, to stigmatize them as an "offender," and to punish them by placing them behind bars. In fact, this is the central premise of deterrence theory—that inflicting such pain would teach offenders that crime does not pay and make them avoid illegal conduct in the future. Labeling theory, however, challenged this commonsense idea. The perspective made the provocative claim that pulling offenders deep into the criminal justice system had the unanticipated consequence of increasing their criminal propensities. In fact, publicly labeling and treating people as serious offenders only served to stabilize their involvement in crime and to create career criminals. As Edwin Lemert (1951) argued, societal reaction could transform potentially transitory, unorganized "primary deviance" into stable, organized "secondary deviance." Importantly, because the labeling perspective appeared well before the advent of formal developmental and life-course theories, it has not often been conceptualized as contributing to our current understanding of how offenders' criminality becomes stabilized. This blind spot is unfortunate because it has led most current life-course and developmental theories to ignore or downplay the role of criminal justice intervention in further entrapping offenders in a criminal trajectory.

Labeling theorists demarcated how state intervention might make matters worse—how it might, like taking the wrong medicine, have iatrogenic effects. For this reason, they called for a policy of "radical non-intervention" (Schur 1973). In essence, they argued that labeling places people on an antisocial pathway on which their exposure to risk factors for crime is increased, not decreased. Thus, when stigmatized and treated by everyone as an offender, individuals will internalize this negative identity, make it part of their self-concept, and then shape their behavior to be consistent with it. Further, especially when imprisoned, offenders are forced into contexts where they interact with other criminals, are cut off from bonds to family and conventional society, and experience social rejection and difficulty finding employment when reentering the community as an "ex-offender" (see also Pager 2007). Any thoughts that crime should be avoided because it does not pay are overwhelmed by the daily realities of public humiliation, social exclusion, and forces pushing them toward rather than away from criminal associations.

Labeling theory lost much of its appeal when it became apparent that people could embark on a criminal career well before being detected and sanctioned by the criminal justice system. If so, then it seemed that the sources of crime lay more fully in other social experiences, including dysfunctional families, delinquent peers, and disorganized or inequitable communities. Further, it was apparent that legal sanctions did not always make offenders more criminal; the empirical research on this issue was unclear. But these observations were taken too far at times. However true, they did not mean that criminal justice labeling is not implicated in stabilizing criminal involvement, at least under some circumstances (Palamara, Cullen, and Gersten 1986).

In this regard, John Braithwaite (1989) has proposed that when offenders are shamed in a reintegrative way—when their bad acts are condemned but they are welcomed back into the community—their criminal involvement lessens. However, stigmatizing shaming—when offenders are condemned and excluded from the community—leads to more crime. Similarly, Lawrence Sherman (1993) notes that criminal sanctions foster defiance and more offending when individuals, with few existing bonds to society, perceive that they are treated unjustly and with disrespect by criminal justice officials. Finally, Don Andrews and James Bonta (2010) reveal that high-quality correctional rehabilitation programs reduce recidivism, but that punitive programs, especially when applied to low-risk offenders, produce high rates of reoffending (see also Cullen and Jonson forthcoming).

Perhaps most important, recent research has reported results supporting the labeling theory claim that justice system processing increases, rather than decreases, criminal involvement (see, e.g., Bernburg and Krohn 2003; Bernburg, Krohn, and Rivera 2006; Chiricos et al. 2007). In particular, several longitudinal studies have shown that imprisonment has a criminogenic rather than a deterrent effect (Spohn and Holleran 2002; Nieuwbeerta, Nagin, and Blokland 2009; see also Nagin, Cullen, and Jonson 2009). Although this finding is typically ignored in summaries of their theory, Sampson and Laub (1993) found that imprisonment increased offending by attenuating offenders' bonds to conventional society. Given the high rate of incarceration in the United States—with approximately 2.4 million offenders behind bars on any given day—the effects of imprisonment and other forms of criminal justice labeling thus clearly warrant consideration. Phrased differently, no understanding of the development of offending over the life course will be complete unless the effects of criminal justice processing—a common experience for most persistent offenders—are systematically taken into account.

VI. Trapped in Crime: Hagan's Theory of Criminal Embeddedness

John Hagan has constructed a developmental theory of street crime in America (Hagan 1991, 1997). His theory is distinguished from most others in the life-course perspective by its explicit emphasis on historically based macro social and economic processes, most notably what he calls "capital disinvestment." Capital disinvestment is something that happened to minority communities and neighborhoods over the course of the latter half of the 20th century.

According to Hagan (1997), in the 1970s the American economy began to slow down after a long period of postwar expansion. During this slowdown, core manufacturing jobs in auto plants and steel mills began to disappear from American cities in the Northeast and Midwest. Jobs in manufacturing had provided a means of economic advancement for African Americans and other minorities. Although the economy eventually created new jobs, these jobs were located in rural and suburban areas where African Americans were not welcome. Policies of residential segregation made it difficult for African Americans to leave inner-city neighborhoods and move to the suburbs, where the economy's new jobs were being created (Hagan 1997, p. 290). Young minority males and females were, in effect, trapped in communities in which there were few opportunities in the legitimate economy (Wilson 1987).

In addition to being located in areas from which African Americans were segregated, the economy's new jobs increasingly required advanced education and high-level technical skills. It was not easy for African Americans to fulfill these requirements. Opposition to affirmative action laws gained strength during the last quarter of the century and restricted the access of African Americans to college and to good jobs in the legitimate economy. Racial differentials in earnings and educational achievement, which had been declining, began to grow again. Race-linked inequality became worse after the mid-1970s. According to Hagan, the rise in racial inequality led to feelings of "resentment, frustration, hopelessness, and aggression" in America's minority youths (Hagan 1997, p. 291).

Residential segregation and racial inequality combined to create hyper-ghettos. In hyper-ghettos, poverty is extreme and extensive. People who are lucky enough to have good jobs and a little money leave as quickly as they can. Only the most disadvantaged and discouraged are left behind. As a result, poverty is concentrated in hyper-ghettos, and the variation in economic resources becomes extremely narrow. Everyone is poor and everyone must struggle to survive.

The processes of capital disinvestment led communities to develop alternative forms of economic organization, called "forms of recapitalization" (Hagan 1997, p. 296). By recapitalization, Hagan means that communities attempt to organize whatever resources are available so that they can be used to help community members achieve their goals. Often, according to Hagan, the only economic resources that disadvantaged communities have at their disposal are illicit. They can offer the outside world something that is not available via the conventional economy. They can offer access to illegal services and commodities, such as prostitution, gambling, and especially narcotic drugs. These communities become deviance service centers for conventional society, places where illicit services and commodities are provided for a price.

Young people who live in disadvantaged communities are drawn to the promise of the deviance service industry. In their eyes, becoming involved in the drug economy or prostitution is a way to get ahead. It is a means for getting money, fine clothes, and fancy cars. Jobs in the legitimate economy are not available to them or to their parents. The prospects of going to college seem dim. The deviance service industry is the most promising employer around, and so young people lacking access to legitimate employment take advantage of what is available. They take positions in the drug economy.

Hagan notes that deviance service centers are not a new urban phenomenon. Indeed, they have a long history in America. Throughout the 19th and early part of the 20th century, different ethnic groups used the deviance service industry as a means of social mobility. Participation in organized crime was a way to acquire the financial resources necessary to move out of the ghetto and into mainstream society. But times have changed, and the deviance service industry is no longer the mobility ladder it once was. Rather than providing a route out of the ghetto and out of a life of crime, participation in deviance and vice is more likely to embed young people in a criminal lifestyle.

The process of criminal embeddedness links the historical community-level processes of capital disinvestments and recapitalization to the life-course trajectories of individuals. Young people, who become involved in the deviance service industry, and especially the drug economy, isolate themselves from conventional employment and educational trajectories. They spend time with other criminals like themselves. Their social contacts are with others in the deviance industry and not with people who might provide access to legitimate employment or who might help them succeed in school. Cutting ties with conventional others is one aspect of criminal embeddedness. The other aspect is the high probability that the individual will eventually be arrested and be officially labeled as a criminal offender. Being labeled a criminal makes it exceedingly difficult, if not impossible, for young minority males and females to ever find a way out of crime and into the middle class. Their life-course trajectories are set in a downward spiral of cumulating disadvantages from which there is little hope of escape.

Overall, Hagan's theory focuses on how broad changes and patterns in the economy and social structure are linked to the life-course trajectories of individuals. Capital disinvestment has created neighborhoods and communities that have relatively little conventional social or cultural capital. The parents of children who grow up in these communities are not well equipped to help their children develop worthwhile skills. Because the parents do not have strong links to the conventional labor market, they also have few resources to help their children find decent jobs in the legitimate economy. Young people see the deviance service industry as the most promising source of employment. Individuals who succumb to the lures of the deviance industry risk becoming embedded in criminal lifestyles that isolate them from conventional educational and employment trajectories. Their trajectories in crime are characterized by continuity into adulthood. Hagan explains the severity and longevity of the criminal trajectories of urban underclass youth by emphasizing the powerful shaping force of personal and neighborhood social disadvantages. Individual-level differences in personal constitutions do not figure prominently in his theory.

VII. FIRMING UP SOCIAL BONDS: SAMPSON AND LAUB'S AGE-GRADED THEORY

Robert Sampson and John Laub have advanced an age-graded theory of informal social control to explain trajectories in crime and delinquency (Sampson and Laub 1993; Sampson 1997; Laub, Nagin, and Sampson 1998; Laub and Sampson 2003). As control theorists, Sampson and Laub start with the assumption that delinquency, crime, and deviance are natural. If people are not somehow controlled or prevented from following their natural inclinations, they will tend to behave in ways that society regards as antisocial or criminal. The theory of age-graded informal social control holds that the most important sources of control come from informal bonds between people.

Sampson and Laub argue that at different stages in the life course, individuals are potentially subject to different forms of informal social control. (Again, this is why their theory is *age-graded*.) For children, family and school bonds are important.

Children who are strongly bonded to their parents and who care about school are less likely to be involved in delinquency than children who have difficult relations with their parents or who do not like school. As children move through the life course, the major sources of informal social control change. Parents and school are not as important for young adults as they are for children and teenagers. For young adults, employment and marriage are potential sources of informal control. Informal social controls influence the likelihood and degree of involvement in crime and deviance at all stages of the life course.

Sampson and Laub recognize that ontogenetic differences between individuals—that is, persistent underlying differences in temperament and criminal potential—may account for some of the variation in criminal behavior. But, unlike Moffitt (1993) or Gottfredson and Hirschi (1990), they place much less emphasis on the idea of stable differences in criminal propensity. Rather, they stress the importance of strong informal social controls based in family, schools, friends, and employment.

As teenagers move into young adulthood, two factors begin operating that shape adult patterns in crime. First, young adults potentially become subject to new forms of informal social control. These new forms of control include employment and marriage. Individuals who are lucky enough to find good jobs or enter good marriages or both become subjugated to new informal controls. According to Sampson and Laub, exposure to these adult forms of social control can redirect the criminal trajectories of individuals who were seriously delinquent as youths.

But the chances that a seriously delinquent youth will find a good job or marry a supportive spouse are less than ideal because of the second factor that begins operating in adulthood. Youths who are seriously delinquent accumulate disadvantages as they age. These cumulative disadvantages snowball, or pile up, over time, making it increasingly more difficult for the individual to exit from a life of crime. These disadvantages are generated most directly by official sanctions, such as arrest, conviction, and incarceration, which label and stigmatize individuals. Being officially labeled as a serious delinquent dramatically reduces future educational and employment opportunities (Sampson and Laub 1993). The individual runs the risk of becoming trapped in a cycle in which crime leads to failure in conventional activities, which in turn motivates further involvement in crime. Thus, Sampson and Laub hypothesize that there is an interaction between early criminal propensities and societal reactions that influences the adult life chances of delinquent youths. Continuity in criminal behavior is not solely the result of underlying criminal propensities; it also is caused by societal reactions.

There are two distinguishing features of Sampson and Laub's theoretical work. The first is their claim that social processes can cause even serious adult criminals to desist from crime. They argue that even for very committed offenders, change is possible and can occur relatively late in life. Developing adult social bonds to work and family can inhibit adult criminality and deviance (Sampson and Laub 1993; Laub, Nagin, and Sampson 1998). The second distinguishing feature is their use of the concept of "human agency" as an important determinant of trajectories in crime (Laub and Sampson 2003). *Agency* refers to our capacity to exercise control over our lives. We are agents when we intentionally make things happen by our own actions (Bandura 2001). The principle of human agency holds that "individuals construct their own life course through the choices and actions they take within the opportunities and constraints of history and social circumstances" (Elder 1998, p. 4).

Sampson and Laub argue that even serious adult criminals can exercise agency. They can make changes in their lives, most notably the change of desisting from crime. A change of this sort is most likely to occur when an offender confronts some sort of turning point that provides an opportunity for the individual to redirect his or her life in a prosocial direction. Such a turning point might be finding a supportive partner of the opposite sex, obtaining a satisfying job, joining the military, or simply moving to a different neighborhood. The important thing is that the turning point presents an opportunity for the offender to "knife off" a way of life conducive to crime—that is, to break away from old patterns of behavior and become involved in new, more structured activities. Gradually this change in the structure of the offender's routine activities, coupled with new informal social controls administered by partners or employers, leads the offender away from a life in crime and toward a life of prosocial conformity.

Sampson and Laub argue that change and desistance can happen to almost all offenders and at any point in the life course. The life course is, in their view, much more indeterminate and random than conceptualized in the more developmental theories proposed by Gottfredson and Hirschi and by Moffitt. They oppose the idea that there are only a small number of fixed trajectories that people follow in regard to crime and deviance. As they see it, change, growth, and development are ever-present features of the life course.

VIII. UNDERSTANDING THE CHANGE PROCESS: COGNITIVE TRANSFORMATION

Sampson and Laub's insights on human agency as an integral part of the desistance process suggests that, beyond life transformations—such as finding a good spouse or job—something occurs inside an offender's mind that prompts change; that is, somehow a cognitive transformation takes place. The construct of human agency seems too broad and amorphous to capture fully this internal process of rethinking one's life that appears to transpire. Other scholars, however, have begun to unravel what might be involved. Two contributions have proven most persuasive.

In his book *Making Good: How Ex-Convicts Reform and Rebuild Their Lives*, Shadd Maruna (2001) confronted this issue when studying and interviewing 65 offenders and ex-offenders in Liverpool, England. These offenders were the living embodiment of the social development and life-course theories described in this chapter. Facing dismal futures, their lives had been marked by "poverty, child abuse, detachment from the labor force, the stigma of social sanctions, low educational attainment, few legitimate opportunities in the community, serious addictions and dependencies, high-risk personality profiles, and, of course, long-term patterns of criminal behavior" (2001, p. 55). Maruna's conundrum was that despite virtually identical backgrounds, some interviewees were continuing in crime (as might be expected) but others were not. The risk factors that fostered and sustained their criminal careers thus could not explain this split in the sample. What, then, distinguished desisters from persisters? Maruna's answer was the narratives or "scripts" they used to describe their lives and futures.

According to Maruna, the persistent offenders thought that they were "doomed to deviance" (p. 74). Thus, they conceptualized their fate by embracing a "condemnation script" in which they felt that they were "condemned" to a life in crime by circumstances beyond their control (p. 73). Although not expressing any attraction to crime, they felt that they had no choice but to continue in their criminal careers. By contrast, those who desisted adopted the "rhetoric of redemption" (p. 85). They reinterpreted their lives through a "redemption script" in which previous criminal conduct was not seen as controlling their future. They denied that past bad acts reflected who they were "deep down"; their "real me" or "true self" was as a decent person (pp. 88–89). Previous difficult days in crime were now seen as making them stronger and as giving them a special calling to do good (e.g., to save juveniles now in trouble). They would no longer waste their lives but seek a higher purpose in helping others (p. 99). In short, the redemption script equipped offenders with a "coherent prosocial identity" that enabled them to resist criminal temptations and to "make good" in society (p. 7).

Peggy Giordano, Stephen Cernkovich, and Jennifer Rudolph (2002) were led to a similar conclusion. They interviewed a sample of 210 males and females, now in their late 20s, who they had first studied 13 years before as serious delinquents. Using both self-report and arrest data, they surprisingly did not find, as had Sampson and Laub (1993), that adult social bonds—job stability and attachment to spouse and children—were strong predictors of desistance. Rather, based on their qualitative interview data, Giordano and colleagues observed a more complex picture of desistance. For them, events such as acquiring a good job and marriage are best seen not as inevitable turning points away from crime but as potential "hooks for change" (p. 1000). These prosocial opportunities either can be latched onto or forfeited (e.g., acting badly can cause one to lose a job or a mate). Human agency, as Laub and Sampson (2003) say, is involved, but it is not a mysterious phenomenon. Rather, taking advantage of hooks for change involves a definable process that tends to involve four "types of intimately related cognitive transformations" (p. 1000).

First, the offender must possess a general openness to change. Second, the person must look favorably upon a specific hook for change and see embracing this hook (e.g., a new relationship) as being "fundamentally incompatible with continued deviation" (Giordano, Cernkovich, and Rudolph 2002, p. 1001). Third, the offender must begin to fashion a new conventional identity, what Giordano and colleagues call a "replacement self" (p. 1001). Fourth, the individual must come to see continued wayward conduct negatively. Thus, a "deviant behavior or lifestyle" is no longer viewed as "positive, viable, or even personally relevant" (p. 1002). In this way, the motivation to deviate vanishes, and the offender's cognitive transformation into a conventional member of society is completed."

Notably, most developmental and life-course theories have been built on data drawn from longitudinal empirical studies that have uncovered the risk factors that contribute to a criminal career. Giordano and colleagues' and Maruna's work suggests, however, that such theories might profit from qualitative projects that seek to illuminate how offenders experience their worlds, in terms of both staying in and finding a way out of their lives in crime.

IX. Conclusion

Developmental and life-course theories of offending have increasingly emerged over the past two decades. It now is clear that no understanding of crime, especially persistent involvement in antisocial conduct, can be achieved without a systematic empirical and theoretical demarcation of how individuals move into and out of crime at different points in their lives (Farrington 2005b; Thornberry and Krohn 2003). As seen in this essay, we are fortunate that scholars have furnished a diversity of important clues about the development of criminality over the life course. However, it is perhaps possible to distill a core insight that underlies the broader theoretical paradigm into which these varied contributions fall.

Thus, upon entering this world, children might be said to board a train. For most, they will be passengers on a train that will head out into life on tracks leading to a prosocial destination. Some of these youngsters, especially in adolescence, will detour off this track. But they will have the individual traits, social supports, and prosocial influences to jump back aboard the train. A smaller group of children, however, will not be so fortunate. They will board a train destined for life-course-persistent offending. Often starting while still in the womb, they will be exposed to an array of criminogenic risk factors. They will be burdened with individual traits, such as a lack of self-control, that will make negotiating their lives challenging. They will be raised by parents with poor child-management skills and be enmeshed in communities where criminal influences are ubiquitous and conventional opportunities are scarce. They may travel through the criminal justice system, which may well just deepen their criminality. As their journey proceeds, they will find it difficult to depart their train, which may well have gathered so much momentum as to make escape unthinkable. Eventually, their train will lose speed and they will step off. But by that time, they will have been carried so far into their lives that they will have experienced much harm and, it must be added, done much harm to others.

Of course, any metaphor has its limitations, but the image of a train heading out into a prosocial or antisocial direction in life's beginning stages has its utility. Theoretically, it tells us that the roots of crime potentially extend to childhood and place youngsters on trajectories in which one bad thing often leads to another. Understanding these pathways is the central challenge for developmental and life-course theories.

Perhaps more important, the train metaphor reminds us that the keys to saving children from a career in crime must extend to the front part of life (Farrington and Welsh 2007). As it turns out, most serious offenders receive very little, if any, intervention prior to being arrested and entering the justice system (Stouthamer-Loeber et al. 1995). It is still possible to intervene with correctional rehabilitation programs at this time; indeed, there is a growing knowledge of how to treat serious juvenile and adult offenders effectively (MacKenzie 2006; Andrews and Bonta 2010). But a developmental perspective provides a compelling rationale for not waiting until criminal careers have matured—for saving youngsters while the train is still in the station or has not ventured too far into life. As Farrington and Welsh (2007, p. 159) tell us, it is "never too early" to assist at-risk children with early intervention programs. Importantly, there is now an array of such programs that evaluation research has demonstrated have the capacity to derail antisocial development and to place youngsters on a pathway with a hopeful future.

REFERENCES

Andrews, D. A., and James Bonta. 2010. *The Psychology of Criminal Conduct,* 5th ed. New Providence, NJ: Anderson/LexisNexis.

Bandura, Albert. 2001. "Social Cognitive Theory: An Agentic Perspective." *Annual Review of Psychology* 52:1–26.

Bernburg, Jon Gunnar, and Marvin D. Krohn. 2003. "Labeling, Life Chances, and Adult Crime: The Direct and Indirect Effects of Official Intervention in Adolescence on Crime in Early Adulthood." *Criminology* 41:1287–318.

Bernburg, Jon Gunnar, Marvin D. Krohn, and Craig J. Rivera. 2006. "Official Labeling, Criminal Embeddedness, and Subsequent Delinquency: A Longitudinal Test of Labeling Theory." *Journal of Research in Crime and Delinquency* 43:67–88.

Braithwaite, John. 1989. *Crime, Shame and Reintegration.* Cambridge, UK: Cambridge University Press.

Catalano, Richard. F., and J. David Hawkins. 1996. "The Social Development Model: A Theory of Antisocial Behavior." In *Delinquency and Crime: Current Theories,* edited by J. David Hawkins. New York: Cambridge University Press.

Catalano, Richard F., Jisuk Park, Tracy W. Harachi, Kevin P. Haggerty, Robert D. Abbott, and J. David Hawkins. 2005. "Mediating Effects of Poverty, Gender, Individual Characteristics, and External Constraints on Antisocial Behavior: A Test of the Social Development Model and Implications for Developmental Life-Course Theory." In *Integrated Developmental and Life-Course Theories of Offending: Advances in Criminological Theory,* vol. 14, edited by David P. Farrington. New Brunswick, NJ: Transaction.

Chiricos, Ted., Kellie Barrick, William Bales, and Stephanie Bontrager. 2007. "The Labeling of Convicted Felons and Its Consequences for Recidivism." *Criminology* 45:547–81.

Cullen, Francis T., and Cheryl Lero Jonson. Forthcoming. "Labeling Theory and Correctional Rehabilitation: Beyond Unanticipated Consequences." In *Empirical Tests of Labeling Theory: Advances in Criminological Theory*, vol. 17, edited by David P. Farrington and Joseph Murray. New Brunswick, NJ: Transaction.

Elder, Glen H., Jr. 1998. "The Life Course as Developmental Theory." *Child Development* 69:1–12.

Farrington, David P. 1996. "The Explanation and Prevention of Youthful Offending." In *Delinquency and Crime: Current Theories*, edited by J. David Hawkins. New York: Cambridge University Press.

Farrington, David P. 2003. "Key Results from the First Forty Years of the Cambridge Study in Delinquent Development." In *Taking Stock of Delinquency: An Overview of Findings from Contemporary Longitudinal Studies*, edited by Terence P. Thornberry and Marvin D. Krohn. New York: Kluwer Academic/Plenum.

Farrington, David P. 2005a. "The Integrated Cognitive Antisocial Potential (ICAP) Theory." In *Integrated Developmental and Life-Course Theories of Offending: Advances in Criminological Theory*, vol. 14, edited by David P. Farrington. New Brunswick, NJ: Transaction.

Farrington, David P., ed. 2005b. *Integrated Developmental and Life-Course Theories of Offending: Advances in Criminological Theory*, vol. 14. New Brunswick, NJ: Transaction.

Farrington, David P., and Brandon C. Welsh. 2007. *Saving Children from a Life in Crime: Early Risk Factors and Effective Interventions*. New York: Oxford University Press.

Giordano, Peggy C., Stephen A. Cernkovich, and Jennifer L. Rudolph. 2002. "Gender, Crime, and Desistance: Toward a Theory of Cognitive Transformation." *American Journal of Sociology* 107:990–1064.

Gottfredson, Michael R., and Travis Hirschi. 1990. *A General Theory of Crime*. Stanford, CA: Stanford University Press.

Hagan, John. 1991. "Destiny and Drift: Subcultural Preferences, Status Attainment, and the Risks and Rewards of Youth." *American Sociological Review* 56:567–82.

Hagan, John. 1997. "Crime and Capitalization: Toward a Developmental Theory of Street Crime in America." In *Developmental Theories of Crime and Delinquency: Advances in Criminological Theory*, vol. 7, edited by Terence P. Thornberry. New Brunswick, NJ: Transaction.

Hawkins, J. David, Richard F. Catalano, Rick Kosterman, Robert D. Abbott, and Karl G. Hill. 1999. "Preventing Adolescent Health-Risk Behaviors by Strengthening Protection During Childhood." *Archives of Pediatrics and Adolescent Medicine* 153:226–34.

Hawkins, J. David, Rick Kosterman, Richard F. Catalano, Karl G. Hill, and Robert D. Abbott. 2005. "Promoting Positive Adult Functioning Through Social Development Intervention in Childhood: Long-Term Effects from the Seattle Social Development Project." *Archives of Pediatrics and Adolescent Medicine* 159:25–31.

Hawkins, J. David, Brian H. Smith, Karl G. Hill, Rick Kosterman, Richard F. Catalano, and Robert D. Abbott. 2003. "Understanding and Preventing Crime: Findings from the Seattle Development Project." In *Taking Stock of Delinquency: An Overview of Findings from Contemporary Longitudinal Studies*, edited by Terence P. Thornberry and Marvin D. Krohn. New York: Kluwer Academic/Plenum.

Hawkins, J. David, Brian H. Smith, Karl G. Hill, Rick Kosterman, Richard F. Catalano, and Robert D. Abbott. 2007. "Promoting Social Development and Preventing Health and Behavior Problems During the Early Elementary Grades: Results from the Seattle Social Development Project." *Victims and Offenders* 2:161–81.

Hawkins, J. David, Elizabeth Von Cleve, and Richard F. Catalano. 1991. "Reducing Early Childhood Aggression: Results from a Primary Prevention Program." *Journal of the American Academy of Child and Adolescent Psychiatry* 30:208–17.

Horney, Julie, D., Wayne Osgood, and Ineke Haen Marshall. 1995. "Criminal Careers in the Short-Term: Intra-Individual Variability in Crime and Its Relation to Local Life Circumstances." *American Sociological Review* 60:655–73.

Laub, John H., Daniel S. Nagin, and Robert J. Sampson. 1998. "Trajectories of Change in Criminal Offending: Good Marriages and the Desistance Process." *American Sociological Review* 63:225–38.

Laub, John H., and Robert J. Sampson. 2003. *Shared Beginnings, Divergent Lives: Delinquent Boys to Age 70.* Cambridge, MA: Harvard University Press.

Lemert, Edwin M. 1951. *Social Pathology: A Systematic Approach to the Theory of Sociopathic Behavior.* New York: McGraw-Hill.

MacKenzie, Doris Layton. 2006. *What Works in Corrections: Reducing the Criminal Activities of Offenders and Delinquents.* New York: Cambridge University Press.

Maruna, Shadd. 2001. *Making Good: How Ex-Convicts Reform and Rebuild Their Lives.* Washington, DC: American Psychological Association.

Moffitt, Terrie E. 1993. "Adolescence-Limited and Life-Course-Persistent Antisocial Behavior: A Developmental Taxonomy." *Psychological Review* 100:674–701.

Moffitt, Terrie E. 1997. "Adolescence-Limited and Life-Course-Persistent Offending: A Complementary Pair of Developmental Theories." In *Developmental Theories of Crime and Delinquency: Advances in Criminological Theory*, vol. 7, edited by Terence P. Thornberry. New Brunswick, NJ: Transaction.

Nagin, Daniel S., Francis T. Cullen, and Cheryl Lero Jonson. 2009. "Imprisonment and Reoffending." In *Crime and Justice: A Review of Research*, vol. 38, edited by Michael Tonry. Chicago: University of Chicago Press.

Nieuwbeerta, Paul, Daniel S. Nagin, and Arjan A. Blokland. 2009. "The Relationship between First Imprisonment and Criminal Career Development: A Matched Samples Comparison." *Journal of Quantitative Criminology* 25:227–57.

Pager, Devah. 2007. *Marked: Race, Crime, and Finding Work in an Era of Mass Incarceration.* Chicago: University of Chicago Press.

Palamara, Francs, Francis T. Cullen, and Joanne C. Gersten. 1986. "The Effect of Police and Mental Health Intervention on Juvenile Deviance: Specifying Contingencies in the Impact of Formal Reaction." *Journal of Health and Social Behavior* 27:90–105.

Sampson, Robert J. 1997. "The Embeddedness of Child and Adolescent Development: A Community-Level Perspective on Urban Violence." In *Violence and Childhood in the Inner City*, edited by Joan McCord. New York: Cambridge University Press.

Sampson, Robert J., and John H Laub. 1993. *Crime in the Making: Pathways and Turning Points Through Life.* Cambridge, MA: Harvard University Press.

Schur, Edwin M. 1973. *Radical Non-Intervention: Rethinking the Delinquency Problem.* Englewood Cliffs, NJ: Prentice-Hall.

Sherman, Lawrence W. 1993. "Defiance, Deterrence, and Irrelevance: A Theory of the Criminal Sanction." *Journal of Research in Crime and Delinquency* 30:445–73.

Spohn, Cassia, and David Holleran. 2002. "The Effect of Imprisonment on Recidivism Rates of Felony Offenders: A Focus on Drug Offenders." *Criminology* 40:329–57.

Stouthamer-Loeber, Magda, Rolf Loeber, Welmoet van Kammen, and Quanwu Zhang. 1995. "Uninterrupted Delinquent Careers: The Timing of Parental Help-Seeking and Juvenile Court Contact." *Studies on Crime and Crime Prevention* 4:236–51.

Thornberry, Terence P., and Marvin D. Krohn, eds. 2003. *Taking Stock of Delinquency: An Overview of Findings from Contemporary Longitudinal Studies*. New York: Kluwer Academic/Plenum.

Wilson, William Julius. 1987. *The Truly Disadvantaged: The Inner City, the Underclass, and Public Policy*. Chicago: University of Chicago Press.

CHAPTER 3

....

RISK AND PROTECTIVE FACTORS FOR OFFENDING

....

DAVID P. FARRINGTON, ROLF LOEBER, AND MARIA M. TTOFI

DURING the 1990s, there was a revolution in criminology, as the risk-factor prevention paradigm became influential (Farrington 2000). The basic idea of this paradigm is very simple: identify the key risk factors for offending and implement prevention methods designed to counteract them. This paradigm was imported into criminology from public health, where it had been used successfully for many years to tackle illnesses such as cancer and heart disease, by pioneers such as Hawkins and Catalano (1992). The risk-factor prevention paradigm links explanation and prevention; fundamental and applied research; and scholars, policymakers, and practitioners. Loeber and Farrington (1998) presented a detailed exposition of this paradigm as applied to serious and violent juvenile offenders.

A risk factor for offending is defined as a variable that predicts a high probability of later offending. Typically, risk factors are dichotomized, so that they are either present or absent. Because of the emphasis of this Handbook, this essay focuses on risk factors that could possibly be changed in intervention studies. Therefore, gender, race/ethnicity, criminal parents, and large family size are not reviewed here, although their links with offending may be explained by changeable factors. For example, Fagan et al. (2007) concluded that boys committed more crimes than girls because boys had higher risk factor scores and lower protective factor scores. In order to determine whether a risk factor is a predictor or possible cause of offending, the risk factor needs to be measured before the offending. Therefore, prospective longitudinal surveys are needed to investigate risk factors.

This paradigm typically also emphasizes protective factors, suggesting that intervention methods to enhance them should also be implemented. However, in the past the term *protective factor* has been used ambiguously. Some researchers have suggested that a protective factor is merely the opposite end of the scale to a risk factor (e.g., White, Moffitt, and Silva 1989). For example, if poor parental supervision is a risk factor, good parental supervision might be a protective factor. However, this seems to be using two terms for the same variable.

Other researchers have suggested that a protective factor interacts with a risk factor to minimize or buffer its effects (e.g., Rutter 1985). Typically, the impact of a protective factor is then studied in the presence of a risk factor. Loeber et al. (2008) suggested a consistent terminology. Following Sameroff et al. (1998), they defined *promotive* factors as variables that predict a low probability of offending and *protective* factors as variables that predict a low probability of offending among persons exposed to risk factors.

In order to disentangle risk and promotive effects, it is important to classify variables into at least three categories (the promotive end, the middle, and the risk end). Stouthamer-Loeber et al. (2002) did this in the Pittsburgh Youth Study (see later). They studied promotive effects by comparing the probability of delinquency in the promotive category versus the middle, and they studied risk effects by comparing the probability of delinquency in the risk category versus the middle. Some variables had promotive effects but not risk effects (e.g., attention deficit-hyperactivity disorder, or ADHD), while others had risk effects but not promotive effects (e.g., peer delinquency in the youngest cohort). There will be a special emphasis on promotive and protective factors in this essay because early crime prevention methods can be based on enhancing promotive and protective factors rather than reducing risk factors. Pollard, Hawkins, and Arthur (1999) argued that focusing on promotive and protective factors and on building resilience of children was a more positive approach, and more attractive to communities, than reducing risk factors, which emphasized deficits and problems.

Within one short essay, it is impossible to review everything that is known about risk, promotive, and protective factors (see also Lösel and Bender 2003; Loeber, Slot, and Stouthamer-Loeber 2006). This essay will review only the most important changeable factors: individual factors such as impulsivity and attainment; family influences such as child-rearing and disrupted families; and social influences such as socioeconomic status, peer, and neighborhood factors. The essay will focus especially on knowledge gained in major prospective longitudinal studies of offending, in which community samples of at least several hundred people are followed up from childhood into adolescence and adulthood, with repeated personal interviews as well as the collection of record data. The emphasis is on the prediction of offending in community samples, not on the prediction of persistence versus desistance in samples of offenders (see Loeber et al. 2007).

There will be a special focus on results obtained in two prospective longitudinal surveys: the Cambridge Study in Delinquent Development and the Pittsburgh Youth Study. The Cambridge Study is a prospective longitudinal survey of over 400

London males from age 8 to age 48 (see Farrington et al. 2006: Farrington, Coid, and West 2009). In the Pittsburgh Youth Study, over 1,500 boys from Pittsburgh public schools were followed up for 12 years (see Loeber et al. 1998, 2008). Initially, 500 were in first grade (age about 7), 500 were in fourth grade (age about 10), and 500 were in seventh grade (age about 13), of public schools in the city of Pittsburgh. See Farrington and Welsh (2007, chap. 2) for more information about these and other prospective longitudinal surveys of offending.

Our main conclusions are as follows:

- The most important factors that should be targeted in intervention research are impulsiveness, school achievement, child-rearing methods, young mothers, child abuse, parental conflict, disrupted families, poverty, delinquent peers, and deprived neighborhoods.
- However, little is known about whether these variables operate primarily as risk or promotive factors or both.
- Similarly, little is known about whether these variables act as causes or what are the important causal mechanisms linking these factors with outcomes such as offending.
- Similarly, little is known about what factors protect children from different types of risky backgrounds against becoming offenders.
- Risk assessment instruments should include promotive and protective factors.
- More research on promotive and protective factors is needed, using prospective longitudinal surveys of community samples with frequent face-to-face interviews.

The organization of this chapter is as follows. Section I reviews the individual factors of hyperactivity/impulsivity and intelligence/attainment. Section II assesses the family factors of child-rearing methods (supervision and discipline), young mothers and child abuse, and parental conflict and disrupted families. Section III reviews the social factors of socioeconomic status, peer influence, and neighborhood factors. Section IV draws conclusions. Throughout, there is a special attempt to review research on promotive and protective factors, as well as research on risk factors, although of course there are many more studies of risk factors.

I. Individual Factors

A. Hyperactivity and Impulsivity

Many studies show that hyperactivity, or ADHD, predicts later offending (see Pratt et al. 2002). In the Copenhagen Perinatal project, hyperactivity (restlessness and poor concentration) at ages 11–13 significantly predicted arrests for violence up to age 22, especially among boys whose mothers experienced delivery complications (Brennan, Mednick, and Mednick 1993). Similarly, in the Orebro longitudinal study in Sweden, hyperactivity at age 13 predicted police-recorded violence up to age 26. The highest rate of violence was among males with both motor restlessness and concentration difficulties (15 percent), compared to 3 percent of the remainder (Klinteberg et al. 1993). In the Seattle Social Development Project, hyperactivity and risk taking in adolescence predicted violence in young adulthood (Herrenkohl et al. 2000).

In the Cambridge Study, boys nominated by teachers as lacking in concentration or restless, those nominated by parents, peers, or teachers as the most daring or taking most risks, and those who were the most impulsive on psychomotor tests at ages 8–10 all tended to become offenders later in life. Daring, poor concentration, and restlessness all predicted both official convictions and self-reported delinquency, and daring was consistently one of the best independent predictors (Farrington 1992b). Interestingly, hyperactivity predicted juvenile offending independently of conduct problems (Farrington, Loeber, and Van Kammen 1990). Lynam (1996) proposed that boys with both hyperactivity and conduct disorder were most at risk of chronic offending and psychopathy, and Lynam (1998) presented evidence in favor of this hypothesis from the Pittsburgh Youth Study.

The most extensive research on different measures of impulsiveness was carried out in the Pittsburgh Youth Study by White et al. (1994). The measures that were most strongly related to self-reported delinquency at ages 10 and 13 were teacher-rated impulsiveness (e.g., acts without thinking), self-reported impulsiveness, self-reported undercontrol (e.g., unable to delay gratification), motor restlessness (from videotaped observations), and psychomotor impulsiveness (on the Trail Making Test). Generally, the verbal behavior rating tests produced stronger relationships with offending than the psychomotor performance tests, suggesting that cognitive impulsiveness (e.g., admitting impulsive behavior) was more relevant than behavioral impulsiveness (based on test performance). A systematic review by Jolliffe and Farrington (2009) showed that early measures of impulsiveness (especially daring and risk-taking) predicted later measures of violence.

The most extensive research on promotive factors predicting a low probability of violence and serious theft was carried out in the Pittsburgh Youth Study by Loeber et al. (2008, chap. 7). They studied predictors over four age ranges in the youngest cohort (7–9, 10–12, 13–16, and 17–19) and over three age ranges in the oldest cohort (13–16, 17–19, 20–25). Predictor variables were trichotomized into the risk end, the middle, and the promotive end. They found that, consistently, low ADHD was a promotive factor for low violence, but high ADHD was not a risk factor. These results replicated the earlier findings of Stouthamer-Loeber et al. (2002) in the same project for predicting persistent serious delinquency. Also, Lynam et al. (2000) showed that a good neighborhood was a protective factor against impulsivity, since impulsivity did not predict offending in good neighborhoods.

B. Intelligence and Attainment

Low intelligence (IQ) and low school achievement also predict offending. In the Philadelphia Biosocial project (Denno 1990), low verbal and performance IQ at ages 4 and 7, and low scores on the California Achievement test at ages 13–14 (vocabulary, comprehension, math, language, spelling), all predicted arrests for violence up to age 22. In Project Metropolitan in Copenhagen, low IQ at age 12 significantly predicted police-recorded violence between ages 15 and 22. The link between low IQ and violence was strongest among lower class boys (Hogh and Wolf 1983).

Low IQ measured in the first few years of life predicts later delinquency. In a prospective longitudinal survey of about 120 Stockholm males, low IQ measured at age 3 significantly predicted officially recorded offending up to age 30 (Stattin and Klackenberg-Larsson 1993). Frequent offenders (with four or more offenses) had an average IQ of 88 at age 3, whereas nonoffenders had an average IQ of 101. All of these results held up after controlling for social class. Similarly, low IQ at age 4 predicted arrests up to age 27 in the Perry preschool project (Schweinhart, Barnes, and Weikart 1993) and court delinquency up to age 17 in the Collaborative Perinatal Project (Lipsitt, Buka, and Lipsitt 1990).

In the Cambridge Study, twice as many of the boys scoring 90 or less on a non-verbal IQ test (Raven's Progressive Matrices) at ages 8–10 were convicted as juveniles as of the remainder (West and Farrington 1973). However, it was difficult to disentangle low IQ from low school achievement because the results were highly intercorrelated and both predicted delinquency. Low nonverbal IQ predicted juvenile self-reported delinquency to almost exactly the same degree as juvenile convictions (Farrington 1992b), suggesting that the link between low IQ and delinquency was not caused by the less intelligent boys having a greater probability of being caught. Also, low IQ and low school achievement predicted offending independently of other variables such as low family income and large family size (Farrington 1990).

The IQ tests are designed to predict later school success (Barchard 2005), and low IQ may lead to delinquency through the intervening factor of school failure. The association between school failure and delinquency has been demonstrated repeatedly in longitudinal surveys (Maguin and Loeber 1996). In the Pittsburgh Youth Study, Lynam, Moffitt, and Stouthamer-Loeber (1993) concluded that low verbal IQ led to school failure and subsequently to self-reported delinquency, but only for African-American boys. An alternative theory is that the link between low IQ and delinquency is mediated by disinhibition (impulsiveness, ADHD, low guilt, low empathy), and this was also tested in the Pittsburgh Youth Study (Koolhof et al. 2007). Felson and Staff (2006) argued that the link between low academic achievement and delinquency was mediated by low self-control.

High school achievement has often been identified as a promotive or protective factor. In the classic longitudinal survey of Werner and Smith (1982) in Kauai, they studied vulnerable children who had four or more risk factors by age 2 (including poverty, low maternal education, a disrupted family, perinatal stress, and low IQ) and compared those who did not develop any serious learning or behavioral problems by age 18 with those who had mental health problems or committed serious delinquencies. Among the most important protective factors were good reading, reasoning, and problem-solving skills at age 10 (Werner and Smith 1992, 2001). Also, high academic achievement was often a promotive factor in the Pittsburgh Youth Study analyses (Loeber et al. 2008).

In the Newcastle Thousand Family Study, Kolvin et al. (1990) followed up children who were deprived at age 5 (based on welfare dependence, overcrowded housing, poor physical care, poor mothering, parental illness, and disrupted families) and found that those who became nonoffenders by age 32 tended to have good reading, spelling, and arithmetic at ages 10–11. Also, Smith et al. (1994) in the Rochester Youth Development Study followed up children with five or more family risk factors (including family on welfare, young mother, child abuse, criminal family member, drug problems of family member, parental unemployment, and poor parental education) and found that those who did not commit serious delinquency tended to have high math and reading ability. Several other longitudinal surveys report that high IQ is a protective factor against offending for high-risk children (e.g. Kandel et al. 1988; White, Moffitt, and Silva 1989; Fergusson and Lynskey 1996; Stattin, Romelsjo, and Stenbacka 1997; Jaffee et al. 2007).

A plausible explanatory factor underlying the link between low IQ and delinquency is the ability to manipulate abstract concepts. Children who are poor at this tend to do badly on IQ tests and in school achievement, and they also tend to commit offenses, mainly because of their poor ability to foresee the consequences of their offending. Delinquents often do better on nonverbal performance IQ tests, such as object assembly and block design, than on verbal IQ tests (Moffitt 1993), suggesting that they find it easier to deal with concrete objects than with abstract concepts.

Impulsiveness, attention problems, low IQ, and low school achievement could all be linked to deficits in the executive functions of the brain, located in the frontal lobes. These executive functions include sustaining attention and concentration, abstract reasoning, concept formation, goal formulation, anticipation and planning, programming and initiation of purposive sequences of motor behavior, effective self-monitoring and self-awareness of behavior, and inhibition of inappropriate or impulsive behaviors (Moffitt and Henry 1991; Morgan and Lilienfeld 2000). Interestingly, in the Montreal longitudinal-experimental study, a measure of executive functioning based on tests at age 14 was the strongest neuropsychological discriminator between violent and nonviolent boys (Seguin et al. 1995). This relationship held independently of a measure of family adversity (based on parental age at first birth, parental education level, broken family, and low social class). In the Pittsburgh Youth Study, the life-course-persistent offenders had marked neurocognitive impairments (Raine et al. 2005).

II. Family Factors

A. Child-Rearing Methods

Many different types of child-rearing methods predict offending. The most important dimensions of child-rearing are supervision or monitoring of children, discipline or parental reinforcement, warmth or coldness of emotional relationships, and parental involvement with children. *Parental supervision* refers to the degree of monitoring by parents of the child's activities, and their degree of watchfulness or vigilance. Of all these child-rearing methods, poor parental supervision is usually the strongest and most replicable predictor of offending (Smith and Stern 1997). In the Cambridge Study, 61 percent of boys who were poorly supervised at age 8 were convicted up to age 50, compared with 36 percent of the remainder (Farrington, Coid, and West 2009).

Many studies show that parents who do not know where their children are when they are out, and parents who let their children roam the streets unsupervised from an early age, tend to have delinquent children. For example, in McCord's (1979) classic Cambridge-Somerville Study in Boston, poor parental supervision in childhood was the best predictor of both violent and property crimes up to age 45. Leschied et al. (2008) found that parental management that was coercive, inconsistent, or lacking in supervision during mid-childhood was a strong predictor of adult criminality, as were parental separation and marital status.

Parental discipline refers to how parents react to a child's behavior. It is clear that harsh or punitive discipline (involving physical punishment) predicts offending (Haapasalo and Pokela 1999). In their follow-up study of nearly 700 Nottingham children, John and Elizabeth Newson (1989) found that physical punishment at ages 7 and 11 predicted later convictions; 40 percent of offenders had been smacked or beaten at age 11, compared with 14 percent of nonoffenders. Erratic or inconsistent discipline also predicts delinquency. This can involve either erratic discipline by one parent, sometimes turning a blind eye to bad behavior and sometimes punishing it severely, or inconsistency between two parents, with one parent being tolerant or indulgent and the other being harshly punitive.

Cold, rejecting parents tend to have delinquent children, as McCord (1979) found in the Cambridge-Somerville Study. She also concluded that parental warmth could act as a protective factor against the effects of physical punishment (McCord 1997). Whereas 51 percent of boys with cold physically punishing mothers were convicted in her study, only 21 percent of boys with warm physically punishing mothers were convicted, similar to the 23 percent of boys with warm nonpunitive mothers who were convicted. The father's warmth was also a protective factor against the father's physical punishment.

The classic longitudinal study by Robins (1979) in St. Louis shows that poor parental supervision, harsh discipline, and a rejecting attitude all predict delinquency. Also, in the Seattle Social Development Project, poor family management (poor supervision, inconsistent rules, and harsh discipline) in adolescence predicted violence in young adulthood (Herrenkohl et al. 2000). Similar results were obtained in the Cambridge Study. Harsh or erratic parental discipline, cruel, passive or neglecting parental attitudes, and poor parental supervision, all measured at age 8, predicted later juvenile convictions and self-reported delinquency (West and Farrington 1973). Generally, the presence of any of these adverse family background features doubled the risk of a later juvenile conviction.

Derzon (2010) carried out a meta-analysis of family factors as predictors of criminal and violent behavior (as well as aggressive and problem behavior). The meta-analysis was based on longitudinal studies, but many predictions were over short time periods (less than four years in 55 percent of cases), many outcome variables were measured at relatively young ages (up to 15 in 40 percent of cases), and many studies were relatively small (less than 200 participants in 43 percent of cases). The strongest predictors of criminal or violent behavior were parental education (r = .30 for criminal behavior), parental supervision (r = .29 for violent behavior), child-rearing skills (r = .26 for criminal behavior), parental discord (r = .26 for criminal behavior), and family size (r = .24 for violent behavior). Notably weak predictors were young parents, broken homes, and low socioeconomic status.

In research on protective factors in the Rochester Youth Development Study, (Smith et al. 1994) found that high-risk children who were resilient (nondelinquent) tended to have good parental supervision and good attachment to parents. In similar research on deprived children who became nondelinquents in the Newcastle Thousand Family Study, Kolvin et al. (1990) reported that the nondelinquent children tended to receive better parental supervision. Also, in the Pittsburgh Youth Study (Loeber et al. 2008), parental supervision, physical punishment by the mother, and involvement of the boy in family activities tended to have promotive rather than risk effects.

Most explanations of the link between child-rearing methods and delinquency focus on attachment or social learning theories. Attachment theory was inspired by the work of Bowlby (1951), and suggests that children who are not emotionally attached to warm, loving, and law-abiding parents tend to become offenders. Social learning theories suggest that children's behavior depends on parental rewards and punishments and on the models of behavior that parents represent (Patterson 1995). Children will tend to become offenders if parents do not respond consistently and contingently to their antisocial behavior and if parents themselves behave in an antisocial manner.

B. Young Mothers and Child Abuse

At least in Western industrialized countries, early child-bearing, or teenage pregnancy, predicts many undesirable outcomes for the children, including low school attainment, antisocial school behavior, substance use, and early sexual intercourse. The children of teenage mothers are also more likely to become offenders. For example, Morash and Rucker (1989) analyzed results from four surveys in the US and UK (including the Cambridge Study) and found that teenage mothers were associated with low-income families, welfare support, and absent biological fathers; that they used poor child-rearing methods; and that their children were characterized by low school attainment and delinquency. However, the presence of the biological father mitigated many of these adverse factors and generally seemed to have a protective effect. Of course, it must be remembered that the age of the mother is highly correlated with the age of the father, and that having a young father may be just as important as having a young mother.

In the Cambridge Study, teenage mothers who went on to have large numbers of children were especially likely to have convicted children (Nagin, Pogarsky, and Farrington 1997). In the Newcastle Thousand-Family Study, mothers who married as teenagers (a factor strongly related to teenage childbearing) were twice as likely as others to have sons who became offenders by age 32 (Kolvin et al. 1990). Also, the deprived children who became offenders were less likely to have older mothers than the deprived children who did not become offenders (Kolvin et al. 1988a). In the Pittsburgh Youth Study (Loeber et al. 2008), an older mother consistently had a promotive effect, rather than a younger mother having a risk effect.

Several researchers have investigated factors that might mediate the link between young mothers and child delinquency. In the Dunedin Study in New Zealand, Jaffee et al. (2001) concluded that the link between teenage mothers and violent children was mediated by maternal characteristics (e.g., intelligence, criminality) and family factors (e.g., harsh discipline, family size, disrupted families). In the Rochester Youth Development Study, Pogarsky, Lizotte, and Thornberry (2003) found that the most important mediating factor was the number of parental transitions (frequent changes in care-givers). Much research suggests that frequent changes of parent figures predict offending by children (e.g., Thornberry et al. 1999; Krohn, Hall, and Lizotte 2009).

A pioneering longitudinal survey in Philadelphia by Maxfield and Widom (1996) found that children who were physically abused up to age 11 were significantly likely to become violent offenders in the next 15 years. Similarly, in the Cambridge-Somerville Study in Boston, McCord (1983) reported that about half of the abused or neglected boys were convicted for serious crimes, became alcoholics or mentally ill, or died before age 35. Child maltreatment before age 12 was one of the most consistent predictors of violence and serious theft in the Pittsburgh Youth Study (Loeber et al. 2008). In the Rochester Youth Development Study, child maltreatment under age 12 (physical, sexual, or emotional abuse or neglect) predicted later self-reported and official offending (Smith and Thornberry 1995). Furthermore, these results held up after controlling for gender, race, socioeconomic status, and family structure. Keiley et al. (2001) reported that maltreatment under age 5 was more damaging than maltreatment between ages 6 and 9. The extensive review by Malinosky-Rummell and Hansen (1993) confirms that being physically abused as a child predicts later violent and nonviolent offending.

Few longitudinal studies on the effects of child abuse by parents have tried to measure promotive or protective factors. However, Herrenkohl et al. (2005), in a longitudinal survey of Pennsylvania children, found that a strong commitment to school, and having parents and peers who disapproved of antisocial behavior, predicted low rates of violence and delinquency among abused children. In the Environmental Risk Study, Jaffee et al. (2007) concluded that maltreated children who did not become antisocial tended to have high intelligence and to live in low-crime neighborhoods with high social cohesion and informal social control.

Possible causal mechanisms linking childhood victimization and adolescent offending have been reviewed by Widom (1994). First, childhood victimization may have immediate but long-lasting consequences (e.g., shaking may cause brain injury). Second, childhood victimization may cause bodily changes (e.g., desensitization to pain) that encourage later aggression. Third, child abuse may lead to impulsive or dissociative coping styles that, in turn, lead to poor problem-solving skills or poor school performance. Fourth, victimization may cause changes in self-esteem or in social information-processing patterns that encourage later aggression. Fifth, child abuse may lead to changed family environments (e.g., being placed in foster care) that have harmful effects. Sixth, juvenile justice practices may label victims, isolate them from prosocial peers, and encourage them to associate with delinquent peers.

C. Parental Conflict and Disrupted Families

There is no doubt that parental conflict and interparental violence predict adolescent antisocial behavior, as the meta-analysis by Buehler et al. (1997) shows. In the Cambridge Study, parental conflict predicted delinquency (West and Farrington 1973). In the Christchurch Study in New Zealand, children who witnessed violence between their parents were more likely to commit both violent and property offenses according to their self-reports (Fergusson and Horwood 1998). Witnessing father-initiated violence was still predictive after controlling for other risk factors such as parental criminality, parental substance abuse, parental physical punishment, a young mother, and low family income.

Many studies show that broken homes or disrupted families predict delinquency. In the Newcastle Thousand-Family Study, Kolvin et al. (1988b) reported that marital disruption (divorce or separation) in a boy's first five years predicted his later convictions up to age 32. Also, the deprived children who became nondelinquents were less likely to have lost their fathers. Similarly, in the Dunedin Study in New Zealand, Henry et al. (1993) found that children who were exposed to parental discord and many changes of the primary care-giver tended to become antisocial and delinquent. In the National Longitudinal Survey of Adolescent Health, Demuth and Brown (2004) concluded that single-parent families predicted delinquency because of their lower levels of parental supervision, closeness, and involvement.

The importance of the cause of the broken home was demonstrated by Wadsworth (1979) in the UK National Survey of Health and Development. Boys from homes broken by divorce or separation had an increased likelihood of being convicted or officially cautioned up to age 21, in comparison with those from homes broken by death or from unbroken homes. Homes broken while the boy was under age 5 especially predicted offending, while homes broken while the boy was between ages 11 and 15 were not particularly criminogenic. Remarriage (which happened more often after divorce or separation than after death) was also associated with an increased risk of offending, suggesting a possible negative effect of stepparents. The meta-analysis by Wells and Rankin (1991) also indicates that broken homes are more strongly related to delinquency when they are caused by parental separation or divorce rather than by death.

Most studies of broken homes have focused on the loss of the father rather than the mother, simply because the loss of a father is much more common. McCord (1982) in Boston carried out an interesting study of the relationship between homes broken by loss of the natural father and later serious offending of the children. She found that the prevalence of offending was high for boys reared in broken homes without affectionate mothers (62 percent) and for those reared in united homes characterized by parental conflict (52 percent), irrespective of whether they had affectionate mothers. The prevalence of offending was low for those reared in united homes without conflict (26 percent) and—importantly—equally low for boys from broken homes with affectionate mothers (22 percent). These results suggest that it is not so much the broken home that is criminogenic as the parental conflict that often causes it, and that a loving mother might in some sense be able to compensate for the loss of a father.

In the Cambridge Study, both permanent and temporary separations from a biological parent before age 10 (usually from the father) predicted convictions and self-reported delinquency, providing that they were not caused by death or hospitalization (Farrington 1992b). However, homes broken at an early age (under age 5) were not unusually criminogenic (West and Farrington 1973). Separation before age 10 predicted both juvenile and adult convictions (Farrington 1992a), and it predicted adult convictions independently of other factors such as low family income or poor school attainment; 60 percent of boys who had been separated from a parent by their tenth birthday were convicted up to age 50, compared with 36 percent of the remainder (Farrington et al. 2009).

Explanations of the relationship between disrupted families and delinquency fall into three major classes. Trauma theories suggest that the loss of a parent has a damaging effect on a child, most commonly because of the effect on attachment to the parent. Life-course theories focus on separation as a sequence of stressful experiences, and on the effects of multiple stressors such as parental conflict, parental loss, reduced economic circumstances, changes in parent figures, and poor child-rearing methods. Selection theories argue that disrupted families produce delinquent children because of preexisting differences from other families in risk factors such as parental conflict, criminal or antisocial parents, low family income, or poor child-rearing methods.

Hypotheses derived from the three theories were tested in the Cambridge Study (Juby and Farrington 2001). While boys from broken homes (permanently disrupted families) were more delinquent than boys from intact homes, they were not more delinquent than boys from intact high-conflict families. Overall, the most important factor was the postdisruption trajectory. Boys who remained with their mother after the separation had the same delinquency rate as boys from intact low-conflict families. Boys who stayed with their father, with relatives, or with others (e.g., foster parents) had high delinquency rates. These living arrangements were more unstable, and other research shows that frequent changes of parent figures predict offending. It was concluded that the results favored life-course theories rather than trauma or selection theories.

III. Social Factors

A. Socioeconomic Status

Numerous indicators of socioeconomic status (SES) were measured in the Cambridge Study, both for the boy's family of origin and for the boy himself as an adult, including occupational prestige, family income, housing, and employment instability. Most of the measures of occupational prestige were not significantly related to offending. Low SES of the family when the boy was ages 8–10 significantly predicted his later self-reported but not his official delinquency. More consistently, low family income and poor housing predicted official and self-reported offending, juvenile and adult (Farrington 1992a, 1992b).

In the Pittsburgh Youth Study, Stouthamer-Loeber et al. (2002) reported that socioeconomic status at age 13 acted as a promotive factor in predicting persistent serious delinquency in the next six years in the oldest cohort. However, in more extensive later analyses by Loeber et al. (2008), socioeconomic status had both risk and promotive effects. In the Newcastle Thousand Family Study, high socioeconomic status was a protective factor against delinquency in the deprived children (Kolvin et al. 1990).

Several researchers have suggested that the link between a low SES family and antisocial behavior is mediated by family socialization practices. For example, Larzelere and Patterson (1990) in the Oregon Youth Study concluded that the effect of SES on delinquency was entirely mediated by parent management skills. In other words, low SES predicted delinquency because low SES families used poor child-rearing practices. In the Christchurch Health and Development Study, Fergusson, Swain-Campbell, and Horwood (2004) reported that living in a low SES family between birth and age 6 predicted self-reported and official delinquency between ages 15 and 21. However, this association disappeared after controlling for family factors (physical punishment, maternal care, and parental changes), conduct problems, truancy, and deviant peers, suggesting that these may have been mediating factors.

B. Peer Influence

Having delinquent friends is an important predictor of later offending. (Battin et al. 1998) showed that peer delinquency predicted self-reported violence in the Seattle Social Development Project. Delinquent acts tend to be committed in small groups (of two or three people, usually) rather than alone. Large gangs are comparatively unusual. In the Cambridge Study, the probability of committing offenses with others decreased steadily with age. Before age 17, boys tended to commit their crimes with other boys similar in age and living close by. After age 17, co-offending became less common (Reiss and Farrington 1991).

The major problem of interpretation is whether young people are more likely to commit offenses while they are in groups than while they are alone, or whether the high prevalence of co-offending merely reflects the fact that, whenever young people go out, they tend to go out in groups. Do peers tend to encourage and facilitate offending, or is it just that most kinds of activities out of the home (both delinquent and nondelinquent) tend to be committed in groups? Another possibility is that the commission of offenses encourages association with other delinquents, perhaps because "birds of a feather flock together" or because of the stigmatizing and isolating effects of court appearances and institutionalization. Thornberry et al. (1994) in the Rochester Youth Development Study concluded that there were reciprocal effects, with delinquent peers causing delinquency and delinquency causing association with delinquent peers.

The absence of delinquent friends, or the presence of prosocial friends, may act as a protective factor. In the Cambridge Study, the boys from criminogenic backgrounds (defined by low family income, large family size, convicted parent, low IQ, and poor child-rearing) who did not become delinquents tended to have few or no friends at age 8 (Farrington et al. 1988a, 1988b). In the Christchurch Health and Development Study in New Zealand, the children from adverse family backgrounds who did not show delinquency, substance use, or school problems tended to have low affiliations with delinquent peers (Fergusson and Lynskey 1996). In the Rochester Youth Development Study, the children from risky family backgrounds who did not commit serious delinquency tended to have peers with prosocial, conventional values. Finally, in a survey of Montreal adolescents, Fergusson et al. (2007) investigated which factors protected children with delinquent peers from themselves becoming delinquents, and concluded that low impulsivity was a major protective factor.

In the Pittsburgh Youth Study, the relationship between peer delinquency and a boy's offending was studied both between individuals (e.g., comparing peer delinquency and offending over all boys at a particular age and then aggregating these correlations over all ages) and within individuals (e.g., comparing peer delinquency and offending of a boy at all his ages and then aggregating these correlations over all boys). Peer delinquency was the strongest correlate of offending in between-individual correlations but did not predict offending within individuals (Farrington et al. 2002). In contrast, poor parental supervision, low parental reinforcement, and low involvement of the boy in family activities predicted offending both between and within individuals. It was concluded that these three family variables were the most likely to be causes, whereas having delinquent peers was most likely to be an indicator of the boy's offending.

It is clear that young people increase their offending after joining a gang. In the Seattle Social Development Project, Battin et al. (1998) found this, and also showed that gang membership predicted delinquency above and beyond having delinquent friends. In the Pittsburgh Youth Study, Gordon et al. (2004) reported not only a substantial increase in drug selling, drug use, violence, and property crime after a boy joined a gang but also that the frequency of offending decreased to pre-gang levels after a boy left a gang. Thornberry et al. (2003) in the Rochester Youth Development Study and Gatti et al. (2005) in the Montreal longitudinal-experimental study also found that young people offended more after joining a gang. Several of these studies contrasted the "selection" and "facilitation" hypotheses and concluded that future gang members were more delinquent to start with but became even more delinquent after joining a gang. Gang membership in adolescence is a risk factor for later violence (Herrenkohl et al. 2000), but this may be because both are measuring the same underlying construct.

C. Neighborhood Factors

Many studies show that living in an urban as opposed to a rural area predicts criminal behavior (Derzon 2010). In the US National Youth Survey, the prevalence of self-reported assault and robbery was considerably higher among urban youth (Elliott, Huizinga, and Menard 1989). Within urban areas, boys living in high-crime neighborhoods are more violent than those living in low-crime neighborhoods. In the Rochester Youth Development Study, living in a high-crime neighborhood significantly predicted self-reported violence (Thornberry, Huizinga, and Loeber 1995). Similarly, in the Pittsburgh Youth Study, living in a bad neighborhood (either as rated by the mother or based on census measures of poverty, unemployment, and female-headed households) significantly predicted official and reported violence (Farrington 1998) and homicide offending (Farrington et al. 2008).

Sampson, Raudenbush, and Earls (1997) studied community influences on violence in the Project on Human Development in Chicago Neighborhoods. The most important community predictors were concentrated economic disadvantage (as indexed by poverty, the proportion of female-headed families, and the proportion of African Americans), immigrant concentration (the proportions of Latinos or foreign-born persons), residential instability, and low levels of informal social control and social cohesion. They suggested that the collective efficacy of a neighborhood, or the willingness of residents to intervene to prevent antisocial behavior, might act as a protective factor against crime. Indeed, in the Enviromental Risk Study, Odgers et al. (2009) found that collective efficacy protected against antisocial behavior, but only in deprived neighborhoods. Sampson, Morenoff, and Raudenbush (2005) concluded that most of the variance between African Americans and Caucasians in violence could be explained by racial differences in exposure to risk factors, especially living in a bad neighborhood. Similar conclusions were drawn in the Pittsburgh Youth Study (Farrington, Loeber, and Stouthamer-Loeber 2003).

It is clear that offenders disproportionately live in inner-city areas characterized by physical deterioration, neighborhood disorganization, and high residential mobility (Shaw and McKay 1969). However, again, it is difficult to determine to what extent the areas themselves influence antisocial behavior and to what extent it is merely the case that antisocial people tend to live in deprived areas (e.g., because of their poverty or public housing allocation policies). Interestingly, both neighborhood researchers such as Gottfredson, McNeil, and Gottfredson (1991) and developmental researchers such as Rutter (1981) have argued that neighborhoods have only indirect effects on antisocial behavior through their effects on individuals and families. In the Chicago Youth Development Study, Tolan, Gorman-Smith, and Henry (2003) concluded that the relationship between community structural characteristics (concentrated poverty, racial heterogeneity, economic resources, violent crime rate) and individual violence was mediated by parenting practices, gang membership, and peer violence.

In the Pittsburgh Youth Study, Wikström and Loeber (2000) found an interesting interaction between types of people and types of areas. Six individual, family, peer, and school variables were trichotomized into risk, middle, or protective categories and added up. Boys with the highest risk scores tended to be delinquent irrespective of the type of area in which they were living. However, boys with high protective scores were more likely to be delinquent if they were living in disadvantaged public housing areas. Hence, the area risk was only important when other risks were not high, and boys in high-risk areas could be protected against delinquency by family, peer, and school factors. Generally, a bad neighborhood was a promotive factor in this survey (Loeber et al. 2008).

One key question is why crime rates of communities change over time, and to what extent this is a function of changes in the communities or in the individuals living in them. Answering this question requires longitudinal research in which both communities and individuals are followed up. The best way of establishing the impact of the environment is to follow people who move from one area to another. For example, in the Cambridge Study, moving out of London led to a significant decrease in convictions and self-reported offending (Osborn 1980). This decrease may have occurred because moving out led to a break-up of co-offending groups or because there were fewer opportunities for crime outside of London.

IV. DISCUSSION AND CONCLUSIONS

A great deal is known about risk factors for offending, and there are many systematic reviews on this topic (e.g., Derzon 2010; Jolliffe and Farrington 2009). In contrast, there are fewer studies of protective factors against offending in high-risk groups and very few studies of promotive factors. More research on protective and promotive factors is needed, using prospective longitudinal surveys of community samples with frequent face-to-face interviews.

Knowledge about promotive and protective factors would have important implications for crime prevention. In risk-focused prevention, efforts are made to reduce risk factors among high-risk children. This is likely to be particularly effective if the targeted factor really acts as a risk factor, but less effective if the targeted factor really acts as a promotive factor. For example, in predicting adult violence in the Pittsburgh Youth Study, it was found that 40 percent of boys who were high on peer delinquency became violent, compared with 11 percent of the middle group and 9 percent of those who were low (Loeber et al. 2008, p. 227). With this pattern of results, targeting boys who are high on peer delinquency and trying to reduce their association with delinquent peers (e.g., mentoring) is entirely logical.

Risk-focused prevention, however, seems less sensible with promotive factors. In the same prediction analysis in the Pittsburgh Youth Study, it was found that 21 percent of boys with low academic achievement became violent, compared with 21 percent of the middle group and 8 percent of those with high academic achievement. In this case, it would be desirable to target not only the high-risk boys (for example, in preschool intellectual enrichment programs; see Schweinhart et al. 2005) but also those in the middle group—or, in other words, three-fourths of all boys. In attempting to reduce violence, it would not be unreasonable to try to enhance the academic achievement of all boys. As mentioned, focusing on enhancing strengths is a more positive and attractive approach to crime prevention than targeting the high-risk boys and trying to reduce their deficits. However, research on risk and promotive factors is needed to establish which approach is likely to be the most effective with different targeted factors.

Similarly, more research on protective factors is needed to indicate which programs are likely to be most effective with which groups of high-risk children. Ideally, a systematic review would indicate which factors were consistently protective against different types of offending outcomes in different categories of high-risk children (e.g., those showing early antisocial behavior, those from deprived backgrounds, those with low academic achievement, etc.). Also, more research is needed on how therapist characteristics interact with risk and protective factors in interventions.

Research on promotive and protective factors also has important implications for risk-assessment instruments, which overwhelmingly focus on risk factors. Several researchers have raised the issue of whether assessment instruments might have higher predictive efficiency if promotive/protective factors were added to them. Loeber et al. (2008) investigated the ability of combined risk-promotive factor scores to predict later violence and serious theft. Rennie and Dolan (2010) found that protective factors in the Structured Assessment of Violence Risk in Youth (SAVRY) assessment instrument were important predictors of later desistance versus persistence of young offenders. More research is needed on the usefulness of promotive/protective factors in risk-assessment instruments.

While a great deal is known about risk factors for offending, less is known about causes, or about causal pathways or mechanisms. Ideally, intervention programs should target causes of offending. The best way of establishing causes is to carry out experimental or quasi-experimental analyses. For example, if an intervention experiment succeeded in reducing impulsivity and if there was a consequent reduction in offending, this would indicate that impulsivity might be a cause of offending (see Robins 1992). Similarly, if changes within individuals in parental supervision were reliably followed by changes within individuals in offending, this would indicate that parental supervision might be a cause of offending (see Farrington 1988).

Based on current knowledge, the following factors should be prime targets for intervention efforts: impulsiveness, school achievement, child-rearing methods, young mothers, child abuse, parental conflict and disrupted families, poverty, delinquent peers, and deprived neighborhoods. Efforts should be made to reduce impulsiveness and/or enhance self-control, to increase school achievement, to improve child-rearing, to encourage young people not to have children at an early age, to discourage child abuse, to increase parental harmony, to decrease poverty, to decrease association with antisocial peers and increase association with prosocial peers, and to improve bad neighborhoods. As other essays in this section of the Handbook demonstrate, many of these types of interventions have already been implemented and rigorously evaluated. Further experimental research informed by more knowledge about promotive and protective factors needs to be conducted.

REFERENCES

Barchard, Kimberly A. 2005. "Does Emotional Intelligence Assist in the Prediction of Academic Success?" *Educational and Psychological Measurement* 63:840–58.
Battin, Sara R., Karl G. Hill, Robert D. Abbott, Richard F. Catalano, and J. David Hawkins. 1998. "The Contribution of Gang Membership to Delinquency Beyond Delinquent Friends." *Criminology* 36:93–115.
Bowlby, John. 1951. *Maternal Care and Mental Health*. Geneva, Switzerland: World Health Organization.

Brennan, Patricia A., Birgitte R. Mednick, and Sarnoff A. Mednick. 1993. "Parental Psychopathology, Congenital Factors, and Violence." In *Mental Disorder and Crime*, edited by Sheilagh Hodgins. Newbury Park, CA: Sage.

Buehler, Cheryl, Christine Anthony, Ambika Krishnakumar, Gaye Stone, Jean Gerard, and Sharon Pemberton. 1997. "Interparental Conflict and Youth Problem Behaviors: A Meta-Analysis." *Journal of Child and Family Studies* 6:233–47.

Demuth, Stephen, and Susan L. Brown. 2004. "Family Structure, Family Processes, and Adolescent Delinquency: The Significance of Parental Absence Versus Parental Gender." *Journal of Research in Crime and Delinquency* 41:58–81.

Denno, Deborah W. 1990. *Biology and Violence: From Birth to Adulthood*. Cambridge, UK: Cambridge University Press.

Derzon, James H. 2010. "The Correspondence of Family Features with Problem, Aggressive, Criminal, and Violent Behavior: A Meta-Analysis." *Journal of Experimental Criminology* 6:263–92.

Elliott, Delbert S., David Huizinga, and Scott Menard. 1989. *Multiple Problem Youth: Delinquency, Substance Use, and Mental Health Problems*. New York: Springer-Verlag.

Fagan, Abigail A., M. Lee Van Horn, J. David Hawkins, and Michael W. Arthur. 2007. "Gender Similarities and Differences in the Association between Risk and Protective Factors and Self-Reported Serious Delinquency." *Prevention Science* 8:115–24.

Farrington, David P. 1988. "Studying Changes Within Individuals: The Causes of Offending." In *Studies of Psychosocial Risk: The Power of Longitudinal Data*, edited by Michael Rutter. New York: Cambridge University Press.

Farrington, David P. 1990. "Implications of Criminal Career Research for the Prevention of Offending." *Journal of Adolescence* 13:93–113.

Farrington, David P. 1992a. "Explaining the Beginning, Progress and Ending of Antisocial Behavior from Birth to Adulthood." In *Facts, Frameworks and Forecasts: Advances in Criminological Theory*, vol. 3, edited by Joan McCord. New Brunswick, NJ: Transaction.

Farrington, David P. 1992b. "Juvenile Delinquency." In *The School Years*, edited by John C. Coleman, 2nd ed. London: Routledge.

Farrington, David P. 1998. "Predictors, Causes, and Correlates of Youth Violence." In *Youth Violence*, edited by Michael Tonry and Mark H. Moore. Chicago: University of Chicago Press.

Farrington, David P. 2000. "Explaining and Preventing Crime: The Globalization of Knowledge—The American Society of Criminology 1999 Presidential Address." *Criminology* 38:1–24.

Farrington, David P., Jeremy W. Coid, Louise Harnett, Darrick Jolliffe, Nadine Soteriou, Richard Turner, and Donald J. West. 2006. *Criminal Careers up to Age 50 and Life Success up to Age 48: New Findings from the Cambridge Study in Delinquent Development*. London: Home Office (Research Study No. 299).

Farrington, David P., Jeremy W. Coid, and Donald J. West. 2009. "The Development of Offending from Age 8 to Age 50: Recent Results from the Cambridge Study in Delinquent Development." *Monatsschrift fur Kriminologie und Strafrechtsreform (Journal of Criminology and Penal Reform)* 92:160–73.

Farrington, David P., Bernard Gallagher, Lynda Morley, Raymond J. St. Ledger, and Donald J. West. 1988a. "Are There any Successful Men from Criminogenic Backgrounds?" *Psychiatry* 51:116–30.

Farrington, David P., Bernard Gallagher, Lynda Morley, Raymond J. St. Ledger, and Donald
    J. West. 1988b. A 24-Year Follow-up of Men from Vulnerable Backgrounds. In *The
    Abandonment of Delinquent Behavior: Promoting the Turnaround*, edited by R. L.
    Jenkins and W. K. Brown. New York: Praeger.
Farrington, David P., Rolf Loeber, Rebecca Stallings, and D. Lynn Homish. 2008. "Early
    Risk Factors for Homicide Offenders and Victims." *In Violent Offenders: Theory,
    Research, Public Policy and Practice*, edited by Matt Delisi and Peter J. Conis. Sudbury,
    MA: Jones and Bartlett.
Farrington, David P., Rolf Loeber, and Magda Stouthamer-Loeber. 2003. "How Can the
    Relationship between Race and Violence be Explained?" In *Violent Crime: Assessing
    Race and Ethnic Differences*, edited by Darnell F. Hawkins. Cambridge, UK:
    Cambridge University Press.
Farrington, David P., Rolf Loeber, and Welmoet Van Kammen. 1990. "Long-term Criminal
    Outcomes of Hyperactivity-Impulsivity-Attention Deficit and Conduct Problems in
    Childhood." In *Straight and Devious Pathways from Childhood to Adulthood*, edited by
    Lee N. Robins and Michael Rutter. Cambridge, UK: Cambridge University Press.
Farrington, David P., Rolf Loeber, Yanming Yin, and Stewart Anderson. 2002. "Are
    Within-Individual Causes of Delinquency the Same as Between-Individual Causes?"
    Criminal Behavior and Mental Health 12:53–68.
Farrington, David P., and Brandon C. Welsh. 2007. *Saving Children from a Life of Crime:
    Early Risk Factors and Effective Interventions*. New York: Oxford University Press.
Felson, Richard B., and Jeremy Staff. 2006. "Explaining the Academic Performance-
    Delinquency Relationship." *Criminology* 44:299–319.
Fergusson, David M., and L. John Horwood. 1998. "Exposure to Interparental Violence in
    Childhood and Psychosocial Adjustment in Young Adulthood." *Child Abuse and
    Neglect* 22:339–57.
Fergusson, David M., and Michael T. Lynskey. 1996. "Adolescent Resiliency to Family
    Adversity." *Journal of Child Psychology and Psychiatry* 37:281–92.
Fergusson, David M., Naomi Swain-Campbell, and L. John Horwood. 2004. "How does
    Childhood Economic Disadvantage Lead to Crime?" *Journal of Child Psychology and
    Psychiatry* 45:956–66.
Fergusson, David M., Frank Vitaro, Brigitte Wanner, and Mara Brendgen. 2007. "Protective
    and Compensatory Factors Mitigating the Influence of Deviant Friends on Delinquent
    Behaviors during Early Adolescence." *Journal of Adolescence* 30:33–50.
Gatti, Uberto, Richard E. Tremblay, Frank Vitaro, and Pierre McDuff. 2005. "Youth Gangs,
    Delinquency and Drug Use: A Test of the Selection, Facilitation and Enhancement
    Hypotheses." *Journal of Child Psychology and Psychiatry* 46:1178–90.
Gordon, Rachel A., Benjamin B. Lahey, Eriko Kawai, Rolf Loeber, Magda Stouthamer-
    Loeber, and David P. Farrington. 2004. "Antisocial Behavior and Youth Gang
    Membership: Selection and Socialization." *Criminology* 42:55–87.
Gottfredson, Denise C., Richard J. McNeil, and Gary D. Gottfredson. 1991. "Social Area
    Influences on Delinquency: A Multilevel Analysis." *Journal of Research in Crime and
    Delinquency* 28:197–226.
Haapasalo, Jaana, and Elina Pokela. 1999. "Child-Rearing and Child Abuse Antecedents of
    Criminality." *Aggression and Violent Behavior* 4:107–27.
Hawkins, J. David, and Richard F. Catalano. 1992. *Communities That Care: Action for Drug
    Abuse Prevention*. San Francisco, CA: Jossey-Bass.
Henry, Bill, Terrie Moffitt, Lee Robins, Felton Earls, and Phil Silva. 1993. "Early Family
    Predictors of Child and Adolescent Antisocial Behavior: Who Are the Mothers of
    Delinquents?" *Criminal Behavior and Mental Health* 3:97–118.

Herrenkohl, Todd I., Eugene Maguin, Karl G. Hill, J. David Hawkins, Robert D. Abbott, and Richard F. Catalano. 2000. "Developmental Risk Factors for Youth Violence." *Journal of Adolescent Health* 26:176–86.

Herrenkohl, Todd I., Emiko A. Tajima, Stephen D. Whitney, and Bu Huang. 2005. "Protection against Antisocial Behavior in Children Exposed to Physically Abusive Discipline." *Journal of Adolescent Health* 36:457–65.

Hogh, Erik, and Preben Wolf. 1983. "Violent Crime in a Birth Cohort: Copenhagen 1953–1977." In *Prospective Studies of Crime and Delinquency*, edited by Katherine T. Van Dusen and Sarnoff A. Mednick. Boston: Kluwer-Nijhoff.

Jaffee, Sara, Avshalom Caspi, Terrie E. Moffitt, Jay Belsky, and Phil A. Silva. 2001. "Why Are Children Born to Teen Mothers at Risk for Adverse Outcomes in Young Adulthood? Results from a 20-year Longitudinal Study." *Development and Psychopathology* 13:377–97.

Jaffee, Sara R., Avshalom Caspi, Terrie E. Moffitt, Monica Polo-Tomas, and Alan Taylor. 2007. "Individual, Family, and Neighborhood Factors Distinguish Resilient from Non-Resilient Maltreated Children: A Cumulative Stressors Model." *Child Abuse and Neglect* 31:231–53.

Jolliffe, Darrick, and David P. Farrington. 2009. "A Systematic Review of the Relationship between Childhood Impulsiveness and Later Violence." In *Personality, Personality Disorder and Violence*, edited by Mary McMurran and Richard Howard. Chichester, UK: Wiley.

Juby, Heather, and David P. Farrington. 2001. "Disentangling the Link between Disrupted Families and Delinquency." *British Journal of Criminology* 41:22–40.

Kandel, Elizabeth, Sarnoff A. Mednick, Lis Kirkegaard-Sorensen, Barry Hutchings, Joachim Knop, Raben Rosenberg, and Fini Schulsinger. 1988. "IQ as a Protective Factor for Subjects at High Risk for Antisocial Behavior." *Journal of Consulting and Clinical Psychology* 56:224–26.

Keiley, Margaret K., Tasha R. Howe, Kenneth A. Dodge, John E. Bates and Gregory S. Pettit. 2001. "The Timing of Child Physical Maltreatment: A Cross-Domain Growth Analysis of Impact on Adolescent Externalizing and Internalizing Problems." *Development and Psychopathology* 13:891–912.

Klinteberg, Britt af, Tommy Andersson, David Magnusson, and Hakan Stattin. 1993. "Hyperactive Behavior in Childhood as Related to Subsequent Alcohol Problems and Violent Offending: A Longitudinal Study of Male Subjects." *Personality and Individual Differences* 15:381–88.

Kolvin, Israel, Frederick J. W. Miller, Mary Fleeting, and Philip A. Kolvin. 1988a. "Risk/Protective Factors for Offending with Particular Reference to Deprivation." In *Studies of Psychosocial Risk: The Power of Longitudinal Data*, edited by Michael Rutter. Cambridge, UK: Cambridge University Press.

Kolvin, Israel, Frederick J. W. Miller, Mary Fleeting, and Philip A. Kolvin. 1988b. "Social and Parenting Factors Affecting Criminal-Offence Rates: Findings from the Newcastle Thousand Family Study (1947–1980)." *British Journal of Psychiatry* 152:80–90.

Kolvin, Israel, Frederick J. W. Miller, David M. Scott, S. R. M. Gatzanis, and Mary Fleeting. 1990. *Continuities of Deprivation? The Newcastle 1000 Family Study*. Aldershot, UK: Avebury.

Koolhof, Roos, Rolf Loeber, Evelyn H. Wei, Dustin Pardini, and Annematt C. D' Escury. 2007. "Inhibition Deficits of Serious Delinquent Boys of Low Intelligence." *Criminal Behaviour and Mental Health* 17:274–92.

Krohn, Marvin D., Gina P. Hall, and Alan J. Lizotte. 2009. "Family Transitions and Later Delinquency and Drug Use." *Journal of Youth and Adolescence* 38:466–80.

Larzelere, Robert E., and Gerald R. Patterson. 1990. "Parental Management: Mediator
    of the Effect of Socioeconomic Status on Early Delinquency." *Criminology*
    28:301–24.
Leschied, Alan, Debbie Chiodo, Elizabeth Nowicki, and Susan Rodger. 2008. "Childhood
    Predictors of Adult Criminality: A Meta-Analysis Drawn from the Prospective
    Longitudinal Literature." *Canadian Journal of Criminology and Criminal Justice*
    50:435–67.
Lipsitt, Paul D., Stephen L. Buka, and Lewis P. Lipsitt. 1990. "Early Intelligence Scores and
    Subsequent Delinquency: A Prospective Study." *American Journal of Family Therapy*
    18:197–208.
Loeber, Rolf, and David P. Farrington. 1998, eds. *Serious and Violent Juvenile Offenders:
    Risk Factors and Successful Interventions*. Thousand Oaks, CA: Sage.
Loeber, Rolf, David P. Farrington, Magda Stouthamer-Loeber, and Welmoet Van Kammen.
    1998. *Antisocial Behavior and Mental Health Problems: Explanatory Factors in Child-
    hood and Adolescence*. Mahwah, NJ: Lawrence Erlbaum.
Loeber, Rolf, David P. Farrington, Magda Stouthamer-Loeber, and Helene R. White. 2008.
    Violence and Serious Theft: Development and Prediction from Childhood to Adulthood.
    New York: Routledge.
Loeber, Rolf, Dustin A. Pardini, Magda Stouthamer-Loeber, and Adrian Raine. 2007. "Do
    Cognitive, Physiological, and Psychosocial Risk and Promotive Factors Predict
    Desistance from Delinquency in Males?" *Development and Psychopathology* 19:867–87.
Loeber, Rolf, Wim Slot, and Magda Stouthamer-Loeber. 2006. "A Three-Dimensional
    Cumulative Developmental Model of Serious Delinquency." In *The Explanation of
    Crime: Contexts and Mechanisms*, edited by Per-Olof H. Wikström and Robert J.
    Sampson. Cambridge, UK: Cambridge University Press.
Lösel, Friedrich, and Doris Bender. 2003. "Protective Factors and Resilience." In *Early
    Prevention of Adult Antisocial Behaviour*, edited by David P. Farrington and Jeremy W.
    Coid. Cambridge, UK: Cambridge University Press.
Lynam, Donald R. 1996. "Early Identification of Chronic Offenders: Who is the Fledgling
    Psychopath? *Psychological Bulletin* 120:209–34.
Lynam, Donald R. 1998. "Early Identification of the Fledgling Psychopath: Locating the
    Psychopathic Child in the Current Nomenclature." *Journal of Abnormal Psychology*
    107:566–75.
Lynam, Donald R., Avshalom Caspi, Terrie E. Moffitt, Per-Olof H. Wikström, Rolf Loeber,
    and Scott Novak. 2000. "The Interaction between Impulsivity and Neighborhood
    Context on Offending: The Effects of Impulsivity are Stronger in Poorer Neighbor-
    hoods." *Journal of Abnormal Psychology* 109:563–74.
Lynam, Donald R, Terrie E. Moffitt, and Magda Stouthamer-Loeber. 1993. "Explaining the
    Relation between IQ and Delinquency: Class, Race, Test Motivation, School Failure or
    Self-Control?" *Journal of Abnormal Psychology* 102:187–96.
McCord, Joan. 1979. "Some Child-Rearing Antecedents of Criminal Behavior in Adult
    Men." *Journal of Personality and Social Psychology* 37:1477–86.
McCord, Joan. 1982. "A Longitudinal View of the Relationship between Paternal Absence
    and Crime." In *Abnormal Offenders, Delinquency, and the Criminal Justice System*,
    edited by John Gunn and David P. Farrington. Chichester, UK: Wiley.
McCord, Joan. 1983. "A Forty Year Perspective on Effects of Child Abuse and Neglect."
    Child Abuse and Neglect 7:265–70.
McCord, Joan. 1997. "On Discipline." *Psychological Inquiry* 8:215–17.
Maguin, Eugene, and Rolf Loeber. 1996. "Academic Performance and Delinquency." In *Crime
    and Justice*, vol. 20, edited by Michael Tonry. Chicago: University of Chicago Press.

Malinosky-Rummell, Robin, and David J. Hansen. 1993. "Long-Term Consequences of Childhood Physical Abuse." *Psychological Bulletin* 114:68–79.

Maxfield, Michael G., and Cathy S. Widom. 1996. "The Cycle of Violence Revisited 6 Years Later." *Archives of Pediatrics and Adolescent Medicine* 150:390–95.

Moffitt, Terrie E. 1993. "Adolescence-Limited and Life-Course-Persistent Antisocial Behavior: A Developmental Taxonomy." *Psychological Review* 100:674–701.

Moffitt, Terrie E., and Bill Henry. 1991. "Neuropsychological Studies of Juvenile Delinquency and Juvenile Violence." In *Neuropsychology of Aggression*, edited by J. S. Milner. Boston: Kluwer.

Morash, Merry, and Lila Rucker. 1989. "An Exploratory Study of the Connection of Mother's Age at Childbearing to her Children's Delinquency in Four Data Sets." *Crime and Delinquency* 35:45–93.

Morgan, Alex B., and Scott O. Lilienfeld. 2000. "A Meta-Analytic Review of the Relation Between Antisocial Behavior and Neuropsychological Measures of Executive Function." *Clinical Psychology Review* 20:113–36.

Nagin, Daniel S., Greg Pogarsky, and David P. Farrington. 1997. "Adolescent Mothers and the Criminal Behavior of their Children." *Law and Society Review* 31:137–62.

Newson, John, and Elizabeth Newson. 1989. *The Extent of Parental Physical Punishment in the UK*. London: Approach.

Odgers, Candice L., Terrie E. Moffitt, Laura M. Tach, Robert J. Sampson, Alan Taylor, and Charlotte L. Matthews. 2009. "The Protective Effects of Neighborhood Collective Efficacy on British Children Growing up in the Deprivation: A Developmental Analysis." *Developmental Psychology* 45:942–57.

Osborn, Stephen G. 1980. "Moving Home, Leaving London, and Delinquent Trends." *British Journal of Criminology* 20:54–61.

Patterson, Gerald R. 1995. "Coercion as a Basis for Early Age of Onset for Arrest." In *Coercion and Punishment in Long-Term Perspectives*, edited by Joan McCord. Cambridge, UK: Cambridge University Press.

Pogarsky, Greg, Alan J. Lizotte, and Terence P. Thornberry. 2003. "The Delinquency of Children Born to Young Mothers: Results from the Rochester Youth Development Study." *Criminology* 41:1249–86.

Pollard, John A., J. David Hawkins, and Michael W. Arthur. 1999. "Risk and Protection: Are Both Necesssary to Understand Diverse Behavioral Outcomes in Adolescence?" *Social Work Research* 23:145–58.

Pratt, Travis C., Francis T. Cullen, Kristie R. Blevins, Leah Daigle, and James D. Unnever. 2002. "The Relationship of Attention Deficit Hyperactivity Disorder to Crime and Delinquency: A Meta-Analysis." *International Journal of Police Science and Management* 4:344–60.

Raine, Adrian, Terrie M. Moffitt, Avshalom Caspi, Rolf Loeber, Magda Stouthamer-Loeber, and Don Lynam. 2005. "Neurocognitive Impairments in Boys on the Life-course Persistent Antisocial Path." *Journal of Abnormal Psychology* 114:38–49.

Reiss, Albert J., and David P. Farrington. 1991. "Advancing Knowledge about Co-offending: Results from a Prospective Longitudinal Survey of London Males." *Journal of Criminal Law and Criminology* 82:360–95.

Rennie, Charlotte E., and Mairead C. Dolan. 2010. "The Significance of Protective Factors in the Assessment of Risk." *Criminal Behavior and Mental Health* 20:8–22.

Robins, Lee N. 1979. "Sturdy Childhood Predictors of Adult Outcomes: Replications from Longitudinal Studies." In *Stress and Mental Disorder*, edited by J. E. Barrett, R. M. Rose, and Gerald L. Klerman. New York: Raven Press.

Robins, Lee N. 1992. "The Role of Prevention Experiments in Discovering Causes of Children's Antisocial Behavior." In *Preventing Antisocial Behavior: Interventions from*

Birth through Adolescence, edited by Joan McCord and Richard E. Tremblay. New York: Guilford.

Rutter, Michael. 1981. "The City and the Child." *American Journal of Orthopsychiatry* 51:610–25.

Rutter, Michael. 1985. "Resilience in the Face of Adversity: Protective Factors and Resistance to Psychiatric Disorder." *British Journal of Psychiatry* 147:598–611.

Sameroff, Arnold J., W. Todd Bartko, Clare Baldwin, and Ronald Seifer. 1998. "Family and Social Influences on the Development of Child Competence." In *Families, Risk, and Competence*, edited by M. Lewis and C. Feiring. Mahwah, NJ: Lawrence Erlbaum.

Sampson, Robert J., Jeffrey D. Morenoff, and Stephen W. Raudenbush. 2005. "Social Anatomy of Racial and Ethnic Disparities in Violence." *American Journal of Public Health* 95:224–32.

Sampson, Robert J., Stephen W. Raudenbush, and Felton Earls. 1997. "Neighborhoods and Violent Crime: A Multilevel Study of Collective Efficacy." *Science* 277:918–24.

Schweinhart, Lawrence, J., Helen V. Barnes, and David P. Weikart. 1993. *Significant Benefits: The High-Scope Perry Preschool Study Through age 27*. Ypsilanti, MI: High Scope Press.

Schweinhart, Lawrence J., Jeanne Montie, Xiang Zongping, W. Steven Barnett, Clive R. Belfield, and Milagros Nores. 2005. *Lifetime Effects: The High/Scope Perry Preschool Study Through Age 40*. Ypsilanti, MI: High Scope Press.

Seguin, Jean, Robert O. Pihl, Philip W. Harden, Richard E. Tremblay, and Bernice Boulerice. 1995. "Cognitive and Neuropsychological Characteristics of Physically Aggressive Boys." *Journal of Abnormal Psychology* 104:614–24.

Shaw, Clifford R., and Henry D. McKay. 1969. *Juvenile Delinquency and Urban Areas*, rev. ed. Chicago: University of Chicago Press.

Smith, Carolyn A., Alan J. Lizotte, Terence P. Thornberry, and Marvin D. Krohn. 1994. "Resilient Youth: Identifying Factors that Prevent High-Risk Youth from Engaging in Delinquency and Drug Use." In *Delinquency and Disrepute in the Life Course*, edited by John L. Hagan. Greenwich, CT: JAI Press.

Smith, Carolyn A., and Susan B. Stern 1997. "Delinquency and Antisocial Behavior: A Review of Family Processes and Intervention Research." *Social Service Review* 71:382–420.

Smith, Carolyn A., and Terence P. Thornberry. 1995. "The Relationship Between Childhood Maltreatment and Adolescent Involvement in Delinquency." *Criminology* 33:451–81.

Stattin, Hakan, and Ingrid Klackenberg-Larsson. 1993. "Early Language and Intelligence Development and their Relationship to Future Criminal Behavior." *Journal of Abnormal Psychology* 102:369–78.

Stattin, Hakan, Anders Romelsjo, and Marlene Stenbacka. 1997. "Personal Resources as Modifiers of the Risk for Future Criminality: An Analysis of Protective Factors in Relation to 18-Year-old Boys." *British Journal of Criminology* 37:198–223.

Stouthamer-Loeber, Magda, Rolf Loeber, Evelyn Wei, David P. Farrington, and Per-Olof H. Wikström. 2002. "Risk and Promotive Effects in the Explanation of Persistent Serious Delinquency in Boys." *Journal of Consulting and Clinical Psychology* 70:111–23.

Thornberry, Terence P., David Huizinga, and Rolf Loeber. 1995. "The Prevention of Serious Delinquency and Violence: Implications from the Program of Research on the Causes and Correlates of Delinquency." In *Sourcebook on Serious, Violent and Chronic Juvenile Offenders*, edited by James C. Howell, Barry Krisberg, J. David Hawkins, and John J. Wilson. Thousand Oaks, CA: Sage.

Thornberry, Terence P., Marvin D. Krohn, Alan J. Lizotte, Carolyn A. Smith, and Kimberly Tobin. 2003. *Gangs and Delinquency in Developmental Perspective*. New York: Cambridge University Press.

Thornberry, Terence P., Alan J. Lizotte, Marvin D. Krohn, Margaret Farnworth, and Soon J. Jang. 1994. "Delinquent Peers, Beliefs and Delinquent Behavior: A Longitudinal Test of Interactional Theory." *Criminology* 32:47–83.

Thornberry, Terence P., Carolyn A. Smith, Craig Rivera, David Huizinga, and Magda Stouthamer-Loeber. 1999. *Family Disruption and Delinquency*. Washington, DC: Office of Juvenile Justice and Delinquency Prevention.

Tolan, Patrick H., Deborah Gorman-Smith, and David B. Henry. 2003. "The Developmental Ecology of Urban Males' Youth Violence." *Developmental Psychology* 39:274–91.

Wadsworth, Michael. 1979. *Roots of Delinquency*. London: Martin Robertson.

Wells, L. Edward, and Joseph H. Rankin. 1991. "Families and Delinquency: A Meta-Analysis of the Impact of Broken Homes." *Social Problems* 38:71–93.

Werner, Emmy E., and Ruth S. Smith. 1982. *Vulnerable but Invincible: A Longitudinal Study of Resilient Children and Youth*. New York: McGraw-Hill.

Werner, Emmy E., and Ruth S. Smith. 1992. *Overcoming the Odds: High Risk Children from Birth to Adulthood*. Ithaca, NY: Cornell University Press.

Werner, Emmy E., and Ruth S. Smith. 2001. *Journeys from Childhood to Midlife*. Ithaca, NY: Cornell University Press.

West, Donald J., and David P. Farrington. 1973. *Who Becomes Delinquent?* London: Heinemann.

White, Jennifer L., Terrie E. Moffitt, Avshalom Caspi, Dawn J. Bartusch, Douglas J. Needles, and Magda Stouthamer-Loeber. 1994. "Measuring Impulsivity and Examining its Relationship to Delinquency." *Journal of Abnormal Psychology* 103:192–205.

White, Jennifer L., Terrie E. Moffitt, and Phil A. Silva. 1989. "A Prospective Replication of the Protective Effects of IQ in Subjects at High Risk for Delinquency." *Journal of Consulting and Clinical Psychology* 37:719–24.

Widom, Cathy S. 1994. "Childhood Victimization and Adolescent Problem Behaviors." In *Adolescent Problem Behaviors*, edited by Robert D. Ketterlinus and Michael E. Lamb. Hillsdale, NJ: Lawrence Erlbaum.

Wikstrom, Per-Olof H., and Rolf Loeber 2000. "Do Disadvantaged Neighborhoods Cause Well-adjusted Children to Become Adolescent Delinquents? A Study of Male Juvenile Serious Offending, Individual Risk and Protective Factors, and Neighborhood Context." *Criminology* 38:1109 –42.

CHAPTER 4

PREVENTING CRIME THROUGH INTERVENTION IN THE PRESCHOOL YEARS

HOLLY S. SCHINDLER AND HIROKAZU YOSHIKAWA

PROBLEM behaviors in early childhood, middle childhood, and adolescence account for considerable costs to the child welfare, juvenile justice, and criminal justice systems, and enormous additional costs in terms of suffering for individuals, families, and other affected parties. One setting for prevention that has shown potential for successfully reducing early behavioral problems, later antisocial behavior, and societal costs related to criminal activity is preschool education. It is widely recognized that children begin learning and acquiring emotional and behavioral capacities long before they enter school and that development proceeds at an astonishingly rapid rate during the first years of life (National Research Council and Institute of Medicine 2000; Knudsen et al. 2006). Research has also documented how complex behavioral and cognitive capacities are built on earlier foundational skills and are strongly shaped by the quality of interactions with caregivers and environments (Knudsen et al. 2006). Some research points to the potency of risk factors as early as the first years of life in predicting later delinquency and crime (e.g., West and Farrington 1977; Caspi et al. 1995; Farrington and Welsh 2007). The life-course-persistent trajectory subtype of antisocial behavior is characterized by first emergence of antisocial behavior as early as in early childhood (Moffitt 1993), and accounts for much of the early-onset, severe delinquency pattern in adolescence (Loeber and Hale 1997). This suggests a developmental rationale for crime prevention in the preschool years.

The timing is also right for preschool interventions to be given serious attention worldwide. The majority of today's generation of children in Organisation for Economic Co-operation and Development (OECD) countries attend some form of child care, with approximately 80 percent of 3–6-year-olds in more affluent countries in some form of early childhood education and care (United Nations Children's Fund 2008). Enrollment is also increasing rapidly in many middle- and low-income countries. Thus, preschool education provides an unprecedented opportunity for implementing prevention programs with an increasingly large portion of the world's early childhood population.

The aim of this essay is to lay out the pathways through which preschool interventions have the potential to prevent crime and to review the evaluation literature of such preschool interventions. While the ultimate goal of this essay is to shed light on how certain kinds of preschool programs may reduce crime later in life, prevention during early childhood can also be viewed more broadly as reducing levels of early behavior problems and improving social-emotional development. We review evidence concerning both short-term and long-term (when available) prevention impacts. We define preschool as center-based care during ages 3–5, but we also include interventions that span longer age ranges and review preschool interventions that incorporate other services, such as parent support services. We focus on programs that represent new directions in the field of prevention research in early childhood. We exclude interventions for children with diagnosed disorders or disabilities, and therefore concentrate on universal and selected prevention programs, not indicated ones. In addition, we emphasize evaluations with randomized controlled designs for the most part, although we include references to those with strong quasi- or nonexperimental designs. Finally, we note the size of effects of programs reviewed, with small indicated by effect sizes between 0.15 and 0.40; medium between 0.40 and 0.70; and large greater than 0.70 (Hill et al. 2008).

From this review, we draw several observations and conclusions:

- Preschool interventions have the potential to target several child and parent characteristics that are risk or protective processes related to behavior problems and crime. Targeting these processes early may be more effective than trying to target them at later points in children's development.
- Indeed, preschool interventions specifically designed to address relevant child processes, such as cognitive skills, behavior problems, or executive functioning, have shown promising results. Similarly, a number of two-generation preschool programs targeting parenting skills or offering comprehensive family services have successfully reduced rates of behavior problems and later crime.
- Understudied, yet important, issues potentially related to preschool programs and behavior problems include teacher education, child-to-staff ratio, and group size, as well as issues of replication, implementation at scale, and policy supports.

- While there have been many advances in preschool interventions and their links to reduced behavior problems, aggression, and crime later in life, for innovative ideas, preschool educators may turn to other fields that have implemented successful interventions. For example, one possibility is for preschools to extend their definition of family support by more seriously considering the intersection of poverty reduction, parent human capital, and crime prevention.

Our essay is laid out as follows. In section I, we review relevant pathways, with a focus on child- and parent-based pathways, through which preschool has the potential to prevent crime and behavior problems. In section II, we review interventions targeting both child-based and parent-based pathways. In section III, we discuss several cross-cutting issues, including structural characteristics, cost-effectiveness, and issues of quality and implementation at scale, that are relevant across multiple intervention strategies in prevention science in preschool. In section IV, we end with a discussion of the findings and suggestions for future directions.

I. PATHWAYS OF PREVENTION

Two pathways through which preschool may prevent behavior problems will be reviewed here: child-based pathways and parent-based pathways.

A. Child-Based Pathways

Preschool is viewed as a way to prepare children for kindergarten or primary school, with often a predominant emphasis placed on academic and cognitive skills as important components for school readiness. While enhanced cognitive skills are one pathway through which children's behavioral problems may be reduced, directly targeting early aggressive behavioral problems themselves may be beneficial as well. In recent years, the importance of early support of emotional and social development for school readiness has received added attention (Raver 2002). As a result, there have been an increased number of preschool interventions focused specifically on improving children's social and emotional skills and reducing problem behaviors. Another pathway through which behavioral problems may be prevented is enhanced executive functioning (e.g., working memory; cognitive flexibility; inhibitory control) (Blair and Diamond 2008). One of the historically debated early childhood questions is whether curricula should be child directed or teacher directed, and how much time should be centered on play (Singer, Golinkoff, and Hirsh-Pasek 2006). Some research suggests that teacher-directed instruction results in better short-term cognitive gains but worse social-emotional outcomes (Schweinhart, Weikart, and Larner 1986), although the evidence is mixed. More promising results have been found for curricula that promote self-regulation through child-constructed activities that include teacher input (Barnett et al. 2008), particularly for promoting children's executive functioning.

Given that relationships with caregivers are another important contributor to children's development, other programs have focused specifically on teacher training. This is especially important in light of the fact that handling children's problem behaviors is cited as one of the biggest training needs by teachers and administrators (Buscemi, Thomas, and Deluca 1996; Yoshikawa and Zigler 2000). We would expect that teacher training would be especially effective in preventing behavior problems and later crime when that training is focused specifically on how to improve children's cognitive functioning, behavioral skills, or executive functioning.

B. Parent-Based Pathways

Developmental theory suggests that home and child care /early education environments exert independent influences on children's behavior (McCall 1981). Such theories have informed the development and implementation of parent-focused services that have often been added to early childhood education. Two parent-based risks for children's later crime that could potentially be targeted by adding parent services to preschool programs are: (1) parenting skills, particularly harshness, severe or inconsistent discipline, and responsiveness; and (2) parent human capital.

Parent-focused components of early childhood education (ECE) can differ on dimensions of content and setting of service delivery, as well as intensity. One common content focus of added parent services is parent education or structured parent-child activities to facilitate responsive interactions and reduce harsh parenting. Such increases in parental responsiveness—represented by contingent responses to child verbal, gestural, and affective communication—have been linked to improved social behavior (Bradley et al. 2001; Landry, Smith, and Swank 2006).

Another content focus of added parent services includes referrals and case management for health or mental health services. Behavioral services such as behavioral screening, therapy, and mental health services can improve socio-emotional development by addressing early and severe behavior problems or by preventing the incidence of such problems (Raver et al. 2009). Long-term effects of some early childhood programs suggest, for example, that the life-course-persistent trajectory of antisocial behavior may be amenable to prevention during early childhood (Moffitt 1993; Yoshikawa, Schindler, and Caronongan 2009). Some of these services affect subgroups of children who qualify (e.g., for early intervention services), while others are more preventive in nature (e.g., immunizations, nutritional services). They vary a great deal across preschool programs.

Programs to increase parent human capital have been less frequently tied to preschool programs; however, there might be opportunities to incorporate such services in future intervention models. The rationale here is the association among parental education, income and employment, and child antisocial behavior, as well as juvenile crime (Yoshikawa, Wiesner, and Lowe 2006). This is discussed in greater detail at the end of the essay.

II. INTERVENTIONS

We organize this section of the review according to two categories of interventions: those targeting child-based pathways and those targeting parent-based pathways. We note in describing particular intervention models a variety of additional characteristics including the setting of the intervention, the level of targeting, and short- versus long-term effects.

A continuing limitation in this literature is the small number of longitudinal studies that follow children into late childhood and adolescence. We therefore have an incomplete picture of which approaches to intervention in the first years of life are most likely to have long-term impacts on behavioral development.

A. Interventions Targeting Child-Based Pathways

A fundamental question in the relationship between early childhood intervention and crime is whether preschool by itself, as most commonly implemented, impacts early antisocial behavior. In a recent meta-analysis of US preschool programs, the largest effect sizes were found for cognitive outcomes; however, preschool programs were also found to have a small positive effect on social skills (early antisocial behavior was not analyzed separately) (Camilli et al. 2010). In a long-term quasi-experimental study of 128 children in Sweden, early childhood education was found to have positive effects on both children's cognitive and social-emotional development into middle childhood (Anderson 2008).

On the other hand, there is some recent nonexperimental evidence that lengthier exposure in the first five years to center-based child care and preschool education may increase behavior problems at the transition to primary schooling in the United States (National Institute of Child Health and Human Development [NICHD Early Child Care Research Network 2003]; Loeb et al. 2007; Magnuson, Ruhm, and Waldfogel 2007). Although these results should be viewed with caution, they appear to be robust to controls for center quality (NICHD Early Child Care Research Network 2003). Thus, specific curricula focused on socio-emotional development and behavior problems may be necessary to achieve impacts on these outcomes in the context of preschool and other center-based programs.

Several preschool classroom curricula have recently been developed and evaluated that target some combination of teacher behavior-management skills, child problem behaviors and social skills, and/or executive functioning skills in young children. All of these provide more intensive supports for these outcomes than typical preschool programs in the United States. The Promoting Alternative Thinking Strategies (PATHS) program aims to strengthen teachers' abilities to create a positive classroom climate, effectively manage children's behavior problems, and increase emotion awareness and self-regulation. This program, in a randomized trial, produced higher levels of emotion knowledge and overall social competence, as rated by both parents and teachers, in a posttest assessment. It also reduced social withdrawal, as rated by teachers (Domitrovich, Cortes, and Greenberg 2007). The Head Start Research Based, Developmentally Informed (REDI) program, which combined the preschool PATHS curriculum with a language and literacy enhancement curriculum, also produced positive impacts on multiple aspects of behavior problems and social skills (specifically, fewer aggressive behaviors; higher social competence; higher social problem solving skills), with effects seen for both teacher and parent-reported scales, with effect sizes ranging from 0.21 to 0.35 (Bierman, Domitrovich, et al. 2008). Two out of five measures of executive function, measuring task orientation and flexible attention, were also significantly improved by the intervention, with effect sizes ranging from 0.20 to 0.30 (Bierman, Nix, et al. 2008). Task orientation partially mediated the effects of REDI on aggressive behaviors.

One curriculum specifically targets multiple domains of self-regulation and executive function in young children. The Tools of the Mind curriculum focuses on increasing deliberate memory, focused attention, regulation of emotions, and cognitions, as well as academic skills such as symbolic thought, literacy, and numeracy. An initial randomized trial testing this program found small to moderate positive effects on reduced behavior problems (Barnett et al. 2006). Similar results were found in two more recent evaluations (Diamond et al. 2007; Barnett et al. 2008). These two evaluations found that children receiving the Tools of the Mind curriculum scored better on inhibitory control and regulation of impulsive and aggressive behaviors than children in control classrooms.

The Chicago School Readiness Project also aims to reduce children's problem behaviors. This program is composed of four main components: (1) teacher training in behavior-management strategies, using the Incredible Years model (Webster-Stratton, Reid, and Hammond 2001); (2) coaching teachers once a week in implementing strategies in the classroom; (3) stress reduction workshops for teachers; and (4) mental health services for selected high-risk children. In an initial cluster-randomized trial of this program implemented in 35 Head Start classrooms, preschoolers receiving the intervention exhibited significantly fewer internalizing and externalizing problem behaviors than children in the control condition by spring of the intervention's academic year (Raver et al. 2009).

These specialized preschool curricula, when successful, provide intensive training and, in some cases, intensive ongoing professional development. For example, both the Head Start REDI program and the Chicago School Readiness Project provided weekly coaching in the classroom as follow-up to intensive training sessions. The Incredible Years program provided teachers with six monthly one-day group training sessions, for a total of 36 hours of training (Webster-Stratton, Reid, and Hammond 2001).

B. Interventions Targeting Parent-Based Pathways

Several program models exist for combining attention to family and child risk and protective processes. The rationale for such "two-generation" programs include the ability to address multiple domains of risk or protective processes at once. Such an approach may have cumulative effects in protecting children against later disorder (Yoshikawa 1994; Gassman-Pines and Yoshikawa 2006). Some target particular issues, such as behavior problems; others are aimed more broadly at children and families in poverty.

For example, a number of programs combine classroom with parent curricula on the same topic, aiming to improve both teachers' and parents' behavior-management skills. The Incredible Years curriculum focuses on positive classroom climate, positive reinforcement of social competence, and effective classroom behavior management. However, this program also includes a parent training component. Tested in a randomized trial in Head Start programs, the program produced reductions in conduct problems as reported by parents, teachers, and peers. In addition, the parenting component reduced the frequency of harsh and critical parenting behaviors, such as spanking, hitting and yelling, and increased positive parenting behaviors such as emotional engagement, at the end of the intervention year (Webster-Stratton, Reid, and Hammond 2001). At a one year follow-up, however, only the effects on positive dimensions persisted; the effect on conduct problems at home was marginal.

The Chicago Parent-Child Centers (CPC) is another example of a program that combines a preschool program with intensive efforts to involve parents. This school-based intervention provides families in selected low-income neighborhoods with a range of education and health services and requires parents to participate in the program for at least a half-day per week in order for their children to be eligible. Long-term outcomes of CPC program participants have been documented through the Chicago Longitudinal Study (Reynolds 2000). Among the long-term benefits demonstrated by participants through age 24 are lower rates of grade retention, special education placement, felony arrests, convictions, and incarcerations (Reynolds et al. 2001, 2007). However, because program participation or eligibility was not randomly assigned, researchers estimate program effects by comparing program participants to similar (in terms of poverty status and Title I eligibility) children in non-CPC schools. As such, results from this evaluation may overestimate the effect of participating in the CPC.

The Perry Preschool program differs from the Chicago Parent-Child Centers in that teachers conducted home visits with each family once a week in the afternoons, after providing a morning preschool program. Thus, despite its influence on many other kinds of preschool programs, the mix of services that the program provided was relatively unique in the early childhood education field. As is very well-known, the Perry Preschool program had impacts into adulthood (e.g., age 27 and age 40 follow-ups), including a higher likelihood of employment, a lower likelihood of being arrested, and higher graduation rates for the treatment group as compared to the control group. In addition, the treatment group was less likely to report having received social services in the past 10 years (Schweinhart 2006).

Other programs with relatively long-term effects on antisocial behavior include the Yale Child Welfare program (Seitz, Rosenbaum, and Apfel 1985), the Syracuse Family Development Program (Lally, Mangione, and Honig 1988), and the Houston Parent-Child Development Center (Johnson and Walker 1987). These programs served low-income families beginning at birth or age 1 for periods ranging from two to five years. Services included home visits, parenting education, and daycare services for children. In addition to targeting low-income families, these programs targeted services based on other risk factors such as low levels of maternal education (Syracuse), or served a particular community, such as Mexican-American families in the case of the Houston program. Program effects were tracked up to 10 years after program participation and demonstrate reductions in antisocial behavior and juvenile arrests.

Head Start has included in its theory of change a range of family and child risk and protective processes, many of which are associated with later antisocial behavior and crime. Among the relevant processes targeted are parent involvement, parenting skills, parent and child mental health, child health and nutrition, and parent educational and vocational progress (Zigler and Styfco 1993). This program thus combines emphases on parenting support, parent involvement, social services, and mental health services for parents as well as children, with an educational child care or preschool experience. However, the parent-focused component is quite a bit less intensive than those that were implemented in the Perry Preschool, Chicago Parent-Child Centers, and other two-generation programs with long-term effects on antisocial behavior. Notably, many state pre-kindergarten programs are lacking in dimensions focused on parents, such as parent involvement, mental health and social services, and even health and nutrition components (Gilliam and Zigler 2001; Gilliam and Leiter 2003).

Data from the National Head Start Impact Study, a large experiment evaluating the effects of Head Start on children and families, show a mixed positive and null pattern of findings. Among the benefits documented for the treatment group after one year of Head Start were less hyperactivity, fewer behavior problems, and better parenting (e.g., lower rates of corporal punishment); however, at the end of first grade, fewer differences were found between the treatment and control group (US Department of Health and Human Services 2010). No impact of Head Start was found for either of two age groups on aggressive or withdrawn behaviors or social skills (Administration for Children and Families 2005; US Department of Health and Human Services 2010). The effect sizes (generally small) were calculated based on an intent-to-treat analysis. In the 2005 report, substantial proportions of the evaluation sample were "crossovers"; over 15 percent of the control group received Head Start for part of the preschool year, and over 10 percent of the experimental group did not, for example. After adjusting for these crossovers using Bloom's (1984) method, Ludwig and Phillips (2007) found that the positive child impacts were in the moderate range. A number of retrospective studies, using family fixed-effects or regression discontinuity designs, have also linked Head Start program attendance to positive outcomes for participants. Such outcomes include reductions in grade repetition, and criminal activity (Currie and Thomas 1995; Garces, Thomas, and Currie 2002; Ludwig and Miller 2007). One reason that these studies may have found longer-term impacts of Head Start while the National Head Start Impact Study did not is that in the National Head Start Impact Study, the child-care experiences of the control group were very similar to those in the Head Start group. For example, approximately half of the control group enrolled in center-based care (National Forum on Early Childhood Policy and Programs 2010).

III. CROSS-CUTTING ISSUES

Cross-cutting issues that are relevant across preschool interventions include structural characteristics, cost-effectiveness, and issues of quality and implementation at scale.

A. Structural Characteristics

Most evaluations of structural characteristics, such as teacher education, child-to-staff ratio, and group size, have been examined only for cognitive and academic skills, with a few exceptions. For teacher education, mixed results have been found. While having teachers with BA degrees does seem to have a positive effect for infants and toddlers, the evidence is not as conclusive for preschool classrooms. Some state pre-k programs, such as Oklahoma's, attribute some of their success to requiring teachers to have a BA degree. However, Early et al. (2006) found few consistent links between teachers' education, major, or credentials and academic outcomes in state-funded preschools. The exceptions were that teachers' education was related to gains in children's math skills and the Child Development Associate (CDA) credential was linked to gains in basic skills. This study did not examine behavioral outcomes, but it is reasonable to hypothesize that teacher education, particularly when it is focused on early childhood development or education, may provide teachers with the tools to better manage children and prevent behavior problems. Several of the successful demonstration projects that have had positive effects on behavior and have reduced adult crime, such as Perry Preschool, Abecedarian, and CPC, required teachers to have BA degrees.

Generally, high-quality preschool programs are also expected to have low child-to-teacher ratios and small group sizes (e.g., National Association for the Education of Young Children [NAEYC] accreditation guidelines). Such characteristics are thought to increase the amount of individual time a teacher can spend with each child and afford teachers the opportunity to interact in warm, responsive environments (NICHD Early Child Care Research Network 2004). In this way, it is reasonable to believe that low ratios and small group sizes may be important in preventing behavior problems for preschoolers. One randomized study that compared two levels of ratios (5.4:1 vs. 7.4:1) did find that children assigned to the classrooms with the lower ratio had improved cooperative behavior and exhibited less hostility and conflict (Ruoppp et al. 1979). However, other nonexperimental studies have not been able to replicate these findings. Mashburn et al. (2008) and Howes et al. (2008) studied state-funded preschool programs and found that neither group size nor staff-to-child ratio predicted children's social competence or problem behaviors.

It is reasonable to hypothesize that each of these structural characteristics may be especially important for behavioral outcomes; however, most of the research has neglected to examine this set of outcomes as they relate to structural characteristics. As research relating preschool interventions to behavior problems and other social-emotional outcomes continues to expand, it will be important to take a closer look at the influence of teachers' credentials, child-to-teacher ratios, and group sizes.

B. Cost-Effectiveness

Very few benefit-cost evaluations of early childhood programs have been conducted. This is due to several reasons, most notably the fact that some of the most expensive societal outcomes of early childhood intervention cannot be measured until adolescence (e.g., juvenile crime). The programs that have been documented and evaluated are also those with the longest-term follow-up, and include some of the most successful programs to date (e.g., Perry Preschool and Chicago Parent-Child Centers). These programs have shown benefit-cost ratios ranging from $4 to $14 (Aos et al. 2004; Karoly, Kilburn, and Cannon 2005; Barnett and Masse 2007; Cunha and Heckman 2007; Duncan, Ludwig, and Magnuson 2007; Temple and Reynolds 2007; Heckman et al. 2009). Among the center-based programs, the degree of parent involvement encouraged in the programs varied considerably, from weekly home visits by teachers in the Perry program to relatively intensive parent involvement efforts in the Chicago program. Of these two studies, only the Chicago Parent-Child Centers can be defined as a program at scale.

Programs utilizing one or more of these models, if implemented at scale in the United States, are likely to have benefit-cost ratios smaller than the $4 to $14 range described above. This is because the overall rate of attendance in center-based care and education has increased dramatically in recent decades. In other nations, with much lower rates of preschool attendance, there may be opportunities to achieve long-term effects on crime with intensive preschool intervention. It is likely that some aspects of the original programs are no longer relevant for families in poverty in the United States, owing to the large increases in maternal employment hours since the time of their original implementation. As such, program components would likely have to be supplemented were they to be implemented in the present day (e.g., half-day program as in the Perry Preschool could be supplemented with wraparound child care; Duncan et al. 2007). However, again aspects of these original programs with long-term effects on antisocial behavior and crime may be relevant and worth testing in other national and economic contexts.

C. Replication, Implementation at Scale, and Policy Supports

The implementation of quality early childhood programs at scale continues to be a vexing problem in the field. Few evaluations have linked implementation quality to the magnitude of impacts on children's socio-emotional outcomes. Some research on quality in at-scale programs has found that Head Start classrooms in general are in the "good" (though not "excellent") range of quality on the Early Childhood Environment Ratings Scale (Zill et al. 2003; Administration for Children and Families 2005). Research on the impacts of thresholds of quality in this and other scales measuring early childhood care and education environments is currently lacking, and the limited research that does exist finds that current quality scales do not predict behavior problems (Howes et al. 2008; Mashburn et al. 2008).

Systems of training and technical assistance are aimed at defining what constitutes membership in a program model, regularly monitoring quality, and intervening with assistance when quality is low. The characteristics of these systems that are most effective in promoting and increasing program-level quality have been understudied in the field of early childhood programs (Yoshikawa, Rosman, and Hsueh 2002). Advances in implementation science, however, hold much promise in identifying at-scale approaches to improving the ability of preschool systems to address antisocial behavior.

Policy supports for quality local implementation include areas of policy that have rarely been evaluated—for example, spending decisions at the program or government levels, union contracts, funding approaches, and auspices of Early Childhood Care and Education (ECCE; Greenberg et al. 2003). One recent study (Currie and Neidell 2007) is an exception. The authors examined associations between Head Start center-level budget information and child outcomes, using matched data from Head Start administrative records and the National Longitudinal Survey of Youth—Child Supplement. The authors found that children who attended Head Start centers with higher proportions of their budgets spent on child-specific categories (education, health, nutrition, and disability) had fewer behavior problems than their counterparts in Head Start centers with lower proportions of such spending. In this study, Currie and Neidell also examined the relationship between county-level Head Start spending and child outcomes, and found that in counties with higher levels of per-capita Head Start spending, children who attended the program had more positive outcomes.

Accountability supports for quality in early childhood programs in the United States have included efforts such as the National Reporting System in Head Start. Most recently, a national panel has been convened to reexamine domains of development and measures assessing them that may be useful in providing a framework for assessing child outcomes in that program (Van Hemel and Snow 2008). As more countries in the majority world begin adopting early childhood programs, accountability supports will be especially important to have in place. However, in the majority world, quality will first need to be defined based on context as opposed to adopting quality measures and accountability supports from OECD countries (Britto et al. 2010).

IV. Discussion and Conclusions

In sum, prevention science in the first years of life has made substantial advances in recent decades. New evidence has emerged on the promise of preschool programs in the prevention of behavioral problems and later crime. For example, social skills curricula that target both teachers and parents for change in preschool settings have proved successful in reducing aggressive behaviors. Particular domains of socio-emotional development have begun to be distinguished as targets of intervention (e.g., social cognitions underlying aggressive behavior problems vs. dimensions of executive function vs. emotion identification). Two-generation programs for families in poverty, targeting both parenting processes and child verbal ability, have shown promise in reducing childhood externalizing behaviors and even in some cases juvenile and adult crime.

Despite these advances in the prevention literature, many challenges remain. These include studies that address cross-cutting issues such as implementation quality and the improvement and maintenance of program quality at scale. Professional development approaches have only begun to be systematically evaluated, with emerging evidence pointing to the potential of on-site, frequent coaching, and assistance in bringing about positive impacts of prevention program curricula. In the rest of this section, we discuss future directions for the field.

A. Overlooked Populations and Global Contexts

Among overlooked populations, few interventions have been successful for higher risk families among families in poverty. These families are exposed to what has been termed "toxic stress"—that is, specific severe forms of stress and risk that have the potential to undermine children's long-term behavioral development (National Scientific Council on the Developing Child 2007). For the population of highest risk families in poverty in the United States, general models of early childhood care and education and family support (as well as two-generation models) appear insufficient (Administration for Children and Families 2007; Alderson et al. 2008). Programs that are targeted not only in their populations but also in their content, addressing particular sources of toxic stress, are urgently needed. Only a very few models exist for such programs, one targeting families in foster care (Fisher and Kim 2007). This holds true in the majority world as well, where sources of toxic stress are more prevalent and basic issues of child survival and health must be integrated with early stimulation and education.

The bulk of the evaluations in prevention science in early childhood have been implemented in North America. However, there have been promising tests of family-focused interventions outside North America. These include innovative interventions such as an attachment-based intervention (Juffer, Bakermans-Kranenburg, and van IJzendoorn 2005) and a home-based educational intervention (Tuijl and Leseman 2004), both conducted in the Netherlands, with effects such as lower rates of disorganized attachment and improved language and math skills. These should be tested in combination with center-based preschool programs to observe whether "two-generation" programs in non-US contexts have more powerful effects on antisocial behavior and its risks than center- or family-based programs alone. In addition, in the poorer countries, interventions with effects on child survival and nutrition may have associated effects on behavior problems and aggression. Some of these programs have demonstrated positive effects on general cognitive abilities, attention, school achievement, and even adult wages, all of which as we have seen are protective processes for antisocial behavior, aggression, and crime (Walker et al. 2000; Attanasio and Vera-Hernandez 2004; Clarke et al. 2008; Hoddinott et al. 2008). Given the very high costs to society of chronic offending across the world, the added costs of prevention programs with both parent and child components may still be worth the price.

B. Poverty Reduction and Human Capital Development

As many countries expand preschool enrollment, more programs should also consider the intersection of poverty reduction, parent human capital, and crime prevention. Evaluations of interventions offering parental income and support in the United States have shown some positive effects for children, with specific effects of income support for children's behavior. This is an additional type of parent support that may be valuable to couple with preschool interventions. A series of experimental evaluations of welfare and employment policy demonstrations conducted in the 1990s in the United States have shown that increases in family income may be modifiable through public policy, and that decreases in externalizing behaviors may result (Morris et al. 2001). This set of 12 experiments were conducted in a variety of states, cities, and counties in the United States, including counties in Minnesota, California, and Florida; and cities in Wisconsin, Michigan, Georgia, and Connecticut. In addition, one experiment targeted families in two provinces in Canada. The programs were of three kinds: those that simply mandated employment, by reducing welfare benefits for those who did not meet work requirements; those that provided financial incentives for employment, through wage supplements or earnings disregards; and those that instituted time limits on welfare receipt. The impacts of these experiments on family income, employment, and child academic and social behaviors were synthesized and summarized in Morris et al. (2001). The four programs that provided earnings supplements (two experimental conditions in the Minnesota Family Investment Program; the New Hope experiment in Milwaukee; and the Self-Sufficiency Project in Canada) were successful in reducing family poverty rates and increasing family income. In addition, the Minnesota and New Hope programs brought about reductions in externalizing behaviors, as reported by parents (the Minnesota program) and by teachers (New Hope; Gennetian and Miller 2000; Huston et al. 2003).

Another successful poverty-reduction program, Oportunidades (formerly known as Progresa), was implemented in Mexico beginning in 1997. The program offered cash income transfers conditioned on certain behaviors focusing on nutrition, education, and health. For example, families received cash transfers only if they participated in certain activities, such as visiting health clinics regularly. Children also received a monthly cash transfer ("scholarship") for attending and completing schooling. In-kind supports, such as school supplies, were also offered to families. Several evaluations of the program have shown positive benefits for children and families. Families who participated in the program had better diets and used more preventive services. Children within the families attended school more regularly and performed better. Finally, the program was successful in reducing the number of households experiencing poverty (Levy 2006). While behavior and crime has not been analyzed in evaluations of the program, this type of human capital intervention has the potential to be successful in a variety of contexts and may be paired with preschool programs in the future in order to decrease problem behaviors and later crime.

Despite challenges to the field, prevention science in preschool has made significant advances. The targeting of new pathways and developmental domains; developments in evaluation science, such as the burgeoning of rigorous, controlled experimental trials (including those at the setting level); and new approaches to the communication of developmental and evaluation science to policymakers all bode well for future developments in the field.

REFERENCES

Administration for Children and Families. 2005. *Head Start Impact Study: First Year Findings.* Washington, DC: US Department of Health and Human Services.

Administration for Children and Families. 2007. *Preliminary Findings from the Early Head Start Prekindergarten Follow-up, Prekindergarten Follow-up.* Washington, DC: US Department of Health and Human Services.

Alderson, Desiree P., Lisa A. Gennetian, Chantelle J. Dowsett, Amy Imes, and Aletha C. Huston. 2008. "Effects of Employment-Based Programs on Families by Prior Levels of Disadvantage." *Social Service Review* 82:361–94.

Anderson, Bentg-Erik. 2008. "Effects of Day-Care on Cognitive and Socioemotional Competence of Thirteen-Year-Old Swedish Schoolchildren, Competence of Thirteen-Year-Old Swedish Schoolchildren." *Child Development* 63:20–36.

Aos, Steve, Roxanne Lieb, Jim Mayfield, Marna Millier, and Annie Penucci. 2004. *Benefits and Costs of Prevention and Early Intervention Programs for Youth*. Olympia, WA: Washington State Institute for Public Policy.

Attanasio, Orazio P., and Marcos Vera-Hernandez. (2004). *Medium and Long Run Effects of Nutrition and Child Care: Evaluation of a Community Nursery Programme in Rural Colombia*. London: Institute for Fiscal Studies.

Barnett, Steven W., Kwanghee Jung, Donald J. Yarosz, Jessica Thomas, Amy Hornbeck, Robert Stechuk, and Susan Burns. 2008. "Educational Effects of the Tools of the Mind Curriculum: A Randomized Trial." *Early Childhood Research Quarterly* 23:299–313.

Barnett, William S., and Leonard Masse. 2007. "Early Childhood Program Design and Economic Returns: Comparative Benefit-Cost Analysis of the Abecedarian Program and Policy Implications." *Economics of Education Review* 26:113–25.

Barnett, William S., Donald J. Yarosz, Jessica Thomas, and Amy Hornbeck. 2006. *Educational Effectiveness of a Vygotskian Approach to Preschool Education: A Randomized Trial*. New Brunswick, NJ: National Institute on Early Education Research.

Bierman, Karen, Celene E. Domitrovich, Robert L. Nix, Scott D. Gest, Janet A. Welsh, Mark T. Greenberg, Clancy Blair, Keith E. Nelson, and Sukhdeep Gill. 2008. "Promoting Academic and Social-Emotional School Readiness: The Head Start REDI Program." *Child Development* 79:1802–17.

Bierman, Karen, Robert L. Nix, Mark T. Greenberg, Clancy Blair, and Celene E. Domitrovich. 2008. "Executive Functions and School Readiness Intervention: Impact, Moderation, and Mediation in the Head Start REDI Program." *Development and Psychopathology* 20:821–43.

Blair, Clancy, and Adele Diamond. 2008. "Biological Processes in Prevention and Intervention: The Promotion of Self-Regulation as a Means of Preventing School Failure, The Promotion of Self-Regulation as a Means of Preventing School Failure." *Development and Psychopathology* 20:899–911.

Bloom, Howard S. 1984. "Accounting for No-Shows in Experimental Evaluation Designs." *Evaluation Review* 8:225–46.

Bradley, Robert H., Robert F. Corwyn, Margaret Burchinal, Harriette Pipes McAdoo, and Cynthia Garcia Coll. 2001. "The Home Environments of Children in the United States Part II: Relationships with Development through Age Thirteen." *Child Development* 72:1868–86.

Britto, Pia R., Hirokazu Yoshikawa, Kimberly Boller, and Cybele Raver. 2010. "Beyond Child Indicators: A Framework to Assess and Evaluate the Quality of Early Childhood Care and Education Settings and Programs in the Majority World." ECCE Conference Proposal.

Buscemi, Leah T., Tess Bennett, Dawn Thomas, and Deborah A. Deluca. 1996. "Head Start: Challenges and Training Needs." *Journal of Early Intervention* 20:1–13.

Camilli, Gregory, Sadako Vargas, Sharon Ryan, and W. Steven Barnett. 2010. "Meta-analysis of the Effects of Early Education Interventions on Cognitive and Social Development." *Teachers College Record* 112(3): 579–620.

Caspi, Avshalom, Bill Henry, Rob O. McGee, Terrie E. Moffitt, and Phil Silva. 1995. "Temperamental Origins and Adolescent Behavior Problems: From Age Three to Age Fifteen." *Child Development* 66:55–68.

Clarke, Sian E., Matthew C.H. Jukes, J. Kiambo Njagi, Lincoln Khasakhala, Bonnie Cundill, Julius Otido, Christopher Crudder, Benson B.A. Estambale, and Simon Brooker. 2008. "Effect of Intermittent Preventive Treatment of Malaria on Health and Education in Schoolchildren: A Cluster-Randomised, Double-Blind, Placebo-Controlled Trial." *Lancet* 372:27–38.

Cunha, Flavio, and James Heckman. 2007. "The Technology of Skill Formation." *American Economic Review* 97:31–47.

Currie, Janet, and Matthew Neidell. 2007. "Getting Inside the "Black Box" of Head Start Quality: What Matters and What Doesn't." *Economics of Education Review* 26:83–99.

Currie, Janet, and Duncan Thomas. 1995. "Does Head Start Make a Difference?" *American Economic Review* 85:341–64.

Diamond, Adele, W. Steven Barnett, Jessica Thomas, and Sarah Munro. 2007. "Preschool Program Improves Cognitive Control." *Science* 318:1387–88.

Domitrovich, Celene E., Rebecca C. Cortes, and Mark T. Greenberg. 2007. "Improving Young Children's Social and Emotional Competence: A Randomized Trial of the Preschool "PATHS" Curriculum." *Journal of Primary Prevention* 28:67–91.

Duncan, Greg J., Jens Ludwig, and Katherine A. Magnuson. 2007. "Reducing Poverty through Preschool Interventions." *The Future of Children* 17:143–60.

Early, Diane M., Donna M. Bryant, Robert C. Pianta, Richard M. Clifford, Margaret Burchinal, Sharon Ritchie, Carollee Howes, and Barbarin Oscar. 2006. "Are Teachers' Education, Major, and Credentials Related to Classroom Quality and Children's Academic Gains in Pre-kindergarten?" *Early Childhood Research Quarterly* 21:174–95.

Farrington, David P., and Brandon C. Welsh. 2007. *Saving Children from a Life of Crime: Early Risk Factors and Effective Interventions*. New York: Oxford University Press.

Fisher, Philip A., and Hyoun K. Kim. 2007. "Intervention Effects on Foster Preschoolers' Attachment-Related Behaviors from a Randomized Trial." *Prevention Science* 8:161–70.

Garces, Eliana, Duncan Thomas, and Janet Currie. 2002. "Longer-term Effects of Head Start." *American Economic Review* 92:999–1012.

Gassman-Pines, Anna., and Hirokazu Yoshikawa. 2006. "The Effects of Anti-Poverty Programs on Children's Cumulative Levels of Poverty-Related Risk." *Developmental Psychology* 42:981–99.

Gennetian, Lisa, and Cynthia Miller. 2000. *Reforming Welfare and Rewarding Work: Final Report on the Minnesota Family Investment Program*, Volume 2, *Effects on Children*. New York: MDRC.

Gilliam, Walter S., and Valerie Leiter. 2003. "Evaluating Early Childhood Programs: Improving Quality and Informing Policy." *Zero to Three* 23:6–13.

Gilliam, Walter S., and Edward F. Zigler. 2001. "A Critical Meta-Analysis of all Impact Evaluations of State-Funded Preschool from 1977 to 1998: Implications for Policy, Service Delivery and Program Evaluation." *Early Childhood Research Quarterly* 15:441–73.

Greenberg, Mark T., Roger P. Weissberg, Mary Utne O'Brien, Joseph E. Zins, Linda Fredericks, Hanks Resnik, and Maurice J. Elias. 2003. "Enhancing School-Based Prevention and Youth Development through Coordinated Social, Emotional, and Academic Learning." *American Psychologist* 58:466–74.

Heckman, James J., Seong Hyeok Moon, Rodrigo Pinto, Peter A. Savelyev, and Adam Yavitz. 2009. *The Rate of Return to the High /Scope Perry Preschool Program*. Chicago: University of Chicago.

Hill, Carolyn J., Howard S. Bloom, Alison Rebeck Black, and Mark W. Lipsey. 2008. "Empirical Benchmarks for Interpreting Effect Sizes in Research." *Child Development Perspectives* 2:172–78.

Hoddinott, John, John A. Maluccio, Jere R. Behrman, Rafael Flores, and Reynaldo Martorell. 2008. "Effects of a Nutrition Intervention during Early Childhood on Economic Productivity in Guatemalan Adults." *Lancet* 371:411–16.

Howes, Carollee, Margaret Burchinal, Robert Pianta, Donna Bryant, Diane Early, Richard
    Clifford, and Oscar Barbarin. 2008. "Ready to Learn? Children's Pre-Academic
    Achievement in Pre-Kindergarten Programs." *Early Childhood Research Quarterly*
    23(1): 27–50.
Huston, Aletha C., Cynthia Miller, Lashawn Richburg-Hayes, Greg J. Duncan, Carolyn A.
    Eldred, Thomas S. Weisner, Edward Lowe, Vonnie C. McLoyd, Danielle A. Crosby,
    Marika N. Ripke, and Cindy Redcross. 2003. *New Hope for Families and Children:
    Five-Year Results of a Program to Reduce Poverty and Reform Welfare.* New York: MDRC.
Johnson, Dale L., and Todd Walker. 1987. "Primary Prevention of Behavior Problems in
    Mexican American Children." *American Journal of Community Psychology* 15:375–85.
Juffer, Femme, Marian J. Bakermans-Kranenburg, and Marinus H. van IJzendoorn. 2005.
    "The Importance of Parenting in the Development of Disorganized Attachment:
    Evidence from a Preventive Intervention Study in Adoptive Families." *Journal of Child
    Psychology and Psychiatry* 46:263–74.
Karoly, Lynn A., M. Rebecca Kilburn, and Jill S. Cannon. 2005. *Early Childhood Interven-
    tions: Proven Results, Future Promise.* Santa Monica, CA: RAND Corporation.
Knudsen, Eric I., James J. Heckman, Judy L. Cameron, and Jack P. Shonkoff. 2006. "Eco-
    nomic, Neurobiological, and Behavioral Perspectives on Building America's Future
    Workforce." *Proceedings of the National Academy of Sciences of the United States of
    America* 103(27): 10155–162.
Lally, J. Ronald, Peter L. Mangione, and Alice S. Honig. 1988. "The Syracuse Family
    Development Project: Long-Range Impact of an Early Intervention with Low-Income
    Children and their Families." In *Parent Education as Early Childhood Intervention,*
    edited by Douglas R. Powell. Norwood, NJ: Ablex.
Landry, Susan H., Karen E. Smith, and Paul R. Swank. 2006. "Responsive Parenting:
    Establishing Early Foundations for Social, Communication, and Independent
    Problem-Solving Skills." *Developmental Psychology* 42:627–42.
Levy, Santiago. 2006. *Progress against Poverty: Sustaining Mexico's Progresa-Oportunidades
    Program.* The Brookings Institute: Washington, DC.
Loeb, Susanna, Margaret Bridges, Daphna Bassok, Bruce Fuller, and Russ Rumberger. 2007.
    "How Much is too Much? The Influence of Preschool Centers on Children's Cognitive
    and Social Development." *Economics of Education Review* 26:52–66.
Loeber, Rolf, and Dale Hay. 1997. "Key Issues in the Development of Aggression and Violence
    From Childhood to Early Adulthood." *Annual Review of Psychology* 48:371–410.
Ludwig, Jens, and Douglas L. Miller. 2007. "Does Head Start Improve Children's Life
    Chances? Evidence from a Regression Discontinuity Design." *Quarterly Journal of
    Economics* 122:159–208.
Ludwig, Jens, and Deborah Phillips. 2007. "The Benefits and Costs of Head Start." *Social
    Policy Report* 21(3): 1–19.
Magnuson, Katherine A., Christopher Ruhm, and Jane Waldfogel. 2007. "The Persistence of
    Preschool Effects: Do Subsequent Classroom Experiences Matter?" *Early Childhood
    Research Quarterly* 22:18–38.
Mashburn, Andrew J., Robert C. Pianta, Bridget K. Hamre, Jason T. Downer, Oscar A.
    Barbarin, Donna Bryant, Margaret Burchinal, Diane M. Early, and Carollee Howes.
    2008. "Measures of Classroom Quality in Prekindergarten and Children's Develop-
    ment of Academic, Language, and Social Skills." *Child Development* 793:732–49.
Moffitt, Terrie E. 1993. "Adolescence-Limited and Life-Course-Persistent Antisocial
    Behavior: A Developmental Taxonomy." *Psychological Review* 100:674–701.

Morris, Pamela A., Aletha C. Huston, Greg J. Duncan, Danielle A. Crosby, and Johannes M. Bos. 2001. *How Welfare and Work Policies Affect Children: A Synthesis of Research.* New York: MDRC.

McCall, Robert B. 1981. "Nature-Nurture and the Two Realms of Development: A Proposed Integration with Respect to Mental Development." *Child Development* 52:1–12.

National Forum on Early Childhood Policy and Programs. 2010. *Understanding the Head Start Impact Study.* Cambridge, MA: Harvard University Center on the Developing Child.

National Research Council and Institute of Medicine. 2000. From Neurons to Neighborhoods: The Science of Early Childhood Development. Washington, DC: National Academies Press.

National Scientific Council on the Developing Child. 2007. *The Science of Early Childhood Development.* Cambridge, MA: Harvard University Center on the Developing Child.

NICHD Early Child Care Research Network. 2003. "Does the Amount of Time Spent in Child Care Predict Socioemotional Adjustment During the Transition to Kindergarten?" *Child Development* 74:976–1004.

NICHD Early Child Care Research Network. 2004. "Does Class Size in First Grade Relate to Children's Academic and Social Performance or Observed Classroom Processes?" *Developmental Psychology* 40:651–64.

Raver, Cybele C. 2002. "Emotions Matter: Making The Case for the Role of Young Children's Emotional Development for Early School Readiness." *Social Policy Report* 16(3): 1–19.

Raver, Cybele C., Stephanie M. Jones, Christine Li-Grining, Fuhua Zhai, Molly W. Metzger, and Bonnie Solomon. 2009. "Targeting Children's Behavior Problems in Preschool Classrooms: A Cluster-Randomized Trial." *Journal of Consulting and Clinical Psychology* 77:302–16.

Reynolds, Arthur J. 2000. *Success in Early Intervention: The Chicago Child-Parent Centers.* Lincoln, NE: University of Nebraska Press.

Reynolds, Arthur J., Judy A. Temple, Suh-Ruu Ou, Dylan Robertson, Joshua Mersky, James W. Topitzes, and Michael Niles. 2007. "Effects of a School-Based, Early Childhood Intervention on Adult Health and Well-being." *Archives of Pediatrics and Adolescent Medicine* 161:730–39.

Reynolds, Arthur J., Judy A. Temple, Dylan L. Robertson, and Emily A. Mann. 2001. "Long- Term Effects of an Early Childhood Intervention on Educational Achievement and Juvenile Arrest: A 15-Year Follow-Up of Low-Income Children in Public Schools." *Journal of the American Medical Association* 285:2339–46.

Ruopp, Richard., J. Travers, F. Glantz, and C. Coelen. 1979. "Children at the Center: Final Report of the National Day Care Study." Cambridge, MA: Abt Associates.

Schweinhart, Larry J. 2006. "The High/Scope approach: Evidence that Participatory Learning in Early Childhood Contributes to Human Development." In *The Crisis in Youth Mental Health: Critical Issues and Effective Programs.* Vol. 4: *Early Intervention Programs and Policies,* edited by Norman F. Watt, Catherine Ayoub, Robert H. Bradley, Jini E. Puma, and Whitney A. LeBoeuf. Westport, CT: Praeger.

Schweinhart, Lawrence J., David P. Weikart, and Mary B. Larner. 1986. "Consequences of Three Preschool Curriculum Models through Age Fifteen." *Early Childhood Research Quarterly* 1:15–46.

Seitz, Victoria, Laurie K. Rosenbaum, and Nancy H. Apfel. 1985. "Effects of Family Support Intervention: A Ten-Year Follow-Up." *Child Development* 56:376–91.

Singer, Dorothy G., Roberta Michnick Golinkoff, and Kathy Hirsh-Pasek, eds. 2006.
    *Play=Learning: How Play Motivates and Enhances Children's Cognitive and Social-Emo-
    tional Growth*. New York: Oxford University Press.
Temple, Judy A., and Arthur J. Renolds. 2007. "The Benefits and Costs of Investments in
    Preschool." *Economics of Education Review* 26:126–44.
Tuijl, Cathy van, and Paul P. M. Leseman. 2004. "Improving Mother-Child Interaction in
    Low-Income Turkish-Dutch Families: A Study of Mechanisms Mediating Improve-
    ments Resulting from Participating in a Home-Based Preschool Intervention Pro-
    gram." *Infant and Child Development* 13:323–40.
United Nation's Children's Fund (UNICEF). 2008. *The Child Care Transition, Innocenti
    Report Card 8*. UNICEF Innocenti Research Centre, Florence.
US Department of Health and Human Services. 2010. *Head Start Impact Study: Final
    Report. January 2010*. Washington, DC: Administration for Children and Families,
    Office of Planning, Research and Evaluation.
Van Hemel, Susan B., and Catherine E. Snow, eds. 2008. *Early Childhood Assessment: Why,
    What and How*. Washington, DC: The National Academy Press.
Walker, Susan P., Sally M. Grantham-McGregor, Christine A. Powell, and Susan M. Chang.
    (2000). "Effects of Growth Restriction in Early Childhood on Growth, IQ, and
    Cognition at Age 11 to 12 Years and the Benefits of Nutritional Supplementation and
    Psychosocial Stimulation." *Journal of Pediatrics* 137:36–41.
Webster-Stratton, Carolyn, M. Jamila Reid, and Mary Hammond. 2001. "Preventing Conduct
    Problems, Promoting Social Competence: A Parent and Teacher Training Partnership in
    Head Start." *Journal of Clinical Child and Adolescent Psychology* 30:283–302.
West, Donald J., and David P. Farrington. 1977. *The Delinquent Way of Life: Third Report of
    the Cambridge Study in Delinquent Development*. London: Heinemann.
Yoshikawa, Hirokazu. 1994. "Prevention as Cumulative Protection: Effects of Early Family
    Support and Education on Chronic Delinquency and its Risks." *Psychological Bulletin*
    115:28–54.
Yoshikawa, Hirokazu, Elisa Altman Rosman, and Joann Hsueh. 2002. "Resolving Paradoxi-
    cal Criteria for the Expansion and Replication of Early Childhood Care and Education
    Programs." *Early Childhood Research Quarterly* 17:3–27.
Yoshikawa, Hirokazu, Holly S. Schindler, and Pia Caronongan. 2009. *Prevention of Mental
    Health Disorders, Delinquency and Problem Behaviors through Intervention in Infancy
    and Early Childhood*. Background paper, Institute of Medicine.
Yoshikawa, Hirokazu, Thomas S. Weisner, and Edward D. Lowe, eds. 2006. *Making it Work:
    Low-Wage Employment, Family Life and Child Development*. New York: Russell Sage
    Foundation.
Yoshikawa, Hirokazu, and Edward Zigler. 2000. "Mental Health in Head Start: New
    Directions for the Twenty-First Century." *Early Education and Development* 11: 247–64.
Zigler, Edward, and Sally J. Styfco. 1993. *Head Start and Beyond: A National Plan for
    Extended Early Childhood Intervention*. New Haven, CT: Yale University Press.
Zill, Nicholas, Gary Resnick, Kwang Kim, Kevin O'Donnell, Alberto Sorongon, Ruth
    Hubbell McKey, Shefali Pai-Samant, Cheryl Clark, Robert O'Brien, and Mary Ann
    D'Elio. 2003. *Head Start FACES 2000: A Whole-Child Perspective on Program Perfor-
    mance*. Fourth Progress Report. Washington, DC: Administration for Children, Youth
    and Families, Head Start Bureau.

CHAPTER 5

PARENT TRAINING AND THE PREVENTION OF CRIME

ALEX R. PIQUERO AND
WESLEY G. JENNINGS

THE majority of longitudinal studies focusing on crime and delinquency show that antisocial and deviant behaviors that are developed and emerge during childhood tend to morph into future antisocial and criminal activities in adolescence and adulthood and reverberate throughout the life course (McCord, Widom, and Crowell 2001; Piquero, Farrington, and Blumstein 2003). This persistent troublesome behavior also has consequences regarding an individual's job, social relationships, and schooling (Moffitt 1993). Thus, as many studies demonstrate that antisocial, delinquent, and criminal behavior originates early in the life course, persists throughout the life course, and permeates many life domains (Sampson and Laub 1997), policies should be directed toward the development and incorporation of early childhood intervention programs that target this problematic conduct (Farrington and Welsh 2007). These preventive services should begin during infancy and target high-risk populations so that they can be more effective, especially because undesirable childhood behaviors are more difficult to correct as a person ages (Frick and Loney 1999; Tremblay 2000).

One particular initiative, parent training programs, was created in an effort to curtail this disruptive behavior in children and prevent future delinquency. These early childhood programs are designed to educate and advise parents in raising their children and teaching them how to manage deviant behaviors such as excessive impulsiveness, defiance, and hostility, thereby improving familial bonds, which should diminish future delinquent activities during adolescence and adulthood (Kazdin, Siegel, and Bass 1992; Tremblay and Craig 1995; Hawkins et al. 1999; Bernazzani and Tremblay 2006).

One recent meta-analysis conducted by Farrington and Welsh (2003) sought to evaluate the efficacy of crime prevention programs directed toward families and included parent training, home/community, home visitation, daycare/preschool, and school-based with both younger children and older adolescents. In order for each of the identified 40 studies to be included in their meta-analysis, they had to have included random assignment and program design, a sample population of more than 50 individuals, a concentration on family-based interventions, and a measure of deviant behavior after the conclusion of the program. The results of their analysis indicated that these early parent training programs diminished problematic childhood behaviors both initially and during follow-up evaluations. Parent training programs were shown to be the most successful in preventing future delinquency with those programs implemented in schools being the least effective. The other program types such as home visitation also had positive effects on child behavior.

Although many parent training programs have had encouraging outcomes in improving children's behavior (Aos et al. 2004, 2006; Greenwood 2006), others have not produced similar findings (Gomby, Culross, and Behrman 1999; Bilukha et al. 2005). Therefore, more research is necessary in order to determine whether parent training programs should be further developed and implemented. For example, in order to measure a program's effectiveness adequately, the study should be well designed and have a clear, measurable goal of preventing deviant childhood behavior.

This essay provides an overview of research on parent training programs with a particular focus on the results of our recent systematic review examining the effectiveness of parent training programs (Piquero et al. 2009). A number of key findings and conclusions are as follows:

- There is a general lack of randomized experimental designs evaluating the effectiveness of parent training programs, and few studies have long-term follow-up data available.
- Of the 55 randomized experimental designs that were identified from our comprehensive systematic review and meta-analysis, the majority were moderately effective in reducing childhood behavior problems.
- Additional results suggested that several factors were identified as significant moderators of the effect size, most notably sample size. As such, it appears that parenting programs are more successful when they target a smaller more manageable number of children rather than large-scale interventions.
- Parent training programs are effective interventions for reducing behavioral problems, and if they are implemented early on in a child's development, then there is likely to be a significant short- and long-term benefit with regard to a reduction in behavior problems.

This essay is organized in the following manner. Section I describes the relevance of parent training programs for policy. Section II provides a brief overview of the prior research on parent training programs with a focus on parental management programs and home visitation programs. Section III specifically focuses on our recent systematic review and meta-analysis. Section IV discusses the implications of the results from our systematic review and meta-analysis with regard to theory and policy. Directions for future research are also identified.

I. Policy Relevance

Currently, family training programs have gained popularity and have been implemented more often in an effort to prevent crime, especially in the Western Hemisphere. Ideally, these programs are directed toward the select few individuals who display antisocial and problematic behavior early and consistently throughout their lives (Piquero 2008). For example, research in Quebec, which focused on males born into high-risk situations (having impoverished, young mothers), showed that these individuals were more likely to become chronic offenders (Nagin and Tremblay 2001). Therefore, Quebec introduced a $70 million program that promotes and initiates parental education and prenatal services to young, underprivileged mothers in an effort to curb future adolescent and adult crime. However, policymakers are hesitant to incorporate expensive parent training programs when the benefits of such initiatives have yet to be rigorously evaluated. As a result, well-designed, scientific research is necessary in order to determine whether such programs are effective in reducing antisocial behavior and its outcomes and whether such programs are cost-effective (Cohen, Piquero, and Jennings 2010).

II. Prior Reviews

A review of early childhood intervention programs (home visitation, daycare, parent training, etc.) aimed at preventing misbehavior and violence conducted by Greenwood (2006) indicated that these program types had other benefits along with crime prevention. Further, family-based programs such as the Nurse Family Partnership (NFP) were seen to be more cost-effective when they were directed toward high-risk youth populations, since they had expensive operational costs (Aos et al. 2004, 2006). Some additional advantages of these programs noticed during follow-up evaluations included improved education and employment attainment, lower levels of substance abuse, and reduced healthcare and welfare expenses.

Based upon a review of previous literature, most parent training programs have concentrated on either educating parents or teaching them proper management techniques. In general, little research has focused on home visitation programs and these studies have produced inconclusive results. Studies on parent management training programs have also displayed mixed findings even though some have been effective in reducing antisocial behavior and delinquency (Serketich and Dumas 1996). Parental education along with daycare initiatives has received more supportive evidence when evaluating its efficacy in preventing future deviant behavior. Further, few studies have included experimental designs (control and experimental groups) and random assignment along with follow-up evaluations and a focus on delinquent behavioral changes. Also, many studies do not separate the results of individual program types (parent training opposed to home visitation), which makes it difficult to determine their effectiveness. Our meta-analysis sought to contribute to this literature by including program interventions directed toward children up to five years old, individually evaluating separate program types, and incorporating newly implemented parent training programs through 2008.

III. Systematic Review of Parent Training Programs

In order for a study to be included within our systematic review and meta-analysis, it had to be quantitative, have an experimental design (random assignment and a control group), include children with a mean age of five years or less at the beginning of the intervention, be primarily focused on parent training, incorporate either delinquent or antisocial behavioral outcomes, provide enough data to calculate an accurate effect size, and be published in English. All of the studies included in our analysis were considered of high quality owing to their research design, although some of the sample sizes were arguably small. Some of the search strategies used to obtain these studies included a key word search of online abstract databases, a bibliographic analysis of previous reviews on parent training programs, a database search of professional agency publications, and consultation with acknowledged experts in the field. After research was identified, full-text versions were obtained through various means.

A. Methods

After the initial 4,000 search results, several methods were used to eliminate ineligible studies. For example, the abstracts of every study were examined to determine if they met the proper criteria for inclusion within the meta-analysis (e.g., study design, age limits). Further, studies using the same original sample population were excluded. After these criteria were applied, 55 studies were determined to meet the criteria for inclusion. Of the 55 studies included in the meta-analysis, 47 were roughly defined as parent training programs, but only eight were considered primarily home visitation programs (Greenwood 2006). Most of the studies had small samples (under 100 children).

Of the studies included in our meta-analysis, most programs were centered on training parents individually or in group environments at a clinic, school, or place within the community. Some of the most well known parent training programs identified through this research were the Triple P-Positive Parenting Program (Sanders, Markie-Dadds, et al. 2000; Sanders, Montgomery, et al. 2000; Leung et al. 2003; Markie-Dadds and Sanders 2006; Morawska and Sanders, 2006,), the Parent-Child Interaction Therapy (Zangwill 1983; McNeil et al. 1991; Eyberg, Boggs, and Algina 1995; Brestan et al. 1997; Schuhmann et al. 1998), and most notably, the Incredible Years Parenting Program, which was implemented in multiple studies (Webster-Stratton 1982, 1984; Webster-Stratton, Kolpacoff, and Hollinsworth 1988; Webster-Stratton 1990, 1992; Tucker 1996; Webster-Stratton and Hammond 1997; Taylor et al. 1998; Webster-Stratton 1998; Scott et al. 2001; Webster-Stratton, Reid, and Hammond 2001; Patterson et al. 2002; Webster-Stratton, Reid, and Hammond 2004; Gardner, Burton, and Klimes 2006; Edwards et al. 2007; Helfenbaum and Ortiz 2007; Kim, Cain, and Webster-Stratton 2008; Reid, Webster-Stratton, and Hammond 2007;). These programs utilized several training techniques, such as videotapes, advice from healthcare providers, and role playing in order to teach parents how to monitor and discipline their child's behavior, improve parent-child relationships, reward compliance, and promote family interaction and school involvement. The programs also targeted different severity levels of child behavior problems.

The intervention programs that utilized home visitation usually began while the child was very young or before he or she was born. In most of these studies, healthcare providers visited a mother's residence and gave her guidance on effectively controlling child conduct (Cullen 1976; Stone, Bendell, and Field 1988; Kitzman et al. 1997; McCarton et al. 1997; Olds, Robinson, Pettitt et al. 1997; Butz et al. 2001; Heinicke et al. 2001; Fergusson et al. 2005).

The nurse home visitation program developed and evaluated by Olds et al. (1986, 1997, 1998) is arguably the most widely recognized example of home visitation programs. In the classic study, Olds et al. recruited 500 pregnant women to enroll in a home visitation program where they were randomly assigned to receive home visits during pregnancy and in the child's first two years of life. In contrast, the control group received standard prenatal care and routine wellness visits at a clinic. Olds et al.'s results demonstrated that the mothers who received both pre- and postnatal visits had fewer instances of child abuse and their children visited the emergency room far less frequently than their counterparts (Olds et al. 1986).

In a long-term follow study, the Elmira youth who had both pre- and postnatal visits reported fewer instances of running away, fewer arrests, fewer convictions and violations of probation, fewer lifetime sex partners, fewer cigarettes smoked per day, and fewer days having consumed alcohol. Olds and his colleagues have since replicated Elmira's study design and a majority of the results in Memphis, Tennessee (Kitzman et al. 1997), and Denver, Colorado (Olds et al. 2004).

B. Results

Effect sizes were calculated by using the means and standard deviations provided by the data in the included studies, thereby computing Cohen's *d*. Each study's effect size was the result of an averaged combination of child behavioral outcome measures and different reporting sources. In order to avoid bias, the effect sizes were then weighted according to the overall sample size so that the results of studies with smaller samples did not have as much credence as those with larger ones (e.g., inverse variance weight; Hedges and Olkin 1985). As displayed in figure 5.1, the effect sizes generated in the study ranged from a large negative effect (-0.97) to an even larger positive effect (2.19). Negative effect sizes indicate that the parent-training program did not favorably influence a child's behavior, whereas positive effect sizes were an indication that the program was successful in reducing a child's behavior problems.

Following a calculation of the individual study effect sizes, a weighted grand mean effect size was calculated. This effect size was estimated to be 0.35, indicating that parent training programs in general were moderately effective. Further, the sign of the effect (e.g., positive) suggested that on average the parent training programs yielded a moderate reduction in childhood behavior problems when the children's behavioral problems after the parent training program were compared with their behavioral problems prior to participation in the parent training program.

1. *Homogeneity Tests and Moderator Analyses.* We determined that the effect sizes were heterogeneous, and as a result we further analyzed the possibility that certain variables may operate as moderators in order to explain the heterogeneity in the effect sizes. These variables were year of publication, country of publication,

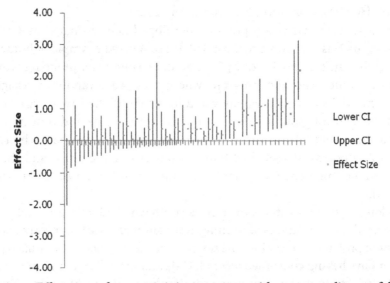

Figure 5.1 Effect sizes of parent training programs with corresponding confidence intervals (CI)

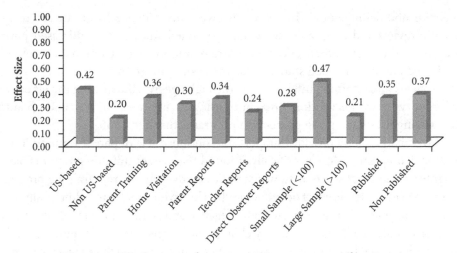

Figure 5.2 Moderators of parent training programs effect sizes

type of program, sample size, and publication bias. The effect sizes of these potential moderators are displayed in figure 5.2.

When comparing studies conducted in the United States to studies done outside of the United States, the effect sizes were greater for US-based studies. Regarding program type, the effect sizes were not significantly different between home visitation studies and parent training programs. When looking at individual reporting methods, effect sizes were greatest for parent reports followed by direct observer reports and teacher reports. However, there was not a significant difference between any of these different outcome measures. In contrast, when examining sample size in relation to effect size, smaller samples had significantly larger effect sizes compared to the effect sizes produced from larger sample studies (over 100 individuals). Finally, there was not a significant difference in the effect sizes of published versus unpublished studies.

2. *Meta-Analysis Regression Results.* Finally, we estimated a weighted least squares regression model using the previously established moderator variables. This analysis provided similar results to the bivariate comparisons in that small samples had the most significant effect sizes. In fact, in this model, when all other variables were controlled for, small samples had the only significant effect in the model.

IV. Discussion and Conclusions

Early parent training has been increasingly acknowledged among social scientists as one of the most effective intervention/prevention methods in addressing delinquency. Despite extensive debate on the success of these programs, scholars support this assertion by demonstrating a correlation between early childhood disruptive

behavior and delinquency. This essay reviewed the evidence from our recent systematic review and meta-analysis, which compiled studies that addressed parent
training and observed their effect on future delinquency by using data from both
published and unpublished studies. Our meta-analysis extended previous research
and reviews by examining interventions through age five, illustrating the efficacy of
different types of interventions (parent training vs. home visitation), and updating
the existing list of parenting prevention programs through 2008.

Overall, this study provides support for continued use of parent training in preventing delinquency. More specifically, it found that parent training programs have a
weighted mean effect size of 0.35, which indicated that early parent training programs
had a small to moderate effect on reducing child behavior problems. Additionally, findings demonstrated that sample size had a negative and significant correlation with the
effect size, with smaller sample sizes yielding much larger effect sizes. Further, studies
with small samples ($n < 100$) and those conducted in the United States produced much
higher effect sizes than studies with large samples ($n > 100$) and those conducted outside the United States. However, there was not a significant difference between the
effect sizes of program types (home visitation vs. parent training), published and
unpublished data, and the source of outcome (parents, teacher, and direct observer).

It is important to further elaborate on the implications of the main finding from
this meta-analysis—specifically the finding that studies with small samples had significantly larger effect sizes. This result may be an indication that when parent
training programs are implemented with a smaller and more manageable number
of children, the likelihood of success is greater. Or stated differently, programs such
as these may not produce the desired effect of reducing childhood behavioral problems when they are attempted as large-scale interventions. Therefore, the evidence
suggests that parent training programs should be implemented in smaller settings.

While some scholars may not be in agreement with some of the coding decisions
or methods used in our study (as is the case with any meta-analysis), this study is the
largest of its kind to date. Given the importance of continued study and the future
funding of effective prevention efforts, it is imperative that the data continue to be
analyzed and updated. Future studies should also include more randomized, experimental designs in order to examine the effects of early parent training programs on
delinquency. Follow-up studies should be conducted so that researchers can identify
the effects of parent training programs on delinquency and crime in individual
cohorts as they progress through adolescence and adulthood. Without continued
study, one cannot be sure of whether these intervention programs will have an indirect effect on other areas of adult life. Studies should also focus on the outcome that
parent training programs have on particular behavioral difficulties in children (such
as antisocial conduct). Finally, studies should attempt to isolate which aspects of
parent training programs are responsible for individual, observed changes in child
behavior instead of having multiple interventions occurring simultaneously.

Moving toward a more consistent theoretical definition of aggression, antisocial behavior, and delinquency would be helpful in future analyses. Currently, a
precise meaning does not exist in the criminal justice field, and more specifically, it

is lacking in the parent training area. Additionally, the inclusion of a sociological understanding of negative child outcomes would be helpful in a more comprehensive analysis of parenting training programs. For example, even effective family/training programs may not be able to influence a child's life-course trajectory where his or her environment may lack legitimate opportunity structures or consist of constant disorganization. Researchers should also make more of an effort to identify the causal link between family interaction and delinquency. In particular, they should better study the relationship between parental socialization and childhood self-control (and as a result, antisocial behavior). This type of research may help identify clues as to which types of family processes are most effective and hence which types of family-based intervention programs should be created. Future studies could control for more variables such as length of program, age of child, and more specific program types to aid in the development of new policies. Finally, a future meta-analysis could incorporate studies outside of the English language and integrate them into the previously established databases of early parent training programs.

The implications of our findings for extant criminological theory are readily apparent and illustrate the significance of early childhood socialization for effective crime prevention. Many criminological theories acknowledge the value of effective parenting in the development of successful social interactions in children. In particular, the quality of parental management in facilitating control over excessive impulsiveness, defiance, and hostility is instrumental in the reduction of troublesome behaviors during adolescence and adulthood. The conclusions of this study support the assertion that the benefits of parental socialization during formative years should be influential in the creation and implementation of policies that encourage parent training and strengthening familial bonds.

The present research demonstrates that policies should attempt to assist families in preventing antisocial and delinquent behavior by providing them with the resources needed to realize effective child development practices. Most of the studies demonstrated that childhood behavioral problems can be partially prevented or lessened with the implementation of the appropriate parent training programs. These same parenting programs have also produced many other benefits outside of crime reduction, including a higher pursuit of education, a decrease in pregnancies during teenage years, better financial security, and improved personal health (Reynolds et al. 2001; Farrington and Welsh 2007). The evidence is clear: parent training programs are effective.

REFERENCES

Aos, Steve, Roxanne Lieb, Jim Mayfield, Marna Miller, and Annie Pennuci. 2004. *Benefits and Costs of Prevention and Early Intervention Programs for Youth.* Olympia, WA: Washington State Institute for Public Policy.

Aos, Steve, Marna Miller, and Elizabeth Drake. 2006. *Evidence-Based Public Policy Options to Reduce Future Prison Construction, Criminal Justice Costs, and Crime Rates.* Olympia, WA: Washington State Institute for Public Policy.

Bernazzani, O., and Richard E. Tremblay. 2006. "Early Parent Training." In *Preventing Crime: What Works for Children, Offenders, Victims, and Places.* Edited by Brandon C. Welsh and David P. Farrington. Dordrecht: Springer.

Bilukha, Oleg, Robert A. Hahn, Alex Crosby, Mindy Fullilove, Akiva Liberman, Eve Moscicki, Susan Synder, Farris, Tuma, Phaedra Corso, Amanda Schofield, Peter Briss, and Task Force on Community Prevention Services. 2005. "The Effectiveness of Early Childhood Home Visitation in Prevention Violence: A Systematic Review." *American Journal of Preventive Medicine* 28(2): 11–39.

Brestan, Elizabeth V, Sheila M. Eyberg, Steven R. Boggs, and James Algina. 1997. "Parent–Child Interaction Therapy: Parents' Perceptions of Untreated Siblings." *Child and Family Behavior Therapy* 19(3): 13–28.

Butz, Andres M., M. Pulsifer, Nadia Marano, Harolyn Belcher, Mark K. Lears, and Richard Royall. 2001. "Effectiveness of a Home Intervention for Perceived Child Behavioral Problems and Parenting Stress in Children with in Utero Drug Exposure." *Archives of Pediatrics & Adolescent Medicine* 155: 1029–37.

Cohen, Mark A., Alex R. Piquero, and Wesley G. Jennings. 2010. "Estimating the Costs of Bad Outcomes for At-Risk Youth and the Benefits of Early Childhood Interventions to Reduce Them." *Criminal Justice Policy Review* 21: 391–434.

Cullen, Kevin J. 1976. "A Six Year Controlled Trial of Prevention of Children's Behavior Disorders." *Journal of Pediatrics* 88(4): 662–66.

Edwards, Rhiannon I., Alan Céilleachair, Tracey Bywater, Dyfrig A. Hughes, and Judy Hutchings. 2007. "Parenting Programme for Parents of Children at Risk of Developing Conduct Disorder: Cost Effectiveness Analysis." *British Medical Journal* 334(7595): 682–685.

Eyberg, Sheila M., Stephen R. Boggs, and James Algina. 1995. "New Developments in Psychosocial, Pharmacological, and Combined Treatments of Conduct Disorders in Aggressive Children." *Psychopharmacology Bulletin* 31(1): 83–91.

Farrington, David P., and Brandon C. Welsh. 2003. "Family-Based Prevention of Offending: A Meta-Analysis." *Australian and New Zealand Journal of Criminology* 36(2): 127–51.

Farrington, David P., and Brandon C. Welsh. 2007. *Saving Children from a Life of Crime: Early Risk Factors and Effective Interventions.* New York: Oxford University Press.

Fergusson, David M., Hildegard Grant, L. John Horwood, and Elizabeth M. Ridder. 2005. "Randomized Trial of the Early Start Program of Home Visitation." *Pediatrics* 116(14): 803–9.

Frick, Paul J., and Bryan R. Loney. 1999. "Outcomes of Children and Adolescents with Oppositional Defiant Disorder and Conduct Disorder." In *Handbook of Disruptive Behavior Disorders,* edited by Herbert C. Quay and Arvin E. Hogan. New York: Kluwer.

Gardner, Francis, Jennifer Burton, and Ivana Klimes. 2006. "Randomised Controlled Trial of a Parenting Intervention in the Voluntary Sector for Reducing Child Conduct Problems: Outcomes and Mechanisms of Change." *Journal of Child Psychology and Psychiatry* 47(11): 1123–32.

Gomby, Deanna S., Patti L. Culross, and Richard E. Behrman. 1999. "Home Visiting: Recent Program Evaluations-Analysis and Recommendations." *Future of Children* 9(1): 4–26.

Greenwood, Peter W. 2006. *Changing Lives: Delinquency Prevention as Crime-Control Policy.* Chicago: University of Chicago Press.

Hawkins, J. David, Richard F. Catalano, Rick Kosterman, Robert Abbott, and Karl G. Hill. 1999. "Preventing Adolescent Health-Risk Behaviors by Strengthening Protection during Childhood." *Archives of Pediatrics and Adolescent Medicine* 153(3): 226–34.

Hedges, Larry V., and Igor Olkin. 1985. *Statistical Methods for Meta-Analysis*. New York: Academic Press.

Helfenbaum-Kun, Eleanor D., and Camilo Ortiz. 2007. "Parent-training Groups for Fathers of Head Start Children: A Pilot Study of Their Feasibility and Impact on Child Behavior and Intra-Familial Relationships." *Child & Family Behavior Therapy* 29:47–64.

Heinicke, Christopher M., Neira R. Fineman, Victoria A. Ponce, and Donald Guthrie. 2001. "Relation-Based Intervention with At-Risk Mothers: Outcome in the Second Year of Life." *Infant Mental Health Journal* 22(4): 431–62.

Kim, Eunjing, Kevin C. Cain, and Carolyne Webster-Stratton. 2008. "The Preliminary Effect of a Parenting Program for Korean American Mothers: A Randomized Controlled Experimental Study." *International Journal of Nursing Studies* 45(9): 1261–73.

Kitzman, Harriet, David L. Olds, Charles R. Henderson, Carole Hanks, Robert Cole, Robert Tatelbaum, Kenneth M. McConnochie, Kimberly Sidora, Dennis W. Luckey, David Shaver, Kay Englehardt, David James, and Kathryn Barnard. 1997. "Effect of Prenatal and Infancy Home Visitation by Nurses on Pregnancy Outcomes, Childhood Injuries, and Repeated Childbearing: A Randomized Controlled Trial." *Journal of the American Medical Association* 278(4): 644–52.

Leung, Cynthia, Matthew R. Sanders, Shirley Leung, Rose Mak, and Joseph Lau. 2003. "An Outcome Evaluation of the Implementation of the Triple P-Positive Parenting Program in Hong Kong." *Family Process* 42(4): 531–44.

McCarton, Cecilia M., Jeanne Brooks-Gunn, Inn F. Wallace, Charles R. Bauer, Forest Bennett, Judy Bernbaum, R. Sue Broyles, Patrick Casey, Marie McCormick, David Scott, Jon Tyson, James Tonasela, and Curtis Meinen. 1997. "Results at Age 8 years of Early Intervention for Low-Birth-Weight Premature Infants: The Infant Health and Development Program." *Journal of the American Medical Association* 277(6): 126–32.

McCord, Joan, Cathy Spatz Widom, and Nancy E. Crowell. 2001. *Juvenile Crime, Juvenile Justice*. Washington, DC: National Academy Press.

McNeil, Cheryl B., Sheila Eyberg, Toni Hembree Eisenstadt, Katherine Newcomb, and Beverly Funderburk. 1991. "Parent—Child Interaction Therapy with Behavior Problem Children: Generalization of Treatment Effects to the School Setting." *Journal of Clinical Child Psychology* 20(2): 140–51.

Markie-Dadds, Carol, and Matthew R. Sanders. 2006. "Self-Directed Triple P (Positive Parenting Program) for Mothers with Children At-Risk of Developing." *Behavioral and Cognitive Psychotherapy* 34(3): 259–75.

Moffitt, Terrie E. 1993. "'Life-Course-Persistent' and 'Adolescence-Limited' Antisocial Behavior: A Developmental Taxonomy." *Psychological Review* 100(4): 674–701.

Morawska, Alina, and Matthew R. Sanders. 2006. "Self-Administered Behavioral Family Intervention for Parents of Toddlers: Part I. Efficacy." *Journal of Consulting and Clinical Psychology* 74(12): 10–19.

Nagin, Daniel S., and Richard E. Tremblay. 2001. "Parental and Early Childhood Predictors of Persistent Physical Aggression in Boys from Kindergarten to High School." *Archives of General Psychiatry* 58(4): 389–94.

Olds, David, John Eckenrode, Charles Henderson, Harriet Kitzman, Jane Powers, Robert Cole, Kimberly Sidora, Pamela Morris, Lisa M. Pettitt, and Dennis Luckey. 1997. "Long- Term Effects of Home Visitation on Maternal Life Course and Child Abuse and Neglect: 15-year Follow-Up of a Randomized Trial." *Journal of the American Medical Association* 278(8): 637–43.

Olds, David, Charles Henderson, Jr., Robert Chamberlin, and Robert Tatelbaum. 1986. "Preventing Child Abuse and Neglect: A Randomized Trial of Nurse Home Visitation." *Pediatrics* 78: 65–78.

Olds, David, Charles Henderson, Robert Cole, John Eckenrode, Harriet Kitzman, Dennis
     Luckey, Lisa Pettitt, Kimberly Sidora, Pamela Morris, and Jane Powers. 1998. "Long-
     Term Effects of Nurse Home Visitation on Children's Criminal and Antisocial
     Behavior: 15-year Follow-Up of a Randomized Controlled Trial." *Journal of the
     American Medical Association* 280:1238–44.

Olds, D. L., JoAnn Robinson, Lisa Pettitt, Dennis Luckey, D., John Holmberg, Rosanna Ng,
     Kathy Isacks, Karen Sheff, and Charles R. Henderson. 2004. "Effects of Home Visits by
     Paraprofessionals and by Nurses: Age 4 Follow-Up Results of a Randomized Trial."
     Pediatrics 114:1560–68.

Patterson, Jacoby, Jane Barlow, Carole Mockford, Ivan Klimes, Cecilia Pyper, and Sarah
     Stewart-Brown. 2002. "Improving Mental Health through Parenting Programmes:
     Block Randomised Controlled Trial." *Archives of Disease in Childhood* 87(6):
     472–77.

Piquero, Alex R. 2008. "Taking Stock of Developmental Trajectories of Criminal Activity
     over the Life Course." In *The Long View of Crime: A Synthesis of Longitudinal Research*,
     edited by Akiva Liberman. New York: Springer.

Piquero, Alex R., David P. Farrington, and Alfred Blumstein. 2003. "The Criminal Career
     Paradigm." In *Crime and Justice: A Review of Research*, vol. 30, edited by Michael
     Tonry. Chicago: University of Chicago Press.

Piquero, Alex R., David P. Farrington, Richard Tremblay, Brandon C. Welsh, and Wesley
     G. Jennings. 2009. "Effects of Early Family/Parent Training Programs on Antisocial
     Behavior and Delinquency." *Journal of Experimental Criminology* 5: 83–120.

Reid, M. Jamila, Carol Webster-Stratton, and Mary Hammond. 2007. "Enhancing a
     Classroom Social Competence and Problem-Solving Curriculum by Offering Parent
     Training to Families of Moderate-to High-Risk Elementary School Children." *Journal
     of Clinical Child and Adolescent Psychology* 35: 605–20.

Reynolds, Arther J., Judy A. Temple, Dylan L. Robertson, and Emily A. Mann. 2001.
     "Long-Term Effects of an Early Childhood Intervention on Educational Achievement
     and Juvenile Arrest: A 15-year Follow-Up of Low-Income Children in Public Schools."
     Journal of the American Medical Association 285(18): 2339–46.

Sampson, Robert J., and John H. Laub. 1997. "A Life-Course Theory of Cumulative Disad-
     vantage and the Stability of Delinquency." In *Developmental Theories of Crime and
     Delinquency*. Advances in Criminological Theory, vol. 7, edited by Terence P. Thorn-
     berry. New Brunswick, NJ: Transaction.

Sanders, Matthew R., Carole Markie-Dadds, Lawrence A. Tully, and William Bor. 2000.
     "The Triple P-Positive Parenting Program: A Comparison of Enhanced, Standard, and
     Self-Directed Behavioral Family Intervention for Parents of Children with Early Onset
     Conduct Problems." *Journal of Consulting and Clinical Psychology* 68(4): 624–40.

Sanders, Matthew R., Danielle T. Montgomery, and Margaret L. Brechtman-Toussaint.
     2000. "The Mass Media and the Prevention of Child Behaviour Problems: The
     Evaluation of a Television Series to Promote Positive Outcome for Parents and Their
     Children." *Journal of Child Psychology and Psychiatry* 41(7): 939–48.

Schuhmann, Elena M., Rebecca C. Foote, Sheila M. Eyberg, Stephen R. Boggs, and James
     Algina. 1998. "Efficacy of Parent-Child Interaction Therapy: Interim Report of a
     Randomized Trial with Short-Term Maintenance." *Journal of Clinical Child Psychology*
     27(1): 34–45.

Scott, Stephen, Quentin Spender, Moira Doolan, Briem Jacobs, and Helen Aspland. 2001.
     "Multicentre Controlled Trial of Parenting Groups for Childhood Antisocial Behav-
     iour in Clinical Practice." *British Medical Journal* 323(7306): 194–97.

Serketich, Wendy J., and Jean E. Dumas. 1996. "The Effectiveness of Behavioral Parent Training to Modify Antisocial Behavior in Children: A Meta-Analysis." *Behavior Therapy* 27(2): 171–86.

Stone, Wendy L., R. Debora Bendell, and Tiffany M. Field. 1988. "The Impact of Socioeconomic Status on Teenage Mothers and Children who Received Early Intervention." *Journal of Applied Developmental Psychology* 9(4): 391–408.

Taylor, Ted K., Fred Schmidt, Debra Pepler, and Christine Hodgins. 1998. "A Comparison of Eclectic Treatment with Webster-Stratton's Parents and Children Series in a Children's Mental Health Center: A Randomized Controlled Trial." *Behavior Therapy* 29(2): 221–40.

Tremblay, Richard E. 2000. "The Development of Aggressive Behavior During Childhood: What Have We Learned in the Past Century?" *International Journal of Behavioral Development* 24(2): 129–41.

Tremblay, Richard E., and Wendy M. Craig. 1995. "Developmental Crime Prevention." In *Crime and Justice: An Annual Review of Research*, edited by M. Tonry and David P. Farrington. Chicago: University of Chicago Press.

Tucker, Stephen J. 1996. "The Long-Term Efficacy of a Behavioral Parent Training Intervention for Families with Two-Year Olds." Dissertation, University of Michigan, Ann Arbor, MI.

Webster-Stratton, Carol. 1982. "Teaching Mothers through Videotape Modeling to Change Their Children's Behavior." *Journal of Pediatric Psychology* 7(3): 279–94.

Webster-Stratton, Carol. 1984. "Randomized Trial of Two Parent-Training Programs for Families with Conduct-Disordered Children." *Journal of Consulting and Clinical Psychology* 52(4): 666–78.

Webster-Stratton, Carol. 1990. "Enhancing the Effectiveness of Self-Administered Videotape Parent Training for Families with Conduct-Problem Children." *Journal of Abnormal Child Psychology* 18(5): 479–92.

Webster-Stratton, Carol. 1992. "Individually Administered Videotape Parent Training: Who Benefits?" *Cognitive Therapy and Research* 16(1): 31–35.

Webster-Stratton, Carol. 1998. "Preventing Conduct Problems in Head Start Children: Strengthening Parent Competencies." *Journal of Consulting and Clinical Psychology* 66(5): 715–30.

Webster-Stratton, Carol, and Mary Hammond. 1997. "Treating Children with Early-Onset Conduct Problems: A Comparison of Child and Parenting Training Interventions." *Journal of Consulting and Clinical Psychology* 65(2): 93–100.

Webster-Stratton, Carol, Mary Kolpacoff, and Terri Hollinsworth. 1988. "Self-Administered Videotape Therapy for Families with Conduct-Problem Children: Comparison with Two Cost-Effective Treatments and a Control Group." *Journal of Consulting and Clinical Psychology* 56(2): 558–66.

Webster-Stratton, Carol, M. Jamila Reid, and Mary Hammond. 2001. "Preventing Conduct Problems, Promoting Social Competence: A Parent and Teacher Training Partnership in Head Start." *Journal of Clinical Child Psychology* 30(3): 283–302.

Webster-Stratton, Carol, M. Jamila Reid, and Mary Hammond. 2004. "Treating Children with Early-Onset Conduct Problems: Intervention Outcomes for Parent, Child, and Teacher Training." *Journal of Clinical Child and Adolescent Psychology* 33(1): 105–124.

Zangwill, William M. 1983. "An Evaluation of a Parent Training Program." *Child and Family Behavior Therapy* 5(4): 1–16.

CHAPTER 6

CHILD SOCIAL SKILLS TRAINING IN THE PREVENTION OF ANTISOCIAL DEVELOPMENT AND CRIME

FRIEDRICH LÖSEL AND DORIS BENDER

THE last two decades have seen a fast-growing interest in developmental prevention of crime, violence, and other forms of antisocial behavior. Numerous prevention and early intervention programs have been implemented in families, preschools, schools, clinical settings, and neighborhoods (Farrington and Welsh 2007). Developmental prevention of antisocial problems also became a key topic of research in criminology, education, psychiatry, psychology, social welfare, and other disciplines. Although research and practice in this field have to cope with many challenges (e.g., Junger et al. 2007), youth crime prevention becomes increasingly important for policy formation (e.g., Ministry of Justice 2010).

Research on antisocial development strongly supports this view: aggression, delinquency and related antisocial behaviors are among the most frequent behavioral problems in childhood. Although Moffitt's (1993) differentiation between life-course-persistent and adolescence-limited antisociality simplifies developmental complexity, nearly all longitudinal studies confirmed the early starting and relatively long-lasting pathway of intensive deviancy (e.g., Sampson and Laub 1993; Frick 1998). Approximately one-third of the early antisocial children continue their problem behavior into youth, and this group has a particularly high risk of serious and persistent offending (Loeber, Farrington, and Waschbusch 1998; Lösel and Bender 2003). Early conduct problems are also a sound predictor of other psychiatric problems in later life (Robins and Price 1991). Saving a high-risk young offender from such a "career" would not only reduce a lot of suffering for parents, teachers, peers, crime victims, and (in the longer run) the youngster himself, but also reduce the costs of approximately $1–5 million on average to society (Muñoz et al. 2004; Cohen and Piquero 2009).

For these and other reasons, numerous studies have addressed the effects of preventing antisocial behavior in children and youth. Developmental crime prevention became a broad field in which programs and research differ in many aspects—for example, with regard to children's age (e.g., early childhood; preschool, elementary, or secondary school age); program participants (e.g., children, parents, teachers, or multiple target groups); type of prevention (e.g., universal for all children of a school or neighborhood, selective for at-risk groups, or indicated for children who already show behavioral problems); content of the program (e.g., child training, parent training, home visits, intensive care, family counseling, multisystemic therapy, whole-school programs, or combinations of measures in multilevel programs); program intensity (e.g., from a few sessions to a duration of several years); institutional context (e.g., family home, preschool, school, guidance center, clinic, or multiple contexts in community prevention); quality of research design (pre-post, quasi-experiment with nonequivalent control group, matched pairs, or RCTs); type of outcome measures (tests on trained contents; parent, teacher, expert or self-reports; behavior observations; archival data); and length of follow-up (from postintervention only over a few weeks/months up to decades).

Given such heterogeneity, it is necessary to analyze and evaluate specific areas of prevention separately and then integrate the findings. Therefore, the present essay concentrates on child social skills training. This is a very popular mode of prevention of antisocial development that has various advantages (Prinz and Miller 1994; Kazdin and Wassell 1999; Lösel 2005). Child social skills training is relatively easy to implement, particularly when delivered by regular teachers in schools or preschools, and programs can be rather inexpensive. Child programs are also less vulnerable to low participation rates than parent-oriented programs. Often they can reach nearly all children of a target population. Last but not least, there is a substantial body of evaluation research on child social skills training. Several observations and conclusions emerge from our review:

- Child skills training is an important and effective developmental approach to preventing crime.
- A number of moderator variables are important to the success of child skills training programs, including evaluation methodology, program type (structured, multimodal, and cognitive-behavioral), targeting of high-risk children, and the age of children.

- There is a need for further large-scale, evidence-based programs with high-quality implementation; more well-controlled, long-term, and independent evaluations; and a systematic and integrated policy in this field.

The organization of this essay is as follows. Section I discusses the conceptual and theoretical background of child social skills training. Section II profiles a few leading child skills programs. Section III involves a systematic evaluation of the effectiveness of such programs. Section IV offers some conclusions and recommendations with respect to future research, practice, and policy.

I. Conceptual and Theoretical Background

Social skills and social competences are often used as interchangeable terms. However, social skills are more specific behavioral manifestations of the complex construct of social competence (Caldarella and Merrell 1997; Gresham 1998). The latter encompasses interpersonal and communication abilities that lead to positively evaluated consequences of social interactions from the perspective of the interacting individuals and important others (e.g., teachers). In general, social competence refers to three levels that interact: (1) cognitive competencies (e.g., effective social information processing and adequate cognitions about self and others); (2) emotional competencies (e.g., age-appropriate development and expression of emotions); and (3) behavioral competencies (e.g., verbal and nonverbal communication and interaction skills). More specific approaches refer to various dimensions of competence, such as initiating relationships, self-disclosure, asserting displeasure with others' actions, providing emotional support, and managing interpersonal conflicts (e.g., Buhrmester et al. 1988).

Social skills are the behavioral targets in social competence training. Such training is recommended for improving social development in general; in anxious, shy, or intellectually less gifted children; and in particular for the prevention and early treatment of antisocial behavior (Durlak and Wells 1997; Kazdin 1998, 2003). Training for the prevention of antisocial development focuses on social skills/ competencies that are particularly relevant for aggressive and delinquent behavior. For example, it aims to promote nonhostile modes of social perception and attribution, identification of own and others' emotions, perspective taking and victim empathy, self-control and anger management, nondeviant attitudes, interpersonal problem solving in conflict situations, and communication skills. Deficits in such competencies are empirical risk factors for antisocial development (Akhtar and Bradley 1991; Crick and Dodge 1994; Lösel and Bender 2006; Farrington and Welsh, 2007), whereas good levels seem to be promotive or even protective when other risks are present (Lösel and Bender 2003; Lösel and Farrington 2010). The social skills targeted in programs should not only correlate with antisocial behavior but also have a causal impact. This is suggested by social-cognitive learning theories (Bandura 1973; Mischel 1973).

Within this framework, concepts of social information processing are an important basis of social skills training (Crick and Dodge 1994; Dodge and Pettit 2003; Lösel and Beelmann, 2005). Such models assume that individuals differ in how they process relevant information in social situations. Within biological and intellectual boundaries these differences develop through learning processes. Cognitive mechanisms mediate between the influences of social contexts, biological dispositions, personality traits, and situational factors. Individuals differ in how they (1) perceive and encode situational and social cues; (2) form a mental representation and interpretation of the situation; (3) clarify and set own goals for the interaction; (4) recall or construct possible reactions; (5) evaluate these reactions; and (6) initiate what they expect to be the most adequate action.

Numerous studies have shown that children with aggressive and other antisocial behavior focus more on aggression-relevant stimuli and remember more of such details (see Akhtar and Bradley 1991; Dodge 2000; Lösel and Bliesener, 2003; Fontaine and Dodge 2009). They are less able to recognize specific motivations of their interaction partners and attribute more hostile intentions to them. Their goal setting is more egocentric and less relationship oriented. They retrieve and generate more aggressive, hostile, and impulsive alternatives for action. These are evaluated more positively and accompanied by expectations of self-efficacy. And finally, there is also a lack of skills for nonaggressive interactions.

The theory assumes that individuals go through these phases more or less automatically. Changing the processes is an important aim of social skills training. The contents of aggression-prone schemes, scripts, and beliefs are mainly learned by experiences of aggression, conflict, abuse, and bad parenting in the family; peer models and reinforcement in groups; or through media consumption (e.g., Crick and Dodge 1994; Lösel, Bliesener, and Bender 2007). The details of such learning processes have not been much investigated. Other questions also need further clarification. For example: Are deficits in social information processing similarly important for various forms of antisocial behavior (e.g., proactive versus reactive aggression; Dodge et al. 1997)? Do they always indicate a lack of skill or are they also plausible approaches in a given social context (Sutton, Smith, and Swettenham 1999)? Is the role of emotions sufficiently incorporated in primarily cognitive concepts (e.g., Denham and Burton 2003)? However, such details can be addressed in more complex models of social information processing (e.g., Huesmann 1998) and are also differently targeted in social skills/competence training.

In practice, there are rather different training concepts (e.g., Webster-Stratton and Taylor 2001; Spence 2003). Historically two main approaches can be differentiated. One is more behavior-oriented and the other focuses on social-cognitive training. Behavior-oriented programs teach children skills for getting in contact with others, making friends, accepting the rights of others, or expressing individual needs appropriately. Often, peers or other social models are used to promote these skills. In contrast, social-cognitive programs target basic cognitive skills for effective social problem solving, such as perspective taking, self-control, and anger management (Chandler 1973; Spivack and Shure 1974; Camp et al. 1977). Over the last two decades, approaches became more similar and often address cognitive and emotional competencies as well as concrete interaction behavior (e.g., Bierman, Greenberg, and Conduct Problems Research Group 1996; Webster-Stratton and Hammond 1997; Frauenknecht and Black 2004).

Most current programs are manual-based and contain a number of structured group sessions. However, there are also approaches that aim to promote social skills by counseling or by buddy systems (e.g., Tierney, Grossman, and Resch 1995). The structured programs use didactic methods such as hypothetical conflict scenarios, model demonstrations, role-plays, reinforcement of adequate behavior, group discussions, social games, concrete instructions, pictures, audio or video material, and home work to improve transfer to real-life situations. Of course, the concepts, materials, and language are adapted to the age, intellectual level, or ethnic background of the respective group. Dependent on whether it is a universal or indicated approach, program length can vary between a few and more than 100 sessions. The framing conditions are also rather different because social skill training may be used as a stand-alone program or integrated into multimodal approaches with parent, teacher, peer-group, or other components.

II. Examples of Programs for Child Social Skills Training

In the following section, we briefly describe five typical child social skills training programs and their related research projects. The examples were not selected because they have particularly large effects. However, they represent various types of universal, selected, and indicated prevention in different contexts. They also demonstrate that social competence training is not only implemented as a silo program but also used with other approaches to prevention. Most importantly, the examples were/are embedded in thorough evaluation projects and had/have a strong impact on the development of the whole field of developmental prevention.

A. I Can Problem Solve (ICPS)

The ICPS is a universal program to promote interpersonal cognitive problem-solving skills in children at kindergarten and elementary school age (Shure and Spivack 1982; Shure 1992a, 1992b). It follows the concept of Spivack and Shure (1989) and two main assumptions: (1) It is important to promote a specific thinking style (problem-solving style) and not specific thought content; (2) Effective social problem solving results from various skills: sensitivity to social problems and identification of emotions (social perception), creating alternative solutions to interpersonal problems (alternative thinking), planning of action steps (means-ends thinking), anticipation of action consequences (consequence thinking), and recognizing the causes of social action (causal thinking, perspective taking).

A previous training program (Spivack and Shure 1974) was adapted and ICPS now consists of three different versions for the ages of 4 to 5, 6 to 8, and 9 to 10 years (Shure 1993). The program consists of 60 to 80 successive exercises that are taught in groups of 5 to 10 children. Sessions last about 20 minutes and are practiced every day for a period of three to six months. Teachers as well as parents are suitable as coaches. The skills are trained in question and answer sessions using images of conflict situations, group interactions, and discussions. Most important is the "problem-solving dialogue" that should support the child's cognitive process to find an appropriate solution. Teachers and parents should also use this dialogue to guide and encourage children to try out different options for action in daily life.

The ICPS has undergone a number of evaluations. For example, Shure and Spivack (1988) showed that it can significantly improve cognitive problem-solving skills and reduce impulsivity or inhibition. Effects lasted through one-year follow-up and could be validated by teachers' behavioral observations (Greenberg, Celene, and Bumbarger 2001). A German adaptation and modification of the program for universal prevention at preschool age was investigated in the Erlangen-Nuremberg Development and Prevention Study (e.g., Lösel et al. 2004). There were positive effects on preschool teacher ratings of social behavior after two to three months and fewer children with multiple problems according to school report cards two years after the training (Lösel et al. 2006, 2009). Not yet published long-term evaluations on self-reported delinquency outcomes suggest a desirable effect after four to five years and even a small effect after nine years when the child skills training had been combined with a parent training (Lösel et al. 2010). However, the outcome patterns over time were not fully consistent and there were no significant effects in parent reports.

B. Promoting Alternative Thinking Strategies (PATHS)

The PATHS curriculum is a comprehensive social training system for children from kindergarten up to the sixth class (Kusché and Greenberg 1994). It was originally developed for deaf children and later expanded and implemented in US regular schools and special classes. There is a preparation unit (Readiness and Self-Control Unit) for kindergarten children or children with special needs (e.g., developmental delays, behavioral or emotional problems). In 12 lessons, children receive a funny introduction to the PATHS content with a focus on readiness skills and developing basic self-control. The PATHS curriculum is based on the ABCD (affective-behavioral-cognitive-dynamic) model of integrated social personality development (Greenberg and Kusché 1993). Objectives of the curriculum are to promote self-control, positive self-esteem, emotional awareness and understanding, interpersonal problem-solving skills, and relationship skills. The program for school-age children includes 120 lessons of 20 to 30 minutes each. It can be implemented as part of the school curriculum. If three to five sessions are carried out per week, the curriculum lasts about two years. The training can be conducted in groups of four to nine children or in whole school classes.

The PATHS curriculum consists of three major units. The Feelings and Relationships Unit (56 lessons) should promote the understanding of emotional and interpersonal processes. It also introduces self-control techniques using the Control Signals Poster. This serves as a visual aid and as a preparation for the Problem-Solving Unit (33 lessons). Here, interpersonal cognitive problem-solving skills are taught and exercised on the basis of 11 steps that are an extension of the Control Signals Poster. Other topics are promotion of self-esteem and relationship skills using discussions and role-plays. Finally, there is a Supplementary Unit that should deepen, transfer, and preserve what was learned (31 lessons). In addition to the basic curriculum there is a PATHS Curriculum for School Age Child Care Providers (Kusché and Greenberg 1992). This is a shorter after-school training program (16 weeks) that can be implemented in various nonschool institutions.

The PATHS curriculum showed positive effects in elementary schools. It promoted problem-solving skills and understanding of other children's feelings (Greenberg, Domitrovich, and Bumbarger 2001), as well as neuropsychological mediators such as inhibitory control (Riggs et al. 2006). Similar effects were found for an adaptation to preschool age (Domitrovich, Cortes, and Greenberg 2007). The PATHS also led to a significant reduction of teacher-rated externalizing and internalizing problems of children from special classes (Greenberg et al. 1995). Eisner et al. (2008) implemented PATHS at grade 1 in elementary schools at Zurich, Switzerland. The experimental evaluation at grade 3 showed some small positive effects in social-cognitive skills and parent-rated aggressive behavior, particularly in schools with good quality of program implementation. An adapted and shortened version of the PATHS after-school program for elementary school children was implemented and evaluated within our Erlangen-Nuremberg Study (Hacker et al. 2007). Outcomes at four months after the training revealed small to medium desirable effects on teacher-rated problem behavior and prosocial behavior.

The most comprehensive evaluation was conducted within the large multisite FAST Track Prevention Trial (FAST = Family and School Together). This project addressed 445 high-risk children and their families, who were selected in a stepwise screening and compared with a random control group (CPPRG; Conduct Problems Prevention Research Group 1992). In addition to PATHS the program included parent training, home visits, parent-child sessions, academic tutoring, peer coaching, and classroom management. After the initial intervention at grade 1, further program elements were delivered according to the family and child needs. The PATHS curriculum was provided in a modified grade-level version in the intervention schools up to grade 5. Through grades 6–10, parent and youth sessions were offered on topics such as sex education or drug abuse.

Owing to the complex multimodal nature of the prevention, it is not possible to estimate the specific effect of PATHS. The whole Fast Track program reduced aggressive and oppositional behavior at school and improved social-cognitive skills of children in the first year after the training. At grade 3, the program group showed less aggression at school and home (Conduct Problems Prevention Research Group 2002). After four years, they revealed better social competence, less contact with deviant peers, and fewer conduct problems outside the school context (Conduct Problems Prevention Research Group 2004). At grade 9, there were lower scores in self-reported delinquency, and from grades 3 to 9, fewer cases with conduct disorder among the highest risk subgroup (Conduct Problems Prevention Research Group 2007). A recent evaluation through age 19 showed a number of desirable effects on official crime such as a lower probability and less severity of arrests (Conduct Problems Prevention Research Group 2010). Differences in self-reported delinquency were mainly nonsignificant. Overall, CPPRG shows positive effects; however, the outcome patterns vary across measures, social contexts, and follow-up times. Children at particularly high risk seem to benefit most.

C. The Montréal Prevention Experiment

This intervention was part of the Montréal Longitudinal and Experimental Study (Tremblay et al. 2003). It contained a selective prevention program for boys from low socioeconomic families who were above the 70th percentile on a measure of disruptive and aggressive behavior (Tremblay 2010; Tremblay et al. 1995). The intervention took place at elementary school age (7–9 years). It included a parent training program that should improve inappropriate parenting behavior and was conducted with parents approximately twice a month over a period of two years. The frequency of sessions (20–46) was adapted to the needs of the respective families. The child social skills training was conducted in a group format during lunchtime breaks at schools. Children at risk were placed in groups with three to five teacher-identified prosocial peers to promote positive modeling and avoid iatrogenic effects. The program consisted of two parts. During the first year, 9 sessions focused on developing and practicing prosocial skills, while 10 sessions in the second year addressed self-control skills. Role-plays, peer modeling, and coaching were typical didactic measures.

The effectiveness of the program was assessed in a randomized trial with three conditions: a treatment group, a control group, and an attention-placebo group (Tremblay et al. 1995, 1996). Results at posttreatment revealed no significant differences between treatment and control groups, but at three year follow-up and in adolescence, there were significant effects. This is an example of potential sleeper effects, which sometimes happen because trained children/parents need time to practice acquired skills. According to teacher ratings, treated boys were less often engaged in fighting, less often had serious difficulties, and were more likely to be rated as well adjusted. Across early adolescence, treated boys reported less gang membership or being drunk or taking drugs compared to controls. At age 16, the program group's delinquency resembled that of the group who was low risk at kindergarten age (Vitaro, Brendgen, and Tremblay 2001). In a 15-year follow-up, more program boys had completed high school and fewer had a criminal record than in the control group (Boisjoli et al. 2007).

D. The Seattle Social Development Project

The Seattle Social Development Project contains a comprehensive universal prevention program that addresses multiple risk and protective factors at the individual, school, and family level (Hawkins et al. 1992, 1999). It is designed to strengthen school and family bonds, to increase school success, and to reduce early signs of physical aggression, as well as school failure and inappropriate parenting practices (e.g., harsh or inconsistent discipline, poor monitoring). Classroom teachers are trained in instructional methods like proactive classroom management, interactive teaching, and cooperative learning. Parents of children in grades 1 to 3 receive parent training that is adapted to the respective developmental stages of children. These approaches are used in combination with classroom based problem-solving training (ICPS; Shure and Spivack 1982) in first grade and assertiveness training for peer pressure and misuse of drugs in the sixth grade. Therefore, the Seattle Project does not provide evaluation of the child social skills program only.

Effects were assessed in quasi-experimental studies addressing three conditions: the full intervention group (package from first to sixth grade), the late intervention group (package in fifth and sixth grade), and a control group with no intervention. Results of the long-term follow-up (six years after intervention) revealed significant positive outcomes for the full-time intervention group. Students committed less violent delinquent acts, had a stronger commitment and attachment to school, had better self-reported academic achievement, showed less self-reported involvement in school misbehavior, had less heavy alcohol use in the past year, and had fewer sex partners by age 18, whereas no effects were shown for life-time prevalence of cigarettes, alcohol, and drug use (Hawkins et al. 1999). Although only the full intervention group showed significant effects, there was a dosage effect on various variables. The fifth grade program package reduced delinquent behavior but not substance use (Hawkins et al. 2008).

E. The Dinosaur Problem Solving Training Program

The Dina Dinosaur Social, Emotional and Problem Solving Child Training Program had been developed by Webster-Stratton and Reid (2004). It is part of The Incredible Years Parents, Teachers, and Children Training Series (Webster-Stratton 2000). These programs aim to prevent, reduce, and treat conduct problems among children ages 2–10, to increase their social, emotional, and academic competence, and to promote parenting competence and strengthen families, as well as to promote teacher competence and strengthen school-home connections. The Dinosaur curriculum is an indicated prevention program to teach positive interaction skills to 4- to 8-year-olds who have conduct problems. It can also be used to address related problems such as attention deficits and peer rejection. The curriculum includes six programs (seven units): Making Friends and Learning School Rules, Understanding and Detecting Feelings, Detective Wally Teaches Problem-Solving Steps (with a unit on anger management), Molly Manners Teaches How to Be Friendly, Molly Explains How to Talk With Friends, and Dina Dinosaur Teaches How to Do Your Best in School. The child training makes use of life and videotape modeling, fantasy play and instruction, role-playing, and creative activities. It also fosters skills maintenance and generalization outside the training context. To promote children's identification, animal puppets are used as models. The training consists of 18 to 22 weekly two-hour lessons and can be delivered by counselors or therapists in a mental health-related field.

The Dinosaur program's effectiveness was assessed in randomized trials with clinic-referred, conduct-disordered children (4–8 years) comparing four groups: child training only, parent training only, combined child and parent training, and waiting list control group (Webster-Stratton and Hammond 1997; Webster-Stratton, Reid, and Hammond 2001, 2004). At post-treatment, all intervention conditions were superior to the control group and the combined parent and child training was most effective. The child training showed significant improvements in observed peer interactions and indicators of social problem solving. Program children had more social skills than the controls and than those whose parents had been trained. One year later, significant effects were maintained, but the combined parent and child intervention showed the most stable effects. Analyses of clinical significance revealed that the combined parent and child training had the most sustained effects on child behavior (Webster-Stratton 2000).

III. Effects of Social Skills Training

As in all areas of research, evidence comes by replication. Therefore, one should not rely too much on single evaluations. This is obvious when one looks at two of the most impressive projects on developmental prevention: the High/Scope Perry Preschool Project (Schweinhart, Barnes, and Weikart 1993; Schweinhart et al. 2005) and the Cambridge-Somerville Youth Study (McCord 1978, 2003). These projects evaluated the efficacy of prevention programs from childhood onwards into middle adulthood. Both studies are outstanding not only with regard to the length of follow-up but also for their methodological quality because they used randomized control trials (RCTs). However, their results tell contradicting stories about the potential of developmental prevention. Whereas the High/Scope Perry Preschool Project showed desirable effects on crime and other outcomes beyond age 40, the findings of the Cambridge-Somerville Youth Study in middle adulthood were zero or even slightly negative.

There are no such long-term evaluations in the field of social skills training, but short-term effects with many outcome measures are also vulnerable to artifacts.

Therefore, our evaluation of the effects of social competence training will focus on reviews and, in particular, quantitative meta-analyses. Over time, a number of systematic reviews have addressed the effects of child social skills training. They cannot be discussed in detail here. At first we present findings from an own comprehensive review of high-quality studies (RCTs) on social skills training. Then we briefly address other reviews in the field and check the consistency of findings.

A. Results of Own Reviews of Randomized Studies

The review of Lösel and Beelmann (2003) contained published and unpublished studies on child social competence training for the prevention of antisocial behavior. It was followed by various more specified analyses (Lösel and Beelmann 2005, Beelmann and Lösel 2006; Lösel and Beelmann 2006). The meta-analysis addressed universal prevention programs as well as selective programs for children from high-risk family backgrounds (e.g., low SES, single mothers) and indicated programs for children with behavioral problems (aggression, conduct disorders, impulsivity). Treatment programs for adjudicated juvenile delinquents were excluded. Only randomized controlled trials were selected as the methodological quality standard; for other eligibility criteria, see Lösel and Beelmann (2003).

After a search of more than 800 documents, 84 research reports met the eligibility criteria. These reports contained 135 treatment-control comparisons and a total of 16,723 children and adolescents. Most studies were carried out in the United States (85 percent), had small sample sizes (73 percent less than 50), and only short time periods for measuring outcome effects (85 percent less than 3 months). Only about 5 percent of the evaluations contained a follow-up period of more than one year. In accordance with the preventive approach, the main target groups were rather young (mean age < 13: 87 percent). Typically, the programs had a group format (78 percent), lasted less than 30 sessions (75 percent), and were implemented within a school context (74 percent).

The program types were coded into four categories: (1) behavioral programs (e.g., focusing on role-play and other behavioral training methods for concrete social skills); (2) cognitive programs (e.g., focusing on self-control, social problem solving, and/or perspective taking without behavioral practice); (3) cognitive-behavioral programs (combining the two aforementioned concepts); and (4) programs based on concepts of counseling, psychotherapy, or other methods that also aimed to improve social skills (e.g., Adlerian counseling, buddy programs). The outcome data were placed in various categories of which two are used here: (1) antisocial behavior (e.g., aggressive, oppositional, or delinquent behavior); and (2) social competence (e.g., social skills such as interaction skills or prosocial behavior and social-cognitive skills such as social problem-solving skills or self-control). The majority of outcomes were measured within two months after the training (posttest); only one-fourth had at least three months follow-up. Table 6.1 presents selected findings.

Overall, the effect of social skills training programs was positive. However, there was a large variation between individual studies and some had even a negative

Table 6.1 Mean effect sizes of child social skills training at post-intervention and follow-up in relation to various study characteristics

	Post-intervention[a]			Follow-up[a]		
	Antisocial behavior	Social competence	Total	Antisocial behavior	Social competence	Total
All programs	.29* (82)	.43* (92)	.39* (127)	.20* (20)	.31* (24)	.28* (34)
Type of program						
Behavioral	.14 (25)	.50* (22)	.34* (37)	.12 (4)	.34* (4)	.17 (5)
Cognitive	.14 (15)	.47* (21)	.41* (25)	-.06 (3)	.41* (8)	.36* (9)
Cognitive-behavioral	.49* (26)	.41* (41)	.43* (48)	.50* (7)	.27* (11)	.37* (14)
Other	.38* (16)	.30 (8)	.37* (17)	.16 (6)	.30 (1)	.17 (6)
Type of prevention						
Universal	.07 (13)	.45* (23)	.36* (30)	-.05 (2)	.14 (4)	.15 (4)
Selective	.12 (27)	.40* (33)	.31* (46)	.15 (10)	.30* (10)	.23* (18)
Indicated	.53* (42)	.44* (36)	.49* (51)	.48* (8)	.40* (10)	.41* (12)
Treatment intensity[b]						
Low	.20 (24)	.43* (39)	.39* (48)	.12 (3)	.22 (5)	.22 (7)
Medium	.31* (49)	.42* (49)	.38* (69)	.17 (11)	.34* (19)	.31* (21)
High	.46* (9)	.60* (4)	.46* (10)	.30* (6)	—	.30* (6)
Age of children						
4–6	.19 (16)	.43* (18)	.33* (24)	.12 (1)	.72* (5)	.60* (6)
7–12	.24* (50)	.40* (61)	.38* (85)	.17 (17)	.24* (19)	.22* (26)
13 and older	.61* (15)	.67* (13)	.51* (18)	.78* (2)	—	.78* (2)

Note: Effect sizes are Cohen's *d*-coefficients; number of primary studies in brackets; underlined study numbers indicate significant heterogeneity in effect sizes;
[a] post-intervention: ≤ 2 months; follow-up: ≥ 3 months;
[b] Low = up to 10 sessions or 2 months duration, medium = 11 to 40 sessions or 3 to 8 months duration, high = more than 40 sessions or 8 months duration;
* effect size differs significantly from zero (*p* <.05).
Source: Adapted from a meta-analysis of randomized evaluations; Beelmann and Lösel 2006.

effect (a better outcome in the control group; see Lösel and Beelmann 2003). According to Cohen's (1988) classification, most mean effects were small to moderate. At postintervention, the effect was larger than at follow-up (*d* = 0.38 vs. 0.28), although—as mentioned—the latter period was also very short in most studies. Owing to the relatively small number of studies with longer follow-ups, the findings on some moderator effects are not as well replicated as in the more frequent short-term evaluations.

Effects on antisocial behavior were smaller than effects on measures of social skills, which are more proximal to the training content. With regard to program types, there were no clear differences at postintervention and in social competence outcomes at follow-up. However, cognitive-behavioral approaches were the only programs with significant effects in terms of reducing antisocial behavior at postintervention and follow-up. As could be expected, behavioral or cognitive approaches had positive effects in the social competence domain, but this did not generalize to antisocial behavior. The most important finding for practice is that only cognitive-behavioral approaches had a substantial effect on antisocial behavior at follow-up. More differentiated analyses (Beelmann and Lösel 2006) also revealed that only cognitive-behavioral approaches had a significant short-term effect on various forms of antisocial behavior (aggressive, oppositional/disruptive, delinquent, and unspecified antisocial behavior). This was particularly notable for delinquency because it was the only field in which at least some studies used official records as the outcome measure. The follow-up data could not be differentiated similarly because the number of studies in subcategories was too small.

Indicated prevention programs revealed larger effects than selected prevention or, in particular, universal programs. This was specifically the case for antisocial and follow-up outcomes. Such a moderator effect is plausible because the target groups of indicated prevention are children who already show some behavior problems and often come from high-risk family backgrounds. If programs are successful, they will have a stronger impact in such groups than in the unselected samples of universal prevention where most children would develop no behavioral problems even without a program. Therefore, effect sizes for universal prevention will normally be smaller. One might assume that the finding of a larger effect in high-risk samples could be an artifact of regression to the mean. However, this is not plausible because the review included only RCTs with equivalent treatment and control groups. Larger effects in high-risk samples are also consistent with findings on offender treatment (e.g., Lipsey and Wilson 1998; Lösel and Schmucker 2005; Lipsey, Landenberger, and Wilson 2007). Similarly, Farrington and Welsh (2003) found larger effects for clinic-based than for school-based family prevention programs. This was probably due to more indicated prevention and higher risk cases in clinical contexts.

Table 6.1 suggests that age of children can also moderate effect size. However, one should not draw too far-reaching conclusions here because there were very few studies in some categories at follow-up. Overall, the review at least suggests that older children can still benefit from social skills training. There was even a tendency for larger effects on antisocial behavior in youth. This finding could be due to more frequent indicated prevention in older children, whereas universal programs are often implemented at preschool or elementary school age. A similar conjoined moderator effect must be assumed for program intensity. Although the most intensive programs showed the largest mean effects, these programs are also often indicated interventions for children with manifest behavior problems. The general problem of confounded moderators in meta-analysis (Lipsey 2003) is particularly relevant for our topic, because there are not enough studies with antisocial outcomes and follow-up data to get substantial cell frequencies in more differentiated categories.

Other moderators are not reported in detail as in table 6.1 because they refer more to evaluation than to program issues. However, they should not be overlooked when planning and implementing child social skills programs. For example, Lösel and Beelmann (2003) found that studies with a relatively large sample size ($n > 150$) had a smaller, and in the follow-up, even a nonsignificant effect. This is in concordance with larger effects in smaller studies of family-oriented prevention (e.g., Farrington and Welsh 2003) or offender treatment (e.g., Lipsey and Wilson 1998; Lösel and Schmucker 2005). One reason for this relation may be a publication bias: larger samples are more likely to reveal the significance of a true small effect (Weisburd, Lum, and Yang 2003). Owing to author or editor decisions, this significant result may be published more frequently than the same, but nonsignificant, effect in a smaller sample. In contrast, studies with small samples may only be published when they have relatively large effects.

Although such a publication bias cannot be ruled out completely, Lösel and Beelmann (2003) found no difference in mean effects between published and unpublished studies. Therefore, issues of program implementation also have to be taken into account. In large studies, difficulties in maintaining program integrity and homogeneity of samples may reduce design sensitivity and thus lead to smaller effects (Lösel and Wittmann 1989; Weisburd, Petrosino, and Mason 1993). Although program integrity is a key factor in prevention (Beelmann and Raabe 2009), too few studies reported sufficient details to explore this explanation of smaller effects in larger samples. A third reason might have been that small studies are often carried out on indicated prevention that had larger effects than universal approaches (see above).

Other potential moderators showed less consistent or nonsignificant results. For example, the dropout rate or the type of control group (no treatment versus attention/placebo) did not reveal a significant effect (Lösel and Beelmann 2003). The same applied to the gender composition of studies. Type of randomization (individual/pairwise versus blockwise/groupwise) had a significant moderator effect, but only at postintervention. The source of information on the outcome seems also to be relevant. Teacher ratings of child behavior showed consistent significant effects at postintervention and follow-up, whereas findings for parent reports were less consistent and self-reports were not significant at both measurement times (Lösel and Beelmann 2006). Contrary to plausible expectations, there were not larger effects in more recent studies. Perhaps, an improvement in program quality may have been compensated by better control conditions or more rigorous study designs.

Last but not least, we need to refer to a potential moderating effect of the researcher. Lösel and Beelmann (2003) found a slightly larger effect when the authors of evaluation studies or their colleagues had also been involved in program development or delivery. Again, this seems to be an issue that is relevant not only for child skills training. In other areas of prevention, effects were also larger when program developers had been involved in the evaluation (Petrosino and Soydan 2005; Eisner 2009). One should not assume intentional faking, but data grouping and analysis contain many decisions that may be carried out more in favor of one's own program. It also needs to be assumed that researchers who evaluate their own program may invest more in high-quality implementation and analysis (Sherman and Strang 2009).

Independence and conflicts of interest are key issues in program evaluation. Although this applies to a much lesser degree to systematic reviews, we now briefly check the consistency of the own meta-analyses with other reviews.

B. Main Results of Selected Other Reviews

In an early systematic review, Denham and Almeida (1987) analyzed 50 studies on social problem-solving interventions in 3–12-year-old children. The programs had a significant impact on various outcome measures. Effects were substantial on measures of interpersonal cognitive problem solving skills ($d = 0.78$), but lower on behavior ratings by teachers ($d = 0.26$). Although there were relatively strong effects in observation data, the authors recommend caution with regard to concrete behavior change.

In a more differentiated meta-analysis of social competence training, Beelmann, Pfingsten, and Lösel (1994) reviewed 49 evaluation studies. This study found substantial effects on social-cognitive skills ($d = 0.77$) and interaction skills ($d = 0.34$). However, effects on social adjustment measures were smaller ($d = 0.18$) and nonsignificant at follow-up. Monomodal programs (i.e., focusing on social-cognitive competencies in conflict scenarios) had no significant impact on measures of either social behavior (e.g., social skills) or adjustment in real life (e.g., behavior problems). In contrast, multimodal programs that combined social problem solving measures with intensive behavioral practice revealed positive effects. Later narrative reviews (e.g., Taylor, Eddy, and Biglan 1999; Webster-Stratton and Taylor 2001) also suggested that children should not just be taught crucial social-cognitive competencies but should also be trained in applying them in concrete behavioral settings.

In a meta-analysis of 38 evaluations of social skills training, Ang and Hughes (2001) found a large mean effect size of $d = 0.62$. At first glance this seems to contradict the typical effects we presented above. However, the focus of the review was indicated prevention that also showed larger effects in Lösel and Beelmann (2003). Most of the outcomes were proximal measures of social skills and not indicators of social behavior in real life. In agreement with table 6.1, the longer term effects were substantially smaller ($d = 0.36$).

A meta-analysis of Wilson, Gottfredson, and Najaka (2001) addressed 165 school-based programs for the prevention of delinquency, drug use, and school dropout (see also Gottfredson, Jones, and Gore 2002). Although this review included a broad range of programs (e.g., individual counseling, behavior modification, and school management), it provides information that is relevant for social skills training. Typical mean effects were significant, but only in the range of d ≈ 0.10 plus/minus 0.05 for outcomes such as delinquency or externalizing behavior. Cognitive-behavioral and behavioral methods to promote social competence showed stronger effects, whereas unstructured mentoring, pure instruction, and counseling programs revealed even slightly negative outcomes. In accordance with Beelmann and Lösel (2006), high-risk groups benefitted most from the programs.

The finding of modest effect sizes was also confirmed by a rare systematic review of single-subject studies (Mathur et al. 1998). The authors found 64 percent of nonoverlapping data (similar to a small d coefficient) for social skills training of children with emotional and behavioral disorders. There were somewhat stronger effects on social interaction skills than on communication skills and young delinquents benefited a little more from the training than other disordered groups.

A systematic review of Mytton et al. (2002) addressed randomized evaluations of school-based programs against violence for children at risk for violence (not specific anti-bullying programs). Twenty-eight studies met the eligibility criteria or provided sufficient data for analysis. The programs were mainly social competence training—for example, interventions to improve relationship skills or skills of nonresponse to aggression. The mean effect on aggression outcomes was $d = 0.36$ and remained similar for the few trials that collected data up to 12 months after treatment. Interventions to improve relationship skills or social context had a larger mean effect ($d = 0.65$). However, only one study on these prevention measures had a follow-up of at least one year.

A meta-analysis of Gansle (2005) reviewed not social skills training in general but school-based anger interventions. Although anger management is a more specific approach, it contains a range of activities including self- and social-focused interventions that are also frequently used in broader social skills training. The review contained 24 studies that addressed universal and indicated prevention for children from 5 to 18 years. The mean effect across all outcome measures was $d = 0.31$ at postintervention and even somewhat larger for externalizing and anger indicators ($d = 0.54$). Follow-up effects in the latter criteria remained stable ($d = 0.53$). However, "follow-up" included every measurement at more than one week after treatment termination. A broader range of behavioral treatment activities, a greater amount of treatment time, and a randomized design were positively related to effect size in externalizing/anger outcomes. The limits of including only published studies and of the small number of real follow-up measurements were rightly mentioned.

Wilson, Lipsey, and Derzon (2003) and, in an updated analysis, Wilson and Lipsey (2007) addressed school-based interventions for aggressive and disruptive behavior. These reviews were not limited to social skills training but also included peer mediation, special classes, and multilevel programs with parent and child training. However, social skills training formed a key part of the interventions. The results of both analyses were consistent with what we reported above. For example, Wilson and Lipsey (2007) found an overall positive effect that was modest in size. Universal programs were most similar to the programs included in Lösel and Beelmann (2003) and had a mean effect of d = 0.20 on aggressive/disruptive behavior. It made no difference whether program modality was more cognitive or more skill oriented. The mean effects for selected/indicated programs were larger (d = 0.29) and behavioral strategies were a significant moderator. In both approaches to prevention, groups at higher risk showed stronger effects. Surprisingly, comprehensive/multilevel approaches to prevention revealed a nonsignificant mean effect. However, this was based on a relatively small number of studies and universal programs with more frequent treatment contacts produced larger reductions of antisocial behavior.

Hahn et al. (2007) carried out a systematic review of 59 studies of universal school-based programs that were intended to prevent violence in high-risk areas (low SES or high crime rate). The meta-analysis included not only control group but also pre/post evaluations. Six studies were of the greatest design suitability and good execution. Although the review included environmental change programs, the majority of interventions focused on cognitive/affective changes and, in particular, concrete social behavior skills. Overall, there was a significant reduction in violence at all school grades (Md = 15 percent relative reduction compared to control population). Effects were larger in high school and preschool (29 and 32 percent, respectively) than in elementary and middle school (18 and 7 percent, respectively). However, the outcomes in the latter grades may be more reliable because of more available studies. Cognitive/affective programs showed an overall violence reduction of 14 percent and social skills training one of 19 percent. This is in the range of the d coefficients presented in table 6.1.

A meta-analysis of Garrard and Lipsey (2007) reviewed 36 controlled evaluations on the impact of conflict-resolution programs on antisocial behavior in US schools. Although these programs represent a special type of social skills training, they contain the main characteristics (e.g., cognitive, emotional, and behavioral self-control; social perspective taking; cooperative interpersonal problem solving; communication and mutual respect). Overall, the programs significantly reduced antisocial behavior among children and youth. The mean effect size was d = 0.26. There were no clear differences between types of programs (e.g., primarily peer mediation, direct skills instruction, etc.), but age was a significant moderator. Effects were larger for youngsters in early and particularly in middle adolescence, whereas 5–9-year-old children benefited less. Programs with no reported implementation difficulties had larger effects. Various other moderators were also significant, but showed no linear relationship with effect size (e.g., intensity of program).

IV. DISCUSSION AND CONCLUSIONS

Although the briefly reported meta-analyses included rather different samples of primary studies, and in some cases not only child skills training, the findings were moderately similar. They also were mostly in accordance with the analyses of

Beelmann and Lösel (2006) on randomized evaluations that were presented in more detail. The main result of all analyses is a desirable effect of child social skills training. As far as follow-up data were available, most mean effects in antisocial or related child behavior varied between d-coefficients of approximately 0.15 and 0.35. This is a small effect in statistical terms (Cohen 1988). However, depending on the prevalence of behavior problems in the control group, a small effect of 0.20 could indicate a reduction of 10 percentage points, or 20 percent of problems. Such an effect would be relevant for practice and cost-benefit analyses show that it could also lead to a financial pay-off for society (e.g., Welsh, Farrington, and Sherman 2001; Aos et al. 2004).

Our overall positive conclusion is supported not only by the various reported reviews on child-oriented prevention but also by a recent comparative meta-evaluation of various types of programs (Beelmann and Raabe 2009). This suggests that social skills training, parent training programs, and early interventions are the most promising developmental prevention strategies. However, one must be aware that any general conclusion requires differentiation. As shown in this essay, the field of social skills training contains a broad range of preventive approaches and study types and accordingly meta-analyses often found significant heterogeneity in over-all effects and moderator variables. Among the many potential outcome modera-tors, the following turned out to be particularly important.

First, evaluation methodology seems to be highly relevant. Studies differed in overall design quality, type of outcome measures, and length of follow-up. Meth-odological features should not be narrowed to the alternative of RCTs versus weaker designs (which was no consistent moderator). Although there are a sub-stantial number of RCTs on child skills training (Lösel and Beelmann 2003), methodological quality is a more complex issue (Lösel and Köferl 1989; Farrington 2003). For example, an RCT on a small sample with no real-life outcome measure and no follow-up will be less informative for practice than a good quasi-experiment with a large sample, sound behavioral effect criteria, and a long-term follow-up. It is a clear deficit that most evaluations of social skills training contain only postinter-vention or very short-term follow-up measurements. This raises the serious question of whether even successful programs are really able to prevent the development of delinquency and violence in the longer term. Although the typical range of follow-up periods is rather narrow, our review shows that effects on children's antisocial behavior at follow-up are smaller than postintervention effects in measures that were similar to the training content (e.g., tests on social-cognitive competences). In addition, many studies contain some inconsistency between multiple effect criteria and bear a risk of fishing for significant results (Gorman 2002).

Second, a relatively consistent moderator was the type of program. Struc-tured, multimodal, cognitive-behavioral approaches revealed the most robust and largest effects. This does not mean that there is only one, single gold standard program. However, research supports basic principles of addressing cognitive, emotional, and behavioral facets of social competence in an integrated manner. Such a multi-modal concept is in line with what we know from longitudinal research on risk factors for delinquent development. Single risk factors often show only small cor-relations with later offending (Lipsey and Derzon 1998; Lösel 2002). Larger effects can be expected when programs target multiple risks or areas of influence. Therefore, as much as possible, programs should not only promote children's cognitive skills and reduce their disruptive behavior but also be complemented by approaches to improve parenting and reduce other risks (e.g., Tremblay and Japel 2003; Lösel 2005).

Third, we found a clear tendency for larger effects in indicated or otherwise targeted prevention for high-risk groups. As discussed, this is a plausible result because universal programs address a large proportion of youngsters who are not at risk for antisocial development and therefore not in need of social skills training. Universal programs often showed a very small or nonsignificant effect, but high-risk participants benefited most. As in public health approaches, even a rather small effect at the population level seems to reduce the average risk and thus impact on the development of high-risk cases (Coid 2003). Universal programs also have the advantage of a more easy outreach and avoidance of potential stigmatization. There-fore, we do not suggest a focus on targeted prevention only. However, one should carefully investigate in a given context whether a universal approach is most appro-priate and then apply stepwise strategies with adequate program intensity for the high-risk cases.

Fourth, a relatively consistent finding was a larger effect in smaller samples. We discussed above that there are various reasons for this result (e.g., publication bias, treatment integrity, demonstration projects). As a practical consequence one should not simply expect that large-scale, routine practice will deliver the same effects as small, well-controlled research projects. In addition, there must be a careful moni-toring of program implementation and quality management.

Fifth, regarding the age of children, here research suggests larger effects in older children/youth or at least not better outcomes at preschool age. As discussed, this result may be due to the confounded effects of risk level and program intensity. Of course, successful prevention at a very young age has the advantage of avoiding problems over several years and related harm for victims, parents, teachers, peers, and the youngsters themselves. However, even the best early programs cannot reach all cases at risk and may have limited effects. Therefore, one should not adopt a pes-simistic view with regard to programs for older children, but follow the basic as-sumption that it is never too early and never too late for sound intervention (Loeber and Farrington 1998; Lösel 2007).

Based on the above and other findings, we conclude with some recommenda-tions for research, policy, and practice (see also Lösel 2005; Junger et al. 2007; Lösel 2007; Beelmann and Raabe 2009):

(1) there is no immediate need for new child social skills programs but knowl-edge on existing approaches should be consolidated and improved;

(2) to investigate the effects of child social skills training on long-term antiso-cial development, we urgently need more well-controlled evaluations with hard behavioral outcomes and long follow-up periods;

(3) there is a clear need of more process evaluation on program implementation and quality management;

(4) research on both process and outcome evaluation must move more from small-scale demonstration projects to large-scale routine prevention in practice;

(5) in addition to the important research of program developers, we need more independent evaluation and less marketing in the field;

(6) although multimodal approaches rightly contain child social skills training, parent training, and other elements, we need more controlled research on the impact of the specific components of such program packages;

(7) social skills training and other developmental crime prevention measures should be integrated in long-term policies and not only be used like fire-brigade interventions after spectacular events of youth crime;

(8) more integrated and long-term policies of developmental crime prevention must be guided by neutral evidence that should be provided by local or nationwide institutions for nonbureaucratic policy guidance and program accreditation (similar to health care);

(9) large-scale implementation of social skills training and related measures of developmental prevention requires financial investment that should be accompanied by cost-benefit analyses (which probably will show a good pay-off); and

(10) developmental crime prevention cannot be achieved by specific programs alone, but requires a careful reflection and perhaps change in how families, schools, neighborhoods, media, and the society as a whole address the real needs of healthy child development.

REFERENCES

Akhtar, Nameera, and E. Jane Bradley. 1991. "Social Information Processing Deficits of Aggressive Children: Present Findings and Implications for Social Skills training." *Clinical Psychology Review* 11:621–44.

Ang, Rebecca P., and Jan N. Hughes. 2001. "Differential Benefits of Skills Training with Antisocial Youth Based on Group Composition: A Meta-Analytic Investigation." *School Psychology Review* 31:164–85.

Aos, Steve, Roxanne Lieb, Jim Mayfiel, Marna Miller, and Annie Pennucci. 2004. *Benefits and Costs of Prevention and Early Intervention Programs for Youth*. Olympia, WA: Washington State Institute for Public Policy.

Bandura, Albert. 1973. *Aggression: A Social Learning Analysis*. New York: Prentice Hall.

Beelmann, Andreas, and Friedrich Lösel. 2006. "Child Social Skills Training in Developmental Crime Prevention: Effects on Antisocial Behavior and Social Competence." *Psicothema* 18:603–10.

Beelmann, Andreas, Ulrich Pfingsten, and Friedrich Lösel. 1994. "Effects of Training Social Competence in Children: A Meta-Analysis of Recent Evaluation Studies." *Journal of Clinical Child Psychology* 23:260–71.

Beelmann, Andreas, and Tobias Raabe. 2009. "The Effects of Preventing Antisocial Behavior and Crime in Childhood and Adolescence: Results and Implications of

Research Reviews and Meta-Analyses." *European Journal of Developmental Science* 3:260–81.

Bierman, Karen L., Mark T. Greenberg, and Conduct Problems Research Group. 1996. "Social Skills Training in the Fast Track Program." In *Preventing Childhood Disorders, Substance Abuse, and Delinquency*, edited by Ray Peters, and Robert J. McMahon. Thousand Oaks, CA: Sage.

Boisjoli, Rachel, Frank Vitaro, Eric Lacourse, Edward C. Barker, and Richard E. Tremblay. 2007. "Impact and Clinical Significance of a Preventive Intervention for Disruptive Boys: 15-year Follow-up." *The British Journal of Psychiatry* 191:415–19.

Buhrmester, Duane, Wyndol Furman, Mitchell T. Wittenberg, and Harry T. Reis. 1988. "Five Domains of Interpersonal Competence in Peer Relationships." *Journal of Personality and Social Psychology* 55:991–1008.

Caldarella, Paul, and Kenneth W. Merrell. 1997. "Common Dimensions of Social Skills of Children and Adolescents: A Taxonomy of Positive Behaviors." *School Psychology Review* 26:264–78.

Camp, Bonnie W., Gaston E. Blom, Frederick Hebert, and William J. van Doorninck. 1977. "'Think Aloud': A Program for Developing Self-Control in Young Aggressive Boys." *Journal of Abnormal Child Psychology* 5:157–69.

Chandler, Michael J. 1973. "Egocentrism and Antisocial Behavior: The Assessment and Training of Social Perspective-Taking Skills." *Developmental Psychology* 9:326–37.

Cohen, Jacob. 1988. *Statistical Power Analysis for the Behavioral Sciences*. New York: Academic Press.

Cohen, Mark A., and Alex R. Piquero. 2009. "New Evidence on the Monetary Value of Saving a High Risk Youth." *Journal of Quantitative Criminology* 25:25–49.

Coid, Jeremy W. 2003. "Formulating Strategies for the Primary Prevention of Adult Antisocial Behaviour: 'High risk' or 'population' strategies?' In *Prevention of Adult Antisocial Behaviour*, edited by David P. Farrington and Jeremy W. Coid. Cambridge, UK: Cambridge University Press.

Conduct Problems Prevention Research Group. 1992. "A Developmental and Clinical Model for the Prevention of Conduct Disorders: The FAST Track Program." *Development and Psychopathology* 4:509–27.

Conduct Problems Prevention Research Group. 2002. "Evaluation of the First 3 Years of the Fast Track Prevention Trial with Children at High Risk for Adolescent Conduct Problems." *Journal of Abnormal Child Psychology* 19:553–67.

Conduct Problems Prevention Research Group. 2004. "The Effects of the Fast Track Program on Serious Problem Outcomes at the End of Elementary School." *Journal of Clinical Child and Adolescent Psychology* 33:650–61.

Conduct Problems Prevention Research Group. 2007. "The Fast Track Randomized Controlled Trial to Prevent Externalizing Psychiatric Disorders: Findings from Grades 3 to 9." *Journal of the American Academy of Child and Adolescent Psychiatry* 46:319–33.

Conduct Problems Prevention Research Group. 2010. "Fast Track Intervention Effects on Youth Arrests and Delinquency." *Journal of Experimental Criminology* 6:131–57.

Crick, Nicki R., and Kenneth A. Dodge. 1994. "A Review and Reformulation of Social Information-Processing Mechanisms in Children's Social Adjustment." *Psychological Bulletin* 115:74–101.

Denham, Susanne A., and M. Connie Almeida. 1987. "Children's Social Problem-Solving Skills, Behavioral Adjustment, and Interventions: A Meta-Analysis Evaluating Theory and Practice." *Journal of Applied Developmental Psychology* 8:391–409.

Denham, Susanne A., and Rosemary Burton. 2003. *Social and Emotional Prevention and Intervention Programming for Preschoolers.* New York: Kluwer Academic/Plenum Publishers.

Dodge, Kenneth A. 2000. "Conduct Disorder." In *Handbook of Developmental Psychopathology*, 2nd ed., edited by Arnold J. Sameroff, Michael Lewis, and Suzanne M. Miller. New York: Kluwer/Plenum.

Dodge, Kenneth A., John E. Lochman, Jennifer D. Harnish, John E. Bates, and Gregory S. Pettit. 1997. "Reactive and Proactive Aggression in School Children and Psychiatrically Impaired Chronically Assaultive Youth." *Journal of Abnormal Psychology* 106:37–51.

Dodge, Kenneth A., and Gregory S. Pettit. 2003. "A Biopsychosocial Model of the Development of Chronic Conduct Problems in Adolescence." *Developmental Psychology* 39:349–71.

Domitrovich, Celene E., Rebecca C. Cortes, and Mark T. Greenberg. 2007. "Improving Young Children's Social and Emotional Competence: A Randomized Trial of the Preschool "PATHS" Curriculum." *The Journal of Primary Prevention* 28:67–91.

Durlak, Joseph A., and Anne M. Wells. 1997. "Primary Prevention Mental Health Programs for Children and Adolescents: A Meta-Analytic Review." *American Journal of Community Psychology* 25:115–52.

Eisner, Manuel. 2009. "No Effects in Independent Prevention Trials: Can We Reject the Cynical View?" *Journal of Experimental Criminology* 5:163–83.

Eisner, Manuel, Denis Ribeaud, Rahel Jünger, and Ursula Meidert. 2008. *Frühprävention von Gewalt. Ergebnisse des Zürcher Interventions-und Präventionsprojektes an Schulen.* Zürich: Rüegger Verlag.

Farrington, David. P. 2003. "Methodological Quality Standards for Evaluation Research." *Annals of the American Academy of Political and Social Science* 587:49–68.

Farrington, David P., and Brandon C. Welsh. 2003. "Family-Based Prevention of Offending: A Meta-Analysis." *Australian and New Zealand Journal of Criminology* 36:127–51.

Farrington, David P., and Brandon C. Welsh. 2007. *Saving Children from a Life of Crime: Early Risk Factors and Effective Interventions.* New York: Oxford University Press.

Fontaine, Reith G., and Kenneth A. Dodge. 2009. "Social Information Processing and Aggressive Behavior: A Transactional Perspective." In *The Transactional Model of Development: How Children and Contexts Shape Each Other*, edited by A. Sameroff. Washington, DC: American Psychological Association.

Frauenknecht, Marianne, and David R. Black. 2004. "Problem-Solving Training for Children and Adolescents." In *Social Problem Solving: Theory, Research, and Training*, edited by Edward C. Chang, Thomas J. D´Zurilla, and Lawrence J. Sanna. Washington, DC: American Psychological Association.

Frick, Paul J. 1998. *Conduct Disorders and Severe Antisocial Behavior.* New York: Plenum.

Gansle, Kristin A. 2005. "The Effectiveness of School-Based Anger Interventions and Programs: A Meta-Analysis." *Journal of School Psychology* 43:321-41.

Garrard, Wendy M., and Mark W. Lipsey. 2007. "Conflict Resolution Education and Antisocial Behavior in U.S. Schools: A Meta-Analysis." *Conflict Resolution Quarterly* 25:9–38.

Gorman, Dennis M. 2002. "Drug and Violence Prevention: Rediscovering the Critical Rational Dimension of Evaluation Research." *Journal of Experimental Criminology* 1:39–62.

Gottfredson, Gary D., Elizabeth M. Jones, and Thomas W. Gore. 2002. "Implementation and Evaluation of a Cognitive-Behavioral Intervention to Prevent Problem Behavior in a Disorganized School." *Prevention Science* 3:43–56.

Greenberg, Mark T., Domitrovic Celene, and Brian Bumbarger 2001. "The Prevention of Mental Disorders in School-Aged Children: Current State of the Field. *Prevention & Treatment* 4(1):1–57.

Greenberg, Mark T., and Carol A. Kusché. 1993. *Promotiong Social and Emotional Development in Deaf Children. The PATHS Project.* Seattle, WA: University of Washington Press.

Greenberg, Mark T., Carol A. Kusché, Elizabeth T. Cook, and Julie P. Quamma. 1995. "Promoting Emotional Competence in School-Aged Children: The Effects of the PATHS Curriculum." *Development and Psychopathology* 7:117–36.

Gresham, Frank M. 1998. "Social Skills Training: Should We Raze, Remodel, or Rebuild?" *Behavioral Disorders* 24:19–25.

Hacker, Stefanie, Friedrich Lösel, Mark Stemmler, Stefanie Jaursch, Daniela Runkel, and Andreas Beelmann. 2007. "Training im Problemlösen TIP: Implementation und Evaluation eines sozial-kognitiven Kompetenztrainings für Kinder [Training in Problem Solving: Implementation and Evaluation of a Social-Cognitive Competence Training for Children]." *Heilpädagogische Forschung* 23:11–21.

Hahn, Robert, Dawna Fuqua-Whitley, Holly Wethington, Jessica Lowy, Alex Crosby, Mindy Fullilove, Robert Johnson, Aktiva Liberman, Eve Moscicki, LeShawndra Price, Susan Snyder, Farris Tuma, Stella Cory, Glenda Stone, Kaushik Mukhopadhaya, Sajal Chattopadhyay, Linda Dahlberg, and Task Force on Community Preventive Services. 2007. "Effectiveness of Universal School-Based Programs to Prevent Violent and Aggressive Behavior: A Systematic Review." *American Journal of Preventive Medicine* 33:114–29.

Hawkins, J. David, Eric C. Brown, Sabrina Oesterle, Michael W. Arthur, Robert D. Abbott, and Richard F. Catalano. 2008. "Early Effects of Communities That Care on Targeted Risks and Initiation of Delinquent Behavior and Substance Use." *Journal of Adolescent Health* 43:15–22.

Hawkins, J. David, Richard F. Catalano, Rick Kosterman, Robert D. Abbott, and Karl G. Hill. 1999. "Preventing Adolescent Health-Risk Behaviors by Strengthening Protection During Childhood." *Archives of Pediatric and Adolescent Medicine* 153:226–34.

Hawkins, J. David, Richard F. Catalano, Diane M. Morrison, Julie O'Donnell, Robert D. Abbott, and L. Edward Day. 1992. "The Seattle Social Development Project: Effects of the First Four Years on Protective Factors and Problem Behaviors." In *Preventing Antisocial Behavior: Interventions from Birth through Adolescence*, edited by Joan McCord and Richard E. Tremblay. New York: Guilford Press.

Huesmann, L. Rowell. 1998. "The Role of Social Information Processing and Cognitive Schemata in the Acquisition and Maintenance of Habitual Aggressive Behavior." In *Human Aggression: Theories, Research, and Implications for Social Policy*, edited by Russell G. Geen and Edward Donnerstein. San Diego, CA: Academic Press.

Junger, Marianne, Lynette Feder, Joy Clay, Sylvana M. Coté, David P. Farrington, Kate Freiberg, Vicente Garrido Genovés, Ross Homel, Friedrich Lösel, Matthew Manning, Paul Mazerolle, Rob Santos, Martin Schmucker, Christopher Sullivan, Carole Sutton, Tom van Yperen, and Richard E. Tremblay. 2007. "Preventing Violence in Seven Countries: Global Convergence in Policy." *European Journal on Criminal Policy and Research* 13:327–56.

Kazdin, Alan E. 1998. "Psychosocial Treatments for Conduct Disorder in Children." In *A Guide to Treatments that Work*, edited by Peter E. Nathan and Jack M. Gorman. New York: Oxford University Press.

Kazdin, Alan E. 2003. "Problem-Solving Skills Training and Parent Management Training for Conduct Disorder." In *Evidence-Based Psychotherapies for Children and Adolescents*, edited by Alan E. Kazdin and John R. Weisz. New York: Guilford Press.

Kazdin, Alan E., and Gloria Wassell. 1999. "Barriers to Treatment Participation and Therapeutic Change Among Children Referred for Conduct Disorder." *Journal of Clinical Child Psychology* 28:160–72.

Kusché, Carol A., and Mark T. Greenberg. 1992. *The PATHS Curriculum for After School Care Providers*. Seattle, WA: Developmental Research and Programs.

Kusché, Carol A., and Mark T. Greenberg. 1994. *The PATHS Curriculum*. Seattle, WA: Developmental Research and Programs.

Lipsey, Mark W. 2003. "Those Confounded Moderators in Meta-Analysis: Good, Bad, and Ugly." *Annals of the American Academy of Political and Social Science* 587:69–81.

Lipsey, Mark W., and James H. Derzon. 1998. "Predictors of Violent or Serious Delinquency in Adolescence and Early Adulthood." In *Serious and Violent Juvenile Offenders: Risk Factors and Successful Interventions*, edited by Rolf Loeber and David P. Farrington. Thousand Oaks, CA: Sage.

Lipsey, Mark W., Nana A. Landenberger, and Sandra Wilson. 2007. Effects of Cognitive-Behavioral Programs for Criminal Offenders. *Campbell Collaboration Crime and Justice Review*. www.campbellcollaboration.org/reviews_crime_justice/index.php.

Lipsey, Mark W., and David B. Wilson. 1998. "Effective Intervention for Serious Juvenile Offenders: A Synthesis of Research." In *Serious and Violent Juvenile Offenders: Risk Factors and Successful Interventions*, edited by Rolf Loeber and David P. Farrington. Thousand Oaks, CA: Sage.

Loeber, Rolf, and David P. Farrington, ed. 1998. *Serious and Violent Juvenile Offenders: Risk Factors and Successful Interventions*. Thousand Oaks, CA: Sage.

Loeber, Rolf, David P. Farrington, and Daniel A. Waschbusch. 1998. "Serious and Violent Juvenile Offenders." In *Serious and Violent Juvenile Offenders: Risk Factors and Successful Interventions*, edited by Rolf Loeber and David P. Farrington. Thousand Oaks, CA: Sage.

Lösel, Friedrich. 2002. "Risk/Need Assessment and Prevention of Antisocial Development in Young People: Basic Issues from a Perspective of Cautionary Optimism." In *Multiproblem Violent Youth: A Foundation for Comparative Research Needs, Interventions and Outcomes*, edited by Ray Corrado, Ron Roesch, Stephen D. Hart and Josef Gierowski. Amsterdam: IOS/NATO Book Series.

Lösel, Friedrich. 2005. "Evaluating Developmental Prevention of Antisocial Behavior: An Example and a Brief Review." In *Forensic Psychology and Law*, edited by Alicja Cerederecka, Teresa Jaskiewicz-Obdydzinska, Ron Roesch and Jozef Wojcikiewicz. Cracow: Forensic Research Publishers.

Lösel, Friedrich. 2007. "It's Never too Early and Never too Late: Towards an Integrated Science of Developmental Intervention in Criminology." *Criminologist* 35(2): 1–8.

Lösel, Friedrich, and Andreas Beelmann. 2003. "Effects of Child Skills Training in Preventing Antisocial Behavior: A Systematic Review of Randomized Evaluations." *Annals of the American Academy of Political and Social Science* 587:84–109.

Lösel, Friedrich, and Andreas Beelmann. 2005. "Social Problem-Solving Programs for Preventing Antisocial Behavior in Children and Youth." In *Social Problem Solving and Offending*, edited by Mary McMurran and James McGuire. Chichester, UK: Wiley.

Lösel, Friedrich, and Andreas Beelmann. 2006. "Child Skills Training." In *Preventing Crime: What Works for Children, Offenders, Victims, and Places*, edited by Brandon C. Welsh and David P. Farrington. Dordrecht, NL: Wadsworth.

Lösel, Friedrich, Andreas Beelmann, Stefanie Jaursch, and Mark Stemmler. 2004. *Soziale Kompetenz für Kinder und Familien* [*Social Competence for Children and Families*]. Berlin: Bundesministerium für Familie, Senioren, Frauen und Jugend.

Lösel, Friedrich, Andreas Beelmann, Mark Stemmler, and Stefanie Jaursch. 2006. "Prävention von Problemen des Sozialverhaltens im Vorschulalter: Evaluation des Eltern-und Kindertrainings EFFEKT. [Prevention of Conduct Problems in Preschool Age: Evaluation of the Parent-and Child-Oriented Program EFFEKT]." *Zeitschrift für Klinische Psychologie und Psychotherapie* 35: 127–39.

Lösel, Friedrich, and Doris Bender. 2003. "Resilience and Protective Factors." In *Prevention of Adult Antisocial Behaviour*, edited by David P. Farrington and Jeremy W. Coid. Cambridge, UK: Cambridge University Press.

Lösel, Friedrich, and Doris Bender. 2006. "Risk Factors for Serious and Violent Antisocial Behaviour in Children and Youth." In *Children Who Commit Acts of Serious Interpersonal Violence: Messages for Best Practice*, edited by Ann Hagell and Renuka Jeyarajah-Dent. London: Jessica Kingsley Publishers.

Lösel, Friedrich, and Thomas Bliesener. 2003. *Aggression und Delinquenz unter Jugendlichen* [*Aggression and Delinquency in Adolescence*]. Neuwied: Luchterhand.

Lösel, Friedrich, Thomas Bliesener, and Doris Bender. 2007. "Social Information Processing, Experiences of Aggression in Social Contexts, and Aggressive Behavior in Adolescents." *Criminal Justice and Behavior* 34:330–47.

Lösel Friedrich, and David P. Farrington. 2010. *Promotive and Protective Factors in the Development of Youth Violence*. Review Paper for the U.S. Centers for Disease Control and Prevention. Atlanta: CDCP.

Lösel, Friedrich, and Peter Köferl. 1989. "Evaluation Research on Correctional Treatment in West Germany: A Meta-Analysis." *Criminal Behavior and the Justice System: Psychological perspectives*, edited by Hermann Wegener, Friedrich Lösel, and Jochen Haisch. New York: Springer.

Lösel, Friedrich, Daniela Runkel, Stefanie Jaursch, and Mark Stemmler. 2010. "Family-Oriented Prevention of Antisocial Development in Children: Long-Term Evaluation of a Parent and Child Training Program." Presentation at the 62th Annual Conference of the American Society of Criminology, San Francisco, November.

Lösel, Friedrich, and Martin Schmucker. 2005. "The Effectiveness of Treatment for Sexual Offenders: A Comprehensive Meta-Analysis." *Journal of Experimental Criminology* 1:117–46.

Lösel, Friedrich, Mark Stemmler, Stefanie Jaursch, and Andreas Beelmann. 2009. "Universal Prevention of Antisocial Development: Short-and Long-Term Effects of a Child-and Parent-Oriented Program." *Monatsschrift für Kriminologie und Strafrechtsreform* 92:289–308.

Lösel, Friedrich, and Werner W. Wittmann. 1989. "The Relationship of Treatment Integrity and Intensity to Outcome Criteria." *New Directions for Program Evaluation* 42:97–108.

McCord, Joan. 1978. "A Thirty-Year Follow-Up of Treatment Effects." *American Psychologist* 33:284–89.

McCord, Joan. 2003. "Cures that Harm: Unanticipated Outcomes of Crime Prevention Programs." *Annals of the American Academy of Political and Social Science* 587:16–30.

Mathur, Sarup R., Kenneth A. Kavale, Mary Magee Quinn, Steven R. Forness, and Robert B. Rutherford Jr. 1998. "Social Skills Interventions with Students with Emotional and Behavioral Problems: A Quantitative Synthesis of Single-Subject Research." *Behavioral Disorders* 23:193–201.

Ministry of Justice. 2010. *Breaking the Cycle: Effective Punishment, Rehabilitation and Sentencing of Offenders* (Green Paper). London: UK Ministry of Justice.

Mischel, Walter. 1973. "Toward a Cognitive Social Learning Reconceptualization of Personality." *Psychological Review* 80:252–83.

Moffitt, Terrie E. 1993. "Adolescence-Limited and Life-Course-Persistent Antisocial Behavior: A Developmental Taxonomy." *Psychological Review* 100:674–701.

Muñoz, Rachel, Judy Hutchings, Rhiannon-Tudor Edwards, Barry Hounsome, and Alan O'Céilleachair. 2004. "Economic Evaluation of Treatments for Children with Severe Behavioral Problems." *Journal of Mental Health Policy Economics* 7:177–89.

Mytton, Julie A., Carolyn DiGuiseppi, David A. Gough, Rod S. Taylor, and Stuart Logan. 2002. "School-Based Violence Prevention Programs: Systematic Review of Secondary Prevention Trials." *Archives of Pediatric and Adolescence Medicine* 156:752–62.

Petrosino, Anthony, and Haluk Soydan. 2005. "The Impact of Program Developers as Evaluators on Criminal Recidivism: Results from Meta-Analyses of Experimental and Quasi-Experimental Research." *Journal of Experimental Criminology* 1:435–50.

Prinz, Ronald J., and Gloria E. Miller. 1994. "Family-Based Treatment for Childhood Antisocial Behavior: Experimental Influences on Dropout and Engagement." *Journal of Consulting and Clinical Psychology* 62:645–50.

Riggs, Nathaniel R., Mark T. Greenberg, Carol A. Kusché, and Mary Ann Pentz. 2006. "The Mediational Role of Neurocognition in the Behavioral Outcomes of a Social-Emotional Prevention Program in Elementary School Students: Effects of the PATHS Curriculum." *Prevention Science* 7:91–102.

Robins, Lee N., and Rumi K. Price. 1991. "Adult Disorders Predicted by Childhood Conduct Problems: Results from the NIMH Epidemiologic Catchment Area Project." *Psychiatry: Interpersonal and Biological Processes* 54:116–32.

Sampson, Robert J., and John H. Laub. 1993. *Crime in the Making: Pathways and Turning Points through Life*. Cambridge, MA: Harvard University Press.

Schweinhart, Lawrence J., Helen V. Barnes, and Daniel P. Weikart. 1993. *Significant Benefits. The High/Scope Perry Preschool Study through Age 27*. Ypsilanti, MI: High/Scope Press.

Schweinhart, Lawrence J., Jeanne Montie, Zongping Xiang, William S. Barnett, Clive R. Belfield, and Milagros Nores. 2005. *Lifetime Effects: The High/Scope Perry Preschool Study through Age 40*. Ypsilanti, MI: High/Scope Press.

Sherman, Lawrence, and Heather Strang. 2009. "Testing for Analysts' Bias in Crime Prevention Experiments: Can We Accept Eisner's One-Tailed Test?" *Journal of Experimental Criminology* 5:185–200.

Shure, Myrna B. 1992a. *I Can Problem Solve. An International Cognitive Problem-Solving Program (Preschool)*. Champaign, IL: Research Press.

Shure, Myrna B. 1992b. *I Can Problem Solve. An International Cognitive Problem-Solving Program (Kindergarten & Primary Grades)*. Champaign, IL: Research Press.

Shure, Myrna B. 1993. "I Can Problem Solve (ICPS): Interpersonal Cognitive Problem Solving for Young Children." *Early Child and Development Care* 96:49–64.

Shure, Myrna B., and George Spivack. 1982. "Interpersonal Problem Solving in Young Children: A Cognitive Approach to Prevention." *American Journal of Community Psychology* 10:341–56.

Shure, Myrna B., and George Spivack. 1988. "Interpersonal Cognitive Problem Solving." In *Fourteen Ounces of Prevention: A Casebook for Practitioners*, edited by Richard H. Price, Emory L. Cowen, Raymond P. Lorion, and Julia Ramos-McKay. Washington, DC: American Psychological Association.

Spence, Susan H. 2003. "Social Skills Training with Children and Young People: Theory, Evidence, and Practice." *Child and Adolescent Mental Health* 8:84–96.

Spivack, George, and Myrna B. Shure. 1974. *Social Adjustment of Young Children: A Cognitive Approach to Solving Real Life Problems*. San Francisco: Jossey-Bass.

Spivack, George, and Myrna B. Shure. 1989. "Interpersonal Cognitive Problem Solving (ICPS): A Competence-Building Primary Prevention Program." *Prevention in Human Services* 6:151–78.

Sutton, Jon, Peter K. Smith, and John Swettenham. 1999. "Social Cognition and Bullying: Social Inadequacy or Skilled Manipulation?" *British Journal of Developmental Psychology* 17:435–50.

Taylor, Ted K., J. Mark Eddy, and Anthony Biglan. 1999. "Interpersonal Skill Training to Reduce Aggressive and Delinquent Behavior: Limited Evidence and the Need for an Evidence-Based System of Care." *Clinical Child and Family Psychology Review* 2:169–82.

Tierney, Joseph P., Jean B. Grossman, and Nancy L. Resch. 1995. *Making a Difference: An Impact Study of Big Brothers/Big Sisters*. Philadelphia, PA: Public/Private Ventures.

Tremblay, Richard E., ed. 2010. *The Montreal Longitudinal and Experimental Study: The Interventions Program and its Long Term Effects*. Montreal: GRIP Research Unit on Children's Psychosocial Maladjustment, University of Montreal.

Tremblay, Richard E., and Christa Japel. 2003. "Prevention during Pregnancy, Infancy and the Preschool Years." In *Early Prevention of Adult Antisocial Behaviour*, edited by David P. Farrington and Jeremy W. Coid. Cambridge, UK: Cambridge University Press.

Tremblay, Richard E., Louise C. Masse, Linda Pagani, and Frank Vitaro. 1996. "From Childhood Aggression to Adolescent Maladjustment: The Montreal Prevention Experiment." In *Preventing Childhood Disorders, Substance Use, and Delinquency*, edited by Ray Peters and Robert J. McMahon. Thousand Oaks, CA: Sage.

Tremblay, Richard E., Linda Pagani-Kurtz, Frank Vitaro, Louise C. Masse, and Robert O. Pihl. 1995. "A Bimodal Preventive Intervention for Disruptive Kindergarten Boys: Its Impact through Mid-Adolescence." *Journal of Consulting and Clinical Psychology* 63:560–68.

Tremblay, Richard E., Frank Vitaro, Daniel Nagin, Linda Pagani, and Jean R. Séguin. 2003. "The Montreal Longitudinal and Experimental Study: Rediscovering the Power of Descriptions." In *Taking Stock of Delinquency: An Overview of Findings from Contemporary Longitudinal Studies*, edited by Terence P. Thornberry. New York: Kluwer Academic/Plenum.

Vitaro, F., Mara Brendgen, and Richard E. Tremblay. 2001. "Preventive Intervention: Assessing its Effects on the Trajectories of Delinquency and Testing for Mediational Processes." *Applied Developmental Science* 5:201–13.

Webster-Stratton, Carolyn. 2000. "The Incredible Years Training Series." *OJJDP Bulletin* (June):1–23.

Webster-Stratton, Carolyn, and Mary Hammond. 1997. "Treating Children with Early-Onset Conduct Problems: A Comparison of Child and Parent Training Interventions." *Journal of Consulting and Clinical Psychology* 65:93–109.

Webster-Stratton, Carolyn, and M. Jamila Reid. 2004. "Strengthening Social and Emotional Competence in Young Children—The Foundation for Early School Readiness and Success." *Infants and Young Children* 17:96–113.

Webster-Stratton, Carolyn, M. Jamila Reid, and Mary Hammond. 2001. "Social Skills and Problem-Solving Training for Children with Early-Onset Conduct Problems: Who Benefits?" *Journal of Child Psychology and Psychiatry* 42:943–52.

Webster-Stratton, Carolyn, M. Jamila Reid, and Mary Hammond, M. 2004. "Treating Children with Early-Onset Conduct Problems: Intervention Outcomes for Parent, Child, and Teacher Training." *Journal of Clinical Child and Adolescent Psychology* 33:105–24.

Webster-Stratton, Carolyn, and Ted Taylor. 2001. "Nipping Early Risk Factors in the Bud: Preventing Substance Abuse, Delinquency, and Violence in Adolescence through Intervention Targeted at Young Children (0-8 years)." *Prevention Science* 2:165–92.

Weisburd, David, Cynthia M. Lum, and Sue-Ming Yang. 2003. "When Can We Conclude that Treatments or Programs 'Don't Work'?" *Annals of the American Academy of Political and Social Science* 587:31–48.

Weisburd, David, Anthony Petrosino, A., and Gail Mason. 1993. "Design Sensitivity in Criminal Justice Experiments." *Crime and Justice* 17:337–80.

Welsh, Brandon C., David P. Farrington, and Lawrence W. Sherman, eds. 2001. *Costs and Benefits of Preventing Crime.* Oxford, UK: Westview Press.

Wilson, David B., Denise C. Gottfredson, and Stacy S. Najaka. 2001. "School-Based Prevention of Problem Behaviors: A Meta-Analysis." *Journal of Quantitative Criminology* 17:247–72.

Wilson, Sandra J., and Mark W. Lipsey. 2007. "School-Based Interventions for Aggressive and Disruptive Behavior: Update of a Meta-Analysis." *American Journal of Preventive Medicine* 33:130–43.

Wilson, Sandra J., Mark W. Lipsey, and James H. Derzon. 2003. "The Effects of School-Based Intervention Programs on Aggressive Behavior: A Meta-Analysis." *Journal of Consulting and Clinical Psychology* 71:136–49.

CHAPTER 7

DEVELOPMENTAL APPROACHES IN THE PREVENTION OF FEMALE OFFENDING

DEBORAH GORMAN-SMITH AND
ALANA M. VIVOLO

SEVERAL reviews of research on aggression and delinquency among girls have been conducted during the last 10 years (e.g., Odgers and Moretti 2002; Daigle, Cullen, and Wright 2007; Zahn et al. 2008). Each review begins in much the same way, highlighting the increasing rates of girls' delinquent involvement, including violent offending, since the late 1980s, as well as the dearth of research on the prediction and prevention of delinquent behavior among girls. Fortunately, as a result of this work, attention to the problem of delinquency and violence among girls has increased, a growing number of studies have been funded, and prevention researchers are considering both biological sex and the construct of gender in the development of interventions and as outcomes are evaluated.

In this essay we review the research on delinquency and offending among girls with the goal of informing prevention efforts. We do so by addressing four broad questions. First, what are the rates and patterns of offending among girls and how have these changed over time? Second, what are the predictors and correlates of involvement among females that should be considered when developing and implementing prevention programs? Third, is there any evidence of program impact of interventions developed specifically for girls? Fourth, for interventions directed toward both boys and girls, is there any evidence of differential impact by sex? Our main conclusions are as follows:

- Although fewer girls than boys are involved in delinquency and violence, rates of girls' involvement has increased significantly over the last two decades.
- The developmental pattern of girls' involvement is somewhat different when compared with boys, with girls both starting and peaking a little earlier than boys.
- While girls are involved in similar types of offending as boys, research suggests that a more complex set of behaviors may need to be considered for girls, particularly relational forms of aggression (e.g., damage or threat of damage to interpersonal relationships).
- Girls involved in delinquent or antisocial behavior as adolescents are at risk for a host of negative health and behavioral outcomes in adolescence and adulthood.
- Although the same list of risk factors appears for girls as for boys, the nature and quality of how these factors relate to outcomes may be different for boys and girls.
- Research on the impact of preventive interventions has been relatively limited, with few studies disaggregating effects by gender. Among those that have been developed specifically for girls, few have been rigorously evaluated and among those few sustained effects have been found.
- Prevention programs need to be developed with the unique risk factors associated with female offending in mind. Evaluations of prevention programs should disaggregate data to identify potential gender differences in effects.

I. Rates and Patterns

A. Sex and Gender Differences

Interest in understanding girls' participation in delinquent and violent offending has grown as data indicate an increase in girls' participation. While the overall rate of youth violence has declined in the past decade, several sources of data suggest that rates among females have declined less or in some cases have been increasing (Poe-Yamagata and Butts 1996; Zahn et al. 2008), with the percentage of female juvenile crime arrests increasing from 20 to 29 percent between 1980 and 2003. Consequently, boys are now approximately twice as likely as girls to be arrested for a crime, whereas in 1980, boys were more than four times as likely as girls to be arrested (Snyder and Sickmund 2006; Steffensmeier et al. 2006). Table 7.1 shows more recent percentage change of juvenile arrests for both males and females from 1999 to 2008.

Partly in response to these increasing trends in female offending, the Office of Juvenile Justice and Delinquency Prevention (OJJDP) convened the Girls Study Group to "gain a better understanding of girls' involvement in delinquency and guide the development, testing, and dissemination of strategies that would reduce incidents of delinquency and violence among girls" (Zahn et al. 2010, p. 1). The initial task of this group was to gather data to examine rates and patterns of girls' delinquent involvement. Using three sources of data—official arrests, self-report, and victimization data—the group examined patterns and trends in girls' participation in violence from 1980 through 2005. While each type of data provides a somewhat different picture of the problem, the pattern that emerges from these and other data sources suggest, as has long been known, that fewer girls are involved in violence than boys, with the greatest difference found for the most serious forms of

Table 7.1 Ten-year arrest trends for males and females

Ten-Year Arrest Trends		
By sex, 1999–2008	Percent change in juvenile arrests	
Offense charged	Male	Female
Violent crime[1]	-8	-10
Property crime[2]	-28	+1
Robbery	+24	+34
Aggravated assault	-22	-17
Simple assault	-6	+12
Burglary	-16	-3
Larceny-theft	-29	+4
Motor vehicle theft	-50	-52
Vandalism	+3	-9
Weapons; carrying, possessing, etc.	-3	-1
Drug abuse violations	-8	-2
DUI	-34	+7
Disorderly conduct	-5	+18

[1] Violent crimes are offenses of murder and nonnegligent manslaughter, forcible rape, robbery, and aggravated assault.
[2] Property crimes are offenses of burglary, larceny-theft, motor vehicle theft, and arson.
Source: Federal Bureau of Investigation 2009, table 33.

physical violence (Snyder and Sickmund 1999; Steffensmeier et al. 2005).While girls are less involved than boys, these data also indicated that rates of girls' arrests for serious violent crimes (i.e., murder, aggravated assault) increased 28 percent between 1991 and 2000 (Snyder 2000) and girls' arrests for simple assault increased 77 percent over that same period of time (Federal Bureau of Investigation 2000). In 2008, females accounted for 30 percent of all juvenile arrests. While juvenile arrests decreased from 1999 to 2008, arrests of females decreased less than arrests of males for most types of offense (e.g., aggravated assault and burglary) and in some cases (e.g., simple assault, larceny-theft, DUI) arrests of girls increased while arrests of boys decreased (Puzzanchera 2009).

In addition to differences in rates of disorders, longitudinal analyses suggest age differences in onset and desistance by sex, particularly for violent offenders (Sommers and Baskin 1992; Cohen et al. 1993; Elliott 1994). The offending careers of violent females both begin and peak a little earlier than those of violent males (Elliott 1994; Snyder and Sickmund 1999). When compared to males in the juvenile justice system, females tend to be younger. In 2003, approximately 50 percent of females in the juvenile justice system were below the age of 15 compared with 33 percent of males (Snyder and Sickmund 2006).

In examining these data, there are several issues that are important to note and have implications for prevention. First, there is a change in the relation between boys' and girls' involvement in antisocial behavior over the course of development, and this gap becomes greater as children get older. There are also differences in the onset and desistance of delinquent behavior for boys and girls. Girls tend to start somewhat younger, peak earlier, and desist earlier. These differences may reflect differences in roles and expectations across development. They may also reflect the greater range of outcomes associated with problem behaviors among girls (Robins 1966; Pajer 1998). Girls may develop other types of problems in adolescence and young adulthood, and there is a need to be cognizant of the range of problems exhibited by girls across development.

It is also important to note contextual differences between offenses of boys and girls. The context of offending refers to issues such as whether the offense was committed with others, the offender's role in initiating and committing the offense, the type of victim, the victim-offender relationship, the value or type of property stolen or damaged, and whether a weapon was used (Steffensmeier 1983; Steffensmeier 1993; Daly 1994; Triplett and Myers 1995; Steffensmeier and Allan 1996). Even when males and females participate in the same types of behaviors, offenses may differ substantially in quality and these differences appear to be greater for more violent offenses.

For minor forms of violent behavior and delinquency, such as hitting others or stealing from stores or schools, girls' prevalence of involvement approaches that of boys. However, girls are less likely to use a weapon or to intend serious injury to their victims (Kruttschnitt 1994). They are also less likely to break into buildings to steal or to steal things that they cannot use (Steffensmeier and Allan 1996). Girls are more likely to steal from somewhere familiar, like a residence, when no one is at home or from work, and they are more likely to steal alone (Steffensmeier 1993). When female offenders do steal with others, they usually act as accomplices (e.g., driving the car) and are less likely to get an equal share of what is taken (Steffensmeier 1983).

Some evidence reports that females are more likely than males to kill someone they know intimately, such as a spouse, child, or other family member (Kruttschnitt 1993; Loper and Cornell 1996). Girls are proportionally more likely than boys to murder very young victims (24 percent of girls' victims are under age three compared with 1 percent of boys' victims; Loper and Cornell 1996). Although committing the same legal category of violent offense, there are often significant sex differences in the nature and quality of the crime committed. Thus, while it is important to understand the rates and patterns of girls' involvement in antisocial behavior, it is crucial to consider these statistics within the context of development, as well as the context within which the crime occurs. These sex and gender differences in offending have important implications for the prevention of male and female delinquent and violent offending.

B. The Complexity of Girls' Aggression

In addition to the data that suggest that girls are increasingly involved in similar types of delinquent and violent activities as boys, research on girls suggests that a more complex set of behaviors may need to be included in assessment of antisocial or aggressive behavior than have been traditionally considered in most studies if we are to adequately understand girls' antisocial behavior and the roles of sex and the construct of gender in antisocial behavior. Particularly for females, aggression and antisocial behavior may not always be represented by the overt and criminal behaviors that have traditionally been measured when referring to antisocial behavior of males (Bjorkqvist and Niemela 1992; Zoccarillo 1993; Cairns and Cairns 1994; Crick 2003; Underwood 2003). A growing body of research has found that girls exhibit forms of aggression that are not common in males, noting that these forms of aggression were often overlooked in much of the early research on girls (Brody 1985; Ostrov and Crick 2005). While aggression is defined as behaviors that are intended to hurt or harm others, there are ways to inflict harm on another person other than through physical aggression.

The ways in which people aggress may be related to their social role which is a function of the gender construct (Brody 1985). The preferred methods of aggression are those that best prevent others from reaching goals that are valued by the aggressive person's gender. Because girls often emphasize qualities of interpersonal relationships more than boys, girls' aggression, particularly early forms of aggression, focuses on relational issues. Thus, girls would be more likely than boys to harm peers through damage or the threat of damage to interpersonal relationships. In contrast, boys would be most likely to harm peers through physical forms of aggression. Examples of relational aggressive behaviors include using social exclusion from a peer group, giving someone the silent treatment, threatening to stop being friends (Crick, Bigbee, and Howes 1996) or increasingly, making these threats public through various forms of technology (e.g., Facebook). In contrast, physical aggression harms through damage to another's physical well-being, such as hitting, kicking, or threatening to beat up someone.

As an early test of this theory, both physical and relational aggression were measured among a sample of third- to sixth-grade children using peer nominations (Crick and Grotpeter 1995). These investigators found that approximately equal numbers of boys and girls were classified as nonaggressive (73 percent of boys and 78 percent of girls). Sixteen percent of boys but only 0.4 percent of girls were classified as overtly aggressive (physically and verbally aggressive). Conversely, 17 percent of girls but only 2 percent of boys were classified as relationally aggressive. Interestingly, 9 percent of boys and 4 percent of girls were classified as both relationally and overtly aggressive. Thus, when both types of aggression were considered, sex differences were not large, but when considering only physically aggressive or only relationally aggressive behavior, they were.

Initially arguments against taking these forms of aggression seriously were made, with some suggesting that the harm caused by relational aggression was not as serious as the harm caused by physical aggression (as victim or perpetrator), and therefore, relational aggression should not be considered a part of aggressive behavior or of equal concern as physical aggression. However, as with other forms of aggression, relationally aggressive children appear to be at risk of serious adjustment problems. Crick and Grotpeter (1995) found that relationally aggressive children were significantly more disliked and rejected by other children than their nonrelationally aggressive counterparts. These children also had significantly elevated rates of depression and reported being lonely and socially isolated. Relational aggression was associated with depression among young adult women (MacDonald and O'Laughlin 1997). Associations between relational aggression and delinquency (Morey 1991; MacDonald and O'Laughlin 1997) and some features of antisocial personality disorder (stimulus-seeking, egocentricity; Morey 1991; Werner and Crick 1999) have been found for both men and women, even after controlling for the contribution of physical aggression. These findings suggest that relational aggression is a serious problem that is associated with other types of disorders during childhood and is related to increased risk of serious psychosocial problems in adolescence and young adulthood.

As relational aggression is associated with serious psychosocial problems in childhood and is related to many forms of antisocial behavior in adulthood, it seems clear that definitions of aggression and antisocial behavior should be expanded to encompass a wider variety of methods of acting aggressively. Both relational and physical aggression need to be considered as early forms of antisocial behavior. In addition, developmental models of antisocial behavior need to be expanded to include sex and gender as major considerations. Specifically, models need to be able to include how development and risk of antisocial behavior may be related to gender roles and social expectations. For example, theories of the development of antisocial behavior should include the centrality of relational concerns observed among women and the way those concerns may affect development. Relational concerns need to be measured for both men and women, so that the focus is not biased in studies of males or female types of aggression.

These findings can have important implications for prevention programs targeting antisocial behavior. For example, general programs may need to be expanded to target other forms of aggression. A greater focus on relational issues, between family members, siblings and peers, seems warranted. In addition, for targeted or indicated prevention programs, it may be important to expand the selection criteria for participant inclusion. If participants are screened only for physical or verbal aggression, a large percentage of children who are at risk, particularly girls, may be missed.

C. Consequences of Girls' Delinquent Involvement

Regardless of the seriousness (or nature) of the violent and/or delinquent acts committed by girls, data suggest that the outcomes for girls may not be so benign. Girls involved in delinquent or antisocial behavior as adolescents are at risk of a host of negative health problems and behaviors, including drug addiction, mental health problems, STI and HIV infection, intimate partner violence, and increased mortality when compared to those not involved in early adolescent delinquent behavior (Bianco and Wallace 1991; Lewis et al. 1991; Haller et al. 1993; Widom and White 1997; Blumenthal 1998; Pajer 1998; Teplin et al. 2002; Battle et al. 2003). These girls appear to be at increased risk, even when compared with girls with other types of adolescent disorders. For example, using data from the Dunedin Multidisciplinary Health and Development Study, investigators found that young adult women with a history of adolescent conduct disorder had more medical problems, poorer self-reported overall health, lower body mass index, alcohol and/or marijuana dependence, tobacco dependence, more lifetime sexual partners, sexually transmitted diseases, and early pregnancy compared with healthy controls, girls with depression, and girls with anxiety (Bardone et al. 1998).

Other studies suggest that 25 to 50 percent of antisocial girls engage in criminal behavior as adults (Robins and Price 1991; Zoccolillo and Rogers 1991; Zoccolillo et al. 1992; Pajer 1998). Cernkovich, Lanctot, and Giordano (2007) found that, in a sample of adult women incarcerated as youth, those who exhibited high levels of past delinquency were 200 percent more likely to be serious adult violent offenders, controlling for individual and family factors.

Antisocial females are also at increased risk for psychiatric problems with rates ranging between 21 and 90 percent (Robins 1966; Lewis et al. 1991; Zoccolillo et al. 1992). When antisocial females become adults, studies suggest that they have deficits in parenting, with about one-third of conduct disordered or delinquent girls having either a family court record or children placed outside of the home because of abuse or neglect (Lewis et al. 1991; Werner and Smith 1992). Adult women with a history of conduct disorder or delinquency had higher rates of dysfunctional and often violent intimate relationships (Lewis et al. 1991; Werner 1992; Bardone et al.

1998) and high rates of service utilization as adults (Bardone et al. 1998). Thus, these data suggest that there are serious long-term risks for girls with antisocial behavior or conduct disorder in childhood and that there may be a broader array of risks for girls than for boys.

Taken together, these data point to the serious problems associated with childhood antisocial behavior for girls. Antisocial girls appear to be as much at risk for problems in adulthood as antisocial boys, and the types of associated problems appear to be less predictable for girls than for boys. Research is needed to understand these divergent patterns in outcome. However, these data clearly point to the critical need for prevention and intervention programs for girls as well as boys. In addition, they emphasize the need for broader consideration of gender in theories of the development of antisocial behavior.

II. RISK FACTORS

A. Gender Differences

Two questions have been explored in research on risk for involvement in delinquency and violence for girls: (1) are the relationships between risk factors and girls' outcomes the same as for boys'?; and (2) are gender-specific factors and models needed to explain girls' involvement? As outlined by Odgers and Moretti (2002), the answers to these two questions appear to depend, to some extent, on the samples used. When examining risk and protection among national or community samples, the consistent finding is that risk factors associated with girls' involvement in antisocial and violent behavior are the same as those associated with involvement among boys (Pepler and Sedighdeilami 1998; Moffitt and Caspi 2001; Fergusson and Horwood 2002). Individual risk factors such as hyperactivity/impulsivity, family factors such as inconsistent or harsh discipline, poor parental monitoring and abuse and neglect, association with delinquent/antisocial peers, poor attachment to school, and living in high-risk urban neighborhoods are just some of the risk factors associated with involvement for both boys and girls when looking within national or community samples (Acoca 1999; Barnow et al. 2002; Hubbard and Pratt 2002; Snyder and Sickmund 2006).

Although the same list of risk factors appears for girls as for boys, the nature and quality of how these factors relate to outcomes may be different for boys and girls. There are certain important ways in which gender is implicated in social relationships that can be obscured or missed when simply looking at whether variables relate to outcomes. For example, because female adolescents are more invested in interpersonal relationships than are male adolescents, girls are more likely to get involved in or be affected by parental conflict (Henggeler, Edwards, and Borduin

1987) or may be pulled into delinquent behavior through involvement in intimate relationships with delinquent males (Steffensmeier and Allan 1996). Given the strong social sanctions against girls' involvement in antisocial behavior, data suggest that it may take a particularly deviant family to increase risk among girls. Although both family and peer influences are related to female antisocial behavior, the nature of the relation may be different and reflect gender differences in relationship development, norms and values, and social control. For example, the greater supervision and control of girls by parents reduces female risk-taking and increases attachment to parents, teachers, and conventional friends, which in turn reduces influence by delinquent peers (Giordano, Cernkovich, and Pugh 1986). Thus, when evaluating psychosocial predictors of antisocial behavior, particularly in regard to informing prevention, elements of social expectations, role, and power as a function of gender need to be considered. Even though the same variables operate as risk factors, the nature and power of associations with outcomes may vary for boys and girls.

B. Role of Victimization

When examining risk factors within samples of youth involved in the justice system, studies have shown similar types of risk factors for both boys and girls, but adjudicated girls have been found to have greater exposure to multiple risk factors and more severe levels of risk factors (Corrado, Odgers, and Cohen 2000). Although it is clear that boys are also at risk, previous childhood victimization experiences, including physical and sexual abuse, has been given a much more central role in risk for antisocial behavior among girls than boys (Poe-Yamagata and Butts 1996; Snyder 2000; Berlinger and Elliott 2002; Hennessy, Swords, and Heary 2008; Smith, Leve, and Chamberlain 2006). Consistent across these samples is the finding that girls are more likely than boys to have experienced severe physical and sexual victimization. Rates of sexual abuse among incarcerated girls range from 45 to 75 percent, compared with 2 to 11 percent for incarcerated males. Rates of physical abuse are also greater for girls, ranging between 40 and 75 percent for girls and 20 to 60 percent for boys (as reported in Odgers and Moretti 2002). Research also finds qualitative differences in the experience of sexual abuse by males and females. Girls' sexual abuse tends to start earlier than boys, and girls are more likely to be assaulted by a family member (Finkelhor and Baron 1986). Girls' abuse tends to last longer and is more likely to last into adulthood (DeJong, Hervada, and Emmett 1983; Snell and Morton 1994). All of these factors (relationship with perpetrator, onset and length of victimization) are associated with more severe trauma (Browne and Finkelhor 1986; Spaccarelli 1994).

In addition to different qualities of the abuse, girls may react differently from boys. Girls are more likely to run away than boys in an attempt to escape continued abuse. Once on the street, they may be forced into delinquent or criminal behavior to survive (Chesney-Lind 1989). Thus, both girls' victimization and their response to it are influenced by their status as a female. However, it is clear that victimization is related to increased risk for boys as well. Only by including both males and females in studies of antisocial behavior can we begin to have a gendered understanding of risk.

C. Neighborhood Context

For both boys and girls, the social ecology of the neighborhood or community must be considered (see Kroneman, Loeber, and Hipwell 2004, for a review of neighborhood context, delinquency, and gender). Across studies, research has clearly demonstrated that the structural characteristics of a neighborhood (e.g., poverty, residential stability, percent of female-headed households) and the social organization of the neighborhood (e.g., cohesion, support) relate to delinquent and violent involvement (Sampson, Morenoff, and Gannon-Rowley 2002) and affect family functioning and its relation to youth risk (Brooks-Gunn, Duncan, and Aber 1997; Gorman-Smith, Tolan, and Henry 1999; Ingoldsby et al. 2006). The differential effect of neighborhood and community factors for girls has not been well studied. Some studies suggest that girls are more closely monitored, kept closer to home, and thus are less exposed to neighborhood risk (Bottcher 2001).

Others have found more similar effects for boys and girls. For example, using data from the Project on Human Development in Chicago Neighborhoods, Molnar and colleagues (2005) found that adolescent girls were more likely to act violently if they had been victims of violence and if they lived in communities with high rates of poverty and/or violent crime. Girls living in economically disadvantaged neighborhoods were 1.5 times as likely to be involved in violence as girls in other neighborhoods. Girls with a history of victimization living in violent, economically disadvantaged neighborhoods were twice as likely to behave violently as nonvictimized girls in similar neighborhoods.

Studies have shown that, across communities that are similar in regard to structural dimensions such as poverty and single-parenthood, there are significant differences in neighborhood social organization and networks that relate to differences in the ways families function and how parents manage their children. For example, in a study of parenting among single mothers in poor, urban neighborhoods, researchers found that those residing in the most dangerous neighborhood adapted to this environment by isolating themselves and their families from those around them (Furstenberg 1993). While this served to increase the mother's sense of safety, it also cut her off from potential social supports. Similarly, others have found that parents in poor neighborhoods often use "bounding" techniques that restrict children to their homes and limit access to neighborhood influences, particularly peers (Jarrett 1997). Other research has pointed to the importance of "precision parenting" in poor, urban neighborhoods (Gonzalez et al. 1996; Mason et al. 1996). That is, in some urban neighborhoods, both too little and too much parental monitoring and involvement are associated with increased behavior problems among youth. This curvilinear relation is not found in studies of families residing in other types of neighborhoods.

Others have found differences in the way parenting practices may relate to youth outcomes depending on community residence. For example, in Chicago, we found that parenting was able to mediate the effects of stress on youth delinquency in poor, but not seriously impoverished or devastated urban communities

(Gorman-Smith, Tolan, and Henry 1999). This was the case, even though there were no differences in average level scores on parenting practices scales between the two community types. We also (Gorman-Smith, Tolan, and Henry 2000) compared the impact of different parenting practices and family relationship patterns in inner-city communities with high and low neighborhood social organization, and in poor but not inner-city urban communities. Overall, families with strong parenting practices but low levels of cohesion and emotional support were more likely than those with both strong parenting and family cohesion to have a child involved in serious and chronic delinquency. However, this was not the case if families with these parenting patterns lived in neighborhoods with high social organization; their children were not more likely to be involved in serious and chronic delinquency. It may be that, when emotional needs, such as a sense of belonging and support, are met by the neighborhood, the risk carried by the family is minimized.

D. A Gendered Approach

Although general theories of delinquency do not specifically exclude females, they often do not include gender issues in the understanding of the development, frequency, seriousness, and context of involvement in antisocial and delinquent behavior. For example, a developmental life-course perspective on crime focuses on career trajectories marked by "turning points" (a change in the life course) from conventional to criminal behavior or vice versa (Sampson and Laub 1994). Transitions such as from school to work or from being single to married are opportunities for change in behavior. Data suggest that, for men, involvement in a stable live-in relationship with a woman decreases risk for continued criminal behavior (Sampson and Laub 1994; Farrington and West 1995) whether this be because of social bonding (Sampson and Laub 1993) or decreased involvement with delinquent peers (Warr 1998). However, it is not clear what effect this type of transition might have for a woman. There is some evidence to suggest that adolescent girls' involvement with male peers serves to increase their risk for antisocial behavior (Caspi et al. 1993). The role of men in initiating women into crime, particularly serious crime, is a consistent finding in the literature (Steffensmeier 1983; Pettiway 1987; Gilfus 1992). Thus, what may be a protective factor for men may, in fact, be a risk factor for women. This does not mean that a developmental life-course perspective might not be useful for understanding antisocial behavior among women. However, it does point to the fact that most theories of delinquent and antisocial behavior fail to consider how risk factors may vary in impact by gender.

Taking a gendered approach is more than just looking at sex differences because gender is a socially defined construct that includes components such as how boys and girls are socialized and what is expected of them based on gender roles. Steffensmeier and Allan (1996) point out several key elements that should be included in a gendered approach to understanding antisocial behavior. Although their work refers more specifically to adult involvement in crime, some elements are transferable to a developmental understanding of antisocial behavior and adolescent delinquency as well. Theory should help explain both male and female involvement by revealing how the organization of gender deters or encourages antisocial behavior in both males and females. Organization of gender refers broadly to things such as "norms, identities, arrangements, institutions, and relations by which human sexual dichotomy is transformed into something physically and socially different" (Steffensmeier and Allan 1996, p. 474).

To be used to inform prevention, risk theory should not just function as a sophisticated tabulation of sex differences in type and frequency of crime but also provide understanding of the developmental and contextual influences that relate the social construct of gender to antisocial behavior. Although the contexts in which mild forms of delinquent behavior occur seem similar for males and females, the contexts for more serious behaviors, particularly violence, are quite different. For example, when involved in peer homicide, girls are more likely to kill as a result of interpersonal conflict and kill alone, whereas boys are more likely to kill with an accomplice (Loper and Cornell 1996). These variations need to be understood or related to gender as an important aspect of development and maintenance of antisocial behavior. On that basis, sound gender encompassing prevention can occur.

III. Prevention

A. Developmental-Ecological Models of Risk

Prevention science increasingly recognizes the importance of considering multiple influences on children's development—influences from different levels of developmental context (Bronfenbrenner 1979; Szapocznik and Coatsworth 1999; Coie, Miller-Johnson, and Bagwell 2000). A central tenet of developmental-ecological theory is that individual development is influenced by the ongoing qualities of the social settings in which the child lives or participates and the extent and nature of the interaction between these settings. Child development is influenced by family functioning, peer relationships, schools, communities, and larger societal influences (e.g., policies, media). This conceptual model also suggests that social systems are "nested" within one another—individuals are nested within families and families in turn are nested within neighborhoods. This model suggests that how families function or how they parent might differ depending on the neighborhood in which they live, and the same level of family functioning may have different effects on children's development depending on neighborhood residence (Sampson 1997; Gorman-Smith, Tolan, and Henry 2000).

The model also incorporates development. That is, as children grow their needs and the demands of the environment change, and the nature and extent of exposure to developmental settings shifts (e.g., influence of schools and peers as children enter those systems, influence of the neighborhood as youth spend more time on their own and in the community). The developmental-ecological model highlights differences in the influences of social settings (e.g., peers, schools, neighborhoods) across child development. The implication is that parenting and family functioning must shift as children age. It also means that the nature of the interaction(s) with other levels of social systems, including peer relationships, will shift over time. Families have to manage not only individual child development but also the influences of other social settings including peers.

The implication of this is that different socializing systems (e.g., families) may be more or less influential at different points in a child's development. A consistent finding is that peer influences are among the strongest predictors of delinquent involvement in adolescence for boys and girls. However, family factors are the strongest predictors of youth involvement with antisocial or delinquent peers. Effective parenting and strong connection/bonding to family are protective and decrease the likelihood of involvement with delinquent peers.

Although it is possible to turn one's life around, and there is never a point in development when it is impossible to effectively intervene to change behavior, "early" preventive intervention appears to have stronger effects on behavior, decreasing the likelihood of any involvement in and other associated consequences of antisocial or criminal behavior.

B. Developmental Trajectories of Risk

Research over the last 15 to 20 years has led to a greater integration of developmental theory into our understanding of risk of involvement in delinquency and violence. A developmental model, based on age of onset of delinquent behavior (middle adolescent onset, early adolescent onset, and preadolescent onset) has been useful in guiding research and prevention efforts (Steinberg 1987). The model suggests that, in general, serious disruptions in parenting and family functioning are related to the early onset of delinquent behavior.

1. *Early Childhood Risk.* Not surprisingly, youth who begin on the path toward aggression and violence very early, those who are defiant and aggressive in early childhood, tend to come from families with multiple problems and of the type that significantly disrupt the parent-child relationship. Typically, this type of parenting involves high levels of coercion and low levels of parental warmth and support (Patterson, Reid, and Dishion 1992; Loeber and Stouthamer-Loeber 1986; Chamberlain and Moore 2002)—sometimes so severe as to constitute abuse or neglect. Over time the pattern may escalate, with the relationship continuing to deteriorate with increasing levels of hostility and discord. As the relationship is disrupted, less monitoring occurs, increasing opportunities for involvement with delinquent or otherwise antisocial peers.

Often, youth who begin early also stand apart from their peers because of other identifiable problems that begin at an early age, such as aggression, impulsivity, problems with self-regulation, and poor social skills (Caspi et al. 1993). These are children who can be very difficult to parent under the best of circumstances. In interaction with problems in parenting, youth are at particularly high risk of involvement in gang or other forms of violence. In these situations, the most effective interventions are those that focus on parenting and family functioning earlier in development.

The disruption in the parent-child relationship may sometimes be less severe or for contextual reasons such as divorce, illness, or other types of stressors. These disruptions may occur early and begin a cycle of struggling and coercive interaction between the parent and child. Disruption in the parent-child relationship is not an inevitable consequence of stress, but stress factors can precipitate disruption without adequate levels of support for both parent and child. Emotional warmth and connection appear to be particularly important and protective in the face of such stressors (Gorman-Smith, Tolan, and Henry 2000).

2. *Adolescent Risk.* Youth who become involved in antisocial behavior during adolescence tend to follow one of two pathways: those who become involved on the margins without involvement in more serious behaviors, and those who become involved later but quickly escalate to serious and violent offending. The second group of individuals, if assessed at a single point in development, may look very similar in regard to level and type of involvement to those starting earlier and who have been chronically involved over the course of childhood.

There is relatively little data available differentiating these two groups of youth, particularly for girls. In general, those who become involved at the fringe and manage to avoid more serious involvement tend to come from families that are functioning well across areas of parenting and family functioning, though they may need additional support during the difficult developmental period of adolescence, particularly around issues of monitoring (i.e., knowing where children are, knowing friends, knowing parents of friends).

C. Impact of Prevention Programs

The limited attention to girls' involvement in delinquent and violent behavior until relatively recently is reflected also in the empirical work on prevention. In 2006, the Girls Study Group (OJJDP) conducted a review of all published evaluations of programs designed to prevent and reduce delinquency among girls. Out of the 61 programs catalogued, they found only that 17 had been evaluated. Applying the criteria used for the Department of Education's "What Works Repository," none of the programs met the criteria to be considered "effective." The large majority of the programs were rated as having insufficient evidence because of poor study design. Of the 17 programs that had been evaluated, seven were no longer in existence, which seems to reflect the cyclical nature of programming—programs often come and go within communities or settings, with little attention paid to issues of sustainability and seldom to evidence of effects or lack of effects.

Often, when girls have been included in preventive interventions, overall effects are reported and analyses are not disaggregated by sex. Some studies report no differences in effects for boys and girls (e.g., Tolan, Gorman-Smith, and Henry 2004). In some cases, when girls have been included, programs have been less effective with girls than with boys (e.g., Kellam et al. 1998; Farrell and Meyer 1997). Other programs have reported some differential effects for boys and girls (e.g., Hawkins, Von Cleve, and Catalano 1991). That is, different behavioral outcomes were found or different moderators of risk were changed. However, there has been little discussion of the meaning of these potential differences.

There are several potential explanations for these gender differences. Some of the programs that have been less effective may not have targeted those risk factors that are most likely to affect change for girls or may not have attended to the particular ways that gender may be a part of the relation with offending. For example, programs that do not focus on management of relationship issues may not be salient for girls and may miss an important path toward modifying risk. In addition, research has demonstrated that programs that include the family as part of the intervention are likely to have the most powerful effects (Tolan and Guerra 1994; Wasserman and Miller 1998). This is true of girls as well as boys, but it may be more important for girls given the research suggesting that girls tend to be more involved with their families and that families of antisocial girls are more dysfunctional than families of antisocial boys (Silverthorn and Frick 1999).

Second, it is possible that programs have been effective, but that programs have not evaluated change in multiple types of outcomes. A focus only on physical aggression or other types of externalizing problems could result in missing important intervention effects. For example, by not considering types of relational aggression, intervention effects (particularly for girls) could be missed. As research suggests that the long-term outcomes for girls with antisocial behavior might be more complex than those of boys, additional outcomes such as internalizing disorders and other indicators of well-being should be considered. Attention to these other types of problems might also result in finding that these outcomes have been affected for boys as well as girls.

If we are to understand why programs are effective for one group and not another, or why programs impact different types of behaviors, sex must be included in analyses, and gender must be included in the development of programs as well as in the interpretation of results. In addition, evaluation of programs should examine mediators of risk and targets of intervention by gender. The same program may decrease risk for both boys and girls, but might do so through different processes. These gender differences may be important for understanding basic risk processes, and they are critical for understanding how to develop appropriate and effective intervention programs. Thus, while it may be possible to design a program that is applicable to both boys and girls, this will only be accomplished by attending to some of the ways in which risk and intervention effects may vary for boys and girls across development.

IV. CONCLUSIONS

Although fewer girls than boys are involved in delinquency and violence, rates of girls' involvement have increased significantly over the last two decades. Girls are involved in similar types of offending as boys, as well as other forms of aggressive behavior (i.e., relational aggression), all of which have serious consequences for both victims and perpetrators. Although the same list of risk factors appears for girls as for boys, the nature and quality of how these factors relate to outcomes may be different for boys and girls. These differences have important implications for prevention and intervention efforts, an area of research that has been relatively limited. We know relatively little about prevention and intervention for girls. Prevention studies rarely disaggregate results by gender. Some programs have been developed specifically for girls, however, among those that have been developed, few have been rigorously evaluated and among those few sustained effects have been found. If we are to make progress in decreasing the rate of girls involved in delinquent and antisocial behavior, continued and increased scientific attention is needed.

NOTE

The findings and conclusions in this report are those of the authors and do not necessarily represent the official position of the Centers for Disease Control and Prevention. No authors have conflicts of interest to report.

REFERENCES

Acoca, Leslie. 1999. "Investing in Girls: A 21st Century Challenge." *Juvenile Justice* 6:3–13.

Bardone, Anna M., Terrie E. Moffitt, Avshalom Caspi, Nigel Dickson, Warren R. Stanton, and Phil A. Silva. 1998. "Adult Physical Health Outcomes of Adolescent Girls with Conduct Disorder, Depression, and Anxiety." *Journal of the American Academy of Child and Adolescent Psychiatry* 37:594–601.

Barnow, Sven, Marc A. Schuckit, Michael Lucht, Ulrich John, and Harald-J. Freyberger. 2002. "The Importance of a Positive Family History of Alcoholism, Parental Rejection and Emotional Warmth, Behavioral Problems and Peer Substance Use for Alcohol Problems in Teenagers: A Path Analysis." *Journal of Studies on Alcohol* 63:305–15.

Battle, Cynthia L., Caron Zlotnick, Lisa M. Najavits, Marysol Gutierrez, and Celia Winsor. 2003. "Posttraumatic Stress Disorder and Substance Use Disorder Among Incarcerated Women." In *Trauma and Substance Abuse: Causes, Consequences, and Treatment of Comorbid Disorders*, edited by Paige C. Ouimette and Pamela J. Brown. Washington, DC: American Psychological Association.

Berlinger, John, and Diana M. Elliott. 2002. "Prevalence and Psychological Sequelae of Self-Reported Childhood Physical and Sexual Abuse in a General Population Sample of Men and Women." *Child Abuse & Neglect* 27:1205–22.

Bianco, Dorothy M., and Susan D. Wallace. 1991. "The Chemically Dependent Female Adolescent: A Treatment Challenge." In *Children of Chemically Dependent Parents: Multiperspectives from the Cutting Edge*, edited by Timothy M. Rivinus. Philadelphia, PA: Brunner/Mazel.

Bjorkqvist, Kaj, and Pirkko Niemela. 1992. "New Trends in the Study of Female Aggression." In *Of Mice and Women: Aspects of Female Aggression*, edited by Kaj Bjorkqvist and Pikko Niemala. San Diego, CA: Academic Press.

Blumenthal, Susan J. 1998. "Women and Substance Abuse: A New National Focus." In *Drug Addiction Research and the Health of Women*, edited by Cora Lee Wetherington and Adele B. Roman. Rockville, MD: National Institute on Drug Abuse.

Bottcher, Jean 2001. "Social Practices of Gender: How Gender Relates to Delinquency in the Everyday Lives of High-Risk Youths." *Criminology* 39:893–932.

Brody, Leslie R. 1985. "Gender Differences in Emotional Development: A Review of Theories and Research." *Journal of Personality* 53:102–49.

Bronfenbrenner, Urie. 1979. *The Ecology of Human Development: Experiments by Nature and Design*. Cambridge, MA: Harvard University Press.

Brooks-Gunn, Jeanne, Greg J. Duncan, and J. Lawrence Aber. 1997. *Neighborhood Poverty: Policy Implications in Studying Neighborhoods*. New York: Russell Sage Foundation.

Browne, Angela, and David Finklehor. 1986. "Impact of Child Sexual Abuse: A Review of Research." Psychological Bulletin 99:66–77.

Cairns, Robert B., and Beverly D. Cairns. 1994. *Lifelines and Risks: Pathways of Youth in Our Time*. Cambridge, UK: Cambridge University Press.

Caspi, Avshalom, Donald Lynam, Terrie E. Moffitt, and Phil A. Silva. 1993. "Unraveling Girls' Delinquency: Biological, Dispositional, and Contextual Contributions to Adolescent Misbehavior." *Developmental Psychology* 29:19–30.

Cernkovich, Stephen A., Nadine Lanctôt, and Peggy C. Giordano. 2007. "Predicting Adolescent and Adult Antisocial Behavior Among Adjudicated Delinquent Females." *Crime & Delinquency* 54:3–33.

Chamberlain, Patricia, and Kevin J. Moore. 2002. "Chaos and Trauma in the Lives of Adolescent Females with Antisocial Behavior and Delinquency." *Journal of Aggression, Maltreatment, and Trauma* 6:79–108.

Chesney-Lind, Meda. 1989. "Girls' Crime and a Woman's Place: Toward a Feminist Model of Female Delinquency." *Crime and Delinquency* 35:5–29.

Cohen, Patricia, Jacob Cohen, Stephanie Kasen, Carmen N. Velez, Claudia Hartmark, James Johnson, Mary Rojas, Judith Brook, and E. L. Streuning. 1993. "An Epidemiological Study of Disorders in Late Childhood and Adolescence—I. Age-and Gender-specific Prevalence." *Journal of Child Psychology and Psychiatry* 34:851–67.

Coie, John D., Shari Miller-Johnson, and Catherine Bagwell. 2000. "Prevention Science." In *Handbook of Developmental Psychopathology*, edited by Arnold J. Sameroff, Michael Lewis, and Suzanne Melanie Miller. Dordrecht, Netherlands: Kluwer.

Corrado, Raymond R., Candice Odgers, and Irwin M.Cohen. 2000. "The Incarceration of Female Young Offenders: Protection for Whom?" *Canadian Journal of Criminology* 42:189–207.

Crick, Nicki R. 2003. "A Gender-balanced Approach to the Study of Childhood Aggression and Reciprocal Family Influences." In *Children's Influence on Family Dynamics: The*

Neglected Side of Family Relationships, edited by Ann C. Crouter and Alan Booth. Mahwah, NJ: Lawrence Erlbaum.

Crick, Nicki R., Maureen A. Bigbee, and Cynthia Howes. 1996. "Gender Differences in Children's Normative Beliefs About Aggression: How Do I Hurt Thee? Let Me Count the Ways." *Child Development* 67:1003–14.

Crick, Nicki R., and Jennifer K. Grotpeter. 1995. "Relational Aggression, Gender, and Social-psychological Adjustment." *Child Development* 66:710–22.

Daigle, Leah E., Francis T. Cullen, and John Paul Wright. 2007. "Gender Differences in the Predictors of Juvenile Misconduct: Assessing the Generality-specificity Debate." *Journal of Youth Violence and Juvenile Justice* 5:254–86.

Daly, Kathleen. 1994. Gender, Crime, and Punishment. New Haven, CT: Yale University Press.

DeJong, Allan R., Arturo R. Hervada, and Gary A. Emmett. 1983. "Epidemiologic Variations in Childhood Sexual Abuse." *Child Abuse and Neglect* 7:155–62.

Elliott, Delbert S. 1994. "Serious Violent Offenders: Onset, Developmental Course, and Termination-the American Society of Criminology 1993 Presidential Address." *Criminology* 32:1–21.

Farrell, Albert D., and Aleta L. Meyer. 1997. "Effectiveness of a School-based Prevention Program for Reducing Violence Among Urban Adolescents: Differential Impact on Girls and Boys." *American Journal of Public Health* 87:979–84.

Farrington, David P., and Donald J. West. 1995. "Effects of Marriage, Separation, and Children on Offending by Adult Males." In *Current Perspectives on Aging and the Life Cycle. Vol. 4: Delinquency and Disrepute in the Life Course*, edited by Zena Smith Blau, and John Hagan. Greenwich, CT: JAI Press.

Federal Bureau of Investigation. 2000. *Uniform Crime Reports: Crime in the United States, 1999*. Washington, DC: US Government Printing Office.

Federal Bureau of Investigation. 2009. *Uniform Crime Reports: Crime in the United States, 2008*. Washington, DC: US Government Printing Office.

Fergusson, David M., and John L. Horwood. 2002. "Male and Female Offending Trajectories." *Development and Psychopathology* 14:159–77.

Finklehor, David, and Larry Baron. 1986. "Risk Factors for Child Sexual Abuse." *Journal of Interpersonal Violence* 1:43–71.

Furstenberg, Frank F. 1993. "How Families Manage Risk and Opportunity in Dangerous Neighborhoods." In *Sociology and the Public Agenda*, edited by William J. Wilson. Newbury Park, CA: Sage.

Gilfus, Mary E. 1992. "From Victims To Survivors to Offenders: Women's Routes of Entry and Immersion Into Street Crime." *Women and Criminal Justice* 4:63–89.

Giordano, Peggy C., Stepehn A. Cernkovich, and M. D. Pugh. 1986. "Friendships and Delinquency." *American Journal of Sociology* 91:1170–202.

Gonzales, Nancy A., Ana Mari Cauce, Ruth J. Friedman, and Craig A. Mason. 1996. "Family, Peer, and Neighborhood Influences on Academic Achievement Among African American Adolescents: One-year Prospective Effects." *American Journal of Community Psychology* 24:365–87.

Gorman-Smith, Deborah, Patrick H. Tolan, and David Henry. 1999. "The Relation of Community and Family to Risk Among Urban Poor Adolescents." In *Historical and Geographical Influences on Psychopathology*, edited by Patricia Cohen, Cheryl Slomkowski, and Lee N. Robins. Mahwah, NJ: Lawrence Erlbaum.

Gorman-Smith, Deborah, Patrick H. Tolan, and David Henry. 2000. "A Developmental-ecological Model of the Relation of Family Functioning to Patterns of Delinquency." *Journal of Quantitative Criminology* 16:169–98.

Haller, Deborah L., Janet S. Knisely, Kathryn S. Dawson, and Sidney H. Schnoll. 1993. "Perinatal Substance Abusers: Psychological and Social Characteristics." *Journal of Nervous and Mental Disease* 181:509–13.

Hawkins, J. David, Elizabeth Von Cleve, and Richard F. Catalano. 1991. "Reducing Early Childhood Aggression: Results of a Primary Prevention Program." *Journal of the American Academy of Child and Adolescent Psychiatry* 30:208–17.

Henggeler, Scott W., James Edwards, and Charles M. Borduin. 1987. "The Family Relations of Female Juvenile Delinquents." *Journal of Abnormal Child Psychology* 15:199–209.

Hennessy, Eilis, Lorraine Swords, and Caroline Heary. 2008. "Children's Understanding of Psychological Problems Displayed by Their Peers: A Review of the Literature." *Child Care, Health and Development* 34:4–9.

Hubbard, Dana J., and Travis C. Pratt. 2002. "A Meta-analysis of the Predictors of Delinquency Among Girls." *Journal of Offender Rehabilitation* 34:1–13.

Ingoldsby, Erin M., Daniel S. Shaw, Emily Winslow, Michael Schonberg, Miles Gilliom, and Michael M. Criss. 2006. "Neighborhood Disadvantage, Parent-child Conflict, Neighborhood Peer Relationships, and Early Antisocial Behavior Problem Trajectories." *Journal of Abnormal and Child Psychology* 34:303–19.

Jarrett, Robin L. 1997. "Resilience Among Low-income African American Youth: An Ethnographic Perspective." *Ethos* 25:218–29.

Kellam, Sheppard G., Lawrence S. Mayer, George W. Rebok, G. W., and Wesley E. Hawkins. 1998. "Effects of Improving Achievement on Aggressive Behavior and of Improving Aggressive Behavior on Achievement Through Two Preventive Interactions: An Investigation of Causal Paths." In *Adversity, Stress, and Psychopathology*, edited by Bruce D. Dohrenwend. New York: Oxford University Press.

Kroneman, Leoniek, Rolf Loeber, and Alison E. Hipwell. 2004. "Is Neighborhood Context Differently Related to Externalizing Problems and Delinquency for Girls Compared to Boys." *Clinical Child and Family Psychology Review* 7:109–22.

Kruttschnitt, Candace. 1993. "Violence By and Against Women: A Cooperative and Cross-national Analysis." *Violence and Victims* 8:253–70.

Kruttschnitt, Candace. 1994. "Gender and Interpersonal Violence." In *Understanding and Preventing Violence. Vol. 3: Social Influences*, edited by Jeffrey Roth and Albert Reiss. Washington, DC: National Academy of Science.

Lewis, Dorothy O., Catherine A. Yeager, Celeste S. Cobham-Portorreal, Nancy Klein, Claudia Showalter, and Adelle Anthony. 1991. "A Follow-up From the Female Delinquents: Maternal Contributions to the Perpetuation of Deviance." *Journal of the American Academy of Child and Adolescent Psychiatry* 30:197–201.

Loeber, Rolf, and Madga Stouthamer-Loeber. 1986. "Family Factors as Correlates and Predictors of Juvenile Conduct Problems and Delinquency." In *Crime and Justice, vol.7*, edited by Michael Tonry and Norval Morris. Chicago, IL: University of Chicago Press.

Loper, Ann B., and Dewey G. Cornell. 1996. "Homicide by Girls." *Journal of Child and Family Studies* 5:321–33.

MacDonald, Christine D., and Elizabeth M. O'Laughlin. 1997. *Relational Aggression and Risk Behaviors in Middle School Students*. Washington, DC: Society for Research in Child Development.

Mason, C. A., Cauce, A. M., Gonzales, N., & Hiraga, Y. 1996. "Neither Too Sweet Nor Too Sour: Problem Peers, Maternal Control, and Problem Behavior in African American Adolescents." *Child Development* 67:2115–30.

Moffitt, Terri E., and Avshalom Caspi. 2001. "Childhood Predictors Differentiate Life-course Persistent and Adolescence-limited Antisocial Pathways Among Males and Females." *Developmental Psychopathology* 13:355–75.

Molnar, Beth E., Angela Browne, Magdalena Cerda, and Stephen L. Buka. 2005. "Violent Behavior by Girls Reporting Violent Victimization: A Prospective Study." *Archives of Pediatrics & Adolescent Medicine* 159:731–39.

Morey, Lesley C. 1991. *The Personality Assessment Inventory: Professional Manual*. Lutz, FL: Psychological Assessment Resources.

Odgers, Candace L., and Marlene M. Moretti. 2002. "Aggressive and Antisocial Girls: Research Update and Future Challenges." *International Journal of Forensic and Mental Health* 2:17–33.

Ostrov, Jamie M., and Nicki R. Crick. 2005. "Current Directions in the Study of Relational Aggression During Early Childhood." *Early Education and Development* 16:109–13.

Pajer, Kathleen A. 1998. "What Happens to "Bad" Girls? Review of the Adult Outcomes of Antisocial Adolescent Girls." *American Journal of Psychiatry* 155: 862–70.

Patterson, Gerald R., John B. Reid, and Thomas J. Dishion. 1992. *Antisocial Boys: A Social Interactional Approach*, vol. 4. Eugene, OR: Castalia.

Pepler, Debra J., and Farrokh Sedighdeilami. 1998. *Aggressive Girls in Canada*. Ottawa, Canada: Applied Research Branch, Strategic Policy, Human Resources Development.

Pettiway, Leon E. 1987. "Arson for Revenge: The Role of Environmental Situation, Age, Sex, and Race." *Journal of Quantitative Criminology* 3:169–84.

Poe-Yamagata, Eileen, and Jeffery A. Butts. 1996. *Female Offenders in the Juvenile Justice System: Statistics Summary*. Pittsburgh, PA: National Center for Juvenile Justice.

Puzzanchera, Charles. 2009. *Juvenile Arrests 2008*. Washington, DC: US Department of Justice, Office of Juvenile Justice and Delinquency Prevention.

Robins, Lee N. 1966. *Deviant Children Grown Up: A Sociological and Psychiatric Study of Sociopathic Personality*. Baltimore: Williams & Wilkins.

Robins, Lee N., and Rumi K. Price. 1991. "Adult Disorders Predicted by Childhood Conduct Problems: Results from the NIMH Epidemiologic Catchment Area Project." *Psychiatry* 54:116–32.

Sampson, Robert J. 1997. "The Embeddedness of Child and Adolescent Development: A Community-level Perspective on Urban Violence." In *Violence and Childhood in the Inner City*, edited by Joan McCord. Cambridge, MA: Cambridge University Press.

Sampson, Robert J., and John H. Laub. 1993. *Crime in the Making: Pathways and Turning Points Through Life*. Cambridge, MA: Harvard University Press.

Sampson, Robert J., and John H. Laub. 1994. "Urban Poverty and the Family Context of Delinquency: A New Look at Structure and Process in a Classic Study." *Child Development* 65:523–39.

Sampson, Robert J., Jeffrey D. Morenoff, and Thomas Gannon-Rowley. 2002. "Assessing "Neighborhood Effects": Social Processes and New Directions in Research." *Annual Review Sociology* 28:443–78.

Silverthorn, Persephanie, and Paul J.Frick. 1999. "Developmental Pathways to Antisocial Behavior: The Delayed-onset Pathway in Girls." *Development and Psychopathology* 11:101–26.

Smith, Dana K., Leslie D. Leve, and Patricia Chamberlain. 2006. "Adolescent Girls' Offending and Health-risking Sexual Behavior: The Predictive Role of Trauma." *Child Maltreatment* 11:346–53.

Snell, Tracy L., and Danielle C. Morton. 1994. *Women in Prison*. Washington, DC: US Bureau of Justice Statistics.

Snyder, Howard N. 2000. *Juvenile Arrest: 2000*. Washington, DC: US Department of
    Justice, Office of Juvenile Justice and Delinquency Prevention.
Snyder, Howard N., and Melissa Sickmund 1999. *Juvenile Offenders and Victims: 1999
    National Report*. Washington, DC: US Department of Justice, Office of Juvenile Justice
    and Delinquency Prevention.
Snyder, Howard N., and Melissa Sickmund. 2006. *Juvenile Offenders and Victims: 2006
    National Report*. Washington, DC: US Department of Justice, Office of Juvenile Justice
    and Delinquency Prevention.
Sommers, Ira, and Deborah R. Baskin. 1992. "Sex, Race, Age, and Violent Offending."
    Violence and Victims 7:191–201.
Spaccarelli, Steve. 1994. "Stress, Appraisal, and Coping in Child Sexual Abuse: A Theoreti-
    cal and Empirical Review." *Psychological Bulletin* 116:340–62.
Steffensmeier, Darrell. 1983. "Sex-segregation in the Underworld: Building a Sociological
    Explanation of Sex Differences in Crime." *Social Forces* 61:1010–32.
Steffensmeier, Darrell. 1993. "National Trends in Female Arrests, 1960–1990: Assess-
    ment and Recommendations for Research." *Journal of Quantitative Criminology*
    9:413–41.
Steffensmeier, Darrell., and Emilie Allan. 1996. "Gender and Crime: Toward a Gendered
    Theory of Female Offending." *Annual Review of Sociology* 22:459–87.
Steffensmeier, Darrell, Hua Zhong, Jeff Ackerman, Jennifer Schwartz, and Suzanne Agha.
    2006. "Gender Gap Trends for Violent Crimes, 1980 to 2003: A UCR-NCVS Compari-
    son." *Feminist Criminology* 1:72–98.
Steffensmeier, Darrell, Jennifer Schwartz, Hua Zhong, and Jeff Ackerman. 2005. "An
    Assessment of Recent Trends in Girls' Violence Using Diverse Longitudinal Sources: Is
    the Gender Gap Closing?" *Criminology* 42:355–406.
Steinberg, Laurence. 1987. "Familial Factors in Delinquency: A Developmental Perspective."
    Journal of Adolescent Research 2:255–68.
Szapocznik, José, and Douglas J. Coatsworth. 1999. "An Ecodevelopmental Framework for
    Organizing the Influences on Drug Abuse: A Developmental Model of Risk &
    Protection." In *Drug abuse: Origins and Interventions*, edited by Meyer D. Glantz and
    Christine R. Hartel. Washington, DC: American Psychological Association.
Teplin, Linda A., Karen M. Abram, Gary M. McClelland, Mina K. Dulcan, and Amy A.
    Mericle. 2002. "Psychiatric Disorders in Youth in Juvenile Detention." *Archives of
    General Psychiatry* 59:1133–43.
Tolan, Patrick H., Deborah Gorman-Smith, and David Henry. 2004. "Supporting Families
    in a High-risk Setting: Proximal Effects of the SAFE Children Preventive Interven-
    tion." *Journal of Consulting and Clinical Psychology* 72: 855–69.
Tolan, Patrick H., and Nancy Guerra. 1994. *What Works in Reducing Adolescent Violence:
    An Empirical Review of the Field*. Boulder, CO: University of Colorado, Center for the
    Study and Prevention of Violence.
Triplett, Ruth, and Laura B. Myers. 1995. "Evaluating Contextual Patterns of Delinquency:
    Gender Based Differences." *Justice Quarterly* 12:59–79.
Underwood, Marion K. 2003. Social Aggression Among Girls. New York: Guilford Press.
Warr, Mark. 1998. "Life-Course Transitions and Desistance from Crime." *Criminology*
    36:183–216.
Wassermann, Gail A., and Laurie S. Miller. 1998. "The Prevention of Serious and Violent
    Juvenile Offending." In *Serious and Violent Juvenile Offenders: Risk Factors and
    Successful Interventions*, edited by Rolf Loeber and David Farrington. Thousand Oaks,
    CA: Sage.

Werner, Emmy E. 1992. "The Children of Kauai: Resiliency and Recovery in Adolescence and Adulthood." *Journal of Adolescent Health* 13:262–68.

Werner, Emily W., and Ruth S. Smith. 1992. *Overcoming the Odds: High-risk Children From Birth to Adulthood*. Ithaca, NY: Cornell University Press.

Werner, Nicole E., and Nicki R. Crick. 1999. "Relational Aggression and Social-psychological Adjustment in A College Sample." *Journal of Abnormal Psychology* 108:615–23.

Widom, Cathy S., and Helene R. White. 1997. "Problem Behaviors in Abused and Neglected Children Grown Up: Prevalence and Co-occurrence of Substance Abuse, Crime, and Violence." *Journal of Criminal Behaviour and Mental Health* 7:287–310.

Zahn, Margaret A., Robert Agnew, Diana Fishbein, Shari Miller, Donna-Marie Winn, Gayle Dakoff, Candace Kruttschnitt, Peggy Giordano, Denise C. Gottfredson, Allison A. Payne, Barry C. Feld, and Meda Chesney-Lind. 2010. *Causes and Correlates of Girls' Delinquency*. Washington, DC: US Department of Justice, Office of Juvenile Justice and Delinquency Prevention.

Zahn, Margaret A., Susan Brumbaugh, Darrell Steffensmeier, Barry C. Feld, Merry Morash, Meda Chesney-Lind, Shari Miller, Allison A. Payne, Denise C. Gottfredson, and Candace Kruttschnitt. 2008. *Violence by Teenage Girls: Trends and Context*. Washington, DC: US Department of Justice, Office of Juvenile Justice and Delinquency Prevention.

Zahn, Margaret A., Stephanie R. Hawkins, Janet Chiancone, and Ariel Whitworth. 2008. *Girls Study Group—Charting the Way to Delinquency Prevention for Girls*. Washington, DC: US Department of Justice, Office of Juvenile Justice and Delinquency Prevention.

Zoccolillo, Mark. 1993. "Gender and the Development of Conduct Disorder." *Development and Psychopathology* 5:65–78.

Zoccolillo, Mark, Andrew Pickles, David Quinton, and Michael Rutter. 1992. "The Outcome of Childhood Conduct Disorder: Implications for Defining Adult Personality Disorder and Conduct Disorder." *Psychological Medicine* 22:971–86.

Zoccolillo, Mark, and Kathy Rogers. 1991. "Characteristics and Outcome of Hospitalized Adolescent Girls With Conduct Disorder." *Journal of the American Academy of Child and Adolescent Psychiatry* 30:973–81.

PART II

COMMUNITY CRIME PREVENTION

CHAPTER 8

COMMUNITY-LEVEL INFLUENCES ON CRIME AND OFFENDING

STEVEN F. MESSNER AND
GREGORY M. ZIMMERMAN

IN an essay on theoretical methods published years ago, Albert Cohen (1985) reflected on the meaning and role of the "environment" in criminological explanations. He initially reminded us of a platitude—namely, that all crime is a product of properties of the actor and properties of the environment in which the actor is situated. That is, crime is not dependent on *either* the individual *or* the environment but, rather, on *who is in what setting* (Wikström 2004, p. 19). Cohen (1985, p. 243) went on to propose that a central challenge in developing sociological explanations of crime is to discover which aspects of the environment are relevant for criminal behavior—in a sense, to *construct* the relevant environment at a theoretical level. In the early years of the 20th century, the classic Chicago School theorists took on this challenge and embraced the notion that one type of environment that is highly relevant for understanding criminal offending is the "community," commonly understood as a localized residential area or "neighborhood." The Chicago School theorists advanced elaborate and insightful arguments about the influences of neighborhood conditions on criminal offending and documented appreciable variation in levels of crime across these territorial units, variation that was correlated with theoretically strategic structural features of neighborhoods. The interest in "neighborhood effects" waned during the 1960s and early 1970s as researchers increasingly shifted their attention away from the neighborhood context to focus on individual-level, social-psychological processes. However, over the course of the past several decades, a keen interest in community- or neighborhood-level influences on crime and offending has reemerged in the discipline (Bursik and Grasmick 1993; Sampson, Morenoff, and Gannon-Rowley 2002; Pratt and Cullen 2005).

The purpose of this essay is to review some of the literature on communities/neighborhoods and crime. Our overarching objectives are to describe the distinguishing features of this macro-sociological approach to understanding crime and to report some of the more important findings that have accumulated in the empirical literature. The following observations and general conclusions emerge from the discussion:

- Research on the interrelationships between community/neighborhood organization and crime has a long and distinguished history in sociology. This field of inquiry has evolved steadily, becoming increasingly sophisticated theoretically and methodologically.
- A major development associated with contemporary work on this topic is an explicit focus on the processes and mechanisms that link the social organization of neighborhoods with varying levels of crime and delinquency. Researchers have directed attention to the important role of social ties and networks, the activation of these ties for purposes of collective social control in the neighborhood, and the emergence of cultural beliefs and attitudes conducive to either conformity on nonconformity.
- Recently developed statistical procedures for multilevel modeling have been applied productively to elucidate the effect of neighborhood conditions on crime. Researchers have made great strides in demonstrating that neighborhood context matters and in explaining why.
- A major challenge for the future is to move beyond simplified models of unidirectional causal processes by incorporating reciprocal causal effects and feedback loops. This will require creative theorizing about neighborhood organization and crime, and innovative data collection procedures to assess novel hypotheses.

Our discussion proceeds as follows. In section I, we identify the core intellectual foundations of this perspective. Section II then explicates the important ways in which contemporary researchers have elaborated and extended earlier work by identifying underlying causal explanations of neighborhood effects. In section III, we discuss the emerging work on reciprocal causation and the role of crime in the stratification of neighborhoods. Section IV concludes with a brief commentary on the lessons to be learned from this body of research and some of the challenges that must be confronted for further development in this field.

I. Intellectual Foundations: Human Ecology and the Chicago School

Researchers in the classic Chicago School of sociology were interested in a wide range of social phenomena, but what gave their work coherence was an underlying analytic framework rooted in insights drawn from the field of "ecology" (this section draws upon Liska and Messner 1999, pp. 55–62). At a general level, ecology refers to the study of the interrelationships between organisms (plant and animal life) and the external environment, including the natural habitat. Ecologists take as their point of departure the premise that organisms must be able to adapt to their environments in order to survive. Moreover, given that other organisms constitute part of the environment, organisms must be able to adapt to each other. These adaptations give rise to discernible patterns of interrelationships among organisms, a so-called web of life, which becomes situated in distinct geographical spaces, or biotic communities and natural areas. Of particular interest to ecologists is how biotic communities and natural areas develop and change. According to the ecological framework, any shock associated with the introduction of a new condition into a biotic community vibrates through the community because of its interdependent organisms. The key elements of such ecological change are the invasion of species, competition among them for resources, and the eventual dominance of a given species over others as a result of this competition.

The Chicago School sociologists applied this general ecological model to social life in Chicago in the early years of the 20th century. They argued that the social order of the city could be understood from an ecological standpoint as a product of social processes such as symbiosis (mutually beneficial relationships), cooperation, competition, and cyclical change. They further argued that humans, unlike other animals, develop a culture (customs, values, norms) that restricts ecological processes. Applying these conceptual and analytic tools, the Chicago School sociologists set out to describe and explain the spatial distribution of persistent patterns of urban activity, such as commerce, industry, residential patterns, and unconventional behaviors including crime and delinquency.

One of the more influential examples of the application of the general ecological model to urban social life was the zonal theory proposed by Ernest Burgess (1925). Burgess argued that the natural development of the city yields a pattern that approximates concentric circles, modified by features of the physical environment (e.g., in the case of Chicago, Lake Michigan serves as a natural barrier). Commerce and industry are concentrated at the center of the city (i.e., the Central Business District), which is bordered by a transitional zone populated by the poor, immigrants, and transients. The socioeconomic status of the surrounding zones increases steadily with distance from the transitional zone. Burgess maintained that the zonal pattern was the outcome of underlying ecological processes, particularly the natural competition over real estate, property, and resources in a newly industrialized and urbanized city.

Two other Chicagoans—Clifford Shaw and Henry McKay (1931, 1942)—adopted Burgess's ecological framework and applied it to describe and understand the spatial patterning of crime and delinquency. Shaw and McKay mapped the residential location of youths who had been referred to juvenile court with data extending over multiple decades. They found that delinquency rates were highest in lower-class neighborhoods concentrated toward the inner city (i.e., in the transitional zone) and decreased as the distance from the city center increased. They also found that the relative rankings of crime rates across the zones of the city remained quite stable over time, regardless of the aggregated properties of the individuals residing there (e.g., their ethnic backgrounds). This observation of stability suggested that something about the area, and not about the characteristics of the individuals living there, was responsible for the crime rates, particularly since the "kinds of persons" living there were constantly changing. Shaw and McKay also identified distinctive structural correlates of crime and delinquency rates. High-crime areas were characterized by residential instability, high percentages of families on public assistance, low median income, low home ownership, high percentages of immigrants, and high percentages of racial and ethnic minorities.

Shaw and McKay theorized that these structural correlates of crime and delinquency were genuine causal factors because they promoted a breakdown of social organization, or social disorganization. In socially disorganized neighborhoods, social controls (both internal and external) were relatively weak, which led to crime and delinquency directly as well as indirectly. For example, weak social controls permitted unstructured socializing among youth, which provided opportunities for deviant behavior (Osgood and Anderson 2004). Because social controls were weak, criminal activity became an organized way of life in these neighborhoods, and once established, these criminal traditions could be "culturally transmitted" from one generation to the next.

The work by the Chicago School sociologists and their followers on social disorganization and crime was criticized on a variety of theoretical and methodological grounds. In a particularly influential but sympathetic critique, Bursik (1988) noted significant conceptual ambiguities in social disorganization theory, and he cited a fundamental confusion pertaining to operationalization that had appeared in much of the literature. Researchers often failed to differentiate clearly "the presumed outcome of social disorganization (i.e., increased rates of delinquency) from disorganization" (Bursik 1988, p. 526). In the absence of indicators of social disorganization that are independent of measures of crime and delinquency, the predictions become tautological, making it impossible to assess empirically the claim that social disorganization leads to high levels of crime and delinquency. Bursik went on to argue, however, that despite the legitimate criticisms of the classical variant of social disorganization theory, the general framework could be reformulated in a way that overcomes the widely recognized limitations, and that in fact such reformulations were already under way. These reformulations have given rise to neighborhood explanations of crime that incorporate and extend insights from classical social disorganization theory. The distinctive feature of the contemporary work that follows in the tradition of social disorganization theory is an explicit theoretical and empirical focus on the underlying *mechanisms* that link features of neighborhoods with levels of crime.

II. Toward Causal Explanations of "Neighborhood Effects": Unpacking Mechanisms

A. The Systemic Model of Crime

A major advancement in the reformulation of classical social disorganization theory was the introduction of the "systemic model of crime" by Bursik and Grasmick (1993). The systemic model of crime follows in the footsteps of the earlier work of the Chicago School theorists in two important respects. First, it adopts the neighborhood as the fundamental unit of analysis in the sociological understanding of crime; that is, the neighborhood serves as the theoretically salient environment. Second, it emphasizes the role of social controls in realizing a goal that is assumed to be widely shared among residents of any neighborhood—namely, securing a relatively crime-free environment. The systemic model of crime also goes beyond the classical variant of social disorganization by explicating the nature of social controls that can effectively limit criminal activity in a neighborhood. Moreover, the systemic model of crime locates the foundation of these social controls in the networks of social relations that exist among neighborhood residents.

Bursik and Grasmick, building on work by Hunter (1985), described three primary forms of social control that operate in neighborhoods. One is "private control," which relies on friendship and kinship ties in the neighborhood. The exercise of this type of control "is usually achieved through the allocation or threatened withdrawal of sentiment, social support, and mutual esteem" (Bursik and Grasmick 1993, p. 16). When effective, residents refrain from criminal behavior to secure reinforcements associated with conformity and to avoid interpersonal sanctions that would accompany criminal behavior. A second type of control is "parochial control." This type of control involves the supervision and monitoring of the public space in the neighborhood, primarily by neighbors. The final type of control is "public control." This entails the application of resources external to the neighborhood for collective purposes. The most important external resources for controlling crime are typically those associated with government and law enforcement agencies, such as vigilant police patrols and swift responses to citizens' reports of criminal behavior.

The systemic model of crime postulates that the effectiveness of these control processes depends on the extensiveness and density of both primary and secondary networks. Primary networks (e.g., social ties among kin and close friends) provide the foundation for effective private control, whereas secondary networks (e.g., social ties among acquaintances in the neighborhood) serve to activate parochial control. Both types of networks facilitate the socialization of youths to conventional norms as well as the exercise of public control. Thus, neighborhoods that are likely to have low levels of crime are those that have strong private, public, and parochial controls. Furthermore, these low-crime neighborhoods are likely to be characterized by extensive and dense relational networks, which serve as the structural foundation for the various forms of control.

The systemic model of crime also postulates that neighborhood conditions such as residential instability, population heterogeneity, and poverty (i.e., the structural covariates of crime identified by the Chicago School sociologists) influence crime rates through their effects on relational networks (and their social controls). Specifically, these networks are likely to be comparatively sparse and loosely connected in poor, heterogeneous neighborhoods with high levels of residential instability. In short, the systemic model of crime "unpacks the mechanisms" of neighborhood effects by highlighting the ways in which relational networks and various forms of social control intervene between structural neighborhood conditions and levels of crime.

After introducing the systemic model of crime, Bursik and Grasmick noted a key difficulty in testing the model's theoretical framework. That is, any such test requires information on relational networks across neighborhoods—information that is not readily available in commonly used secondary data sources such as the US Census. Bursik and Gramick (1993, pp. 38–45) cited several studies that were able to address elements of the systemic model by combining data from secondary sources and surveys. These studies offered mixed support for hypotheses derived from the systemic model. The evidence from subsequent research, however, has indicated that the relationship between neighborhood social ties and levels of crime is more complicated than depicted in the systemic model. For example, there is evidence that certain social ties may actually inhibit rather than enhance social controls aimed at reducing crime (Wilson 1987). To illustrate, Warner and Rountree (1997) and Pattillo-McCoy (1998) reported that strong social ties between gang members and drug dealers impede efforts to achieve social control. Thus, when considering the influence of the extensiveness and density of ties among neighbors on crime, it is evidently important to pay attention *to whom* the ties connect (Patillo-McCoy 1999; see also Browning, Feinberg, and Dietz 2004).

Research also suggests that it may be possible to achieve high levels of informal social control and to fight crime in the absence of strong neighborhood ties. For example, studies by Bellair (1997) and Hampton and Wellman (2003) found benefits of infrequent associations and weak nonpersonal ties (e.g., contacts via email, Internet chatrooms, and list-serves). This is in contrast to the strong frequent interactions and intimate bonds among neighbors emphasized in the systemic model.

These findings raise questions about the "idyllic notion of local communities as 'urban villages' characterized by dense personal networks" (Sampson 2006, p. 150). Moreover, social ties and the resources associated with them (sometimes referred to as "social capital") may be necessary but not sufficient for social control. That is, the intended effects (e.g., fighting crime) might not be achieved just through the presence of interpersonal bonds and potential resources; rather, social ties might need to be activated and resources mobilized in order to achieve social control (Kubrin and Weitzer 2003a, p. 377).

B. Collective Efficacy

Largely in response to the issues raised about the adequacy of the systemic model of crime, Robert Sampson and colleagues introduced the concept of collective efficacy to the neighborhood effects literature (Sampson, Raudenbush, and Earls 1997; Sampson 2006). *Collective efficacy* refers to the linkage of social cohesion in a neighborhood, which depends on high levels of trust and mutual support, with shared expectations among neighbors to intervene for the common good. Collective efficacy at the neighborhood level is an analogue to the concept of self-efficacy at the individual level. As such, it is situated rather than global; that is, it is relative to a specific task: the realization of the goal of social control in the neighborhood.

The processes associated with collective efficacy differ from those depicted in the systemic model of crime and related approaches that emphasize social capital in several significant respects. First, collective efficacy does not depend primarily on the strength of direct social ties in the community; rather, it relies on a basic level of working trust among neighbors. Thus, collective efficacy "recognizes the transformed landscape of modern urban life, holding that while community efficacy may depend on working trust and social interaction, it does not require that my neighbor . . . be my friend" (Sampson 2006, p. 153). Second, collective efficacy incorporates the key factor of purposeful action that is often assumed in other "social capital" interpretations. It does so by uniting trust and mutual support among neighbors with shared expectations for social control, or the willingness to intervene for the common good. Collective efficacy emphasizes that social networks and public resources ultimately need to be activated in order to be meaningful. In the absence of social action, strong social ties mean little for crime control. Third, by pairing mutual trust and solidarity with expectations for social action, collective efficacy underscores that cohesion and control are about repeated interactions and therefore expectations about the future. In other words, neighborhood residents will be reluctant to engage in efforts for social control when they anticipate mistrust with other residents. Conversely, the willingness to intervene for the common good is enhanced under conditions of trust and solidarity.

Research has demonstrated that collective efficacy is a robust predictor of neighborhood crime rates and that it mediates much of the effects of structural neighborhood characteristics on crime. For example, Sampson, Raudenbush, and Earls (1997) demonstrated that: (1) collective efficacy is inversely associated with rates of violence (measured by official homicide counts and self-reported victimization), controlling for prior violence, demographic variables, structural neighborhood characteristics, and community social process variables; and (2) collective efficacy reduces the effects of concentrated disadvantage and transiency on rates of violence (see also Sampson, Morenoff, and Earls 1999; Morenoff, Sampson, and Raudenbush 2001). In addition, researchers have documented the wide-reaching effects of collective efficacy. Spatial analysis has revealed that levels of collective efficacy in one neighborhood are positively associated with levels of collective efficacy and inversely associated with rates of crime in surrounding neighborhoods (Sampson, Morenoff, and Earls 1999; Morenoff, Sampson, and Raudenbush 2001). In addition, collective efficacy has been extended to explain social behaviors such as community well-being, health, and public disorder (Sampson and Raudenbush 1999; Morenoff 2003; Sampson 2003).

C. Bringing Culture Back In

Our review thus far has revealed that much of the contemporary research on neighborhood effects following in the tradition of social disorganization theory has focused primarily on social controls: the regulatory capacity of neighborhood social ties and the activation of these ties for collective purposes. In doing so, this research has largely neglected the role that culture can play in facilitating social control, or conversely, in promoting antisocial behavior (Warner 2003, p. 73). Yet, as noted earlier, Shaw and McKay (1931, 1942) argued that high rates of crime and delinquency in socially disorganized areas are not entirely the result of weakened controls; they also reflect exposure to criminal cultures. Shaw and McKay maintained that concentrated disadvantage isolates lower-class neighborhoods from middle- and upper-class resources and opportunities (also see Sampson and Wilson 1995). In turn, social, economic, and political isolation not only weakens residents' conventional value systems but also causes some residents to embrace an alternative set of norms that condone delinquent behavior and criminal activity. As a result, residents of these areas face divergent value systems that are "culturally transmitted" through successive generations.

The classical cultural transmission thesis has been resurrected in somewhat modified form in the "cultural attenuation" approach to explaining criminal behavior. This approach maintains that most residents in high-crime areas do not condone crime per se; rather, informal social control is compromised in these areas because residents' commitment to conventional value systems are weakened or attenuated. Proponents of this approach (e.g., Warner and Rountree 1997; Warner 2003) contend that individuals do not vary appreciably in how they view the moral legitimacy of conventional values embedded in basic social institutions such as the family, school, and religion. Instead, the strength of the attachments to these conventional values varies. When these attachments are weak, neighborhoods lose their ability to realize common goals such as crime control. Researchers have theorized about social conditions that are conducive to cultural attenuation. For example,

Wilson (1987, 1996) argued that decreasing job opportunities and patterns of middle-class migration out of inner cities isolate poor neighborhoods with heavy concentrations of minority populations from middle-class values, thereby weakening attachment to conventional value systems.

Another prominent example of the "rediscovery" of culture that is highly consistent with the earlier studies of the Chicago School theorists is the work by Anderson (1990, 1997, 1999) on conflicting cultural orientations in highly disadvantaged neighborhoods with large minority populations. Drawing upon his ethnographic research in Philadelphia, Anderson proposed that two distinct orientations can be detected in these neighborhoods. One can be characterized as a "decent" orientation. This orientation embraces mainstream goals, norms, and values. It emphasizes hard work and self-reliance. The other orientation embodies an "oppositional culture" with norms that are directly opposed to those of mainstream society. The rules of this oppositional culture are manifested in a "code of the streets." At the core of this street code is a preoccupation with respect and deference. One gains respect through toughness and by dominating others, which often involves violence, theft, insults, and vengeance. While the preoccupation with respect might appear to be irrational to an outsider, it is quite understandable within the context of these neighborhoods because someone who lacks respect (i.e., someone who has been "disrespected") is likely to be viewed as an easy target vulnerable to victimization.

Anderson stressed that only a relatively small portion of the population fully endorses the "code of the streets"; the decent orientation is typically the more common one. Nonetheless, this code shapes the behaviors of everyone living in these neighborhoods because knowledge of the code is essential for survival. Decent parents, for example, like street parents, teach their children to retaliate when provoked, challenged, or insulted for self-protection; for even the most decent child in these neighborhoods must at some point project toughness in order to survive (Anderson 1999, p. 99). Anderson also hypothesized that the origins of the code of the street can be traced to alienation from mainstream society and, in particular, to a lack of faith in the police and the judicial system. Under such conditions, residents believe that they have to take personal security into their own hands.

Anderson's observations based on his ethnographic inquiry have received support in some quantitative research. For example, using data from a longitudinal study of African-American adolescents and their primary caregivers in two Southern states, Stewart and Simons (2006) reported that youths who scored high on a scale reflecting socialization into the core elements of the code of streets exhibited relatively high levels of self-reported violent delinquency (also see Stewart and Simons 2009). In addition, in a study of St. Louis youths, Kubrin and Weitzer (2003b) found that belief in retribution for disrespect, analogous to a street code orientation, was an essential part of the local subculture that led to and rationalized aggressive and violent responses to provocation.

Other researchers have extended the street code to outcomes such as victimization and have examined the causes of retaliatory cultural beliefs. Stewart, Schreck, and Simons (2006) investigated Anderson's claim that the code of the street encourages individuals to be aggressive and tough in order to gain respect among one's peers and potential attackers, thereby reducing subsequent victimization. Contrary to the anticipated benefits of the street code, they found that its adoption resulted in higher levels of victimization than would otherwise have been experienced in violent, disorganized neighborhoods. Brezina et al. (2004) investigated both the predictors and outcomes of Anderson's code-related beliefs in an examination of a male subsample of the National Youth Survey (NYS). They found that youths who perceived a lack of structural opportunity "were more likely to view physical retaliation as an acceptable and necessary response to real or perceived slights" (Brezina et al. 2004, p. 322). In turn, the endorsement of retaliation in line with the code of the streets was positively correlated with an array of violent behaviors. The authors also reviewed a number of additional studies that reported results consistent with Anderson's ethnographic research.

D. Multilevel Analysis

As noted above, classical social disorganization theory was informed by ecological perspectives. It is therefore not surprising that much of the early and subsequent research in this general tradition has adopted geographic areas as the primary units of analysis—that is, neighborhoods operationalized in various ways. Recently, researchers have attempted to integrate insights about individual-level and neighborhood-level processes to formulate more comprehensive explanations of crime. These approaches involve "multilevel analysis," which is a natural extension of hierarchical data structures that exist naturally in time and space. For example, individuals are nested within families and peer groups, and these social networks are nested within social contexts such as communities.

Besides multilevel analysis, two general approaches have been used to analyze hierarchical data structures: disaggregated analysis and aggregated analysis. By assigning neighborhood-level values to all individuals within a particular neighborhood, disaggregated analysis is used to investigate the influence of community-level factors on individual-level variations in offending. Conversely, aggregated analysis takes the average of the individual characteristics in each neighborhood to examine the effects of individual-level factors on area crime rates. Standard multiple regression is then performed to examine the effects of all predictors simultaneously (the most widely used technique is "ordinary least squares regression," or OLS). While these regression techniques have allowed researchers to avoid making faulty conclusions based on inappropriate units of analysis, they are not without problems. For example, estimates from disaggregated analysis based on OLS can lead to problematic inferences because the assumption of independence of observations is violated. That is, individual observations tend to supply less information than assumed because individuals nested within the same neighborhoods tend to share certain characteristics (i.e., not be independent). This violation of the assumption of independence can lead to an array of statistical problems (e.g., inefficient slope estimates; biased standard errors and intercepts; and Type I errors—i.e., rejecting the null hypotheses more often than appropriate). Similarly, aggregated analysis disregards individual-level variability in the outcome variable and therefore biases the effects of the higher-level variables upward (Raudenbush and Bryk 2002).

Multilevel analysis adjusts for these problems by nesting individuals within their social contexts. As a result, multilevel analysis has bridged the gap between theory and empiricism by linking levels of analysis and providing researchers the opportunity to more accurately model a realistic view of criminal offending. Multilevel analysis allows researchers to assess empirically the following: the percentage of variation in the dependent variable explained by individual- and community-level variables (i.e., partition variance-covariance components); the effects of individual characteristics on crime, controlling for relevant features of the environment (i.e., "controlling out" clustering); the effects of environmental factors on crime, controlling for compositional differences (i.e., the relative proportion of persons with specified characteristics) across contexts (i.e., contextual effects); and the effects of variables at one level of analysis on relationships occurring at another level (i.e., moderating or cross-level interaction effects).

The vast majority of studies considering individual and contextual factors simultaneously has been concerned with "controlling out" higher-level clustering in individual-level studies, proving that community-level effects on area crime rates exist after controlling for compositional differences, or demonstrating that community-level effects on individual variation in offending exist after controlling for individual risk factors. For example, at the neighborhood level of analysis, Sampson, Raudenbush, and Earls (1997) demonstrated that collective efficacy predicts neighborhood violence after controlling for the aggregated characteristics of individuals in the neighborhoods. At the individual level of analysis, researchers have found that neighborhood characteristics are significantly, albeit weakly, correlated with offending (see, e.g., Lizotte et al. 1994).

Fewer studies have been concerned with how community factors moderate the effects of individual factors on criminal behavior (Wikström and Loeber 2000). The basic conceptual argument is that crime is not about "kinds of individuals" or "kinds of settings" but about "kinds of individuals in kinds of settings" (Wikström 2004, p. 19). This presupposes that a full understanding of criminal behavior requires a consideration of how individual and community characteristics interact to produce offending behavior.

Some of the studies comparing the effects on offending of key individual and community factors have found that the relationship between individual traits and offending is invariant to neighborhood context. That is, the highest rates of offending are found for the highest-risk individuals (i.e., those psychologically/situationally disposed to offending) living in the highest-risk areas (e.g., areas with high poverty, disadvantage), while the lowest rates of offending are found for the lowest-risk individuals living in the lowest-risk areas (e.g., Reiss and Rhodes 1961; Vazsonyi, Cleveland, and Wiebe 2006). However, there are also studies suggesting that the relationship between individual risk factors and offending is modified by neighborhood context. For example, research by Sampson and Laub (1994) indicated that the level of protection afforded by the family may be more important in disadvantaged neighborhoods than in advantaged neighborhoods, where the community acts as a safety net for inadequate parents; and Wikström and Loeber (2000) found that neighborhood socioeconomic context had the strongest effects on rates of serious offending for the most well-adjusted youths, while neighborhood context had no effect on youths with the highest risk scores (also see Lynam et al. 2000; Simons et al. 2005).

Multilevel analysis has also been expanded to accommodate three-level structures, predict latent variables from repeated observations, examine individual growth over time, study the consistency of results across studies (i.e., meta-analysis), and investigate the importance of spatial dynamics in the study of neighborhood effects on crime and delinquency. The study of spatial dynamics stems from research on ecological differentiation (see Massey and Denton 1993) and the fact that neighborhoods overlap within a larger socioeconomic system such as a city. For example, a neighborhood has been loosely defined as a geographical and social subsection of a larger community in which residents share a common sense of identity that persists over time (see Bursik and Grasmick 1993, pp. 5–12). If neighborhoods are part of a larger community, it follows that these neighborhoods are inextricably linked, share similar characteristics and can influence one another socially, economically, and politically. That is, "research that considers neighborhoods as islands unto themselves misses the theoretical point" (Sampson, Morenoff, and Earls 1999, p. 637). Accordingly, research suggests that a neighborhood's proximity to violence and poverty (in surrounding neighborhoods) has as much of an effect on social processes within that neighborhood as social structural characteristics within the neighborhood (Morenoff and Sampson 1997). Thus, it appears that individuals are nested within neighborhoods, which are themselves situated near other theoretically strategic neighborhoods within a broader social context.

III. Rethinking the Causal Structure of Mechanisms

Much of the work on neighborhood-level influences on crime reviewed above is based on a fairly straightforward causal model of "intervening effects": $X \to T \to Y$. Features of social structure X (e.g., concentrated disadvantage, population heterogeneity, residential instability) are depicted as causing relevant social processes T (e.g., the operation of informal controls, collective efficacy), which in turn are regarded as the proximate determinants of levels of crime Y. In the formal language of statistical modeling, social structural variables are assumed to be exogenous to social process variables, and social processes variables are assumed to be exogenous to crime rates. These assumptions underlie the standard application of regression techniques. Increasingly, however, researchers have raised questions about this model of one-way causal effects and have pointed to the possibility of reciprocal relationships and feedback processes.

These feedback processes can involve all three types of variables. To illustrate, research has indicated that levels of crime can affect features of social structure ($Y \rightarrow X$). In a pioneering study based on panel data for large US cities from 1950 to 1990, Liska and Bellair (1995) proposed that the widely observed positive association between the percent of the nonwhite population and violent crime rates for areal units might overstate the causal impact of the former on the latter due to reciprocal effects. They hypothesized that the level of crime affects decisions about residential location (i.e., to move out of or into a city, and by extension, movement across neighborhoods) and that the resources to migrate are differentially distributed by race (i.e., whites are more likely to be able to relocate). Accordingly, high crime rates at one point in time are likely to lead to relatively high percentages of minorities at a later point in crime. They reported that violent crime rates (especially robbery) had the expected effect on change in racial composition across all four decades for their sample of cities.

Studies at the neighborhood level have also provided evidence suggestive of feedback loops involving the theorized proximate determinants of crime and levels of crime ($Y \rightarrow T$). For example, Markowitz et al. (2001) developed a causal model incorporating a feedback effect of crime on social cohesion. Specifically, decreased social cohesion is hypothesized to increase crime, consistent with conventional versions of social disorganization theory, but increases in crime are expected to foster high levels of fear among residents, which in turn weakens social cohesion. Longitudinal analyses based on three waves of data from the British Crime Survey for 151 neighborhoods supported these hypotheses. Bellair (2000) similarly advanced a causal model of feedback effects, but with a focus on the "surveillance" predictor of crime rather than social cohesion. His model is based on a rather complex process whereby crime might either attenuate or amplify prior levels of informal surveillance depending on the relative impact of crime on perceptions of risk versus reactions of moral outrage. He assessed his hypotheses with data on robbery/stranger assault rates and burglary rates for 100 US Census tracts in Seattle, which served as proxies for neighborhoods. The results of his analyses revealed the widely observed negative effect of informal surveillance on rates of both types of crime. He further discovered that increases in robbery/stranger assaults were associated with reduced surveillance via perceptions of risk, whereas increases in burglary were associated with enhanced surveillance. In other words, the nature of the feedback processes varied for different types of offenses.

Sampson (2006, pp. 158–59) offered an example of how the "social process" variable of collective efficacy might exert a causal influence on the "social structural" variable of neighborhood poverty ($T \rightarrow X$) rather than serving exclusively as an intervening variable in the prediction of crime rates. Neighborhoods with widespread mistrust and low social cohesion among residents (components of collective efficacy) are likely to be undesirable. Accordingly, as residents of such neighborhoods acquire more financial resources, they are likely to move to more attractive neighborhoods—that is, those with higher levels of collective efficacy. Such out-migration would tend to produce a negative association between poverty and collective efficacy, but the causal process would be the reverse of that typically inferred. The degree of collective efficacy would be causing the observed level of poverty rather than vice versa. Sampson reported some preliminary evidence in support of this speculation with data for neighborhoods in Chicago. In a model predicting future poverty levels of neighborhoods, the prior degree of collective efficacy exhibited a strong negative coefficient, controlling for prior poverty, racial composition, and the violent crime rate.

The limited but highly suggestive theorizing and evidence about reciprocal causal processes among social structural variables, social process variables, and crime rates call for the reconsideration of an issue in the study of neighborhood effects that has typically been viewed in purely methodological terms—that is, the issue of "selection bias." Researchers have long recognized that correlations between features of neighborhoods and levels of crime can be produced by both the impact of the neighborhood conditions on the residents residing therein ("context effects") and the choices of individuals to live in neighborhoods with different characteristics ("selection effects"). Most commonly, the selection processes are regarded as a "statistical nuisance" to be controlled in order to evaluate accurately the importance of neighborhood context (Sampson 2008, p. 227). However, as Sampson (2008, p. 217) has observed, "neighborhood selection is part of a process of stratification that situates individual decisions within an ordered, yet constantly changing, residential landscape." The reciprocal effects described above imply that levels of crime are likely to play a prominent role in this stratification process.

IV. DISCUSSION AND CONCLUSIONS

Since the classic work of Shaw and McKay (1931, 1942), researchers have consistently documented appreciable differences in levels of crime across neighborhoods. These differences tend to persist over time, regardless of the aggregate properties of the individuals residing there, lending credibility to the basic insight that ecological determinants contribute to observed levels of crime. Yet early research focused on correlating criminal/delinquent behavior with static neighborhood characteristics rather than with neighborhood "causal processes." That is, early research "tended toward a risk-factor rather than an explanatory approach" to crime (Sampson 2006, p. 149). In response to this criticism, research over the past several decades has identified theoretically relevant neighborhood mechanisms: social ties and cohesion, social capital, and collective efficacy.

There is a growing awareness that the interconnections among these factors are complex and that social behavior depends on how individuals and ecologies symbiotically exist and interact. As a result, current research is wrestling with understanding linkages across levels of social structure, as well as dynamic causal systems with feedback loops. For example, progress has been made toward integrating selection processes with contextual effects. However, important challenges remain.

Theoretically, criminological and sociological inquiry must focus on linking individual-level and community-level processes, rather than "controlling out" the variance of one level of analysis when studying the other. Some research examining cross-level moderating effects has made strides in this direction. Nevertheless, criminologists need to *theorize* more explicitly and comprehensively about how selection processes and neighborhood-level influences act in concert to structure the observed residential landscape of different communities. Methodologically, researchers should continue to develop and embrace analytical programs and techniques that make it possible to study some of the complex interrelationships that have been hypothesized about for decades. Multilevel analysis is becoming more commonplace, but obstacles prevent it from becoming more widely used. Perhaps the most formidable impediment to methodological progress is the paucity of data sources that take into account the naturally occurring hierarchical social structure. Although researchers have made significant theoretical and methodological progress, further advancements are needed in order to disentangle the complex relationships among individuals and the social contexts in which they are imbedded.

REFERENCES

Anderson, Elijah. 1990. *Streetwise: Race, Class, and Change in an Urban Community*. Chicago: University of Chicago Press.

Anderson, Elijah. 1997. "Violence and the Inner-city Street Code." In *Violence and Children in the Inner City*, edited by Joan McCord. New York: Cambridge University Press.

Anderson, Elijah. 1999. *Code of the Streets: Decency, Violence, and the Moral Life of the Inner City*. New York: W.W. Norton.

Bellair, Paul E. 1997. "Social Interaction and Community Crime: Examining the Importance of Neighbor Networks." *Criminology* 35:677–703.

Bellair, Paul E. 2000. "Informal Surveillance and Street Crime: A Complex Relationship." *Criminology* 38:137–70.

Brezina, Timothy, Robert Agnew, Francis T. Cullen, and John Paul Wright. 2004. "The Code of the Street: A Quantitative Assessment of Elijah Anderson's Subculture of Violence Thesis and its Contribution to Youth Violence Research." *Youth Violence and Juvenile Justice* 2:303–28.

Browning, Christopher, Seth L. Feinberg, and Robert D. Dietz. 2004. "The Paradox of Social Organization: Networks, Collective Efficacy, and Violent Crime in Urban Neighborhoods." *Social Forces* 83:503–34.

Burgess, Ernest. 1925. "The Growth of the City." In *The City*, edited by Robert E. Park and Ernest Burgess. Chicago: University of Chicago Press.

Bursik, Robert J. 1988. "Social Disorganization and Theories of Crime and Delinquency: Problems and Prospects." *Criminology* 26:519–51.

Bursik, Robert J., and Harold G. Grasmick. 1993. Neighborhoods and Crime. New York: Lexington Books.

Cohen, Albert K. 1985. "The Assumption that Crime is a Product of Environments: Sociological Approaches." In *Theoretical Methods in Criminology*, edited by Robert F. Meier. Beverly Hills, CA: Sage.

Hampton, Keith N., and Barry Wellman. 2003. "Neighboring in Netville: How the Internet Supports Community and Social Capital in a Wired Suburb." *City and Community* 2:277–311.

Hunter, Albert J. 1985. "Private, Parochial and Public Orders: The Problem of Crime and Incivility in Urban Communities." In *The Challenge of Social Control: Citizenship and Institution Building in Modern Society*, edited by Gerald D. Suttles and Mayer N. Zald. Norwood, NJ: Ablex.

Kubrin, Charis E., and Ronald Weitzer. 2003a. "New Directions in Social Disorganization Theory." *Journal of Research in Crime and Delinquency* 40: 374–402.

Kubrin, Charis E., and Ronald Weitzer. 2003b. "Retaliatory Homicide: Concentrated Disadvantage and Neighborhood Culture. *Social Problems* 50: 157–80.

Liska, Allen E., and Paul E. Bellair. 1995. "Violent-crime Rates and Racial Composition: Convergence Over Time. *American Journal of Sociology* 101: 578–610.

Liska, Allen E., and Steven F. Messner. 1999. *Perspectives on Crime and Deviance*, 3rd ed. Upper Saddle River, NJ: Prentice Hall.

Lizotte, Alan J., Terence P. Thornberry, Marvin D. Krohn, Deborah C. Chard-Wierschem, and David. McDowall. 1994. Neighborhood context and delinquency: A longitudinal analysis. In *Cross-National Longitudinal Research on Human Development and Criminal Behavior*, edited by E. Weitekamp and Hans-Jurgen. Netherlands: Academic Publishers.

Lynam, Donald R., Per-Olof H. Wikström, Avshalom Caspi, Terrie E. Moffitt, Rolf Loeber, and Scott Novak. 2000. "The Interaction Between Impulsivity and Neighborhood Context on Offending: The Effects of Impulsivity are Stronger in Poorer Neighbor-hoods." *Journal of Abnormal Psychology* 109:563–74.

Markowitz, Fred E., Paul E. Bellair, Allen E. Liska, and Jianhong Liu. 2001. "Extending Social Disorganization Theory: Modeling the Relationships Between Cohesion, Disorder, and Fear." *Criminology* 39:293–320.

Massey, Douglas S., and Nancy Denton. 1993. *American Apartheid: Segregation and the Making of the Underclass*. Cambridge, MA: Harvard University Press.

Morenoff, Jeffrey D. 2003. "Neighborhood Mechanisms and the Spatial Dynamics of Birth Weight. *American Journal of Sociology* 108:976–1017.

Morenoff, Jeffrey D., and Robert J. Sampson. 1997. "Violent Crime and the Spatial Dynamics of Neighborhood Transition: Chicago, 1970–1990. *Social Forces* 76: 31–64.

Morenoff, Jeffrey D., Robert J. Sampson, and Stephen Raudenbush. 2001. "Neighborhood Inequality, Collective Efficacy, and the Spatial Dynamics of Homicide. *Criminology* 39:517–60.

Osgood, D. Wayne, and Amy L. Anderson. 2004. "Unstructured Socializing and Rates of Delinquency. *Criminology* 42:519–49.

Pattillo-McCoy, Mary E. 1998. "Sweet Mothers and Gangbangers: Managing Crime in a Black Middle-class Neighborhood." *Social Forces* 76:747–74.

Pattillo-McCoy, Mary E. 1999. *Black Picket Fences: Privilege and Peril Among the Black Middle Class*. Chicago: University of Chicago Press.

Pratt, Travis C., and Francis T. Cullen. 2005. "Assessing the Relative Effects of Macro-level Predictors of Crime: A Meta-analysis." In *Crime and Justice: A Review of Research,* vol. 32, edited by Michael Tonry. Chicago: University of Chicago Press.

Raudenbush, Stephen W., and Anthony S. Bryk. 2002. *Hierarchical Linear Models: Applications and Data Analysis Methods.* London: Sage.

Reiss, Albert J., and Albert Lewis Rhodes. 1961. "The Distribution of Juvenile Delinquency in the Social Class Structure." *American Sociological Review* 26: 720–32.

Sampson, Robert J. 2003. "The Neighborhood Context of Well Being." *Perspectives in Biology and Medicine* 46:S53–73.

Sampson, Robert J. 2006. "Collective Efficacy Theory: Lessons Learned and Directions for Future Inquiry." In *Taking Stock: The Status of Criminological Theory, Advances in Criminological Theory,* vol. 15, edited by Francis T. Cullen, John Paul Wright, and Kristie R. Blevins. New Brunswick, NJ: Transaction.

Sampson, Robert J. 2008. "Moving to Inequality: Neighborhood Effects and Experiments Meet Social Structure. *American Journal of Sociology* 114:189–231.

Sampson, Robert J., and John H. Laub. 1994. "Urban Poverty and Family Context of Delinquency: A New Look at Structure and Process in a Classic Study. *Child Development* 65:523–40.

Sampson, Robert J., Jeffrey D. Morenoff, and Felton Earls. 1999. "Beyond Social Capital: Spatial Dynamics of Collective Efficacy for Children. *American Sociological Review* 64:633–60.

Sampson, Robert J., Jeffrey D. Morenoff, and Thomas Gannon-Rowley. 2002. "Assessing "Neighborhood Effect": Social Processes and New Directions in Research." *Annual Review of Sociology* 28:443–78.

Sampson, Robert J., and Stephen Raudenbush. 1999. "Systematic Social Observation of Public Spaces: A New Look at Disorder in Urban Neighborhoods." *American Journal of Sociology* 105:603–51.

Sampson, Robert J. Stephen Raudenbush, and Felton Earls. 1997. "Neighborhoods and Violent Crime: A Multilevel Study of Collective Efficacy." *Science* 277: 918–24.

Sampson, Robert J., and William J. Wilson. 1995. "Toward a Theory of Race, Crime, and Urban Inequality." In *Crime and Inequality*, edited by John Hagan and Ruth D. Peterson. Stanford, CA: Stanford University Press.

Shaw, Clifford, and Henry D. McKay. 1931. *Social Factors in Delinquency*. Chicago: University of Chicago Press.

Shaw, Clifford, and Henry D. McKay. 1942. *Juvenile Delinquency and Urban Areas*. Chicago: University of Chicago Press.

Simons, Ronald L., Leslie G. Simons, Callie H. Burt, Gene H. Brody, and Carolyn Cutrona. 2005. "Collective Efficacy, Authoritative Parenting and Delinquency: A Longitudinal Test of a Model Integrating Community-and Family-level Processes." *Criminology* 43:989–1029.

Stewart, Eric A., Christopher J. Schreck, and Ronald L. Simons. 2006. ""I Ain't Gonna Let No One Disrespect Me:" Does the Code of the Street Reduce or Increase Violent Victimization Among African American Adolescents?" *Journal of Research in Crime and Delinquency* 43:427–58.

Stewart, Eric A., and Ronald L. Simons. 2006. "Structure and Culture in African American Adolescent Violence: A Partial Test of the 'Code of the Street' Thesis." *Justice Quarterly* 23:1–33.

Stewart, Eric A., and Ronald L. Simons. 2009. *The Code of the Street and African-American Adolescent Violence*. Washington, DC: US Department of Justice, Office of Justice Programs, National Institute of Justice. NCJ223509.

Vazsonyi, Alexander T., H. Harrington Cleveland, and Richard P. Wiebe. 2006. "Does the
    Effect of Impulsivity on Delinquency Vary by Level of Neighborhood Disadvantage?"
    Criminal Justice and Behavior 33:511–41.
Warner, Barbara D. 2003. "The Role of Attenuated Culture in Social Disorganization
    Theory." *Criminology* 41:73–97.
Warner, Barbara D., and Pamela Rountree. 1997. "Examining Informal Social Ties in a
    Community and Crime Model: Questioning the Systemic Nature of Informal Social
    Control." *Social Problems* 44:520–36.
Wikström, Per-Olof H. 2004. "Crime as Alternative: Towards a Cross-level Situational
    Action Theory of Crime Causation." In *Beyond Empiricism*, edited by Joan McCord.
    New Brunswick, NJ: Transaction.
Wikström, Per-Olof H., and Rolf Loeber. 2000. "Do Disadvantaged Neighborhoods Cause
    Well-adjusted Children to Become Adolescent Delinquents? A Study of Male Juvenile
    Serious Offending, Individual Risk and Protective Factors, and Neighborhood
    Context." *Criminology* 38:1109–42.
Wilson, William J. 1987. *The Truly Disadvantaged: The Inner-City, the Underclass and Public
    Policy*. Chicago: University of Chicago Press.
Wilson, William J. 1996. *When Work Disappears: The World of the New Urban Poor*. New
    York: Knopf.

CHAPTER 9

DISORDER AND CRIME

WESLEY G. SKOGAN

THE idea of disorder first burst into public consciousness in an article by academic experts George Kelling and James Q. Wilson (1982) that examined the merits of order maintenance policing. Describing the conditions that foot patrol officers faced in a run-down section of Newark, New Jersey, Kelling and Wilson inventoried open gambling and drug sales, public drinking, street prostitution, congregations of idle men, rowdy teenagers, the mentally disturbed, and panhandlers. In research since, the list of challenges has grown to include "urban campers" living in parks under cardboard tents, verbal harassment of women passing on the street, noise, abandoned cars, trash on the streets and sidewalks, people rummaging through trash receptacles in search of cigarette butts, "kerb crawling" (looking for a prostitute, with a British spelling), and even "joyriding up and down residential streets with loud music playing as late as 3:00 a.m." (Novak et al. 1999, p. 177).

"Disorder" was my term for all of this (Skogan 1990); Kelling and Wilson's metaphor summarizing them was "broken windows." The argument that broken windows demanded their attention because they attracted and even created additional crime rapidly became one of the most influential ideas in policing. In the almost 30 years of research that followed, others have referred to them as "incivilities." This is sometimes appropriate, but does not, in my view, capture the malevolence and destructiveness of some of the actions it encompasses. The British government has been tackling what they term "anti-social behaviour," and while their list of proscribed activities covers many described here, it does not include the visible consequences of neglect and sheer negligence that are widely taken as disorderly as well.

What all of these conditions have in common, and one feature that makes them of interest to policymakers and researchers, is that they have a long list of documented consequences for individuals, communities, and cities. These include undermining the stability of urban neighborhoods, undercutting natural processes of informal social control, discouraging investment, and stimulating fear of crime. The role of disorder in causing other forms of crime is another reason to look at it carefully, but it is just an additional checkmark on a long list of reasons for concern.

Several observations and conclusions emerge:

- Studying disorder is challenging because the concept includes a wide range of activities and conditions. Researchers have used surveys, police records, and field observations to measure the extent of disorder. While each approach has advantages, each has disadvantages as well.
- Disorder is heavily concentrated in disadvantaged communities. The various approaches that have been used to measure disorder are in broad agreement as to where disorder is concentrated. While some critics contend that disorder merely reflects middle-class conventionalism, it tends to be high in the same generally poor places, whether it is assessed by outside observers or by the people who live in the community.
- Disorder is closely associated with many forms of common crime. Because research has not identified many high-disorder but low-crime neighborhoods, it is difficult to tease out why they are so closely related. It could be because both are dependent upon poverty, racial exclusion, and disinvestment; because disorder undermines the social processes that help constrain neighborhood crime; or because disorder actually attracts and generates other forms of crime.
- Disorder, independently but in tandem with other conventional crime, plays a role in undermining the stability of urban neighborhoods, undercutting natural processes of informal social control, discouraging investment, and stimulating fear of crime. Understanding that disorder could play an important role in the dynamics of neighborhood stability and change is what led researchers to expand the range of the concept to include many conditions and events that lie at, or beyond, the boundaries of criminal law, an idea that has gained traction in many fields of social science. This justifies the attention that policymakers around the world have given to disorder reduction.

This essay began by reviewing the variety of ways in which disorder has been defined. Section I discusses approaches to the measurement of disorder. The methods that are employed to study disorder are more diverse than those used in many other branches of criminology, and their various advantages and disadvantages reveal something of the complexities involved in understanding the magnitude and distribution of disorder. Section II summarizes what we know about the role of disorder as an engine of neighborhood destabilization and decline, and section III offers a few concluding comments.

I. Measuring Disorder

The list of disorders that researchers have examined is long and untidy. Some of the issues considered here are clearly illegal, and the public can hope to get the police interested in them. Activities in this category include prostitution and the sale of drugs. But other items are not so clearly breaking the law and may even be legally protected. Noisy neighbors and accumulating trash are in the first category, and begging and congregating bands of idle youths are in the other. A great deal of disorderly behavior potentially falls into ambiguous and contested legal categories, such as "disturbing the peace," "loitering," and "vagrancy." Many other disorders do not fall into the domain of the criminal law at all, but are municipal service delivery problems or call for civil legal action by health and building code enforcers. Furthermore, some forms of disorder present seemingly intractable enforcement problems for police because they are conditions rather than events. Many disorders (an exception being residential vandalism) do not have individual victims. While these disorders often lead to complaints that the authorities "do something," the source of the public's concern is often the anticipation of further disorderly behavior or the possible consequences of growing disorder for the community, rather than a specific criminal incident. Because of the tenuous legal status of such complaints, and the fact that many disorders are not conventionally defined as serious problems, getting the attention of the police or other municipal agencies can be difficult. Albert Reiss (1985) captured the flavor of disorderly conditions lying near the edges of the law when he dubbed them "soft crimes."

Researchers conventionally subdivide this untidy list, distinguishing between "social" and "physical" disorders. Social disorders are unsettling or potentially threatening and perhaps unlawful public behaviors. Kelling and Wilson (1982, p. 2) described them as involving "disreputable or obstreperous or unpredictable people." In addition to those listed above, this sublist has expanded to include school truancy, "squeegee men" looking for tips in return for cleaning car windshields, "dumpster divers" in search of food, public urination, people sleeping in public on hot-air grates or under layers of cardboard, squatters in abandoned buildings, nuisance neighbors, and men fixing their cars (and perhaps draining their radiators and oil pans) at the curb. To measure the effectiveness of its antisocial behavior initiative, the British Home Office focuses on a list of 60 activities grouped in 16 major categories. They add to our inventory activities such as "letting down tyres," making false calls to the fire service, setting fires, skateboarding in pedestrian areas, and setting vehicles on fire (Home Office 2004).

Physical disorders include the overt signs of negligence or unchecked decay as well as the visible consequences of malevolent misconduct. These include abandoned, boarded up, or severely dilapidated buildings; abandoned, stripped, and burned-out cars; collapsing garages; broken streetlights; junk-filled and unmowed vacant lots; street litter; loose syringes and condoms laying on the pavement; illegal dumping; garbage-strewn alleys; graffiti; and of course, broken windows. By-and-large, physical disorder involves visible conditions, while many social disorders appear as brief but sometimes frequent events. I am not sure in which category a few other disorders fall, including rats in the alley and packs of wild dogs running loose, but these present serious concerns for people as well.

Many of the studies described here maintain the distinction between social and physical disorders. However, depending on what is relevant and included in the research, measures of specific disorders may not neatly cluster along physical and social lines. Raudenbush and Sampson (1999) gathered observational data at the block level in Chicago. They found that a long list of observed conditions formed distinct physical and social clusters that were only moderately correlated (0.58), and thus could be considered separately. On the other hand, Ross and Mirowsky (1999) found that survey-based measures of vandalism and graffiti problems clustered with other measures of both physical and social disorder, which may befit their status as the visible residue of malevolent behavior. They recommend aggregating measures of specific disorders into one index, and in a number of studies subclusters of disorders prove to be highly intercorrelated. Some reasons this should be the case are discussed below.

Research on disorder uses methods that are more varied than those employed in many other branches of criminology. Researchers make frequent use of sample surveys to gauge the views and experiences of individuals regarding their neighborhood, nearby shopping precincts, or downtown areas. Because of the close association between many disorders and the things that people complain about to the authorities, data from police call centers and municipal complaint hotlines provide a second view of the extent and distribution of forms of disorder. Finally, because disorders by definition involve behaviors that take place in public space, and many leave behind a trail of visible physical consequences, observers can systematically record them in the field. Each of these approaches to measuring the extent and distribution of disorder has its strengths and weaknesses, and can tell us things that the others cannot.

A. Surveys

In a typical neighborhood-focused survey, respondents are asked something like "how much of a problem" ("a big problem," "somewhat of a problem," or "not a problem") they consider each of a list of events or conditions. A few studies have instead asked if they have observed or experienced the problems on the list, or the volume or frequency of each, rather than calling for an assessment of their impact, but exactly how these questions are asked seems to have little practical effect on the findings (Sampson and Raudenbush 2004). The lists, which best are tailored to the issues and communities being studied, commonly include questions concerning a mix of physical and social disorders. In effect, surveys use residents or users of the space as observers of the local scene, in numbers large enough that the results can be averaged in order to characterize the area as a whole.

These measures usually reveal a great deal of internal consistency, at both the individual and the neighborhood level. At the individual level, survey respondents who recognize one problem usually rate several others as serious as well. This could be because they share the same causes or because they affect each other over time and thus "grow together." For example, there may be reciprocal relationships among building abandonment, squatting, casual fire-setting, and vandalism. At the area level, respondents who live in the same neighborhood usually give relatively consistent high or low ratings to the problems that are described to them, indicating that they have experienced them (or not) in similar fashion. For example, Sampson and Raudenbush (2004) found that survey samples as small as about 10 respondents per area can produce useful measures due to of high levels of agreement (or "reliabilities," which in their study ranged from 0.65 to 0.70) about the extent of disorder within neighborhoods. Across communities, ratings typically vary widely. For example, in a large citywide survey that I conducted in Chicago, average within-neighborhood ratings on a mix of social disorder questions ranged from places in which essentially none of those interviewed thought they were a problem to areas where 66 percent of adults thought that local disorder fell, on average, in the "big problem" category. Survey measures of social disorder in particular have a relatively high between-neighborhood, as opposed to between-individuals within-neighborhood, component (Sampson and Raudenbush 1999).

A strength of the survey approach to assessing the extent of disorder is that it relies on the assessments of local knowledgeables—people who live in or use the area on a regular, and often around-the-clock, basis. Surveys use the expertise of substantial numbers of them, often in the range of 40 or so to several hundred respondents for each area being studied. Of course, survey respondents do not always agree on conditions even in their own neighborhoods, and there has been research on why views of the same area differ and the kinds of respondents who stand out from the crowd (see Hipp 2010). Some of this seems due to differences in exposure. Those who go out frequently at night observe things that stay-at-homes do not. For example, I found that young adults, those under age 25, reported more social disorder than did their older neighbors. One might anticipate that older people would be less tolerant of deviance and more often be unsettled by things going on around them, but—surprisingly—in several studies, older residents (but not very strongly) reported *less* physical and social disorder than did younger people living in the same area. Disorders may also vary in their impact, and thus salience, depending on who is reporting on "how big a problem" they constitute. Another example: homeowners may worry about things that renters do not typically worry about. Female respondents report more disorder (and more crime and fear) than do their neighbors. There is mixed evidence on whether better-off people feel more threatened by disorder around them; Hipp (2010) found the effects of income and education to be small (and none of the others were very large). He also found that whites tended to perceive more disorder than did Hispanics or African Americans living in the same small neighborhood, in the limited number of areas where such racial diversity could be found. There is also an effect of social isolation: survey respondents who are more "distant" from their neighbors (based on an aggregation of their race, age, marital status, and household composition) tend to report more social and physical disorder. However, because we understand how many of these differences occur, by statistically adjusting for them, surveys can produce even better estimates of small-area disorder.

A disadvantage of surveys is that they are costly to conduct. They require large numbers of respondents in order to characterize many small geographical areas with any accuracy. There has been some research on the optimal size of areas to be studied, and it turns out that the best estimates of the extent of disorder come from a focus on very small ones—places the size of city blocks or clusters of a few blocks. Unlike conventional crime, which circulates around somewhat larger areas because offenders are mobile and tend to go where they are not recognized, many disorders are firmly fixed in place and have their impact quite locally (Hipp, 2007). To date, surveys have not been used to gather detailed reports concerning specific disorders, including such factors as when they occur, exactly where in the community they surface, how many people are involved, or who seems to be responsible for them, but instead have focused on general assessments of their frequency or impact.

B. Complaints to the Police

Complaints by the public to police, via either the emergency call system or alternative hotlines, provide another picture of the extent and distribution of disorder. Unlike survey reports of the extent of problems, these complaints are filtered by residents' decisions that particular events or conditions are a public matter, and that they are important enough to warrant making a complaint. They also may be filtered by people's views of the efficacy of calling the police and involving themselves with the authorities. However, compared to incidents that are later investigated and might be deemed to have been crimes, telephone complaints provide relatively unfiltered depictions of immediate concern about disorder. They are "things about which something needs to be done," although doubtless many of them would not pass legal muster. They certainly can be frequent. For example, during 2009, call takers at Chicago's emergency telephone center recorded 73,000 complaints about graffiti and other forms of vandalism, 13,500 reports of gambling or prostitution, almost 11,000 complaints about truancy or curfew violations by youths, more than 25,000 trespassing incidents, 45,000 calls reporting gang disturbances or gang loitering, and 108,000 drug-market related complaints.

An advantage of complaint data on disorder is that it can be tied to specific, and small, geographical areas throughout the city, for callers are hoping that someone will come to the scene and do something about the problem. The date and time of a complaint—which provide indirect evidence of *when* it presented a problem—are also precisely registered, and city data systems capture them over an extended period of time. As a result it is possible to address questions about seasonal and day-night differences in the distribution of reports of disorder—something for which one-time surveys and (as we will see) observational studies are not well suited. Complaint data are also useful for monitoring or evaluating intervention programs focusing on disorder because they are independent of police crime recording and can accommodate season and time trends while comparing specific program and comparison areas. For example, Weisburd et al. (2006) used disorder calls (along with on-site observations) in an evaluation of drug market and prostitution interdiction efforts, and found large declines in both, which were associated with the program and did not spill over into other, nearby areas due to displacement. Complaints data were critical to the study because crime had been steadily falling all over the city they studied and the intervention took place during a particular season of the year, while the "before-program" period fell in another season.

Not surprisingly, disorder complaints are very highly seasonal, peaking in the summer months. During 2009 in Chicago, more than 70 percent of complaints about prostitution, gambling, and general "disturbance" calls (which are left to the police to sort out on the scene) came between April and October, as did about two-thirds of the calls in every other category. Depending on the category, 50 to 60 percent of disorder calls throughout the year occurred during evening and late-night hours. Survey and observational studies do not often examine seasonal or timing issues, but when it comes to location, complaints turn out to be distributed in much the same fashion as the findings of other methods. At the neighborhood level, all three disorder measures are strongly correlated with concentrated poverty, and residents of predominately African-American neighborhoods are far more likely than others to perceive, and complain about, all forms of disorder.

C. Observation

A third approach to measuring the extent of disorder is to dispatch observers trained to make note of disorderly behaviors and conditions when they see them. Perhaps the best of these studies is reported by Sampson and Raudenbush (1999). For their project, which was conducted in Chicago, a pair of video recorders taped activities and the physical features of both sides of a large sample of blocks, while researchers drove down them at random time points during the day and early evening. Observers sitting next to the cameras also recorded their observations and judgments, based on what they could see and interpret. Later, all of this material was reviewed and coded by teams of independent raters. The physical disorders they counted included the presence or absence of cigarettes or cigars in the street or gutters, garbage or litter on street or sidewalk, empty beer bottles visible in the street, graffiti of various kinds, abandoned cars, condoms on the sidewalk, needles/syringes on the sidewalk, and political message graffiti. They also noted vacant houses and boarded-up or abandoned commercial and industrial buildings, and badly deteriorated structures. Social disorder was indexed by the presence of adults loitering or congregating, drinking alcohol in public, youth groups evidencing gang indicators, apparent public intoxication, adults fighting or arguing in a hostile manner, visible drug sales, and street prostitution.

Observational studies are obviously appealing. Their public character is part of the definition of disorder, and many of them leave behind a trail of observable consequences for the community. Observation also provides measures that are independent of the personal experiences and judgments of survey respondents, providing a reality check on their views, and they can examine aspects of the social and physical environment that respondents have difficulty describing in response to the relatively simple questions that surveys demand (Sampson and Raudenbush 1999). For example, observers can count the number of people involved and assess their sex and apparent age.

One limitation of studies like that in Chicago is that observers typically do not work, or videotape, very late into the evening. That is the time, however, when a great deal of disorderly behavior takes place. To examine this, I calculated the percentage of calls to Chicago's police emergency number that took place after 7 p.m. and before 7 a.m., a period when their observers were not in the field. Calls made during the later hours of the evening and early morning constituted 59 percent of all complaints about disturbances, 54 percent of all complaints about gang activity, 55 percent of prostitution complaints, and 58 percent of calls regarding public drinking. A great deal of activity takes place on the streets after dark (which was also when 67 percent of all calls reporting people shot and shots fired were made), but this is a period during which it can be difficult—and dangerous—to conduct observations. Likewise, the high degree of seasonal variation in disorder means that when, as well as where, observations are conducted has an important impact on the resulting data. In contrast, surveys of residents and counts of emergency calls reflect events that take place late on Saturday nights, and in the winter as well as the summer months.

Observational studies can also be quite expensive to conduct, and (like surveys) they grow more costly as the size of the areas to be observed goes down and the number of them (and the times of the day they need to be observed) goes up. The transient nature of many social disorders presents a particular problem. During their daytime observations, Raudenbush and Sampson (1999) spotted public drinkers on only 36 of the 15,111 block faces they observed, only 12 locations hosting street drug dealing, and 11 apparent prostitutes, making this a very expensive way to spot disorders. In their study, systematic observation could produce highly reliable estimates of social and physical disorder at the level of the census tract, but for smaller areas, agreement among observers on the extent of physical disorder dropped to 0.37 for physical disorder and to 0.00 for social disorder. By contrast, Sampson and Raudenbush's (2004) survey of Chicagoans found the reliability for social disorder ratings to be 0.67 at the block group level, and Perkins and Taylor (1996) reported very high agreement among survey respondents (0.77) at the level of city blocks, in Baltimore. Because of the cost, typical observational studies have been more modest in scope than the Chicago project, using two-person teams of trained (often student) observers rather than video equipment and follow-up ratings, and gathering data on many fewer blocks. A few survey studies conducting in-person interviews have trained interviewers to also make observations from the doorsteps of sample households while they are there. This is an approach that yields survey and observational data that can be matched for analysis, but these studies rely on the reports of one observer at one particular, and non-random, point in time.

D. Agreement Among Measures

As I noted, the race and class correlates of neighborhood-level disorder tend to be quite similar, regardless of how disorder is measured. There have been only a few studies of the correspondence between disorder measures themselves, for this requires running parallel (and thus even more expensive) data collection efforts. However, these have found moderate to high agreement between different measures of disorder for the same areas. This indicates that they are reflecting—each imperfectly and with unique biases and sources of error—an underlying reality about variations in conditions among urban neighborhoods. Perkins and Taylor (1996) reported a correlation of 0.76 between survey and observational measures of the extent of decaying residential buildings. After some statistical controls, Perkins, Meeks, and Taylor (1992) found perceived teen group problems correlated 0.31 with observers' counts of groups of males hanging out. The large-scale Chicago observational study described above found a correlation of 0.56 between neighborhood measures of social disorder and the findings of a huge survey that could be aggregated to the same level. For physical disorder, the correlation between the two indices was 0.55 (Sampson and Raudenbush 1999). In my Chicago data, which was collected independently (Skogan 2006), correlations between aggregated small area survey data and measures of disorder based on emergency call data range from the 0.70s (for concern about drugs and gangs) to 0.48 (for public drinking).

The methodological research described here, and the agreement among measures of disorder across methods, also speaks to the question of whether disorder is "really there," or if instead it largely rests "in the eye of the beholder." Does it represent anything other than narrow-mindedness and intolerance for all but conventional middle-class views of how people ought to behave? Harcourt (2001), for example, thinks that claims that things are disorderly merely reflects the distribution of white, middle-class views about public deportment, and that important subcultures are far less "uptight" about many of the same conditions. He is concerned that the idea of disorder confounds eccentricity, difference, and criminality. He sees discussion of disorder, as defined by the better-off, as justifying classifying people considered the "losers" of society—vagrants, drunks, drug addicts, loiterers, and panhandlers—as criminals. However, we have seen that agreement among survey respondents reporting about the same neighborhood tends to be substantial, with some of the largest differences being attributable to factors like differential exposure to public disorders or enhanced vulnerability to their consequences. Some important economic cleavages do not seem to independently affect views of local disorder at all. Neighborhoods where residents take the initiative and complain to the police tend to be the same ones where they complain to survey interviewers, and when independent observers drop by they tend to spot visible instances of disorder in the same places. Further, in each case it is not the better-off who are most "uptight," and in many instances the disorders in question involve serious, victimizing consequences for households and communities, and are not exercises disparaging eccentricity.

So, which is the "best" measure of disorder? As John Hipp (2007) has argued, all of these methods for assessing the extent of disorder have strengths and weaknesses, and the answer to that question is probably that it depends on the nature of the research question and the resources that are available to address it. Each approach is fallible, and disorder itself can be of a transitory nature. Disorder ebbs and flows with the weather and by season and time of day, and broken windows can be fixed. Observable disorderly behavior can be particularly transient and concentrated in the hard-to-study late-night hours. On the other hand, stereotypes of individuals and whole neighborhoods may be reined in when teams of trained observers compare notes about what they are seeing, and when they remain focused on relatively unambiguous conditions and behaviors. Data on telephone complaints are cheap and provide an around-the-clock flow of information, at the expense of being filtered by the decision to make a formal (albeit free and easy) complaint to the police. It is also not required that they be legally actionable in order to be registered, which suits the fuzzy status of many disorders. Surveys also handily provide measures that help *explain* the distribution of disorder, including such factors as neighborhood solidarity and individual involvement in efforts to control crime and disorder, but at the cost of potentially building in associations between these factors that are produced by the method rather than causal relations in the real world.

II. THE IMPACT OF DISORDER

Each of the specific disorders considered here—and the list is a long one—has interesting features. They have diverse origins and present different problems with different potential cures. However, disorder is of interest here because it has consequences for individuals, neighborhoods, and entire cities. This section describes recent research on the consequences of disorder; Skogan (1990) summarizes earlier work, and Hipp (2010) recent research.

First, disorder has a negative effect on many of the processes that sustain healthy neighborhoods. My earliest work on this topic showed a sizable impact of disorder on neighborhood satisfaction and moving intentions. It helps drive out those for whom stable community life is important, and it discourages people from moving in. In particular, family households desire to move elsewhere in the face of disorderly conditions, and disorder also affects school choice. Because people can move only if they have the financial means to do so, disorder contributes to the sorting of residential communities by income, with the less well-off being left behind in increasingly concentrated poverty. All of this affects rents and house prices, through the decisions of prospective residents, real estate and insurance agents, and investors, about neighborhood quality. As a result, disorder is frequently associated with building vacancies and abandonment. Fewer people will want to shop as well as live in areas stigmatized by visible signs of disorder, so business conditions deteriorate and store operators consider relocating (Fisher 1991). Over time these problems feed upon one another, threatening to push neighborhoods deeper down a spiral of decline.

Disorder is also associated with declining trust in neighbors and declining participation in community life. This in turn undercuts resident-based supervision of local spaces and natural processes of social control in neighborhoods. Withdrawal tends to reduce supervision of youths, undermines any general sense of mutual responsibility among area residents, and weakens informal social control. Residents of disorderly neighborhoods also are more likely to report that other people cannot be trusted, to be suspicious, and to think that others are out to harm them (Ross and Mirowsky 1999; Taylor 2010). Perceived disorder is associated with the erosion of social ties. People who describe their neighborhoods as disorderly report lower levels of informal contact with those living around them. Residents of disorderly neighborhoods are less likely to chat with one another, visit each other's homes, or lend things to one another (Liska 1987). They are also less likely to report participating in neighborhood or community service organizations. Those who cannot physically leave withdraw psychologically, finding friends elsewhere or simply isolating themselves. One hope of community organizers is that, in troubled neighborhoods, consciously created community organizations can serve as at least a partial substitute for weakened informal social control. But like informal cohesion, formal collaboration is lower in disorderly neighborhoods, further diminishing their capacity for collective action. In short, disorder helps erode what control neighborhood residents can maintain over local events and conditions.

Fear of crime is an issue close to the traditional concerns of criminologists, and there is a huge inventory of studies pointing to a very large impact of disorder on fear. Unlike many crimes, disorder is visible to all, and unlike many serious crimes, disorder can be observed on a frequent, even daily basis; both of these features help magnify its consequences. In surveys, residents of disorderly areas are more likely to fear that they or other family members will be victimized, they more frequently report being afraid to leave their home, and they worry that their homes will be broken into. Where people report high levels of disorder, they also are more likely to perceive higher levels of crime and increasing neighborhood crime. Robinson and associates (2003) went further than most by interviewing Baltimore residents on two occasions. This enabled them to examine the impact of changes in perceived disorder over time between the two interviews. They found that changes in disorder drove changes in fear of crime and changes in worry about victimization (a somewhat different measure), as well as satisfaction with the neighborhood. Further, statistically embedding respondents in the context of their street block revealed that when disorder changed at the micro-neighborhood level, neighborhood satisfaction and fear of crime shifted in response. There is evidence that perceived disorder has a special effect on fear in less affluent areas, where residents appear to take them most seriously as signals of danger (Taylor, Schumaker, and Gottfredson 1985).

Studies of the impact of disorder range beyond residential neighborhoods. In a project on schools, perceived school disorder was the major factor associated with students' fear of crime. The authors concluded that disorderliness may "serve to signal to students a lack of consistent adult concern and oversight that can leave them feeling unsafe" (Mijanovich and Weitzman 2003, p. 400). Further afield, a growing body of research concludes that disorder is psychologically distressing and undermines personal health. Daily exposure to disorderly conditions can be psychologically distressing, contributing to anxiety and depression. In turn, disorder appears to lead to increased alcohol consumption as a means of tension reduction and escape (Hill, Ross, and Angel 2005). In survey studies, perceived disorder has been linked with a range of mental health conditions, ranging from depression, psychological distress, hostility, and mistrust to perceived powerlessness (for a review see Sampson, Morenoff, and Gannon-Rowley 2002).

As the list of the consequences of disorder should suggest, neighborhood levels of disorder are also closely related to crime rates. The two go together tightly, and because research has not identified many high-disorder but low-crime neighborhoods, the task of teasing out the direct and indirect relationships between the two remains to be completed. The close link between crime and disorder could come about in at least three ways. First, as the review above suggests, research indicates disorder has a strong, negative effect on many factors that discourage crime, ranging from neighborhood solidarity and civic engagement to investment and stability. Disorder undermines the processes by which communities ordinarily maintain social control and preserve their character. Disorder also generates fear, and another very large body of research has documented that fear of crime has an independent, destabilizing effect on neighborhoods (Markowitz et al. 2001). From this vantage point, disorder causes crime via a set of very well understood, mediating causal mechanisms that have been the subject of a half-century or more of criminological research.

Second, levels of disorder and crime could appear to go together because both are dependent upon some third set of factors, including poverty and discrimination. Racial exclusion and concentrated poverty are deeply implicated in every aspect of crime, so it would not be surprising that this is the case here as well (for a review, see Hipp, 2007). Sampson and Raudenbush (2004) implicate stereotyping in this process. In their view, beliefs about the distribution and significance of disorder arise in part because of the historical association of segregated minority areas with concentrated poverty and disinvestment. These views become self-confirming when they influence (as we have seen above) future housing and investment decisions, law enforcement policies, and civic engagement. These decisions in turn further increase the statistical association between race and disorder.

They also note that widespread cultural stereotyping probably influences the measurement of neighborhood disorder even when gauged systematically using video cameras and trained observers. The social meaning attached to race and class (presumably even self-attached, when disorder is assessed by residents' opinions or calls to emergency numbers) may be confounded to some extent with the "reality" of disorder, whatever that may be. Sampson (2009) sees evidence of this in his finding that neighborhood race and concentrated poverty are statistically related to perceived disorder, as measured by surveys of area residents, even after controlling for observed disorder, as measured by cameras and observers. He also reports that perceived disorder measured in the past is a strong predictor of disorder measured in a follow-up survey, after controlling for observed disorder. He interprets all of this as evidence that cultural cues provided by race and class shape how Americans assess disorder, in this case in their own communities, and how it further disadvantages neighborhoods over time. However, the data are also consistent with the possibility that resident surveys provide more encompassing and nuanced measures of neighborhood problems, so that statistical controlling for counts of observed disorder does not fully account for the underlying extent of disorder.

More contentiously, Kelling and Wilson (1982) argued for a third link between disorder and crime (but I have no doubt they would have agreed there is an important role for the first two as well). This is their famous "broken windows" thesis. They described a sequence in which visible decay (those windows) and minor but unchecked rule-breaking invites more conventionally serious crime by attracting serious criminals. Criminals are drawn to such areas because they offer opportunities for crime. Where disorder is common and the ability of communities to intervene is at a minimum, criminals will feel their chances of being interrupted are low. Areas that tolerate (or cannot effectively counter) rowdy taverns, sex and drug-oriented paraphernalia shops, public drinking, prostitution, roving bands of young men, and similar disorders will quickly be inundated by crime. Gambling and drinking lead to robberies and fights; prostitution and drug sales attract those who prey upon the consumers of vice.

This variant of the disorder-causes-crime connection has not been carefully examined by researchers. It would require careful attention to the origins of offenders and their destination neighborhoods, but research of that nature has to date focused on issues like travel time between the two points and the availability of attractive targets for burglary, and has not focused on the role of disorder (and other community factors, for that matter) in creating a viable habitant for serious but imported criminals.

One crime-generating process that has been investigated is the role of disorder in lowering the *inhibitions* that discourage people from committing crimes. A component of the broken-windows argument is that visible manifestations of social disorganization provide a signal to outsiders that "anything goes" here, for the signs of disorder signal the unwillingness of residents to confront strangers, intervene in a crime, or call the police. As a result, potential lawbreakers grow bolder when the environment communicates that an area is defenseless. This argument has been the subject of the only randomized experiments in the disorder-and-crime domain, and they firmly support the broken-windows thesis.

The study was conducted in the Netherlands. Six different experiments tested the hypothesis that visible public disorder encourages other forms of crime. In each experiment, visibly disorderly conditions were created in one area, while another matched area remained in its normal, orderly state. The disorders ranged from massive graffiti to piles of abandoned grocery carts and the sound of fireworks going off. Opportunities for rule-breaking (ranging from littering to theft) were created in each study area, so passers-by could choose (or not) to break the law. Hidden observers recorded what they did as people came upon the scene. The question was, would the opportunities that were presented for rule-breaking be taken up more frequently when they were presented in a disorderly rather than in an orderly context? The findings were strong and consistent in their support of the disorder hypothesis. As is typical with arranged field experiments, the opportunities for crime that were presented were minor; at most, passers-by could choose to steal an envelope visibly containing five euros. However, in the two envelope-theft versions of the experiment, those who encountered this temptation under disorderly conditions were twice as likely to be observed stealing what was available (Keizer, Lindenberg, and Steg 2008).

III. Discussion and Conclusions

This chapter has argued that disorder—an untidy collection of conditions and events that often fall on the fringe of issues that have traditionally concerned the criminal justice system—has important implications for the fate of households, neighborhoods, and cities. The broken-windows argument was a rationale for selective order-maintenance policing. However, the understanding that disorder could play an important role in the dynamics of neighborhood stability and change led researchers to quickly expand the range of the concept to include many conditions and events that lie at, or beyond, the boundaries of criminal law, an idea that has gained traction in many fields of social science. Studying disorder is methodologically demanding because of the wide range of phenomena it encompasses and their often transitory character. Researchers use sample surveys, administrative records, and observations in the field in order to assess the magnitude and differential distribution of disorder across neighborhoods, because each has particular advantages and disadvantages. However, the findings of this research are in general agreement regardless of method. Disorder, independently but always in tandem with other conventional crime, plays a role in undermining the stability of urban neighborhoods, undercutting natural processes of informal social control, discouraging investment, and stimulating fear of crime. This, plus perhaps its independent role in generating conventional crime, amply justifies the attention that policymakers around the world have given to social and physical disorder reduction.

REFERENCES

Fisher, Bonnie. 1991. "A Neighborhood Business Area is Hurting: Crime, Fear of Crime, and Disorders Take their Toll." *Crime & Delinquency* 37:363–73.

Harcourt, Bernard. 2001. *Illusion of Order: The False Promise of Broken Windows Policing*. Cambridge, MA: Harvard University Press.

Hill, Terrence D, Catherine E. Ross, and Ronald J. Angel. 2005. "Neighborhood Disorder, Psychophysiological Distress, and Health." *Journal of Health and Social Behavior* 46:170–86.

Hipp, John R. 2007. "Block, Tract, and Levels of Aggregation: Neighborhood Structure and Crime and Disorder as a Case in Point." *American Sociological Review* 72: 659–80.

Hipp, John R. 2010. "Resident Perceptions of Crime and Disorder: How Much is 'Bias' and How Much is Social Environmental Differences." *Criminology* 48: 475–508.

Home Office. 2004. *Defining and Measuring Anti-social Behaviour*. Home Office Development and Practice Report no. 26. London: Research, Development and Statistics Directorate.

Keizer, Kees, Siegwart Lindenberg, and Linda Steg. 2008. "The Spreading of Disorder." *Science* 322:1681–85.

Kelling, George, and James Q. Wilson. 1982. "Broken Windows: The Police and Neighborhood Safety." *The Atlantic* (March):29–38.

Liska, Alan E. 1987. Perspectives on Deviance, 2nd ed. Englewood Cliffs, NJ: Prentice-Hall.

Markowitz, Fred E., Paul E. Bellair, Allen E. Liska, and Jianhong Liu. 2001. "Extending Social Disorganization Theory: Modeling the Relationships between Cohesion, Disorder, and Fear." *Criminology* 39:293–320.

Mijanovich, Todd, and Beth C. Weitzman. 2003. "Which 'Broken Windows' Matter?: School, Neighbourhood, and Family Characteristics Associated with Youths' Feelings of Unsafety." *Journal of Urban Health* 80:400–15.

Novak, Kenneth J., Jennifer L. Hartman, Alexander M. Holsinger, and Michael G. Turner. 1999. "The Effects of Aggressive Policing of Disorder on Serious Crime." *Policing: An International Journal of Police Strategies & Management* 22:171–90.

Perkins, Douglas D., and Ralph B. Taylor. 1996. "Ecological Assessments of Community Disorder: Their Relationship to Fear of Crime and Theoretical Implications." *American Journal of Community Psychology* 24:63–107.

Perkins, Douglas D., John W. Meeks, and Ralph B. Taylor. 1992. "The Physical Environment of Street Blocks and Resident Perceptions of Crime and Disorder: Implications for Theory and Measurement." *Journal of Environmental Psychology* 12:21–34.

Raudenbush, Stephen W., and Robert J. Sampson. 1999. "'Ecometrics': Toward a Science of Assessing Ecological Settings, with Application to the Systematic Social Observation of Neighborhoods." *Sociological Methodology* 29:1–41.

Reiss, Albert J. Jr. 1985. "Policing a City's Central District: The Oakland Story." *National institute of Justice Research Paper*. Washington, DC: US Government Printing Office.

Robinson Jennifer B., Brian A. Lawton, Ralph B. Taylor and Douglas D. Perkins. 2003. "Multilevel Longitudinal Impacts of Incivilities: Fear of Crime, Expected Safety, and Block Satisfaction." *Journal of Quantitative Criminology* 19:237–74.

Ross, Catherine E., and John Mirowsky. 1999. "Disorder and Decay: The Concept and Measurement of Perceived Neighborhood Disorder." *Urban Affairs Review* 34: 412–32.

Sampson, Robert J. 2009. "Disparity and Diversity in the Contemporary City: Social (Dis) order Revisited." *British Journal of Sociology* 60:1–31.

Sampson, Robert J., and Stephen W. Raudenbush. 1999. "Systematic Social Observation of Public Spaces: A New Look at Disorder in Urban Neighborhoods." *American Journal of Sociology* 105:603–51.

Sampson, Robert J., and Stephen W. Raudenbush. 2004. "Seeing Disorder: Neighborhood Stigma and the Social Construction of 'Broken Windows.'" *Social Psychology Quarterly* 67:319–42.

Sampson, Robert J., Jeffrey D. Morenoff, and Thomas Gannon-Rowley. 2002. "Assessing 'Neighborhood Effects': Social Processes and New Directions in Research." *Annual Review of Sociology* 28:443–78.

Skogan, Wesley G. 1990. *Disorder and Decline: Crime and the Spiral of Decay in American Cities.* New York: Free Press.

Skogan, Wesley G. 2006. *Police and Community in Chicago: A Tale of Three Cities.* New York: Oxford University Press.

Taylor, Ralph B. 2010. "Physical Environment and Crime." In *Encyclopedia of Criminological Theory*, edited by Francis T. Cullen and Pamela Wilcox. Thousand Oaks, CA: Sage.

Taylor, Ralph B., Sally Ann Schumaker, and Stephen D. Gottfredson. 1985. "Neighborhood-level Links Between Physical Features and Local Sentiments: Deterioration, Fear of Crime and Confidence." *Journal of Architectural Planning and Research* 21:261–75.

Weisburd, David, Laura A. Wyckoff, Justin Ready, John E. Eck, Joshua C. Hinkle, and Frank Gajewski. 2006. "Does Crime Just Move Around the Corner? A Controlled Study of Spatial Displacement and Diffusion of Crime Control Benefits." *Criminology* 44:549–91.

CHAPTER 10

....

POVERTY DECONCENTRATION AND THE PREVENTION OF CRIME

....

JENS LUDWIG AND JULIA BURDICK-WILL

CRIME rates vary dramatically across neighborhoods and communities in developed and developing countries. Consider, for example, that in the American city of Chicago, over half of all crime occurred in just 18 of the city's 77 designed Community Areas. Just two of the city's community areas account for more than 10 percent of the city's violent crimes (Chicago Police Department 2008).

The dramatic variation across neighborhoods in crime rates has led to a great deal of scientific and policy interest in whether something about the neighborhood physical or social environment might itself contribute causally to criminal behavior. Dating back at least to the 1940s with the work of the University of Chicago sociologists Clifford Shaw and Henry McKay, social scientists have developed a number of candidate explanations for why there might be "neighborhood effects" on crime, including the possibility that ethnic heterogeneity, residential instability, and poverty lead to the breakdown of the dense social and family ties that socialize youth and encouraged them to avoid trouble. These theories raise the possibility that community-level interventions may provide an opportunity for targeted crime prevention.

A large body of nonexperimental evidence suggests that youth and adults are more likely to engage in crime when they live in poor, racially segregated, or highly socially disordered neighborhoods even after some statistical adjustment is made for the individual's own socio-demographic characteristics and other risk factors. Yet the key concern with the available nonexperimental literature on neighborhood effects stems from the fact that most families have at least some degree of choice as to where they live and with whom they associate. As a result, there necessarily remains some uncertainty about the degree to which nonexperimental studies are able to isolate the causal effects of neighborhood environments themselves on criminal behavior from whatever hard-to-measure individual or family attributes may be associated with residential selection. The one randomized experiment that has been carried out in this area is the US Department of Housing and Urban Development's (HUD) Moving to Opportunity (MTO) experiment, which randomly assigned a sample of 4,600 public housing families to receive housing vouchers to move from high-poverty, dangerous neighborhoods to less distressed areas. The purpose of this essay is to discuss the results of the MTO randomized experiment and their implications for neighborhood effects on crime in general, and for the design of specific public policies that target crime prevention or may inadvertently have implications for criminal behavior. Our essay does not discuss either the previous theoretical or the empirical literatures about neighborhood effects on crime because these are the topics of extensive discussion in other essays in the volume. Instead, the essay focuses on the following key results of MTO on youth criminal behavior:

- MTO-induced moves appear to reduce violent criminal offending for all youth in the sample, especially during the first few years after the move.
- Nonviolent offending patterns, on the other hand, vary by gender. Female youth show reductions in arrests and increases in prosocial behavior postmove, while males appear to increase their likelihood of property crime arrest and antisocial behavior.
- These gender differences appear to be the result of gender differences in adaptation to their destination neighborhoods, rather than differing patterns of mobility.
- Instrumental variable analysis finds no evidence for the epidemic model of violent offending, in which the largest decreases in violent offending should occur in the cities where MTO movers experienced the largest changes in their neighborhood violent crime rates. Instead, the largest reductions in violent crime occurred when the youth were moved to neighborhoods with the lowest concentration of minority residents, perhaps because high-minority neighborhoods also tend to be areas with substantial drug markets.
- Another similar experiment in Chicago, known as CHAC, replicates the violent crime reduction findings of MTO, as well as showing that these effects appear to hold for adults as well as adolescents.
- Despite offsetting effects of increased property crime, the moves induced by MTO and CHAC appear to reduce the social cost of offending for youth living in high concentrations of poverty. However, without a better understanding of the "general equilibrium" and the externalities that these moves may cause in both the sending and receiving neighborhoods, it is impossible to calculate the total social cost or benefit of such programs.

The organization of the essay is as follows. Section I describes the MTO experiment, section II presents the main MTO findings, section III discusses the source of the gender difference on crime, section IV discusses the results of a "natural experiment" that essentially replicates the MTO experiment in Chicago, and section V discusses the implications of these results for theory and policy.

I. THE MOVING TO OPPORTUNITY EXPERIMENT

The Moving to Opportunity (MTO) experiment was designed to test the impact of moving families living in public housing projects in the most disadvantaged neighborhoods in American cities into neighborhoods with much lower poverty rates using private housing vouchers. By design, eligibility was limited to families living at baseline in public housing, which are housing units that are operated by local government housing authorities. In 1994, HUD began randomly assigning eligible low-income families with young children who volunteered to participate in MTO into three different groups: experimental, Section 8, and control. The experimental group was offered a housing voucher[1] that could only be used in neighborhoods where the poverty rate was 10 percent or less according to the 1990 census. This group was also given counseling to help locate an appropriate unit and neighborhood. Families assigned to the "Section 8" housing group were offered standard housing vouchers that could be used for any unit that met basic standards, but were not restricted geographically. Lastly, the control group did not receive any special MTO funding, but could receive any of the regularly available social services for which they would have been eligible regardless of the experiment.

In total, 4,600 families signed up between 1994 and 1997 to be randomly assigned to one of the three groups. Tables 10.1 and 10.2 describe the characteristics of the adults who were assigned to the three different groups. The participants were approximately two-thirds African American, and one-third Hispanic. However, in two of the sites, Chicago and Baltimore, the participating families were overwhelmingly African American (Kling, Ludwig, and Katz 2005). Approximately one-fourth of the household heads has been arrested at some point before randomization. About half of the adults who signed up for the program felt unsafe in their current neighborhoods at night, and around 40 percent reported living with someone who had been victimized in the last six months. Three-quarters of the respondents reported a desire to get away from drugs and gangs and half reported that they wished to find better schools for their children as their primary or secondary reason for moving (Kling, Liebman, and Katz 2007, pp. 110–12). The young adults in the program are described in tables 10.1 and 10.3.

Assignment to the experimental group had a significant impact on the participants' neighborhood characteristics. Table 10.4 describes the mobility outcomes for each group. The mobility outcomes did not vary substantially by either gender or age. Since the goal of the program was to move families to lower poverty neighborhoods, it makes sense that the largest changes are found in the census tract poverty rates. The changes in percent minority, however, are significant but more modest in magnitude. The experimental vouchers also appear to have a greater impact on neighborhood violent crime rates than property crime rates (Ludwig and Kling 2007, p. 497).

Table 10.1 Baseline descriptive statistics for Moving to Opportunity (MTO) adult and youth samples

	Females			Males		
	Experimental	Section 8	Control	Experimental	Section 8	Control
ADULTS:						
Black	0.65	0.646	0.657	0.359	0.364	0.386
Hispanic	0.294	0.297	0.298	0.505	0.494	0.487
HH on AFDC at baseline	0.739	0.752	0.756	0.579	0.586	0.491
Moved because:						
Drugs and/or crime	0.767	0.755	0.783	0.739	0.755	0.764
Schools	0.468	.521*	0.465	0.469	0.577	0.489
Age at end of 2001	39	39.4	39.1	43	43.4	44.8
Any before RA arrest	0.258	0.231	0.26	0.375	0.423	0.354
N	1,483	1,013	1,102	224	153	166
YOUTH:						
Black	0.647	0.606	0.64	0.609	0.605	0.612
Hispanic	0.296	0.318	0.304	0.329	0.333	0.339
HH on AFDC at baseline	0.732	0.744	0.749	0.743	0.706	0.727
Moved because:						
Drugs and/or crime	0.807	0.732	0.782	0.78	0.76	0.791
Schools	0.46	0.524	0.483	0.511	0.549	0.505
Age at end of 2001	19.1	18.9	18.9	19	18.9	19
Any before RA arrest	0.062	0.041	0.048	0.147	0.122	0.131
N	966	651	716	988	691	739

Note: HH = Household Head, RA = Random Assignment.
*p <.05 on experimental versus control or Section 8 versus control difference.
Source: Adapted from Ludwig and Kling 2007, p. 496.

Table 10.2 MTO adult baseline characteristics

	Experimental	Section 8	Control
ECONOMIC AND EDUCATION:			
Working	0.29	0.25	0.25
In school	0.16	0.16	0.16
High school diploma	0.41	0.41	0.38
General equivalency diploma	0.18	0.19	0.21
HOUSEHOLD:			
Household member victimized by crime during past 6 months	0.42	0.43	0.41
NEIGHBORHOOD AND HOUSING:			
Lived in neighborhood 5 or more years	0.61	0.63	0.62
Moved more than 3 times in past 5 years	0.08*	0.09	0.11
Very dissatisfied with neighborhood	0.46	0.47	0.46
Streets very unsafe at night	0.48	0.49	0.49
Chats with neighbors at least once a week	0.52	0.5	0.55
Respondent very likely to tell neighbor if saw neighbor's child getting into trouble	0.53	0.55	0.56
No family living in neighborhood	0.65	0.62	0.65
No friends living in neighborhood	0.4	0.38	0.41
Very sure would find an apartment in another part of city	0.45	0.48	0.45
To get away from gangs or drugs was primary or secondary reason for moving	0.77	0.75	0.78
Better schools was primary or secondary reason for moving	0.47	0.52	0.48
N	1,453	993	1,080

*p <.05 on experimental versus control or Section 8 versus control difference.
Source: Adapted from Kling, Liebman, and Katz 2007, pp. 110–12.

Table 10.3 MTO youth baseline characteristics

	Females			Males		
	Experimental	Section 8	Control	Experimental	Section 8	Control
African American	0.68	0.64	0.67	0.64	0.65	0.59
Special class for gifted students or did advanced work	0.15	0.17	0.17	0.17*	0.15*	0.27
Special school, class, or help for learning problem in past 2 years	0.13	0.13	0.12	0.29	0.25	0.3
Special school, class, or help for behavioral or emotional problems in past 2 years	0.07	0.08	0.05	0.18	0.17	0.11
Problems that made it difficult to get to school and/or to play active games	0.03	0.06	0.06	0.11*	0.08	0.05
Problems that required special medicine and/or equipment	0.05	0.07	0.05	0.13	0.14	0.09
School asked to talk about problems child having with schoolwork or behavior in past 2 years	0.19	0.23	0.19	0.41	0.37	0.33
Suspended or expelled from school in past 2 years	0.09	0.1	0.07	0.23	0.2	0.15

Note: Baseline data were collected at random assignment, during 1994–97. Surveys were completed in experimental, Section 8, and control groups with 749, 510, and 548 respondents, respectively, ages 15–20 on 12/31/2001 for a total sample size of 1,807.
*p <.05 on experimental versus control or Section 8 versus control difference.
Source: Adapted from Kling, Liebman, and Katz 2007, p. 113.

Table 10.4 Mobility outcomes by mobility treatment group, age group, and sex

	Females			Males		
	Experimental	Section 8	Control	Experimental	Section 8	Control
ADULTS:						
Tract poverty rate	.326*	.351*	0.439	.329*	.339*	0.417
0%–20%	.363*	.212*	0.11	.333*	.235*	0.121
21%–40%	0.266	.409*	0.292	0.261	0.407	0.32
Over 40%	.371*	.379*	0.598	.406*	.359*	0.559
% Tract black	.532*	.537*	0.566	0.389	0.454	0.402
% Tract minority	.816*	.868*	0.89	.833*	0.887	0.883
Beat violent crime rate	224.3*	228.3*	264	171.9	185	194.4
Beat property crime rate	520.2*	522.9*	561.2	403.7	465.6	440.6
YOUTH:						
Tract poverty rate	.335*	.356*	0.444	.338*	.358*	0.448
0%–20%	.329*	.215*	0.104	.330*	.208*	0.098
21%–40%	0.29	.399*	0.29	0.274	.403*	0.282
60% and over	.382*	.386*	0.606	.396*	.390*	0.62
% Tract black	0.536	0.527	0.555	0.524	0.531	0.542
% Tract minority	.831*	0.88	0.899	.831*	.875*	0.903
Beat violent crime rate	223.2*	228.2*	260.1	225.4*	231.0*	260.3
Beat property crime rate	531.9	518.2	574.9	535.4	540.6	547

Note: Tract data are based on duration-weighted averages of tract characteristics, interpolating between and extrapolating from 1990 and 2000 censuses. Police beat rates are crimes per 10,000 residents in the beat.
*p <.05 on experimental versus control or Section 8 versus control difference.
Source: Adapted from Ludwig and Kling 2007, p. 497.

II. MTO Effects on Crime

Early results from the MTO experiment measured two to three years after baseline seemed to be quite consistent with the predictions of the existing theoretical and nonexperimental empirical literature.[2]

Follow-up data measured around five years after baseline for MTO families in all five demonstration sites reveal a more complicated picture. What is clear is that parents and children are safer, and victimization rates seem to decline. Around 69

percent of the experimental group families report feeling safe in their neighborhoods at night, compared to just 55 percent of the control group. Around 17 percent
of the experimental group households had someone victimized by a crime in the six
months prior to the follow-up surveys, a large proportional change compared to the
21 percent victimization rate among control group households (Orr et al. 2003;
Kling, Ludwig, and Katz 2005, p. 88).

In terms of criminal behavior by MTO youth, when we look at male and female
youth pooled together, we see statistically significant declines in violent crime arrests,
but not for arrests for other types of offenses (Kling, Ludwig, and Katz 2005, p. 98).
Table 10.5 makes clear that this impact on violent crime seems to occur among both
male and female youth, with ITT impacts that are large for both genders as a share of
the relevant control means (-0.077 for females compared to a control mean of 0.241, and
-0.045 for males relative to a control mean of 0.537). But MTO impacts on arrests for
other offenses, and for other types of behavioral measures more generally, vary greatly
by gender. In general, female behavior becomes more prosocial after moving through
MTO. Males, on the other hand, appear to become more antisocial after MTO moves
relative to the control group, at least for measures other than violent-crime arrests. This
does not seem to be due just to differences in policing practices in low-poverty areas,
since we also see some increase in the behavior problem index that is self-reported.

How do we reconcile these five-year impacts using data from all five sites with
those from the two- to three-year follow-up of MTO families in Baltimore? Kling,
Ludwig, and Katz (2005) estimate the effect of the experimental vouchers on annual
arrests one to two years after random assignment and three to four years after random assignment separately. Table 10.6 shows that they find significant decreases in
annual violent arrests during the first two years for males; but the increase in property arrests for MTO boys does not seem to occur until three to four years after
randomization. The results by year since randomization do not appear to vary much
for females. This indicates that the differences between the earlier site-specific
results of MTO are more likely due to changes in the treatment effect over time than
differences between the effects in different cities (Kling, Ludwig, and Katz 2005).

III. Causes of the Gender Difference in
Offending Responses to MTO Mobility

Kling, Ludwig, and Katz (2005) also explore some of the explanations for these gender gaps. They are able to rule out gender differences in mobility patterns by showing
that a qualitatively similar pattern of results occurs when the sample is limited to
male and female pairs of siblings in the same household.

Another possible explanation for the gender differences in arrest rates could be differences in discrimination against minority males and females. Arrest rates for males
could be higher than for females either if they were unfairly targeted for arrest in their new
neighborhoods or if increased perceptions of discrimination led to increased antisocial

Table 10.5 MTO effects on arrests, delinquency, and problem behavior
        by gender

	Females		Males		Male-Female
	Control Mean	ITT	Control Mean	ITT	ITT
A. EXP-CONTROL, AGES 15–25					
Lifetime violent arrests	0.241	-.077*	0.537	-0.045	0.031
N = 4475		(0.031)		(0.051)	(0.057)
Lifetime property arrests	0.164	-.057*	0.474	.150*	.207*
N = 4475		(0.026)		(0.055)	(0.06)
Lifetime drug arrests	0.087	-0.06	0.597	0.047	0.106
N = 4475		(0.034)		(0.071)	(0.076)
Lifetime total arrests	0.611	-.225*	0.021	0.16	.385*
N = 4475		(0.071)		(0.15)	(0.16)
B. EXP-CONTROL, AGES 15–20					
Lifetime total arrests	0.531	-.186*	0.382	0.279	.465*
N = 3079		(0.078)		(0.15)	(0.164)
Ever arrested	0.245	-0.029	0.39	0.053	.082*
N = 3079		(0.025)		(0.028)	(0.036)
Ever arrested [SR]	0.126	-0.015	0.289	0.013	0.028
N = 1790		(0.028)		(0.041)	(0.049)
Delinquency index [SR]	0.07	-0.008	0.136	0.002	0.009
N = 1795		(0.011)		(0.018)	(0.02)
Behavior prob index [SR]	0.34	-0.019	0.343	.064*	.082*
N = 1795		(0.023)		(0.025)	(0.033)

SR = self-report. ITT = Intent-to-Treat.
*p value <.05.
Source: Adapted from Kling, Ludwig, and Katz 2005, p. 100.

behavior. However, a postrandomization survey shows no gender differences in the perception of discrimination by male and females in the experimental group.

On the other hand, the moves did increase the experimental groups' contact with affluent and "high-status" neighbors (which makes sense given the requirement to move to nonpoor census tracts). Interviews with youth participants in MTO in

Table 10.6 Effects on annual arrests by year since random assignment, ages 15–20 (MTO)

	Females		Males	
	Control Mean	Experimental-Control	Control Mean	Experimental-Control
A. *Violent arrests*				
1–2 years since RA	0.0282	-0.0091	0.0725	-.0248*
		(0.007)		(0.012)
3–4 years since RA	0.0375	-0.0071	0.073	-0.0099
		(0.008)		(0.012)
1–4 years since RA	0.0332	-0.008	0.0728	-0.0168
		(0.006)		-(0.010)
B. *Property arrests*				
1–2 years since RA	0.0225	-0.012	0.0614	-0.0107
		(0.006)		(0.012)
3–4 years since RA	0.0299	-0.0135	0.0707	.0374*
		(0.008)		(0.014)
1–4 years since RA	0.0265	-.0132*	0.0664	0.0149
		(0.005)		(0.010)
C. *Total arrests*				
1–2 years since RA	0.0707	-.0311*	0.2296	-0.0262
		(0.013)		(0.026)
3–4 years since RA	0.1025	-0.0295	0.3018	0.0479
		(0.017)		(0.035)
1–4 years since RA	0.0877	-.0308*	0.2681	0.0133
		(0.012)		(0.026)

RA = Date of random assignment.
*p value <.05. Sample size is 2,252 females and 2,221 males.
Source: Adapted from Kling, Ludwig, and Katz 2005, p. 104.

Chicago and Baltimore provide some support for the hypothesis that male youth may have been clashing culturally with affluent neighbors more often than did female youth. Males in the experimental group were far more likely to feel harassed by the police than either boys in the control group or girls in any group and report conflicts with neighbors over the use of public space, which the boys saw as just hanging out, but neighbors described as loitering (Clampet-Lundquist et al. 2006, pp. 23–24). Therefore, while there is not much evidence for social class discrimination in the

Kling, Ludwig, and Katz analysis, the possible role of social class discrimination in new neighborhoods should not be completely discounted.

Gender differences in adaptation to new settings more generally seems like the most plausible explanation for the gender difference in MTO impacts on behavior, although again it is important to emphasize that the data available to directly test this hypothesis are limited. It is possible that male youth in the MTO-mover groups increased their property offending because of a "comparative advantage in exploiting the set of theft opportunities" (Kling, Ludwig, and Katz 2005, p. 114) that these youth enjoyed in their new neighborhoods. Given that experimental movers on average attended schools with higher test scores than they did prerandomization, but did not experience increases in test scores (Sanbonmatsu et al. 2006), it is likely that these youths suddenly found themselves lower in the distribution of academic ability relative to their new peers. At the same time, coming from high-crime neighborhoods, they might also have been relatively advantaged compared to those same new peers when it came to levels of criminal activity.

Kling, Ludwig, and Katz (2005) argue, further, that boys would be more prone to this comparative advantage than girls for a variety of reasons. First, male youth in the experimental group had substantially lower test scores than the girls in the sample, and would therefore be even more disadvantaged in an academic setting. Second, the males in the MTO study were subject to much lower levels of supervision than their female counterparts, allowing for more opportunities to commit crimes. Third, adolescent males, in general, are more likely to be risk-taking than females at the same age, and therefore may be more willing to become criminally entrepreneurial. Fourth, gender differences in population-wide propensities toward criminal activity may give male youth more opportunities to recruit peers who are willing to engage in criminal activity with them. The availability of these confederates has been shown in other work to be a particularly important predictor of youth criminal activity (Kling, Ludwig, and Katz 2005, p. 115).[3]

To learn more about the mechanisms behind the MTO effects on violent crime, Ludwig and Kling (2007) used city by treatment group interactions to measure the effect of neighborhood violence, poverty and concentration of minority residents on the size of the treatment effect. Ludwig and Kling applied an instrumental variables (IV) analysis to the MTO data that still tried to capitalize as much as possible on the key strength of MTO's randomized experimental design. The analysis exploited the fact that random assignment to the two MTO groups produced different types of neighborhood changes across the five MTO sites. For example, assignment to the experimental, rather than control, group had an unusually large effect in reducing neighborhood violent crime rates for participants in the Chicago MTO site. If local crime rates were the most important mechanism through which neighborhood environments influence criminal behavior by individual neighborhood residents, we would expect the experimental-control difference in violent crime arrests of MTO participants to also be larger (more negative) in Chicago than at the other MTO sites. Mechanically, these instrumental variable estimates were generated by using interactions of indicators for MTO site and treatment group assignment as instruments for specific neighborhood characteristics, including tract poverty or minority share, and police beat–level violent crime rates.

Table 10.7 presents the results of these instrumental variable estimates and, for comparison to highlight the biases that can result from nonexperimental results, estimates from ordinary least squares regressions that condition on a rich set of baseline characteristics, including prerandomization arrest histories. Ludwig and Kling found no evidence for the epidemic model of violent crime in which large changes in neighborhood violence should accompany the largest declines in violent arrests. Nor did they find evidence that changes in the concentration of poverty predict larger declines in violent crime. Instead, they found that the largest treatment effects are evident in the cities in which the MTO experimental group experienced the largest changes in percent minority (Ludwig and Kling 2007, p. 508). Based on the postmove survey of MTO participants, Ludwig and Kling hypothesized that this was due to the increased presence of drug markets, and the violence that accompanies them, in neighborhoods with a high concentration of minorities. In fact, the interaction between high drug use or selling and percent minority in a neighborhood significantly predicts an increase in young male violent arrests (Ludwig and Kling 2007, p. 511).

IV. A CHICAGO REPLICATION

Social policy should never be decided on the basis of a single study. For that reason and others, we are fortunate that a "natural experiment" that occurred in Chicago provides an opportunity to replicate the MTO design and compare the results.

In 1997, for the first time in about 12 years, the Chicago Housing Authority (CHA) through a local firm, CHAC, Inc., opened the city's housing voucher waiting list. Far more families applied than there were vouchers available, so CHAC randomly assigned the 82,607 eligible families to the voucher program wait list. This lottery number provides exogenous variation in voucher receipt, so we can compare average outcomes essentially of families who are randomly assigned "good" versus "bad" lottery numbers. By focusing on families who were living in public housing when they applied for a voucher, we can basically replicate the MTO results, at least in Chicago.

As with the Chicago MTO sample, families in the CHAC program are almost all African-American female-headed households. Using social service records, Ludwig and colleagues (2007) matched the household heads on the CHAC housing application to their children's names and then matched those names to administrative data from the Illinois State Police from 1995 to 2005 (Ludwig et al. 2007).

Analysis of the CHAC data (table 10.8) shows that youth ages 12 to 18 in 1997 appear to have about one-quarter fewer violent crime arrests per quarter than those who did not receive a voucher. However, none of the other types of crime appears to be reduced by the voucher offer. When the results are divided by gender, none of the results for females is statistically significant, but for males, the violent crime reductions

Table 10.7 Experimental and nonexperimental estimates of neighborhood characteristics on arrest rates (MTO)

Model:		OLS	IV
Instrument:		None	E/S*Site
		Full Sample	Full Sample
Explanatory Variable	Controls		
Beat Violent Crime Rate		0.017	-0.016
		(0.017)	(0.070)
Beat Violent Crime Rate	Tract Share Minority	0.01	-0.137
		(0.018)	(0.095)
Beat Violent Crime Rate	Tract Share Poverty	0.015	-0.111
		(0.020)	(0.124)
Beat Violent Crime Rate	Tract Share Poverty and Tract Share Minority	0.013	-0.118
		-0.02	(0.125)
Tract Share Minority		.016*	.067*
		(0.008)	(0.033)
Tract Share Minority	Tract Share Poverty	0.016	.115*
		(0.010)	(0.051)
Tract Share Minority	Beat Violent Crime Rate	0.012	.110*
		(0.009)	(0.046)
Tract Share Minority	Beat Violent Crime Rate and Tract Share Poverty	0.014	.115*
		(0.010)	(0.053)
Tract Share Poverty		0.007	0.008
		(0.008)	(0.020)
Tract Share Poverty	Tract Share Minority	-0.002	-0.041
		(0.010)	(0.030)
Tract Share Poverty	Beat Violent Crime Rate	0.002	0.037
		(0.010)	(0.034)

continued

Table 10.7 (continued)

Model:		OLS	IV
Tract Share Poverty	Beat Violent Crime Rate and Tract Share Minority	-0.004	-0.009
		(0.011)	(0.039)

Note: Values presented are coefficients (standard errors) from a separate two-stage least squares estimation with rows. For example, in the first row, the model contains only neighborhood violent crime rate; in the second row, the model contains neighborhood violent crime rate controlling for tract share minority, and the coefficient reported is for violent crime rate. Endogenous variables are expressed in standard deviation units relative to the standard deviation in the control group for that variable. The control group standard deviations are 17% for tract share minority, 14% for tract share poverty, 185% for beat violent crime rate, and 525% for beat property crime rate.
[+]p <.10,
[*]p <.05.
Source: Adapted from Ludwig and Kling 2007, pp. 501, 505.

remain significant. Changes in property crime arrests for either gender are never statistically significant from zero (Ludwig et al. 2007).

One extra benefit of the CHAC study is its ability to at least partially rule out one of the possible mechanisms through which neighborhoods might affect criminal activity. Along with the youth in the program, Ludwig et al. (2007) also analyze the effect of voucher receipt on the younger household heads in the sample, ages 18–30. They find substantial reductions in violent crime associated with voucher receipt that mirror those of the youth participants. This suggests that the behavioral mechanisms driving these results must be something that is not unique to teenagers, such as the quality of local schools or parental supervision, which would not pertain to adults (Ludwig et al. 2007).

V. Discussion and Conclusions

Both the MTO and the CHAC experimental data suggest that living in a more disadvantaged neighborhood increases an individual's risk of involvement with violent criminal behavior. Neighborhood minority composition seems to be the strongest attribute associated with violent crime—more so than neighborhood poverty (which is also correlated with social process measures like disorder) or local-area crime rates. This may be due to the increased use and sale of drugs, and the violence that accompanies them, in areas with high concentration of minorities.

The MTO data also provide some suggestive evidence that the effect of moving people to lower poverty areas among boys might generate at least some partially offsetting effect, in the form of higher property crime offending. Gender differences in arrest rates and the increase in property offending by males are most plausibly explained by gender differences in adaptation to a new neighborhood. Even if the findings on property crimes from the MTO experiment prove to be generalizable to a

Table 10.8 Effects of housing vouchers on arrest (CHAC)

	Control Mean	ITT
Youth 12–18		
Violent crime arrests	0.017	-0.004**
		(0.002)
Property crime arrests	0.007	-0.001
		(0.001)
Drug crime arrests	0.024	-0.002
		(0.003)
Other crime arrests	0.031	-0.004
		(0.004)
Total arrests	0.079	-0.011
		(0.007)
Male youth 12–18		
Violent crime arrests	0.026	-0.006*
		(0.003)
Property crime arrests	0.009	-0.002
		(0.001)
Drug crime arrests	0.047	-0.006
		(0.005)
Other crime arrests	0.058	-0.007
		(0.009)
Total arrests	0.14	-0.021
		(0.014)
Female youth 12–18		
Violent crime arrests	0.008	-0.002
		(0.001)
Property crime arrests	0.005	0
		(0.001)
Drug crime arrests	0.003	0
		(0.001)
Other crime arrests	0.007	-0.001
		(0.002)

continued

204 COMMUNITY CRIME PREVENTION

Table 10.8 (continued)

	Control Mean	ITT
Total arrests	0.024	-0.002
		(0.004)

Notes: The unit of observation is person-year-quarter. The sample is limited to households with lottery numbers above 35,000 or below 18,103. ITT = Intent-to-Treat. See text for discussion of these estimates. Robust standard errors clustered at household level.
** = significant at 5% level,
* = significant at 10% level.
Source: Adapted from Ludwig et al. 2007, p. 35.

larger portion of the urban population living in poor neighborhoods, the overall results of these experiments suggest that there is, on balance, a decline in the amount of social harm from criminal behavior among the youth who move. Using the social costs of different crimes calculated in Miller, Cohen, and Wiersema (1996), Kling, Ludwig, and Katz (2005) estimate the overall social savings from the changes in crimes committed by the MTO experimental movers. The Miller, Cohen, and Weirsema social cost index takes into account the dollar values of property damage, medical costs, lost productivity, and damages awarded by juries for reductions in quality of life. The cost of each primary offense is summed for each of the youth's arrests through 2001 to estimate the total cost of their criminal activity. The MTO moves reduce the social costs of criminal behavior by youth in the program by 15 to 33 percent of the control mean social costs, most of which is driven by the early changes in criminal behavior in the few years after the move. However, it is important to remember that this only represents the reduction of social cost due to the crimes committed by MTO participants. A full analysis of social welfare costs would have to take into account the externalities of those youth's criminal behavior on the youth in both their neighborhoods of origin and destination (Kling, Ludwig, and Katz 2005, pp. 124–25).

The MTO and CHAC data provide randomized experimental evidence that neighborhood environments are relevant for the criminal behavior of at least very disadvantaged urban populations in the United States, but fall short of providing sharp guidance about the effects of potential policy interventions. The MTO data to date provide, at best, suggestive evidence about which specific neighborhood attributes are most relevant in affecting criminal behavior, complicating efforts to guide the design of place-based community interventions. The MTO and CHAC data only identify effects on people who move, and are not informative about the effects of residential mobility interventions on people in origin and destination areas. If, for example, peer influences on criminal behavior were constant and linear in peer characteristics, then re-sorting people across community areas may simply redistribute crime, rather than reduce an area's overall crime rate. Answering this sort of "general equilibrium" question for mobility interventions, as well as developing a better understanding of which specific neighborhood attributes are relevant for criminal behavior, seems to us to be the highest priorities for developing community-oriented interventions to help prevent crime.

NOTES

1. Olsen (2003, pp. 365–441) offers an excellent review of the housing voucher program, which provides families with a subsidy to live in private-market housing. The maximum voucher subsidy is determined by the Fair Market Rent (FMR), which is a function of family size, the gender mix of adults and children in the home, and the local rent distribution. For a family of four, the FMR is between 40 and 50 percent of the local metropolitan area private-market rent distribution. For example, the FMR for a two-bedroom apartment in the Chicago area was equal to $699 in 1994, $732 in 1997, and $762 in 2000. Families are expected to pay 30 percent of their income (adjusted by family size, childcare expenses, and medical expenses) toward their rent. Note that in the United States, housing assistance is not an entitlement, so housing voucher (and other housing) programs usually have long wait lists. Olsen (2003) estimates that only around 28 percent of income-eligible families in the United States receive any housing assistance.

2. More specifically, in Baltimore, on average there were 3 arrests per 100 teens in the control group. The intent to treated (ITT) effect, controlling for pre-voucher arrests and calendar quarter dummies, was estimated to be 1.6 fewer arrests per 100 teens per quarter in the experimental group. There were no statistically significant reductions in the incidence of any other crimes, or for all crimes in general (Ludwig, Duncan, and Hirschfield 2001). Early results of the MTO experiment in Boston support these findings with reductions in general behavior problems for teens in the experimental group compared to the control group (Katz, Kling, and Liebman 2001).

3. Another gender difference is in the peer networks of experimental youth. Girls in the study tended to make more friends in their newer school, whereas experimental youth tended to continue to cite pre-move friends from elementary or middle school as their closest ties (Clampet-Lundquist et al. 2006). These close ties to the old neighborhood could provide extra resources, in terms of knowledge or willing confederates, for criminal activity in their new target-rich neighborhoods. However whether these MTO gender differences in peer affiliations are a cause or an effect of the gender difference in MTO's impact on criminal behavior is not clear.

REFERENCES

Chicago Police Department. 2008. 2007 *Annual Report: A Year in Review*. Chicago: Chicago Police Department.

Clampet-Lundquist, S., K. Edin, J. R. Kling, and G. J. Duncan. 2006. "Moving At-Risk Teenagers Out of High-Risk Neighborhoods: Why Girls Fare Better than Boys." Working Paper, Princeton University Industrial Relations, Section 509.

Katz, Lawrence. F., Jeffrey R. Kling, and Jeffrey B. Liebman. 2001. "Moving to Opportunity in Boston: Early Results of a Randomized Mobility Experiment." *Quarterly Journal of Economics* 116(2): 607–54.

Kling, Jeffrey R., Jeffrey B. Liebman, and Lawrence F. Katz. 2007. "Experimental Analysis of Neighborhood Effects." *Econometrica* 75(1): 83–119.

Kling, Jeffrey R., Jens Ludwig, and Lawrence F. Katz. 2005. "Neighborhood Effects on Crime for Female and Male Youth: Evidence from a Randomized Housing Voucher Experiment." *Quarterly Journal of Economics* 120(1): 87–130.

Ludwig, Jens, Greg J. Duncan, and Paul Hirschfield. 2001. "Urban Poverty and Juvenile
    Crime: Evidence from a Randomized Housing-Mobility Experiment." *Quarterly
    Journal of Economics* 116(2): 655–80.
Ludwig, Jens, Brian A. Jacob, Greg J.Duncan, James Rosenbaum, and Michael Johnson.
    2007. "Neighborhood Effects on Crime: Evidence from a Randomized Housing-
    Voucher Lottery." Unpublished manuscript. Chicago: University of Chicago.
Ludwig, Jens, and Jeffrey R. Kling. 2007. "Is Crime Contagious?" *Journal of Law & Eco-
    nomics.* 50(3): 491–518.
Miller, Ted R., Mark A. Cohen, and Brian Wiersema. 1996. *Victim Costs and Consequences:
    A New Look.* Washington, DC: US Department of Justice, Office of Justice Programs,
    National Institute of Justice.
Olsen, Edgar. 2003. "Housing Programs for Low-Income Households." In *Means-Tested
    Transfer Programs in the United States. A National Bureau of Economic Research
    Conference Report,* edited by Robert A. Moffitt. Chicago: University of Chicago Press.
Orr, Larry L., US Department of Housing and Urban Development, Office of Policy
    Development and Research, Abt Associates, National Bureau of Economic Research,
    and Urban Institute. 2003. *Moving to Opportunity Interim Impacts Evaluation.*
    Washington, DC: US Department of Housing and Urban Development, Office of
    Policy Development and Research.
Sanbonmatsu, Lisa, Jeffrey R. Kling, Greg J. Duncan, and Jeanne Brooks-Gunn. 2006.
    "Neighborhoods and Academic Achievement: Results from the Moving to Opportu-
    nity Experiment." *Journal of Human Resources* 41(4): 649–91.

CHAPTER 11

....

PEER INFLUENCE, MENTORING, AND THE PREVENTION OF CRIME

....

CHRISTOPHER J. SULLIVAN AND DARRICK JOLLIFFE

MANY criminological theories either implicitly or explicitly acknowledge that criminal behavior is influenced by those to whom we have close contact. For example, Differential Association theory (Sutherland 1947), Social Learning theory (Akers 1973) and Social Control Theory (Hirschi 1969) all suggest that criminal behavior is more or less likely depending upon those with whom we share the immediate environment, and importantly, the value we place on the relationships that are shared. The impact of the presence and value of others on the likelihood of crime is also supported by more contemporary risk-focused approaches. Numerous prospective longitudinal studies have identified that the presence of certain relationships (e.g., delinquent friends) and the absence of others (e.g., single-parent families) can have a considerable impact on the likelihood of later offending (Farrington and Welsh 2007).

Crime prevention strategies focused on peer influence and mentoring are broadly based on these associations. This essay will first explore the nature and impact of programs designed to resist developing attachments to undesirable peers and then move on to explore the nature and impact of programs designed to create attachments to desirable prosocial models. Several main conclusions emerge in reviewing these two types of programming:

- Several evaluations within the broader areas suggest potentially promising results in reducing delinquent behavior for both peer risk and mentoring programs. The evidence base is slightly more extensive for the latter.

- There are a number of methodological shortcomings in study designs and execution that make it difficult to draw firm conclusions as to the extent of the effectiveness of these programs.
- Although both types of programs make specific assumptions about social influences and delinquent behavior, those theoretical foundations are only sparingly operationalized in their evaluation. This creates difficulty in the appropriate attribution of effects (or lack thereof)—even in otherwise rigorous evaluations.

Section I of this essay offers a brief overview of the theoretical suppositions that provide a foundation for the anticipated impact of peer risk and mentoring programs. It then moves into a general overview of peer risk interventions in section II. This is then carried forward into a consideration of the characteristics of such programs and the methods used to evaluate them before drawing some general conclusions about this area of research. The general shortcomings of studies of programs directed at peer risk are also discussed. Section III considers the impact of mentoring based on research in that area. As with peer risk interventions, this section also analyzes key characteristics of the research in terms of how they might contextualize the observed findings. Section IV provides an overview of future research needs and presents a brief conclusion with respect to the two programmatic areas of interest.

I. Peer Influence, Mentoring, and Delinquency

Peers are essential influences for youth as they progress through adolescence (Giordano 2003; Smetana, Campione-Barr, and Metzger 2006). The study of juvenile delinquency is one of a variety of research areas where peer effects are considered (Warr 2002). Although there may be some methodological artifacts at work (Haynie and Osgood 2005), extant empirical findings generally suggest that peers do in fact play a substantial role in delinquent behavior. A number of studies, for instance, have identified "co-offending" as a major component of the generally observed prevalence and pattern of delinquency (McCord and Conway 2005; Reiss and Farrington 1991).

While the social nature of juvenile delinquency has been borne out in a number of empirical studies, the mechanisms by which this relationship holds are less clear. Warr (2002) outlined several potential mechanisms by which a person's associates might contribute to their delinquent behavior (see also van Lier, Vitaro, and Eisner 2007). The fear of ridicule, loyalty to friends, acquisition and maintenance of status, diffusion of responsibility, learning and reinforcement processes, and presentation of opportunity are among potential explanations offered in studies of the relationship between peers and delinquent behavior. Peers are central to any number of criminological theories that purport to explain delinquent behavior, and a number of perspectives have laid claim to this empirically observed effect. They range from foundational, long-held and tested theories in the field (e.g., social learning, differential association) to recently developed integrated theories that blend multiple perspectives (e.g., interactional theory, the social development model). Still, other views suggest that the "peer effect" is spurious and the observed relationship can better be attributed to youths' penchant for spending time and forming relationships with similar others (e.g., Glueck and Glueck 1950; Gottfredson and Hirschi 1990).

Each of these mechanisms connotes a distinct path by which social interactions might facilitate or cause delinquency. Understanding this process is important as different perspectives may suggest vastly different intervention approaches. For example, the social learning view of the peer-delinquency relationship suggests that it would be fruitful to provide youths with skills designed to help in resisting deviant influences, whereas the situational perspective perceives "idle hands as the devil's tools" and suggests youth involvement in structured social activities may be effective in limiting delinquency.

Mentoring programs also derive from notions of how association with others might impact individual behavior. The general theme of all mentoring programs is the exposure of a less experienced or "at-risk" individual to a more experienced and often older role model in a one-on-one relationship. The mentor is often considered to act as a role model for the mentee while providing guidance, advice, and encouragement aimed at developing the youth's competence and character (Rhodes 1994). The mentee is usually perceived to be "at risk" for various reasons, including individual factors (e.g., acting out in school, offending, substance use, gang membership) and/or social circumstances (e.g., single-parent family, socially excluded).

Given the general theme of mentoring, it is not surprising that it is often considered an attractive option to use to prevent crime. In a criminal justice context, mentoring is usually viewed as being capable of reducing the likelihood of offending by increasing positive life outcomes, such as leaving a gang, improving education, or gaining employment (e.g., O'Donnell, Lydgate, and Fo 1979; Grossman and Tierney 1998; Newburn and Shiner 2005).

There are a number of potential mechanisms whereby mentoring might have an impact on crime. For example, the mentor could provide assistance to the mentee that reduces the likelihood of offending. The assistance could be either direct (e.g., helping to fill in job applications, locating appropriate housing or benefits) or indirect (e.g., encouragement, acting as a positive role model), but might otherwise be unavailable to most offenders or youths who are "at risk" because of their family or social background. This would suggest that mentoring programs that offer trained and informed mentors skilled in providing assistance would be more successful at preventing crime.

Mentoring might also have an effect on crime through the attachment or social bond that is formed between the mentor and mentee. According to Hirschi (1969), the social bonds established in close relationships to conventional others should act

Table 11.1 Summary results of peer intervention articles

Study	Sample	Study Design	Evaluation of Skills	Outcome Measure	Results
Sharkey 1998	171 elementary and middle school students	Single group, pre/post test	SR attitudes toward gangs, refusal skills, and decision making	n.a.	No observed effects on gang attitudes, decision making, refusal skills
Esbensen and Osgood 1999	5935 8th-grade students in 11 sites	Nonequivalent group, post-test only	SR peer delinquency/prosocial behavior, commitment to prosocial peers	SR delinquency	Positive effects on peer related measures, delinquency at 1-yr follow-up
Harrell et al. 1999	874 high-risk adolescents from 11–13	Randomized experiment	n.a.	Positive peer support, association with delinquent youths, peer pressure, SR and official delinquency	Positive effects on peer-related measures, self-reported violence and drug sales; no effect on property offenses, official delinquency
DuRant et al. 2001	563 urban, middle school students	Nonequivalent group	n.a.	SR weapon carrying, use of violence	No effect on use of violence at post-test
Esbensen et al. 2001	2503 junior high school students in 6 sites	Nonequivalent group	SR peer delinquency/prosocial behavior, commitment to prosocial peers	SR delinquency (longitudinal)	Small, nonsignificant effect on peer delinquency, commitment; significant effect on prosocial peers, small nonsignificant effect on delinquency
Farrell, Meyer, and White 2001	510 urban, middle school students	Randomized experiment	SR knowledge of intervention skills	SR violence, school disciplinary records	Effects found on intervention knowledge; effects on school infractions, violence at post-test but not 6, 12 mos.

Farrell, Meyer, et al. 2003	350 urban, middle school students	Randomized experiment	SR knowledge of intervention skills, attitudes	SR violence, school delinquency	Mixed, positive effect on violence
Farrell, Valois, et al. 2003	809 rural, middle school students	Nonequivalent group	SR perceived peer support for nonviolence, knowledge of intervention skills	SR aggression, delinquency, school disciplinary records	Effects found on intervention knowledge; mixed findings on aggression, delinquency
Flay et al. 2004	1155 students in grades 5–8	Randomized experiment	n.a.	SR violence, school delinquency	Sizable effects on violence, delinquency
Ngwe et al. 2004	571 African-American students in an urban area in grades 5–8	Randomized experiment	SR estimates of peer behavior, perceptions of friend's behavior, peer encouragement to engage in delinquent behavior	SR violence (longitudinal)	Significant effect on violence trends, mediated by peer variables
Wright et al. 2004	129 urban, middle school students	Single group, pre/post test	Utilization of different refusal skills in recorded role-playing	SR delinquency	Mixed, favored divergent skills
Cho, Hallfors, and Sánchez 2005	1004 urban, high school students	Randomized experiment	SR connection to positive peers, reduce bonding to deviant peers	SR delinquency	Mixed, immediate post-intervention effects were positive for delinquency, effects on peer risk were negative
Johnson et al. 2008	129 urban youths, transitioning to high school	Nonequivalent group, main results analyzed by BL risk level	SR ability to resist peer pressure	SR school-related misconduct	Effects for high-risk students on resisting peer pressure, school-related misconduct

Note: SR = Self-Report

as a deterrent to crime because the individual will take these relationships into account before committing a crime. Committing a crime risks the disapproval, or even the loss, of the valued mentor. This would suggest that mentoring programs in which strong emotional relationships are developed between the mentor and mentee will have a particularly salient impact in reducing crime.

Another potential way in which mentoring might reduce crime is through the reduction of opportunity for crime. Regular and lengthy meetings between mentors and mentees not only provide less time for the mentee to offend but might also disrupt their established relationships with delinquent friends. This would suggest that mentoring programs that had consistent and regular meetings between mentors and mentees would reduce the likelihood of crime.

II. PEER RISK INTERVENTIONS

While a great deal of empirical and theoretical literature has focused on the presence of peer influence on delinquency, far less work has been done to explicitly operationalize and test those findings in the programming and policy realm. In early work, Gottfredson (1987) reviewed several studies of peer group interventions that fell into the category of guided group interaction (GGI), which is meant to prevent a variety of problematic outcomes (e.g., truancy, delinquency). Many of the evaluations examined in that review were inconclusive and focused on populations that were already involved in the juvenile justice system. Gottfredson suggested that it is plausible that, given theoretical views and empirical evidence regarding peer risk factors, addressing this domain might prevent delinquency but further study was needed.

Although evidence on programs specifically geared toward counteracting peer risk has advanced since that review was published, the research base is still somewhat narrow. The body of evidence for programs aimed explicitly at the potential negative impacts of peers are considered here. This may include those based on peer-group interventions as well as those that use some other mechanism to reduce the risk of delinquency posed by peers (e.g., skills training). The scope of the body of evidence surrounding these programs expands or contracts depending on the outcome of interest. The current focus on delinquency and violence restricts the pool of available studies as much of the extant research on peer risk prevention has an explicit focus on substance use. Using a search method that encompassed a number of bibliographic databases across social science fields (e.g., Criminal Justice Abstracts, National Criminal Justice Reference Service, PsychInfo, ERIC, and Sociological Abstracts) and search terms such as "peer pressure," "peer influence," and "peer refusal skills," a number of studies that focused specifically on the prevention of delinquency and violence through an emphasis on reducing peer risk were identified and removed. Table 11.1 presents key methodological features and summarizes results for the identified studies.

A. Targeted Youths and the Nature of Intervention

Thirteen studies focused on peer risk, published since Gottfredson's (1987) work, were identified. Nearly all studies were school-based and most were directed at middle-school-age youths. The programs tended to be implemented in urban school districts and many were targeted at areas expected to have a disproportionate number of high-risk youths. Although the interventions were often implemented in high-risk areas, they generally targeted all youths in those settings. The intervention modality typically involved a skill-building, curriculum-based approach. Some utilized role-playing and feedback to participants. In all cases, a stated objective of the program was to target associations and decision making within the context of peer interactions. In most cases, peer relationships were only one focus of a multi-dimensional prevention program.

A prototypical intervention program in this area is presented by Wright et al. (2004), who report on an intervention designed to inculcate youths with "peer pressure refusal skills" in order to provide resistance to continued peer pressure for engagement in problem behaviors. The researchers recorded and coded a series of role-playing interactions with participants to determine how well they applied peer refusal skills. They then assessed their performance on these tasks in relation to self-reported delinquency in the subsequent school year (seventh to eighth grade).

The Responding in Peaceful and Positive Ways (RIPP) program offers another example of an intervention approach common in this area (Farrell, Meyer, and White 2001; Farrell, Meyer, et al. 2003; Farrell, Valois, et al. 2003). This program used an intervention specialist to present a curriculum designed to teach youths problem-solving and violence-prevention skills. The curriculum was delivered using an experiential learning model. There were a total of 25 cumulative lessons implemented in social studies or health classes (Farrell, Meyer, and White 2001).

A third intervention identified was the Aban Aya Youth project, which was implemented in the Chicago metropolitan area (Flay et al. 2004; Ngwe et al. 2004). The program entailed two treatment conditions, the first a social development curriculum and the second a school-based social development curriculum plus community interventions. The curriculum was delivered via classroom teaching and accompanying role-playing exercises. Content areas included focus on communication skills, problem solving, decision making, social networking, and refusal skills.

B. Characteristics of Evaluation Methods

This brief inventory of the research literature on programs aimed at mitigating risk for delinquency and violence from peer relationships identified both commonalities and differences. Methodologically, the studies vary from small, uncontrolled designs to more rigorous experimental trials. Two studies used single group, pre/post test designs and five used nonequivalent group designs. Authors of these studies did typically use controls for measured confounding variables in the analysis of program effects. The remaining six studies utilized randomized experimental designs. As these were school-based interventions, the typical unit of assignment was the classroom. Most studies utilized large samples, with a range from 129 to 5,935. The majority of studies have samples of over 500 youths, some coming from multiple schools. Most studies utilized short-term follow-up periods (one year or less), but some report on outcomes measured at several time periods following program participation.

The selection criteria required that the research report results for delinquency or violence variables. In general, these outcomes were measured based on self-reports and focused on general delinquency and/or violence. Two studies utilized records of school misconduct in assessing intervention outcomes (Farrell, Meyer, and White 2001; Farrell, Meyer, et al. 2003) and another was able to draw on official juvenile justice records (Harrell, Cavanagh, and Sridaharan 1999). As peer risk is perceived as a mediator between the intervention and delinquency and/or violence outcomes, it is important that this domain is measured in this type of evaluation. In three cases, peer-related risk was not measured after program participation, precluding an assessment of proximal effects. In one case, researchers established the mediator variables through observation of role-playing exercises. Generally, the studies that did measure peer risk as a proximal outcome of program participation utilized pencil-and-paper tests to assess relative knowledge of the curriculum among participants and comparison cases. Some utilized scale-based assessment of contact with deviant peers, peer delinquency, and perceived ability to resist peer pressure to more formally consider those objectives. Generally, these measures were assessed as a distinct outcome of the intervention and were not utilized in a formal assessment of their role as mediating variables between the intervention and the delinquency/violence outcome.

C. General Conclusions from the Research

Several preliminary findings emerge from this review of the extant research. First, in general, the studies report positive short-term effects on peer-related risk and intervention knowledge where that was measured. Peer risk was measured somewhat infrequently, but several studies did show positive intervention impacts on variables such as peer delinquency and peer refusal skills. Cho, Hallfors, and Sánchez (2005), however, evaluated an interactive, peer-group-based intervention that demonstrated a negative impact on peer risk, which was attributed to the aggregation of high-risk youths. Similar findings have been observed in other studies (Ang and Hughes 2001), with Dodge, Dishion, and Lansford (2006) suggesting that programs targeted to all youths (e.g., general, school-based) are likely to be less problematic on this front than those that separate youths based on risk level.

The programs considered here were aimed at producing reductions in delinquency and violence. On that score, this body of research shows mixed effects. A few studies show effects that decidedly favor the intervention groups. Most studies presented here, however, tend to find positive outcomes on some measures but no effects on others. Moderated effects based on risk level were observed as well. Among those studies reporting effect sizes, Flay and colleagues' (2004) work stands out because it showed a strong positive effect on multiple outcomes of interest. Otherwise, these studies did not present unequivocal support for interventions targeting peer risk. Still, it is helpful to examine some of these studies in more depth to consider key findings in the context of their substantive aims and research designs.

Probably the most deleterious form of peer influence on delinquency is the gang. Among the studies identified based on the criteria used here were evaluations of the Gang Resistance Education and Training (GREAT) program (Esbensen and Osgood 1999; Esbensen et al. 2001). Those studies focused on a multisite, school-based curriculum delivered by law enforcement in several sessions. Inoculating students against delinquency and gang involvement through conveyance of key life skills (e.g., conflict resolution, strategies for deflecting negative peer influence) was among the program's key aims. The results suggest that there were small positive effects on peer-risk measures and delinquent behaviors in both the short and longer-term evaluations.

Ngwe and colleagues' (2004) study utilized a randomized experimental design and also followed youths over multiple time periods. This study affirmed the findings from Flay et al (2004) regarding the Aban Aya Youth Project, which suggested sizable program effects on violence and school delinquency. Going beyond the basic effects, Ngwe and colleagues' work tested a mediation model around proximal program effects on peer behaviors and peer group pressure. Their findings suggest that the Aban Aya program had an impact on growth in violence that was mediated by its effect on peer risk. This was the only study that fully tested the underlying theory presumed in these interventions. Coupled with the initial results of Flay and colleagues, this research indicates that a program directed at this chain of relationships can have an impact on later delinquency and violence.

The line of research on the Responding in Peaceful and Positive Ways (RIPP) intervention by Farrell and colleagues (Farrell, Meyer, and White 2001; Farrell, Meyer, et al. 2003; Farrell, Valois, et al. 2003) is instructive in demonstrating some features of this body of literature. The three studies considered here constitute two randomized and one quasi-experimental design; each had a fairly large sample size (350 plus youths). All interventions were implemented in school settings (two urban, one rural with sixth- to eighth-grade students). In all three studies, observed effects were somewhat mixed, with intervention youths tending to have better outcomes on school disciplinary problems captured in records but fairly similar outcomes on self-reported behavior. The authors also highlight the potential for moderation of program effects by the level of risk demonstrated by participants, an issue that comes up multiple times in this literature. While the program did have an impact on a variable derived from a survey-based test of intervention knowledge, other key mediators (e.g., willingness to stop a fight despite peer pressure) were not affected by RIPP.

D. Shortcomings in the Research

Although we can learn from the findings of extant research on interventions targeted at peer risk, most of the research reviewed here took place in school settings where there may be difficulties in implementing programs with fidelity (Johnson et al. 2008), owing to compromises in evaluation design (see, for example, Esbensen et al. 2001). Consequently, a variety of methodological issues may affect the conclusions reached in these studies. These problems include the fact that most studies do not have randomized control groups. Also, assignment of the treatment is typically made at the class or school level with assessment of outcomes at the individual level (Ngwe et al. 2004). Within-school designs may also encounter a diffusion of effects across students and classrooms (Farrell, Meyer, and White 2001). There are also some common measurement problems in this research area. First, despite their clear relevance as a proximal outcome, there tends to be an exclusion of (or weak) measures of peer-risk mediator variables in these studies and a lack of thorough analysis of the theory underlying the intervention. Additionally, the almost exclusive use of self-report measures might raise the specter of social desirability bias in the context of an intervention (Wynn et al. 1997). Although some studies accounted for these potential problems in design or analysis, the identified methodological difficulties tended to appear in multiple studies in this area.

III. THE IMPACT OF MENTORING

There have been a number of evaluations of the impact of mentoring on later life outcomes. However, as pointed out by Newburn and Shiner (2005), many of these have been based on limited research designs, such as case studies, small-scale qualitative studies, and evaluations that did not include a control group (e.g., St. James-Roberts and Singh 2001; Tarling, Burrows, and Clarke 2001). The results of these studies are almost uniformly positive; unfortunately, these types of evaluations do not allow the effectiveness of mentoring programs to be adequately tested. This makes it difficult for researchers and policymakers to interpret the results of these studies.

Recently, however, two systematic reviews (including meta-analyses) of the relationship between mentoring and offending have been published. It should be noted that high-quality evidence about the relationship between mentoring and offending was available, but not accessible, before the production of these two reviews. The exact impact of mentoring could not easily be assessed as it was included alongside a number of other interventions in larger systematic reviews that were designed to quantify the overall impact of intervention on delinquency and offending (Lipsey and Wilson 1998; Aos et al. 2004).

Jolliffe and Farrington (2008) undertook a review of the impact of mentoring on reoffending. The inclusion/exclusion criteria for this review specified that mentoring was considered to have taken place if a nonprofessional person spent time with an at-risk individual in a supportive manner acting as a role model or advocate. The mentor could have been acting in a paid or unpaid capacity, but could not be acting as a member of a professional group or in a professional capacity. In addition, this mentoring had to have been provided to individuals who were either convicted offenders or individuals at risk of offending (e.g., youths acting out in school). To be included in the review, the evaluation of the mentoring program also needed to be at least Level 3 on the Maryland Scientific Scale (Sherman et al. 1997; i.e., include a control group or a group similar to those mentored, but who did not receive a mentor), include a total of 50 individuals, and have sufficient quantitative information so that the study could be included in a meta-analysis. From the 49 potentially relevant evaluations, a total of 18 independent evaluations were identified. Below are two examples of studies that were included in the review.

In a large-scale randomized trial, Grossman and Tierney (1998) investigated the impact of the Big Brothers and Big Sisters mentoring program on a number of outcomes, including self-reported violence, theft, and vandalism, for a group of 959 youths (ages 10–16) from eight areas across the United States. Of these 959 youths, 487 were randomly allocated to receive an adult "big brother" or "big sister" and 472 were allocated to a control condition (waiting list). The mentors and mentees were matched based on gender and race (where possible) and met at least once a month for an average of 3.6 hours per meeting. The results suggested that those in the experimental condition were significantly less likely than those in the control condition to initiate illegal drug and alcohol use over the study period (about 11 months). However, there were no significant differences in the prevalence of self-reported violence, theft, or vandalism between the treatment and control groups.

O'Donnell, Lydgate, and Fo (1979) evaluated the Buddy System, a program in Hawaii that matched "at-risk" youths with adult "buddies." The youths were referred to the program for behavior and academic problems primarily by public schools and were randomly allocated either to receive an adult buddy (n = 335) or to be in a control condition (n = 218), which involved not being invited to participate in the buddy program. Two years after the program arrest rates were compared for the two conditions. The results suggested that those in the buddy program had significantly fewer arrests for major offenses compared to controls, but this applied only to those who had no arrests at the commencement of the program. Those who had arrests prior to being allocated a buddy were significantly more likely to be arrested than those in the control group. This could possibly have reflected the negative effect of associating with other disruptive children (see McCord 2003). Overall, there was no significant difference in rearrest rates between experimental and control conditions.

Meta-analysis was used to obtain an overall picture of the impact of mentoring on offending across the 18 included evaluations. Combining effect sizes suggested that mentoring was associated with a significant reduction in offending in the range of 4 to 10 percent. Compared to other individual-level interventions (e.g., Lipsey and Landenberger 2006), the effect of mentoring appeared small to moderate.

Another systematic review on the impact of mentoring was completed by Tolan et al. (2008). This review included a wider range of outcomes than that included in the review by Jolliffe and Farrington (2008)—for example, delinquency, aggression, drug use, school failure—and benefitted from a more comprehensive searching strategy. The authors were able to identify 112 studies, of which 39 met the inclusion criteria. Of the 20 outcomes studied, 6 reported aggression outcomes, 6 reported drug use outcomes, and 19 reported academic achievement outcomes.

The results suggested that, across the studies, mentoring was associated with a decrease in offending of about 12 percent, a decrease in aggression of about 20 percent, a decrease in drug use of about 7 percent, and an increase in academic achievement of about 4 percent. However, much like the review of Jolliffe and Farrington (2008), Tolan et al. (2008) noted significant variation within studies of delinquency, as well as those of aggression and drug use.

Both reviews attempted to investigate the potential sources of variation and in turn uncover the features of successful mentoring programs. The reviews were concordant in indicating that the relationship between mentor and mentee was an important feature. For example, Tolan et al. (2008) demonstrated that mentoring programs that focused on emotional support had significantly greater effects. Similarly, Jolliffe and Farrington (2008) found a significant positive relationship between the impact of the mentoring program and the duration per contact between the mentor and mentee (i.e., time spent together per meeting). Furthermore, mentoring that took place weekly or more often was more successful. While these two features of mentoring programs could perhaps be considered as having their impact through reducing the opportunity for offending, the finding that the duration of the mentoring program (i.e., the longer the program went on) was negatively related to the impact suggests that this did not appear to be the case. Alternatively, this finding could have been because more troublesome persons were given mentoring for longer time periods, or that mentoring was terminated when it appeared to be successful.

The two reviews also differed with respect to some conclusions. For example, the Jolliffe and Farrington (2008) review found a strong relationship between methodological quality of the evaluation and the effect of the mentoring program. That is, the finding that mentoring was related to a reduction in offending was limited to those evaluations of lower quality (i.e., those at Level 3 on the SMS scale). Studies of higher quality (which provide a more valid assessment of the relationship between mentoring and offending) found no relationship. However, the review of Tolan et al. (2008) identified no such impact of the methodological quality of the evaluations. In fact, randomized controlled trials (Level 5 on the SMS) were found to have higher effects than quasi-experimental studies.

Another difference between the reviews was related to the finding of the differential impact of mentoring as a sole intervention. Some mentoring programs include the one-to-one relationship between a mentor and mentee as the only intervention (e.g., Grossman and Tierney 1998), while others include mentoring as part of a multimodal intervention. Other common interventions included alongside mentoring were employment (e.g., Buman and Cain 1991), behavioral treatment (e.g., Davidson and Redner 1988), and counseling and tutoring (Frazier, Richards, and Potter 1981). The review by Tolan et al. (2008) found no difference in offending whether or not mentoring was used as the sole intervention, whereas Jolliffe and Farrington (2008) found that only those evaluations that used mentoring and additional interventions had an impact.

These differences in the findings of the review might be a result of the different inclusion criteria in each review or their different methods of analysis. For example, the Tolan et al. (2008) review included only studies of higher methodological quality (e.g., Level 4 and Level 5 on the SMS), and analyses included all outcomes (delinquency, aggression, drug use, and academic achievement), making it difficult to interpret the impact of mentoring on offending.

Despite these differences, it is clear that the bulk of evidence suggests that unlike some interventions (e.g., Scared Straight; Petrosino, Buehler, and Turpin-Petrosino 2007), mentoring is not harmful. Furthermore, there is some evidence to suggest that mentoring might be beneficial, especially if a strong relationship can be fostered (through persistent contact) between a mentor and mentee. Unfortunately, however, the studies that have been conducted leave many questions unanswered.

Perhaps the most important question concerns how mentoring is generating the observed positive impacts. The general theme and purpose of mentoring seem clear, but even some of the most basic components, such as the one-to-one relationship, don't necessarily exist in mentoring programs that have successfully reduced offending (e.g., Hanlon et al. 2002). Uncovering the mechanism has proved difficult because, as noted by Tolan et al. (2008), there seems to be little interest by either program managers or evaluators in specifying exactly what constitutes mentoring or what takes place in a typical meeting between a mentor and mentee. This might be because no one meeting is like another (e.g., joint recreational activities one day, providing a ride to a job interview the next), but even the impact of this variation could be examined if the information were collected appropriately.

Mentoring as an intervention has been used and evaluated with numerous types of individuals. This includes established "offenders" (e.g., young and adult offenders leaving prison; Barnoski 2002; Johnson and Larson 2003), those diverted from the criminal justice system (Davidson and Redner 1988), and those at risk of becoming offenders because of their personal circumstances (Grossman and Tierney 1998). It isn't clear, however, who would benefit the most from mentoring and at what point in their criminal careers. Given the open remit of many mentoring programs, on the surface it would appear that mentoring might not be sufficiently structured or focused to remediate the more common factors (e.g., thinking skills) associated with entrenched criminal behavior. In fact, the idea of mentoring appears somewhat at odds with the "risk principle," which argues that interventions should be targeted at those more likely to reoffend (Andrews and Bonta 2006). However, even with those more advanced in their criminal careers, there is some emerging evidence that mentoring might be efficacious (e.g., Maguire et al. 2010), perhaps through its ability to keep established offenders engaged with concurrent interventions (e.g., Gur and Miller 2004).

IV. DISCUSSION AND CONCLUSIONS

It is promising that a number of the studies reviewed here used strong designs in assessing peer-risk intervention and, in addition, some of the better studies on mentoring are finding their way into comprehensive reviews of evidence. Although some of the better implemented programs and controlled studies in both areas suggest positive effects, there is a need for more high-quality research to ensure that appropriate inferences are made regarding the size and nature of the intervention effects. At this point there are a host of suggestions for future research that may help in strengthening the ability of researchers to appropriately discern the ideal population, application, and outcome measure to maximize the effects of these programs.

Several points should be strongly considered in future studies of peer-risk interventions. These suggestions cut across research design, measurement, and analytic issues. First, it is important that research more thoroughly investigate issues of targeting in terms of age of youths and risk levels and consider the degree to which findings are replicated across targeted samples and implementation settings (e.g., school/community, urban/rural). Given the fact that many of these programs are currently implemented as part of broader prevention initiatives in school settings, it is also important that there is proper study of the attribution of effects in multifaceted treatment programs, use of appropriate analytic approaches in school-based interventions with multiple units of analysis, and investigation of the potential for underrepresentation of the highest risk youths (Johnson et al. 2008). Researchers should also ensure that they fully measure and analyze the relationship between intervention and peer-risk outcome and more thoroughly investigate the theory underlying these interventions (Howe, Reiss, and Yuh 2002; Weiss 1995). Lastly, further study of the potential for iatrogenic effects (Ang and Hughes 2001; Cho, Hallfors, and Sánchez 2003; Dodge, Dishion, and Lansford 2006; Welsh and Farrington 2007) and analysis of the cost and benefit of such programs are necessary.

As with the literature on peer-risk programs, it is clear that in order to increase the knowledge surrounding mentoring more high-quality research, especially randomized controlled trials, is needed. Ideally, this would include contact diaries completed by both mentors and mentees, follow-up interviews with mentees, information about a number of outcome measures (e.g., self-reported and official offending), and longer follow-up periods. It would also be useful to study the effects of mentoring on reoffending separately for males and females and for different ethnic groups.

Also, future research should make efforts to disentangle the specific influence of mentoring in reducing reoffending. Mentoring may reduce reoffending, but because most interventions apply mentoring along with educational classes, employment, and counseling, it is difficult to disentangle the specific role of mentoring or its interactive effects with other features. This could be addressed by undertaking a randomized controlled trial where individuals were allocated to mentoring or mentoring plus an additional intervention.

It would also be useful to examine the "dose-response" relationship between mentoring and reoffending. If mentoring reduces reoffending by developing strong social bonds between mentors and mentees, then mentoring at a high frequency in the beginning (to facilitate bonding) followed by lower frequency contact later may be sufficient to achieve the desired effect. If, however, mentoring reduces reoffending by removing offending opportunities, then continued high-frequency contact between the mentor and the mentee for a longer duration might be required.

Cost-benefit analyses (see Welsh, Farrington, and Sherman 2001) of these programs would help policymakers evaluate the true benefit of mentoring. The overall evidence appears to suggest that mentoring is moderately beneficial, but there is also evidence to suggest that mentoring programs are challenging to run, and significant resources are needed to recruit mentors who are willing to volunteer (e.g., Newburn and Shiner, 2005; St. James-Roberts et al. 2005). It seems sensible to know the expected benefit of a mentoring program before widespread implementation.

Our review of the impact of peer influence and mentoring programs suggests that these are potentially promising crime-prevention approaches, with the evidence appearing somewhat stronger for mentoring. It is clear, however, that the evidence base surrounding both programs would benefit from additional high-quality research. This should include large-scale randomized controlled trials, but these should be designed with embedded controls and appropriate measurement so that the various underlying mechanisms implicit in the interventions can be adequately tested. Once the more probable mechanisms have been identified, both the design and delivery of peer influence and mentoring programs could be refined to target these, and this might allow the graduation of these two intervention methods from potentially promising to clearly effective.

NOTE

We are grateful to Michael Chou for his research assistance.

REFERENCES

Aos, Steve, Roxanne Lieb, Jim Mayfield, Marna Miller, and Ann Pennucci. 2004. *Benefits and Costs of Prevention and Early Intervention Programs for Youth.* Olympia, WA: Washington State Institute for Public Policy.

Akers, Ronald L. 1973. *Deviant Behavior: A Social Learning Approach.* Belmont, CA: Wadsworth.

Andrews, Don A., and James Bonta. 2006. *The Psychology of Criminal Conduct.* Cleveland, OH: Anderson Publishing.

Ang, Rebecca P., and Jan N. Hughes. 2001. "Differential Benefits of Skills Training with Antisocial Youth Based on Group Composition: A Meta-Analytic Investigation." *School Psychology Review* 31:164–85.

Barnoski, Robert. 2002. *Preliminary Findings for the Juvenile Rehabilitation Administration's Mentoring Program.* Research Report No. 02-07-1202. Olympia, WA: Washington State Institute for Public Policy.

Buman, Bobbi, and Ruth Cain. 1991. *The Impact of Short Term, Work Oriented Mentoring on the Employability of Low-Income-Youth.* Minneapolis, MN: Minneapolis Employment and Training Program.

Cho, Hyunsan, Denise Dion Hallfors, and Victoria Sánchez. 2005. "Evaluation of a High School Peer Group Intervention for High Risk Youth." *Journal of Abnormal Child Psychology* 33:363–74.

Davidson, William S., and Robin Redner. 1988. "Prevention of Juvenile Delinquency: Diversion from the Juvenile Justice System." In *Fourteen Ounces of Prevention: A Casebook for Practitioners,* edited by Richard H. Price, Emory L. Cowen, Raymond P. Lorion, and Julia Ramos-McKay. Washington, DC: American Psychological Association.

Dodge, Kenneth, Thomas J. Dishion, and Jennifer E. Lansford. 2006. "Deviant Peer Influences in Intervention and Public Policy for Youth." *Society for Research in Child Development, Social Policy Report* 20:3–19.

DuRant, Robert H., Shari Barkin, and Daniel P. Krowchuk. 2001. "Evaluation of A Peaceful Conflict Resolution and Violence Prevention Curriculum For Sixth Grade Students." *Journal of Adolescent Health* 28:386–93.

Esbensen, Finn-Aage, and D. Wayne Osgood. 1999. "Gang Resistance Education and Training: Results From the National Evaluation." *Journal of Research in Crime and Delinquency* 36:194–225.

Esbensen, Finn-Aage, D. Wayne Osgood, Terrance J. Taylor, Dana Peterson, and Adrienne Freng. 2001. "How Great is G.R.E.A.T.? Results From a Longitudinal Quasi-Experimental Design." *Criminology and Public Policy* 1:87–118.

Farrell, Albert D., Aleta Meyer, Terri N. Sullivan, and Eva M. Kung. 2003. "Evaluation of the Responding in Peaceful and Positive Ways (RIPP) Seventh Grade Violence Prevention Curriculum." *Journal of Child and Family Studies* 12:101–20.

Farrell, Albert D., Aleta Meyer, and Kamila S. White. 2001. "Evaluation of Responding in Peaceful and Positive Ways (RIPP): A School-Based Prevention Program for Reducing Violence Among Urban Adolescents." *Journal of Clinical Child Psychology* 30:451–63.

Farrell, Albert D., Robert F. Valois, Aleta Meyer, and Ritchie P. Tidwell. 2003. "Impact of the RIPP Violence Prevention Program on Rural Middle School Students." *Journal of Primary Prevention* 24:143–67.

Farrington, David P., and Brandon C. Welsh. 2007. *Saving Children from a Life of Crime: Early Risk Factors and Effective Intervention*. New York: Oxford University Press.

Flay, Brian R., Sally Graumlich, Eisuke Segawa, James L. Burns, Michelle Y. Holiday, and Aban Aya. 2004. "Effects of Two Prevention Programs on High-Risk Behaviors Among African-American Youth." *Archives of Pediatric and Adolescent Medicine* 158:377–84.

Frazier, Charles E., Pamela J. Richards, and Roberto H. Potter. 1981. *Evaluation of the Florida Project Diversion—September 1, 1980—January 31, 1981: Final Report*. Rockville, MD: National Institute of Justice. NCJRS Document Reproduction Service No 81816.

Giordano, Peggy C. 2003. "Relationships in Adolescence." *Annual Review of Sociology* 29:257–81.

Glueck, Sheldon, and Eleanor Glueck. 1950. *Unraveling Juvenile Delinquency*. New York: Commonwealth Fund.

Gottfredson, Gary. 1987. "Peer Group Interventions to Reduce the Risk of Delinquent Behavior: A Selective Review and a New Evaluation." *Criminology* 25:671–714.

Gottfredson, Michael R, and Travis Hirschi. 1990. *A General Theory of Crime*. Stanford, CA: Stanford University Press.

Grossman, Jean Baldwin, and Joseph P. Tierney. 1998. "Does Mentoring Work? An Impact Study of the Big Brothers Big Sisters Program." *Evaluation Review* 22: 404–26.

Gur, Merav, and Lisa Miller. 2004. "Mentoring Improves Acceptance of a Community Intervention for Court-Referred Male Persons in Need of Supervision (PINS)." *Child and Adolescent Social Work Journal* 21:573–91.

Hanlon, Thomas E., Richard W. Bateman, Betsy D. Simon, Kevin E. O'Grady, and Steven B. Carswell. 2002. "An Early Community-Based Intervention for the Prevention of Substance Abuse and Other Delinquent Behavior." *Journal of Youth and Adolescence* 31:459–71.

Harrell, Adele, Shannon Cavanagh, and Sanjeev Sridaharan. 1999. *Evaluation of the Children at Risk Program: Results 1 Year After the End of the Program*. Washington, DC: National Institute of Justice, Office of Justice Programs.

Haynie, Dana, and D. Wayne Osgood. 2005. "Reconsidering Peers and Delinquency: How Do Peers Matter?" *Social Forces* 84:1109–30.

Hirschi, Travis (1969). *Causes of Delinquency*. Berkeley, CA: University of California Press.

Howe, George W, David Reiss, and Jongil Yuh. 2002. "Can Prevention Trials Test Theories of Etiology?" *Development and Psychopathology* 14:673–94.

Johnson, Byron R. and David B. Larson. 2003. *Inner Change Freedom Initiative: A Preliminary Evaluation of a Faith-Based Prison Program*. Huntsville, TX: Center for Research on Religion and Urban Civil Society.

Johnson, Valerie L., Laura J. Holt, Brenna Bry, and Sharon Powell. 2008. "Effects of an Integrated Prevention Program on Urban Youth Transitioning into High School." *Journal of Applied School Psychology* 24:225–46.

Jolliffe, Darrick, and David P. Farrington (2008). *The Influence of Mentoring on Reoffending*. Stockholm, Sweden: Swedish National Council on Crime Prevention.

Lipsey, Mark. W., and Nana A. Landenberger. 2006. "Cognitive-Behavioral Interventions." In *Preventing Crime: What Works for Children, Offenders, Victims, and Places*, edited by Brandon C. Welsh and David. P. Farrington. Dordrecht, The Netherlands: Springer.

Lipsey, Mark, and David Wilson. 1998. "Effective Interventions for Serious Juvenile Offenders: A Synthesis of Research." In *Serious and Violent Juvenile Offenders: Risk Factors and Successful Interventions*, edited by Rolf Loeber and David. Farrington. Thousand Oaks, CA: Sage.

McCord, Joan. 2003. "Cures that Harm: Unanticipated Outcomes of Crime Prevention Programs." *Annals of the American Academy of Political and Social Science* 587: 16–30.

McCord, Joan, and Kevin P. Conway. 2005. *Co-Offending and Patterns of Juvenile Crime.* Washington, DC: National Institute of Justice.

Maguire, Mike, Katy Holloway, Mark Liddle, Fionn Gordon, Paul Gray, Alison Smith, and Sam Wright. 2010. *Evaluation of the Transitional Support Scheme (TSS).* Final Report for the Welsh Assembly Government. Pontypridd, Wales: University of Glamorgan.

Newburn, Tim, and Michael Shiner. 2005. *Dealing with Disaffection: Young People, Mentoring and Social Inclusion.* Cullompton, UK: Willan.

Ngwe, Job E., Li C. Liu, Brian R. Flay, Eisuke Segawa, and Aban Aya Investigators. 2004. "Violence Prevention Among African American Adolescent Males." *American Journal of Health Behaviors* 28(Suppl.): S24–37.

O'Donnell, Clifford R., Tony Lydgate, and Walter S.O. Fo. 1979. "The Buddy System: Review and Follow-up." *Child Behavior Therapy* 1:161–69.

Petrosino, Anthony, John Buehler, and Corolyn Turpin-Petrosino. 2007. *Scared Straight and other Juvenile Awareness Programs for Preventing Juvenile Delinquency.* Oslo, Norway: Campbell Systematic Reviews.

Reiss, Albert J., and David P. Farrington. 1991. "Advancing Knowledge About Co-Offending: Results From A Prospective Longitudinal Survey Of London Males." *Journal of Criminal Law and Criminology* 82:360–95.

Rhodes, Jean E. 1994. "Older and Wiser: Mentoring Relationships in Childhood and Adolescence." *Journal of Primary Prevention* 14:187–96.

St. James-Roberts, Ian, Ginny Greenlaw, Antonia Simon, and Jane Hurry. 2005. *National Evaluation of Youth Justice Board Mentoring Schemes 2001–2004.* London: Youth Justice Board.

St. James-Roberts, Ian, and Clifford S. Singh. 2001. *Can Mentors Help Primary School Children with Behavior Problems?* Research Study No. 233. London: Home Office.

Sharkey, Suzanne. 1998. *Project YES! Pilot Program.* Austin, TX: Austin Independent School District, Office of Program Evaluation.

Sherman, Lawrence W., Denise Gottfredson, Doris MacKenzie, John Eck, Peter Reuter., and Shawn Bushway. 1997. *Preventing Crime: What works, What doesn't, What's Promising. Report to the U.S. Congress.* Washington, DC: US Department of Justice.

Smetana, Judith G., Nicole Campione-Barr, and Aaron Metzger. 2006. "Adolescent Development in Interpersonal and Societal Contexts." *Annual Review of Psychology* 57:255–84.

Sutherland, Edwin H. 1947. *Principles of Criminology*, 4th ed. Philadelphia, PA: Lippincott.

Tarling, Roger, John Burrows, and Alan Clarke. 2001. *Dalston Youth Project Part II (11–14): An Evaluation.* Research Study No. 232. London: Home Office.

Tolan, Patrick, David Henry, Michael Schoeny, and Arin Bass (2008). *Mentoring Interventions to Affect Juvenile Delinquency and Associated Problems.* Oslo, Norway: Campbell Systematic Reviews.

van Lier, Pol, Frank Vitaro, and Manuel Eisner. 2007. "Preventing Aggressive and Violent Behavior: Using Prevention Programs to Study the Role of Peer Dynamics in Maladjustment Problems." *European Journal of Criminal Policy and Research* 13:297–300.

Warr, Mark. 2002. *Companions in Crime: The Social Aspects of Criminal Conduct.* Cambridge, UK: Cambridge University Press.

Weiss, Carol H. 1995. "Nothing as Practical as Good Theory: Exploring Theory Based Evaluation for Comprehensive Community-Based Initiatives for Children and Families." In *New Approaches to Evaluating Community Initiatives. Vol. 1: Concepts,*

Methods and Contexts, edited by James P. Connell, Anne C. Kubisch, Lisbeth B. Schorr, and Carol H. Weiss. Washington, DC: Aspen Institute.

Welsh, Brandon, and David P. Farrington. 2007. "Key Challenges and Prospects in Peer-Based Delinquency Prevention Programs: Comment on van Lier, Vitaro, and Eisner." *European Journal of Criminal Policy and Research* 13:297–300.

Welsh, Brandon C., David P. Farrington, and Lawrence W. Sherman, eds. 2001. *Costs and Benefits of Preventing Crime.* Boulder, CO: Westview Press.

Wright, A. Jordan, Tracy R. Nichols, Julia A. Graber, Jeanne Brooks-Gunn, and Gilbert J. Botvin. 2004. "It's Not What You Say, It's How Many Ways You Can Say It: Links Between Divergent Peer Resistance Skills and Delinquency a Year Later." *Journal of Adolescent Health* 35:380–91.

Wynn, Sheri R., John Schulenberg, Deborah D. Kloska, and Virginia B. Letz. 1997. "The Mediating Influence of Refusal Skills in Preventing Adolescent Alcohol Misuse." *Journal of School Health* 67:390–95.

CHAPTER 12

....

COMPREHENSIVE COMMUNITY PARTNERSHIPS FOR PREVENTING CRIME

....

DENNIS P. ROSENBAUM AND AMIE M. SCHUCK

SCHOLARS of crime prevention argue that programs and policies will achieve maximum effectiveness if they are built on scientific knowledge regarding the nature and causes of crime and delinquency and on knowledge of what works, or "best practices." Over the past two decades, a careful look at this issue has drawn many scholars and practitioners away from singular law-enforcement responses to drugs and violence to endorse coordinated community-wide strategies that address a combination of known risk factors at the individual, family, and neighborhood levels.

We have chosen to define the subject matter as "comprehensive community partnerships." Although scholars of community health and other fields have offered a wide range of definitions, theoretical models, and underlying assumptions (e.g., Merzel and D'Afflitti 2003; Stevenson and Mitchell 2003; Brown et al. 2008), we are seeking parsimony with three terms. The terms that define this approach for us—*community, comprehensive*, and *partnerships*—each has its own empirical and theoretical foundation.

Community approaches to crime are based on the fundamental notion that crime rates at the community level are controlled more by neighborhood context and informal social control processes than by formal social control mechanisms

(Rosenbaum 1988). Neighborhood stability influences the level of social organization among residents, which in turn, determines their capacity to regulate neighborhood crime and delinquency via informal social control (Sampson and Groves 1989; Bursik and Grasmick 1993). Social disorganization—a diminished capacity of local institutions such as families, schools, and community groups to regulate social behavior—is a central problem in urban life. Community crime-prevention strategies, especially social prevention approaches, are based on this reality and are designed to strengthen community capacity to fight back against crime and disorder (Hope 1995; Rosenbaum, Lurigio, and Davis 1998). Studies have shown that crime rates are lower in neighborhoods where residents feel more attached to the neighborhood, report more cohesion, feel more responsible for events that occur in the neighborhood, report a greater willingness to intervene when problems occur, are less prone to avoidance and social withdrawal, and participate more in crime-prevention activities (see Rosenbaum 1988; Skogan 1990, for reviews). At the micro level of street encounters, Wilkinson (2003) has carefully documented how peer social networks contribute to youth gun violence, thus underscoring the potential for community-based prevention to alter these social dynamics. Cullen (1994) argues that social control may not be the only community process operating to prevent urban violence. The signs of neighborhood social disorganization—family disruption, weak friendship networks, and low rates of participation—are also indicators of weak social support. In essence, Cullen argues that to prevent crime, communities need stronger helping networks that provide services and support to youth and families at risk rather than simply stronger punitive controls.

Numerous criminal justice reform efforts over the past two decades have adopted a community oriented approach to solving neighborhood problems. Community policing (Greene and Mastrofksi 1988; Rosenbaum 1994; Skogan and Hartnett 1997), community prosecution (Kelling and Coles 1996), and community justice models (Clear and Karp 1999) all recognize the fundamental importance of community involvement in preventing crime and achieving justice. Furthermore, broader community development and community organizing efforts *outside* the criminal justice/criminology field are designed to economically stabilize neighborhoods and empower local residents to address a wide range of local problems which, in turn, should have crime-prevention benefits. Finally, the rationale for community-based approaches in public health models is grounded in epidemiological notions about the spread of disease. As Rose's (1992) analysis suggests, population-based strategies (i.e., trying to reach large numbers of low-risk individuals) will have a larger impact than high-risk strategies (i.e., targeting a smaller number of high-risk individuals). As Merzel and D'Afflitti (2003, p. 562) note, "even a small shift at the peak of a risk curve can have sizable population effects."

Comprehensive is the second defining feature of these community interventions. The common assumption underlying these diverse initiatives is that crime and other community problems are complex and not easily reduced or prevented by a single strategy or tactic. Comprehensive strategies seek to attack the problem on all fronts (or as many as resources will allow). This requires the identification and targeting of multiple causal mechanisms. Research on adolescent substance abuse, for example, has identified a wide range of risk factors, including individual, family, peer, school, and community influences (see Hawkins, Catalano, and Miller 1992). Similarly, researchers have uncovered a host of developmental, social, and environmental risk factors for criminal behavior that point to different types of prevention programs (see Sherman et al. 2002). Ecological and developmental prevention models also recognize the importance of targeting different structures and sources of influence at different stages in the life cycle (e.g., Bronfenbrenner 1977; Laub and Sampson 2003; Farrington and Welsh 2007). All of these perspectives are consistent with the comprehensive approach to crime prevention, suggesting that a single intervention at a particular point in time will be less effective than carefully targeted multiple interventions over time.

In a nutshell, we are suggesting that because of the multiple and complex causes of crime and substance abuse, comprehensive models are promising because they seek to address these problems from multiple angles, addressing multiple risk factors. As we have argued previously (Rosenbaum 2002; Schuck and Rosenbaum 2006), comprehensive programs can, in theory, target multiple domains of influence (e.g. individuals, families, peers, schools, neighborhood groups, businesses, community norms), multiple causal mechanisms (e.g., public education, parenting skills, opportunity reduction), multiple targets (e.g., at-risk youth at different ages, parents, known gang members), and multiple service providers (e.g., police, schools, social/health service agencies, community groups).

Partnership is the third defining feature of these initiatives. Engaging multiple agencies and organizations in a partnership structure is the most common method of achieving the comprehensiveness described above. While there is no universal definition for partnership, in this essay we are essentially referring to synergistic working relationships between two or more organizations that are designed to achieve common community goals. Many authors have articulated the benefits of partnerships and community coalitions (Prestby and Wandersman 1985; Butterfoss, Goodman, and Wandersman 1993; Cook and Roehl 1993; Kubisch et al. 1995; Rosenbaum 2002; Wandersman 2003; Brown et al. 2008). Partnerships are assumed to bring together diverse agencies and individuals, leverage more resources to address the problem, and coordinate the development and application of interventions. In theory, therefore, partnerships are expected to be more inclusive and responsive to community priorities than single agencies; achieve a greater understanding of risk factors; develop more diverse, creative, and comprehensive strategies; reduce duplication of services and provide better coordination of strategies across agencies; increase agency accountability; strengthen local community organizations; and provide more political clout to garner additional resources. These advantages are expected to result in larger and more sustained impacts on target problems. Larger effects are expected as a result of better targeting of risk factors, a higher dosage of the treatment (more resources), and/or the synergistic effects of exposure to interacting treatments.

After summarizing and assessing the literature, this essay draws several conclusions:

- Comprehensive community partnerships have broad appeal but are difficult to implement because of their complexity. When implemented well, there is some evidence that they can have desired effects on substance abuse and violence for individuals at risk and for larger target populations.
- To be effective, comprehensive community crime-prevention programs require a supportive start-up environment that includes adequate funding and preferably a history of collaborative partnerships; a common purpose or mission that unifies all participating stakeholders; a lead agency that is respected by other agencies and can champion the cause; and a formalized structure, including steering and working committees.
- The most effective partnerships also demonstrate a commitment to evidence-based practice and prevention science, and provide access to training and technical assistance that are needed to build competency at the individual, organizational, programmatic, and relational levels.
- Community involvement is considered important to produce larger effect sizes and establish legitimacy for particular interventions, strategies, and agencies. The challenges to community engagement, however, are enormous, including representativeness, differential power in decision making and funding, and cultural and political differences in styles of interacting.
- Evaluations of comprehensive community prevention initiatives also face a host of unique obstacles and challenges, including difficulty isolating causal factors in complex settings and the time required for prevention processes to show results. We encourage the use of multisite randomized control trials to increase confidence that the observed changes are attributable to collaborative partnerships.
- Despite the many challenges to both implementation and evaluation, these obstacles are not insurmountable. Indeed, comprehensive community initiatives have been implemented with high fidelity, and rigorous community-level randomized trials have been successfully conducted to estimate community-wide effects.

This essay examines comprehensive community initiatives to prevent crime, violence, and drug abuse, giving special attention to the role of partnerships/coalitions as the primary vehicle for conceiving, executing, and maintaining these crime-prevention strategies. Section I summarizes and interprets a substantial literature on coalitions largely outside the public safety domain. Here, we review the evidence regarding program impact and identify factors that determine partnership effectiveness, with an eye toward lessons that can be transferred to crime prevention. Turning to crime prevention, section II summarizes a wide array of efforts in the United States to prevent youth violence by introducing comprehensive community strategies. Section III provides a discussion of the common themes and conclusions to emerge from these literatures and underscores some of the central challenges to both implementation and evaluation of comprehensive coalitions.

I. Comprehensive Approaches to Community Capacity Building

Before examining community-based violence prevention, there is much that we can learn from a substantial body of research on comprehensive community initiatives in the public health field. In the United States, there have been several large-scale community-based collaborative partnerships that involve careful documentation and evaluation. These include the Fighting Back Initiative in 15 communities (Saxe et al. 1997), the Midwest Prevention Project in 26 communities (Pentz 1998), the Community Partnership program in 24 communities (Yin et al. 1997), and the Communities That Care program in 24 communities (Hawkins, Catalano, and Associates 1992). Some of these evaluations have yielded promising impact results. For example, an evaluation of the Midwest Prevention Project found that significant reductions in adolescents' use of cigarettes, alcohol, and marijuana were associated with a comprehensive approach that included mass-media education, school-based education, parent education and organizing, community organizing, and changes in health policy (Pentz et al. 1989). Communities That Care is another good example of success, illustrating how a coordinated community-wide program can prevent early alcohol and drug use by tackling risk factors in the family, school, and community (Hawkins et al. 2009).

These programs are impressive, but they are not typical. Despite the enthusiasm for comprehensive collaborative partnerships, the research literature paints a less rosy picture. In one major review of 68 studies of public health collaboratives (Kreuter, et al. 2000), the authors identified only a half dozen in which significant changes in health status or health systems could be attributed to the collaborative. Roussos and Fawcett (2000), however, offer a slightly more positive conclusion after reviewing 34 studies of public health collaboratives mostly involving quasi-experimental or experimental designs. The health concerns were quite diverse, including substance abuse, adolescent pregnancy, heart disease, violence, health services, HIV/AIDS, immunization, infant mortality, lead poisoning, and nutrition. Ten of the 34 studies showed some improvement in distant population-level outcomes relative to controls (e.g., lead poisoning, infant mortality, teen pregnancy, alcohol-involved vehicle crashes). Also, improvements in behavioral outcomes were observed for many of the 15 studies that included such measures, including tobacco use, alcohol use, illicit drug use, physical activity, and safer sexual practices.

Some of the larger and more rigorous studies, however, have not yielded these positive effects. A large smoking cessation study, with random assignment of communities, did not change the rate of quitting among heavy smokers and had only weak effects on light smokers after four years (COMMIT Research Group 1995). The Community Partnership program in 24 communities showed no real effects on reported use of alcohol and illicit drugs over a one-year period when the data were pooled (Yin et al. 1997). The Fighting Back program in 12 sites produced no effects on youth and community outcomes and resulted in negative effects on adults relative to matched controls (Hallfors et al. 2002).

There have been many large-scale studies and literature reviews regarding community-based coalitions in the public health field (see Yin et al. 1997; Kreuter, Lezin, and Young 2000; Pentz 2000; Roussos and Fawcett 2000; Berkowitz 2001; Hallfors et al. 2002; Merzel and D'Afflitti 2003; Stevenson and Mitchell 2003; Brown et al. 2008). The overall conclusion is this: there is some evidence that collaborative partnerships are associated with desired community outcomes and system changes such as new programs, policies, and practices. These effects have been achieved by building community capacity, by increasing service integration, and by influencing policy change (Stevenson and Mitchell 2003). Collectively, however, this body of work suggests that community-level outcomes are weak—that is, that effect sizes are small for community partnerships. By asking why, we can learn a lot about the strengths and weaknesses of this approach.

A. Explanations for Limited Effectiveness

Researchers have offered a variety of explanations for the modest effects of collaborative community-based partnerships: (1) this approach is truly ineffective and based on a poorly developed theoretical model; (2) designers have failed to utilize scientific evidence regarding prevention; (3) partnerships are not well implemented or well functioning; (4) programs developed by these collaboratives suffer from weak implementation and short duration; (5) evaluation methods and measures are inadequate and insensitive to partnership effects. There is some truth to each of these alternative explanations. In terms of the evaluations, the paucity of randomized control trials, interrupted time series designs, low statistical power, specific measures of mediating processes, and precise partnership theories make it more difficult to interpret existing results. Given the complexity of collaborative partnerships and community-level interventions, researchers are constrained in their ability to isolate the effects of any particular strategy or component.

The delivery of community-wide interventions within collaborative partnerships can be fraught with problems that limit the size of program effects. These delivery problems include limited duration of the program, inadequate tailoring to particular conditions or segments of the community, limited community penetration into the overall population, and inability to reach different targeting levels. Merzel and D'Afflitti (2003) refer to the latter as "limited ecological reach." Ecological theory encourages the targeting of multiple levels (individual, social networks, community environments) and the use of multiple interventions; but often, community-based initiatives are unable to achieve this ecological reach. Instead, they focus on individual-level change rather than community change.

B. Partnership Implementation Success

From case studies to multisite analyses, we have learned a great deal about partnership implementation issues and why some collaboratives flourish while many others do not (Gray, 1989; Butterfoss, Goodman, and Wandersman 1993; Chavis et al., 1993;

Kreuter, Lezin, and Young 2000). One review (Foster-Fishman et al., 2001) suggests that to achieve maximum effectiveness, capacity building needs to occur at different levels—individual member level capacity, relational capacity, organizational capacity, and programmatic capacity. Each level carries a long list of recommendations to achieve competency. In another review (Kreuter, Lezin, and Young 2000) researchers argue that community colloboratives move through different stages—preformation, formation, implementation, and maintenance—and need special attention/training in the early stages to prevent common problems (e.g., conflicts over power, cultural differences).

Stevenson and Mitchell (2003, p. 384) summarize the factors that are cited frequently as predictors of successful implementation and survival of community-based partnerships:

> a supportive social context in the formative stages (e.g., funding streams coordinated to provide an incentive to collaborate rather than compete; a history of collaborative power-sharing); an initial structure designed purposefully (lead agency with credibility and resources; leadership with process skills and vision; size of group and level of organizational representation appropriate to tasks); formalized structure and task-focused work groups (to aid a sense of instrumental effectiveness and promote continued participation); anticipation of turnover in membership and leadership; and processes to deal with the inevitability of external change, conflict, and competition.

Indeed, research has shown that successful implementation of key components is associated with successful outcomes and community change. A systematic review by Roussos and Fawcett (2000) of 34 studies covering 252 community health collaborative partnerships identified seven factors (each with empirical support) that determine a partnership's capacity to make a difference in community and system outcomes. These are: (1) having a clear vision and mission; (2) engaging in action planning for community and system change; (3) developing and supporting strong leadership; (4) documenting and providing feedback; (5) having access to technical assistance and support; (6) securing financial resources for the work; and (7) making sure that outcomes are a priority that matter to the core partners.

In addition to the importance of team dynamics, research suggests that community-level factors are predictive of partnership functioning. A review by Feinberg, Ridenour, and Greenberg (2008) indicates that coalitions located in low-income communities with fewer institutional supports are more likely to experience mistrust, low functioning, and failure.

Many writers have expressed concern about the long-term survival of community-wide coalitions and how to achieve institutionalization. Certainly, continued financial support has been shown repeatedly to be important for survival (Hallfors et al. 2002; Gomez, Greenberg, and Feinberg 2005), as well as many of the factors listed above. Also, a review of large-scale substance abuse demonstrations by Pentz (2000) finds that longevity is a function of whether organizations are able to move successfully from planning to implementation within two years and whether they are able to successfully make policy changes as part of the prevention program, including fund raising and institutionalizing services. To achieve these objectives, they need a "champion." Pentz (2000) concludes that institutionalization of community-wide drug prevention is problematic because community leaders do not feel empowered to continue prevention work and are not prepared to utilize evidence-based programs. But programs can be sustained with careful planning, leadership, training and technical assistance.

C. Evidence-based Practice

There is widespread agreement in the literature on the importance of research and evaluation data to help plan, document, and evaluate partnership activities. Many studies have concluded that the failure to translate prevention science knowledge into practice has played a major role in limiting the effectiveness of comprehensive community collaborations (Pentz 2000; Wandersman 2003; Brown et al. 2008). Hence, there has been a push to close this gap and test the role of science in community-based initiatives.

When we talk about an "evidence-based" or "prevention science" paradigm, we are talking about a process that involves: (1) the identification and assessment of a community problem with research tools; (2) an analysis of the nature of the problem, especially a determination of risk and protective factors; (3) the development and implementation of strategies that are based on these local identified factors and/or evidence-based practices elsewhere ("best practices"); and (4) the scientific evaluation of implementation processes and outcomes with feedback to the participating parties.

The fundamental question here is, will adding a scientific/research component to community programming make a difference? More specifically, will the evidence-based model help in the creation, maintenance, or effectiveness of collaborative partnerships? One of the few efforts to test the contribution of prevention science within a collaborative framework is the Communities That Care (CTC) program, which is designed to prevent adolescent substance abuse and delinquency (Hawkins, Catalano, and Associates 1992; Hawkins et al. 2008). The Community Youth Development Study (CYDS) is a community-level randomized trial of the CTC system, with 24 small towns matched within seven states prior to random assignment.

Several conclusions are possible to date. First, we have learned that the model can be successfully implemented. The 12 CTC communities significantly out-performed 12 control communities between 2001 and 2004 in terms of their adoption of science-based approach, collaboration across sectors, and collaboration on specific prevention activities (Brown et al., 2007). Second, we have learned that the model can lead to significant changes in key community-level outcomes. While the CTC and control communities were equivalent on baseline outcome measures (Hawkins et al. 2008), annual student survey data ($N = 4407$) revealed that rates of alcohol, cigarette, and smokeless tobacco initiation and delinquent behavior were significantly lower in CTC communities than control communities for each grade level from fifth through eighth (Hawkins et al. 2009).

The results suggest that community prevention colloboratives can make a difference in the community when they adopt a scientific evidence-based model and when they are supported by extensive training, technical assistance, and guiding materials. Several studies have examined coalition processes in 21 CTC boards in Pennsylvania. One study found that "community readiness" increases internal coalition functioning (e.g., less infighting) which in turn increases perceived effectiveness (Feinberg, Greenberg, and Osgood 2004). Another study found that board activities were more likely to be sustained after three years when members reported greater knowledge of prevention, when coalition internal functioning was higher, and when the processes were more true to the original CTC model (Gomez, Greenberg, and Feinberg 2005).

II. Comprehensive Approaches
to Gang Violence

Youth gangs have been part of the urban landscape for more than a century and have emerged in cities and communities around the world (Hagedorn 2010). In the 21st century, virtually all US cities serving populations greater than 250,000 have reported a gang problem, and gangs have spread to many smaller communities as well (Egley 2005). The problem is that youth gangs account for a sizable percentage of urban violence (e.g., Rosenbaum and Stephens 2005). Longitudinal studies indicate that gang-involved youth are substantially more delinquent and violent than youth not affiliated with gangs (Hawkins et al. 1998; Thornberry, Huizinga, and Loeber 2004). Thus, the sheer volume and severity of the gang problem demands that communities develop effective strategies to reduce/prevent gang violence.

Over the past century, communities have sought to reduce gang problems by improving community conditions (primary prevention), improving services for at-risk youth (secondary prevention), persuading/helping gang members to give up gang-related activity (intervention), or using legal/social controls to reduce gang crime (suppression). Comprehensive community approaches to youth gangs are not new. The comprehensive model implemented in the 1931 Chicago Area Project included the prevention of juvenile delinquency (Shaw and McKay 1942). The Boston Mid-City project of the 1950s and the Mobilization for Youth program in the 1960s also sought to increase public safety though the partnering of government and non-profit organizations with community involvement (Miller 1962; Marris and Rein 1967). In the 1980s and 1990s, suppression by law enforcement agencies became the dominant strategy for combating gang violence in the United States, but this approach, by itself, has not been successful (Reed and Decker 2002; Sherman et al. 2002). In part, the ineffectiveness of police suppression programs can be attributed to a failure to address the underlying individual, family, and community factors that contribute to gang activity and the need for coordinated responses.

From the early days of research on gangs (Thrasher 1927), we have known that gangs arise when family, schools, and communities are ineffective at socializing youth and meeting their needs, especially in the context of neighborhood poverty. Risk of gang violence and gang membership are associated with economic and racial segregation, lack of employment, inadequate education, and inadequate parenting, among other factors (see Curry and Spergel 1992). High levels of neighborhood social disorganization, violence, and drug markets provide a fertile environment for the growth of gangs (see Howell 1998; Thornberry 2001). Collectively, these factors weaken the capacity of families, schools, and communities to exercise social control and social support and to create self-regulating neighborhoods.

This knowledge of gang etiology and program effectiveness set the stage for the development of more comprehensive models in the late 1980s and early 1990s. To effectively address the problem of gang violence, communities would need to reach beyond the criminal justice system to address risk factors. Although macro-structural factors can seem insurmountable (e.g., reducing poverty), programs can reasonably expect to strengthen individual, family, and community capacities via social services, crisis intervention, community empowerment, and suppression. Prior research suggests that some service components can make a difference. Positive impacts on individual gang members have been shown by offering employment and individual outreach, and serious juvenile offenders appear to benefit from counseling, behavioral interventions, and interpersonal skill building (Howell 2000; Cullen 2005; Lipsey, Wilson, and Cothern 2000). An important remaining question is whether comprehensive, integrated initiatives could be developed and implemented with sufficient integrity to effectively impact the gang violence problem.

A. The Comprehensive Gang Model

After conducting a national study of gang problems and existing programs in the United States, Irving Spergel and his colleagues at the University of Chicago proposed a comprehensive intervention model (Spergel et al. 1994). This approach—now called the Spergel Model or the Office of Juvenile Justice and Delinquency Prevention (OJJDP) Comprehensive Gang Model—was first tested in Chicago, and has since gone through several iterations and refinements. Here, we provide a brief overview of this evolution of demonstration programs and their impact on the target problem (see also Cahill et al. 2008; Office of Juvenile Justice and Delinquency Prevention 2008). Although the impact evaluations are typically quasi-experiments with only moderate internal validity, they have nevertheless yielded a wealth of information.

The Spergel Model can be distilled into five key intervention strategies:

1. *Suppression*: Using formal social controls by criminal justice agencies (e.g., arrest, imprisonment, monitoring) in conjunction with informal social controls by community-based agencies and organizations (reporting gang activity, supervision of youth) to deter gang-involved individuals.
2. *Social Intervention*: Reaching out to gang-involved youth and their families and other at-risk youth and linking them to services tailored to their individual needs.
3. *Opportunities Provision*: Offering a range of education, training, employment, and social opportunities for gang-involved youth.

4. *Community Mobilization*: Efforts to engage local residents (including former gang members), community groups, and various agencies in a comprehensive and coordinated set of services and interventions.
5. *Organizational Change and Development*: Creating a planning and development process that maximizes the effective use of current and future resources. This involves building community capacity, especially the capacity of organizations to work together in a coordinated partnership.

The Spergel/OJJPD model is distinctive in several ways. First, it focuses on individual youth and seeks to provide each one with a tailored cocktail of services to meet their specific needs. Second, it seeks to introduce a comprehensive coordinated approach that involves a network of partners including various criminal justice agencies, the schools, social service agencies, youth agencies, businesses, community groups and the entire local community. Although each of the component models could represent a different agency, the model is flexible and can be adapted to community needs. (The only required agencies are police, grassroots organizations, and a jobs program.) Third, the model proposes a problem-solving and consensus-building process with a series of steps to achieve successful implementation and build community capacity. These steps include the community acknowledging the gang problem, assessing the nature and causes of the gang problem, identifying the target problem, identifying existing resources, and developing programs and policies to strengthen current responses or introduce new coordinated interventions. Key structural elements include a lead agency to manage the initiative, a steering committee representing partner agencies, and policies/mechanisms to encourage communication and coordination within the network. The participation of former gang-involved individuals on crisis intervention and service teams is also a distinctive feature of the Spergel/OJJDP model. Finally, we should note that, for the demonstration sites, this model has been accompanied by extensive training and technical assistance from a team of experts.

1. *Demonstration Projects and Outcomes*

a. *Early Demonstrations.* The comprehensive gang model was first tested in 1993 in Chicago's Little Village neighborhood, a Mexican-American community with a serious gang problem. The evaluation results were encouraging, as members of the two targeted gangs reported fewer violent and property offenses in a pre/post design and fewer arrests relative to controls that received minimal or no services (Spergel 2007). Although the overall pattern of results was mixed, the Little Village demonstration provided the impetus for OJJDP to fund an additional five cities and provide a larger test of the comprehensive model from 1995 to 1998. The key goals were to reduce gang crime and build community capacity to respond effectively to gang problems. The evaluation (Spergel, Wa, and Sosa 2006) found that the comprehensive model was able to show reductions in gang-related violence and/or arrests among the target population relative to controls in three of six locations: Chicago, Meza (Arizona), and Riverside (California); no changes were found in Bloomington-Normal (Illinois), San Antonio (Texas), and Tucson

(Arizona). Based on considerable field work, the evaluators explain the difference in out-comes in terms of implementation success. The three sites with successful outcomes were judged to have substantially higher levels of program implementation on an 18-dimen-sion index. Success was attributed to well-integrated and collaborative interventions, highly skilled staff, and a balanced approach that did not rely entirely on suppression. Also, increased treatment "dosage" for the targeted gang members (defined by more fre-quent and lengthy services by multiple providers) was associated with fewer arrests for violent crime, especially for older gang members and females. In sum, the early demon-strations suggest that a combination of prevention, intervention, and suppression strat-egies, when implemented with fidelity, can make a difference in gang violence. But for many sites, creating a fully-functioning multi-organization, multi-strategy initiative proved to be too difficult, even with considerable training and technical assistance; thus, they pursued one or two anti-gang strategies with limited or no interagency cooperation.

   b. *Safe Futures Program.* Using the Spergel model as a springboard, OJJDP funded six Safe Futures sites in 1995—Seattle (WA), St. Louis (MO), Boston (MA), Fort Belknap (ND), Contra Costa County (CA), and Imperial Valley (CA). Each site was given sub-stantial funding to engage in a more extensive assessment and planning process than previous demonstrations. The preliminary results of the national assessment indicate that implementation of the comprehensive model remains problematic despite addi-tional time and resources, but most sites were successful at creating interagency partnerships and deciding on appropriate youth services. Impact results are available only for St. Louis (Decker et al. 2002), and they show that the control group outper-formed the treatment group in terms of having fewer court referrals and police con-tacts. The evaluators were not surprised given that the model was not well implemented and that most targeted youth did not receive multiple services.

   c. *Rural Demonstrations.* Between 1999 and 2002, OJJDP decided to test the Comprehensive Gang Model in four rural communities. Two did not have a gang problem, but two did try to implement the model with mixed success. No impact data were collected, but an interim process evaluation (National Council on Crime and Delinquency 2000) concluded that the project coordinator was essential to suc-cess and that achieving an inclusive and diverse steering committee was directly related to the level of effort expended. Assessing the problem and developing a plan of action was a significant challenge for the steering committees, suggesting the need for technical assistance with research-related tasks.

   d. *Gang Reduction Program.* In 2003, OJJDP continued to build on its strong history of comprehensive gang initiatives by introducing the Gang Reduction Pro-gram (GRP). Funded in four cities (Los Angeles, Milwaukee, North Miami Beach, and Richmond), the GRP model was defined by OJJDP as "comprehensive, inte-grated and coordinated." (See Cahill et al. 2008, p. 17, for details). The GRP model shares many of the central features of prior generations of comprehensive gang pro-grams (e.g., collaborative planning and implementation), but reaches beyond the pri-mary target group of gang-involved youth and extends the strategic options. The range of approaches includes primary prevention (e.g., health and social services), secondary prevention (e.g., services for at-risk youth), intervention (e.g., outreach to gang-involved youth), gang suppression (targeted enforcement and graduated sanctions), and reentry (e.g., services to gang members returning home after incarceration). In addition to individual needs, the GRP seeks to address community needs. The GRP also incorporates the data-based planning process found in other criminal justice partnership models, such as the Strategic Approaches to Public Safety Initiative and Project Safe Neighborhoods (see Rosenbaum and Roehl 2010).

The impact evaluation showed that in Los Angeles the Gang Reduction Program was associated with a significant reduction in crime, gang-related serious crime, and citizen reports of shots fired with no evidence of displacement effects (Cahill et al. 2008). But positive results were not observed in all program sites. The authors found that in two of the Gang Reduction Program sites (Milwaukee and North Miami Beach), there were no significant reductions on key public safety measures; and in one site (Richmond), serious violence and gang-related problems actually increased. Researchers suggest that fractured implementation of the program, as well as strategies that increased awareness and crime reporting, may help explain why the partnerships were not effective at these sites. The program was discontinued in Milwaukee where leadership was the weakest, but institutionalized in Los Angeles as part of a citywide gang initiative.

e. *CeaseFire.* The latest adaptation of the Spergel model is the CeaseFire program, which started in Chicago in 1999. It has received national attention and has been adopted in other US cities. As a partnership that involves churches, community organizations, law enforcement, and staff program, CeaseFire seeks to change the behavior of high-risk youth on the streets who are likely gunshot victims or offenders and to change community norms about violence by using a public health model. Using outreach workers and "violence interrupters" on the street (often former gang members), the program interrupts retaliations and offers gang members alternative ways of thinking about their future. An evaluation by Skogan et al. (2008) found that the Chicago CeaseFire program was reaching its target audience with a range of services. Furthermore, the impact evaluation revealed that shootings and/or homicides declined in most of the target areas being studied relative to comparison areas and that the size and intensity of the shooting hot spots decreased in more than half of the sites. A similar program in Baltimore has yielded positive preliminary results (Webster, Vernick, and Mendel 2009), yet a comparable program in Pittsburgh has had no impact on homicides and is associated with increased rates of aggravated assaults and gun assaults (Wilson, Chermak, and McGarrell 2010). Implementation failures (i.e., targeting the wrong youth) may account for the lack of effects in Pittsburgh.

f. *Strategic Criminal Justice Partnerships.* Finally, gangs and gun violence have been approached through the development of problem-solving partnerships among community organizations, social service agencies, and law enforcement. In the early 1990s, the Boston Gun Project (also called Operation Ceasefire) was created as a result of university researchers' teaming up with practitioners to address the problem of juvenile gang homicides and gun violence in Boston. Research, strategic problem solving, and multi-agency collaboration were the key elements of the approach. A "pulling levers" intervention was eventually implemented, which focused resources on a small group of gang-involved repeat offenders. The Boston program was associated with substantial reductions in youth homicides, shots fired, and gun assaults (see Braga et al. 2001). The Department of Justice sought to replicate this planning process on a larger scale by funding the Strategic Approaches to Community Safety Initiative (SACSI) in 10 cities and, eventually, Project Safe Neighborhoods (PSN) in nearly all federal jurisdictions. Both SACSI and PSN build upon the Boston experience by creating a steering committee of federal and local law enforcement agencies, service providers, community leaders, and researchers to introduce a "carrot and stick" approach with known gun users (McGarrell et al. 2009; Klofas, Hipple, and McGarrell 2010). These initiatives often combine suppression and deterrence strategies (e.g., threats of federal prosecution for gun crimes) with risk-factor reduction services (e.g., employment, housing, substance abuse treatment, and educational services).

The evidence suggests that strategic criminal justice partnerships can be effective in reducing crime. In a national multisite study of PSN in the United States, McGarrell et al. (2009) found an 8 percent drop in violent crime in the target cities and no change in comparison cities. In the cross-site study of SACSI, researchers found that intervention sites experienced larger decreases in homicides than comparison sites (Roehl et al. 2005; Rosenbaum and Roehl 2010). One Chicago study found that offender notification meetings (where offenders are offered help to change their lifestyle while being threatened with federal prosecution for future gun crimes) was the most effective partnership strategy for reducing violence (Papachristo, Meares, and Fagan 2006). National PSN data suggest that effective partnerships were more likely to have a lead agency that was viewed as trustworthy and able to get things done, such as the US Attorney's office. McGarrell et al (2009) concluded that when the PSN partnerships were functioning well and able to "fully adopt" the strategic process, the effects were stronger than when the model was only partially adopted or not at all. Similar to the community health initiatives, PSN and SACSI encouraged evidence-based strategic planning with a defined role for researchers. A primary concern, however, regarding these criminal justice partnership models is making sure that community participation and viewpoints are incorporated and respected (Rosenbaum 2002).

III. Discussion and Conclusions

Comprehensive community partnerships have been widely employed in public health and now in criminal justice as a vehicle to effect change in individuals, organizations, and communities. Despite their theoretical and political appeal, collaborative partnerships are very difficult to implement. When implemented well, there is some evidence that they can have desired effects on substance abuse and violence for individuals at risk and for larger target populations. More typically, however, the model is not fully implemented and program effects are small or nonsignificant.

Several decades of research across a wide range of social problems point to a common set of conditions that are needed to create and sustain effective comprehensive community partnerships. These conditions include: (1) a supportive start-up environment with adequate funding and a history of collaborative partnerships; (2) a common purpose or mission that unifies all participating stakeholders; (3) a lead agency that is respected by other agencies; (4) leadership that can champion the cause, stimulate problem solving, resolve conflicts, and maintain group cohesiveness; (5) a formalized structure, including a steering committee (with appropriate community representation) that can develop strategies, make decisions, and leverage resources for implementation, and a working group that can fully execute action plans and strategies; (6) a commitment to evidence-based practice and prevention science; and (7) access to training and technical assistance to build competency at the individual, organizational, programmatic, and relational levels.

We emphasize the importance of three interdependent factors in this list that contribute to success by building organizational capacity in the early stages of development. First, the partnership should be committed to evidence-based practice and a research-grounded strategic planning process to facilitate an understanding of risk and protective factors and to identify best practices in the field. Second, the partnership should be willing to receive technical assistance on prevention science, problem solving and strategic planning, and the management of relations in multi-agency partnerships. Third, the partnership should have a strong leader who promotes this commitment to evidence, encourages technical assistance, and has the full trust and confidence of the partnership members.

One of the themes in collaborative community initiatives is the need to be inclusive and representative and serve as an empowering mechanism for the community. For initiatives that define a role for the community or seek to implement population-wide interventions, community involvement is critical and can produce larger effect sizes, as has been shown in the case of HIV community programming (see Merzel and D'Afflitti 2003). However, the challenges of community engagement are enormous, including achieving representativeness (which is difficult to define); giving community members a voice in the process; resolving cultural and political differences in styles of interacting; distributing funds equitably; and being sensitive to differential power in decision making and resources. Community engagement is a substantial problem in partnerships that involve criminal justice agencies with a history of distrust from minority communities (for a fuller discussion of community issues, see Rosenbaum 2002).

We would be remiss if we did not mention that *evaluations* of comprehensive community prevention initiatives, especially with multisite demonstrations, face a host of unique obstacles and challenges that threaten valid conclusions (Kaftarian and Hansen 1994; Murray, Moskowitz, and Dent 1996; Rosenbaum 2002). First, comprehensive interventions—because they are comprehensive—make it especially difficult to isolate causal mechanisms when so much is going on at the same time. Second, multisite interventions, although sharing some common features, are frequently characterized as having a predominance of localized treatments (or unique operationalizations of the same constructs), thus making it difficult to estimate program effects across sites and establish both construct validity and external validity. Third, the nested structure of the data (i.e., individuals clustered within communities) requires additional statistical attention and multilevel (hierarchical) analysis. Fourth, prevention programs seek to modify individual and community processes that, in theory, require many years to change either because of the time required to impact youth developmental processes or the stability of the macro-level structures being targeted.

In the absence of randomized control trials, we cannot be sure that observed changes are attributable to collaborative partnerships (internal validity). More research is needed to estimate the effects of collaboratives per se on community outcomes. With respect to construct validity, the "black box" of comprehensive community partnerships must be opened, as "comprehensive" often means something different in different settings. Clear logic models should be articulated and tested to identify specific causal mechanisms and pathways (Rosenbaum 2002). Stevenson and Mitchell (2003) propose four elements that must be defined in order to adequately assess the impact of collaboratives: (1) intervention mechanisms; (2) structure, membership, and engagement; (3) intermediate indicators of collaborative activity; and (4) long-term outcomes. More work is needed to determine whether observed outcomes are related to the type, intensity, duration, or penetration of the treatment across settings. Also, more research is needed to document the effects of partnerships on community and organizational outcomes given that much of the current research is limited to individual-level effects. Finally, research measuring the political, economic, and organizational context in which partnerships operate is needed to help determine the probability that such collaboratives will be institutionalized.

As the reader can deduce, the challenges to both implementation and evaluation are numerous but, we would argue, not insurmountable. In fact, comprehensive community initiatives have been implemented with high fidelity, and rigorous community-level randomized trials have been successfully conducted to estimate community-wide effects. With the continued collaboration of researchers and practitioners, we have every reason to expect future gains in the prevention of crime as a result of comprehensive community partnerships.

REFERENCES

Berkowitz, Bill. 2001. "Studying the Outcomes of Community-Based Coalitions." *American Journal of Community Psychology*, 29:213–27.

Braga, Anthony A., David M. Kennedy, Elin J. Waring, and Anne M. Piehl. 2001."Problem-Oriented Policing, Deterrence, and Youth Violence: An Evaluation of Boston's Operation Ceasefire." *Journal of Research in Crime and Delinquency*, 38(3): 195–225.

Bronfenbrenner, Urie. 1977. "Toward an Experimental Ecology of Human Development." *American Psychologist* (July): 513–31.

Brown, Eric C., David J. Hawkins, Michael W. Arthur, Robert D. Abbott., and M. Lee Van Horn. 2008. "Multilevel Analysis of a Measure of Community Prevention Collaboration." *American Journal of Community Psychology*, 41:115–26.

Brown, Eric C., David J. Hawkins, Michael W. Arthur, John S. Briney, and Robert D. Abbott. 2007. "Effects of 'Communities That Care' on Prevention Services Systems:

Findings from the Community Youth Development Study at 1.5 Years." *Prevention Science* 8(3): 180–91.

Bursik, Robert J., and Harold G. Grasmick. 1993. *Neighborhoods and Crime: The Dimensions of Effective Community Control.* New York: Lexington.

Butterfoss, Frances D., Robert. M. Goodman, and Abraham Wandersman. 1993. "Community Coalitions for Prevention and Health Promotion." *Health Education Research* 8:315–30.

Cahill, Meagan, Mark Coggeshal, David Hayeslip, Ashley Wolff, Erica Lagerson, Michelle L. Scott, Elizabeth Davies, Kevin Roland, and Scott Decker. 2008. *Community Collaboratives Addressing Youth Gangs: Interim Findings from the Gang Reduction Program.* Washington, DC: The Urban Institute.

Chavis, David M., Paul Speer, Ira Resnick, and Allsion Zippay. 1993. "Building Community Capacity to Address Alcohol and Drug Abuse: Getting to the Heart of the Problem." In *Drugs and the Community: Involving Community Residents in Combatting the Sale of Illegal Drugs,* edited by Robert C. Davis, Arthur J. Lurigio, and Dennis. P. Rosenbaum. Springfield, IL: Charles C. Thomas.

Clear, Todd R., and David R. Karp. 1999. *The Community Justice Ideal: Preventing Crime and Achieving Justice.* Boulder, CO: Westview Press.

COMMIT Research Group. 1995. "Community Intervention Trial for Smoking Cessation I. Cohort Results from a Four-Year Community Intervention." *American Journal of Public Health* 85:183–91.

Cook, Royer F., and Janice A. Roehl. 1993. "National Evaluation of the Community Partnership Program: Preliminary Findings." In *Drugs and the Community: Involving Community Residents in Combatting the Sale of Illegal Drugs,* edited by Robert C. Davis, Arthur J. Lurigio, and Dennis. P. Rosenbaum. Springfield, IL: Charles C. Thomas.

Cullen, Francis T. 1994. "Social Support as an Organizing Concept for Criminology: Presidential Address to the Academy of Criminal Justice Sciences." *Justice Quarterly* 11:527–59.

Cullen, Francis T. 2005. "The Twelve People Who Saved Rehabilitation: How the Science of Criminology Made a Difference." *Criminology* 43:1–42.

Curry, G. David, and Irving A. Spergel 1992. "Gang Involvement and Delinquency among Hispanic and African American Adolescent Males." *Journal of Research in Crime and Delinquency* 29:273–91.

Decker, Scott H., G. David Curry, H. Arlen Egley, Eric Baumer, Maria Weldle, and Adam Bossler. 2002. *Evaluation of the St. Louis Safe Futures Program.* St. Louis, MO: University of Missouri-St. Louis.

Dunworth, Terence, Gregory Mills, Gary Cordner, and Jack Greene. 1999. *National Evaluation of Weed and Seed: Cross-Site Analysis.* Washington, DC: US Department of Justice, Office of Justice Programs, National Institute of Justice.

Egley, Arlen, Jr. 2005. *Highlights of the 2002–2003 National Youth Gang Survey.* Washington, DC: US Department of Justice, Office of Justice Programs, Office of Juvenile Justice and Delinquency Prevention.

Farrington, David P., and Brandon C. Welsh. 2007. *Saving Children from a Life of Crime: Early Risk Factors and Effective Interventions.* New York: Oxford University Press.

Feinberg, Mark E., M. T. Greenberg, and Dwayne W. Osgood. 2004. "Readiness, Functioning, and Perceived Effectiveness in Community Prevention Coalitions: A Study of Communities That Care." *American Journal of Community Psychology* 33(3/4): 163–76.

Feinberg, Mark E., Ty A. Ridenour, and Mark T. Greenberg. 2008. "The Longitudinal Effect of Technical Assistance Dosage on the Functioning of Communities That Care Prevention Boards in Pennsylvania." *Journal of Primary Prevention* 29(2): 145–65.

Foster-Fishman, Pennie G., Shelby L. Berkowitz, David W. Lounsbury, Stephanie Jacobson, and Nicole A. Allen. 2001. "Building Collaborative Capacity in Community Coalitions: A Review and Integrative Framework." *American Journal of Community Psychology* 29:241–61.

Gomez, Brendan J., Mark T. Greenberg, and Mark E. Feinberg. 2005. Sustainability of Community Coalitions: An Evaluation of Communities That Care. *Prevention Science* 6(3): 199–202.

Gray, Barbara. 1989. *Collaborating: Finding Common Ground for Multiparty Problems*. San Francisco: Jossey-Bass.

Greene, Jack R., and Stephen D. Mastrofski, eds. 1988. *Community Policing: Rhetoric or Reality?* New York: Praeger.

Hagedorn, John M. 2010. *A World of Gangs: Armed Young Men and Gangsta Culture*. Minneapolis: University of Minnesota Press.

Hallfors, Denise, Hyunsan Cho, D. Livert, and Charles Kadushin. 2002. "Fighting Back Against Substance Abuse: Are Community Coalitions Winning?" *American Journal of Preventive Medicine* 23:237–45.

Hawkins, J. David, Richard F. Catalano, Michael W. Arthur, Elizabeth Egan, Erica C. Brown, Robert D. Abbott, and David M. Murray. 2008. "Testing Communities That Care: The Rationale, Design and Behavioral Baseline Equivalence of the Community Youth Development Study." *Prevention Science* 9:178–90.

Hawkins, J. David, Richard F. Catalano, and Associates. 1992. *Communities that Care: Action for Drug Abuse Prevention*. San Francisco: Jossey-Bass, Inc.

Hawkins, J. David, Richard. F. Catalano, and J. Y. Miller. 1992. "Risk and Protective Factors for Alcohol and Other Drug Problems in Adolescence and Early Adulthood: Implications for Substance Abuse Prevention." *Psychological Bulletin* 112:64–105.

Hawkins, J. David, Todd Herrenkohl, David P. Farrington, Devon Brewer, Richard F. Catalano, and Tracy W. Harachi. 1998. "A Review of Predictors of Violence." In *Serious and Violent Juvenile Offenders: Risk Factors and Successful Interventions*, edited by Rolf Loeber and David P. Farrington. Thousand Oaks, CA: Sage.

Hawkins, J. David, Sabrina Oesterle, Erica C. Brown, Michael W. Arthur, Robert D. Abbott, Abigail A. Fagan, and Richard F. Catalano. 2009. "Results of a Type 2 Translational Research Trial to Prevent Adolescent Drug Use and Delinquency: A Test of Communities That Care." *Archives of Pediatrics and Adolescent Medicine* 163:789–98.

Hope, Tim. 1995. "Community Crime Prevention." In *Building a Safer Society: Strategic Approaches to Crime Prevention. Crime and Justice: A Review of Research*, vol. 19, edited by Michael Tonry and David. P. Farrington. Chicago: University of Chicago Press.

Hough, Michael, and Nick Tilley. 1998. *Auditing Crime and Disorder: Guidance for Local Partnerships*. Crime Detection and Prevention Series Paper 91. London: Home Office.

Howell, James C. 1994. "Recent Gang Research: Program and Policy Implications." *Crime and Delinquency* 40:495–515.

Howell, James C., ed. 1995. *Guide for Implementing the Comprehensive Strategy for Serious, Violent, and Chronic Juvenile Offenders*. Washington, DC: US Department of Justice, Office of Justice Programs, Office of Juvenile Justice and Delinquency Prevention.

Howell, James C. 1998. *Youth Gangs: An Overview. Bulletin*. Washington, DC: US Department of Justice, Office of Justice Programs, Office of Juvenile Justice and Delinquency Prevention.

Howell, James C. 2000. *Youth Gang Programs and Strategies*. Washington, DC: US Department of Justice, Office of Justice Programs, Office of Juvenile Justice and Delinquency Prevention.

Kaftarian, Shakeh J., and Hansen, W. B. 1994. "Improving methodologies for the evaluation of community-based substance abuse prevention programs." *Journal of Community Psychology* (Special issue): 3–6.

Kelling, George L., and Catherine M. Coles. 1996. *Fixing Broken Windows*. New York: Free Press.

Klofas, John M., Natalie K. Hipple, and Edmund F. McGarrell. 2010. *The New Criminal Justice*. New York: Routledge.

Kreuter, Marshall W., Nichole A. Lezin, and Laura A. Young. 2000. "Evaluating Community-based Collaborative Mechanisms: Implications for Practitioners." *Health Promotion Practice* 1:49–63.

Kubisch, Anne C., Carol. H. Weiss, Lisbeth. B. Schorr, and James. P. Connell (1995). Introduction. In *New Approaches to Evaluating Community Initiatives: Concepts, Methods, and Contexts*, edited by J. P. Connell, A. C. Kubisch, L. B. Schorr, and C. H. Weiss. Washington, DC: The Aspen Institute.

Laub, John H., and Robert J. Sampson. 2003. *Shared Beginnings, Divergent Lives: Delinquent Boys to age 70*. Cambridge, MA: Harvard University Press.

Lipsey, Mark W., David B. Wilson, and Lynn Cothern. 2000. *Effective Intervention for Serious Juvenile Offenders*. Washington, DC: US Department of Justice, Office of Justice Programs, Office of Juvenile Justice and Delinquency Prevention.

Marris, Peter, and Martin Rein. 1967. *Dilemmas of Social Reform: Poverty and Community Action in the United States*. New York: Atherton Press.

McGarrell, Edmund F., Natalie Kroovand Hipple, Nicholas Corsaro, Timothy S. Bynum, Heather Perez, Carol A. Zimmerman, and Melissa Garmo. 2009. *Project Safe Neighborhoods—A National Program to Reduce Gun Crime: Final Report*. Washington, DC: US Department of Justice, Office of Justice Programs, National Institute of Justice.

Merzel, Cheryl, and Joanna D'Afflitti. 2003. "Reconsidering Community-based Health Promotion: Promise, Performance, and Potential." *American Journal of Public Health* 93:557–74.

Miller, Walter B. 1962. "The Impact of a Total Community: Delinquency Control Project." *Social Problems* 10(2): 168–91.

Murry, David M., Joel M. Moskowitz, and Clyde W. Dent 1996. "Design and Analysis Issues in Community-Based Drug Abuse Prevention." *American Behavioral Scientist* 39:853–67.

National Council on Crime and Delinquency. 2000. *National Evaluation of the First Year of the OJJDP Rural Gang Initiative: Cross-Site Analysis*. Unpublished draft report submitted to the Office of Juvenile Justice and Delinquency Prevention. Oakland, CA: National Council on Crime and Delinquency.

Office of Juvenile Justice and Delinquency Prevention. 2008. *Best Practices to Address Community Gang Problems: OJJDP's Comprehensive Gang Model*. Washington, DC: US Department of Justice, Office of Justice Programs, Office of Juvenile Justice and Delinquency Prevention.

Papachristo, Andrew, Tracey Meares, and Jeffrey Fagan. 2006. *Attention Felons: Evaluating Project Safe Neighborhoods in Chicago*. Working Paper 06–06. Institute for Social and Economic Research and Policy, Columbia University.

Pentz, Mary Ann. 1998. "Preventing Drug Abuse Through the Community: Multi-component Programs Make the Difference." In *NIDA Research Monograph*, No. 98-4293edited by Zili Sloboda and William B. Hansen.

Pentz, Mary Ann. 2000. "Institutionalizing Community-based Prevention Through Policy Change." *Journal of Community Psychology* 28(3): 257–70.

Pentz, Mary Ann, James H. Dwyer, David P. MacKinnon, Brian R. Flay, William B. Hansen, Eric Yu I. Wang, and C. Anderson Johnson. 1989. "A Multicommunity Trial for Primary Prevention of Adolescent Drug Abuse: Effects on Drug Use Prevalence." *Journal of the American Medical Association* 261(22): 3259–66.

Prestby, John E., and Abraham Wandersman. 1985. "An Empirical Exploration of a Framework of Organizational Viability: Maintaining Block Organizations." *Journal of Applied Behavior Science* 21:287–305.

Reed, Winifred, L., and Scott H. Decker, eds. 2002. *Responding to Gangs: Evaluation and Research.* Washington, DC: US Department of Justice, Office of Justice Programs, National Institute of Justice.

Roehl, Jan, Dennis P. Rosenbaum, Sandra K. Costello, James R. Coldren, Amie M. Schuck, and Laura Kunard 2005. *Strategic Approaches to Community Safety Initiatives (SACSI) in 10 U.S. Cities: The Building Blocks for Project Safe Neighborhoods.* Washington, DC: US Department of Justice, National Institute of Justice, Office of Justice Programs.

Rose, Geoffrey. 1992. *The Strategy of Preventive Medicine.* New York: Oxford University Press.

Rosenbaum, Dennis P. 1988. "Community Crime Prevention: A Review and Synthesis of the Literature." *Justice Quarterly* 5:323–95.

Rosenbaum, Dennis P., ed. 1994. *The Challenge of Community Policing: Testing the Promises.* Newbury Park, CA: Sage.

Rosenbaum, Dennis P. 2002. "Evaluating Multi-Agency Anti-crime Partnerships: Theory, Design, and Measurement Issues." *Crime Prevention Studies* 14:171–225.

Rosenbaum, Dennis P., Arthur J. Lurigio, and Robert C. Davis. 1998. *The Prevention of Crime: Social and Situational Strategies.* Belmont, CA: Wadsworth.

Rosenbaum, Dennis P., and Jan Roehl. 2010. "Building Successful Anti-Violence Partnerships: Lessons from the Strategic Approaches to Community Safety Initiative (SACSI) Model." In *The New Criminal Justice: American Communities and the Changing World of Crime Control*, edited by John M. Klofas, Natalie Kroovand Hipple, and Edmund F. McGarrell. New York: Routledge.

Rosenbaum, Dennis P., and Cody Stephens. 2005. *Reducing Public Violence and Homicide in Chicago: Strategies and Tactics of the Chicago Police Department.* Chicago, IL: Illinois Criminal Justice Information Authority.

Roussos, Stergios Tsai, and Stephen B. Fawcett. 2000. "A Review of Collaborative Partnerships as a Strategy for Improving Community Health." *Annual Review of Public Health* 21:369–402.

Sampson, Robert J., and W. Byron Groves. 1989. "Community Structure and Crime: Testing Social-Disorganization Theory." *American Journal of Sociology* 94:774–802.

Saxe, Leonard, Emily Reber, Denise Hallfors, Charles Kadushin, Delmos Jones, David Rindskopf, and Andrew Beveridge. 1997. "Think Globally, Act Locally: Assessing the Impact of Community-Based Substance Abuse Prevention." *Evaluation and Program Planning* 20(3): 357–66.

Schuck, Amie. M., and Dennis P. Rosenbaum. 2006. "Promoting Safe and Healthy Neighborhoods: What Research tells us about Intervention." In *Community Change: Theories, Practices and Evidence*, edited by K. Fulbright-Anderson. Washington, DC: The Aspen Institute.

Scott, Kamela. K., Joseph. J. Tepas, Eric Frykberg, Pamela M. Taylor, and A. J. Plotkin. 2002. "Rethinking Violence—Evaluation of Program Efficacy in Reducing Adolescent Violent Crime Recidivism." *Journal of Trauma: Injury, Infection and Critical Care* 53(1): 21–27.

Shaw, Clifford R., and Henry D. McKay. 1942. *Juvenile Delinquency and Urban Areas.* Chicago, IL: University of Chicago Press.

Sheppard, D., W. Rowe, H. Grant, and N. Jacobs. 2000. "Fighting Juvenile Gun Violence" *Juvenile Justice Bulletin.* Washington, DC: US Department of Justice, Office of Justice Programs, Office of Juvenile Justice and Delinquency Prevention.

Sherman, Lawrence W., David P. Farrington, Brandon C. Welsh, and Doris Layton MacKenzie, eds. 2002. *Evidence-Based Crime Prevention*, rev. ed. New York: Routledge.

Sherman, Lawrence W., Denise Gottfredson, Doris Layton MacKenzie, John Eck, Peter Reuter, and Shawn Bushway. 1997. *Preventing Crime: What Works, What Doesn't, What's Promising.* Washington, DC: US Department of Justice, Office of Justice Programs, National Institute of Justice.

Skogan, Wesley. G. 1990. *Disorder and Decline: Crime and the Spiral of Decay in American Neighborhoods.* New York: Free Press.

Skogan, Wesley G., and Susan M. Hartnett, 1997. *Community Policing, Chicago Style.* New York: Oxford University Press.

Skogan, Wesley G., Susan M. Hartnett, Natalie Bump, and Jill DuBois. 2008. *Evaluation of CeaseFire-Chicago Final Report.* US Department of Justice, Office of Justice Programs, National Institute of Justice.

Spergel, Irving A. 2007. *Reducing Youth Gang Violence: The Little Village Gang Project in Chicago.* Lanham, MD: AltaMira Press.

Spergel, Irving A., Ron Chance, Kenneth Ehrensaft, Thomas Regulus, Candice Kane, Robert Laseter, Alba Alexander, and Sandra Oh. 1994. *Gang Suppression and Intervention: Community Models.* Washington, DC: US Department of Justice, Office of Justice Programs, Office of Juvenile Justice and Delinquency Prevention.

Spergel, Irving A., Kwai Ming Wa, and Rolando Villarreal Sosa. 2006. The Comprehensive, Community-wide, Gang Program Model: Success and Failure. In *Studying Youth Gangs,* edited by J. F. Short and L. A. Hughes. Lanham, MD: Alta Mira Press.

Stevenson, John F., and Roger E. Mitchell. 2003. "Community-level Collaboration for Substance Abuse Prevention." *Journal of Primary Prevention* 23:371–404.

Tatem-Kelley, B. 1994. *A Comprehensive Response to America's Gang Problem.* Washington, DC: US Department of Justice, Office of Justice Programs, Office of Juvenile Justice and Delinquency Prevention.

Thornberry, Terence P. 2001. "Risk Factors for Gang Membership." In *The Modern Gang Reader,* 2nd ed., edited by Cheryl L. Maxson, Jody Miller, and Malcolm W. Klein. Los Angeles, CA: Roxbury.

Thornberry, Terence P., David Huizinga, and Rolf Loeber. 2004. "The Causes and Correlates Studies: Findings and Policy Implications." *Juvenile Justice* 9:3–19.

Thrasher, Frederic M. 1927. *The Gang: A Study of 1,313 Gangs in Chicago.* Chicago: University of Chicago Press.

Wandersman, Abe. 2003. "Community Science: Bridging the Gap between Science and Practice with Community-centered Models." *American Journal of Community Psychology* 31:227–42.

Webster, Daniel W., Jon S. Vernick, and Jennifer Mendel. 2009. *Interim Evaluation of Baltimore's Safe Streets Program.* Baltimore, MD: Johns Hopkins Bloomberg School of Public Health, Center for the Prevention of Youth Violence.

Welsh, Brandon C., and David P. Farrington, eds. 2006. *Preventing Crime: What Works for Children, Offenders, Victims, and Places.* New York: Springer.

Wilkinson, Deanna. L. 2003. *Guns, Violence and Identity among African-American and Latino Youth.* New York: LFB Scholarly Publishing.

Wilson, Jeremy M., Steven Chermak, and Edmund F. McGarrell. 2010. *Community-Based Violence Prevention: An Assessment of Pittsburgh's One Vision One Life Program.* Santa Monica, CA: Rand.

Yin, Robert K., Shakeh J. Kaftarian, Ping Yu, and Mary A. Jansen. 1997. "Outcomes from CSAP's Community Partnerships Program: Findings from the National Cross-site Evaluation." *Evaluation and Program Planning* 20:345–56.

CHAPTER 13

COMMUNITY-BASED SUBSTANCE USE PREVENTION

ABIGAIL A. FAGAN AND
J. DAVID HAWKINS

RATES of youth drug use are substantial. In the 2007 Monitoring the Future study (Johnston et al. 2008), 46 percent of 12th-grade students reported smoking cigarettes at least once in their lifetime, 72 percent reported lifetime alcohol use, 26 percent reported binge drinking (i.e., having five or more drinks on one occasion), and 42 percent reported lifetime marijuana use. While numerous prevention programs have been found to reduce alcohol use among minors (Spoth, Greenberg, and Turrisi 2008), the impact of an intervention is likely to be compromised if the environments in which youth live are unfavorable to or do not support program goals and activities (Wagenaar and Perry 1994; Flay 2000). Community-based efforts offer much potential for impacting rates of youth substance use because, in contrast to single prevention programs operating in a single context, they typically utilize multicomponent strategies that seek to change a variety of factors that place youth at risk for substance use (Wandersman and Florin 2003). They attempt to alter not only the immediate or situational risk factors but also the long-term, structural, and environmental influences that are associated with drug use and abuse (Wagenaar and Perry 1994). By targeting multiple risks faced in multiple contexts and saturating the environment with prevention strategies and messages, community-based efforts have the potential to achieve population-level reductions in youth substance use.

Another advantage of community-based strategies is their reliance on members of the local community to plan, implement, and monitor prevention activities, usually via coalitions of stakeholders from diverse organizations and backgrounds. By pooling information and resources, community coalitions can enhance community support for prevention initiatives, minimize duplication of services, and potentially offer more cost-effective services that are better implemented and more likely to be sustained (Hawkins, Catalano, and Arthur 2002; Stevenson and Mitchell 2003; Wandersman and Florin 2003). Community-level prevention helps to ensure that services are a good fit with local needs, resources, and norms. What is most needed in one community to reduce youth drug use may not be what is needed in another community, and these differences are best assessed and addressed through community-level mechanisms (Hawkins, Catalano, and Arthur 2002).

Despite having many advantages, community-based prevention services are not easy to implement, evaluate, or sustain. Ensuring the adoption and high-quality implementation of a single prevention strategy is difficult, and problems are likely to be multiplied when adopting a multiple-component strategy enacted in a variety of settings by numerous service providers (Wandersman and Florin 2003). It is challenging to engage and ensure collaboration among community members from diverse backgrounds who may have different skills, needs, resources, and ideas about what is needed to prevent youth substance use (Merzel and D'Afflitti 2003; Stith et al. 2006). Compared to single prevention programs, community-level strategies may be costlier to implement and evaluate, in part because longer term solutions are needed to achieve community-wide outcomes (Merzel and D'Afflitti 2003). Additional methodological challenges include difficulties in recruiting communities, ensuring a large enough sample to allow for multilevel analysis (which is desired when schools or communities are randomized to conditions and effects on youth are analyzed), and adequately measuring community-level processes and changes (Merzel and D'Afflitti 2003; Wandersman and Florin 2003; Stith et al. 2006).

Despite these challenges, community-focused prevention initiatives have produced significant reductions in youth substance use. This essay reviews scientific evidence of the effectiveness of these prevention strategies and draws the following conclusions regarding the potential of community-based mechanisms to reduce youth drug use:

- Successful community-based initiatives have relied on local coalitions to select and implement with fidelity preventive interventions that have evidence of effectiveness.
- The incorporation of universal, school-based drug prevention curricula into community-based efforts to prevent drug use among those under the age of 18 is associated with effectiveness, while a *sole* focus on changing environmental risk factors is not.
- Additional evaluation of community-based strategies is needed, particularly studies that employ an experimental design, analyze effects for population subgroups, compare the effectiveness of discrete prevention strategies, and assess costs versus benefits of the initiative.

The organization of this essay is as follows. Section I describes the methods used to identify the interventions included in this review. Section II provides information regarding each of the included interventions and their effects on youth substance use. Section III identifies the components of community-based strategies that are most strongly linked to positive outcomes and makes recommendations for future research in this area.

I. METHODS

Prior reviews of community-based preventive interventions targeting youth substance use (Flay 2000; Wandersman and Florin 2003; Gates et al. 2006; Cheon 2008; Biglan and Hinds 2009) have produced somewhat different lists of best practices, primarily due to variations in defining "community-based drug prevention." The current review conceptualizes community-based interventions as those that seek to change the larger environment in which youth reside using approaches that are owned and operated by the local community.[1] Community-based efforts may involve a variety of specific strategies. Some focus on decreasing risk factors and enhancing protective factors related to drug use via the implementation of multiple, discrete prevention programs and practices. They may also attempt to transform the larger environment by seeking changes in local ordinances, norms, and policies related to youth drug use. Some community-based efforts rely on a combination of such strategies and many utilize coalitions of community stakeholders to collaboratively plan and coordinate prevention activities.

In order to be included in the current review, interventions had to include a substantial[2] community-based component as defined above. While interventions could seek change in drug use among adults, they also had to include and measure changes in drug use among youth less than 21 years old.[3] Interventions that restricted analyses to tobacco use or to problems associated with drug use, such as driving while impaired or drug-related accidents/deaths, were not included. Evaluations had to employ a quasi-experimental or true experimental design, including, at a minimum, one experimental and one comparison group and two waves of data collection. Published studies meeting all of these criteria were included in the review, except in cases in which the two authors agreed that the evaluation was subject to significant threats to internal validity or used inadequate statistical techniques.[4]

A comprehensive literature search was conducted to identify published evaluations in this area, including searches on PsycINFO, Medline, and the Social Sciences Citation Index databases. The bibliographies of relevant articles were used to generate additional studies, and evaluations of programs identified in other systematic reviews of community-based programs were reviewed. We also consulted lists of best practices related to youth drug use, including the Blueprints for Violence Prevention database (Center for the Study and Prevention of Violence 2010), the Communities

That Care Prevention Strategies Guide (www.communitiesthatcare.net), the Model Programs Guide (Office of Juvenile Justice and Delinquency Prevention 2010), and the National Registry of Evidence-based Programs and Practices (NREPP) (Center for Substance Abuse Prevention 2010).

II. Community-Based Interventions

Our review identified 12 community-based initiatives targeting reductions in youth substance use. About half of the evaluations of these initiatives employed quasi-experimental research designs and half employed randomized controlled trials. Table 13.1 provides information on the sample size(s) and demographic characteristics, research design, drug use measures, significant outcomes, attrition rate (when applicable), and significant limitations of each of the primary studies reviewed. Only findings demonstrated to be statistically significant using two-tailed tests and conventional level of significance ($p < .05$) are reported in the table and this level of significance was necessary in order to be considered an effective intervention.

All of the identified community-based initiatives involved the use of coalitions to plan and implement prevention activities, although the structure and goals of these coalitions varied across initiatives. The first two community-based efforts reviewed involved quasi-experimental research designs assessing the effectiveness of largely self-directed coalitions that emphasized local empowerment; the coalitions aimed to find their own solutions to local problems rather than employ prevention strategies created outside the community. The evaluation of the Fighting Back initiative (Hallfors et al. 2002) compared coalitions in 14 communities across the United States to 29 communities with similar demographic characteristics. Coalitions served portions of mid-sized or larger cities, created their own prevention programs to address needs identified by the coalition, and were well funded, receiving $3 million to 4 million each. Interviews with randomly selected youth ages 16–20 indicated no significant differences in changes of drug use in youth from intervention versus comparison communities over a four-year period.

In the Community Partnership Program (Yin et al. 1997), 251 coalitions were funded by the Center for Substance Abuse Prevention (CSAP) to design and implement their own interventions to reduce youth and adult drug use. An evaluation of this initiative compared 24 communities served by coalitions (randomly selected from a larger pool of 251 coalitions) to 24 demographically matched communities that did not receive funding. Repeated, cross-sectional surveys of eighth- and tenth-grade students showed no significant ($p < .05$) differences between intervention and comparison communities in changes in past-month or past-year alcohol or other drug use after one year. Additional analysis indicated gender differences in the findings among eighth graders, with significant effects favoring boys in the intervention communities for two of the eight outcomes (past-month alcohol and other drug use), and one marginally significant ($p < .10$) iatrogenic effect for girls in the intervention communities (increased past-month other drug use).

Two evaluations examined the effectiveness of employing coalitions to reduce the availability and distribution of alcohol via changes in community-level policies, practices, and norms. In the A Matter of Degree (AMOD) (Weitzman et al. 2004) study, coalitions comprising community members and university students sought to limit access to alcohol by under-age college students by requiring keg registrations, conducting responsible beverage service training, increasing legal and academic sanctions for alcohol violations, creating substance-free student housing, planning alcohol-free social events, restricting alcohol-related advertising in student news outlets, and educating faculty about the consequences of under-age drinking. A quasi-experimental evaluation of AMOD (Weitzman et al. 2004) matched 10 intervention colleges/communities, identified from a national survey as having high rates of drinking by college students, with 32 control colleges/communities also identified as having high rates of college drinking. Four years after the start of the intervention, rates of alcohol use (including drinking, binge drinking, frequent drinking, and getting drunk) reported by randomly selected college students did not differ between intervention and comparison sites.

A randomized, controlled evaluation of the Communities Mobilizing for Change on Alcohol (CMCA) program involved 15 school districts in 15 medium-size communities, 7 of which were randomly assigned to enact CMCA and 8 of which were control sites (Wagenaar et al. 2000). The CMCA program seeks to reduce under-age drinking via prevention activities coordinated by a local mobilizer and community agencies, including educating alcohol sales establishments about the penalties for selling to minors, tracking keg sales, restricting alcohol sales in venues easily accessible to youth, increasing enforcement of community laws and policies related to youth alcohol use, prohibiting alcohol advertising and promotions at public events that include youth, offering youth more alcohol-free events and activities, and increasing media coverage about the consequences of under-age drinking. The evaluation did not show any significant ($p < .05$) differences in the proportion of 12th grade students in CMCA and non-CMCA sites who reported alcohol use (including past month drinking and binge drinking) 2.5 years after the study began. Among 18- to 20-year-olds, CMCA young adults were significantly less likely to have provided alcohol to minors in the past month, but they did not demonstrate reductions in drinking.

These two studies suggest that coalitions focusing *solely* on changing environmental risk factors in order to reduce access to and the availability of alcohol are not effective in reducing alcohol use among high school students or young adults. However, as described next, there is evidence that combining environmental strategies with the implementation of a school-based prevention curriculum can significantly reduce rates of youth drug use.

The Midwestern Prevention Project (MPP) (Pentz et al. 1989) sought reductions in adolescent drug use by implementing a five-year, sequenced set of prevention activities including: (1) a two-year middle school curriculum that promotes students'

Table 13.1 Studies assessing the effectiveness of community-based initiatives intended to reduce youth substance use

Study	SAMPLE (Baseline)			Study Design	Measures[1]	Follow-up Period (post-baseline)	Significant Results[2] Favoring Treatment at Follow-up	Study Design and Analysis Notes
	Number of Schools or Communities	Number of Youth	Demographics					
Hallfors et al. 2002 *Fighting Back*	N=43 communities across the U.S. (14E, 29C)	16–20-year-olds[3]	City size: 100–250,000	Quasi-experimental. Repeated cross-sectional phone interviews	4 outcomes: past-month smoking; past-month marijuana use or binge drinking; past-year other drug use; binge drinking	4 years	None	Intent-to-treat analysis compromised: data were not analyzed for 2 intervention sites due to data collection or implementation problems
Yin et al. 1997 *Community Partnership Program*	N=48 communities across the U.S. (24 E, 24C)	4,151 8th-graders 12,842 10th-graders	Not reported	Quasi-experimental. Repeated cross-sectional school-based surveys	4 outcomes in each grade: past-month and past-year drinking, other drug use	1 year	None	Intent-to-treat analysis compromised: data were not collected in 3 pairs of communities
Weitzman et al. 2004 *A Matter of Degree*	N=42 colleges across the U.S. (10E, 32C)	N=14,700 college students	Not reported	Quasi-experimental. Repeated, cross-sectional mail surveys of randomly selected students	7 outcomes: past-year drinking, frequent (10+ times) past-month drinking, frequent (3+ times) past-month drunkenness, 4 outcomes related to binge drinking	4 years	None	Multilevel analyses were not conducted

Study	Sample	Demographics	Design	Outcomes	Duration	Effects	Notes
Wagenaar et al. 2000 *Communities Mobilizing for Change on Alcohol*	N=15 school districts in MN and WI (8E, 7C)	4,506 12th-graders 3,095 18–20-year-olds	District size: 30,836 (range 8,029–64,797) 12th-graders: 52% female 6% nonwhite 18–20 year olds: 49% female, 4% nonwhite	Experimental. Repeated cross-sectional surveys of 12th-graders and telephone surveys of 18–20-year-olds	5 outcomes for each age: past month drinking, binge drinking, number of drinks consumed, number of drinking occasions in past month, providing alcohol to a minor Alcohol purchase attempts by minors	2.5 years	Grade 12: none 18–20-year-olds: less likely to provide alcohol to minors. Alcohol sales to minors: none	63% of invited school districts agreed to participate
Pentz et al. 1989 *Midwestern Prevention Project*	N=42 schools in Kansas City (24E, 18C)	5,065 6th- and 7th-graders	51% female, 21% nonwhite	Quasi-experimental. Repeated, cross-sectional school surveys with an embedded longitudinal sample	6 outcomes: past-week and past-month smoking, drinking, marijuana use	1.5 years	2 effects: past-month smoking, drinking	Attrition: 16% multilevel analyses were not conducted
Biglan et al., 2000 *Project SixTeen*	N=16 communities in OR (8E, 8C)	2,187 7th-graders 2,251 9th-graders	City size: 1,700–13,500 48% female, 15% nonwhite	Experimental. Repeated, cross-sectional school-based surveys	4 outcomes: past-week use of smokeless tobacco, tobacco, alcohol, marijuana	4 years	3 effects: smoking (pre/post), marijuana (pre/post), drinking (change over time; 9th grade only)	Assessed pre/post differences and changes in drug use over time
Perry et al., 2002 *Project Northland*	N=24 school districts in MN (14E, 10C)	N=2,953 6th-graders	47% female, 7% nonwhite	Experimental. Longitudinal sample followed from grades 6–12	3 drug use outcomes: past-week drinking, past-month drinking, binge drinking. Alcohol purchase attempts by minors	6.5 years	2 effects: binge drinking, alcohol sales to minors	Growth curve analysis examined change over time in drug-use rates

continued

Table 13.1 (continued)

Study	SAMPLE (Baseline)			Study Design	Measures[1]	Follow-up Period (post-baseline)	Significant Results[2] Favoring Treatment at Follow-up	Study Design and Analysis Notes
	Number of Schools or Communities	Number of Youth	Demographics					
Komro et al. 2008 *Project Northland Chicago*	N=61 schools in Chicago (29E, 32C)	5,698 6th- graders	50% female, 87% nonwhite, 72% free or reduced lunch	Experimental. Repeated cross-sectional school surveys with an embedded longitudinal sample	2 outcomes: alcohol use (count of 5 drugs: past- year, past- month and past-week drinking, binge drinking, been drunk); drug use (count of 9 drugs: 5 alcohol, 2 smoking, 2 marijuana)	2.5 years	None	Attrition: 39%
Schinke et al. 2000 *Native American Project*	N=27 tribal and public schools in the Midwest	1,396 3rd- to 5th- graders	49% female, 100% Native American	Experimental (schools randomly assigned to three conditions). Longitudinal sample followed from grades 3–5 to 6–8	4 outcomes: past-week smokeless tobacco, smoking, drinking, marijuana	3-5 years	School program vs. control: 3 effects: smokeless tobacco, drinking, marijuana. School + community vs. control: none	Multilevel analyses were not conducted. Attrition: 14%
Perry et al. 2003 *DARE Plus*	N=24 schools in MN	7,261 7th- graders	48% female, 33% nonwhite	Experimental (schools randomly assigned to three conditions). Longitudinal sample followed from grades 7–8	4 outcomes: current smoking, past-year and past-month drinking, ever been drunk	1.5 years	Boys: 3 sig effects (DARE Plus vs. control): past-year and past-month drinking, smoking. Girls: one effect (DARE Plus vs. DARE only): ever been drunk	No effects for DARE only vs. control. Attrition: 16%

Spoth et al. 2007 *PROSPER*	N=28 communities in IA and PA (14E, 14C)	12,022 6th-graders	City size: 6,975–44,510. 51% female, 15% non-white, 31% free or reduced lunch	Experimental. Longitudinal sample of two consecutive 6th-grade cohorts followed to grade 7	Initiation of: cigarettes, alcohol, drunkenness, marijuana inhalants, meth, ecstasy (7 outcomes). Lifetime use of gateway drugs (=cigarettes, alcohol, or marijuana). Lifetime use of other drugs (marijuana, meth, ecstasy, prescription drugs or opiates). Past-year drunkenness, marijuana, inhalants (3 outcomes). Past-month smoking, drinking (2 outcomes).	1.5 years	4 effects: initiation of marijuana, inhalants, meth, ecstasy. 4 effects: lifetime use of gateway drugs, lifetime use of other illicit drugs, past year marijuana use, past year inhalant use	Attrition: 9%
Collins et al. 2007 KY *Incentives for Prevention*	N=20 coalitions in KY. N=175 schools (110E, 65C)	13,612 8th-graders, 11,420 10th-graders	50% female, 13% non-white	Quasi-experimental. Repeated cross-sectional school-based surveys	6 outcomes in each grade: past month smokeless tobacco, smoking, drinking, marijuana, inhalants; binge drinking	3 years	8th grade: 1 iatrogenic effect: inhalant use 10th grade: 3 effects: smoking, drinking, binge drinking	Intent-to-treat analysis compromised: data were not analyzed for one coalition that dropped out in Year 1
Flewelling et al. 2005 *New Directions*	N=23 coalitions in VT (matched to the rest of the state)	24,932 8–12th graders	City size: 15K (range: 4–60K). 50% female, 10% non-white	Quasi-experimental. Repeated cross-sectional school-based surveys	9 outcomes: lifetime and past-month smoking, drinking, marijuana, other drugs; binge drinking	3 years	2 effects: past-month smoking, marijuana use	Analyses based on data available at all time points, which excluded 3 coalitions

continued

Table 13.1 (continued)

Study	SAMPLE (Baseline)			Study Design	Measures[1]	Follow-up Period (post-baseline)	Significant Results[2] Favoring Treatment at Follow-up	Study Design and Analysis Notes
	Number of Schools or Communities	Number of Youth	Demographics					
Feinberg, Greenberg, et al. 2007 *Communities That Care*	N=79 school districts in PA (41E, 38C)	38,107 6th, 8th, 10th, and 12th graders	6% non-white, 6% below poverty	Quasi-experimental. Repeated cross-sectional school-based surveys	5 outcomes: past-month smoking, drinking, any drug use; binge drinking; past-year drunk/high at school	1–3 years	6th grade: drinking, smoking 8th and 10th grade: no effects 12th grade: drinking, any drug use, binge drinking	
Hawkins et al. 2009 *Communities That Care*	N=24 communities in 7 states (12E, 12C)	4,407 5th-graders	City size: 1,578 to 40,787; 50% female, 10% non-white, 37% free or reduced lunch	Experimental. Longitudinal sample followed from grades 5–8	5 outcomes: initiation of smokeless tobacco, cigarettes, alcohol, marijuana, inhalants 8 outcomes: past-month use of the 5 drugs above, binge drinking, prescription drugs, other drugs	3 years	3 effects: initiation of smokeless tobacco, smoking, alcohol. 3 effects: past-month smokeless tobacco, drinking, binge drinking	Attrition: 4%

[1] Nearly every study that assessed binge drinking defined it as having 5 or more drinks on one (or more) occasion in the last two weeks.

[2] Only results demonstrated to be significant at p < .05, based on two-tailed tests, are presented, even if the original evaluation used a different standard.

[3] The sample size for the youth respondents was not provided; 12,113 interviews were conducted with individuals aged 16–44.

drug resistance skills; (2) homework assignments to increase parent support for youth drug prevention; (3) media campaigns using television, radio, and print media to reinforce anti-drug messages; and (4) local policy changes to reduce demand and supply of drugs (e.g., ordinances restricting cigarette smoking in public settings, increasing alcohol pricing, and creating drug-free zones). A quasi-experimental evaluation of MPP in Kansas City (Pentz et al. 1989) involved 24 MPP schools ($N = 3,011$ students) and 18 comparison schools ($N = 2,054$ students). After one year, seventh-grade students in the MPP conditions demonstrated significant ($p < .05$) reductions in past month smoking and alcohol use compared to students in control schools. Effects for past month marijuana, and past week smoking, drinking, and marijuana were marginally significant ($p < .10$) and favored intervention students (Pentz et al. 1989). A longer term follow-up of students in eight of the schools (Johnson et al. 1990) indicated favorable intervention effects on past-month tobacco and marijuana use, but not alcohol use, when students were in grades 9–10. These effects were generalizable to students considered at both high and low risk for drug use, as defined by their levels of drug use and exposure to a variety of risk factors at baseline.

In Project SixTeen (Biglan et al. 2000), eight pairs of small communities (population 1,700–13,500) in Oregon were matched on size and socioeconomic status, then randomly assigned to intervention and control conditions. Students in grades 6–12 in both conditions received a five-session school-based program previously shown to reduce tobacco use. In experimental communities, a full-time staff person working with youth and adult volunteers also conducted: (1) media advocacy to increase adult support of youth tobacco prevention via newspaper articles, presentations to local civic groups, and fact sheets mailed to community leaders; (2) youth activities with anti-tobacco themes; (3) pamphlets mailed to homes and parent quizzes given by students to encourage parent support of tobacco prevention; and (4) reductions in youth access to tobacco via a "reward and reminder" program that included merchant education and compliance checks, with rewards (e.g., positive publicity) to clerks and store owners when tobacco was not sold to minors and reminders/warnings when it was sold that such actions were illegal. Intervention effects were assessed using five annual cross-sectional surveys of 4,438 students in grades 7 and 9. The evaluation showed a significant reduction in past week smoking and marijuana use for seventh- and ninth-grade students in intervention compared to control communities at Time 5 versus baseline. No intervention effects were found for smokeless tobacco use or for alcohol use among seventh-grade students, but ninth-grade students in the control communities had a significantly greater increase in alcohol use compared to students in the intervention sites.

Project Northland utilizes school- and community-based interventions similar to those employed in Project Sixteen, with the goal of reducing drug use—primarily drinking—among adolescents. The middle-school intervention includes a three-year school curriculum with homework assignments and booklets mailed to parents to foster parent-child discussions about alcohol, three years of alcohol-free recreational and social events planned by students, and changes in local policies and practices associated with youth alcohol use planned by coalitions, such as increased identification checks by retail liquor establishments and legal consequences for selling alcohol to minors (Wagenaar and Perry 1994; Perry et al. 1996). An evaluation of the middle school program (Perry et al. 1996) involved 24 school districts in Minnesota randomly assigned to intervention ($N = 14$) and control ($N = 10$) conditions and a longitudinal sample of 2,351 sixth-grade students followed through eighth grade. The evaluation showed significantly lower rates of past-month and past-week alcohol use among eighth graders receiving the program compared to those in the control group, but no significant differences for lifetime tobacco or smokeless tobacco use or past-year marijuana use. The program was more effective for students who had not initiated alcohol use at baseline, with significant intervention effects on four of the five drugs assessed (excluding smokeless tobacco),while no significant intervention effects were found among students who had already begun using alcohol at baseline.

A second evaluation followed Project Northland and control group students into high school. Intervention activities were minimal in grades 9 and 10, and at the end of grade 10, intervention students reported *greater* increases in past month alcohol use and binge drinking compared to control youth (Perry et al. 2002). In grade 11, a six-session school curriculum focused on the legal and social consequences of using alcohol, and parent education continued via the mailing of postcards describing program activities. In grades 11 and 12, community coalitions planned youth activities and implemented environmental strategies including responsible beverage training and media campaigns to change community norms favorable to alcohol use (Perry et al 2000). Analyses demonstrated significantly smaller increases in binge drinking from grades 10 to 12 among students in Project Northland schools compared to those in control schools, and marginally significant ($p < .10$) intervention effects on past-month drinking.

Project Northland was replicated in 61 schools in Chicago to determine if the positive outcomes demonstrated for white youth in Minnesota would be shown for urban, ethnically diverse youth from primarily low-income families (Komro et al. 2008). Adaptations to the original program included more home activities, youth community service projects rather than social activities, and community mobilization efforts that focused on specific neighborhoods. The experimental evaluation involved random assignment of blocks of schools to Project Northland ($N = 10$ blocks, 29 schools) and control ($N = 12$ blocks, 32 schools) conditions, with annual surveys of students in grades 6 through 8 ($N = 5,812$ students, including a subset of youth who were followed longitudinally, with a relatively high attrition rate of 39 percent). The evaluation found no significant intervention effects on drug use or on alcohol sales to minors.

The Native American Project (Schinke, Tepavac, and Cole 2000) involved 1,396 Native American students attending grades 3–5 in 27 tribal and public schools. Schools were randomly assigned to one of three conditions, receiving: (1) a school-based curriculum; (2) the school curriculum and a community-based intervention; and (3) control schools implementing services as usual. The three-year school curriculum was the Life Skills Training program, previously demonstrated to reduce youth drug use, which was culturally tailored for Native American students. The community intervention component involved a media campaign (flyers and posters distributed to community organizations) and meetings held at schools to inform parents, neighbors, and teachers about the importance of preventing substance use among Native American youth. The evaluation was based on past-week drug use reported by students at baseline ($N = 1,396$) and annually through grades 6–8. Analyses were conducted at the individual level and did not control for clustering of students in schools. At the last follow-up period, no significant differences were found between conditions for tobacco use. Smokeless tobacco use was significantly lower for students receiving the school program only compared to those in the combined intervention group and students in the control condition. Students in the school program only also had significantly lower rates of alcohol use and marijuana use compared to students in the control condition. There were no differences in drug use rates for students receiving the school- and community-based intervention compared to those in the school-only and control groups, which was unexpected.

The evaluation of the Drug Abuse Resistance Education (DARE) Plus program (Perry et al. 2003) randomized 24 schools to one of three conditions: (1) the DARE program only (eight schools); (2) the DARE Plus program (eight schools); and a wait-list control (eight schools) condition. The DARE program involved 10 sessions taught in school by police officers to bolster students' ability to resist drug offers and respond to violent situations. The DARE Plus curriculum added: (1) four classroom sessions taught by classroom teachers and peer leaders, (2) homework activities to increase parents' support for prevention messages, and (3) community and extracurricular activities planned by coalitions including neighborhood watch groups, patrols of school grounds and/or community neighborhoods, graffiti removal, and community meetings to discuss youth drug use (Perry et al. 2000; Komro et al. 2004). The program evaluation involved a longitudinal panel of 7,261 students followed from fall of grade 7 to spring of grade 8. No significant intervention effects were found for students in the DARE-only condition compared to those in the control group. For boys, those in DARE Plus condition had significantly smaller increases in past-year drinking, past-month drinking, and current smoking compared to boys in control schools, but not compared to those in the DARE-only condition. Among girls, those in DARE Plus schools were less likely to report increases in ever having been drunk, compared with girls in the DARE-only schools, but not compared to girls in the control schools (Perry et al. 2003).

The PROmoting School-community-university Partnerships to Enhance Resilience (PROSPER) project (Spoth et al. 2004) also emphasizes the importance of embedding school curricula in larger community efforts to prevent substance use among youth. In this model, local university Cooperative Extension Service agents and school district personnel jointly oversee local coalitions of youth, parents, and community members from diverse organizations. Coalitions select and monitor the implementation of universal, school-based prevention programs, as

well as programs that seek to improve parenting practices and parent-child interactions. Unlike the initiatives described above, PROSPER does not advocate for the
implementation of particular school- and family-focused programs; rather, community coalitions select programs from a menu of interventions that have previously been evaluated and shown to be effective at reducing drug use among youth
(Spoth et al. 2004).

An evaluation of this model (Spoth et al. 2007) involved the random assignment of 28 rural and suburban communities to implement PROSPER ($N = 14$) or to
conduct prevention services as usual ($N = 14$). Drug-use outcomes were assessed
among two consecutive cohorts of sixth-grade students ($N = 12,022$ students) who
were followed for 18 months. In grade 6, about 17 percent of students in the intervention communities participated in a universal parent-training program with their
parents, and most received a school-based prevention curriculum in grade 7. The
analysis demonstrated significant ($p < .05$) effects favoring students in the intervention communities for 8 of the 14 outcomes assessed. Based on data from students
who had never used drugs prior to grade 6, significantly fewer students in the
PROSPER communities had initiated use of marijuana, inhalants, methamphet-
amine, and ecstasy (but not cigarettes, alcohol, or having been drunk) by the spring
of grade 7. Students in the intervention communities were also less likely than those
in the control communities to report lifetime use of gateway drugs (having ever
used alcohol, cigarettes, or marijuana) and lifetime use of any illicit drug (having
ever used marijuana, methamphetamines, ecstasy, drugs prescribed for another
person, or opiates). Students in the PROSPER communities reported significantly
less marijuana and inhalant use in the past year compared to students in the control
communities, but no significant intervention effects were found for drinking or
smoking in the past month.

The final three studies included in this review evaluated the effectiveness of
coalition-led, community-based prevention efforts similar to those used in the
PROSPER model, in that coalitions select prevention strategies from a menu of
options that includes only strategies that have been previously found to be effective,
but unlike PROSPER, choices include more than just school- and family-focused
programs. Two evaluations assessed the effectiveness of coalitions funded by State
Incentive Grants (SIGs) in Kentucky ($N = 19$) and Vermont ($N = 23$) to assess local
prevention needs and address them using discrete, effective programs (in Kentucky)
or a combination of school-based prevention programs, environmental strategies,
and activities for high-risk youth (in Vermont). The evaluation in Kentucky
(Collins, Johnson, and Becker 2007) compared data from cross-sectional surveys of
students in 8th and 10th grade in 110 schools served by the coalitions to data from
students in 65 comparison schools, with schools matched by size and location in an
urban area. Three years after funding began, a meta-analysis of pair-by-pair comparisons found no significant effects favoring 8th grade students in the schools
served by coalitions. One significant iatrogenic effect was found, with increased
rates of inhalants reported by intervention students compared to students in the
comparison sites. For 10th graders, significant effects favoring intervention sites

were reported for past month smoking, drinking, and binge drinking. The evaluation of coalitions funded in Vermont (Flewelling et al. 2005) involved analysis of
data from cross-sectional, repeated surveys of students in grades 9–12 in schools
served by the 23 funded coalitions compared to responses from students in all
other schools in the state that completed the survey. Of the nine outcomes assessed,
significant declines over the three-year period favoring the intervention students
were shown for smoking and marijuana use in the past month, and marginal effects
($p < .10$) favoring the intervention students were demonstrated for lifetime smoking
and marijuana use.

The Communities That Care prevention system is similar to that used by the
SIG coalitions but provides communities with more structure and guidance to
conduct prevention work and places more emphasis (and more rigorous standards)
on using effective prevention strategies to target community needs. CTC involves
five phases: (1) assessing community readiness to undertake collaborative prevention efforts; (2) forming a diverse and representative prevention coalition; (3) using
epidemiologic data to assess prevention needs, focusing on the identification of
elevated risk factors and depressed protective factors that are associated with youth
substance use; (4) choosing evidence-based prevention policies and programs that
target local needs; and (5) implementing the new policies and programs with monitoring to ensure fidelity and evaluation to ensure that goals are being met. The
CTC coalitions are to be structured, ideally with chairs, co-chairs, and workgroups;
should employ at least a half-time coordinator, and should be broad-based,
involving representation from law enforcement, health and human service agencies,
schools, youth-service groups, local or state government, business, religious
groups, youth, and parents. Tested and effective prevention activities selected and
implemented by communities can take place in a variety of settings and target risk
or protective factors in the individual, family, school, peer, or community domains
(Hawkins, Catalano, and Arthur 2002).

Feinberg, Greenberg, and colleagues (2007) evaluated the use of the CTC system
in Pennsylvania in a quasi-experimental study relying on data from repeated,
cross-sectional surveys of students in grades 6, 8, 10, and 12 in school districts served
by CTC coalitions ($N = 41$ in 2001 and 102 in 2003) compared to students in demographically comparable school districts not served by CTC coalitions ($N = 38$ in 2001
and 52 in 2003). Total sample sizes were approximately 38,000 students in 2001 and
nearly 97,000 in 2003. In 2001, prior to the start of prevention activities in most CTC
sites, no differences in self-reported rates of five types of drug use were found in
intervention compared to comparison schools for any grade. In 2003, one to five
years after CTC activities had begun in intervention communities, 6th and 12th
grade students in CTC communities reported significantly less alcohol use in the
past month, 6th graders reported less cigarette use in the past month, and 12th
graders reported less binge drinking and less past-month overall drug use, compared
to students in comparison schools (Feinberg, Greenberg, et al. 2007). A follow-up
evaluation with data collected in 2005 (Feinberg et al. 2010) indicated no significant
changes in drug use for students in intervention sites versus comparison sites.

The Community Youth Development Study (CYDS) evaluated the efficacy of CTC in a randomized controlled trial in which freestanding towns (with a mean population of 14,646 residents) were assigned to either implement the CTC system (N = 12) or to serve as control communities (N = 12) in which prevention services were conducted as usual. Intervention sites received training in the CTC model, proactive and intensive technical assistance, and funding for five years to plan and implement tested and effective prevention strategies. According to information from a longitudinal panel of 4,407 students from all 24 communities surveyed annually from grades 5 to 8, changes in student drug use favoring CTC sites were achieved (Hawkins et al. 2009). Using data from students who had never used drugs prior to grade 5, reductions in the initiation of drug use were found for three of the five drugs assessed, with 17 percent of students in CTC communities initiating alcohol use by eighth grade, compared to 25 percent in control communities, 8 percent initiating cigarette smoking versus 12 percent in control communities, and 4 percent initiating smokeless tobacco use versus 6 percent in control communities. Based on data from all students, there were significant reductions in recent drug use for students in CTC communities compared to the control communities for three of the eight drugs assessed. In eighth grade, students in CTC communities reported less alcohol use than students in control communities (with 16.4 percent of CTC youth reporting past-month alcohol use, compared to 21.4 percent of control youth), less binge drinking (9 percent versus 5.7 percent), and reduced smokeless tobacco use (4.3 percent versus 2.2 percent). Additional analyses (Oesterle et al. 2010) found some gender differences in the effects of CTC on recent drug use. Reductions in past month drinking, binge drinking, and smokeless tobacco use among students in intervention compared to control communities were significant for boys but not girls, as was an additional outcome—past-month marijuana use. The strength of the intervention effects did not vary according to baseline levels of drug use: for both users and nonusers of drugs at grade 5, the main effects on current drug use were significant.

III. Discussion and Conclusions

As evidenced in this review, some community-based strategies have been found in well-conducted research trials to prevent the initiation of drug use and/or reduce rates of smoking, drinking, and use of marijuana and other drugs. While all of the effective interventions involved the use of community-based coalitions to plan and implement activities, it is clear that simply gathering local stakeholders and asking them to do their best to solve local drug problems is not enough to prevent adolescent substance use, even if they are provided with significant resources (Hallfors et al. 2002). In the Fighting Back and Community Partnership coalition initiatives, which produced no significant changes in youth drug use, coalitions received insufficient guidance in how to enact prevention strategies, varied widely in the nature and amount of prevention services provided, and largely relied on locally created prevention strategies that likely had not been previously evaluated for effectiveness in reducing drug use. In contrast, the CTC and PROSPER models, which were found to lower rates of youth drug use in well-controlled, randomized trials (Spoth et al. 2007; Hawkins et al. 2009), provide proactive training and technical assistance to community coalitions to ensure that they select and implement with fidelity prevention strategies that have been previously demonstrated as effective in reducing youth drug use and other problem behaviors.

Existing evidence does *not* indicate that coalitions focused explicitly and solely on changing alcohol policies are effective in preventing alcohol use among youths under the age of 18, although additional research is warranted given that only two studies in this review employed such methods (Wagenaar et al. 2000; Weitzman et al. 2004). However, combining environmental strategies with the implementation of universal, school-based drug prevention curricula to target more proximal influences on drug use does appear to be related to successful drug-use prevention among adolescents. School-based programs may be particularly important to the success of community-based prevention efforts given their potential to reach a large proportion of the youth population.

To be successful, community-based interventions have to be well implemented and intensive. Perry and colleagues (2002) found that effects of Project Northland in Minnesota decayed over time, and additional services were needed to sustain effects through high school. The replication of Project Northland in Chicago failed to produce effects, however, leading Komro et al. (2008) to recommend that in lower income, urban populations, in which problems other than youth drug use (e.g., gangs, violence, and housing) may take precedence, longer term and more intense community-based strategies may be needed. This study and others (Yin et al. 1997; Hallfors et al. 2002; Collins, Johnson, and Becker 2007; Feinberg, Greenberg, et al. 2007) also noted that implementation challenges, such as difficulty in engaging community members in the initiative and challenges in moving from planning to action, may compromise the ability of community-based efforts to produce significant effects. Nonetheless, evaluations of the Communities That Care and PROSPER models have shown that achieving implementation fidelity of multicomponent, coalition-based efforts is possible (Spoth et al. 2007; Fagan et al. 2009) and can be enhanced through the provision of high-quality training and technical assistance to local coalitions (Feinberg, Chilenski, et al. 2007; Feinberg, Ridenour, and Greenberg 2008).

While effective community-based prevention models were identified in this review, additional evaluations of community-based strategies are warranted, particularly studies that employ a true experimental design. Future research should also employ methodologies that allow comparison of the relative effectiveness of specific components of community-based interventions. We also recommend that evaluations continue to analyze differential effectiveness—that is, the extent to which interventions may have different effects for different groups of individuals—because some of the programs reviewed did identify variation in effects for subgroups. More complete information about how and for whom interventions work can reveal whether or not programs have iatrogenic effects for some, can aid in the selection of programs by communities, and can be used by program developers to refine their interventions.

Finally, further research is needed to provide information on the costs versus benefits of community-based efforts. The National Center on Addiction and Substance Abuse (CASA) (2009) estimated that over $467 billion was spent in the United States in 2005 in responding to the negative consequences of drug abuse and addiction. Only two of the programs included in this review have been rigorously evaluated for cost-effectiveness, and in both cases, fiscal savings were demonstrated. According to the Washington State Institute for Public Policy (Aos et al. 2004), for every dollar spent on Project Northland in Minnesota, the program produced a savings of $2.45 in later treatment, morbidity, mortality, and criminal justice costs, while the Midwestern Prevention Project produced a savings of $1.27. Given that cost is a major factor influencing community decisions to adopt new programs, information on financial benefits may help to increase the dissemination of effective community-based prevention strategies, and, in turn, their potential to substantially reduce rates of drug use among young people.

NOTES

This work was supported in part by a research grant from the National Institute on Drug Abuse (R01 DA015183–03), with co-funding from the National Cancer Institute, the National Institute of Child Health and Human Development, the National Institute of Mental Health, the Center for Substance Abuse Prevention, and the National Institute on Alcohol Abuse and Alcoholism.

1. Although some changes to state or national laws (e.g., raising the age at which youth can legally consume alcohol) have been found to reduce youth substance use, these practices are not considered "community-based" in the current review because the mechanism that produces change is not conducted at the local level.

2. Decisions regarding whether or not programs had a "substantial" community-based prevention component were made jointly by the two authors based on program descriptions. As an example, the Aban Aya Youth Project (Flay et al. 2004) is not described because the primary intervention involved a school curriculum and the community component largely focused on changing the school environment, not the larger community.

3. For example, although programs such as the Community Trials Project (Grube 1997) and the Sacramento Neighborhood Alcohol Prevention Project (Treno et al. 2007) sought to reduce under-age drinking using community-based strategies, their evaluations did not assess under-age alcohol consumption; as a result, these programs are not included in this review.

4. Studies were not automatically excluded when statistical procedures failed to account for the clustering of individuals in schools or communities when such units were the basis for randomization to conditions.

REFERENCES

Aos, Steve, Roxanne Lieb, Jim Mayfield, Marna Miller, and Annie Pennucci. 2004. *Benefits and Costs of Prevention and Early Intervention Programs for Youth.* Olympia, WA: Washington State Institute for Public Policy.

Biglan, Anthony, Dennis V. Ary, Keith Smolkowski, Terry Duncan, and Carol Black. 2000. "A Randomised Controlled Trial of a Community Intervention to Prevent Adolescent Tobacco Use." *Tobacco Control* 9:24–32.

Biglan, Anthony, and Erika Hinds. 2009. "Evolving Prosocial and Sustainable Neighborhoods and Communities." *Annual Review of Clinical Psychology* 5: 169–96.

Center for the Study and Prevention of Violence. 2010. "Blueprints for Violence Prevention." http://www.colorado.edu/cspv/blueprints/index.html.

Center for Substance Abuse Prevention. 2010. "The National Registry of Evidence-based Programs and Practices (NREPP)." http://www.nrepp.samhsa.gov/index.asp.

Cheon, Jeong Woong. 2008. "Best Practices in Community-Based Prevention for Youth Substance Reduction: Towards Strengths-Based Positive Development Policy." *Journal of Community Psychology* 36(6): 761–79.

Collins, David, Knowlton Johnson, and Betsy Jane Becker. 2007. "A Meta-Analysis of Direct and Mediating Effects of Community Coalitions That Implemented Science-Based Substance Abuse Prevention Interventions." *Substance Use and Misuse* 42:985–1007.

Fagan, Abigail A., Koren Hanson, J. David Hawkins, and Michael W. Arthur. 2009. "Translational Research in Action: Implementation of the Communities That Care Prevention System in 12 Communities." *Journal of Community Psychology* 37(7): 809–29.

Feinberg, Mark, Sarah Meyer Chilenski, Mark T. Greenberg, Richard L. Spoth, and Cleve Redmond. 2007. "Community and Team Member Factors That Influence the Operations Phase of Local Prevention Teams: The PROSPER Project." *Prevention Science* 8(3): 214–26.

Feinberg, Mark E., Mark T. Greenberg, D. Wayne Osgood, Jennifer Sartorius, and Daniel Bontempo. 2007. "Effects of the Communities That Care Model in Pennsylvania on Youth Risk and Problem Behaviors." *Prevention Science* 8(4): 261–70.

Feinberg, Mark E., Damon Jones, Mark T. Greenberg, D. Wayne Osgood, and Daniel Bontempo. 2010. "Effects of the Communities That Care Model in Pennsylvania on Change in Adolescent Risk and Problem Behaviors." *Prevention Science* 11:163–71.

Feinberg, Mark E., Ty A. Ridenour, and Mark T. Greenberg. 2008. "The Longitudinal Effect of Technical Assistance Dosage on the Functioning of Communities That Care Prevention Boards in Pennsylvania." *Journal of Primary Prevention* 29:145–65.

Flay, Brian R. 2000. "Approaches to Substance Use Prevention Utilizing School Curriculum Plus Social Environment Change." *Addictive Behaviors* 25(6): 861–85.

Flay, Brian R., Sally Graumlich, Eisuke Segawa, James L. Burns, and Michelle Y. Holliday. 2004. "Effects of 2 Prevention Programs on High-Risk Behaviors Among African American Youth: A Randomized Trial." *Archives of Pediatric and Adolescent Medicine* 158:377–84.

Flewelling, Robert L., David Austin, Kelly Hale, Marcia LaPlante, Melissa Liebig, Linda Piasecki, and Lori Uerz. 2005. "Implementing Research-Based Substance Abuse Prevention in Communities: Effects of a Coalition-Based Prevention Initiative in Vermont." *Journal of Community Psychology* 33(3): 333–53.

Gates, Simon, Jim McCambridge, Lesley A. Smith, and David Foxcroft. 2006. "Interventions for Prevention of Drug Use by Young People Delivered in Non-School Settings." *Cochrane Database of Systematic Reviews*, Issue 1, Article No. CD005030.

Grube, Joel W. 1997. "Preventing Sales of Alcohol to Minors: Results From a Community Trial." *Addiction* 92(S2): S251–260.

Hallfors, Denise, Hyunsan Cho, David Livert, and Charles Kadushin. 2002. "Fighting Back Against Substance Use: Are Community Coalitions Winning?" *American Journal of Preventive Medicine* 23(4): 237–45.

Hawkins, J. David, Richard F. Catalano, and Michael W. Arthur. 2002. "Promoting Science-Based Prevention in Communities." *Addictive Behaviors* 27:951–76.

Hawkins, J. David, Sabrina Oesterle, Eric C. Brown, Michael W. Arthur, Robert D. Abbott, Abigail A. Fagan, and Richard F. Catalano. 2009. "Results of a Type 2 Translational Research Trial to Prevent Adolescent Drug Use and Delinquency: A Test of Communities That Care." *Archives of Pediatric Adolescent Medicine* 163(9): 789–98.

Johnson, C. A., M. A. Pentz, M. D. Weber, J. H. Dwyer, D. P. MacKinnon, Brian R. Flay, N. A. Baer, and William B Hansen. 1990. "The Relative Effectiveness of Comprehensive Community Programming for Drug Abuse Prevention with High Risk and Low Risk Adolescents." *Journal of Consulting and Clinical Psychology* 58(4): 447–56.

Johnston, Lloyd D., Patrick M. O'Malley, Jerald G. Bachman, and John E. Schulenberg. 2008. *Monitoring the Future National Survey Results on Drug Use, 1975–2007. Vol. I: Secondary School Students.* NIH Publication No. 08–6418A. Bethesda, MD: National Institute on Drug Abuse.

Komro, Kelli, Cheryl L. Perry, Sara Veblen-Mortenson, Kian Farbakhsh, Traci L. Toomey, Melissa H. Stigler, Rhonda Jones-Webb, Kari C. Kugler, Keryn Pasch, and Carolyn L Williams. 2008. "Outcomes from a Randomized Controlled Trial of a Multi-Component Alcohol Use Preventive Intervention for Urban Youth: Project Northland Chicago." *Addiction* 103:606–18.

Komro, Kelli, Cheryl L. Perry, Sara Veblen-Mortenson, Melissa H. Stigler, Linda M. Bosma, Karen A. Munson, and Kian Farbakhsh. 2004. "Violence-Related Outcomes of the DARE Plus Project." *Health Education and Behavior* 31:335–54.

Merzel, Cheryl, and Joanna D'Afflitti. 2003. "Reconsidering Community-Based Health Promotion: Promise, Performance, and Potential." *American Journal of Public Health* 93(4): 557–74.

National Center on Addiction and Substance Abuse. 2009. "Shoveling Up II: The Impact of Substance Abuse on Federal, State, and Local Budgets." New York: Columbia University.

Oesterle, Sabrina, J. David Hawkins, Abigail A. Fagan, Robert D. Abbott, and Richard F. Catalano. 2010. "Testing the Universality of the Effects of the Communities That Care Prevention System for Preventing Adolescent Drug Use and Delinquency." *Prevention Science* 11:422–23.

Office of Juvenile Justice and Delinquency Prevention. 2010. "OJJDP Model Programs Guide." http://www2.dsgonline.com/mpg/Default.aspx.

Pentz, Mary Ann, James H. Dwyer, David P. MacKinnon, Brian R. Flay, William B. Hansen, Eric Yu I. Wang, and C. Anderson Johnson. 1989. "A Multicommunity Trial for Primary Prevention of Adolescent Drug Abuse." *Journal of the American Medical Association* 261:3259–66.

Perry, Cheryl L., Kelli Komro, Sara Veblen-Mortenson, Linda M. Bosma, Kian Farbakhsh, Karen A. Munson, Melissa H. Stigler, and Leslie A. Lytle. 2003. "A Randomized

Controlled Trial of the Middle and Junior High School D.A.R.E. And D.A.R.E. Plus Programs." *Archives of Pediatric and Adolescent Medicine* 157:178–84.

Perry, Cheryl L., Kelli Komro, Sara Veblen-Mortenson, Linda M. Bosma, Karen A. Munson, Melissa H. Stigler, Leslie A. Lytle, Jean L. Forster, and Seth L. Welles. 2000. "The Minnesota DARE PLUS Project: Creating Community Partnerships to Prevent Drug Use and Violence." *Journal of School Health* 70(3): 84–88.

Perry, Cheryl L., Carolyn L. Williams, Kelli A. Komro, Sara Veblen-Mortension, Melissa H. Stigler, Karen A. Munson, Kian Farbakhsh, Resa M. Jones, and Jean L. Forster. 2002. "Project Northland: Long-Term Outcomes of Community Action to Reduce Adolescent Alcohol Use." *Health Education Research* 17(1): 117–32.

Perry, Cheryl L., Carolyn L. Williams, Sara Veblen-Mortenson, Traci L. Toomey, Kelli Komro, Pamela S. Anstine, Paul G. McGovem, John R. Finnegan, Jean L. Forster, Alexander C. Wagenaar, and Mark Wolfson. 1996. "Project Northland: Outcomes of a Communitywide Alcohol Use Prevention Program During Early Adolescence." *American Journal of Public Health* 86:956–65.

Schinke, S. P., L. Tepavac, and K. C. Cole. 2000. "Preventing Substance Use Among Native American Youth: Three-Year Results." *Addictive Behaviors* 25(3): 387–97.

Spoth, Richard L., Mark Greenberg, Karen Bierman, and Cleve Redmond. 2004. "PROSPER Community-University Partnership Model for Public Education Systems: Capacity-Building for Evidence-Based, Competence-Building Prevention." *Prevention Science* 5(1): 31–39.

Spoth, Richard L., Mark T. Greenberg, and Robert Turrisi. 2008. "Preventive Interventions Addressing Underage Drinking: State of the Evidence and Steps Towards Public Health Impact." *Pediatrics* 121(S4): S311–36.

Spoth, Richard L., Cleve Redmond, Chungyeol Shin, Mark Greenberg, Scott Clair, and Mark Feinberg. 2007. "Substance Use Outcomes at Eighteen Months Past Baseline from the PROSPER Community-University Partnership Trial." *American Journal of Preventive Medicine* 32(5): 395–402.

Stevenson, John F., and Roger E. Mitchell. 2003. "Community-Level Collaboration for Substance Abuse Prevention." *Journal of Primary Prevention* 23(3): 371–404.

Stith, Sandra, Irene Pruitt, JEMEG Dees, Michael Fronce, Narkia Green, Anurag Som, and David Linkh. 2006. "Implementing Community-Based Prevention Programming: A Review f the Literature." *Journal of Primary Prevention* 27(6): 599–617.

"The Community That Care Prevention Strategies Guide." http://ncadi.samhsa.gov/features/ctc/resources.aspx.

Treno, Andrew J., Paul J. Gruenewald, Juliet P. Lee, and Lillian G. Remer. 2007. "The Sacramento Neighborhood Alcohol Prevention Project: Outcomes from a Community Prevention Trial." *Journal of Studies on Alcohol and Drugs* 68:197–207.

Wagenaar, Alexander C., David M. Murray, John P. Gehan, Mark Wolfson, Jean L. Forster, Traci L. Toomey, Cheryl L. Perry, and Rhonda Jones-Webb. 2000. "Communities Mobilizing for Change on Alcohol: Outcomes from a Randomized Community Trial." *Journal of Studies on Alcohol* 61:85–94.

Wagenaar, Alexander C., and Cheryl L. Perry. 1994. "Community Strategies for the Reduction of Youth Drinking: Theory and Application." *Journal of Research on Adolescence* 4(2): 319–45.

Wandersman, Abraham, and Paul Florin. 2003. "Community Intervention and Effective Prevention." *American Psychologist* 58(6–7): 441–48.

Weitzman, Elissa R., Toben F. Nelson, Hang Lee, and Henry Wechsler. 2004. "Reducing Drinking and Related Harms in College: Evaluation of the "A Matter of Degree" Program." *American Journal of Preventive Medicine* 27(3): 187–96.

Yin, Robert K., Shakeh J. Kaftarian, Ping Yu, and Mary A. Jansen. 1997. "Outcomes from CSAP's Community Partnership Program: Findings from the National Cross-Site Evaluation." *Evaluation and Program Planning* 20(3): 345–55.

CHAPTER 14

SCHOOLS AND PREVENTION

DENISE C. GOTTFREDSON,
PHILIP J. COOK, AND CHONGMIN NA

SCHOOL violence, drug use, vandalism, gang activity, bullying, and theft are costly and interfere with academic achievement. Student misbehavior interferes with teaching and learning and is one of the primary sources of teacher turnover in our nation's schools. Gallup polls from the past 20 years show that the percentage of parents who report being concerned about the physical safety of their children while at school has ranged from 15 to 55 percent, with the highest percentages registering just after the infamous school shootings at Columbine High School in 1999. Reducing crime rates has become an increasingly high priority for America's schools.

Middle and high schools aggregate youths who are in their peak crime years. Hence, it is not surprising that crime rates in schools are high. Victimization rates are about the same in school as out, despite the fact that youths spend only about one-fifth of their waking hours in school. And other things equal, youth violence rates tend to be higher when school is in session than not.

However, since 1993 schools have enjoyed a strong downward trend in crime of all types that mimics the downward trend in overall youth victimization. That coincidence reflects one of the important findings in the school crime literature: school crime is linked closely to community crime rates. The schools have benefited from the remarkable crime drop in America.

There has also been an important trend in the official response to school crime. The response has become increasingly formal over the last 20 years, with greater recourse to arrest and the juvenile courts rather than school-based discipline—a trend that has been dubbed the "criminalization" of student misbehavior (Hirschfield 2008). To some extent this trend has been furthered by federal law that has imposed zero-tolerance rules for some offenses, and has subsidized the hiring of uniformed officers to police the schools. The shift has been from administrative discretion to mandatory penalties, and from in-school discipline to increasing use of suspension or arrest. At the same time, there has been a considerable investment in the use of surveillance cameras and metal detectors.

While the increasing formality in school response to crime has coincided with the declining crime rates, there is no clear indication of whether the new approach gets any of the credit. Indeed, the evaluation literature that we review here has very little to say about the likely effects of these changes. As so often happens, there appears to be a disconnect between policy and research.

There are alternatives to the get-tough approach with its reliance on deterrence and exclusion. We know that some schools do a much better job than others in controlling the behavior of their students. Characteristic of successful schools in this respect is that they are close-knit communities where rules of acceptable behavior are clearly communicated and consistently (if not harshly) enforced. In addition to good management practices, there is much that can be done in the classroom that has demonstrated effectiveness in improving behavior.

In this essay, we consider how schools can be organized and managed, and what practices and policies they can adopt to reduce levels of crime, victimization, violence, and substance use both in and out of schools. We find that which school a student attends matters for these outcomes. Characteristics of the way schools are operated are reliably related to crime and disorder in the schools. Some specific findings include:

- Many instructional programs have been demonstrated to be effective for reducing crime. In particular, those that teach self-control or social competency skills using cognitive-behavioral or behavioral instructional methods are effective. These programs are most effective when targeted at youths who are at elevated risk for subsequent problem behavior.
- School discipline management policies and practices are important determinants of school crime. Schools in which rules are clearly stated, fair, and consistently enforced, and in which students have participated in establishing mechanisms for reducing misbehavior, experience less disorder. Programs that employ behavioral strategies to monitor and reinforce student behavior are effective both for controlling behavior in school and for reducing subsequent crime.
- Perceptions of social norms for behavior are related as expected to problem behavior, net of individuals' personal beliefs. Schools can intervene to change perceptions of norms and expectations for behavior and doing so reduces delinquency, although attempts to do so sometimes backfire.

- In schools in which students feel an emotional attachment to the adults in the school, their misbehavior is restrained. Several strategies that might increase communal social organization show promise for increasing youths' sense of connection to the school. More work is needed to develop and test the full potential of this type of school-based prevention strategy.
- The field lacks strong evidence of the effectiveness of most school policies and practices designed to reduce levels of crime, victimization, violence, and substance use. The tendency is to launch major initiatives in response to high-profile events without doing a high-quality evaluation. This limits schools' effectiveness for reducing these problems.

Section I contains a summary of research on the effectiveness of curriculum-based prevention programs. Section II summarizes evidence showing that how the school is organized and managed also influences problem behavior and school safety. Sections III and IV discuss two aspects of school organizational climate—discipline management and school culture, respectively—and how they can be manipulated to reduce crime and related problem behaviors. Section V concludes with recommendations to guide future evaluation research on school-based interventions. Throughout the essay, our focus is on how schools can and do influence the behavior of students while they are enrolled.

I. Prevention Curricula

Gottfredson and Gottfredson (2001) reported results from the National Study of Delinquency Prevention in Schools (NSDPS) showing that 76 percent of schools use at least one prevention curriculum to reduce problem behavior or increase school safety. These programs can be effective. D. Gottfredson, Wilson, and Najaka's (2002) review of studies of school-based prevention found that certain types of curricular change are effective for reducing problem behaviors. They reported average effect sizes ranging from 0.05 ($p < .05$) for alcohol and drug use to 0.30 ($p < .05$) for antisocial behavior and aggression due to instructional programs that teach self-control or social competency using cognitive-behavioral or behavioral instructional methods. This category of intervention seeks to develop students' skills in recognizing situations in which they are likely to get into trouble, controlling or managing their impulses, anticipating the consequences of their actions, perceiving accurately the feelings or intentions of others, or coping with peer influence that may lead to trouble. These interventions use instructional methods that explicitly teach principles for self-regulation and recognize antecedents of problem behavior. They provide cues to help young people remember and apply the principles, use modeling to demonstrate the principles and associated behavior, encourage goal setting, provide opportunities for rehearsal and practice of the behavior in social situations (role-playing), provide feedback on student performance, and promote self-monitoring and self-regulation.

A closely related type of school-based intervention teaches similar cognitive content, but often couples instruction with behavior change strategies (to be discussed in greater detail later) and most often targets higher risk youths rather than entire classrooms. This type of school-based program also has positive effects on measures of antisocial behavior and aggression (D. Gottfredson, Wilson, and Najaka 2002). More recent reviews of school-based prevention curricula (Hahn et al. 2007; Wilson and Lipsey 2007) concur that this type of prevention curriculum is moderately effective for reducing a variety of forms of problem behavior. Also of interest is the conclusion from these reviews (Wilson, Gottfredson, and Najaka 2001; Wilson and Lipsey 2007); that school-based interventions targeting more at-risk populations produced larger effect sizes on measures of delinquent, disruptive, and aggressive behaviors than those targeting the general population.

More than a dozen narrative reviews and meta-analyses of school-based interventions aimed at reducing conduct problems and delinquent behavior other than those summarized above have been published in the last fifteen years (Dryfoos 1990; Lipsey 1992; Lipsey and Wilson 1993; Institute of Medicine 1994; Durlak 1995; Tremblay and Craig 1995; Stage and Quiroz 1997; Catalano et al. 1998; Hawkins, Farrington, and Catalano 1998; Samples and Aber 1998; Gottfredson and Gottfredson 2001; Wilson, Gottfredson, and Najaka 2001). Readers are referred to these sources for more detailed discussions of a large number of programs of the general type found to be effective. These effective programs are heterogeneous in terms of age group (ranging from pre-K through high school), duration, and targeting strategies.

II. Does School Organization Matter?

How the school is organized and managed also influences problem behavior and school safety. In an early national study of school disorder, Gottfredson and Gottfredson (1985) showed that even after controlling for input characteristics of students and communities in which schools were located, characteristics of schools accounted for an additional 12 percent (junior high) and 18 percent (senior high) of variance in teacher victimization rates. More recent national studies have replicated these findings and extended them to show that school characteristics account for a substantial amount of variance not only in teacher victimization but also in student reports of victimization and delinquency (G. Gottfredson et al. 2005).

Which aspects of the way schools are organized and managed influence crime and disorder? Cook, Gottfredson, and Na (2010) discuss school system decisions that influence the demographic composition of schools and the number and types of other students to whom a child is exposed. Schools and school districts have a good deal of control over the makeup of the student body. Schools can be based on neighborhood residential patterns or integrated across race and class. The grade span for elementary and middle schools can be adjusted. Truancy and dropout prevention programs can be pursued with more or less vigor, and troublesome students reassigned. Whether failing students are retained in grade or given a social promotion influences the extent of age homogeneity within classrooms. Students who are enrolled in the school can be tracked on the basis of academic potential or mixed together. These decisions influence the characteristics of other students to whom youths will be exposed. Importantly, these decisions determine the pool of youths from which highly influential peers will be selected, as well as the dominant peer culture in the school.

School and school district decisions about curricular content and teaching methods are also important. These decisions determine student success in school and decisions to persist in school, and, as summarized earlier, the use of specialized prevention curricula directly influences the level of problem behavior. Below we discuss two additional characteristics of schools that influence crime and disorder: (1) policies and procedures governing discipline management that directly affect the extent to which formal sanctions are applied and the effectiveness of these sanctions, and (2) aspects of the school social organization that affect the nature of interactions among teachers and students (and hence the application of social controls), and the school culture.

III. Discipline Management

Cook, Gottfredson, and Na (2010) summarize findings from 12 studies that looked at the association of discipline management practices with school crime. The results show remarkable consistency: when schools monitor students and control access to the campus, and when students perceive that school rules are fair and consistently enforced, schools experience lower levels of problem behavior. Inclusion of students in establishing school rules and policies for dealing with problem behaviors has also been found to be related to lower levels of problem behavior, most likely because students are apt to internalize school rules if they have helped to shape them. On the other hand, severity of sanctions is not related to a reduction in problem behaviors. These findings conform to the main findings from deterrence research that the certainty of punishment has greater deterrent effect than the severity of punishment (Cook 1980; Nagin 1998).

Of course, there has been considerable policy attention to school disciplinary practices, especially in response to the spate of school shootings experienced in the 1980s and 1990s. Most schools employ security and surveillance strategies aimed at keeping intruders out and preventing weapons from coming into the schools. Common practices include controlled entry and identification systems, metal detectors, security personnel or volunteers who challenge intruders, or doors fitted with electromagnetic locks. The NSDPS described earlier showed that over half of schools in the United States employ one or more such procedure (Gottfredson and Gottfredson 2001). Unfortunately, our search for evidence on the effectiveness of these practices yielded only one outcome study of reasonable scientific rigor—a study of metal detectors in high schools in New York City. Ginsberg and Loffredo (1993) compared the frequency of weapon carrying in schools with and without metal detectors and found that students in schools with metal detectors were half as likely to carry a weapon to school as students in schools without metal detectors.

Since the late 1990s, school resource officers (SROs) have been especially popular in secondary schools as a way to prevent violence, encouraged by federal subsidies. Kochel, Laszlo, and Nickles (2004) reported that as of October 2004, the US Department of Justice had invested $746 million to place more than 6,500 SROs in schools and an additional $20 million to train them to implement community policing in schools. According to the School Crime Supplement to the National Crime Victimization Survey, the percentage of students ages 12–18 who reported the presence of security guards and/or assigned police officers at their schools increased from 54 percent in 1999 to 68 percent in 2005. A *New York Times* article (January 4, 2009) reported that more than 17,000 police officers are now placed in the nation's schools. As with other security strategies, little high-quality evaluation research has been conducted to assess SRO effectiveness, but it seems reasonable that the increased presence of SRO officers in schools at the very least increases the referral of problem behaviors to law enforcement agencies. Cook, Gottfredson, and Na (2010) report on an analysis of School Crime and Safety data (Guerino et al. 2006) showing that the presence of an officer in the school results in a doubling of the rate of referrals to law enforcement for the most common crime perpetrated by students in schools—simple assault without a weapon.

We do not know if the increase in referrals to law enforcement deters future crime. Regardless of the impact, the cost of adding SROs to schools is high, not only in personnel costs but also in extra costs related to formal processing of misbehaviors that would otherwise be handled in the school. There are also civil liberties issues to be considered. As reported in the *New York Times* (January 4, 2009), an A.C.L.U inquiry into school-based arrests in Hartford, Connecticut, found that they disproportionately involved minority youths. Clearly, research is needed to assess the effectiveness of popular but costly security and surveillance practices, especially in light of the high potential for net-widening and disproportionality in the consequences of their use.

A closely related discipline strategy is the use of zero-tolerance policies in schools—another "tough on crime" practice engendered by the epidemic of youth violence in the late 1980s and the school rampage shootings of that decade and the next. The US Congress adopted the Gun-Free Schools Act in 1994, mandating that students be suspended for one year if they brought a gun to school. A large majority of school districts adopted zero-tolerance policies for alcohol, tobacco, drugs, and violence (Simon 2006). The use of suspension, especially long-term suspension, is thought to have disproportionate impact on minority and special education populations (McFadden and Marsh 1992; Gregory 1995), whose behavior places them more at risk for suspension. Civil liberties advocates have argued that zero-tolerance policies rob youths of their right to a public education (Skiba 2000).

As with the other security-related school polices, little high-quality evidence is available to guide decisions about which discipline management policies produce the most desirable outcomes. The issue is complex, requiring consideration of the trade-offs between in-school and out-of-school crime, the welfare of the youths who perpetrate the school-based offenses versus that of the other youths in the school, and long-term versus short-term outcomes. Clearly, removing troublemakers from school helps to maintain an environment more suitable for learning for these remaining students. But the costs of doing so for the offenders and society are not well understood (but see Kinsler 2009). A complete analysis of the effect of zero-tolerance policies on youth crime would consider the displacement of crime from school to the community, as well as the consequences for the suspended youths' long-term criminal and academic careers. As youths lose more days of school to suspension, promotion to the next grade becomes less likely. And as youths fall further behind grade, they become much less likely to graduate (Alexander, Entwisle, and Horsey 1997; Entwisle, Alexander, and Olson 1997; Lee and Burkam 2003; Jimerson et al. 2006), and more likely to drop-out, which is likely to increase subsequent crime. Clearly, although zero-tolerance policies benefit the classmates of troublesome youths, a rational discipline policy would also have to consider the broader consequences of such policies for the community.

More consistent with the research on effective crime deterrents are school discipline polices that emphasize the certainty of response to misbehavior over the severity of the response. Among the most effective school-based strategies for reducing youth violence, aggression, and problem behavior are behavioral interventions that target specific behaviors, systematically remove rewards for undesirable behavior, and apply contingent rewards for desired behavior or punishment for undesired behavior. These interventions are often applied to the high-risk youths who are most at risk for being suspended from school under zero-tolerance policies, and as such could be incorporated into school routines for discipline management. Gottfredson, Wilson, and Najaka's (2002) meta-analysis reported average effect size on measures of antisocial behavior and aggression of 0.34 ($p < .05$) across 12 studies of this type of behavioral intervention.

Examples of particularly effective behavioral interventions currently in use in schools are the "Good Behavior Game" (GBG; Dolan et al. 1993; Kellam et al. 1994, 2008) and "home-based reinforcement" (Schumaker, Hovell, and Sherman 1977). The GBG is a classroom-based application of behavioral principles in which elementary school children are divided into small teams, and the teams are rewarded when the classroom behavior of the entire team meets or exceeds a pre-established standard. The GBG is played several times per week throughout the school year. The intervention was evaluated through a randomized trial involving 19 schools in Baltimore, with posttests conducted immediately following the intervention, as well as 6 and 14 years later. The results of this study indicate that participation in GBG is related to immediate reductions in aggressive behavior, rates of diagnosed antisocial personality disorder, and long-term effects (14 years later) on drug and alcohol use and smoking.

Home-based reinforcement (HBR), applied to individual students displaying behavior problems, requires cooperation between teachers and parents in the management of the child's behavior. After agreeing upon specific child behaviors to be extinguished or encouraged and establishing a baseline for these behaviors, teachers systematically record data on the target behavior on a "daily report card" that goes home to the parents. The parents, who generally have access to a wider array of reinforcers and punishments than do the teachers, use the teacher's information to guide the application of rewards and punishments. As the desired behavior emerges, the frequency of reports home is reduced, and the schedule of contingencies is relaxed. In the earliest research on HBR, application of this technique to junior high school students showed that school rule compliance, teacher satisfaction with the student, and academic performance improved as a result of participation in an HBR program (Schumaker, Hovell, and Sherman 1977). A recent review of 18 empirical studies of "school-home collaboration" interventions (Cox 2005) concluded that behavioral interventions using the daily report card strategy had the strongest effects on problem behavior. Lasting effects on crime are unknown.

These relatively simple and inexpensive behavioral interventions represent a potentially potent school-based prevention strategy that might be incorporated into routine school practice. The 1997 reauthorization of the Individuals with Disabilities Education Act (IDEA; P.L. 105–17) required functional assessment and behavioral intervention procedures to be implemented in the disciplining of students with disabilities. The evidence-based programs described here would meet these federal requirements.

Behavioral principles have also been incorporated into school-wide discipline management systems. These systems are typically designed to clarify expectations for behavior. They establish school and classroom rules, communicate these rules as well as consequences for breaking them clearly to parents and students, establish systems for tracking both youth behavior and consequences applied by the schools, and monitor the consistency of the application of consequences for misbehavior. School-wide discipline management efforts, most often implemented by a school-based team of educators, are highly consistent with the research summarized earlier suggesting that students' perceptions of school rules as fair and consistently enforced is related to reductions in problem behavior.

The meta-analysis described earlier (D. Gottfredson, Wilson, and Najaka 2002) also examined the effectiveness of this type of school-wide effort to improve discipline management and reported average effect size on measures of crime (0.27, $p < .05$) and alcohol and other drug use (0.24, $p < .05$). Among the studies included in the meta-analysis are two early studies of the effects of school-wide discipline management systems on problem behavior outcomes. Students in the intervention schools in the first of these efforts (Project PATHE implemented in nine Charleston, South Carolina, schools) reported less delinquent behavior and drug use and fewer punishments in school relative to the students in the comparison schools (D. Gottfredson 1986).

A similar intervention was tested in a troubled Baltimore, Maryland, junior high school, with a special emphasis on replacing the school's reliance on out-of-school suspension with a wider array of consequences for misbehavior. This intervention, which added positive reinforcement for desired behavior to the mix of consequences routinely used, also showed positive effects on student delinquency and rebellious behavior (D. Gottfredson 1987). This early research, although based on relatively small numbers of schools and lacking randomization to condition, suggested that behavioral principles could be incorporated into "normal" school disciplinary practices, and that an emphasis on consistency of rule enforcement as opposed to severity of punishment provided an effective deterrent.

Contemporary approaches to discipline management incorporate behavioral principles into comprehensive systems that include school-wide discipline policies and practices as well as targeted behavioral interventions. One popular approach is School-Wide Positive Behavior Support (SWPBS), a "whole-school approach emphasizing effective systemic and individualized behavioral interventions for achieving social and learning outcomes while preventing problem behaviors" (Sugai and Horner 2008). This system, adopted by over 5,600 schools throughout the United States, uses a school-team approach to apply behavioral interventions at different levels of intensity for students at different levels of need. Universal interventions focus on clarity of school and classroom rules and consistency of enforcement, and on screening for more serious behavior disorders. Group-based behavioral interventions are employed with the 5 to 10 percent of youths who do not respond to the universal interventions. In addition, intensive, individualized behavioral interventions are employed to manage the behavior of the small segment of the population that is especially at risk. Unfortunately, the research on the effectiveness of SWPBS is not as sophisticated as it should be for such a widely disseminated program. Although dozens of studies have demonstrated that problem behavior decreases after the intervention is put in place, only one (Sprague et al. 2001) compared change in the intervention school(s) with the change that might be expected in the absence of an intervention. Even this study is not useful for isolating the effects of the behavior management strategies because it also included the introduction of a prevention curriculum along with the school-wide behavioral supports. Higher quality research is needed to assess the effects of this promising approach on crime both in and out of school.

IV. SCHOOL CULTURE

School culture is potentially the most potent aspect of school climate because it involves proximal interpersonal influences on student behavior. *School culture* refers to the quality of human relationships in the school and includes both peer culture and the extent to which the organization is communally organized. All of these dimensions influence youth crime and can be successfully manipulated to reduce it.

A. Behavioral Norms

Cultural norms, expectations, and beliefs influence all behaviors. Early research on characteristics of effective schools documented that schools have a distinctive ethos that influences students' academic and social behaviors (Rutter et al. 1979). More recent research on school culture (summarized in Cook, Gottfredson, and Na 2010) concurs that norms and expectations for behavior, of both peers and adult, are powerful determinants of behavior, net of the individual's own beliefs.

Of course, school "inputs" are key determinants of the predominant cultural beliefs in the school. School desegregation and retention policies, as well as the grade span, of the school can influence school culture by altering the mix of students in the school. But several more programmatic attempts to alter school culture have also been studied. These programs have in common a focus on clarifying behavioral norms. That is, in contrast to the instructional programs described in the previous section that focus on teaching youths specific social competency skills, these normative change programs focus on clarifying expectations for behavior. Some signal appropriate behavior through media campaigns or ceremonies; others involve youths in activities aimed at clarifying misperceptions about normative behavior; and still others increase exposure to prosocial models and messages.

Several studies of attempts to clarify norms for behavior have been reported. D. Gottfredson, Wilson, and Najaka (2002) summarized effects reported in 13 studies and concluded that such programs are effective for reducing crime, substance use, and antisocial behavior. Two of the better known examples of programs in this category are the Bullying Prevention Program (Olweus, Limber, and Mihalic 1999), and the Safe Dates Program (Foshee et al. 1996; 1998).

Olweus's anti-bullying program includes school-wide, classroom, and individual components. School-wide components include increased adult supervision at bullying "hot spots" and school-wide discussions of bullying. Classroom components focus on developing and enforcing rules against bullying. Individual counseling is also provided to children identified as bullies and victims. A large-scale evaluation of this program in Norwegian schools demonstrated that it led to reductions in student bullying and victimization and decreases in the incidence of vandalism, fighting, and theft (Olweus, Limber, and Mihalic 1999). A very recent review of anti-bullying programs summarizing results from 59 studies conducted between 1983 and 2008 (Farrington and Ttofi 2009) confirmed that anti-bullying programs are effective for reducing bullying and student victimization, and that Olweus's program is particularly effective.

The Safe Dates Program targets norms for dating violence among adolescents. The school portion of the intervention includes a theater production performed by peers; a 10-session curriculum addressing dating violence norms, gender stereotyping, and conflict management skills; and a poster contest. The community portion of the intervention includes services for adolescents experiencing abuse and training for community service providers. Foshee et al. (1998) found that intervention students reported less psychological abuse and violence against dating partners than did control students.

Based on these and other relatively rigorous evaluations, D. Gottfredson, Wilson, and Najaka (2002) concluded that interventions aimed at establishing norms or expectations for behavior can be effective in preventing substance use, delinquency, aggression, and other problem behaviors. It should be noted, however, that evaluations of these programs seldom provide clean tests of the proposition that culture matters, since the programs more often than not combine attempts to alter norms with other components aimed at increasing levels of supervision and enforcement (e.g., Olweus) or improving social competency skills (Foshee).

We would be remiss if we failed to mention that sometimes school-based practices that seek to clarify norms for behavior backfire. One example is a peer counseling program that deliberately mixed delinquent and nondelinquent youths in counseling sessions in which youths were encouraged to share their problems. The intent was that the negative beliefs and attitudes voiced by the delinquent youths would be corrected through interaction with the nondelinquent youths. A randomized experiment testing this program as implemented in the Chicago Public Schools (G. Gottfredson 1987) reported predominantly harmful effects for high school students: high school treatment youths reported significantly *more* delinquent behavior than controls. A more recent large-scale evaluation of the Reconnecting Youth program (Cho, Hallfors, and Sánchez 2005) also found negative effects for a group counseling program for at-risk high school students. This program sought to "re-connect" truant, underachieving high school students (and to reduce their deviance and substance use) by developing a positive peer-group culture. Students were grouped together in classes of 10 to 12 students for a full semester during which a trained group leader (following a standardized curriculum) attempted to develop a climate conducive to building trust. The evaluation reported only negative effects six months following the end of the intervention. Treatment students showed greater bonding to high-risk peers, lower bonding to school and conventional peers, lower GPA, and higher anger than control students at the six-month follow-up.

B. Communal Social Organization

A second aspect of school culture that has been studied extensively pertains to the affective bonds between students and teachers and among adults in the school. The concept of "communal social organization" (CSO) was first introduced as part of the effective schools debate in the 1980s (e.g., Purkey and Smith 1983; Firestone and Rosenblum 1988) and studied by Bryk and colleagues (Bryk and Dirscoll 1988) mostly in the context of predictors of school achievement. Communally organized schools are schools in which "members know, care about, and support one another, have common goals and sense of shared purpose, and . . . actively contribute and feel personally committed" (Solomon et al. 1997). This aspect of school culture is especially important for school crime research because we know that individual-level student affective bonds are an important predictor of delinquency (Hirschi 1969), and it seems reasonable to hypothesize that schools high on CSO would produce higher levels of student bonding to school.

Research suggests that average student attachment to school and CSO more generally do inhibit student problem behaviors. The most comprehensive test of this linkage was provided by Payne, Gottfredson, and Gottfredson (2003) using data from the NSDPS. This study demonstrated that more communally organized schools experience less student delinquency and teacher victimization, and that the effect of communal school organization on student delinquency is mediated by average student bonding.

This survey research dovetails nicely with an ambitious ethnographic study of school violence conducted for the National Research Council. In 2003, the Committee to Study Youth Violence in Schools of the National Research Council published its report on the circumstances surrounding several incidents involving extreme lethal violence that had occurred in the nation's schools (National Research Council 2003). The report was based on detailed case studies of six schools and communities that had experienced school shootings resulting in death. Among the committee's several insights into the factors leading to the incidents is the following:

> the sense of community between youth and adults in these schools . . . was lacking. In the worst example, the school allowed a school newspaper to print an article that humiliated one of the students who became a shooter. The adults involved may have been too distant from the students to prevent some social processes leading to the potential for violence or resulting in an intolerable humiliation from some potentially vulnerable youth. (p. 256)

This observation is consistent with the research on more mundane forms of school violence just summarized. It suggests that strategies that increase social bonds between students and others in their schools will reduce misbehavior by increasing informal controls. Students who care what adults in the school think about them will be less likely to act in ways that jeopardize their positive regard. More concretely, students who have close ties to the adults in the school will be more likely to report on rumors of impending attacks. But how can such bonds be built or maintained? Possibilities include organizing the school so that the typical teacher interacts with fewer students, reducing class size, and creating more "communal" social environments in which members are more tightly joined together by common goals and in which members are held in place by the support and positive regard of others in the organization. Reorganizing schools to create a smaller feel to the schooling experience is an effective strategy for increasing youths' sense of connection, and that enhanced connectedness should hold criminal behavior in check.

A less drastic intervention with the same objectives is mentoring. Youth mentoring programs often target youths at risk of behavioral problems, assigning them to an adult mentor who spends time with the young person, provides support and guidance, and offers general guidance. Evaluations of such programs have been mixed, but often null or weak results can be attributed to implementation failure. As with any voluntary program, mentoring programs in practice are often not as intensive as intended (e.g., Karcher 2008). However, a recent meta-analysis of mentoring programs (Eby et al. 2007) demonstrated small but positive effects of mentoring programs on several behaviors of interest in this chapter: withdrawal behaviors (e.g., school drop-out, truancy—18 studies), deviance (e.g., suspension from school, aggressive behavior, property crime—15 studies), and substance use (7 studies). This review included a wide range of types of mentoring programs, but outcomes for youth mentoring programs were as strong on these outcomes as were the other types of mentoring programs (academic and workplace mentoring) included in the review.

One of the better-known models for adult mentoring, the Big Brothers–Big Sisters program (BBBS) is a community-based program evaluated in a large-scale randomized trial that found that mentored youths were 46 percent less likely than control youth to initiate drug use, 27 percent less likely to initiate alcohol use, and almost one-third less likely to hit someone during the study period (Tierney, Grossman, and Resch 1995). Community-based mentoring involves meetings between the mentor and mentee at times and places selected by the pair. Many schools now provide "school based mentoring," (SBM), which involves meetings primarily in school during the school day. A recent evaluation of the BBBS SBM model, also involving random assignment of a large number of youths, showed that although it is not as effective as the community-based alternative, SBM does improve academic performance, reduce truancy, and reduce serious school infractions (Herrera et al. 2007) at least during the first year of mentoring. Consistent with results from smaller scale randomized trials of SBM showing positive effects on increasing connectedness to school (Karcher 2005) and perceived social support (Karcher 2008), Herrera et al. (2007) found that mentored youths reported more often than controls the presence of a nonparental adult in their life who provides social supports. At the end of the second year of the study during which minimal SBM was provided, the positive program effect on truancy was sustained but the other positive effects were not. Herrera et al. (2007) conclude that although the SBM model is promising, it needs to be strengthened to ensure longer and higher quality mentor/mentee matches than are typically found in schools.

V. Discussion and Conclusions

In this brief essay, we reviewed what is known about the effectiveness of prevention curricula for reducing problem behaviors. We summarized evidence showing that instructional programs that teach self-control or social competency using cognitive-behavioral or behavioral instructional methods are effective, and that the largest crime-prevention potential results when youths who are at elevated risk for subsequent problem behavior are targeted for such school-based programs.

We also summarized research on school discipline management policies and practices and showed that they are important determinants of school crime. Research consistently shows that in schools in which students report that the school rules are clearly stated, fair, and consistently enforced, and in schools in which students have participated in establishing mechanisms for reducing misbehavior, students are much less likely to engage in problem behaviors. We showed that evaluations of specific school-based programs that employ behavioral strategies to monitor and reinforce student behavior are effective both for controlling behavior in school and for reducing subsequent crime. Also, altering school-wide discipline management policies and practices to incorporate behavioral principles, clarify expectations for behavior, and consistently enforce rules reduces problem behavior. We discussed popular "get tough" approaches to school discipline, including zero-tolerance policies and the use of law enforcement officers in schools. Although the effects of these polices on crime are not known, we argued that they might actually increase crime outside of school. There is a clear need for rigorous research on the effects of these policies.

Finally, we summarized research showing that perceptions of social norms for behavior are related as expected to problem behavior, net of individuals' personal beliefs. In schools in which the prevailing norm is to condone delinquent activities, students are more likely to do so regardless of their own personal dispositions to engage in these behaviors. But we showed that schools can intervene to change perceptions of norms and expectations for behavior and that doing so reduces delinquency, although attempts to do so sometimes backfire. We also reported on evidence suggesting that in schools in which students feel an emotional attachment to the adults in the school, their misbehavior is restrained. We discussed several strategies that might increase communal social organization and that show promise for increasing youths' sense of connection to the school. We reviewed research on school-based mentoring programs and showed that they also hold considerable promise for crime prevention. Although research documents positive effects of these programs on social relations outcomes, more work is needed to test the full potential of more potent models of school-based mentoring than have been tested to date.

Given the limitations of the evidence base, we are more confident in making recommendations about research priorities than about effective policy. Indeed, this field is burdened by a lack of timely policy research, and a tendency to launch major initiatives without first (or ever!) doing a high-quality evaluation. Note in this regard the various "get tough" policies that have been encouraged by the federal government and adopted nationwide since the 1990s, the widespread use of SROs, or the School-Wide Positive Behavior Support package that has been adopted by 5,500 schools.

We have several recommendations to guide evaluation research on interventions. The first recommendation is to actually do such research, as suggested above. Given the tens of millions that are being spent on school resource officers, it seems criminal that we do not have good evidence on the effects on how infractions are dealt with, whether crime is suppressed, and more generally whether there is a positive or negative effect on attitudes of students toward school. An impediment to learning about the effects of many school reforms is that the reforms tend to be implemented in all schools in the affected jurisdiction at once. This hinders rigorous evaluation because it leaves no schools in which to measure what would happen in the absence of the reform. A smarter approach would be to randomly assign schools to different phase-in periods, allowing for comparison during the first few years of the schools who implement the reform early and those who will implement it in the future.

Other recommendations are to measure effects on crime and other forms of misbehavior in evaluations conducted of interventions intended to improve academic performance, to capture the most serious forms of crime in evaluations rather than only less serious misbehavior, and to assess effects of prevention practices and policies on the entire student population rather than only on the students who are targeted.

Finally, it is important to identify programs to create more cohesive, communal, personalized environments. Many approaches to creating such environments seem plausible, but no rigorous research has yet established that such changes can be accomplished and that doing so results in a reduction in crime. This appears to be the next large challenge facing research on school-based prevention.

NOTES

This essay is based on a more detailed chapter (Cook, Gottfredson, and Na 2010) that reviews statistics on crime in school and youth crime more generally, documents trends and patterns, summarizes research on school effects, and discusses organizational characteristics of schools that might influence crime. These characteristics include school size, composition of the student body, school discipline, delinquency prevention curricula, and school culture.

REFERENCES

Alexander, Karl L., Doris R. Entwisle, and Carrie S. Horsey. 1997. "From First Grade Forward: Early Foundations of High School Dropout." *Sociology of Education* 70:87–107.

Bryk, Anthony S., and Mary E. Driscoll. 1988. *The High School as Community: Contextual Influences and Consequences for Students and Teachers*. Madison: University of Wisconsin, National Center on Effective Secondary Schools.

Catalano, Richard F., Michael W. Arthur, J. David Hawkins, Lisa Berglund, and Jeffrey J. Olson. 1998. "Comprehensive Community-and School-Based Interventions to Prevent Antisocial Behavior." In *Serious and Violent Juvenile Offenders: Risk Factors and Successful Interventions*, edited by Rolf Loeber and David P. Farrington. Thousand Oaks, CA: Sage.

Cho, Hyunsan, Denise D. Hallfors, and Victoria Sánchez. 2005. "Evaluation of a High School Peer Group Intervention for At-Risk Youth " *Journal of Abnormal Child Psychology* 33:363–74.

Cook, Philip J. 1980. "Research in Criminal Deterrence: Laying the Groundwork for the Second Decade." In *Crime and Justice: An Annual Review of Research*, edited by Norval Morris and Michael Tonry. Chicago: University of Chicago.

Cook, Philip J., Gottfredson, Denise C., and Na, Chongmin. 2010. "School Crime Control and Prevention." In *Crime and Justice: A Review of Research*, vol. 39, edited by Michael Tonry. Chicago: University of Chicago Press. Available at http://papers.ssrn.com/sol3/papers.cfm?abstract_id=1368292.

Cox, Diane D. 2005. "Evidence-based Intervention Using Home-school Collaboration." *School of Psychology Quarterly* 20:473–97.

Dolan, Lawrence J., Sheppard G. Kellam, C. Hendricks Brown, Lisa Werthamer-Larsson, George W. Rebok, Lawrence S. Mayer, Jolene Laudolff, Jaylan S. Turkkan, Carla Ford, and Leonard. Wheeler. 1993. "The Short-Term Impact of Two Classroom-Based Preventive Interventions on Aggressive and Shy Behaviors and Poor Achievement." *Journal of Applied Developmental Psychology* 14:317–45.

Dryfoos, Joy G. 1990. *Adolescents at Risk: Prevalence and Prevention*. New York: Oxford University Press.

Durlak, Joseph A. 1995. *School-Based Prevention Programs for Children and Adolescents*. Thousand Oaks, CA: Sage.

Eby, Lillian T., Tammy D. Allen, Sarah C. Evans, Thomas Ng, and David L. DuBois. 2007. "Does Mentoring Matter? A Multidisciplinary Meta-Analysis Comparing Mentored and Non-Mentored Individuals." *Journal of Vocational Behavior* 72:254–67.

Entwisle, Doris R., Karl L. Alexander, and Linda S. Olson. 1997. *Children, Schools, and Inequality*. Boulder, CO: Westview.

Farrington, David P., and Maria M. Ttofi. 2009. "Reducing School Bullying: Evidence-Based Implications for Policy." In *Crime and Justice: A Review of Research*, vol. 38, edited by Michael Tonry. Chicago: University of Chicago Press.

Firestone, William A., and Sheila Rosenblum. 1988. "Building Commitment in Urban High Schools." *Educational Evaluation & Policy Analysis* 10:285–99.

Foshee, Vangie A., Karl E. Bauman, Ximena B. Arriaga, Russell W. Helms, Gary G. Koch, and George F. Linder. 1998. "An Evaluation of Safe Dates, an Adolescent Dating Violence Prevention Program." *American Journal of Public Health* 88:45–50.

Foshee, Vangie A., George F Linder, Karl E. Bauman, Stacey A. Langwick, Ximena B. Arriaga, Janet L. Heath, Pamela McMahon, and Shrikant Bangdiwala. 1996. "The Safe Dates Project: Theoretical Basis, Evaluation Design, and Selected Baseline Findings." *American Journal of Preventive Medicine* 12:39–47.

Ginsberg, C., and L. Loffredo. 1993. "Violence-Related Attitudes and Behaviors of High School Students—New York City 1992." *Journal of School Health* 63:438–40.

Gottfredson, Denise C. 1986. "An Empirical Test of School-Based Environmental and Individual Interventions to Reduce the Risk of Delinquent Behavior." *Criminology* 24:705–31.

Gottfredson, Denise C. 1987. "An Evaluation of an Organization Development Approach to Reducing School Disorder." *Evaluation Review* 11:739–63.

Gottfredson, Denise C. 2001. *Schools and Delinquency*. New York: Cambridge University Press.

Gottfredson, Denise C., David B. Wilson, and Stacy S. Najaka. 2002. "School-Based Crime Prevention." In *Evidence-Based Crime Prevention*, edited by Lawrence W. Sherman, David P. Farrington, Brandon Welsh, C., and Doris L. MacKenzie. London: Routledge.

Gottfredson, Gary D. 1987. "Peer Group Interventions to Reduce the Risk of Delinquent Behavior: A Selective Review and a New Evaluation." *Criminology* 25:671–714.

Gottfredson, Gary D., and Denise C. Gottfredson. 1985. *Victimization in Schools*. New York: Plenum Press.

Gottfredson, Gary D., and Denise C. Gottfredson. 2001. "What Schools Do to Prevent Problem Behavior and Promote Safe Environments." *Journal of Educational and Psychological Consultation* 12:313–44.

Gottfredson, Gary D., Denise C. Gottfredson, Allison A. Payne, and Nisha C. Gottfredson. 2005. "School Climate Predictors of School Disorder: Results from a National Study of Delinquency Prevention in Schools." *Journal of Research in Crime and Delinquency* 42:412–44.

Gregory, James. F. 1995. "The Crime of Punishment: Racial and Gender Disparities in the Use of Corporal Punishment in U.S. Public Schools." *Journal of Negro Education* 64:454–62.

Guerino, Paul, Michael D. Hurwitz, Margaret E. Noonan, and Sarah M. Kaffenberger. 2006. *Crime, Violence, Discipline, and Safety in U.S. Public Schools: Findings from the School Survey on Crime and Safety: 2003–04.* NCES 2007–302rev. Washington, DC: US Department of Education, National Center for Education Statistics.

Hahn, Robert A., Dawna S. Fuqua-Whitley, Holly Wethington, Jessica Lowy, Alex Crosby, Mindy Fullilove, Robert Johnson, Akiva Liberman, Eve Moscicki, LeShawndra Price, Susan Snyder, Farris Tuma, Stella Cory, Glenda Stone, Kaushik Mukhopadhaya, Sajal Chattopadhyay, and Linda Dahlberg,. 2007. "A Review of the Effectiveness of Universal School-Based Programs for the Prevention of Violence." *American Journal of Preventive Medicine* 33:S114–29.

Hawkins, J. David, David P. Farrington, and Richard F. Catalano. 1998. "Reducing Violence through the Schools." In *Violence in American Schools*, edited by Delbert S. Elliott, Beatrix A. Hamburg, and Kirk R. Williams. New York: Cambridge University Press.

Herrera, Carla, Jean B. Grossman, Tina J. Kauh, Amy F. Feldman, Jennifer McMaken, and Linda Z. Jucovy. 2007. *Making a Difference in Schools: The Big Brothers Big Sisters School-Based Mentoring Impact Study*. Philadelphia: Public/Private Ventures.

Hirschfield, Paul J. 2008. "Preparing for Prison? The Criminalization of School Discipline in the USA." *Theoretical Criminology* 12:79–101.

Hirschi, Travis. 1969. *Causes of Delinquency*. Berkeley, CA: University of California Press.

Institute of Medicine. 1994. *Reducing Risks for Mental Disorders: Frontiers for Preventive Intervention Research*. Washington, DC: National Academy Press.

Jimerson, Shane R., Sarah M.W. Pletcher, Kelly Graydon, Britton L. Schnurr, Amanda B. Nickerson, and Deborah K. Kundert. 2006. "Beyond Grade Retention and Social Promotion: Promoting the Social and Academic Competence of Students." *Psychology in the Schools* 43:85–97.

Karcher, Michael J. 2005. "The Effect of Developmental Mentoring and High School Mentors' Attendance on Their Younger Mentees' Self-Esteem, Social Skills, and Connectedness." *Psychology in the Schools* 42:65–77.

Karcher, Michael J. 2008. "The Study of Mentoring in the Learning Environment (SMILE): A Randomized Evaluation of the Effectiveness of School-Based Mentoring." *Prevention Science* 9:99–113.

Kellam, Sheppard G., C. Hendricks Brown, Jeanne Poduska, Nick Ialongo, Wei Wang, Peter Toyinbo, Hanno Petras, Carla Ford, Amy Windham, and Holly C. Wilcox. 2008. "Effects of a Universal Classroom Behavior Management Program in First and Second Grades on Young Adult Behavioral, Psychiatric, and Social Outcomes." *Drug and Alcohol Dependence* 95:S5–28.

Kellam, Sheppard G., George W. Rebok, Nick Ialongo, and Lawrence S. Mayer. 1994. "The Course and Malleability of Aggressive Behavior from Early First Grade into Middle School: Results of a Developmental Epidemiologically-Based Preventive Trial." *Journal of Child Psychology and Psychiatry* 35:259–81.

Kinsler, Josh. 2009. "School Discipline: A Source or Salve for the Racial Achievement Gap?" Unpublished manuscript. New York: University of Rochester.

Kochel, Tammy R., Anna T. Laszlo, and Laura B. Nickles. 2004. *Outcome-Oriented SRO Performance Measures: Learning from a Pilot Study.* Washington, DC: US Department of Justice, Office of Community Oriented Policing Services.

Lee, Valerie E., and David T. Burkam. 2003. "Dropping out of High School: The Role of School Organization and Structure." *American Educational Research Journal* 40:353–93.

Lipsey, Mark W. 1992. "Juvenile Delinquency Treatment: A Meta-Analytic Inquiry into the Variability of Effects." In *Meta-analysis for Explanation*, edited by Thomas D. Cook, Harris Cooper, David S. Cordray, Heidi Hartman, Larry V. Hedges, Richard J. Light, Thomas A. Louis, and Fredrick Mosteller. New York: Russell Sage Foundation.

Lipsey, Mark W., and David B. Wilson. 1993. "The Efficacy of Psychological, Educational, and Behavioral Treatment: Confirmation from Meta-Analysis." *American Psychologist* 48:1181–209.

McFadden, Anna C, and George. E. Marsh. 1992. "A Study of Racial and Gender Bias in the Punishment of School Children." *Education and Treatment of Children* 15:140–46.

Nagin, Daniel S. 1998. "Criminal Deterrence Research at the Outset of the Twenty-First Century." In *Crime and Justice: An Annual Review of Research*, edited by Michael Tonry. Chicago: University of Chicago Press.

National Research Council. 2003. *Deadly Lessons: Understanding Lethal School Violence.* Washington, DC: National Academy Press.

New York Times. 2009. "The Principal's Office First." Editorial, January 4.

Olweus, Dan, Sue Limber, and Sharon Mihalic. 1999. *Blueprints for Violence Prevention: Bullying Prevention Program.* Boulder, CO: Center for the Study and Prevention of Violence.

Payne, Allison A., Denise C. Gottfredson, and Gary D. Gottfredson. 2003. "Schools as Communities: The Relationships among Communal School Organization, Student Bonding, and School Disorder." *Criminology* 41:749–77.

Purkey, Stewart C., and Marshall S. Smith. 1983. "Effective Schools: A Review." *Elementary School Journal* 83:427–52.

Rutter, Michael, Barbara Maughan, Peter Mortimore, Janet Ouston, and Alan Smith. 1979. *Fifteen Thousand Hours: Secondary Schools and Their Effects on Children.* Cambridge, MA: Harvard University Press.

Samples, Faith, and J. Lawrence Aber. 1998. "Evaluations of School-Based Violence Prevention Programs." In *Violence in American Schools*, edited by Delbert S. Elliott, Beatrix A. Hamburg, and Kirk R. Williams. New York: Cambridge University Press.

Schumaker, Jean B., Melbourne F. Hovell, and James A. Sherman. 1977. "An Analysis of Daily Report Cards and Parent-Managed Privileges in the Improvement of Adolescents' Classroom Performance." *Journal of Applied Behavioral Analysis* 10:449–64.

Simon, Jonathan. 2006. *Governing Through Crime: How the War on Crime Transformed American Democracy and Created a Culture of Fear.* New York: Oxford University Press.

Skiba, Russell J. 2000. *Zero Tolerance, Zero Evidence: An Analysis of School Disciplinary Practices. Policy Research Report.* Bloomington, IN: Indiana Education Policy Center.

Solomon, Daniel, Victor Battistich, Dong-il Kim, and Marilyn Watson. 1997. "Teacher Practices Associated with Students' Sense of the Classroom as a Community." *Social Psychology of Education* 1:235–67.

Sprague, Jeffrey, Hill Walker, Annemieke Golly, Kathy White, Dale Myers, and Tad Shannon. 2001. "Translating Research into Effective Practice: The Effects of a Universal Staff and Student Intervention on Key Indicators of School Safety and Discipline." *Education and Treatment of Children* 24:495–511.

Stage, Scott A., and David R. Quiroz. 1997. "A Meta-Analysis of Interventions to Decrease Disruptive Classroom Behavior in Public Education Settings." *School Psychology Review* 26:333–68.

Sugai, George, and Robert H. Horner. 2008. "What We Know and Need to Know about Preventing Problem Behavior in Schools." *Exceptionality* 16:67–77.

Tierney, Joseph P., Jean B. Grossman, and Nancy L. Resch. 1995. *Making a Difference: An Impact Study of Big Brothers Big Sisters*. Philadelphia: Public/Private Ventures.

Tremblay, Richard E., and Wendy M. Craig. 1995. "Developmental Crime Prevention." In *Crime and Justice: A Review of the Research: Building a Safer Society: Strategic Approaches to Crime Prevention*, edited by Michael Tonry and David P. Farrington. Chicago: University of Chicago Press.

Wilson, David B., Denise C. Gottfredson, and Stacy S. Najaka. 2001. "School-Based Prevention of Problem Behaviors: A Meta-Analysis." *Journal of Quantitative Criminology* 17:247–72.

Wilson, Sandra J., and Mark W. Lipsey. 2007. "School-Based Interventions for Aggressive and Disruptive Behavior: Update of a Meta-Analysis." *American Journal of Preventive Medicine* 33:S130–43.

PART III

SITUATIONAL CRIME PREVENTION

....

CHAPTER 15

SITUATIONAL CRIME PREVENTION: CLASSIFYING TECHNIQUES USING "GOOD ENOUGH" THEORY

....

MARTHA J. SMITH AND RONALD V. CLARKE

SITUATIONAL crime prevention (SCP) attempts to limit the harm caused by crime events by altering the more immediate causes of crimes. In particular, this approach looks to the situational components of crime events. These situational components are frequently referred to as crime "opportunities" (e.g., Clarke 2008). More recently, the types of situational components included have been expanded by some to include the potential for situations to provide precipitating conditions for offending (Wortley 2001; cf. Cornish and Clarke 2003). The SCP focus on situational components differs from the approach taken by more traditional crime-prevention strategies that seek to reduce crime by changing the offender's motivation for offending, often considered as a more or less stable "disposition" to offend. The SCP approach to crime prevention developed, in part, from research findings questioning the effectiveness of treatments aimed at changing offender motivation (Clarke and Cornish 1983). The SCP seeks generally to alter the "near" or proximal causes of crime, rather than the "distant" or distal causes (Clarke 2008). These proximal causes are, by definition, closest in time to the crime event and may be more amenable to being changed.

The success of this situational approach is well documented (see, e.g., Clarke 1992, 1997; Guerette 2009; Guerette and Bowers 2009), and as this evidence demonstrates, preventing offending without changing deep-seated offender motivation does not inevitably lead to displacement. The view that SCP can and does work is not lost on all scholars who work within traditional criminology (see, e.g., Hirschi and Gottfredson 2001, pp. 92–93, for a discussion of the comparative efficiency of offense-specific prevention aimed at the situational components of offending and offender-focused efforts aimed at incapacitation, treatment, and deterrence). Nevertheless, the general failure of mainstream criminology to focus on crime reduction—either by limiting crime events or by capturing offenders—is one of the influences behind the movement to develop "crime science," a broadly scientifically based, multidisciplinary alternative to traditional criminology (see Clarke 2008). Not surprisingly, SCP is one of the core approaches incorporated in this potential realignment of perspectives.

Over the past 30 years, Clarke has written a number of reviews of SCP (e.g., Clarke 1980, 1992, 1995, 2009). This essay differs from many of these because it does not seek to provide a broad overview of this area of crime-prevention practice. Other chapters in this volume will cover much of this ground. Instead, we will confine ourselves to discussing some of the more theoretical aspects of SCP. The emphasis in this essay is on developments in crime-events theories that influence SCP and in the changes to the SCP classification scheme from the early to mid-1990s until the present. Theory and practice in this area have expanded significantly in the past 15 years or so. General observations about these developments include the following points.

- The three key theoretical perspectives used by those working in this area of research and practice are the rational choice perspective (RCP), the routine activity approach (RAA), and crime pattern theory (CPT).
- The RCP, which was developed in part to explain how SCP operates to prevent crime, has retained its emphasis on purposive decision making by potential offenders who use bounded rationality. This theoretical perspective continues to look at decision making using models that focus on the crime event (the original, basic model and the crime script approach) and on three different stages of involvement (initial, continuance, and desistence). It has employed the perspective of being a "good enough" theory—that is, one that has practical utility for explaining preventive policy and can adapt to the changing needs of practice in relation to this policy.
- The RAA has continued to expand from its initial emphasis on explaining macro-level crime rates to a more general theory of crime events. In terms of SCP, it has developed a wide area of explanatory power by focusing on the context of the crime event, particularly in terms of the roles of key actors and places, as well as the people and factors that influence and control these actors and settings.
- The CPT represents a broad area of theorizing in relation to the occurrence of crime events in time and space, and to the routine behaviors of potential offenders and victims, particularly those related to convergences that result in crimes. The movement patterns of offenders and the diverse ways in

which hot spots develop are two key areas of CPT that are specifically relevant to understanding SCP and to designing successful initiatives.

- The SCP has also benefited from the proposals of Wortley (2001, 2002) in relation to situational precipitators, which developed from research on the strategies used to control the behavior of prisoners.
- The SCP has used these theories to assist in classifying SCP measures. These classification schemes—which provide a useful means of summarizing SCP theory so that it can be easily disseminated to practitioners and to other academics in the field—have been changed through an iterative process to reflect developments in both theory and practice.
- The SCP classification schemes, and their associated explanations using case studies and drawing on relevant theories, have produced a "good enough" theory of how SCP operates—one that is parsimonious and simple, yet has a great deal of heuristic power. SCP will continue to be a "good enough" theory as long as it meets the needs of SCP practice.

This essay is organized into three main sections. Section I looks at the general features of RCP, RAA, and CPT, focusing on those that have had the most influence on the development of the SCP classification schemes and on its use in crime prevention practice. Section II discusses the initial presentation of, and changes to, the classification systems of prevention measures developed by Clarke and a series of colleagues (Hough, Clarke, and Mayhew 1980; Clarke 1992; Clarke and Homel 1997; Cornish and Clarke 2003) and by Wortley (2001, 2002). Section III briefly points out some of the key theoretical concepts of the main three theories that have influenced SCP and discusses whether the underlying theoretical aspects of SCP can be considered as "good enough" theory—that is, whether it employs theory that has responded to challenges from research and practice, as well as guiding practice in this area.

I. Key Situational Theories

A number of situational theories and approaches for understanding and preventing crime events have been very influential within the general area of crime analysis and environmental criminology in the past several decades (Clarke 2010). Situational crime prevention is only one of these approaches. Likewise, there have been a number of theoretical innovations in the past ten years, including Ekblom's (2000) discussion of the conjunction of criminal opportunity and Wortley's (2001, 2002) proposals concerning situational precipitators. These recent contributions, as well as earlier theories such as CPTED (Jeffery 1971), situational deterrence (Cusson 1993), and the criminology of place (Sherman, Gartin, and Buerger 1989)—all of which adopt a broadly situational approach—provide further insights for those working in the area of SCP. The discussion in this essay will, however, concentrate on the three theories that have had the most noticeable effects on, and which provide the widest theoretical scope for understanding, SCP: the rational choice perspective (RCP), the routine activity approach (RAA), and crime pattern theory (CPT). In this section, we will look at general features of these theories and at the theoretical tools they provide for understanding and using SCP.

A. Rational Choice Perspective

The rational choice perspective (RCP) in criminology was set out formally and systematically by Clarke and Cornish in 1985 to cover a wide variety of criminal behaviors, situations, and types of decisions. They analyzed existing criminological theories in terms of their utility for crime control and looked at then-current research on residential burglary in terms of a series of four models of offender decision making. These models looked at the factors affecting different types of decisions, three related to different types of involvement (initial involvement, habituation or continuance, and desistance) and one devoted to the crime event (Clarke and Cornish 1985).[1] The three general influences that were seen as important across the models related to the risks, rewards, and efforts of alternative courses of action. The RCP used the concept of reasoned decision making to help explain why and how opportunity-reduction measures operate to reduce crime. A choice model was chosen over other possibilities for its advantages in mirroring the way that people usually describe their actions and because it is the model used when describing legal culpability (Clarke 2008).

The RCP does not require that criminals be wholly rational in the manner in which they seek to achieve these purposes, only that their behavior is in many respects broadly rational (Cornish and Clarke 2008). Simon (1983, cited in Clarke and Cornish 1985) used the term "bounded rationality" to describe the process of solving complex tasks in less than completely rational ways. The everyday constraints on perfect rationality can include limitations of time, ability, and knowledge about the circumstances in which decisions are made. Jacobs (2010) argued that bounded rationality may aid offenders in quickly taking advantage of unexpected crime opportunities when they are confronted with them. Furthermore, as Clarke and Cornish (1985) pointed out, when undue attention is paid to the impulsive, expressive, and other apparently irrational elements in a complex sequence of behavior, such as those involved in crime-commission behaviors, this can result in the neglect of the rational elements that enable the crime in question to be carried out successfully (cf. Hayward's 2007 view of rational choice theory's ability to explain emotive crimes and Farrell's 2010 response).

The twin assumptions of purposiveness and bounded rationality serve very important functions for SCP—and are assumptions shared by RAA and CPT.[2] By assuming that offenders are acting with bounded rationality, preventers can gain and build knowledge about crime-prevention measures that attempt to prevent these offenders from carrying out their purposes. This manner of gaining knowledge is consistent with the position taken by the eminent philosopher Karl Popper, who argued that it was important to see human action as rational because of the methodological advantages this provides when seeking to understand behavior, even if that assumption was not always correct (Tilley 2004; see also Knepper 2007). Interestingly, Tilley (2004) has challenged the use of rational choice models across all actors, situations, and interventions and has asserted that this may potentially limit the scope of measures considered by those working in SCP. Nevertheless, at this point, we think that pragmatic considerations suggest that the assumption of bounded rationality may be very useful for SCP practice. For example, in trying to prevent the most purposive and rational offenders from completing their crimes, other less committed offenders may also be discouraged. Also, assuming minimal rationality may keep preventers from giving up too soon, allowing them to continue to look for ways to block crime events even if one set of responses proves ineffective.

Another important, or core, concept of RCP that affects the practice of SCP is the exhortation to be crime specific when analyzing crime events and criminal involvement, and when devising responses to crimes. To understand why this is important, particularly when thinking about crime prevention, it is useful to consider what Cornish and Clarke (1987, p. 935) called the "choice structuring properties of crime." Offenders may seek a variety of rewards from crime, both expressive (such as fun or excitement) and instrumental (such as money, power, or control) and crimes are not all alike in what they offer in these respects to a potential offender. Even crimes that share the same legal category, such as burglaries of suburban houses and of apartments in inner-city areas, may fulfill different purposes and require different types of skills to carry out. Likewise, not all situations are equal in the opportunities they provide for carrying out a particular type of crime. The RCP assists those involved in preventing crime by pointing out that each type of crime has components that fit particular purposes and that those who seek to carry them out will make decisions to do so with bounded rationality—that is, making decisions that are limited by their knowledge, skills, and the situational factors of the setting.

The RCP also includes crime scripts, developed by Cornish in 1993 (see Cornish 1994a, 1994b) but formally added as a core concept of the perspective in 2008 (Cornish and Clarke 2008). The concept of the crime script aids SCP through its formal elaboration of the stages of the crime event. By setting out all of the stages of a crime, it becomes easier for preventers to see possible intervention points for situational measures. This is particularly important for crimes like residential burglary, where it is unlikely that a single measure could be designed and implemented that would block an essential action needed to complete the crime. In addition to emphasizing the temporal processes of the crime event, crime scripts require information about the types of actors and the instrumentalities (or props) needed, or often used, to complete a crime successfully.

The RCP was developed primarily as a working theoretical framework—that is, as a "good enough" theory of criminal behavior (Clarke and Cornish 1983). As Clarke and Cornish (1985) noted, "simple and parsimonious accounts of criminal behavior—such as those provided by dispositional or situational theories—can have considerable heuristic value. They do not have to be 'complete' explanations of criminal conduct, but only ones 'good enough' to accommodate existing research and to suggest new directions for empirical enquiry or crime control policy" (p. 149). This suggests that theories that are good enough at a particular point in time might subsequently have to be modified to accommodate new findings or serve as guides for new policy directions. This perspective is a useful one not only for understanding RCP but also for examining the development of SCP theory and its use of all three key event theories described in this section.

B. Routine Activity Approach

The routine activity approach (RAA) was developed as a macro-level victimization theory by Cohen and Felson in 1979 to explain the rise in direct-contact predatory crime in the period after World War II in the United States. At the micro level, it focused on the crime event and it identified three factors that needed to be present for this crime event to occur: a likely (motivated) offender, a suitable target for the offense, and the absence of a capable guardian to prevent the crime from occurring. These theorists also looked at the day-to-day, or routine, activities of offenders, targets (or victims), and potential guardians, seeing these as crucial for understanding the likelihood that they would be present together, or converge, at a particular time and place and so bring about a specific crime event. In addition, they studied why some targets might be more suitable than others, noting the importance of four factors—value, visibility, accessibility, and inertia (or VIVA)—decision-making concepts that neatly overlap with some aspects of risk, reward, and effort, which were used a few years later in the RCP models of Clarke and Cornish (1985) (discussed above).

Felson has continued to develop the theory in a variety of ways in the 30 years since it was initially set out. He has included crimes other than direct-contact predatory crimes and discussed the importance of place (Felson 1987); added the concept of "handler" as someone who may exert social control over an offender (Felson 1986; see also Tillyer and Eck 2011); explored the process of co-offender generation in a convergence setting (Felson 2003); and provided numerous examples of the ways that the changing conditions of modern life provide opportunities for crime (e.g., Felson and Clarke, 1998; Felson, 2002)

Eck and his colleagues have also built on this theory by expanding the number and types of elements to be considered in crime events, focusing on the control of crime opportunities through the control of actors and settings. The first step in the expansion of RAA, as noted above, came when Felson identified handlers as those who could potentially control offenders—as part of a "web of informal crime control" (Felson 1986, p. 122)—and then included "place" as part of the convergence event. Next, Eck (1995) identified those who control places as "place managers." Eck (2003) then developed what he referred to as routine activity theory's crime triangles, also now known as the "problem analysis triangle" (Clarke and Eck 2005); see figure 15.1). This device helps explain the relationships between elements of crime events (or problems) and their controls by using two triangles, one inside another. As figure 15.1 shows, the economy of presentation and the visual pneumonic provided by these double triangles of oversight, or social control, over key elements of the crime event make clear the relationships between the actors who can control and the elements of a crime event that should be controlled.

More recently, Sampson, Eck, and Dunham (2010) have added another level to the embedded triangles, making three levels of relationships in total. This third level includes the more abstract concept of "super controllers" to refer to the types of incentives that handlers, guardians, and managers have to block, observe, cajole, distract, or other otherwise exert some measure of social control over offenders, targets, and places in ways that may make crime less likely to occur.

The RAA and its expansions are important because they allow SCP preventers to see (1) that there are at least three factors associated with a crime event that can be controlled situationally; (2) who some of the actors who have some potential to control these factors might be; (3) which aspect of the crime event they might exert control over; and (4) what incentives might be used to get them to act. Just what they seek to do to control the situation is what Clarke and his colleagues cover in the SCP classification schemes (discussed below).

C. Crime Pattern Theory

Crime pattern theory (CPT) represents a rich blend of theoretical insights and empirical observations about human behaviors that show regularities when viewed across time and space (Brantingham and Brantingham 2008). These regularities can be seen in terms of individual offenders—alone, with others in a network, or aggregated—and in terms of decision rules, movement patterns related to places, and crime concentrations. The descriptions of patterns in CPT are usually made at the aggregate level since this is where regularities become more discernable. In terms of

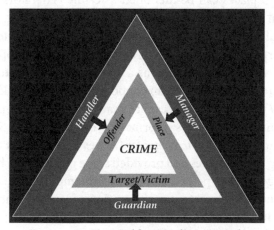

Figure 15.1 The problem analysis triangle
Source: Clarke and Eck 2005.

crime prevention, CPT shares with RAA two key ideas: (1) crime events and criminal opportunities can result from routine, noncriminal patterns of behavior; and (2) crime events can occur when possible offenders and their targets or victims converge in time and space.

Although Brantingham and Brantingham had published work on crime patterns in the 1970s, their broad theorizing in the area of environmental criminology is usually seen as dating from 1981, with the publication of an edited book on the subject, including their chapter on the "geometry of crime." In 1993 they began articulating a specific "crime pattern theory" using many of the terms they had adopted previously, such as *template, backcloth, nodes, paths,* and *edges.* Pattern analysis can be used to help understand crimes for which movement patterns of all types are important, such as target selection in residential burglary, the locations of crimes on public transport, the density of potential crime targets in urban public spaces, and the journey to crime for crimes occurring in decaying urban neighborhoods or in suburban shopping malls.

The types of crime patterns that have influenced SCP practice most directly involve the clustering of crimes into hot spots. The SCP measures are often targeted at areas in which crimes cluster (see Clarke and Eck 2005). The CPT can be used to look for patterns in the development of hot spots (Brantingham and Brantingham 2008). Some of the eight types of patterns that may converge and produce hot spots relate to: (1–2) the residential and activity spaces of offenders and of potential victims, (3–4) the spatial and temporal features of other potential crime targets and of security and guardianship, (5–6) the presence of a broad mix of activities and land uses, and (7–8) the modes and structures of transportation and the patterns of actual movement. Paying attention to these convergences can assist preventers in understanding how to achieve the prevention effects desired when using measures in specific places to prevent specific crimes.

The CPT also looks at the reasons that offenders go to activity nodes, one example of how routine movement patterns of offenders can result in crime events. According to CPT, places can be identified as crime generators, crime attractors, and crime neutral places (Brantingham and Brantingham 1995). A place (such as a transportation hub) is a *crime generator* if offenders and targets tend to come there for noncrime purposes, but offenders are able to find crime opportunities while they are there. *Crime attractors* (such as areas known for prostitution) are places that offenders go to because of the crime opportunities that they know will be there, and *crime neutral* places (those places that draw little police attention) are those in which crime events are rare. This information can be used in SCP. For example, Clarke and Eck (2005) added *crime enabler* (places that have few controls in operation) to this group of place types and provided some guidance on how to link crime-prevention strategy to the type of crime place. By comparing the number of crimes and the number of crime targets at each location of interest, one can establish the number of crime incidents and the crime rates at each particular location. It is then possible to identify whether each place is: (a) a crime generator (high number of crime incidents, low rate), (b) a crime attractor (high number of incidents, high rate), (c) a crime enabler (high or low number of incidents, high rate), or (d) crime neutral (low number of incidents, low rate). In terms of prevention, crime generators have many unprotected targets, so protection for these targets should be increased. Crime attractors, as the name implies, attract offenders, so they should be discouraged from coming there. Places that enable crime have lost controls, so that all three types of controls—handling, guardianship, and management—could be increased there.

II. Classifications of Prevention Measures

A classification system is a useful way of organizing crime-prevention techniques since it frames the discussion of individual measures in terms of the shared general, and more specific, mechanisms by which each operates to limit crime opportunities. In so doing, it systematizes knowledge in the area, clarifies links between theory and prevention practice, and can highlight gaps in the case studies of particular techniques. It also provides a checklist for practitioners dealing with new problems. They can use it to consider measures set out in the classification scheme that might be usefully applied to their situation.

This section discusses the four classification systems of situational crime prevention measures set out over the past 30 years by Clarke and his colleagues and one complementary scheme proposed by Wortley (2001, 2002).[3] Over this time, Clarke has moved from a simple two-category, eight-technique classification system (Hough, Clarke, and Mayhew 1980) to a five-category, 25-technique system (Cornish and Clarke 2003).[4] The classification schemes have changed primarily because of theoretical developments and because novel measures emerged that did not fit into the existing classification system. Theoretical developments led to the inclusion of additional general categories, describing the manner (or broad mechanism) by which SCP measures in that category tend to operate to prevent crime. New measures often required the identification of a new "technique" or narrowly tailored description of a specific operating mechanism. In addition, when a scheme was expanded, some measures and techniques were reclassified so that they were explained in different ways, emphasizing different aspects of the mechanisms that were considered likely to be operating. The classification schemes were designed as evolving tools to assist in planning and understanding active crime-prevention projects. Their development can be seen as a continual adaptation to the practice of SCP and its theoretical underpinnings. In other words, they demonstrate how SCP theory has continually changed under pressure to be "good enough" to incorporate the developing insights of the three key crime event theories and to meet the needs of crime-prevention practice. By classifying and clarifying practice, these schemes also can be seen as challenging event theories to continue to evolve to meet the needs of practice.

A. The Original Classification Scheme

Although SCP measures were studied and discussed in earlier research by the Home Office Research Unit in the UK (e.g., Clarke 1978), the first classification of SCP techniques was published in 1980 in a compendium of early research on SCP (Hough, Clarke, and Mayhew 1980). This classification scheme distinguished two groups of measures: (a) those that make it physically harder to commit crime; and (b) those that manipulate the costs and benefits, as well as the material conditions, of crime. The first group included: (1) target hardening, (2) target removal, and (3) removing the means of crime. The second group of techniques included: (4) reducing the pay-off, (5) formal surveillance, (6) natural surveillance, (7) surveillance by employees, and (8) environmental management.

This classification represented the interaction of empirical observations about specific measures that had been used with success and the move toward generalization and theory building. More important, however, it provided information on potential mechanisms that were common across individual techniques and, therefore, could be used to assist preventers in thinking about how the technique could be applied in a particular situation. Nevertheless, it was not as clearly tied to theoretical foundations as the classification schemes that followed. The discussion was not devoid of references to relevant existing theories, however. For example, the section on natural surveillance acknowledged the theoretical roots of the concept in the writing of Jane Jacobs and Oscar Newman, but also noted some of the potential limitations of using it alone to bring about either social cohesion (as Jacobs 1961 had predicted) or high levels of crime reduction (as Newman 1972 reported).

B. Twelve-Techniques Table

Clarke (1992) set out the second classification of SCP techniques (see table 15.1) in the first edition of his edited book on successful case studies. This classification scheme marked a sea change in terms of category classification, with theoretical concepts derived from the decision models of RCP—risk, reward, and effort (see Clarke and Cornish 1985; Cornish and Clarke 2008). Although effort is a cost under a more traditional rational choice cost-benefit approach, separating it from other costs that are more closely related to the risk of detection (and possibly capture) allows more techniques and individual measures to be identified and grouped by common mechanism. In total, examples of 84 SCP measures were grouped according to 12 techniques (or specific types of mechanism), with these 12 techniques divided according to one of the three categories of general means or broader mechanisms by which they were expected to limit crime events—increasing the effort, increasing the risk, or decreasing the rewards. This classification scheme was expanded shortly after it was proposed.

Table 15.1 Comparison of the Twelve-Techniques Table of Clarke (1992) and the Sixteen-Techniques Table of Clarke and Homel (1997)[1]

Clarke's (1992) Twelve Techniques of Situational Prevention

INCREASING THE EFFORT	INCREASING THE RISKS	REDUCING THE REWARDS
Target Hardening	*Entry/Exit Screening*	*Target Removal*
Steering locks	Border searches	Removable car radios
Bandit screens	Baggage screening	Exact change fares
Access Control	*Formal Surveillance*	*Identifying Property*
Locked gates	Police patrols	Cattle branding
Fenced yards	Security guards	Property marking
Deflecting Offenders	*Surveillance by Employees*	*Removing Inducements*
Bus stop placement	Bus conductors	"Weapons effect"
Tavern location	Park attendants	Graffiti cleaning
Controlling Facilitators	*Natural Surveillance*	*Rule Setting*
Spray-can sales	Pruning hedges	Drug-free school zone
Gun control	"Eyes on the street"	Public park regulations

Clarke and Homel's (1997) Sixteen Techniques of Situational Prevention

INCREASING PERCEIVED EFFORT	INCREASING PERCEIVED RISKS	REDUCING ANTICIPATED REWARDS	INDUCING GUILT OR SHAME[2]
1. Target hardening	*5. Entry/exit screening*	*9. Target removal*	*13. Rule setting*
Slug-rejector device	Automatic ticket gate	Removable car radio	Customs declaration
Steering locks	Baggage screening	Women's refuges	Harassment codes
2. Access control	*6. Formal surveillance*	*10. Identifying property*	*14. Strengthening moral condemnation*
Parking lot barriers	Speed cameras	Property marking	Roadside speedometers
Fenced yards	Burglar alarms	Vehicle licensing	"Shoplifting is stealing"
3. Deflecting offenders	*7. Surveillance by employees*	*11. Reducing temptation*	*15. Controlling disinhibitors*
Bus stop placement	Pay phone location	Gender-neutral phone listings	Drinking-age laws
Tavern location	Parking attendants	Off-street parking	Ignition interlock
4. Controlling facilitators	*8. Natural surveillance*	*12. Denying benefits*	*16. Facilitating compliance*
Credit card photo	Defensible space	Ink merchandise tags	Improved library checkout
Gun controls	Street lighting	PIN for car radios	Public lavatories

[1] Only the first two examples of techniques given in each table have been included here.

[2] This category was called "removing excuses" in Clarke (1997).

Source: Adapted from Clarke (1992) and Clarke and Homel (1997).

C. The 16-Techniques Table

The classification scheme developed by Clarke and Homel (1997) retained the core structure of Clarke's (1992) previous scheme; yet, it also:

1. Increased the number of techniques identified to 16.
2. Included another general mechanism category—inducing guilt or shame— which was based on a more expansive view of RCP.
3. Moved from an objective view of the operation of the mechanisms in SCP measures to one that was subjective—that is, as perceived from the offender's point of view.
4. Addressed not just street crimes but also crimes involving disorder, with corresponding differences in the types of offenders targeted.
5. Expanded the focus from measures that were primarily "physical" to those that were social and psychological (see table 15.1).

In increasing the number of techniques, the changes were designed to provide greater precision about the definitions of the specific mechanisms employed and to encompass a more complete set of techniques used in practice. These are largely empirical concerns that focus on the utility of the classification scheme for SCP practice.

On a more theoretical level, the additional category of techniques (inducing guilt or shame) was seen as being consistent with four different strains of criminological research about offending: (a) the importance of moral commitment as a shield against offending; (b) Sykes and Matza's (1957) idea that guilt must be neutralized prior to offending, and Bandura's (1976) similar views about forms of self-exoneration; (c) the importance of peer influences; and (d) the influence of public shaming on behavior.

D. Situational Precipitators

Wortley (2001, 2002) proposed an expansion in the types and number of techniques included in SCP to take account of recent research on the control of prisoners. In his view, offender decision making should be seen as a two-stage process, beginning with "situational precipitators"—environmental conditions that can motivate an actor to do a crime—and followed in some situations by conditions that provide acceptable opportunities for the crime to be carried out at that time and place. He identified different sets of SCP strategies as affecting these different types of person-situation interactions. Ignoring these differences could, according to Wortley, result in more crime because the use of traditional SCP measures, in the prison context, sometimes created conditions that prompted otherwise nonmotivated prisoners to offend. He identified two different types of situational influences on prisoner behavior: what he termed "tightening up" measures (using the traditional SCP opportunity-reduction techniques involving risk, reward, and effort and the inclusion of a new category designed to increase anticipated punishments) and "loosening up" measures (using techniques designed to address the existing situational precipitators).

Adopting the approach developed by Clarke for categorizing SCP's opportunity-reduction measures and generalizing from prison research to other types of situational contexts, Wortley presented an additional classification of 16 strategies designed to address situational precipitators of criminal behavior. Table 15.2 presents this classification system, provides one example from Wortley (2001) of each strategy, and provides a brief description of the mechanism by which each strategy is likely to operate to control a precipitating condition. The four precipitating conditions addressed in Wortley's table were derived from psychological research and theory. Each theoretical tradition appears as a separate column in the table and is linked to a particular type of precipitating condition: (1) the social learning tradition—prompts, (2) social psychology—pressures, (3) social cognitive theory (or neutralization theory)—permissibility, and (4) environmental psychology—provocations (Wortley 2008).[5] Four strategies for addressing these conditions are set out in each column. Most of these techniques and examples of measures were new to SCP; however, two of the permissibility strategies (rule setting and clarifying responsibility) had been included, in part, within the inducing guilt or shame category of Clarke and Homel (1997).

E. The 25-Techniques Table

1. *Theoretical Background.* In response to a "series of carefully reasoned" papers setting out Wortley's view of situational precipitators, Cornish and Clarke (2003, p. 42) examined the practical and theoretical case for broadening the number and type of SCP measures to include situational precipitators as part of a two-stage model of offender decision making, with situational precipitators and opportunities as co-equal aspects of SCP. For Cornish and Clarke, Wortley's proposal was not seen just as an expansion of SCP, but as one that required a reevaluation of the relationship between SCP and RCP, despite their agreement with Wortley on nine key issues (see pp. 50–51). Using the device of setting out three "ideal types" of offenders with different levels of motivation and different types of experience—the antisocial predator (SCP's default assumption) (pp. 56–61), the mundane offender (pp. 61–68), and the provoked offender (pp. 69–79), Cornish and Clarke explored the implicit assumptions of SCP as it has developed and broadened its scope over the years. They then compared these to Wortley's positions, assessing the implications of his critique for the future theory and practice of SCP.

In general, Cornish and Clarke's view about the utility of theory in relation to the SCP classification scheme was that, pragmatically, it is best to have a broad set of assumptions about offending that are based on RCP—one of which is the default assumption of an unknown motivated offender with few moral scruples (basically the antisocial offender) who enters a setting ready to do crime. In this view, offenders will make decisions about whether to do crime there based primarily on the risks, rewards, and efforts involved. Despite the utility of having broad default assumptions, Cornish and Clarke saw that there were situations in which it is possible to expand these decision factors to include mechanisms involving excuse and provocation. This expansion,

Table 15.2 Wortley's 2001 Classification of Precipitation-Control Strategies with one example of each strategy and a proposed mechanism by which each strategy works

CONTROLLING PROMPTS (Based on learning theory view of stimulus-response principle related to responses to cues in immediate environment)	CONTROLLING PRESSURES (Based on social psychology view that the expectations and demands of others influence behavior)	REDUCING PERMISSIBILITY (Based on view in neutralization theory that distortions to moral reasoning provide excuses that facilitate involvement in crime)	REDUCING PROVOCATIONS (Based on environmental psychology view that frustration related to environmental factors can produce aversive emotional arousal)
Controlling triggers	*Reducing inappropriate conformity*	*Rule setting*	*Reducing frustrations*
▪ Gun control	▪ Dispersing gang members	▪ Harassment codes	▪ Inmate control of comfort settings
MECHANISM: Limits automatic or reflex responses to eliciting stimuli	MECHANISM: Addresses tendency to adopt group norms	MECHANISM: Addresses the clarity of the moral principle involved	MECHANISM: Allows individuals to pursue tasks absent stressful stimuli
Providing reminders	*Reducing inappropriate obedience*	*Clarifying responsibilities*	*Reducing crowding*
▪ Warning signs	▪ Support for whistle-blowers	▪ Server intervention	▪ Limiting nightclub patron density
MECHANISM: Gives situational reminders of appropriate behavior through use of discriminative stimuli	MECHANISM: Supports someone acting against those with only illegitimate authority	MECHANISM: Promotes personal accountability for the behavior	MECHANISM: Eliminates perceptions of spatial limitations and associated responses
Reducing inappropriate imitation	*Encouraging compliance*	*Clarifying consequences*	*Respecting territory*
▪ Rapid repair of vandalism	▪ Persuasive signs	▪ Copyright messages	▪ Identifiable territories for residents
MECHANISM: Promotes exposure to pro-social models or restricts anti-social models	MECHANISM: Promotes conforming responses to direct commands	MECHANISM: Promotes appropriate view of the seriousness of crime outcomes	MECHANISM: Provides sense of territorial possession and limits invasion of territorial space
Setting positive expectations	*Reducing anonymity*	*Personalizing victims*	*Controlling environmental irritants*
▪ Pub gentrification	▪ School dress codes	▪ Humanizing conditions for prisoners	▪ Smoke-free nightclubs
MECHANISM: Involves use of expectancy cues to prompt appropriate responses	MECHANISM: Limits ability to submerge identity in a crowd, avoiding possible disinhibition of potential offender	MECHANISM: Sensitizes offenders to humanity of victims, avoiding possible derogation of potential crime targets	MECHANISM: Limits aversive environmental conditions

Source: Adapted from Wortley (2001).

however, involves making other assumptions about offenders and offending that limit the application of these techniques to particular types of crimes, in particular types of settings, and for particular types of offenders—and these will generally be more constraining, and perhaps less effective, than those produced from the traditional SCP assumptions. Therefore, because of these differences, Cornish and Clarke proposed a more limited role for precipitators than that taken by Wortley, not the equal contributors to the offender's decision making that he had suggested. Nevertheless, they recommended adopting a revised table of 25 techniques that incorporated some of the strategies proposed by Wortley, although they cautioned that preventers should be careful not to be drawn into designing initiatives that are aimed primarily at trying to change criminal "dispositions" (or long-term offender motivation; pp. 88–89). The original table in Cornish and Clarke (2003),[6] sets out five general categories of broad crime-prevention mechanisms, with five techniques each, and lists 75 (25 × 3) individual measures as examples.[7]

2. *The Techniques.* To provide a clearer picture of how each of these 25 techniques has incorporated aspects of the theory and practice of SCP, we have included a modified 25-technique table here (see table 15.3). This table does not include any examples of measures but sets out a general description of how each technique can operate to reduce crime. The descriptions explicitly take into account theoretical concepts from the three main crime-event theories—the rational choice perspective (RCP), the routine activity approach (RAA), and crime pattern theory (CPT).

The first column (increase effort) of table 15.3 includes techniques that block the offender's actions or movement, thereby increasing the effort he or she would have to exert to do this crime in this place at this time against this target. The five techniques listed here are: (1) target harden (proximity), (2) control access to facilities (setting), (3) screen exits (setting), and (4) deflect offenders (offender movement), (5) control tools/weapons (instrumentalities). Setting is an important aspect of the three main theoretical traditions used in SCP. RAA and CPT focus on place and activity spaces, respectively, and the crime script of RCP is, of course, carried out in a setting. Proximity and offender movement are key aspects of RAA and CPT, with their emphases on the convergence of offenders and victims (or suitable targets) and on these actors' routine activities. The idea of controlling facilitators (as props) was incorporated in the script approach in 1993 (Cornish 1994a), soon after it appeared in Clarke's 1992 classification scheme, demonstrating the interaction between the development of the classification scheme and the elaboration of RCP.

The second column (increase risks) of table 15.3 sets out techniques associated with increasing the extent, or improving the quality, of guardianship for potential victims and, more generally, the potential targets and management of places. Both aspects are intended to increase the risks for offenders, primarily risks of detection. These techniques include: (6) extend guardianship (more unofficial guardians), (7) assist natural surveillance (to see better), (8) reduce anonymity (to identify better), (9) utilize place managers (use existing employees), and (10) strengthen formal surveillance (provide effective formal guardians). The techniques related to surveillance were initially included with the acknowledgment of the link between natural

Table 15.3 Explanations for the Twenty-five Techniques of Situational Prevention

INCREASE THE EFFORT	INCREASE THE RISK	REDUCE THE REWARDS	REDUCE PROVOCATIONS	REMOVE EXCUSES
Block or limit **offender** actions or movements	Provide more or better **guardianship** to increase the likelihood of detection	Limit the value of a **target (or victim)** for an offender or the offender's ability to find target/ victim in situation	Limit the introduction or intensification of **situational stimuli** that may lead to criminal actions	Present/explain/remind about/ facilitate/implement **situational controls** that clarify offender responsibility
1. Target harden	*6. Extend guardianship*	*11. Conceal targets*	*16. Reduce frustrations and stress*	*21. Set rules*
Make it more difficult for the offender to get to or use the **target** to achieve the criminal purpose	Provide incentives to encourage unofficial **guardians to act** or to be more effective	Encourage those guarding or controlling crime targets to **limit offenders' ability to see** these targets	Encourage **settings that are calming** or contain procedures that are efficient	Provide information about **unacceptable behaviors** in setting
2. Control access to facilities	*7. Assist natural surveillance*	*12. Remove targets*	*17. Avoid disputes*	*22. Post instructions*
Block access to **places** where a criminal action may be carried out	Increase likelihood that potential **guardians will see** any criminal actions occurring in places	**Take potential targets away** from places or remove the valuable aspects of them	Limit **situations that promote conflicts** or disputes or encourage their escalation	Provide detailed information about **how to meet the behavioral requirements** of setting

3. Screen exits
Make it more difficult for the offender to leave a **place** after a criminal action (to complete the action or to remove proceeds)

4. Deflect offenders
Change existing or potential offender **movement patterns**

5. Control tools/weapons
Limit offender access to or use of **instrumentalities** associated with particular *modus operandi*

8. Reduce anonymity
Increase likelihood that potential **guardians will identify** features of offenders

9. Utilize place managers
Use existing or new employees or managers as **potential guardians** or change the setting to limit crime opportunities

10. Strengthen formal surveillance
Provide official or **formal guardians** or increase their ability to be effective in situations with potential crime opportunities

13. Identify property
Mark potential targets to make them **traceable** to the owner or to reduce ability of the offender to claim ownership

14. Disrupt markets
Make it **difficult to transfer** proceeds of crime to others

15. Deny benefits
Make it difficult for offenders to use crime targets **for intended purposes**

18. Reduce emotional arousal
Remove or limit **emotional or insulting behaviors** or stimuli in setting

19. Neutralize peer pressure
Remove or lessen **desire to gain acceptance** through criminal action or remove from setting those who might encourage this behavior

20. Discourage imitation
Seek to limit **access to details of crime-commission processes** that potential offenders may copy

23. Alert conscience
Provide **situational reminders** about the unacceptable aspects of certain behaviors in the setting

24. Assist compliance
Make it **easier to carry out acceptable behavior** in a setting

25. Control drugs and alcohol
Make it **easier to limit** the ingestion of substances that distort thinking or act as behavioral disinhibitors

Source: Adapted from Cornish and Clarke 2003.

surveillance and Newman's (1972) defensible space concept (Hough, Clarke, and Mayhew 1980). In this scheme the different aspects of surveillance are distinguishable primarily according to who carries them out, with an explicit acknowledgment of the role of place managers. The variety of techniques related to guardianship implicitly demonstrates that this response may not be an easily achievable intervention even if onlookers are present. Nevertheless, the techniques in this classification provide guidance for practitioners about how to approach the task of increasing risk by providing a wider variety of approaches than with previous classification schemes. This classification also stresses the risk aspect of the "reduce anonymity" technique adapted from Wortley's (2001) scheme.

The third column included in this scheme straightforwardly focuses on reducing the rewards of the crime for the individual offender: (11) conceal targets (limit offender's ability to see), (12) remove targets (remove them or their value), (13) identify property (make them traceable), (14) disrupt markets (make them difficult to transfer), and (15) deny benefits (make them difficult to use for intended purpose). The targets are either hard to find in a particular setting or the value of the target, or proceeds of the projected crime, have been reduced for that offender. With these techniques, potential victims may be called upon to act as guardians of their own property or manufacturers may be able to design-in features in goods that will incorporate the technique's proposed mechanism for limiting the rewards of potential crimes. Legal requirements and market forces may operate as "super controllers" (Sampson, Eck, and Dunham 2010) to encourage potential guardians to act.

The fourth column (reduce provocations) reflects the influence of Wortley's (2001) expansion of SCP to include situational inducements. The techniques included here are: (16) reduce frustrations and stress (encourage calming settings), (17) avoid disputes (limit situations that promote conflicts), (18) reduce emotional arousal (limit emotional or insulting behaviors), (19) neutralize peer pressure (limit the desire to gain acceptance through criminal behavior), and (20) discourage imitation (limit access to details of crime-commission processes). Limiting some of these provoking situations can be seen as overlapping with traditional SCP concerns related to cues about risk, reward, and effort. For example, measures that discourage imitation may increase the efforts for offenders seeking to do a particular type of crime, and measures that avoid disputes may limit offender rewards in relation to assaults. However, these techniques were included primarily to reduce situational motivators in relation to the more limited cases discussed by Cornish and Clarke, including: (a) life-threatening situations, and (b) settings in which there are repeated exposures to these provoking stimuli, such as those found in isolated environments (e.g., prisons). Many of the measures included in these techniques will be carried out by some type of place manager, guardian, or handler, and these actors may be influenced by the variety of incentives described as "super controllers."

The last column (remove excuses) in table 15.3 sets out techniques that clarify offender responsibility for actions in a setting. These include strategies adapted from Clarke and Homel (1997) and Wortley (2001). The techniques are: (21) set rules (about unacceptable behavior), (22) post instructions (about how to meet the behavioral requirements), (23) alert conscience (provide situational reminders), (24) assist compliance (make it easier to carry out acceptable behaviors), and (25) control drugs and alcohol (limit ingestion of substances that distort thinking). Again, these techniques can be seen as providing cues about risks, rewards, and efforts, but they are included primarily as situational reminders about the wrongness of doing particular types of behaviors in this setting. Place managers of particular settings, such as bars, train stations, and libraries, are most likely to control the measures employed with each technique. Often the targeted behaviors in these settings involve ambiguously criminal or antisocial acts or include offenders who are new to crime or do not routinely engage in serious types of crime. Nevertheless, the inclusion of these warnings and controls makes it difficult for any offender to claim ignorance about the legality or appropriateness of particular behaviors in particular settings and addresses some of the concerns raised by Wortley's (2001) critique.

F. The Next Iteration of the Classification Scheme

It seems likely that each of the theoretical traditions described in this essay will expand to include new insights about crime commission and its prevention, and that SCP practice will increase as new areas of application are recognized. For these reasons, it is probable that the present classification scheme will come to be seen as incomplete. Further iterations, however, will have to take into consideration three potential barriers to expansion. The first potential barrier relates to the inclusion of a sixth column of measures. This is a substantive concern related to the underlying theoretical structure of the current classification system (see table 15.3). In the current scheme, each column represents a different aspect of the crime event: (a) increasing the effort by blocking or limiting offender actions; (b) increasing the risk by providing more or better guardianship; (c) reducing the rewards by limiting the value of a target for an offender; (d) reducing provocations by limiting particular types of situational stimuli; and (e) removing excuses by using situational controls that clarify offender responsibility. Developing a sixth column would require including an aspect of the crime event that is not covered in the other five columns and is both situational in focus and not aimed at trying to change an offender's long-term motivation or "disposition" to offend (as discussed in Cornish and Clarke 2003).

The second potential barrier is also a substantive one that centers on the completeness of the present cells within each column. To expand the scheme by adding techniques within one of the five existing category columns requires that additional considerations appear through practice or from theory to justify the addition of another technique that uses the same general mechanism as the other techniques in that column. This second type of expansion possibility leads to a third potential barrier to expansion, which is more formalistic and relates to the symmetry of the schemes. Each iteration of the classification system after the first in Hough, Clarke, and Mayhew (1980) has had the same number of rows across all of the columns (3×4, 4×4, and 5×5, respectively). Although there is no reason theoretically to require this type of symmetry, it does allow for a clean and clear presentation of information, which is important when complex information is being disseminated to a broad and diverse audience. In addition, the desire to retain symmetry can provide an incentive to think hard about the need to include additional techniques in the other categories in the table.

Thus, it is difficult to predict at this point whether there will be a new classification scheme of situational techniques despite the probable pressures for expansion. What does appear likely, however, is that it will occur when theory and practice considerations provide the necessary guidance for what these changes should be.

III. DISCUSSION AND CONCLUSIONS

The dynamic nature of the development of the field of SCP is clearly illustrated in its borrowing from a wide variety of theoretical approaches.[8] Crime-event theories and SCP practice have expanded significantly over the past 15 years and the classification schemes developed by Clarke and his colleagues represent one aspect of the evolving view of the linkage between theory and practice in this area of crime prevention. Crime analysts and other practitioners need to understand the particular crime problems present at particular types of places or linked to particular types of targets so that they can recommend strategies for preventing these crimes. The rational choice perspective (RCP), routine activity approach (RAA), and crime pattern theory (CPT) provide many tools for doing this. For example, RCP was conceived as a "good enough" theory to help explain how SCP operates to limit the rewards associated with the crime event and to increase the risks and efforts involved in carrying it out. But RCP also included decision models that were initially seen as wider than was necessary for explaining SCP. However, more recently, the inclusion of the involvement model has allowed RCP to provide an alternative explanation for the situational precipitators that have been identified by Wortley (2001, 2002) as potentially important motivational precursors for a variety of crimes (see Cornish and Clarke 2003). The development of the script approach has allowed SCP to link preventive measures directly to the actions of offenders, and thus provides a way for even inexperienced practitioners to understand important aspects of SCP practice, such the need to be crime specific and to employ more than one measure in a setting.

Similarly, RAA has expanded the scope of the types of crime it seeks to explain and the descriptions of the types of controls and actors that are involved in crime events and in preventing them. These theoretical insights can be employed by preventers to understand the potential reach of situational constraints on crime events, and link controls to potential actors in a particular setting. The expansion of CPT to include patterns to help explain the movement of potential offenders and crime targets, as well as patterns of use and historical development of places, allows crime analysts to identify patterns that may not be clear when viewed at a single place or a single time. Identifying patterns allows preventers to intervene in strategic ways that are not possible when crime events are seen as purely localized phenomena.

These theories have also directly influenced the evolution of SCP theory and practice, through the type of iterative process characteristic of "good enough" theory. It has grown organically, and only when necessary to respond to challenges to it—such as claims about displacement, where research and theory were used to present counter evidence (e.g., Cornish and Clarke 1987; Clarke 1992). It has continually changed to explain in better ways how measures operate and how best to understand how a potential offender is most likely to view a situation in which a particular technique is used. It holds the promise of continuing to adapt to theory and practice through possible expansions of its classification scheme and through the use of case studies that explain the operation of measures in the situational context.

NOTES

1. These models have changed little since they were first developed. The largest changes were made in the initial involvement model in 2001, when the causal paths were reordered, the role of current circumstances, routines and lifestyles were explicitly included, and the place of risk, reward, and effort was highlighted by placing these factors as part of the final set of "solutions evaluated" prior to "readiness" to offend, the last factor in the model (see Clarke and Cornish 2001, p. 28; Cornish and Clarke 2008, p. 30). To the extent that the incorporation of "crime scripts" (Cornish 1994b) into RCP (Cornish and Clarke 2008) can be seen as an elaboration of the event model, this additional model represents a change to the original scheme.

2. These shared assumptions provide support for Cornish's (1993) view of RCP as a meta-theory, a unifying theory of human action.

3. See also Lab (2010) for a detailed discussion of the evolution in the SCP classification systems.

4. Table 15.3 sets out descriptions of the operating mechanisms for the 25-technique scheme. Because most of the techniques included here were included in earlier versions of the classification schemes, descriptions of the techniques are not provided for earlier classification schemes. Each classification scheme described in this section includes the names of all techniques in that scheme either in the text or in the associated table.

5. Wortley (2002) sets out more detailed explanations of the theoretical underpinnings of the strategies.

6. This table can also be found on the www.popcenter.org Web site. This table provides descriptions of the general categories of broad mechanisms and the more specific techniques, as well as examples of measures within each of these techniques.

7. This table did not include "perceived" in the description of each general mechanism. While offender perceptions of conditions may be important in terms of their criminal decision making, real conditions, even if not perceived by a potential offender, may also affect his or her ability to carry out a crime.

8. Additional evidence of SCP's dynamic nature at this stage of its development is the resistance of those working in the field to adopt a single view about whether SCP should be considered part of traditional criminology or is better seen as a separate academic discipline called "crime science" (Clarke 2010).

REFERENCES

Bandura, Albert. 1976. "Social Learning Analysis of Aggression." In *Analysis of Delinquency and Aggression*, edited by Emilio Ribes-Inesta and Albert Bandura. Hillside, N.J.: Lawrence Erlbaum.

Brantingham, Patricia, and Paul Brantingham. 1993. "Environment, Routine, and Situation: Toward a Pattern Theory of Crime." In *Routine Activity and Rational Choice*, edited by Ronald V. Clarke and Marcus Felson. Vol. 5 of Advances in Criminological Theory, edited by Freda Adler and William Laufer. New Brunswick, NJ: Transaction.

Brantingham, Patricia, and Paul Brantingham. 1995. "Criminality of Place: Crime Generators and Crime Attractors." In *Crime Environments and SituationalPrevention*, edited by Mike Hough and Jane Marshall. *European Journal of Criminal Policy and Research* 3(3): 5–26.

Brantingham, Paul J., and Patricia L. Brantingham, eds. 1981. *EnvironmentalCriminology*. Beverly Hills, CA: Sage.

Brantingham, Paul, and Patricia Brantingham. 2008. "Crime Pattern Theory." In *Environmental Criminology and Crime Analysis*, edited by Wortley, Richard, and Lorraine Mazerolle. Cullompton, UK: Willan.

Clarke, R. V. G., ed. 1978. *Tackling Vandalism. Home Office Research Study 47*. London: Her Majesty's Stationery Office.

Clarke, R. V. G. 1980. "'Situational' Crime Prevention: Theory and Practice." *British Journal of Criminology* 20:136–47.

Clarke, Ronald V., ed. 1992. *Situational Crime Prevention: Successful Case Studies*. Albany, NY: Harrow and Heston.

Clarke, Ronald V. 1995. "Situational Crime Prevention." In *Building a Safer Society: Strategic Approaches to Crime Prevention*, edited by Michael Tonry and David P. Farrington. Vol. 19 of *Crime and Justice: A Review of Research*, edited by Michael Tonry. Chicago: University of Chicago Press.

Clarke, Ronald V., ed. 1997. *Situational Crime Prevention: Successful Case Studies*, 2nd ed. Guilderlands, NY: Harrow and Heston.

Clarke, Ronald V. 2008. "Situational Crime Prevention." In *Environmental Criminology and Crime Analysis*, edited by Wortley, Richard, and Lorraine Mazerolle. Cullompton, UK: Willan.

Clarke, Ronald V. 2009. "Situational Crime Prevention: Theoretical Background and Current Practice." In *Handbook on Crime and Deviance*, edited by Marvin D. Krohn, Alan J, Lizotte, and Gina Penly Hall. New York: Springer Science + Business Media.

Clarke, Ronald V. 2010. "Crime Science." In *The Sage Handbook of Criminal Theory*, edited by Eugene McLaughlin and Tim Newburn. London: Sage.

Clarke, Ronald V. G., and Derek B. Cornish, eds. 1983. *Crime Control in Britain: A Review of Policy Research*. Albany, NY: State University of New York Press.

Clarke, Ronald V., and Derek B. Cornish. 1985. "Modeling Offenders' Decisions: A Framework for Research and Policy." In *Crime and Justice: An Annual Review of Research*, vol. 6, edited by Michael Tonry and Norval Morris. Chicago: University of Chicago Press.

Clarke, Ronald V., and Derek B. Cornish. 2001. "Rational Choice." In *Explaining Criminals and Crime: Essays in Contemporary Criminological Theory*, edited by Raymond Paternoster and Ronet Bachman. Los Angeles, CA: Roxbury.

Clarke, Ronald V., and John E. Eck. 2005. *Crime Analysis for Problem Solvers in 60 Small Steps*. Washington, DC: US Department of Justice, Community Oriented Policing Service.

Clarke, Ronald V., and Ross Homel. 1997. "A Revised Classification of Situational Crime Prevention Techniques." In *Crime Prevention at a Crossroads*, edited by Steven P. Lab. Highland Heights, KY, and Cincinnati: Academy of Criminal Justice Sciences and Anderson.

Cohen, Lawrence E., and Marcus Felson. 1979. "Social Change and Crime Rates: A Routine Activity Approach." *American Sociological Review* 44:588–608.

Cornish, Derek B. 1993. "Theories of Action in Criminology: Learning Theory and Rational Choice Approaches." In *Routine Activity and Rational Choice*, edited by Ronald V. Clarke and Marcus Felson. Vol. 5 of *Advances in Criminological Theory*, edited by Freda Adler and William Laufer. New Brunswick, NJ: Transaction.

Cornish, Derek B. 1994a. "Crimes as Scripts." In *Proceedings of the International Seminar on Environmental Criminology and Crime Analysis, University of Miami, Coral Gables, Florida, 1993*, edited by Diane Zahm and Paul Cromwell. Coral Gables, FL: Florida Statistical Analysis Center, Florida Criminal Justice Executive Institute.

Cornish, Derek B. 1994b. "The Procedural Analysis of Offending and Its Relevance for Situational Prevention." In *Crime Prevention Studies*, vol. 3, edited by Ronald V. Clarke. Monsey, NY: Criminal Justice Press.

Cornish, Derek B., and Ronald V. Clarke. 1987. "Understanding Crime Displacement: An Application of Rational Choice Theory." *Criminology* 25:933–47.

Cornish, Derek B., and Ronald V. Clarke. 2003. "Opportunities, Precipitators and Criminal Decisions: A Reply to Wortley's Critique of Situational Crime Prevention." In *Theory for Practice in Situational Prevention*, edited by Martha J. Smith and Derek B. Cornish. Vol. 16 of *Crime Prevention Studies*, edited by Ronald V. Clarke. Monsey, NY, and Cullompton, UK: Criminal Justice Press and Willan.

Cornish, Derek B., and Ronald V. Clarke. 2008. "The Rational Choice Perspective." In *Environmental Criminology and Crime Analysis*, edited by Richard Wortley and Lorraine Mazerolle. Devon, UK: Willan.

Cusson, Maurice. 1993. "Situational Deterrence: Fear during the Criminal Event." In *Crime Prevention Studies*, vol. 1, edited by Ronald V. Clarke. Monsey, NY: Criminal Justice Press.

Eck, John E. 1995. "Examining Routine Activity Theory: A Review of Two Books." *Justice Quarterly* 12:783–97.

Eck, John. 2003. "Police Problems: The Complexity of Problem Theory, Research and Evaluation." In *Problem-oriented Policing: From Innovation to Mainstream*, edited by Johannes Knutsson. Vol. 15 of *Crime Prevention Studies*, edited by Ronald V. Clarke. Monsey, NY, and Cullompton, UK: Criminal Justice Press and Willan.

Ekblom, Paul. 2000. "The Conjunction of Criminal Opportunity." In *Key Issues in Crime Prevention, Crime Reduction and Community Safety*, edited by Scott Ballintyne, Ken Pease, and Vic McLaren. London: Institute for Public Policy Research.

Farrell, Graham. 2010. "Situational Crime Prevention and Its Discontents: Rational Choice and Harm Reduction Versus 'Cultural Criminology.'" *Social Policy and Administration* 44:40–66.

Felson, Marcus. 1986. "Linking Criminal Choices, Routine Activities, Informal Control, and Criminal Outcomes." In *The Reasoning Criminal: Rational Choice Perspectives on Offending*, edited by Derek B. Cornish and Ronald V. Clarke. New York: Springer-Verlag.

Felson, Marcus. 1987. "Routine Activity and Crime Prevention in the Developing Metropolis." *Criminology* 25:911–31.

Felson, Marcus. 2002. *Crime and Everyday Life*, 3rd. ed. Thousand Oaks, CA: Sage.

Felson, Marcus. 2003. "The Process of Co-offending." In *Theory for Practice in Situational Prevention*, edited by Martha J. Smith and Derek B. Cornish. Vol. 16 of *Crime Prevention Studies*, edited by Ronald V. Clarke. Monsey, NY, and Cullompton, UK: Criminal Justice Press and Willan.

Felson, Marcus, and Ronald V. Clarke. 1998. *Opportunity Makes the Thief: Practical Theory for Crime Prevention*. Police Research Series Paper 98. London: Home Office Research, Development and Statistics Directorate.

Guerette, Rob T. 2009. "The Pull, Push, and Expansion of Situational Crime Prevention Evaluation: An Appraisal of Thirty-seven Years of Research." In *Evaluation of Crime Reduction Initiatives*, edited by Johannes Knutsson and Nick Tilley. Vol. 24 of *Crime Prevention Studies*, edited by Ronald V. Clarke. Monsey, NY, and Devon, UK: Criminal Justice Press.

Guerette, Rob T., and Kate J. Bowers. 2009. "Assessing the Extent of Crime Displacement and Diffusion of Benefits: A Review of Situational Crime Prevention Evaluations." *Criminology* 47:1331–68.

Hayward, Keith. 2007. "Situational Crime Prevention and Its Discontents: Rational Choice Theory Versus the 'Culture of Now.'" *Social Policy and Administration* 41:232–50.

Hirschi, Travis, and Michael R. Gottfredson. 2001. "Self-control Theory." In *Explaining Criminals and Crime*, edited by Raymond Paternoster and Ronet Bachman. Los Angeles, CA: Roxbury.

Hough, J. M., R. V. G. Clarke, and P. Mayhew. 1980. "Introduction." In *Designing Out Crime*, edited by R. V. G. Clarke and P. Mayhew. London: Her Majesty's Stationery Office.

Jacobs, Bruce A. 2010. "Serendipity in Robbery Target Selection." *British Journal of Criminology* 50:514–29.

Jacobs, Jane. 1961. *The Death and Life of Great American Cities*. New York: Random House.

Jeffery, C. Ray. 1971. *Crime Prevention Though Environmental Design*. Beverly Hills, CA: Sage.

Knepper, Paul. 2007. "Situational Logic in Social Science Inquiry: From Economics to Criminology." *Review of Austrian Economics* 20(1): 25–41.

Lab, Steven P. 2010. *Crime Prevention: Approaches, Practices, and Evaluations*, 7th ed. Albany, NY: Lexis-Nexis/Anderson.

Newman, Oscar. 1972. *Defensible Space: Crime Prevention Through Urban Design*. New York: Macmillan.

Sampson, Rana, John E. Eck, and Jessica Dunham. 2010. "Super Controllers and Crime Prevention: A Routine Activity Explanation of Crime Prevention Success and Failure." *Security Journal* 23:37–51.

Sherman, Lawrence W., Patrick R. Gartin, and Michael E. Buerger. 1989. "Hot Spots of Predatory Crime: Routine Activity and the Criminology of Place." *Criminology* 27:27–55.

Sykes, Gresham M., and David Matza. 1957. "Techniques of Neutralization: A Theory of Delinquency." *American Sociological Review* 22:664–70.

Tilley, Nick. 2004. "Karl Popper: A Philosopher for Ronald Clarke's Situational Crime Prevention?" In *Tradition and Innovation in Crime and Justice*, edited by Schlomo Shoham and Paul Knepper. Vol. 8 of *Israel Studies in Criminology*. Ontario, Canada: de Sitter.

Tillyer, Marie Shuback, and John E. Eck. 2011. "Getting a Handle on Crime: A Further Extension of Routine Activities Theory." *Security Journal* 24(2): 179–93. [doi:10.1057/sj.2010.2]

Wortley, Richard. 2001. A Classification of Techniques for Controlling Situational Precipitators of Crime." *Security Journal* 14(4): 63–82.

Wortley, Richard. 2002. *Situational Prison Control: Crime Prevention in Correctional Institutions*. Cambridge, UK: Cambridge University Press.

Wortley, Richard. 2008. "Situational Precipitators of Crime." In *Environmental Criminology and Crime Analysis*, edited by Richard Wortley and Lorraine Mazerolle. Cullompton, UK: Willan.

CHAPTER 16

HIGH CRIME PLACES, TIMES, AND OFFENDERS

ANTHONY A. BRAGA

CRIME is highly concentrated at a small number of very specific places within communities, often happens during very particular days of the week and hours of the day, and is disproportionately committed by a few high-rate offenders. These concentrations are present across a wide variety of crime types. For instance, much of the devastating toll of urban gun violence can be linked to dynamics and situations generated by a small number of high-rate offenders committing shootings at specific places and times. In his up-close portrait of gun violence in Boston, public health researcher John Rich (2009) describes the elevated victimization risks experienced by young African-American men from disadvantaged neighborhoods who tragically get wounded and killed by being in the "wrong place" at the "wrong time."

Empirical analyses of recurring gun violence problems in Boston support his qualitative work on high-risk places, times, and people. Some 5 percent of Boston's street corners and block faces generated 74 percent of fatal and nonfatal shootings between 1980 and 2008, with the most active 65 locations experiencing more than 1,000 shootings during this time period (Braga, Papachristos, and Hureau 2010). The bulk of Boston shootings take place immediately after school dismissal and during the weekend evening hours, and tend to increase during summer months (Braga 2004). In 2006, roughly 1 percent of Boston youth between the ages of 15 and 24 participated in gangs, but these gang dynamics generated more than half of all homicides and gang members were involved in roughly 70 percent of fatal and nonfatal shootings as either a perpetrator and/or a victim (Braga, Hureau, and Winship 2008).

This essay reviews the empirical and theoretical evidence on the concentration of crime at a small number of places and times, and the concentration of offending among a small number of very active offenders. Key observations and conclusions include:

- Crime is highly concentrated at a small number of specific places across urban landscapes. Even within so-called high-crime neighborhoods, crime clusters at particular street corners and blocks and the remainder of the neighborhood experiences very little crime. Research has linked the uneven spatial distribution of crime to risky characteristics, situations, and dynamics that create compelling criminal opportunities at specific places.
- Crime also exhibits an uneven temporal distribution. Research has revealed that crime tends to be higher during particular hours of the day, days of the week, and months of the year. These temporal variations can be linked to daily and seasonal activities in the lifestyles of individuals and temporal rhythms that arise from the situational characteristics and dynamics of places.
- A very small number of high-rate offenders generate a disproportionate amount of crime. When trying to understand crime problems involving repeat offenders, an important consideration is co-offending, or the commission of crimes by groups of offenders. Nearly half of all robberies are committed by groups of offenders. Ongoing disputes among street gangs and other criminally active street groups usually account for a large share of serious violent crime problems.
- While concerning, these patterns represent important opportunities for more effective crime prevention and control. If municipalities can organize themselves to control the small number of risky places, risky times, and risky people who generate the bulk of their crime problems, they can more effectively manage citywide crime trends. A growing body of evidence suggests that crime-prevention strategies tailored to specific places, such as hot spots policing, and addressing groups of chronic offenders, such as focused deterrence strategies, can be effective in reducing these recurring crime problems. These near-term strategies should be accompanied by longer term prevention approaches.

This essay is organized as follows. Section I documents the concentration and stability of crime at a very small number of "micro places" within communities, presents relevant criminological theories and perspectives to explain the situational factors and dynamics that give rise to high-crime places, briefly acknowledges the link between crime hot spots and repeat victimization, and examines the relationship between high-crime times and place dynamics. Section II documents the concentration of offending among a small number of very high rate offenders, describes the salience of co-offending to serious crime problems, and explores some of the group dynamics that drive the bulk of urban violence. Section III concludes the essay with observations on the prospects of controlling citywide crime rates by focusing crime-prevention resources on high-crime places, times, and offenders.

I. High Crime Places and Times

A. Places and Crime Hot Spots

For most of the last century criminologists have focused their understanding of crime on individuals and communities (Nettler 1978; Sherman 1995; Weisburd, Bernasco, and Bruinsma 2009). In the case of individuals, criminologists have sought to understand why certain people as opposed to others become criminals (e.g. see Hirschi 1969; Akers 1973; Gottfredson and Hirschi 1990; Raine 1993), or to explain why certain offenders become involved in criminal activity at different stages of the life course or cease involvement at other stages (e.g., see Moffitt 1993; Sampson and Laub 1993). In the case of communities, criminologists have often tried to explain why certain types of crime or different levels of criminality are found in some communities as contrasted with others (e.g., see Shaw and McKay 1942; Sampson and Groves 1989; Bursik and Grasmick 1993; Agnew 1999) or how community-level variables, such as relative deprivation, low socioeconomic status, or lack of economic opportunity may affect individual criminality (e.g., see Merton 1938; Cloward and Ohlin 1960; Wolfgang and Ferracuti 1967; Agnew 1992). In most cases, research on communities has focused on the "macro" level, often studying states (Loftin and Hill 1974), cities (Baumer et al. 1998), and neighborhoods (Sampson 1985; Bursik and Grasmick 1993).

While concern with the relationship between crime and place goes back to the founding generations of modern criminology (Guerry 1833; Quetelet 1842), the "micro" approach to places emerged only in the last few decades (e.g., see Duffala 1976; Rengert 1980, 1981; Brantingham and Brantingham 1981; LeBeau 1987). With the advent of powerful computer systems and software packages in the late 1980s, two well-known studies found that over 50 percent of citizen calls for service to the police were generated by only 5 percent of the addresses in Boston (Pierce, Spaar, and Briggs 1988) and Minneapolis (Sherman, Gartin, and Buerger 1989). Places in this "micro" context are specific locations within the larger social environments of communities and neighborhoods (Eck and Weisburd 1995). They are sometimes defined as buildings or addresses (see Sherman, Gartin, and Buerger 1989; Green 1996), block faces or street segments (see Sherman and Weisburd 1995; Taylor 1997), and clusters of addresses, block faces, or street segments (see Block, Dabdoub, and Fregly 1995; Weisburd and Green 1995; Weisburd, Morris, and Groff 2009).

Even within the worst neighborhoods, research suggests that crime clusters at a few discrete locations, leaving blocks of areas relatively crime free (Sherman, Gartin, and Buerger 1989). Further, research by Taylor and Gottfredson (1986) revealed conclusive evidence that links this spatial variation to the physical and social characteristics of particular blocks and multiple dwellings within a neighborhood. Crime clustering at specific locations within specific neighborhoods has been reported in studies of a variety of crimes, including burglary (Forrester, Chatterton, and Pease 1988; Farrell 1995), convenience store robberies (Crow and Bull 1975; Hunter and Jeffrey 1992), gun crimes (Sherman and Rogan 1995), and drug selling (Weisburd and Green 1994).

The study of places as a means to explain the variation of crime within communities has developed from an interest in improving crime control policies (Weisburd, Maher, and Sherman 1992). The attributes of a place are viewed as key factors in explaining clusters of criminal events. For example, a poorly lit street corner with an abandoned building, located near a major thoroughfare, provides an ideal location for a drug market. The lack of proper lighting, an abundance of "stash" locations around the derelict property, a steady flow of potential customers on the thoroughfare, and a lack of defensive ownership (informal social control) at the place all generate an attractive opportunity for drug sellers. In many such cases, the police spend considerable time and effort arresting sellers without noticeably affecting the drug trade. The compelling criminal opportunities at the place attract sellers and buyers, and thus sustain the market. If the police want to disrupt the market, they should focus on the features of the place that cause the drug dealing to cluster at that particular location. This approach to focusing on the characteristics of high-crime locations is considered to be a radical departure from traditional criminological theories, which centered prevention efforts on the individual and ignored the importance of place (Sherman, Gartin, and Buerger 1989).

An important issue in the potential benefit of policing places is whether high-rate locations tend to remain high rate for a long time. The "criminal careers" of high-activity places have been found to be relatively stable, suggesting that place-oriented interventions do have potential crime-prevention value. Spelman (1995) analyzed calls for service at high schools, housing projects, subway stations, and parks in Boston, and found that the risks at these public places remained fairly constant over time. Any changes in risks over time at these locations were attributable to random processes or seasonal changes. In Spelman's analyses, 50 percent of calls at hot spots were generated by long-run risks at these places. Long-run risks were characterized as the unique characteristics of those locations that create criminal opportunities, such as the presence of bars, abandoned buildings or valuable goods, and a lack of proper management. Although long-run risks at the place were the most important source of variation, Spelman (1995) cautions against identifying crime hot spots based on short time periods (such as one month). This is because random errors (i.e., a chance cluster of crime that suddenly appears and never recurs) and short-run changes in risk (i.e., a place may look especially hot at a particular time, such as during the summer months, but all locations were hot) were also important in explaining the clustering of crime at the place.

Taylor (1999) also reported evidence of a high degree of stability of crime at place over time, examining crime and fear of crime at 90 street blocks in Baltimore, Maryland, using a panel design with data collected in 1981 and 1994 (see Taylor 2001; Robinson et al. 2003). Data included not only official crime statistics but also measures of citizen perceptions of crime and observations of physical conditions at the sites. Although Taylor and his colleagues observed significant deterioration in physical conditions at the blocks studied, they found that neither fear of crime nor crime showed significant or consistent differences across the two time periods. In Seattle, an analysis of crime trends at specific street segments over a 14-year period suggested that places have stable concentrations of crime events over time (Weisburd et al. 2004). The study also found that a relatively small proportion of places could be grouped as having steeply rising or declining crime trends, and this sub-group of places was primarily responsible for overall city crime trends. Weisburd et al. (2004) observed that city crime trends could be better understood as strong changes generated by a relatively small group of micro places over time rather than a general process evenly spread across the city landscape. Similar findings on the concentration and stability of crime at specific places over time have been reported for fatal and nonfatal shootings (Braga, Papachristos, and Hureau 2010) and rob-beries (Braga, Hureau, and Papachristos 2011) in Boston.

Beyond this observed clustering of criminal events, Eck and Weisburd (1995) identified four other types of research evidence that illuminate the role of place in crime. Facilities—such as bars, churches, and apartment buildings—have been found to affect crime rates in their immediate environment depending on the type of people attracted, the way the space is managed, or the possible crime controllers present such as owners, security, or police. For example, Spelman (1993) found the presence of unsecured, abandoned buildings on city blocks was positively associ-ated with criminal activity. Felson (2006) identified multiple ways that abandoned sites, such as shells of factories, closed businesses, abandoned residences, and empty lots, can feed crime problems. Much research points to the relationship between bars and crime in proximate areas (Roncek and Meier 1991; Block and Block 1995). However, most bars experience little crime while a few may be hot spots of crime (Sherman, Schmidt, and Velke 1992; Homel and Clark 1994). As Eck (1997, p. 7:10) suggests, "the behavior of bartenders and bouncers may contribute to violence in these places and changes in bar management practices (from server training and changes in legal liability of bartenders) may reduce assaults, drunk driving, and traffic accidents." As Clarke and Eck (2007) observe, only a small proportion of any type of facility will account for the majority of crime and disorder problems experi-enced or produced by the group of facilities as a whole.

The variety of physical and social characteristics known as site features can enhance or diminish the attractiveness of a place to offenders (Taylor 1997). Eck (1994) found evidence to suggest that crack and powder cocaine dealers prefer buildings with physical features that control access and prevent burglary. However, Eck (1994) also found that crack and powder cocaine dealers seem to prefer small apartment buildings with weak management. Apartment buildings with drug dealing are often encumbered with debt, have lost value, and are often losing money or just breaking even for the owner. Landlords at such locations tend to not know how to control the behavior of their drug-selling residents or cannot afford to do much about drug selling. Likewise, the presence of attendants (Laycock and Austin 1992) and closed-circuit television (Poyner 1988) has been found to reduce the number of auto thefts in parking lots. In short, features such as easy access, lack of guardians, inept or improper management, and the presence of valuable items influence the decisions that offenders make about the places they choose to commit their crimes (Eck and Weisburd 1995).

In a similar vein, studies of offender mobility have been interpreted as evidence of "rational and deliberate target searching behavior and the influence of personal characteristics and the distribution of crime targets on this behavior" (Eck and Weisburd 1995, p. 16). Weisburd and Green (1994) argued that drug markets within close proximity to each other have clear and defined boundaries, and they reported a high degree of territoriality for local drug sellers. Repeat arrestees were more likely to be arrested in a different district in the city than in a drug market a block or two away. In San Diego, Eck (1994) found a high proportion of drug dealers arrested at their home address. Offender mobility also seems to vary across gender, age, race, and crime types. For instance, robbers who victimize individuals do not seem to travel as far from home as robbers who attack commercial facilities (Capone and Nichols 1976). Brantingham and Brantingham (1981) show that target selection is a direct outgrowth of offender mobility patterns. Thus, offenders are attracted to areas with many potential targets and move from places with few targets to places with many targets (Rhodes and Conley 1991).

Studies of offender interviews have concluded that their target selection decision-making processes exhibit bounded rationality (Eck and Weisburd 1995). Rengert and Wasilchick's (1990) research on residential burglars revealed that these offenders seek places with cues that indicate acceptable risks and gains, such as homes that are located on the outskirts of affluent neighborhoods. Such places are found during both intentional target searches and during offenders' daily legitimate routines.

B. Theoretical Perspectives Supporting the Importance of Place in Crime Problems

The study of crime events at places is influenced and supported by three complementary theoretical perspectives: rational choice, routine activities, and environmental criminology. The importance of focusing crime-prevention resources on crime hot spots is also informed by the "broken windows" thesis on the relationship between disorder and more serious crimes.

The rational choice perspective assumes that "crime is purposive behavior designed to meet the offender's commonplace needs for such things as money, status, sex, and excitement, and that meeting these needs involves the making of (sometimes quite rudimentary) decisions and choices, constrained as these are by limits of time and ability and the availability of relevant information" (Clarke 1995, p. 98; see also Cornish and Clarke 1986; Smith and Clarke this volume). Rational choice makes distinctions between the decisions to initially become involved in crime, to continue criminal involvement, and to desist from criminal offending, as well as the decisions made to complete a particular criminal act. This separation of the decision-making processes in the criminal event from the stages of criminal involvement allows the modeling of the commission of crime events in a way that yields potentially valuable insights for crime prevention. Of particular importance to situational crime prevention, the decision processes and information utilized in committing criminal acts can vary greatly across offenses; ignoring these differences and the situational contingencies associated with making choices may reduce the ability to effectively intervene (Clarke 1995). In the case of places, modeling an offender's choice of committing crimes at one place over another may provide avenues for intervention. For example, a robber may choose a "favorite" spot because of certain desirable attributes that facilitate an ambush, such as poor lighting and untrimmed bushes. One obvious response to this situation would be to improve the lighting and trim the bushes.

Rational choice is often combined with routine activity theory (Cohen and Felson 1979) to explain criminal behavior during the crime event (Clarke and Felson 1993). Rational offenders come across criminal opportunities as they go about their daily routine activities and make decisions whether to take action. The source of the offender's motivation to commit a crime is not addressed (it is assumed that offenders commit crimes for any number of reasons); rather, the basic ingredients for a criminal act to be completed are closely examined. (For more on this theory, see Smith and Clarke this volume.)

Environmental criminology, also known as crime pattern theory, explores the distribution and interaction of targets, offenders, and opportunities across time and space (Brantingham and Brantingham 1981). According to Eck and Weisburd (1995, p. 6):

> This occurs because offenders engage in routine activities. Environmental
> criminology is important in understanding the nature of crime at places because
> it combines rational choice and routine activity theory to explain the distribution
> of crime across places.

Understanding the characteristics of places, such as facilities, is important as these attributes give rise to the opportunities that rational offenders will encounter during their routine activities. Environmental criminologists unravel crime problems through studying offender decision-making processes and small (e.g., shopping mall or housing project) and intermediate-level (e.g., neighborhood or city) analyses of very specific types of crimes occurring at very particular locations in these areas (Brantingham and Brantingham 1981).

Studies of environmental factors of crime have shown that commercial properties located near main roads have an increased risk of robbery, and affluent homes located adjacent to poorer areas are more likely to be burglarized. In both cases, the offenders' "journey to work" was greatly reduced by the proximity of the targeted places to the offenders' homes or to a major thoroughfare. A key insight from these studies was that the offender's target search time—the amount of effort expended by the offender to locate a suitable target—was related to risk of victimization at that place (as described by Clarke 1995). According to Marcus Felson (2006), offenders find suitable targets through personal knowledge of the victim (your neighbor's son might know when you are away from your house), work (a burglar working as a telephone engineer might overhear that you will be taking vacation next week), and overlapping activity spaces (where people live, work, shop, or seek entertainment).

In their seminal "broken windows" article, Wilson and Kelling (1982) argue that social incivilities (e.g., loitering, public drinking, and prostitution) and physical incivilities (e.g., vacant lots, trash, and abandoned buildings) cause residents and workers in a neighborhood to be fearful. Fear causes many stable families to move out of the neighborhood and the remaining residents isolate themselves and avoid others. Anonymity increases and the level of informal social control decreases. The lack of control and escalating disorder attracts more potential offenders to the area and this increases serious criminal behavior (see also Kelling and Coles, 1996). Wilson and Kelling (1982) argued that serious crime developed because the police and citizens did not work together to prevent urban decay and social disorder.

At the neighborhood level, the available research evidence on the connections between disorder and more serious crime is mixed (Skogan 1990; Harcourt 1998; Sampson and Raudenbush 1999; Jang and Johnson 2001; Taylor 2001). Research on crime hot spots, however, suggests that disorder often clusters in space and time with more serious crimes. In their closer look at crime in Minneapolis hot spots, Weisburd, Maher, and Sherman (1992) found that assault calls for service and robbery of person calls for service were significantly correlated with "drunken person" calls for service. In Jersey City, New Jersey, Braga et al. (1999) found that violent crime hot spots also suffered from serious disorder problems. Yang (2010) reports some evidence of positive relationships between high-levels of disorder and violent crime in her longitudinal analysis of street segments in Seattle over a 16-year period. Her analyses revealed that, like violent crime, disorder was concentrated in a relatively small number of hot spot areas in the city. However, while disorder and violent crime were found to be correlated in these relatively small areas over time, the relationship was not perfect with some high-disorder places experiencing low levels of violence over time.

A recent study of crime hot spot areas in Chicago found some support for both broken windows and collective efficacy theories in explaining the concentration of specific crime types at places (St. Jean 2007). However, this research also found that different kinds of crime occur most often in locations that offer perpetrators specific "ecological advantages." For instance, drug dealers and robbers were primarily attracted to locations with businesses like liquor stores, fast-food restaurants, and check-cashing outlets (St. Jean 2007). In St. Jean's research, interviews with offenders revealed that criminals found certain facilities and site features at specific places provided compelling opportunities to commit crimes.

C. Repeat Victimization and its Relevance to High-Crime Places

Crime hot spots are often populated by specific targets that repeatedly attract offenders. For instance, an apartment building could have a particular unit that is burglarized over and over again. The same apartment building could have another unit that generates a large number of calls to the police as a result of violent husband who repeatedly abuses his wife and children. The growing body of research that seeks to understand and prevent repeat victimization has much to offer in developing our understanding of the underlying conditions and situations that cause particular places to be crime hot spots.

Criminological research has demonstrated that small proportions of the population, and of victims, suffer large proportions of all criminal victimizations. In the United States, 10 percent of the victims are involved in 40 percent of the victimizations (Spelman and Eck 1989). Using data from the 1992 British Crime Survey, Farrell and Pease (1993) reported that 4 percent of people experience 44 percent of all victimizations. In his review of the international research evidence on repeat victimization, Farrell (1995) found that the 2 or 3 percent of victim survey respondents who are most commonly victimized report between a quarter and a third of all incidents. As such, preventing repeat victimization may stop a large percentage of all crimes. Focusing on repeat victims also provides an opportunity to detect more serious offenders, as well as addressing specific problems within crime hot spots. Louise Grove and Graham Farrell (this volume) address this important related topic in their essay in this book.

D. The Link Between High-Crime Places and High-Crime Times

Crime also exhibits an uneven temporal distribution. Research has demonstrated concentrations of crime during certain months of the year, particular days of the week, and specific hours of the day. For example, as described earlier, most Boston youth gun violence occurred in the afternoon hours immediately following school release, as well as during weekend evenings (Braga 2004). The Boston research also noted higher levels of youth gun violence during the summer months and in October. Felson and Poulsen (2003) reviewed 406 robberies in Albany, New York, in 2000 and reported tremendous variation over the course of a day. For the entire year, only one robbery occurred between 7:00 a.m. and 7:59 a.m. In contrast, 35 robberies occurred between 8:00 p.m. and 8:59 p.m. Felson and Poulsen (2003) revealed that the number of robberies rose slightly in the morning, dipped, and then accelerated in the early afternoon. The number of robberies then dipped again during rush hour (between 5:00 p.m. and 5:59 p.m.) and accelerated again with nightfall.

Situational theories, such as environmental criminology, rational choice, and routine activities, are often applied to understand the temporal dynamics of crime. The temporal variation of crime suggests that the opportunities for crime vary over the course of months, days, and hours. Some researchers have linked temporal variations to weather patterns that influence criminal opportunities (see, e.g., Cohn 1990). Indeed, as described earlier, routine activities theory explicitly examines the interactions among likely offenders, capable guardians, and suitable targets in space and time (Cohen and Felson 1979). These temporal variations can be linked to daily and seasonal activities in the lifestyles of individuals (Hindelang, Gottfredson, and Garofalo 1978) and temporal rhythms that arise from the situational characteristics and dynamics of places. As Marcus Felson (2006, p. 7) describes in his discussion of crime rhythms and movement:

> We must study these rhythms of life if we wish to understand crime, for the energy of crime draws from the energy of life. Residential burglars depend on weekday flows of people away from home. Certain robbers rely on the motion of people near money machines. Offenders have their own metabolism, perhaps sleeping late to recover from a late night's partying. Residential burglars depend on the rhythmic shift of residents away from home in the morning, and they better watch out for their return later. Each community breathes both illegal and legal activity, with offenders, targets, and guardians all moving with respect to one another.

These temporal patterns of crime can be powerfully tied to the place-level dynamics of "activity spaces" (Felson 2006) and the idea of crime hot spots. Juveniles, for instance, are attracted to very specific activities, such as "hanging out" at malls and movie theaters. The timing of school hours and business hours of popular hangout places can lead to concentrations of potential offenders and potential targets in space and time. Weisburd, Morris, and Groff's (2009) research on juvenile crime in Seattle provides strong confirmation of the relevance of juvenile activity spaces to understanding the concentration of juvenile arrests over time at specific places. The highest rate trajectories of juvenile crime hot spots were much more likely to have arrest incidents committed at schools and/or youth centers, and shops/malls and restaurants, as compared to low-rate trajectory juvenile crime hot spot groups.

II. HIGH-CRIME OFFENDERS

It is important to note here that this section does not address the various individual-level, family-level, and neighborhood-level factors that are associated with the initiation to, continuation of, or desistance from the criminal careers of high-crime offenders. Indeed, there are many well-known volumes on this topic (e.g., Blumstein et al. 1986; Laub and Sampson 2003; Piquero, Farrington, and Blumstein 2007) and interested readers can consult this broader literature or peruse the essays in this book by Cullen, Benson, and Makarios (this volume) and by Farrington, Loeber, and Ttofi (this volume). Rather, this section has a less ambitious objective: it simply documents the concentration of offending among a small number of very high rate offenders, describes the salience of co-offending to serious crime problems, and explores some of the group dynamics that drive the bulk of urban violence.

Police officers have long known from experience that a small number of criminals account for a large share of the crime problem, and some detectives have attempted to prevent crimes by "working" particular criminals rather than particular crimes (see, e.g., Lane 1971). Research has confirmed that a small number of chronic offenders generate a disproportionate share of crime. In their classic study of nearly 10,000 boys in Philadelphia, Wolfgang, Figlio, and Sellin (1972) revealed that the most active 6 percent of delinquent boys were responsible for more than 50 percent of all delinquent acts committed. Laub and Sampson's (2003) close examination of a small set of persistent violent offenders revealed that these men were arrested on average 40 times over the course of their criminal career (the most active offender had been arrested 106 times) and spent an inordinate amount of times in prison and jails. Over their full life course, these men were incarcerated on average 75 days each year. Similarly, the RAND Corporation's survey of jail and prison inmates in California, Michigan, and Texas revealed that, in all three states, the most recidivist 10 percent of active offenders committed some 50 percent of all crimes and 80 percent of crimes were committed by only 20 percent of the criminals (Chaiken and Chaiken 1982). Moreover, the worst 1 percent of offenders committed crimes at an extremely high rate—more than 50 serious offenses per year (Rolph, Chaiken, and Houchens 1981).

In his review of the literature on repeat offenders, Spelman (1990) observes that frequent offenders do not specialize, are usually drug addicts, and are more persistent. In the RAND survey in three states, about two-thirds of all offenders specialized in either violent or property crimes; however, crime "generalists" committed about twice as much property crime as the property-crime specialists and about twice as much violent crime as the violent-crime specialists (Chaiken and Chaiken 1982). Although most criminals are specialists, most crimes are committed by highly active "violent predators" (Spelman 1990).

In his review of data from the US Department of Justice (DOJ) Arrestee Drug Abuse Monitoring (ADAM) system, Kleiman (1997) concludes that the population of heavy drug users consists mainly of frequent offenders. Kleiman (1997) further notes that among offenders, the use of expensive drugs predicts both high-rate offending and persistence in crime. Chaiken and Chaiken (1982) find that most frequent offenders also deal drugs in high volume. Frequent offenders also have longer "criminal careers" than the typical offender. While the average criminal career for an adult offender lasts no more than six or seven years (Blumstein et al. 1986), frequent offenders persist for between nine and ten years (Spelman 1986). Finally, as frequent offenders gain more experience they become more difficult to apprehend. Spelman's (1990) analysis of the probability of arrest per crime among offenders who commit crimes at different rates revealed that high-rate offenders run substantially lower risks of arrests than others. This pattern was true for both property and personal crimes.

These studies suggest that focusing on the worst offenders is a particularly efficient use of limited crime-prevention resources. As Spelman (1990, p. 7) suggests:

> The offense rates show the typical criminal to be a casual, low-rate offender, committing only a few crimes each year. For them, crime probably supplements a low-paying, legitimate job. But the 90th percentile offender is a full-time criminal, committing one or more crimes per day. Thus a few offenders commit

crimes 40 or 50 times as often as the average active criminal, assuming all other factors equal, incarcerating one of them should be 40 to 50 times more effective in reducing crime.

Given that prisons have become increasingly overcrowded, if municipalities can effectively focus their crime-prevention efforts on a small number of highly active offenders, then crime can be reduced without further burdening the limited resources of the criminal justice system.

A. The Salience of Co-Offending to High-Rate Youth Offenders

When considering the prospects of focusing on repeat offenders, an important dimension to consider is "co-offending," or the commission of crimes by groups of offenders. In his analyses of victimization data in the United States for 2000 through 2005, Cook (2009) notes that nearly half of all robberies were committed by groups of offenders and the chances of a successful robbery were greatly enhanced when a gun was used or when there were accomplices involved in the commission of the robbery. Felson (2003, p. 151) describes how access to accomplices is inherently criminogenic:

> Likely co-offenders not only reinforce one another's criminal impulses, but also provide each other with information and direct assistance in carrying out illegal acts. The information they can provide includes what crime targets are located where, as well as how to attack these targets, avoid apprehension, escape with loot, dispose of stolen goods, and/or win physical contests. These are simple lessons, but a little shared crime knowledge can go a long way.
>
> Not only can co-offenders exchange knowledge, but they can also provide one another with several types of direct assistance in carrying out offenses. It is easier to carry out a property crime with someone to monitor, distract, or thwart particular guardians against the crime. Accomplices can bring different skills to the scene—one is more powerful, another runs faster, another has a keener eye. With criminal violence, two can intimidate or overpower more readily than one. Even individuals who are going to commit crime anyway can be more efficient when they act together. In short, easy access to each other under suitable circumstances causes offenders to commit more crimes.

Youth, in particular, commit crimes, as they live their lives, in groups (Zimring 1981). This observation is particularly important because youth offenders account for a disproportionate share of the most serious crimes. In his review of juvenile self-report survey data studies, Warr (2002) reports that most studies find between 50 and 75 percent of juvenile crimes are committed in the company of others.

In urban areas, gun violence takes a particularly heavy toll, as vastly disproportionate numbers of young minority males are killed and injured, and increasing fear drives out businesses and disrupts community social life. Research has linked urban youth gun violence to gang conflicts, street drug markets, and gun availability (see, e.g., Blumstein and Cork 1996; Kennedy, Piehl, and Braga 1996; Cook and Laub

2002). Youth gun violence is usually concentrated among groups of serious offenders, and conflicts between youth street gangs have long been noted to fuel much
of the serious street violence in major cities (Miller 1975; Klein and Maxson 1989;
Curry, Ball, and Fox 1994). City-level studies have found gang-related motives in
more than one-third of homicides in Chicago (Block and Block 1993), 50 percent of
the homicides in Los Angeles' Boyle Heights area (Tita, Riley, and Greenwood
2003), and 75 percent of homicides in Lowell, Massachusetts (Braga, McDevitt, and
Pierce 2006).

Even in neighborhoods suffering from high rates of youth gun violence, most
youth are not in gangs and criminally active groups. In addition, some gangs are
more dangerous than others. To better understand Boston's gang problem during
the 1990s, Harvard University researchers mapped gang turf and estimated gang
size (Kennedy, Braga, and Piehl 1997). They identified 61 different crews with
around 1,300 members. Gang members represented less than 1 percent of all Boston
youth, and less than 3 percent of youth in high-risk neighborhoods. The mapping
also documented rivalries and alliances among gangs. Gangs had identifiable
"beefs" with particular rival gangs, not all rivalries were active (i.e., shots were not
currently being fired), and certain gangs were much more involved in conflicts than
others. In Minneapolis, researchers identified some 2,650 people in 32 active street
gangs as being central to youth gun violence; they represented less than 3.5 percent
of Minneapolis residents between the ages of 14 and 24 (Kennedy and Braga 1998).
The gangs tended not to be territorial; they operated fluidly across Minneapolis and
nearby jurisdictions. In Boyle Heights, researchers identified 37 criminally active
street gangs as being involved in youth gun violence (Tita, Riley, and Greenwood
2003).

However, gangs are not always behind youth gun violence. In some cities, criminally active groups who are not considered "gangs" are major gun offenders. In
Baltimore, violent groups active in street drug markets were involved in numerous
homicides in 1997 (Braga, Kennedy, and Tita 2002). Most of the murders occurred
in or near a street drug market, and many victims and suspects were part of a drug
organization or a recognized neighborhood criminal network. Researchers identified 325 drug groups that ranged in nature from rather sophisticated organizations,
to structured neighborhood groups, to loose neighborhood groups. While drug disputes and street drug robberies contributed to Baltimore's gun violence problem,
homicides often resulted from ongoing, non-drug-related disputes among people in
drug-selling groups.

In thinking about the nature of youth gun violence problems, it is important to
recognize that the direct links among youth gangs, drugs, and violence are usually
overstated (Block and Block 1993; Howell and Decker 1999). Even in Baltimore,
where most youth gun violence occurs in a drug-market setting, most youth gun
homicide was not drug related (Braga, Kennedy, and Tita 2002). Gang and group
violence is usually retaliatory or expressive (defending gang honor, status, and
members). Today's offenders are often tomorrow's victims, and vice versa. Youth
gun violence victims treated in Boston emergency rooms during the 1990s often

had scars from past gun and knife wounds (Rich and Stone 1996). Youth gun violence in many cities appears to be a self-sustaining cycle among a relatively small
number of criminally active youth. They are at high risk of being confronted by gun
violence, so they tend to try to protect themselves by getting, carrying, and using
guns; forming and joining gangs; acting tough; and so forth (Kennedy, Piehl, and
Braga 1996). This behavior adds to the cycle of street violence.

When considering youth crime, the strategy of focusing resources on a lone offender who participates in several groups may do little to prevent crimes given the
continuation of the co-offending groups (Sherman 1992). As such, offender-based
prevention strategies targeting youthful offenders should think about focusing on
groups rather than particular individuals. Reiss (1988) observes that both adults and
juveniles may be vulnerable to the suggestive influence of "Typhoid Marys," or people
who accumulate high numbers of co-offenders. These people serve as "carriers" of
criminal ideas across social networks and their presence in particular groups could
facilitate criminal action. Sherman (1992) suggests that identifying and incarcerating
these "idea men" may produce greater crime prevention benefits then apprehending
lone offenders who do not spread criminal ideas around.

III. DISCUSSION AND CONCLUSIONS

The available empirical and theoretical evidence suggests that crime is highly concentrated at a small number of high-risk places during high-risk times and generated by a small number of very risky people. The existing research also points to
important place-level dynamics and situational factors and the daily activities and
behaviors of people who constitute offender and victims populations in understanding the concentration of crime at specific small places during very specific
months of the year, days of the week, and hours of the day. Similarly, for high-crime
offenders, research documents the salience of co-offending patterns and the central
role of group-based dynamics and norms in persistent violent crime problems in
urban settings.

While these patterns are very concerning, they also represent important opportunities for more effective crime prevention and control. If municipalities can organize themselves to control the small number of risky places, risky times, and risky
people that generate the bulk of their crime problems, they can more effectively
manage citywide crime trends. This orientation will obviously put a premium on
data collection and analysis systems. By virtue of their recurring patterns in commonly available criminal justice data systems (such as arrest data, crime incident
data, and calls for service data), these risks are easily identifiable through simple
analysis. Through the collection of other data (such as offender and victim interviews) and closer analysis, the underlying conditions and dynamics associated with
the genesis and continuation of these recurring problems can be understood.

Practical prevention frameworks, such as situational crime prevention and problem-oriented policing approaches, can be used to diagnose and respond to high-crime places, times, and offenders (Goldstein 1990; Clarke 1997; Braga 2008) in the near term. A growing body of evidence suggests that crime-prevention strategies tailored to specific places, such as hot spots policing (Braga 2001; Braga and Weisburd 2010), and addressing group of chronic offenders, such as focused deterrence strategies (Braga et al. 2001; Kennedy 2008), can be effective in reducing these recurring crime problems. Ideally, these interventions should be implemented in conjunction with complementary, longer term approaches that seek to prevent the development of children into high-crime offenders, such as child skills training programs and parent education programs (Farrington and Welsh 2007), and minimize the presence and continuity of crime hot spots in neighborhoods through building informal social control and the collective efficacy of residents and business owners in these areas (Sampson 2002).

REFERENCES

Agnew, Ronald. 1992. "Foundation for a General Strain Theory of Crime and Delinquency." *Criminology* 30:47–84.

Agnew, Ronald. 1999. "A General Strain Theory of Community Differences in Crime Rates." *Journal of Research in Crime and Delinquency* 36:123–55.

Akers, Ronald. 1973. *Deviant Behavior: A Social Learning Approach*. Belmont, CA: Wadsworth.

Baumer, Eric, Janet Lauritsen, Richard Rosenfeld, and Richard Wright. 1998. "The Influence of Crack Cocaine on Robbery, Burglary, and Homicide Rates: A Cross-city, Longitudinal Analysis." *Journal of Research in Crime and Delinquency* 35:316–40.

Block, Carolyn R., and Richard Block. 1993. "Street Gang Crime in Chicago." *Research in Brief Series*. Washington, DC: US Department of Justice, National Institute of Justice.

Block, Carolyn R., Margaret Dabdoub, and Suzanne Fregly, eds. 1995. *Crime Analysis through Computer Mapping*. Washington, DC: Police Executive Research Forum.

Block, Richard, and Carolyn R. Block. 1995. "Space, Place and Crime: Hot Spot Areas and Hot Places of Liquor-Related Crime." In *Crime and Place*, edited by John Eck and David L. Weisburd. Vol. 4 of *Crime Prevention Studies*, edited by Ronald V. Clarke. Monsey, NY: Criminal Justice Press.

Blumstein, Alfred, Jacqueline Cohen, Jeffrey Roth, and Christy Visher (Eds.). 1986. *Criminal Careers and Career Criminals*. Washington, DC: National Academy Press.

Blumstein, Alfred, and Daniel Cork 1996. "Linking Gun Availability to Youth Gun Violence." *Law and Contemporary Problems* 59:5–24.

Braga, Anthony A. 2001. "The Effects of Hot Spots Policing on Crime." *Annals of the American Academy of Political and Social Science* 578:104–25.

Braga, Anthony A. 2004. *Gun Violence Among Serious Young Offenders*. Problem-Oriented Guides for Police Series, Problem-Specific Guide Number 23. Washington, DC: US Department of Justice, Office of Community Oriented Policing Services.

Braga, Anthony A. 2008. *Problem-Oriented Policing and Crime Prevention,* 2nd ed. Monsey, NY: Criminal Justice Press.

Braga, Anthony A., David M. Hureau, and Andrew V. Papachristos. 2011. "The Relevance of Micro Places to Citywide Robbery Trends: A Longitudinal Analysis of Robbery Incidents at Street Corners and Block Faces in Boston." *Journal of Research in Crime and Delinquency* 48:7–32.

Braga, Anthony A., David M. Hureau, and Christopher Winship. 2008. "Losing Faith? Police, Black Churches, and the Resurgence of Youth Violence in Boston." *Ohio State Journal of Criminal Law* 6:141–72.

Braga, Anthony A., David M. Kennedy, and George Tita. 2002. "New Approaches to the Strategic Prevention of Gang and Group-Involved Violence." In *Gangs in America*, 3rd ed. edited by C. Ronald Huff. Thousand Oaks, CA: Sage.

Braga, Anthony A., David M. Kennedy, Elin J. Waring, and Anne M. Piehl. 2001. "Problem-Oriented Policing, Deterrence, and Youth Violence: An Evaluation of Boston's Operation Ceasefire." *Journal of Research in Crime and Delinquency* 38:195–225.

Braga, Anthony A., Jack McDevitt, and Glenn L. Pierce. 2006. "Understanding and Preventing Gang Violence: Problem Analysis and Response Development in Lowell, Massachusetts." *Police Quarterly* 9:20–46.

Braga, Anthony A., Andrew V. Papachristos, and David M. Hureau. 2010. "The Concentration and Stability of Gun Violence at Micro Places in Boston, 1980–2008." *Journal of Quantitative Criminology* 26:33–53.

Braga, Anthony A., and David L. Weisburd. 2010. *Policing Problem Places: Crime Hot Spots and Effective Prevention*. New York: Oxford University Press.

Braga, Anthony A., David L. Weisburd, Elin J. Waring, Lorraine Green Mazerolle, William Spelman, and Francis Gajewski. 1999. "Problem-Oriented Policing in Violent Crime Places: A Randomized Controlled Experiment." *Criminology* 37: 541–80.

Brantingham, Patricia L., and Paul J. Brantingham 1981. "Notes on the Geometry of Crime." In *Environmental Criminology*, edited by Paul J. Brantingham and Patricia L. Brantingham. Beverly Hills, CA: Sage.

Bursik, Robert, and Harold Grasmick. 1993. *Neighborhoods and Crime: The Dimensions of Effective Community Control*. Lexington, MA: Lexington.

Capone, Donald L., and Woodrow Nichols. 1976. "Urban Structure and Criminal Mobility." *American Behavioral Scientist* 20:199–213.

Chaiken, Jan, and Marcia Chaiken. 1982. *Varieties of Criminal Behavior*. Santa Monica, CA: RAND.

Clarke, Ronald V. 1995. "Situational Crime Prevention." In *Building a Safer Society: Strategic Approaches to Crime Prevention*, edited by Michael Tonry and David Farrington. Vol. 19 of *Crime and Justice: A Review of Research*, edited by Michael Tonry. Chicago: University of Chicago Press.

Clarke, Ronald V., ed. 1997. *Situational Crime Prevention: Successful Case Studies*, 2nd ed. Albany, NY: Harrow and Heston.

Clarke, Ronald V., and John E. Eck. 2007. *Understanding Risky Facilities*. Problem-Oriented Guides for Police, Problem Solving Tools Series, No. 6. Washington, DC: US Department of Justice, Office of Community Oriented Policing Services.

Clarke, Ronald V., and Marcus Felson. 1993. "Introduction: Criminology, Routine Activity, and Rational Choice." In *Routine Activity and Rational Choice, Advances in Criminological Theory*, vol. 5, edited by Ronald V. Clarke and Marcus Felson. New Brunswick, NJ: Transaction.

Cloward, Richard, and Lloyd Ohlin. 1960. *Delinquency and Opportunity*. Glencoe, IL: Free Press.

Cohen, Lawrence E., and Marcus Felson. 1979. "Social Change and Crime Rate Trends: A Routine Activity Approach." *American Sociological Review* 44: 588–605.

Cohn, Ellen G. 1990. "Weather and Crime." *British Journal of Criminology* 30:51–64.

Cook, Philip J. 2009. "Robbery." In *The Oxford Handbook of Crime and Public Policy*, edited by Michael Tonry. New York: Oxford University Press.

Cook, Philip J., and John Laub. 2002. "After the Epidemic: Recent Trends in Youth Violence in the United States." In *Crime and Justice: A Review of Research,* vol. 29, edited by Michael Tonry. Chicago: University of Chicago Press.

Cornish, Derek, and Ronald V. Clarke, eds. 1986. *The Reasoning Criminal: Rational Choice Perspectives on Offending*. New York: Springer-Verlag.

Crow, Wayman J., and James L. Bull. 1975. *Robbery Deterrence: An Applied Behavioral Science Demonstration-Final Report*. La Jolla, CA: Western Behavioral Sciences Institute.

Curry, G. David, Richard Ball, and Robert Fox. 1994. *Gang Crime and Law Enforcement Record Keeping*. Washington, DC: US Department of Justice, National Institute of Justice.

Duffala, Dennis C. 1976. "Convenience Stores, Robbery, and Physical Environmental Features." *American Behavioral Scientist* 20:227–46.

Eck, John E. 1994. "Drug Markets and Drug Places: A Case-Control Study of the Spatial Structure of Illicit Dealing." Ph.D. Dissertation, University of Maryland, College Park.

Eck, John E. 1997. "Preventing Crime at Places." In *Preventing Crime: What Works, What Doesn't, What's Promising*, edited by University of Maryland, Department of Criminology and Criminal Justice. Washington, DC: US Department of Justice, Office of Justice Programs.

Eck, John E., and David L. Weisburd (1995). "Crime Places in Crime Theory." In *Crime and Place*, edited by John Eck and David L. Weisburd. Vol. 4 of *Crime Prevention Studies*, edited by Ronald V. Clarke. Monsey, NY: Criminal Justice Press.

Farrell, Graham. 1995. "Preventing Repeat Victimization." In *Building a Safer Society: Strategic Approaches to Crime Prevention*, edited by Michael Tonry and David Farrington. Vol. 19 of *Crime and Justice: A Review of Research*, edited by Michael Tonry. Chicago: University of Chicago Press.

Farrell, Graham, and Kenneth Pease. 1993. *Once Bitten, Twice Bitten: Repeat Victimization and its Implications for Crime Prevention*. Crime Reduction Research Series Paper Number 5. London: Home Office.

Farrington, David, and Brandon Welsh. 2007. *Saving Children from a Life of Crime*. New York: Oxford University Press.

Felson, Marcus. 2003. "The Process of Co-Offending." In *Theory for Practice in Situational Crime Prevention*, edited by Martha Smith and Derek Cornish. Vol. 16 of *Crime Prevention Studies*, edited by Ronald V. Clarke. Monsey, NY: Criminal Justice Press.

Felson, Marcus. 2006. *Crime and Nature*. Thousand Oaks, CA: Sage.

Felson, Marcus, and Erika Poulsen. 2003. "Simple Indicators of Crime by Time of Day." *International Journal of Forecasting* 19:595–601.

Forrester, Donald, Michael Chatterton, and Kenneth Pease. 1988. *The Kirkholt Burglary Prevention Project*. Home Office Crime Prevention Unit Paper 13. London: Home Office.

Goldstein, Herman. 1990. *Problem-Oriented Policing*. Philadelphia, PA: Temple University Press.

Gottfredson, Michael, and Travis Hirschi. 1990. *A General Theory of Crime*. Stanford, CA: Stanford University Press.

Green, Lorraine. 1996. *Policing Places with Drug Problems*. Thousand Oaks, CA: Sage.

Guerry, Andre-Michel. 1833. *Essai sur la Statistique Morale de la France*. Paris: Crochard.

Harcourt, Bernard. 1998. "Reflecting on the Subject: A Critique of the Social Influence of Deterrence, the Broken Windows Theory, and Order-Maintenance Policing New York Style." *Michigan Law Review* 97:291–389.

Hindelang, Michael J., Michael Gottfredson, and James Garofalo. 1978. *Victims of Personal Crime: An Empirical Foundation for a Theory of Personal Victimization*. Cambridge, MA: Ballinger.

Hirschi, Travis. 1969. *Causes of Delinquency*. Berkeley, CA: University of California Press.

Homel, Ross, and Jeff Clark. 1994. "The Prevention of Violence in Pubs and Clubs." In *Crime Prevention Studies*, Vol. 3, edited by Ronald V. Clarke. Monsey, NY: Criminal Justice Press.

Howell, James, and Scott Decker. 1999. *The Gangs, Drugs, and Violence Connection*. Washington, DC: US Department of Justice, Office of Juvenile Justice and Delinquency Prevention.

Hunter, Ronald, and C. Ray Jeffrey. 1992. "Preventing Convenience Store Robbery through Environmental Design." In *Situational Crime Prevention: Successful Case Studies*, edited by Ronald V. Clarke. Albany, NY: Harrow and Heston.

Jang, Sung J., and Byron Johnson. 2001. "Neighborhood Disorder, Individual Religiosity, and Adolescent Use of Illicit Drugs: A Test of Multilevel Hypotheses." *Criminology* 39:109–44.

Kelling, George, and Catherine Coles. 1996. *Fixing Broken Windows: Restoring Order and Reducing Crime in Our Communities*. New York: Free Press.

Kennedy, David M. 2008. *Deterrence and Crime Prevention: Reconsidering the Prospect of Sanction*. London: Routledge.

Kennedy, David M., and Anthony A. Braga. 1998. "Homicide in Minneapolis: Research for Problem Solving." *Homicide Studies* 2:26390.

Kennedy, David M., Anthony A. Braga, and Anne M. Piehl. 1997. "The (Un)Known Universe: Mapping Gangs and Gang Violence in Boston." In *Crime Mapping and Crime Prevention*, edited by David L. Weisburd and J. Thomas McEwen. Vol. 8 of *Crime Prevention Studies*, edited by Ronald V. Clarke. Monsey, NY: Criminal Justice Press.

Kennedy, David M., Anne M. Piehl, and Anthony A. Braga. 1996. "Youth Violence in Boston: Gun Markets, Serious Youth Offenders, and a Use-Reduction Strategy." *Law and Contemporary Problems* 59:147–96.

Kleiman, Mark A. R. 1997. "Coerced Abstinence: A Neopaternalist Drug Policy Initiative." In *The New Paternalism: Strategic Approaches to Poverty*, edited by Lawrence Mead. Washington, DC: Brookings Institution.

Klein, Malcolm, and Cheryl Maxson. 1989. "Street Gang Violence." In *Violent Crimes, Violent Criminals*, edited by Neil A. Weiner. Beverly Hills, CA: Sage.

Lane, Roger. 1971. *Policing the City: Boston 1822–1855*. New York: Antheneum.

Laub, John, and Robert Sampson. 2003. *Shared Beginnings, Divergent Lives: Delinquent Boys to Age 70*. Cambridge, MA: Harvard University Press.

Laycock, Gloria, and Claire Austin. 1992. "Crime Prevention in Parking Facilities." *Security Journal* 3:154–60.

LeBeau, James. 1987. "The Methods and Measures of Centrography and the Spatial Dynamics of Rape." *Journal of Quantitative Criminology* 3:125–41.

Loftin, Colin, and Robert Hill. 1974. "Regional Subculture and Homicide: An Examination of the Gastil-Hackney Thesis." *American Sociological Review* 39: 714–24.

Merton, Robert K. 1938. "Social Structure and Anomie." *American Sociological Review* 3:672–82.

Miller, Walter B. 1975. *Violence by Youth Gangs and Youth Groups as a Crime Problem in Major American Cities*. Washington, DC: US Government Printing Office.

Moffitt, Terrie. 1993. "Adolescence-Limited and Life-Course Persistent Antisocial Behavior: A Developmental Taxonomy." *Psychological Review* 4:674.

Nettler, Gwynne. 1978. *Explaining Crime*, 2nd ed. New York: McGraw-Hill.

Pierce, Glenn L., Susan Spaar, and LeBaron Briggs. 1988. *The Character of Police Work Strategic and Tactical Implications*. Boston, MA: Northeastern University, Center for Applied Social Research.

Piquero, Alex, David Farrington, and Alfred Blumstein. 2007. *Key Issues in Criminal Career Research*. New York: Cambridge University Press.

Poyner, Barry. 1988. "Video Cameras and Bus Vandalism." *Security Administration* 11: 44–51.

Quetelet, Adolphe J. 1842. *A Treatise of Man*. Gainesville, FL: Scholar's Facsimiles and Reprints [1969].

Raine, Adrian. 1993. *The Psychopathy of Crime*. New York: Academic Press.

Reiss, Albert. 1988 "Co-Offending and Criminal Careers." In *Crime and Justice: A Review of Research,* vol. 10, edited by Michael Tonry and Norval Morris. Chicago: University of Chicago Press.

Rengert, George. 1980. "Theory and Practice in Urban Police Response." In *Crime: A Spatial Perspective*, edited by Daniel Georges-Abeyie and Keith Harries. New York: Columbia University Press.

Rengert, George. 1981. "Burglary in Philadelphia: A Critique of an Opportunity Structure Model." In *Environmental Criminology*, edited by Paul J. Brantingham and Patricia L. Brantingham. Beverly Hills, CA: Sage.

Rengert, George, and John Wasilchick. 1990. "Space, Time, and Crime: Ethnographic Insights into Residential Burglary." Report submitted to US Department of Justice, National Institute of Justice.

Rhodes, William, and Catherine Conley. 1991. "Crime and Mobility: An Empirical Study." In *Environmental Criminology*, 2nd ed. edited by Paul J. Brantingham and Patricia L. Brantingham. Beverly Hills, CA: Sage.

Rich, John A. 2009. *Wrong Place, Wrong Time: Trauma and Violence in the Lives of Young Black Men*. Baltimore: Johns Hopkins University Press.

Rich, John, and David Stone. 1996. "The Experience of Violent Injury for Young African-American Men: The Meaning of Being a 'Sucker.'" *Journal of General Internal Medicine* 11:77–82.

Robinson, Jennifer, Brian Lawton, Ralph Taylor, and Douglas Perkins. 2003. "Multilevel Longitudinal Impacts of Incivilities: Fear of Crime, Expected Safety, and Block Satisfaction." *Journal of Quantitative Criminology* 19:237–74.

Rolph, John, Jan Chaiken, and Robert Houchens. 1981. *Methods for Estimating the Crime Rates of Individuals*. Santa Monica, CA: RAND.

Roncek, Dennis, and Pamela Meier. 1991. "Bar Blocks and Crimes Revisited: Linking the Theory of Routine Activities to the Empiricism of 'Hot Spots.'" *Criminology* 29:725–55.

Sampson, Robert. 1985. "Neighborhood and Crime: The Structural Determinants of Personal Victimization." *Journal of Research in Crime and Delinquency* 22:7–40.

Sampson, Robert. 2002. "The Community." In *Crime*, edited by James Q. Wilson and Joan Petersilia. Oakland, CA: ICS Press.

Sampson, Robert, and W. Byron Groves. 1989. "Community Structure and Crime: Testing Social Disorganization Theory." *American Journal of Sociology* 94: 774–802.

Sampson, Robert, and John Laub. 1993. *Crime in the Making: Pathways and Turning Points through Life*. Cambridge, MA: Harvard University Press.

Sampson, Robert, and Stephen Raudenbush. 1999. "Systematic Social Observation of Public Spaces: A New Look at Disorder in Urban Neighborhoods." *American Journal of Sociology* 105:603–51.

Shaw, Clifford, and Henry McKay. 1942. *Juvenile Delinquency in Urban Areas*. Chicago: University of Chicago Press.

Sherman, Lawrence. 1992. "Attacking Crime: Police and Crime Control." In *Modern Policing*, edited by Michael Tonry and Norval Morris. Vol. 15 of *Crime and Justice: A Review of Research*, edited by Michael Tonry. Chicago: University of Chicago Press.

Sherman, Lawrence. 1995. "Hot Spots of Crime and Criminal Careers of Places." In *Crime and Place*, edited by John Eck and David L. Weisburd. Vol. 4 of *Crime Prevention Studies*, edited by Ronald V. Clarke. Monsey, NY: Criminal Justice Press.

Sherman, Lawrence, Patrick Gartin, and Michael Buerger. 1989. "Hot Spots of Predatory Crime: Routine Activities and the Criminology of Place." *Criminology* 27:27–56.

Sherman, Lawrence, and Dennis Rogan. 1995. "Effects of Gun Seizures on Gun Violence: 'Hot Spots' Patrol in Kansas City." *Justice Quarterly* 12:673–94.

Sherman, Lawrence, Janell Schmidt and Robert Velke. 1992. *High Crime Taverns: A RECAP Project in Problem Oriented Policing*. Final Report to the National Institute of Justice. Washington, DC: Crime Control Institute.

Sherman, Lawrence, and David L. Weisburd. 1995. "General Deterrent Effects of Police Patrol in Crime Hot Spots: A Randomized Controlled Trial." *Justice Quarterly* 12:625–48.

Skogan, Wesley. 1990. *Disorder and Decline: Crime and the Spiral of Decay in American Neighborhoods*. New York: Free Press.

Spelman, William. 1986. "*The Depth of a Dangerous Temptation: Crime Control and the Dangerous Offender*." Final Report to the National Institute of Justice. Washington, DC: Police Executive Research Forum.

Spelman, William. 1990. *Repeat Offender Programs*. Washington, DC: Police Executive Research Forum.

Spelman, William. 1993. "Abandoned Buildings: Magnets for Crime?" *Journal of Criminal Justice* 21:481–95.

Spelman, William. 1995. "Criminal Careers of Public Places." In *Crime and Place*, edited by John Eck and David L. Weisburd. Vol. 4 of *Crime Prevention Studies*, edited by Ronald V. Clarke. Monsey, NY: Criminal Justice Press.

Spelman, William, and John E. Eck. 1989. "Sitting Ducks, Ravenous Wolves, and Helping Hands: New Approaches to Urban Policing." *Public Affairs Comment* 35:1–9.

St. Jean, Peter K. B. 2007. *Pockets of Crime: Broken Windows, Collective Efficacy, and the Criminal Point of View*. Chicago: University of Chicago Press.

Taylor, Ralph. 1997. "Social Order and Disorder of Street-Blocks and Neighborhoods: Ecology, Micro-ecology, and the Systematic Model of Social Disorganization." *Journal of Research in Crime and Delinquency* 34:113–55.

Taylor, Ralph. 1999. "The Incivilities Thesis: Theory, Measurement, and Policy." In *Measuring What Matters: Proceedings from the Policing Research Institute Meetings*, edited by Robert Langworthy. Washington, DC: US Department of Justice, National Institute of Justice.

Taylor, Ralph. 2001. *Breaking Away from Broken Windows: Baltimore Neighborhoods and the Nationwide Fight Against Crime, Grime, Fear, and Decline*. Boulder, CO: Westview.

Taylor, Ralph, and Stephen Gottfredson. 1986. "Environment Design, Crime, and Prevention: An Examination of Community Dynamics." In *Communities and Crime*, edited by Albert J. Reiss and Michael Tonry. Vol. 8 of *Crime and Justice: A Review of Research*, edited by Michael Tonry and Norval Morris. Chicago: University of Chicago Press.

Tita, George, Kevin J. Riley, and Peter Greenwood. 2003. "From Boston to Boyle Heights: The Process and Prospects of a 'Pulling Levers' Strategy in a Los Angeles Barrio." In *Policing Gangs and Youth Violence*, edited by Scott H. Decker. Belmont, CA: Wadsworth.

Warr, Mark. 2002. *Companions in Crime: The Social Aspects of Criminal Conduct*. New York: Cambridge University Press.

Weisburd, David L., Wim Bernasco, and Gerben Bruinsma, eds. 2009. *Putting Crime in its Place: Units of Analysis in Geographic Criminology*. New York: Springer.

Weisburd, David L., Shawn Bushway, Cynthia Lum, and Sue-Ming Yang. 2004. "Trajectories of Crime at Places: A Longitudinal Study of Street Segments in the City of Seattle." *Criminology* 42:283–322.

Weisburd, David L., and Lorraine Green. 1994. "Defining the Drug Market: The Case of the Jersey City DMAP System." In *Drugs and Crime: Evaluating Public Policy Initiatives*, edited by Doris L. MacKenzie and Craig Uchida. Newbury Park, CA: Sage.

Weisburd, David L., and Lorraine Green. 1995. "Policing Drug Hot Spots: The Jersey City DMA Experiment." *Justice Quarterly* 12:711–36.

Weisburd, David L., Lisa Maher, and Lawrence Sherman. 1992. "Contrasting Crime General and Crime Specific Theory: The Case of Hot Spots of Crime." *Advances in Criminological Theory* 4:45–69.

Weisburd, David L., Nancy Morris, and Elizabeth Groff. 2009. "Hot Spots of Juvenile Crime: A Longitudinal Study of Arrests Incidents at Street Segments in Seattle, Washington. *Journal of Quantitative Criminology* 25:443–67.

Wilson, James Q., and George Kelling. 1982. "Broken Windows: The Police and Neighborhood Safety." *Atlantic Monthly* (March): 29–38.

Wolfgang, Marvin, and Franco Ferracuti. 1967. *The Subculture of Violence: Toward an Integrated Theory in Criminology*. New York: Tavistock.

Wolfgang, Marvin, Roberto Figlio, and Thorsten Sellin. 1972. *Delinquency in a Birth Cohort*. Chicago: University of Chicago Press.

Yang, Sue-Ming. 2010. "Assessing the Spatial-temporal Relationship between Disorder and Violence." *Journal of Quantitative Criminology* 26:139–63.

Zimring, Franklin. 1981. "Kids, Groups, and Crime: Some Implications of a Well-Known Secret." *Journal of Criminal Law and Criminology* 72:867–85.

CHAPTER 17

CRIME DISPLACEMENT AND DIFFUSION OF BENEFITS

SHANE D. JOHNSON,
ROB T. GUERETTE, AND
KATE J. BOWERS

ONE criticism of situational crime prevention is that it does not address the so-called root causes of crime. In the extreme, such causes would be explained entirely in terms of influences that (for example) lead to some people being unable to achieve desired goals through legitimate means (Merton 1938) or enduring psychological (e.g., Yochelson and Samenow 1976) dispositions. These types of explanations suggest a hydraulic view of crime whereby changes to the physical environment would have no net effect on levels of crime. That is, those people who would have committed offenses in the absence of intervention will continue to do so at the same rate. All that would change is how, when or where they commit those offenses; crime would be displaced.

For some time, five forms of displacement have been identified (Repetto 1976): those that result in offenders' changing *how* they commit offenses, *when* they commit them, the specific types of *targets* they select (e.g., certain types of homes in the case of burglary), *where* they commit them, and the *types* of offenses committed. Later, Barr and Pease (1990) introduced the idea that incapacitated offenders—or those who desist from crime—might be replaced by others if opportunities are not reduced. With the exception of the latter, each form of displacement describes one way in which an existing population of offenders might be anticipated to adapt to the blocking of opportunities.

The hydraulic view of crime requires that a series of assumptions be met. For example, where opportunities are blocked, that alternatives exist that are more or less substitutive; that offenders are aware of such opportunities and have the motivation and ability to exploit them; and unless accessible substitutive opportunities are abundant, that offenders are unconcerned with the effort associated with discovering new opportunities, the potential risks associated with exploiting them in unfamiliar areas (see Weisburd et al. 2006), or that they have no preferences for particular types of target or ways of committing offenses (Cornish and Clarke 1986).

In contrast to dispositional theories, opportunity theories more explicitly consider the interaction between the offender and the immediate situation and how this might influence the likelihood of crime occurrence. To illustrate, consider that research suggests that crime is concentrated in space (e.g., Johnson 2010). However, it is not just concentrated, but there is also often a sharp discontinuity in risk apparent at very fine levels of resolution, including street segments (Johnson and Bowers 2010), individual households (Pease 1998) or facilities (Eck, Clarke, and Guerette 2007). For example, using trajectory analysis, Weisburd et al. (2004) show that in Seattle, a small fraction of street segments account for the majority of crime. Moreover, that the same street segments consistently do so over the 15-year period observed. This has led Weisburd (2010) to suggest that crime is strongly *coupled* to place. That is, just as offender motivations play a role in crime occurrence so, too, does the environment, and it would appear that offenders are not indifferent to the varied choices available to them but that their collective choices reveal preferences. If this view is accepted, then one has to think differently about the inevitability of crime displacement and how crime patterns might change following intervention.

The opposite of crime displacement is a diffusion of benefit, whereby the positive effects of an intervention extend beyond the operational range of intervention. Clarke and Weisburd (1994) discuss two mechanisms through which crime-control benefits might be diffused, rather than criminal action displaced. In the first instance, they discuss deterrent effects—that is, where offenders perceive that the risk of identification or apprehension has increased. As offenders will rarely be aware of the operational boundary of an intervention, they may easily overestimate the actual coverage. While perhaps more appropriate to intense police activity, some situational crime-prevention interventions may also diffuse crime-control benefits in this way. For example, Poyner (1992) evaluated how closed circuit television (CCTV) cameras were used on a university campus to reduce vehicle crime and vandalism in three car parks covered by cameras. His findings suggested that crime was reduced in all three locations, but also in a fourth that was not covered by the cameras. That is, rather than displacing crime to the car park not protected by the cameras, the crime-control benefit experienced in those that were appeared to have been diffused. Poyner suggests that the success of the intervention was partly attributable to the fact that early detections associated with the cameras were publicized, thereby shaping offender perceptions of risk, effort, and reward in the areas that were and were not covered by the cameras.

A second mechanism through which crime-control benefits might be diffused is discouragement (Clarke and Weisburd 1994). In this case, as a result of blocking opportunities within offender awareness spaces, offenders may perceive the effort associated with seeking out new opportunities or with targeting those that are more difficult to attack outweigh the perceived benefits.

Other reasons for not expecting displacement to occur as a consequence of situational crime-prevention measures exist. For example, consider that the immediate situation may facilitate crime by influencing the decision-making process of an already motivated offender, or it may actually precipitate criminal action by provoking what otherwise might not have occurred (Wortley 1997). For example, Wortley (2008) discusses how the cumulative effect of the various frustrations that may be experienced during a night out—crowded conditions, excess heat caused by ineffective ventilation or other factors, poor door policies, and so on (all of which are situational factors)—might provoke a violent response in someone who would not normally behave this way. In this case, there is an interaction between the actor and the environment, but the latter plays a central role in shaping behavior. Where situational facilitators or precipitators that contribute to a problem are removed, not only should this prevent crime but also there is no reason to expect prevented crimes to be displaced.

Further, when displacement is considered, many who advocate its likelihood no doubt consider crime as being committed solely by a population of prolific offenders. However, while some offenders will be prolific, others will not (e.g., Cornish and Clarke 2003). With this in mind, it does not seem unreasonable to suggest that different types of offenders will be deterred or discouraged from offending by situational modifications to differing degrees. For some, the blocking of opportunities may have little effect, but for others it may lead to a reduction in offending or even a cessation.

The aim of this essay is to provide a review of research concerned with crime displacement and to discuss the challenges encountered in evaluations designed to examine this. The following conclusions emerge:

- Many evaluations do not collect sufficient data to examine displacement using quantitative methods.
- Few studies employ a random allocation strategy, and few attempt to identify the precise crime-control mechanisms through which interventions might affect levels of crime.
- Spatial displacement is by far the most commonly considered form of displacement in the evaluation literature.
- The available evidence suggests that for situational crime-prevention interventions, a diffusion of benefit is at least as likely as crime displacement.
- When displacement does occur, it rarely is greater than the reduction observed in the treatment area.

The essay is organized as follows. Section I provides an overview of previous reviews concerned with crime displacement. Section II describes the search strategy employed to identify studies for inclusion in the meta-analysis that follows.

In section III, we discuss the approach to analysis and methodological challenges for studies concerned with crime displacement. In section IV, we present the results of the meta-analysis, and in section V, we draw conclusions and suggest future directions for research.

I. Summary of Prior Reviews

Many studies have been conducted and a number of reviews completed to assess the extent to which situational crime-prevention interventions displace crime or diffuse benefits. Unfortunately, until recently evaluators had not routinely estimated the extent of displacement using quantitative methods and so early reviews (e.g., Hesseling 1994) were limited to vote counting methods.

In the most recent review, Guerette and Bowers (2009) identified 102 evaluation studies in which the possible side effects (displacement or diffusion of benefit) of situational crime-prevention interventions were considered. For the majority, quantitative data were unavailable or not in a form that facilitated quantitative analyses. A vote-counting exercise indicated that for about half of the studies, neither displacement nor a diffusion of benefit was reported by the study authors. Of the remainder, for the six forms of side effect considered, a diffusion of benefit was just as likely to be reported as displacement.

Of course, caution is required in the interpretation of findings based on a vote-counting methodology (Petticrew and Roberts 2006). Fortunately, for 13 of the studies, raw data—published in the form of area crime rates—were available for analysis. Consequently, Guerette and Bowers (2009) were able to quantify the extent to which spatial displacement or diffusion occurred. The conclusion from that analysis, and from the earlier reviews, was that rather than displacement being an inevitable outcome of intervention, a diffusion of benefit was equally likely to occur.

Since that review, other studies have been published for which crime counts as well, or instead of, crime rates are available. Thus, the current essay represents an update to the review conducted by Guerette and Bowers (2009). It also represents an opportunity to use an alternative statistical approach (see below) for which crime *counts* rather than *rates* are analyzed, to help determine if the previous conclusions are robust to variations in methodology.

II. Search Strategy and Data

The current study examined the evaluations identified by Guerette and Bowers (2009) plus those conducted since. The original search revealed 261 evaluations that broadly assessed interventions that entailed a prominent or exclusive situational component that could be classified according to Cornish and Clarke's (2003) classification of situational crime-prevention techniques. Of these, 206 were published reports of original research (see Guerette and Bowers 2009). The updated search resulted in the identification of an additional 27 possible studies for inclusion.

Studies included in the current review were those that satisfied the following criteria: (1) the evaluation constituted a dominant or exclusive situational intervention; (2) it reported original research findings; (3) it used a quantitative outcome measure of crime; (4) the findings reported both pre- and post-count data; and (5) the study design included the use of at least three areas of measurement: a target/intervention area, a buffer, and a control. Thirteen studies met these criteria.[1]

A summary of the 13 studies is provided in table 17.1. Only two studies employed a random allocation strategy, with most ($N = 11$) adopting a quasi-experimental design. Only the former used independent catchment areas for both treatment and control areas. In some studies, data were collected for more than one catchment area ($N = 2$), or for a variety of control areas ($N = 2$). In another, while there were data for multiple treatment sites, the control areas were not independent. Consequently, it was possible to calculate more than one odds ratio for some of the studies. We discuss how we addressed this issue later.

Across studies, the follow-up periods used post-intervention ranges from 6 to 36 months, with 14 months being about the average. Slightly more than half of the studies ($n = 7$) assessed outcomes for a range of crime types, while six examined changes in a single crime type, either burglary or theft.

The locations where the 13 evaluations were conducted were divided mostly between the United Kingdom ($n = 7$) and the United States ($n = 5$), with one study taking place in Australia (Cummings 2005). Overall, the interventions were applied most frequently in residential areas ($n = 6$), with the remainder being carried out in public places ($n = 3$); some combination of multiple environments ($n = 3$; such as public, residential, and recreational, for instance); and one study where the intervention took place in both a retail and a residential setting (Cameron et al. 2008). Most of these place types were situated in urban geographical areas ($n = 9$), with a smaller portion of studies having been carried out in what could be considered rural ($n = 2$) and suburban ($n = 1$) locales. For one study, the specific location was anonymized (Waples, Gill. and Fisher 2009).

The most common situational techniques used were those that increase formal surveillance ($n = 7$), followed by target hardening ($n = 3$) and methods to extend guardianship ($n = 2$). Other types of situational measures evaluated included methods to control access, assist natural surveillance, and the identification of property ($n = 1$ for each). One study used a variety of situational techniques implemented as part of a problem-oriented policing project (Braga and Bond 2008). All of the studies included data from police records and five supplemented this with data from interviews, surveys, or social observations.

The geographical area in which evaluators search for displacement or diffusion is an important element of the research design, and its definition can influence whether effects are detected or not. While there is some guidance in the literature concerning the identification of catchment areas (e.g., Weisburd and Green 1995),

Table 17.1 Details of the studies included in the meta-analysis

Author*	Year	Publication Type	Location	Environment	SCP techniques	Data Source	Research design	Time Period	Outcome Measures
Allatt (4)	1984	Journal	Northumbria, UK	Residential	Control access	Police records; survey	Time series; Quasi exp. Pre/post with control	5-year trend; 1-year post	Attempted & completed burglary
Bowers et al. (1)	2003	Government report	Liverpool, UK	Residential	Target hardening; identify property	Police records	Quasi exp. Pre/post with control	2 years pre and post	Burglary
Bowers et al. (1)	2004	Journal	Liverpool, UK	Residential	Target hardening	Police records	Time series; Quasi exp. Pre/post with control	2 years pre, 3 years post	Burglary
Braga and Bond (17)+	2008	Journal	Massachusetts, USA	Multiple	Various	Calls for service, social observation	Randomized controlled exp. Pre/post with control	6 months pre and post	Multiple
Cameron et al. (2)	2008	Organizational report	Los Angeles, USA	Retail and residential	Strengthen formal surveillance (CCTV)	Police records	Quasi exp. Pre/post with control	25 months pre and 14 months post; 45 months pre and 16 months post	Multiple
Cummings (2)	2005	Government report	Bentley and Morley, AUS	Residential	Target harden; extend guardianship	Interview; police records	Time series; Quasi exp. Pre/post with control	12-month period	Burglary
Laycock & Austin (2)	1992	Journal	Basingstoke, UK	Residential	Strengthen formal surveillance	Police records	Quasi-exp. Pre/post with control	12 month pre and post	Theft of and from cars

Study	Year	Source	Location	Setting	Intervention	Data	Design	Observations*	Crime type
Ratcliffe et al. (8)	2009	Journal	Philadelphia, USA	Multiple	Strengthen formal surveillance (CCTV)	Police records	Time series; Quasi exp. Pre/post with control	18 month pre and 14 months post; 21 months pre and 11 months post; 22 months pre and 10 months post; 23 months pre and 8 months post	Multiple
Sarno et al. (5)	1999	Organizational report	London, UK	Public areas	Assist natural surveillance	Police records; survey; interviews	Quasi exp. Pre/post with control	2 years pre and post	Multiple
Seldon (1)	1978	Dissertation	Kalamazoo, MI, US	Residential	Strengthen formal surveillance (Neighborhood watch)	Police records	Quasi exp. Pre/post with control	1-year pre and post	Burglary
Skinns(4)	1998	Book chapter	Redton, UK	Public areas	Strengthen formal surveillance	Police records; surveys; interviews	Quasi exp. Pre and post with control	1-year pre and post	Multiple
Waples et al. (6)	2009	Journal	Unknown, UK	Multiple	Strengthen formal surveillance	Police records	Quasi exp. Pre and post with control	1-year pre and post	Multiple
Weisburd &Green (1)+	1995	Journal	Jersey City, USA	Public areas	Strengthen formal surveillance; extend guardianship	Police records	Randomized Control exp. Pre/post with control	7 months pre and post	Multiple

Notes: *Number of observations per study shown in parentheses; +Only aggregated data available for analysis.

when reviewing studies, what becomes clear is that no systematic method is used to identify them. However, by far the most commonly used approach is to create a concentric "buffer" of the treatment area, which is an area directly adjacent and completely surrounding it. In a limited number of studies a separate catchment area was also identified for the control area.

III. META-ANALYSIS

Across the 13 studies, the most consistently reported findings were counts of crime for the periods pre- and post-intervention for (at least) one treatment area, one control area, and one catchment area that surrounded the treatment area. In the previous review, Guerette and Bowers (2009) computed a measure of effect size known as the weighted displacement quotient (Bowers and Johnson 2003), a form of differences in differences statistic that uses crime rates. To complement that review, here we follow the approach typically used in systematic reviews of place-based interventions (e.g., Weisburd et al., 2008) and estimate mean effect sizes and associated confidence intervals for each study using odds ratio (OR) calculations (Lipsey and Wilson 2001, pp. 52–54).

In contrast to reviews that focus only on outcomes directly associated with intervention, our primary interest concerned changes observed in the *catchment* areas that surrounded them and into which crime would be most likely to displace or benefits diffuse. Of course, to put observed changes into context, it was necessary to also examine outcomes in the treatment areas. Thus, for each study, ORs were calculated for both the treatment and the catchment areas. In addition to computing individual estimates of effect size for each study, mean effect sizes were calculated across studies to allow general inferences to be made.

The OR is a point estimate of effect size and is subject to sampling error. Confidence intervals (CIs) are, therefore, computed to provide an indication of the error associated with the estimate and the range of values within which the actual value is likely to be found. The approach taken to estimate the confidence intervals for the OR is the same as that adopted in previous meta-analyses of place-based interventions. This is not without controversy (Marchant 2004). One concern is the extent to which the parametric assumptions on which the approach is based are reasonable (Farrington et al. 2007). For instance, one assumption is that the data-generating process is a Poisson process. This may be reasonable for studies for which the units of analysis are independent (e.g., unrelated people), but is probably unreasonable for those in which they are not (Farrington et al. 2007), such as the count of crime in an area before and after intervention. A consequence of this is that the standard error derived using the standard equations is likely to underestimate the actual variance, meaning that the estimated confidence intervals will be too small. For this reason, we adopt the approach used elsewhere (Farrington et al. 2007) and multiply the standard error by an inflation factor (of 2) when calculating confidence intervals.

As discussed, for a number of studies, there were multiple observations for the same treatment area(s). While this is unproblematic where effect sizes are considered independently, it is a problem where they are combined. That is, if all of the data were included in the calculation of a mean effect size, this would lead to dependency in the data and would violate a central assumption of the approach. On the other hand, to exclude observations would be to lose useful data and would require an unbiased approach to observation selection. A compromise is to estimate the mean effect size using those observations that reflect the best- and worst-case scenarios (e.g., Weisburd et al. 2008). However, as this approach uses only two possible permutations of the data, conclusions may be sensitive to outlying observations. An alternative is to compute the mean effect size for every possible permutation of the available data, which allows the distribution of all possible mean effect sizes to be examined.

IV. RESULTS

Figure 17.1 shows the individual effect sizes and CIs for the best-case scenario for both the treatment and catchment areas for all 13 studies. Where there were multiple observations, the observations used were those for which the treatment (and catchment) effect was most positive (i.e., in favor of a treatment effect).

For some studies, data were available for catchment control areas as well as treatment control areas. When calculating the ORs for the catchment areas, we used the best available control area—that is, where there is a separate catchment control area we used that.

Where the OR is greater than 1, this indicates that the outcome favors treatment. Values less than 1 indicate that crime increased in the area considered (treatment or catchment) at a rate that exceeded that observed in the control area (in relative terms). Considering the general trend, we computed the Q statistic (Lispey and Wilson 2001) to determine if the variation in effect sizes indicated variation above and beyond that which would be expected for sampling error alone. For the treatment and catchments areas, the respective values of 26.5 ($df = 12$) and 32.7 ($df = 12$) were statistically significant ($p < .05$). Consequently, to calculate the weighted mean effect, we used a random effects model (Lipsey and Wilson 2001).

Overall, the weighted mean OR of 1.23 (CI: 1.12–1.35) suggests a positive significant effect at the treatment sites ($p < .05$). In interpreting this finding, the reader should recall that we included in this review only those studies for which data were available for treatment, catchment, and control areas. Consequently, other studies that examined changes in treatment and control areas alone are excluded from the analysis. Accordingly, the reader should not interpret the effect-size estimate for the

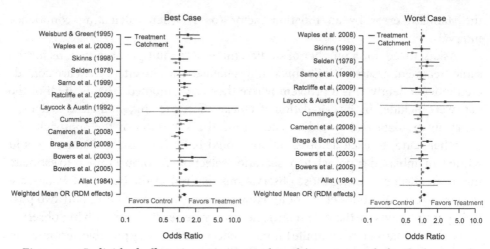

Figure 17.1 Individual effect-size estimates and confidence intervals for the best- and worst-case scenarios.

Note: In the case of Weisburd and Green (1995), count data were only available for the treatment and catchment areas for public morals disorder, for which reductions were observed in both the treatment and catchment areas. Data for the other types of offenses, for which reductions were not observed in both areas, were unavailable. Hence, the data for this study are included in the best-case, but not worst-case, scenario.

treatment areas as representing the treatment effect for situational crime-prevention interventions in general, but just for the subset of studies for which changes in catchment areas as well as the treatment and control areas were considered. For the catchment areas, the weighted mean OR of 1.03 (CI:.97–1.10) suggests a positive but nonsignificant effect.

Figure 17.1 also shows the results for the worst-case scenario.[2] In this case, the Q statistic was again statistically significant for both the treatment (Q = 21.5, df = 12, p <.05) and catchment (Q = 27.7, df = 12, p <.05) areas and so we use a random effects model to compute the overall weighted mean effect sizes. The weighted mean OR for the treatment areas of 1.13 (CI: 1.03–1.23) suggests a positive impact of intervention (p <.05). For the catchment areas, the weighted mean OR of .96 (CI:.90–1.03) suggests a negative but nonsignificant effect.

One issue with presenting data for the best- and worst-case scenarios alone is that they may be sensitive to the presence of outliers. An alternative is to not only compute the best- and worst-case scenarios but also all of those in between. Considering all studies, there are 8,192 possible permutations. Instead of computing every mean effect size, we sample 1,000 using a Monte Carlo simulation. For each (re) sample, we use a random effects model to compute the weighted mean effect sizes and CIs. Figure 17.2 shows the results of this analysis. The point estimates and CIs at the top of the two Forest plots are the 1,000 permutations (included for the purposes of illustration). The point estimates and CIs at the bottom of the plot summarize the distribution. Those shown in black represent the mean of the mean effect sizes and the mean of the upper and lower CIs. Those shown in gray are the upper

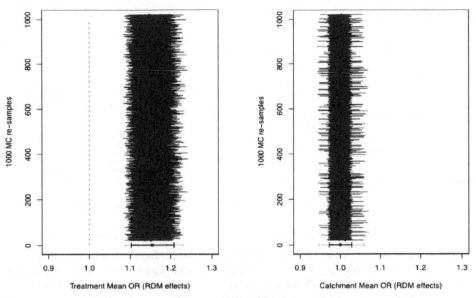

Figure 17.2 Weighted mean effect-size estimates and confidence intervals for 1,000 permutations of the available data.

and lower 95 percent CIs for the mean of the upper and lower CIs. Consistent with the results discussed above, the analysis suggests that relative to the control areas, reductions were observed in the treatment areas, but no changes were apparent in the catchment areas.

A. Accounting for Research Design

For evaluations that employ quasi-experimental designs, causal inference will be weaker than for those that use a random allocation strategy to assign units to treatment and control conditions (Campbell and Stanley 1963). This is because for the former differences between groups (treatment, catchment, and control), other than the assignment to conditions, may explain trends in any changes observed. In such cases, an increase (decrease) in crime in the catchment area may indicate displacement (diffusion of crime-control benefit), but it may also be explained by other factors. For the studies available, only two used a random allocation protocol. In both cases, there was evidence of a treatment effect and either no evidence of displacement or evidence in favor of a diffusion of benefit.

As threats to internal validity weaken causal inferences, it seems sensible to apply stricter criteria when estimating the extent to which crime might have been displaced or benefits diffused when examining quasi-experimental studies. One such criterion is that the search for displacement should be conditional on the demonstration of an intervention effect in the treatment area (e.g., Weisburd & Green 1995). That is, when there is some evidence to suggest that an intervention has led to a change in offending behavior, the search for displacement makes sense and a

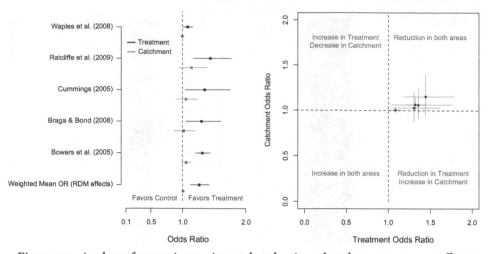

Figure 17.3 Analyses for quasi-experimental evaluations that show a treatment effect.
Note: Figures present treatment effects and confidence intervals (left panel), and a scatter plot to show the effect-size estimates and confidence intervals for the treatment areas plotted against those for the catchment areas (right panel)

causal link to the intervention would seem more probable. Moreover, it seems logical to suggest that any evidence of displacement should be most apparent for those interventions that the evidence suggests that opportunities were blocked in the area where activity was focused.

Of the 11 quasi-experimental studies, significant reductions were observed (one observation per study) for five of the evaluations.[3] The results shown in figure 17.3 suggest that where crime declined (OR = 1.27, CI = 1.13–1.43) in the treatment area(s), there was no change in the catchment area(s) (OR = 1.01, CI =.99–1.04). The right panel of figure 17.3 shows the same data but with the effect size (and CIs) for one type of area plotted against the other. Put simply, it does not appear to be the case that for those situations where we might most expect it, crime is displaced to nearby areas.

V. DISCUSSION AND CONCLUSIONS

The aim of this essay was to review the available evidence regarding the extent to which situational crime-prevention interventions displace crime or diffuse crime-control benefits geographically. For the studies for which data were available, the results are clear: geographic displacement is not an inevitable consequence of this type of intervention. In fact, across the studies examined, rarely was it the case that crime increased in the catchment areas following intervention. Rather, in line with previous reviews, crime appears just as likely (or perhaps slightly more so) to decrease in the areas that surround a treatment area following intervention.

The results are based on a relatively small sample of studies and hence there is a need for more data. Moreover, with respect to the types of situational interventions considered, most evaluations focused on those that involve some form of improvement to surveillance (e.g., CCTV). Consequently, at this point it would be unwise to speculate as to whether some types of interventions are more likely to diffuse benefits or displace crime than others. Before such analysis can be meaningfully conducted there is a need to examine the potential side effects of other types of situational crime prevention.

As a result of conducting the current review, a number of other issues regarding the evaluation of situational crime-prevention interventions were identified (see also Guerette 2009). First, for only a limited number of evaluations were data collected that allowed a quantitative analysis of the extent to which displacement or diffusion of benefit occurred, although this is becoming more commonplace. And, while six types of displacement have been identified, spatial displacement was by far the most frequently considered. Consequently, at the current time it is not possible to systematically estimate the extent to which situational crime-prevention tactics diffuse benefits or displace crime in ways other than that considered here.

Second, as for research designs, only two of the studies used a random allocation strategy to assign units to treatment and control groups, and only those studies collected data for catchment areas that surrounded both the treatment and control areas. For many interventions—new ones in particular—nonrandomization will generally be appropriate, as it is useful to gauge the extent to which an intervention might work before trying to implement a randomized controlled trial that will require much more effort to arrange. The same can be said for interventions that are specifically tailored to a particular context where the intervention(s) would not be expected to work across all times and places. Quasi-experimental designs are also helpful because they can be used to estimate the crime-prevention effects of interventions retrospectively, whereas randomization must be done prospectively. In such cases, the lack of randomization might not outweigh the benefits of having more data (Eck 2006).

However, for those types of interventions that are rather generic in nature (e.g., property marking), are large in scale, and for which there is considerable commercial profit, evidence from randomized control trials (RCTs) would be beneficial. Such evidence would be useful not only in establishing causality but also in estimating more accurately the likely crime-reductive effect of a particular intervention net of any crime that may have been displaced or benefits diffused. Such evidence would enable practitioners to compare particular interventions with more confidence than they may do so at present.

Equally, however, it is important to consider that while RCTs reduce threats to internal validity unless they are carefully designed they do not necessarily enhance understanding of how things work. For the studies reviewed, it was evident that few of them collected data on intermediate outcomes that would allow an evaluator to examine the mechanisms through which an intervention might affect change (see Pawson and Tilley 1997) in the treatment areas and those nearby. Thus, more effort is required to understand how interventions might bring about change and how mechanisms might operate (or not) across different contexts.

On a different note, estimating the extent to which displacement may or may not have occurred is a nontrivial exercise associated with a number of methodological concerns. In terms of spatial displacement, analyses are generally limited to the examination of changes in a catchment area that immediately surrounds a treatment area. While this is logical from what the evidence suggests about offender mobility, it precludes the possibility of detecting displaced activity that might occur outside of such an area.

The size of the catchment area can also affect the sensitivity with which displacement or a diffusion of benefit might be detected. An area too large might result in any changes being lost in the background variation expected for a large area. An area too small may mean that the crime counts considered are small and that anything other than a large change is assumed to reflect random variation. Consequently, Barr and Pease (1990) have commented that even the evaluator with unlimited resources would be unable to perform a study sensitive enough to ensure that all possible evidence of displacement was examined in a single study; the same can be said for the diffusion of crime-control benefit.

In closing, we suggest that there are several methodological issues surrounding the estimation of the extent to which interventions might displace crime or diffuse benefits. At present only a fraction of studies provide the data necessary to examine these side effects in a systematic way. Nevertheless, the results of the current study, like those before it, suggest that situational crime-prevention tactics are as likely to diffuse benefits as they are to displace crime. Given this, it seems practical to suggest that the agenda for future research should no longer be whether or not such interventions displace crime but, rather, under what conditions and for what types of interventions displacement is most likely, and when is it possible to enhance the impact of an intervention by increasing the likelihood that benefits will be diffused.

NOTES

The authors would like to thank Johannes Knuttson and Richard Wortley for discussions on the topic of crime displacement over the years, and Anthony Braga for providing data for the Braga and Bond (2008) study. We would also like to thank the editors for helpful comments on an earlier draft of this chapter.

1. Note that these are not the same 13 studies used in the review by Guerette and Bowers (2009). In the current study, evaluations were included only if they reported crime counts. If a meta-analysis using crime counts had been conducted by Guerette and Bowers, in that review only 7 studies would have been eligible for analysis.

2. Where there was only one observation available for a study, this was used in both the best- and worst-case scenarios.

3. A number of other studies showed a trend in the right direction but using the inflated confidence intervals, the effect was nonsignificant.

REFERENCES

(* studies included in meta-analysis)

*Allat, Patricia. 1997. "Residential Security: Containment and Displacement of Burglary." *Howard Journal of Criminal Justice* 23(2): 99–116.

Barr, Robert, and Ken Pease. 1990. "Crime Placement, Displacement and Deflection." In *Crime and Justice: A Review of Research*, vol. 12, edited by Michael Tonry and Norval Morris. Chicago: University of Chicago Press.

Bowers, Kate J., and Shane D. Johnson. 2003. "Measuring the Geographical Displacement and Diffusion of Benefit Effects of Crime Prevention Activity." *Journal of Quantitative Criminology* 19(3): 275–301.

*Bowers, Kate J., Shane D. Johnson, and Alexander F. G. Hirschfield. 2003. "Pushing Back the Boundaries: New Techniques for Assessing the Impact of Burglary Schemes." Home Office Online Report 24/03. Home Office: London.

*Bowers, Kate J., Shane D. Johnson, and Alexander F. G. Hirschfield. 2004. "Closing off Opportunities for Crime: An Evaluation of Alleygating." *European Journal on Criminal Policy and Research* 10(4): 283–308.

*Braga, Anthony, and Brenda J. Bond. 2008. "Policing Crime and Disorder Hot Spots: A Randomized Controlled Trial." *Criminology*, 46(3): 577–607.

Campbell, Donald T., and Julian C. Stanley. 1963. *Experimental and Quasi-Experimental Designs for Research*. Boston: Houghton Mifflin.

*Cameron, Aundreia, Elke Kolodinski, Heather May, and Nicholas Williams. 2008. "Measuring the Effects of Video Surveillance on Crime in Los Angeles." Report to the Califonia Research Bureau. Available at www.library.ca.gov/crb/08/08-007.pdf.

Clarke, Ronald V., and Derek Cornish. 1985. "Modelling Offenders' Decisions: A Framework for Research and Policy." In *Crime and Justice: A Review of Research*, vol. 6, edited by Michael Tonry and Norval Morris, Chicago: University of Chicago Press.

Clarke, Ronald V., and David Weisburd. 1994. "Diffusion of Crime Control Benefits: Observations on the Reverse of Displacement." In *Crime Prevention Studies*, vol. 2, edited by Ronlad V. Clarke. Monsey, NY: Criminal Justice Press.

Cornish, Derek B., and Ronald V. Clarke. 1986. *The Reasoning Criminal*. New York: Springer-Verlag.

Cornish, Derek B., and Ronald V. Clarke. 2003. "A Reply to Wortley's Critique of Situational Crime Prevention." In *Crime Prevention Studies*, vol. 16, edited by Martha J. Smith and Derek B. Cornish. Cullompton, UK: Willan.

*Cummings, Rick. 2005. *Operation Burglary Countdown November 2003–October 2004: Evaluation Study Final Report*. Perth: Estill & Associates.

Eck, John E. 2006. "When Is a Bologna Sandwich Better than Sex? A Defense of Small-N Case Study Evaluations." *Journal of Experimental Criminology* 2(3): 345–62.

Eck, John E., Ronald V. Clarke, and Rob T. Guerette. 2007. "Risky Facilities: Crime Concentration in Homogeneous Sets of Establishments and Facilities." In *Crime Prevention*

Studies, vol. 21, edited by Graham Farrell, Kate J. Bowers, Shane D Johnson, and Michael Townsley. Cullompton, UK: Willan.

Farrington, David P., Martin Gill, Sam J. Waples, and Javier Argomaniz. 2007. "The Effects of Closed-Circuit Television on Crime: Meta-Analysis of an English National Quasi Experimental Multi-Site Evaluation." *Journal of Experimental Criminology* 3(1): 21–38.

Guerette, Rob T. 2009. "The Pull, Push and Expansion of Situational Crime Prevention Evaluation: An Appraisal of Thirty-Seven Years of Research." In *Crime Prevention Studies*, vol. 24, edited by Johannes Knutsson and Nick Tilley. Cullompton, UK: Willan.

Guerette, Rob T., and Kate J. Bowers. 2009. "Assessing the Extent of Crime Displacement and Diffusion of Benefits: A Review of Situational Crime Prevention Evaluations." *Criminology* 47(4): 1331–68.

Hesseling, Rene B. P. 1994. "Displacement: A Review of the Empirical Literature." In *Crime Prevention Studies*, vol. 3, edited by Ronald V. Clarke. Monsey, NY: Criminal Justice Press.

*Johnson, Shane D. 2010. "A Brief History of the Analysis of Crime Concentration." *European Journal of Applied Mathematics* 21(4): 349–70.

Johnson, Shane D., and Kate J. Bowers. 2010. "Permeability and Crime Risk: Are Cul-de-sacs Safer?" *Journal of Quantitative Criminology* 26(1): 89–111.

Laycock, Gloria, and Claire Austin. 1992. "Crime Prevention in Parking Facilities." *Security Journal* 3:154–59.

Lipsey, Mark W., and David B. Wilson. 2001. *Practical Meta-Analysis*. Thousand Oaks, CA: Sage.

Marchant, Paul R. 2004. "A Demonstration that the Claim That Brighter Lighting Reduces Crime Is Unfounded." *British Journal of Criminology* 44(3): 441–47.

Merton, Robert K. 1938. "Social Structure and Anomie." *American Sociological Review* 3(5): 672–82.

Pawson, Ray, and Nick Tilley. 1997. *Realistic Evaluation*. London: Sage.

Pease, Ken. 1998. *Repeat Victimization: Taking Stock*. Crime Detection and Prevention Paper Series Paper 90. London, UK: Home Office.

Petticrew, Mark, and Helen Roberts. 2006. *Systematic Reviews in the Social Sciences: A Practical Guide*. Oxford: Blackwell.

Poyner, Barry. 1992. "Situational Crime Prevention in Two Parking Facilities." In *Situational Crime Prevention: Successful Case Studies*, edited by Ronald V. Clarke. New York: Harrow and Heston.

*Ratcliffe, Jerry H., Travis Taniguchi, and Ralph B. Taylor. 2009. "The Crime Reduction Effects of Public CCTV Cameras: A Multi-Method Spatial Approach." *Justice Quarterly* 26(4): 746–70.

Reppetto, Thomas A. 1976. "Crime Prevention and the Displacement Phenomenon." *Crime and Delinquency* 22(2): 166–77.

*Sarno, Chris, Michael Hough, and Majorie Bulos. 1999. *Developing a Picture of CCTV in Southwark Town Centres: Final Report*. London: Criminal Policy Research Unit, South Bank University.

*Seldon, Paul Hubert III. (1978). *Using a Neighborhood Crime Prevention Program to Reduce Residential Breaking and Entering*. Dissertation, Western Michigan University. Ann Arbor.

*Skinns, David. 1998. "Crime Reduction, Diffusion and Displacement: Evaluating the Effectiveness of CCTV." In *Surveillance, Closed Circuit Television and Social Control*, edited by Clive Norris, Jade Moran, and Gary Armstrong. Aldershot, UK: Ashgate.

*Waples, Sam, Martin Gill, and Peter Fisher. 2009. "Does CCTV Displace Crime?" *Criminology and Criminal Justice* 9(2): 207–24.

Weisburd, David. 2010. "Location, Location, Location: Hot Spots of Crime and Crime Prevention." Stockholm Criminology Prize Address, June 15. Stockholm, Sweden.

Weisburd, David, Shawn Bushway, Cynthia Lum, and Sue-Ming Yang. 2004. "Trajectories of Crime at Places: A Longitudinal Study of Street Segments in the City of Seattle." *Criminology* 42(2): 283–321.

*Weisburd, David, and Lorraine Green. 1995. "Measuring Immediate Spatial Displacement: Methodological Issues and Problems." In *Crime and Place, Crime Prevention Studies*, vol. 4, edited by John Eck and David Weisburd. Monsey, NY: Criminal Justice Press.

Weisburd, David, Cody W. Telep, Joshua C. Hinkle, and John E. Eck. 2008. "The Effects of Problem Oriented Policing on Crime and Disorder." *Criminology and Public Policy* 9(1): 139–72.

Weisburd, David, Laura A. Wyckoff, Justin Ready, John E. Eck, Joshua C. Hinkle, and Frank Gajewski. 2006. "Does Crime Just Move around the Corner? A Controlled Study of Spatial Displacement and Diffusion of Crime Control Benefits." *Criminology* 44(3): 549–91.

Wortley. Richard. 1997. "Reconsidering the Role of Opportunity in Situational Crime Prevention." In *Rational Choice and Situational Prevention*, edited by Graham Newman, Ronald V. Clarke and Shlomo G. Shohan. Aldershot, UK: Ashgate.

Wortley, Richard. 2008. "Situational Precipitators of Crime." In *Environmental Criminology and Crime Analysis*, edited by Richard Wortley and Lorraine Mazerolle. Cullompton, UK: Willan.

Yochelson, Samuel, and Stanton E. Samenow. 1976. *The Criminal Personality, Vol. 1: A Profile for Change*. New York: Jason Aronson.

CHAPTER 18

PLACE-BASED CRIME
PREVENTION: THEORY,
EVIDENCE, AND POLICY

JOHN E. ECK AND ROB T. GUERETTE

THE 1990s were an exciting time for new policies to reduce crime. Crime was declining (Zimring 2006); police innovations such as problem-oriented policing (Goldstein 1990) and community policing (Maguire and Katz 2002) were taking hold; and new police innovations, such as COMPSTAT (Silverman 1999) and intelligence-led policing (Ratcliff 2008) were getting started. Opportunity blocking as a crime-prevention approach became more common (Clarke 1992). The importance of repeat victimization was (re)discovered and led to numerous applications (Farrell 1995). Research clearly implicated places as focal points of crime (Sherman, Gartin, and Buerger 1989) and police and crime researchers became interested in crime prevention at very specific places (Eck and Weisburd 1995).

All of these developments are connected. The police reforms provided a platform to experiment with new crime research developments and research into crime patterns stimulated police reforms. Place-based prevention, the topic of this essay, developed in this environment.

Crime prevention at places makes specific locations unattractive for offenders to commit crimes. These interventions do not necessarily result in the arrest and incarceration of offenders, nor do they usually assist in the rehabilitation of offenders. They may not even keep offenders away. They just make offenders less willing to choose to commit crimes at the location where these interventions are deployed. Place-based crime prevention blocks opportunities for crime by making offending riskier, less rewarding, more difficult, less excusable, or less likely to be provoked (Clarke 2008). The people who implement these techniques are usually place managers: owners of places or designated representatives of owners (Eck 1994).

Is this useful? Should policymakers pay attention to place-based prevention? Should governments require place managers to implement specific measures to curb crime? Evidence suggests that when police focus on specific, small high-crime areas—hot spots—that they can reduce crime (Braga 2001, 2005), at least in the short term (Sherman 1990). But what about other forms of curbing crime at places—interventions that alter the physical and social environment of the place and do not necessarily involve police?

Theory and research on places and place-based prevention lead to a number of conclusions, the first global and the remaining supportive.

- Focusing prevention efforts on high-crime places is a productive approach to reducing crime.
- Places are useful for examining the distribution of crime and organizing prevention efforts, and they are conceptually different from neighborhoods and larger geographical units.
- Crime and disorder are concentrated in a few places and virtually absent from most.
- Applying situational crime prevention at places often reduces crime or disorder at these places.
- The threat of crime displacement to other places not receiving prevention is relatively low and seldom overwhelms prevention gains.
- Prevention at places can reduce crime or disorder in the surrounding areas.
- Places have owners who are responsible for implementing place-based prevention.
- Tailor-making place-based prevention maybe more effective than implementing off-the-shelf place-based interventions.
- Government strategies to reduce crime should include holding place managers accountable for crime and disorder at their locations.

This essay is organized as follows. Section I clarifies what we mean by "place." Section II gives four reasons that places are important: the concentration of crime and disorder; the lack of a displacement threat; the spread of prevention benefits from places; and the prospect of holding owners accountable for high-crime places. These reasons hinge on place-based prevention working, so in sections III and IV we explore this question by examining 149 evaluations of place-based crime prevention. Section III describes the methods used to select studies for analysis. Section IV looks at the evidence for place-based prevention effectiveness at five common place types: residences, outside/public, retail, transportation, and recreation. Section V contains our conclusions, implications, and extensions, with eight summary tables. The appendix at the end of this essay includes five additional tables that support our conclusions and implications.

I. What Is a Place?

To understand why places are important for reducing crime, we need to first be clear on what we mean by "place." Common to all notions of place is that it is a geographic unit. But it is more than that. Place is a concept imbedded within Routine Activity Theory (Cohen and Felson, 1979; Sherman, Gartin, and Buerger 1989). Places are locations where offenders and targets meet. This requires that a place be sufficiently small that an offender can control the target and manage the immediate situation. Sherman and colleagues define a place as "a fixed physical environment that can be seen completely and simultaneously at least on its surface, by one's naked eye" (1989, p. 31). These authors then go on to operationalize places by addresses and street corners.

Places have five related features: location, boundaries, function, control, and size (Eck 1994, p. 10). First, the place must have a known geographical location in space. Second, a place must have boundaries so we can identify features and events that are inside and outside of it. Third, a place has a principal function—such as living, recreation, work, transport, and so forth. Sorting places by their major functions creates functionally homogeneous sets of places called "facilities" (Eck and Weisburd 1995; Eck, Clarke, and Guerette 2007). Fourth, places are legally controlled by a person or organization. This is the source of place management and the implementation of prevention at places. And finally, consistent with Sherman and colleagues (1989), a place must be small: the time a healthy adult takes to traverse a place is measured in seconds rather than hours, or even minutes, and place size is measured in feet and meters rather than miles and kilometers.

These are not hard-and-fast criteria, and each may be loosened for practical reasons. The first requirement can be waived for the study of buses, trains, planes, and ships, for example. The third requirement can be relaxed for some mixed-use places—a hotel, though a residential place, may contain a public bar (recreation) and stores (shopping), for example. Outside locations may serve numerous functions over the course of a day. The fourth requirement can be tempered for shopping centers and other locations where legal responsibility is sometimes mixed—that is, we can allow for multiple overlapping place management. And size can vary—from the location of an automatic teller machine to a sports stadium.

It is also helpful to describe what we do *not* mean by places. First, they are not neighborhoods, communities, police beats or districts, or any other heterogeneous collections of many addresses and street segments. Function, ownership, and size criteria are violated, and in the cases of neighborhoods and communities, the boundaries are often too vague.

Crime hot spots are not necessarily places. It depends on how they are identified. Hot spots are unlikely to be places if they have been identified by geographical analysis techniques such as kernel density estimation (Chainey 2005). These show a landscape of crime frequency or risk. Such a hot spot may contain one or more high-crime places, but the hot spot itself may not be a place. This is because kernel density estimation is highly sensitive to the analyst's choices of bandwidth and cell sizes, so hot spots do not have a fixed location. Neither is there a clear boundary—rather, there is a gradual transition from inside to outside the hotspot. And they do not have clear functions or owners. On the other hand, other hot spot mapping techniques, such as repeat address mapping (Eck, Gersh, and Taylor 2000) identify addresses with multiple crime events, so hot spots identified in this way may qualify as places.

Street segments are ambiguous. They meet some of the criteria, but often fail on function, ownership, and sometimes size. Many street segments contain locations with very different functions. Similarly, ownership is heterogeneous along most street segments. Even on a street segment with one type of facility—houses or apartments, for example—the owners of each parcel often differ. Further, the street and sidewalks are owned by one entity (often a government) and the parcels by other entities (often private individuals and businesses). Nevertheless, street segments are located in space and have definite insides and outsides.

Street segments are still of practical value to crime-place research. It is sometimes difficult to locate crimes at precise locations because of errors in citizen reports to the police and in police recording of crimes. It is not uncommon for a police officer to record an event at a corner location, when it occurred elsewhere on the block. This is particularly the case with crimes that move—street robberies, drug dealing, or prostitution. When the crimes in question are clearly occurring on public streets and sidewalks, the ownership concern is less because the owner is often the local government. Further, the function criterion is also met, as the principal function of streets and sidewalks is transportation. But when studying crimes that are likely to occur off streets and sidewalks, inside buildings and parcels, findings from street segment analysis will be ambiguous. So, while it is theoretically better to measure crime at the address level (or even at the scale of rooms and hallways), in practice our tools are insufficient for the task and we have to make do with courser distinctions, such as street segments.

Facilities are places with a single function (Eck, Clarke, and Guerette 2007). The utility of place-based prevention depends on the type of facility in which it is applied: CCTV is feasible in stores and parking areas, but not in public restrooms, for example. Homes operate differently from bars, so comparing them to bars seems inappropriate. But comparisons among residences or among bars can be meaningful.

What kinds of facilities are there? There is no easy way to answer this question. In part it depends on the level of precision that one is interested in. For example, are bars and night clubs the same sort of facility or different forms? Are high-rise apartment complexes the same type of facility as high-rise condominiums or garden apartments? The finer the gradation of facilities we use, the more precise our conclusions. But again, pragmatic considerations arise. The number of studies of crime-place prevention is limited: too fine a gradation will leave us with no ability to draw conclusions. So we will use a very coarse typology derived from Eck and Clarke (2003). They proposed 11 environments. However, there are insufficient studies to examine all, so here we will only focus on 5 very common types: residential, public, retail, transportation, and recreation. This should give us a reasonable perspective on what sorts of place-based preventions work in typical facilities.

II. Why Are Places Important?

Earlier essays in this volume by Smith and Clarke, Braga, and Johnson, Guerette, and Bowers established some of the main reasons places are important. These can be summarized as follows:

1. A few of places contain a very large proportion of crime. This is true over a wide variety of crimes and a wide variety of place types. If we can substantially reduce crime in these few places, we can have a large impact on crime overall.
2. Displacement of crime following prevention is not a serious threat. The evidence for this is now incontrovertible. Displacement happens on occasion, but it never fully overwhelms the prevention benefits.
3. Reducing crime at high-crime places can often reduce crime at nearby locations. There is strong evidence for the diffusion of crime-prevention benefits.

There is a fourth reason places are important. This is the matter of control and accountability. Every place is owned by someone or some organization that has authority over activities at the location. The owner makes decisions about the physical and social environment of places. Eck (1994) christened these people and organizations, and the people they employ, "place managers." Place managers are interested in the functioning of their places. Place managers have four principal functions: they organize the physical environment; they regulate conduct; they control access; and they acquire resources (Madensen 2007). None of these functions is exclusively or even largely about crime control. Rather, these functions are about business: how the place should be organized so that it enables permitted behavior by desired people, and it improves the acquisition of resources (taxes, user fees, sales, donations, and so forth). *The crime prevention aspects of place management grow out of this business.* This is just as true of a church as of a bar, of a jail as of a school, of a store as of a library, or of an apartment building as of a bank.

Because place management is situated within Routine Activity Theory (Felson 2008) it is common to think of place managers as either a form of guardianship or an alternative form of surveillance—that one can choose between having place managers or using other forms of crime prevention. This is wrong. All places have managers, so it is not a case of installing them or not. The concern is what place managers may do (or fail to do) that produces crime and what they could do differently that could reduce crime.

Importantly, all crime prevention at places is implemented with the consent of the place managers. This includes the use of locks, lights, signage, CCTV, rules of conduct, space reconfiguration, and any form of crime prevention through environmental design (CPTED). There are legal methods for compelling place managers to implement measures to reduce crime. This is sometimes called "third party policing" (Mazerolle and Ransley 2005), though others besides the police can mobilize civil law for this purpose. In fact, premise liability lawsuits are often brought against owners of the crime places. To avoid these suits, place managers implement many crime-prevention techniques (Eck 1996). Two randomized experiments (Eck and Wartell 1998; Mazerolle, Roehl, and Kadleck 1998) and one strong quasi-experiment (Green 1995) tested whether threatening owners with civil sanctions would reduce drug dealing and crime at their places. All three studies showed that this approach has merit. Most efforts to control disorder and crime in bars involves getting place managers—owners, bartenders, wait staff, and bouncers—involved in controlling crime (Madensen and Eck 2008). These efforts invoke the full panoply of situational techniques: increasing risk or effort, decreasing rewards, and reducing provocations or excuses. One way of understanding the ubiquitous influence of place management on crime is to reconsider the first point in this section: most places have little or no crime. One reason may be that the place managers of these locations are doing something differently from their neighbors with substantial crime problems.

If we bring together the three points made in earlier chapters with this discussion of place management, we have four reasons places are important for prevention: (1) the concentration of crime at a relatively few places and prospects of obtaining substantial crime drops if these few places are targeted for prevention; (2) the relative unimportance of spatial displacement of crime if prevention is carried out at these few places; (3) the nontrivial possibility producing diffusion of crime-prevention benefits to surrounding places if high crime places are targeted; and (4) the ability to identify and hold accountable for implementing prevention those people and organizations that control high-crime places.

Of course, the importance of these points hinges on answering the question: does blocking crime opportunity at places reduce crime? And if it does, what sorts of things work to reduce what sorts of crime? An earlier systematic review of 89 evaluations found that they were quite effective at reducing crime. There is an important caveat: most of the studies used weak research designs, so we are left with greater uncertainty than we would desire (Eck 2002). Since this review, researchers have evaluated numerous other interventions at places. Welsh and Farrington (2009), in particular, have carefully examined the utility of CCTV, lighting, and other interventions designed to increase offender risk in public places. With this additional evidence, should we still be optimistic about the effectiveness of place-based interventions?

III. How Were Prevention Evaluations Selected?

Evaluations of interest to answering this question must fulfill two broad criteria. They must test the implementation of some form of situational crime prevention and this prevention must be at a place. We located studies for this review by following the same procedures used by Guerette and Bowers (2009). Briefly, this systematic procedure identified several thousand abstracts, of which 276 described an assessment of a situational measure. Of these 276 articles, 216 were published reports of original research findings showing the quantitative impact of a situational crime-prevention intervention (excluding targeted law enforcement operations) on crime or disorder. These 216 studies were then reviewed and coded. The full searchable database of these studies is freely available at the Center for Problem-Oriented Policing (2010).

Since we were only interested in place-based applications for this essay, we eliminated studies that were primarily evaluations of neighborhood or larger interventions (e.g., neighborhood watch schemes, mass-media campaigns, or public information efforts). We also removed evaluations of product design modifications (e.g., steering wheel lock in vehicles) or other nongeographic-based prevention. In some circumstances mixed interventions—for example, place and neighborhood—were evaluated. We included the study if, in our judgment, the dominant thrust of the prevention effort was place based; otherwise we eliminated it.

IV. What Works to Prevent Crime at Places?

Table 18.1 presents a summary of the overall conclusion reported by the study author(s) disaggregated by place. The appendix at the end of this essay explains how this and the following tables were created. There were a total of 149 evaluations across the five place types.[1] There is variation in effectiveness among place types, though for no place type did reported effectiveness dip below 60 percent. Though all recreational interventions appear successful, the number of these is too small to inspire confidence in this finding: more evaluations will likely turn up some failures. Looked at from the negative perspective, situational efforts in public outdoor settings and in residences had the most failures, but even in these settings ineffective interventions were relatively rare compared to successes and mixed successes.

There are several possible explanations for the relatively lesser success of situational interventions at public places compared to other settings: they are more open

Table 18.1 Effectiveness of place-based intervention evaluations by place type

Place Type	Percent of Authors' Conclusions for Each Place Type (n)			
	Effective	Not Effective	Mixed Findings	Inconclusive
Residential (39)	77 (30)	10 (4)	10 (4)	3 (1)
Public ways (52)	62 (32)	12 (6)	19 (10)	8 (4)
Retail (25)	88 (22)	4 (1)	4 (1)	4 (1)
Transport (26)	88 (23)		8 (2)	4 (1)
Recreational (7)	100 (7)			
Total (149)	77 (114)	7 (11)	11 (17)	5 (7)

and less contained; they may have a wider variety of deviance; or implementation may be weaker. In the concluding section we will consider a fourth hypothesis: government use of off-the-shelf techniques.

Our positive assessment of the utility of place-based interventions must be tempered by the nature of the evaluations used. Stronger evaluation designs eliminate more alternative explanations for a change in crime following an intervention (Shadish, Cook, and Campbell 2002). Weak evaluations leave open more possibilities that the observed change in crime was due to factors other than the intervention being tested.

Table 18.2 ranks designs roughly according to their ability to eliminate rival explanations. Evaluations of place-based interventions are, on average, modest in terms of their ability to eliminate alternative explanations for crime changes. The strongest evaluations—randomized experiments—are rare and have been applied only to residential and retail settings. At the other extreme, studies that have neither control groups nor take advantage of changes over time, and have simple pre/post evaluations, are distributed over most types of settings. So while the consistency of the findings in table 18.1 gives us reason to be optimistic about the use of place-based interventions, table 18.2 suggests that our confidence can be improved by stronger evaluations.

Importantly, the precision of the study estimates of crime or disorder changes cannot be reliably or accurately determined from most of the evaluations. We can make gross conclusions about whether place-based interventions work, particularly when we have numerous studies in the same settings, using the same form of intervention, or where there is outcome consistency among diverse studies. But precise numerical estimates of the magnitude of impacts from place-based evaluations are unlikely to be reliable. So we will simply give the basic conclusions of studies, based on the interpretations of these studies' authors.

The following sections inspect in more detail specific findings of prevention evaluations in these five place types in response to an array of crime problems.

Table 18.2 Evaluation designs used by place type

	Percent of Designs for Each Place Type					
Evaluation Design	Total	Residential	Public	Retail	Transport	Recreation
Randomized	3 (5)	60 (3)		40 (2)		
Time Series w/control	10 (15)	20 (3)	33 (5)	20 (3)	13 (2)	13 (2)
Time Series	20 (30)	27 (8)	23 (7)	20 (6)	30 (9)	
Before-After w/control	36 (53)	28 (15)	47 (25)	8 (4)	13 (7)	4 (2)
Before-After	26 (38)	18 (7)	34 (13)	24 (9)	16 (6)	8 (3)
Other	5 (8)	38 (3)	25 (2)	13 (1)	25 (2)	
Total	100 (149)	(39)	(52)	(25)	(26)	(7)

A. Residential Places

Residential places include locations where people live. Though hotels and motels could be in this category, we found no examples of evaluations of interventions at such places. Instead, these are all interventions at apartment buildings or single family homes.

The 39 evaluations summarized in table 18.3 tested seven different types of interventions (including "other"). Most were effective, though evaluators found that property marking was not effective in two of three tests. This is the only intervention tested multiple times that fails more often than it succeeds (though with three evaluations this finding is not definitive).

We grouped prevention evaluations in residential settings into four categories of crime based on what the crime or disorder the evaluator used to measure effectiveness: drug, burglary and theft, violence, and multiple crime types (see table 18.3). Researchers have examined a wide variety of prevention techniques to address crime in these places. Though we have tried to categorize evaluations by the dominant intervention, typically several things were done at the same time. This makes it difficult to isolate the specific causal mechanism responsible for any observed crime change.

Of the 39 interventions evaluated at residential locations, most were to address burglary or other forms of theft. Authors of these evaluations found them successful about 80 percent of the time. Though a number of methods for addressing burglary have been examined, the majority of these interventions used some form of access control or alarms.

Drug problems have also been examined. The primary types of intervention evaluated were forms of compelling improved place management by threatening civil court action against the owner or inducing a change of owners. These efforts were very successful. Two of the five randomized experiments were of these sorts of interventions, so we can be more confident of the success of these measures than most others. The one evaluation not applying this form of place management was a multi-pronged effort in a public housing project.

Here, CCTV was used extensively. Six of the multiple crime evaluations, one violence evaluation, and two of the burglary-theft evaluations examined CCTV. Though more successful than not, CCTV had more negative or ambiguous evaluation outcomes than the norm for residential place interventions. As CCTV has been extensively studied elsewhere (Welsh and Farrington 2009), we will not describe it in detail. We will see, however, that CCTV is one of the most frequently evaluated interventions at places.

Table 18.3 Residential place intervention outcomes

Problem type	Authors' Conclusions			
Intervention	Effective	Not Effective	Mixed	Inconclusive
Burglary /theft (24)	79 (19)	13 (3)	4 (1)	4 (1)
Access controls & alarms (14)	93 (13)			7 (1)
CPTED (4)	75 (3)		25 (1)	
CCTV (2)	50 (1)	50 (1)		
Property marking (3)	33 (1)	67 (2)		
Other (1)	100 (1)			
Drugs (6)	83 (5)		17 (1)	
Place management (5)	80 (4)		20 (1)	
Multiple (1)	100 (1)			
Violence (2)	50 (1)		50 (1)	
POP (1)	100 (1)			
CCTV (1)			100 (1)	
Multiple (7)	71 (5)	14 (1)	14 (1)	
Access control (1)	100 (1)			
CCTV (6)	67 (4)	17 (1)	17 (1)	
Total (39)	77 (30)	10 (4)	10 (4)	3 (1)

B. Public Places

More evaluations have been conducted of outside locations open to the public than any other facility type examined. However, relatively few types of interventions were studied. We would expect outside public settings to have a wider variety of problems and require a greater diversity of interventions than residences, but that was not the case. Of the 52 evaluations summarized in table 18.4, three interventions were the topic of 87 percent of the studies: lighting (20), CCTV (19), and street closure or redesign (6). Of the 7 evaluations remaining, 3 were of target hardening of phones and parking meters to prevent vandalism.

Table 18.4 Public place intervention outcomes

Problem type	Authors' Conclusions			
Intervention	Effective	Not Effective	Mixed	Inconclusive
Burglary /theft (6)	50 (3)		33 (2)	17 (1)
Lighting (4)	50 (2)		25 (1)	25 (1)
CCTV (1)			100 (1)	
Mixed (1)	100 (1)			
Alcohol /Drugs (8)	88 (7)		13 (1)	
CCTV (2)	100 (2)			
Street closure/ redesign (3)	67 (2)		33 (1)	
Other (3)	100 (3)			
Disorder/ vandalism (3)	100 (3)			
Mixed target hardening (3)	100 (3)			
Violence (1)	100 (1)			
Street closure/ redesign (1)	100 (1)			
Multiple (34)	53 (18)	18 (6)	21 (7)	9 (3)
Lighting (16)	57 (9)	19 (3)	13 (2)	13 (2)
CCTV (16)	50 (8)	17 (3)	31 (5)	
Street closure/ redesign (2)	50 (1)			50 (1)
Total (52)	62 (32)	12 (6)	19 (10)	8 (4)

Most of these evaluations described in table 18.4 measured effectiveness by reductions in multiple forms of crime. It is notable that these 34 interventions were less likely to be effective than the single crime evaluations. This finding supports Clarke's (1992) admonition to be crime specific when applying situational crime prevention.

C. Retail

Crime problems occurring in retail settings predominantly involve burglary and theft but also frequently frauds and robbery (see table 18.5). Retail businesses are a common host to these monetary-driven crimes because they regularly hold reasonably large sums of cash and many contain products that are desirable for thieves and fraudsters.

Five intervention types were evaluated for this setting, but "other" was the dominant type of intervention. Perhaps merchants (or evaluators) are being more crime specific than is the case with authorities in charge of outdoor public settings. The number of evaluations is too small to draw strong conclusions, however. It is notable that, as a whole, prevention in retail settings is more likely to be successful than prevention in public settings. Maybe public decision makers, relative to retailers, are not particularly adept at selecting the best prevention practices.

Table 18.5 Retail place intervention outcomes

Problem type	Authors' Conclusions			
Intervention	Effective	Not Effective	Mixed	Inconclusive
Burglary & theft (17)	88 (15)		6 (1)	6 (1)
CCTV (6)	67 (4)		17 (1)	17 (1)
Electronic article surveillance (3)	100 (3)			
Other (8)	100 (8)			
Frauds (4)	100 (4)			
ID checks (2)	100 (2)			
Other (2)	100 (2)			
Robbery (3)	67 (2)	33 (1)		
Mixed (3)	67 (2)	33 (1)		
Multiple (1)	100 (1)			
CPTED	100 (1)			
Total (25)	88 (22)	4 (1)	4 (1)	4 (1)

D. Transport

Transportation places include trains, buses, planes, taxies, and the specialized infra-structure used to support them. Most are government owned, but not all. Eight different types of interventions were evaluated, more than for any other setting (see table 18.6). While CCTV was applied in three of the five categories, it was not the dominant strategy. In fact, there does not seem to be a dominant intervention over-all, or within any crime category. The one exception is the use of guardianship to prevent thefts in parking areas associated with transport. As we saw with retail set-tings, this diversity of approaches is associated with greater than average success (and fewer clear failures).

Table 18.6 Transportation place intervention outcomes

Problem Type	Authors' Conclusions			
Intervention	Effective	Not Effective	Mixed	Inconclusive
Burglary /theft (7)	100 (7)			
CCTV (1)	100 (1)			
Guardianship & patrols (4)	100 (4)			
Other (2)	100 (2)			
Frauds (6)	83 (5)		17 (1)	
Physical changes & redesign (6)	83 (5)		17 (1)	
Disorder (5)	100 (5)			
CCTV (1)	100 (1)			
Cleanup (1)	100 (1)			
Mixed (3)	100 (3)			
Violence (5)	100 (5)			
Barriers (2)	100 (2)			
CCTV (1)	100 (1)			
Entrance screening (1)	100 (1)			
Exact fares (1)	100 (1)			
Multiple (3)	33 (1)		33 (1)	33 (1)
Mixed (3)	33 (1)		33 (1)	33 (1)
Total (26)	88 (23)		8 (2)	4 (1)

E. Recreational

Four types of interventions were evaluated in recreational settings (see table 18.7). Though this is the fewest for any place category, there were only seven evaluations (less than a third of the next smallest place category, retail). Five of the seven evaluations of prevention at recreational settings describe efforts to stem problems associated with bars, pubs, and taverns. With the exception of cash removal in betting parlors, all involved engaging place managers to change the way they handled patrons: how bouncers were used, the way drinks were served, and other place practices. All were effective, according to the studies' authors.

V. Discussion and Conclusions

Our review of the place-based prevention evidence must be optimistic. Place-based prevention works, and it works in a variety of place types and against many forms of crime and disorder. But these 149 evaluations are not a representative sample of place-based interventions and many of the evaluations used weak designs, so for many crime types and most interventions we have very thin evidence. Nevertheless, the overall evidence certainly does not support skepticism over whether place based interventions work.

What, then, should we conclude about place-based prevention? Let's review the four earlier points and add a fifth.

Table 18.7 Recreation residential place intervention outcomes

Problem Type	Authors' Conclusions			
Intervention	Effective	Not Effective	Mixed	Inconclusive
Alcohol (2)	100 (2)			
Regulation (1)	100 (1)			
Mixed (1)	100 (1)			
Violence (4)	100 (4)			
Cash removal (1)	100 (1)			
Mixed (3)	100 (3)			
Vehicle accidents (1)	100 (1)			
Server training (1)	100 (1)			
Total (7)	100 (7)			

1. Crime is concentrated at a relatively few places.
2. When crime is prevented at places, it is unlikely to displace.
3. When crime is prevented at places, it is likely to reduce crime nearby.
4. Place managers are responsible for what occurs at their places.
5. There are numerous place-based interventions that work, at least at some places against some crime.

While place-based prevention is effective, we cannot say precisely how useful it is. There are a number of reasons for this, including the methods used to evaluate these interventions. But a more important reason is that places are quite varied—we examined only 5 settings out of 11, and the diversity of places within these settings is quite broad. The number of possible interventions is extensive. Clarke (2008) describes 25 categories of situational crime-prevention techniques, so let us assume we have 11 types of places and 25 techniques. We also need to be crime specific. Eck and Clarke (2003) suggest six broad crime categories, and though this is not very specific, it is a start. Also, we should replicate each test, and assuming we only need five replications (a very low number), this suggests 8,250 (= 11 * 25 * 6 * 5) evaluations. Even if every evaluation we examined for this essay were a well-conducted randomized trial, we would still have to also assume that the 149 evaluations were a representative sample of this hypothetical population. Even with these extremely charitable assumptions, this is clearly not the case. So our conclusions must be tempered by the fact that there is much we do not know.

Typically, this is where authors suggest more research is needed. However, we want to make two different suggestions. The first suggestion is directed primarily toward public settings and other places where government agencies have a strong role in place management. Place-prevention practitioners in the public sector should be evidence-based *before* they even think about what to implement. That is, they should understand the crime problem at the place before looking for solutions, and then pick solutions that fit. We can draw an analogy to bridge building: civil engineers do not simply build bridges following a list of "bridges that work." Instead, they survey the terrain and then select and modify a design that fits the needs (Petroski 1997). This approach should be used to select crime prevention at places. This is in keeping with the principles of Situational Crime Prevention (Clarke 1992) and Problem-Oriented Policing (Goldstein 1990).

Consider table 18.8. Seven interventions account for 79 percent of the 149 evaluations. When one considers the variety of places and crimes examined, this concentration of interventions seems peculiar. We would expect to see a greater variety of interventions in these circumstances. Table 18.8 ranks these interventions in decreasing order of use (totals column) and shows (in the rows) the percent of each intervention type that had various outcomes. Though all interventions listed in table 18.8 were more effective than not, the least effective interventions are the most commonly used.

Maybe lighting and CCTV attract more evaluation dollars. Or maybe decision makers are not as careful about when to use them because they are well known; they are more likely to be "selected off the rack." Perhaps the lesser used interventions

Table 18.8 Effects of the most used interventions

Intervention	Totals	Authors' Conclusions			
		Effective	Not Effective	Mixed	Inconclusive
CCTV	25 (37)	59 (22)	14 (5)	24 (9)	3 (1)
Lighting	14 (20)	55 (11)	15 (3)	15 (3)	15 (3)
CPTED	11 (16)	94 (15)			6 (1)
Mixed /other	10 (16)	93 (14)	7 (1)		
Access control	9 (14)	92 (13)			8 (1)
Place management	6 (9)	89 (8)		11 (1)	
Street redesign	4 (6)	67 (4)		17 (1)	17 (1)
Total	79 (118)	74 (87)	7 (8)	12 (14)	6 (7)

were selected after analyses of local situations, so they were more likely to fit local circumstances. An objection to this argument is that lighting comes off poorly because several older and less rigorous evaluations confound these results. Perhaps, but this cannot be argued for CCTV, a much newer technology. In short, we cannot reject the hypothesis that broad use of any place-prevention technique will be less effective than using tailor-made techniques that fit the evidence of the specific circumstances.

If these conclusions are roughly correct, then an evidence-based policymaker cannot simply ask, "What works to reduce crime?" Instead, the policymaker should ask, "Given the specific conditions at these places, what is likely to work to reduce the crime I am most concerned with?" In short, general evidence about effectiveness should be applied in the context of specific evidence about a place's crime problem. This means that it is critical to strengthen the capacity of government agencies, including the police, to analyze problems, form partnerships with other stakeholders, and find situational specific solutions.

The second suggestion we want to make concerns how government agencies reduce crime at private places. Government policymakers need to consider who is responsible for places, and hold these people and organizations accountable for the crimes occurring at their locations. Crime has traditionally been thought of as a public concern that the public tax dollars should address. As long as we consider the offender as the principal cause of crime and the criminal justice system as the hallmark of crime reduction, this is unlikely to change. Once we start considering crime opportunities, however, and once we start preventing crimes at places, we must consider that the owners of these locations control these crime opportunities. Further, no one else has the authority to control these opportunities without first getting place managers' compliance (either through cooperation, threat, or replacement).

Evaluation of what works is expensive and largely supported by the taxpayer. These expenses are worth it if the costs of the prevention and the risk of failure are high. But if, instead of having government agencies implement crime-prevention practices at places, we shifted the responsibility to place owners, then they and their customers would bear the costs and reap the rewards of prevention. Perhaps governments' principal role in crime prevention at places is to set limits for crime that place managers cannot exceed and then hold them accountable. The place managers choose the interventions (within broad legal bounds). And rather than have governments pay for 8,259 or more high-quality evaluations to discover what works at what places for specific crimes, perhaps we should have place owners pay. If owners choose to fund the necessary evaluations, that is their choice. If they choose to use trial and error to discover what works, then this too is their choice. In short, we should consider whether governments should simply focus on setting crime and disorder caps for places, and let place managers figure out how to meet these limits. Most will have no trouble—they do not have much crime now.

In conclusion, we know that a small proportion of places are the sites of most crime at places, regardless of what types of places we examine. We also have sufficient information to be confident that crime can and should be reduced at these high-crime places. Not only does it work, but it often reduces crime around targeted high-crime places. We have less information about what specific interventions are best in specific circumstances. But the cost of getting this type of information is high, and the information will not come soon, even if the money were available. It may be better social policy to shift the crime-prevention burden from the police and other elements of the criminal justice system to those who own and control locations that produce most of the crime. In short, we should explore a policy of "If you own the place, you own the crime."

APPENDIX

The following tables summarize the specific studies we examined. Tables 18.A3 through 18.A7 correspond to earlier tables 18.3 through 18.7. Tables 18.1, 18.2, and 18.8 can be reconstructed from these appendix tables as well. Complete information on the studies examined can be found at Center for Problem Oriented Policing (2010).

NOTES

1. Twenty-four evaluations either entailed larger scale interventions that occurred in a variety of place types or evaluated measures that were implemented in places other than the five reported here (e.g., educational, human service, industrial, etc.). Another 43 evaluations examined nonplace-based interventions, in neighborhoods and larger areas, such as neighborhood watch and public information campaigns.

Table 18.A3 Residential

Study	Intervention	Design	Conclusion
Burglary & Theft			
Chatterton & Frenz 1994	CCTV; warning notices	Before-after	Effective
Musheno et al. (1978)	CCTV	Before-after w/ comparison	Not effective
Allatt (1984)	Secured entry points	Time series; Before-After w/ comparisons	Effective
Beedle & Stangier (1980)	Door locks	Before-after	Effective
Bowers et al. (2003)	Locks; property marking	Before-after w/ comparison	Effective
Bowers, Johnson & Hirschfield (2004)	Alley-gating	Before-after w/ comparisons	Effective
Bozkurt (1994)	Secured entry; police patrol; lighting; other	Time series w/ comparison	Effective
Casey et al. (2004)	Deadbolts; window locks; alarms	Post analysis	Inconclusive
Sturgeon & Adams 2005	Alley gates; property marking; locks; education/awareness; lighting	Before-after w/ comparison	Effective
Tilley & Webb (1994)	Improved window and door security	Before-after w/ comparison	Effective
West (2001)	Locks/bolts; lighting; community awareness and involvement; security audit	Before-after	Effective
WRI (2003)	Security audits; Locks; Alarms	Before-after w/ comparison	Effective
Armitage (2000)	Secured by design (CPTED)	Before-after; cross sectional comparisons	Effective
Bones (1994)	CPTED	Cross-sectional w/ comparison	Mixed findings
Poyner (1994)	Entry changes	Time series	Effective
Shaftoe (1994b)	Secured by design (CPTED)	Before-after	Effective

Study	Intervention	Design	Conclusion
Chenery et al. (1997)	Tiered package of measures; alarms, locks, etc.	Time series; Before-after	Effective
Farr & Moynihan (1994)	Concierge w/ electronic controls	Before-after w/ comparison	Effective
Haywood et al. (2009)	Alley Gating	Before-after w/ comparison	Effective
Kendrick (1994b)	Concierge w/ electronic controls	Before-after w/ comparison	Effective
Alcohol & Drugs			
Eck & Wartell (1998)	Improve property management	Before-after w/controls (randomized)	Effective
Green (1995)	Civil abatement	Before-after w/ comparisons	Effective
Hope (1994)	Closing or selling property	Before-after w/ comparison	Effective
Violence			
King et al. (2008)	CCTV	Before-after w/ comparison	Mixed findings

Study	Intervention	Design	Conclusion
Gabor (1981)	Property marking	Time series w/ comparison	Not effective
Knutsson (1984)	Property marking	Time series	Not effective
Laycock, 1985, 1991	Property marking and publicity	Before-after w comparisons	Effective
Forrestal et al. (1988)	Various-cocoon neighborhood watch	Before-after w/ comparison	Effective
Lurigio et al. (1998)	Civil abatement	Cross sectional w/ comparison	Mixed findings
Mazerolle et al. (1998)	Civil remedies	Before-after w/ comparison (randomized)	Effective
Popkin et al. (1999)	Multipronged crime prevention program in public housing estate	Time series	Effective
Braga et al. (1999)	Police led, various POP projects	Before-after w/controls (randomized)	Effective

continued

Table 18.A3 (continued)

Multiple

Study	Intervention	Design	Conclusion	Study	Intervention	Design	Conclusion
Arthur Young & Co (1978)	CCTV; alarms; locks; resident patrol; security guards	Before-after w/ comparisons	Effective	Kendrick (1994a)	Security; controlled entry; CCTV	Time series	Effective
Davidson & Farr (1994)	CCTV; single, controlled entry point; lighting; police patrol; other	Time series	Effective	Knight (1994)	Security; controlled entry; CCTV	Time series	Effective
Gill et al. (2005)	CCTV	Before-after w/ comparison	Mixed findings	Newman (1996)	Restricting access and other changes	Before-after	Effective
Greenberg & Roush (2009)	CCTV; Door alarms; Card access	Time series w/ comparison	Not Effective				

Table 18.A4 Public Places

Study	Intervention	Design	Conclusion
Burglary & Theft			
Lentz et al. (1977)	Street lighting	Time series; Before-after w/ comparison	Inconclusive
Payne & Gardiner (2003)	Street lighting	Before-after	Effective
Griswold (1984)	Street lighting; crime surveys	Time series w/ comparison	Effective
Alcohol & drugs			
Mazerolle et al. (1999)	CCTV	Time series w/ comparison	Effective
Young et al. (2006)	CCTV; Gated community; Focused policing	Time series w/ comparison	Effective
Madensen & Morgan (2005)	Street barricade	Before-after w/ comparison	Mixed findings
Matthews (1993)	Street barricades and closures; neighbor. watch; police surveillance	Before-after	Effective
Kushmuk & Whittemore (1981)	Street lighting; security survey	Time series	Mixed findings
Maguire & Wood (1998)	CCTV	Before-after	Mixed findings
Pascoe & Harrington-Lynn (1998)	Establish residence; CCTV; alarms	Cross-sectional	Effective
Matthews (1986)	Road Closures/ barricades; Police crackdown	Before-after w/ comparison	Effective
Ramsay (1990)	Alcohol free zone	Before-after	Effective
Knutsson (1997)	Police surveillance; park redesign	Before-after w/ comparison	Effective
Bjor, Knutson & Kuhlhorn (1992)	Various	Case study/cross-sectional	Effective

continued

Table 18.A4 (continued)

Study	Intervention	Design	Conclusion	Study	Intervention	Design	Conclusion
Disorder/Vandalism				Wilson (1990)	Secure change box; Strengthened glass	Time series	Effective
Bridgeman (1997)	Various	Time series	Effective				
Challinger (1991)	Various	Time series	Effective				
Violence							
Lasley (1998)	Street barricades and closures	Before-after w/ comparison	Effective				
Multiple				Goodwin (2002)	CCTV	Before-after	Not effective
Atlanta Regional Commission (1974)	Street lighting	Before-after w/ comparison	Not effective	Griffiths (2003)	CCTV	Before-after w/ comparisons	Effective
Barr & Lawes (1991)	Street lighting	Before-after	Effective	KPMG (2000)	CCTV	Time series w/ comparisons	Effective
Davidson & Goodey (1991)	Street lighting	Before-after	Effective	Ratcliffe & Taniguchi (2008)	CCTV	Before-after w/ comparison	Effective
Ditton, Nair & Bannister (1996)	Street lighting	Before-after	Effective	Serno et al. (1999)	CCTV	Before-after w/ comparisons	Effective
Herbert & Moore (1991)	Street lighting	Before-after	Inconclusive	Sivarajasingam & Shepherd (1999)	CCTV	Before-after w/ comparisons	Mixed Findings
Lewis & Sullivan (1979)	Street lighting	Before-after	Mixed findings				

Study	Intervention	Design	Conclusion
Morrow & Hutton (2000)	Street lighting	Before-after w/ comparison	Not effective
Nair & Ditton (1994)	Street lighting	Before-after	Inconclusive
Painter (1994)	Street lighting	Before-after	Effective
Painter (1988)	Street lighting	Before-after	Effective
Painter & Farrington (2001)	Street lighting	Before-after w/ comparisons	Effective
Painter & Farrington (1999)	Street lighting	Before-after w/ comparisons	Effective
Painter & Farrington (1997)	Street lighting	Before-after w/ comparisons	Effective
Quinet & Nunn (1998)	Street lighting	Before-after w/ comparison	Effective
Shaftoe (1994)	Street lighting	Time series w/ comparison	Not effective
Wright et al. (1974)	Street lighting	Before-after w/ comparison	Mixed findings
Cameron et al. (2008)	CCTV	Before-after w/ comparisons	Mixed Findings

Study	Intervention	Design	Conclusion
Sivarajasingam et al. (2003)	CCTV	Before-after w/ comparisons	Mixed Findings
Skinns (1998)	CCTV	Before-after w/ comparisons	Effective
Squires (2003)	CCTV	Before-after; time series	Not effective
Squires (2000)	CCTV	Before-after w/ comparison	Mixed Findings
Squires (1998)	CCTV	Before-after w/ comparison	Effective
Armitage, Smyth & Pease (1999)	CCTV	Before-After w/ comparisons; time series	Effective
Brown (1995)	CCTV	Before-after w/ comparisons	Effective
Ditton (2000)	CCTV	Before-after w/ comparisons	Not effective
Ditton & Short (1999)	CCTV	Before-after w/ comparisons	Mixed Findings
Atlas & LeBlanc (1994)	Street barricades and closures	Before-After w/ comparison	Effective
Wagner (1997)	Street closures	Before-after w/ comparison	Inconclusive

Table 18.A5 Retail

Study	Intervention	Design	Conclusion
Burglary & Theft			
Beck & Willis (1999)	CCTV	Before-after	Effective
Gill & Turbin (1998)	CCTV	Before-after w/12. Removed intervention	Mixed Findings
Berkowitz (1975)	Alarms; CCTV	Before-after w/ comparisons	Inconclusive
Bowers (2001)	Security survey; locks; alarms; CCTV	Time series; Before-after w/ comparison	Effective
Taylor (1999)	Alarms; CCTV guided by repeat victimization	Before-after	Effective
Wallis & Ford (1980)	Fencing; CCTV; Lighting; Patrols	Time series w/ comparison	Effective
Bamfield (1994)	Electronic Article Surveillance	Before-After w/ comparison	Effective
DiLonardo (1996)	Electronic Article Surv.	Time series; before-after	Effective
Laycock (1984)	Securing of pharmacy medicine	Cross sectional w/ comparisons	Effective
Masuda (1992)	Intensive inventorying	Time series w/ comparison	Effective
McNees et al. (1980)	verbalization of non-theft	Before-after w/Removed intervention	Effective
McNees et al. (1976)	Posting signs; ID high risk theft items; Awareness Campaign	Before-after w/Removed intervention	Effective
Pearson (1980)	Security survey	Before-after w/ comparison; time series	Effective
Dilonardo & Clarke (1996)	Ink tags	Before-after w/ comparisons	Effective
Tilley & Hopkins (1993)	Information packs/ education-awareness	Before-after	Effective
Touche Ross (1976)	Media campaign; security survey; property marking	Before-after	Effective

Study	Intervention	Design	Conclusion
Farrington et al. (1993)	T1: Electronic Article Surv.; T2: store redesign; T3 security guard	Before-after w/controls (randomized)	Effective
Frauds			
Challinger (1996)	Restrictive refund policy	Time series	Effective
Masuda (1993)	Cashier training; procedural safeguards	Before-after	Effective
Robbery			
Clifton (1993)	Lighting; clear windows; CCTV; low cash volume; Clerk location	Before-after	Effective
Schnelle et al. (1979)	Alarms	Before-after w/ comparison	Not effective
Multiple			
Lavrakas & Kushmuk (1986)	CPTED	Time series w/ comparison	Effective

Study	Intervention	Design	Conclusion
Webb (1996)	Photo on check cards; awareness campaign	Time series	Effective
Knutsson & Kuhlhorn (1997)	Require ID with check use	Time series	Effective
Whitcomb (1979)	Hidden cameras	Before-after w/control (randomized)	Effective

Table 18.A6 Transport Settings

Study	Intervention	Design	Conclusion	Study	Intervention	Design	Conclusion
Burglary & Theft							
Barclay et al. (1996)	Bike patrol	Before-After w/comparisons; Time series	Effective	Poyner (1991)	CCTV; barriers; lighting	Before-after w/comparison	Effective
Clarke & Goldstein (2003)	Police Patrol; lighting; fencing; attendants; CCTV	Before-after w/comparison	Effective	Smith et al. (2003)	Various parking lot security measures	Cross sectional	Effective
Laycock & Austin (1992)	Parking attendants	Before-after w/comparisons	Effective	Tseng et al. (2004)	Lighting; Exit location; increased visibility	Before-after	Effective
Mayhew et al. (1976)	bus attendant visibility	Study 1: Before-after; Time series w/comparison; Study 2: cross sectional	Effective				
Frauds							
Bichler & Clarke (1996)	Various	Time series; Before-after w/comparison	Effective	Decker (1977)	Slug rejecters; transparent window; warning signs	Times series; Before-after w/comparisons	Mixed findings
Clarke (1993)	Automatic gates/Automated ticketing	Before-after	Effective	DesChamps, Brantingham & Brantingham (1992)	Fare Evasion Audit; increase train attendants	Before-after	Effective

Study	Intervention	Design	Conclusion
Clarke, Cody & Natarajan (1994)	machine modification	Case study; Time series comparisons	Effective
Disorder			
Carr & Spring (1993)	Increased lighting; CCTV; cleanup system	Before-after	Effective
Felson et al. (1996)	Various	Time series; Before-after	Effective
Poyner (1988)	CCTV	Time series	Effective
Violence			
Burrows (1980)	CCTV	Before-after w/ comparison	Effective
Chaiken et al. (1974)	Increased police patrol; exact fare system; cash boxes	Time series	Effective
Landes (1978)	Airline passenger screening; air marshals	Time series	Effective
Multiple			
Kenney (1986)	Guardian Angels	Before-after w/ comparisons	Inconclusive
LaVigne (1996)	Subway design; CCTV; lighting; fare cards	Cross sectional w/ comparisons; time series	Effective
Weidner (1996)	High wheel turnstiles	Before-after w/ comparison	Effective
Sloan-Howitt & Kelling (1990)	Graffiti cleaning	Time series	Effective
Van Andel (1989)	Various	Before-after	Effective
Poyner & Warner (1986)	Protective screens for drivers	Before-after	Effective
Stone & Stevens (1999)	Taxi cab partitions	Before-after w/ comparison	Effective
Webb & Laycock (1992)	CCTV; Police; improved communication	Time series w/ comparisons	Mixed findings

Table 18.A7 Recreation

Study	Intervention	Design	Conclusion
Alcohol & Drug			
Felson et al. (1997)	Various	Time series w/ comparisons	Effective
Homel et al. (1997)	increased regulation of bars & taverns	Before-after	Effective
Violence			
Clarke & McGrath (1990)	Cash removal; time lock safes	Time series w/ comparisons	Effective
Putram, et al (1993)	Server training and police enforcement	Before-after w/ comparison	Effective
Hauritz et al. (1998)	Safety Initiative	Before-after	Effective
Veno & Veno (1993)	Various	Before-after	Effective
Vehicle crashes			
Saltz (1987)	Server training	Before-after w/ comparison	Effective

REFERENCES

Braga, Anthony A. 2001. "The Effects of Hot Spots Policing on Crime." *Annals of the American Academy of Political and Social Science* 578:104–25.

Braga, Anthony A. 2005. "Hot Spots Policing and Crime Prevention: A Systematic Review of Randomized Controlled Trials." *Journal of Experimental Criminology* 1:317–42.

Center for Problem-Oriented Policing. 2010. "Situational Crime Prevention Evaluation Database." http://www.popcenter.org/library/scp/.

Chainey, Spencer. 2005. "Methods and Techniques for Understanding Crime Hotspots." In *Mapping Crime: Understanding Hot Spots*, edited by John E. Eck, Spencer Chainey, James G. Cameron, Michael Leitner, and Ronald E. Wilson. Washington, DC: US Department of Justice, National Institute of Justice.

Clarke, Ronald V., 1992. *Situational Crime Prevention: Successful Case Studies*. Albany, NY: Harrow and Heston.

Clarke, Ronald V., 2008. "Situational Crime Prevention." In *Environmental Criminology and Crime Analysis*, edited by Richard Wortley and Lorraine Mazerolle. Cullompton, UK: Willan.

Cohen, Richard, and Marcus Felson. 1979. "Social Change and Crime Rate Trends: A Routine Activity Approach." *American Sociological Review* 44:588–605.

Cornish, Derek, and Ronald V. Clarke. 2003. "Opportunities, Precipitators and Criminal Decisions: A Reply to Wortley's Critique of Situation Crime Prevention." In *Theory for Practice in Situational Crime Prevention*, edited by Martha J. Smith and Derek B. Cornish. Vol. 16 of *Crime Prevention Studies*, edited by Ronald V. Clarke. Monsey, NY: Criminal Justice Press.

Eck, John E. 1994. "Drug Markets and Drug Places: A Case-Control Study of the Spatial Structure of Illicit Drug Dealing." Ph.D. dissertation, University of Maryland.

Eck, John E. 1996. "Do Premises Liability Suits Promote Business Crime Prevention." In *Business and Crime Prevention*, edited by Ronald V. Clarke and Marcus Felson. Monsey, NY: Criminal Justice Press.

Eck, John E. 2002. "Preventing Crime at Places." In *Evidence-Based Crime Prevention*, edited by Lawrence W. Sherman, David Farrington, Brandon Welsh, and Doris Layton MacKenzie. New York: Routledge.

Eck, John E., and Ronald V. Clarke. 2003. "Classifying Common Police Problems: A Routine Activity Approach." In *Theory for Practice in Situational Crime Prevention*, edited by Martha J. Smith and Derek B. Cornish. Vol. 16 of *Crime Prevention Studies*, edited by Ronald V. Clarke. Monsey, NY: Criminal Justice Press.

Eck, John E., Ronald V. Clarke, and Rob T. Guerette. 2007. "Risky Facilities: Crime Concentration in Homogeneous Sets of Establishments and Facilities." In *Imagination for Crime Prevention*, edited by Graham Farrell, Kate J. Bowers, Shane D. Johnson, and Michael Townsley. Vol. 19 of *Crime Prevention Studies*, edited by Ronald V. Clarke. Monsey, NY: Criminal Justice Press.

Eck, John E., Jeffery Gersh, and Charlene Taylor. 2000. "Finding Hotspots Through Repeat Address Mapping." In *Analyzing Crime Patterns: Frontiers of Practice*, edited by Victor Goldsmith, Philip G. McGuire, John Mollenkopf, and Timothy Ross. Thousand Oaks, CA: Sage.

Eck, John E., and Julie Wartell. 1998. "Improving the Management of Rental Properties with Drug Problems: A Randomized Experiment." In *Civil Remedies and Crime Prevention*, edited by Lorraine Mazerolle and Jan Roehl. Vol. 9 of *Crime Prevention Studies*, edited by Ronald V. Clarke. Monsey, NY: Criminal Justice Press.

Eck, John E., and David Weisburd. 1995. *Crime and Place*. Vol. 4 of *Crime Prevention Studies*, edited by Ronald V. Clarke. Monsey, NY: Criminal Justice Press.

Farrell, Graham. 1995. "Preventing Repeat Victimization." In *Building a Safer Society: Strategic Approaches to Crime Prevention*, edited by David Farrington. Chicago: University of Chicago Press.

Felson, Marcus. 2008. "Routine Activity Theory." In *Environmental Criminology and Crime Analysis*, edited by Richard Wortley and Lorraine Mazerolle. Cullompton, UK: Willan.

Goldstein, Herman. 1990. *Problem-Oriented Policing*. New York: McGraw-Hill.

Green, Lorraine. 1995. "Policing Places with Drug Problems: The Multi-Agency Response Team Approach." In *Crime and Place*, edited by John E. Eck and David Weisburd. Vol. 4 of *Crime Prevention Studies*, edited by Ronald V. Clarke. Monsey, NY: Criminal Justice Press.

Guerette, Rob T., and Kate J. Bowers. 2009. "Assessing the Extent of Crime Displacement and Diffusion of Benefits: A Systematic Review of Situational Crime Prevention Evaluations." *Criminology* 47:1331–68.

Madensen, Tamara D. 2007. *"Bar Management and Crime: Toward a Dynamic Theory of Place Management and Crime Hotspots."* Ph.D. dissertation, University of Cincinnati.

Madensen, Tamara D., and John E. Eck. 2008. "Violence in Bars: Exploring the Impact of Place Manager Decision-Making." *Crime Prevention and Community Safety* 10:111–25.

Maguire, Edward R., and Charles M. Katz. 2002. "Community Policing, Loose Coupling, and Sensemaking in American Police Agencies." *Justice Quarterly* 19: 503–36.

Mazerolle, Lorraine, and Janet Ransley. 2005. *Third Party Policing*. New York. Cambridge University Press.

Mazerolle, Lorraine G., Jan Roehl, and Colleen Kadleck. 1998. "Controlling Social Disorder Using Civil Remedies: Results from a Randomized Field Experiment in Oakland, California." In *Civil Remedies and Crime Prevention*, edited by Lorraine Green Mazerolle and Jan Roehl. Vol. 9 of *Crime Prevention Studies*, edited by Ronald V. Clarke. Monsey, NY: Criminal Justice Press.

Petroski, Henry. 1997. *Design Paradigms: Case Histories of Error and Judgment in Engineering*. New York: Cambridge University Press.

Ratcliff, Jerry. 2008. *Intelligence Led Policing*. Cullompton, UK: Willan.

Shadish, William R., Thomas D. Cook, and Donald T. Campbell. 2002. *Experimentation and Quasi-Experimental Designs for General Causal Inference*. New York: Houghton Mifflin.

Sherman, Lawrence W. 1990. "Police Crackdowns: Initial and Residual Deterrence." In *Crime and Justice: A Review of Research*, vol. 12, edited by Michael Tonry and Norval Morris. Chicago: University of Chicago Press.

Sherman, Lawrence W., Patrick R. Gartin, and Michael E. Buerger. 1989. "Hot Spots of Predatory Crime: Routine Activities and the Criminology of Place." *Criminology* 27:27–55.

Silverman, Eli B. 1999. *NYPD Battles Crime: Innovative Strategies in Policing*. Boston: Northeastern University Press.

Welsh, Brandon C., and David P. Farrington. 2009. *Making Public Places Safer: Surveillance and Crime Prevention*. New York: Oxford University Press.

Zimring, 2006. *The Great American Crime Decline*. New York: Oxford University Press.

CHAPTER 19

THE PRIVATE SECTOR AND DESIGNING PRODUCTS AGAINST CRIME

PAUL EKBLOM

DESIGN is a field with enormous scope. Design itself is, in brief, creativity deployed to a specific end (HM Treasury 2005). It is a generic process of creating some new or improved product that is materially or logically possible to make; is fit or fitter than its predecessors; is for some specified principal purpose; and does not significantly interfere with subsidiary purposes or with wider requirements of social and economic life and the environment (adapted from Booch 1993).

Most practitioners, in situational crime prevention or crime prevention through environmental design (Cozens, Saville, and Hillier 2005), view design in terms of its fruits, whether secure laptops or safe buildings. However, a more fundamental view of design and its contributions to prevention is in terms of the design process and the design way of thinking. Design incorporates a problem-solving aspect, with affinities to problem-oriented policing (Ekblom 2008), but equally covers problem formulation or problem finding (Cropley 2010). Much effort is required to give designers a "think thief" mindset (Ekblom 1997)—they tend to assume people are honest and won't abuse or misuse their products. But there are potentially enormous benefits from getting crime-prevention practitioners to "draw on design" (Ekblom 2008) when developing practical interventions of whatever kind. This may be in the theoretical design of a youth inclusion program (how the intervention principles are intended to combine to reduce the risk of offending), industrial design of a youth shelter, environmental design of a housing estate (Home Office/Office of Deputy Prime Minister 2004), procedural design of a secure Internet registration sequence, graphic/communications design of a crime-prevention publicity poster, system design of a secure financial system or CCTV facility, educational design of an anger-management course, knowledge design of a schema for capturing and transferring good practice (Ekblom 2011), and of course, the more familiar research design of a sample survey or impact evaluation, as well as adjunct aspects such as the layout of survey forms or design of the database.

This essay focuses on product design, meaning three-dimensional objects, whether portable (like handbags), mobile (e.g., bikes) or fitted (e.g., bike stands), and generally up to vehicle-size in scale. A number of key points emerge:

- Design of products against crime is closely related to situational crime prevention in theory and practice, though it poses challenges to that field; but a broader design-based approach may benefit all kinds of prevention.
- Design of products against crime has a concern with risk factors and risk reduction, but designers and engineers need clearer language than that which is commonly used in crime prevention.
- It is possible to develop a systematic and generic way for describing the security function of a given product in terms of purpose, security niche, causal mechanisms, and technology.
- Design of products against crime must be proportionate to other require-ments—user friendly while abuser unfriendly, and respecting a range of noncrime values. Focused creativity and iterative trials and improvements, addressing the conflicts and contradictions inherent in crime, can maximize all benefits and minimize undesired side effects.
- Design must anticipate adaptive offenders who will seek to circumvent security. Given this, and more general social, commercial, and technological changes, designers can cope by incorporating into their products flexibility and upgradeability of the security function.
- Strategically, the arms-race issue requires designers to be given the capacity and the motivation to out-innovate offenders over the medium to long term.
- Diverse parties in society bear some civil responsibility for the design, manufacture, installation, and use of products that are secure. Businesses in particular relate to crime and the civil responsibility for prevention in diverse ways.
- Where self-protection of businesses' own assets is not at stake, motivating them to address crime is a challenge for governments seeking to remedy this market failure for product security. A range of initiatives have been taken in research, legislation, and direct action, and various policy levers have been applied, but intermittent government attention and funding undermine achievements.
- More generally, mobilizing people and organizations to use secure designs is as much of a challenge as the technical design task itself (though both tasks should proceed in step).

- Evaluation of the research and development kind is embedded in product design, but that of the impact on crime is limited. Evidence of impact/ cost-effectiveness is mainly correlational, self-evident, or reliant on intermediate outcome measures. Various practical challenges face those seeking to supply harder evidence.

The essay is organized as follows. Section I establishes theoretical links between design against crime and situational prevention. Section II identifies empirical links with risk-factor approaches. Section III uses illustrations from practice to show how the security function of products can be described in depth. Section IV covers diverse issues in the secure design of products, including contradictions and trade-offs, adaptive offenders, anticipation of new crime problems, and co-evolution between offenders and preventers. Section V considers the question of responsibility for secure design, especially the roles of business and government. Section VI examines the (limited) evidence of effectiveness and difficulties of evaluation, and section VII presents discussion and conclusions.

I. Theoretical Links: Situational Crime Prevention

Product design (as well as some of its close relations such as environmental design) connects quite closely with and can apply most of the 25 techniques of situational prevention (see Smith and Clarke this volume). It can even extend this list—for example, with the concept of target softening. Here, say, can be found the lock whose bolt is free to swivel in its housing, thereby denying hacksaw blades purchase.

More theoretically, product design engages with the risk, effort, and reward (as encountered or perceived by the offender) of rational choice theory (Cornish and Clarke 1986): the Karrysafe handbag[1] has a Velcro opening that increases the risk of the owner's hearing or feeling the thief's action. An anchor cable designed to clip laptop to library table leg increases the effort and resources (a cutter is needed to release it). The Puma folding bike[2] has a down-tube (the diagonal part of the frame) made of tensioned steel cable that unfastens and doubles as a locking device that can wrap round a bike stand—cut the cable and the released bike is now useless. This reduces the reward.

Situational prevention also encompasses Wortley's (2008) crime precipitators, which combine emotional/motivational/perceptual influences with opportunity to act out the emotion or realize the criminal goal thus awakened. For example, a difficult-to-operate door entry system can provoke damage from "machine rage"; a glittering new mobile phone can prompt thoughts of theft. Such processes connect with Norman's (2004) concept of emotional design.

Finally, product design engages with the guardians of routine activities theory (Cohen and Felson 1979). The caMden bike stand's M-shaped design[3] nudges cyclists to lock their bikes by both wheels and frame, known to be the most secure method.

II. Empirical Links: Risk Factors

At an empirical level, Clarke (1999) introduced the concept of hot products—those shown to be at especial risk of theft owing to their being concealable, removable, available, valuable, enjoyable, and disposable (CRAVED). The archetypical example is the mobile phone, which later acquired its own acronym (topping CRAVED for esoteric elegance) of design factors predicting theft risk: IN SAFE HANDS— identifiable, neutral, seen, attached, findable, executable, hidden, automatic, necessary, detectable, and secure (Whitehead et al. 2008). Armitage and Pease (2007) drew on CRAVED and further ideas by Clarke and Newman (2005a) to explore an approach to systematic crime proofing of domestic electronic products at the design stage (Project MARC). This involved getting manufacturers to match the level of inbuilt security to an advance estimate of the level of theft risk to which a product might be exposed in its natural environment.

Theft is only one kind of crime risk to which products are exposed or can contribute. This approach, which parallels the risk and protective factor approach in potential offenders' lives (see Farrington, Loeber, and Ttofi this volume), can be generalized using the Misdeeds and Security framework (Ekblom 2005b, 2008). Originally developed to forecast crime risks and crime-prevention opportunities from new scientific advances or technological applications, misdeeds offers a ready framework for anticipating broad crime possibilities that may happen to, or be caused by, a given product. A camera phone, say, can be misappropriated or stolen; mistreated or deliberately damaged; mishandled—smuggled; misbegotten counterfeited; misused as a tool for crime in anonymous drug deals; or misbehaved with (filming of humiliating attacks).

In this domain, to avoid confusing designers and engineers, it is important to employ clear language. Unfortunately, clarity is not the norm. *Risk* is used loosely in situational crime prevention (generally relating to probability alone, and implicitly meaning risk of harm to offender). *Risk* can be decomposed into *possibility, probability,* and *harm* (Ekblom, forthcoming). Eliminating the possibility includes, for example, the remedial design of railway carriage ends to remove footholds for youths to ride the couplings at mortal peril (a sloping plastic housing covers the ledges where they once perched). Reducing the probability includes converting the mushroom-shaped locking buttons inside car doors (easy to snag with a wire noose introduced via the rubber door seal) into ones with asparagus-shaped tips. Reducing the harm includes designing an easy-to-use back-up system for the numbers stored on stolen mobile phones, which would otherwise be lost, or the bike stand that, if

vandalized, does not leave dangerous jagged edges for passers-by to injure themselves on.

Armitage and Pease (2007) were conscious of difficulties of language in Project
MARC. With more scope to address the problem, Ekblom and Sidebottom (2007)
distinguished four different ways in which the term vulnerability had been used in
that project, then developed a complete, consistent, and systematic glossary that
attempted to bridge the disciplinary divide between situational prevention and
security. For example, they distinguished between criminogenic products (associated with increased probability of crime to/from themselves) and their opposite,
criminocclusive. Also between the value of a product (the potential to gratify some
motivation of the offender—including enjoyment, status display, misuse, or resale)
and its vulnerability (where its own properties enable it to be seen and taken by the
offender)—vulnerability incorporating all criminogenic factors associated with
theft of product except the motivation it engenders.

Both Misdeeds and Security, and the security glossary, have a dual face: understanding and anticipating crime risk; and describing prevention through design.

III. Describing the Security Function of a Product

The diversity of products, and the preventive approaches they embody, tend toward
confusion. But a way of systematically describing the security function of any product has emerged in the course of practical projects to design antitheft clips to secure
the bags of customers sitting in bars and restaurants,[4] and to design and develop
standards for bike parking facilities (www.bikeoff.org; Ekblom 2009; Thorpe et al.
2009). Further motivation for this approach has come from the author's experience
in judging design against crime competitions (like the Student Design Awards of the
Royal Society of Arts) and participating in briefing/critique sessions for studio classes
in an MA Industrial Design course. In both cases, it proved hard to get the student
designers to be clear about the rationale for the design—what it's for, how it works,
and how its construction and materials support both of these. The Security Function
framework (Ekblom 2012a; Ekblom et al. 2012; Meyer and Ekblom forthcoming)
attempts to remedy this. It enables a product to be described in four parallel but distinct discourses: purpose, security niche, preventive mechanisms, and technology.

A. Purpose

Describing purpose covers several distinct aspects. What is the designed product
for? A car is for transport, a chair is for sitting; an ink tag is for preventing shoplifting; an offender tag (a wireless monitoring device strapped to a curfewed offender's
ankle) is for keeping the individual at home. This is the product's principal purpose,

but it also has subsidiary ones. Crime prevention (reducing possibility, probability, or harm) can feature in either purpose. What other "desire" requirements must it meet, which are beneficial to the immediate users and manufacturers, such as aesthetics, economy, and user-friendliness? What "hygiene" or social responsibility requirements must it meet (referring to societal values/goals that the product should not interfere with, or should positively boost, such as social inclusion or energy efficiency)? In all this, note that different stakeholders may vest different purposes and priorities in the product—criminal purposes are a special case. Designers are generally paid to take certain stakeholders' perspectives; in private industry, of course, the aim is to maximize the manufacturer's profit, which may or may not simultaneously give maximum benefit to the purchaser/user or to other parties, as will be seen below.

B. Security Niche

The concept of security niche attempts to characterize how the security function within a given product relates to other products, people, and places in the human/ technological ecosystem. Where the risk to or from criminogenic products is sufficiently high, action may be taken to reduce that risk. This could be in line with a desire requirement—the owner doesn't want to lose it. It could be a hygiene requirement—collectively, we don't want it to generate police and criminal justice costs by being stolen. Crime risks could be multiple (a product could be misappropriated, mistreated, and/or misused), and certain risks may be more important than others to particular stakeholders. Consider some product, such as a laptop-carrier backpack, which is at risk of being a target of, or a tool for, crime. Security can be conferred in several ways, singly or in combination (cf. Ekblom 2005a):

- The bag could be safe—not in itself needing explicit security because it is used only in secure environments, protected by enclosures and/or people acting as crime preventers such as guardians or place managers (Clarke and Eck 2003). In practice, complete safety occurs only in relatively rare circumstances.
- A bag that was in fact exposed to significant risk could be protected by separate security products or securing products. A security product's principal purpose is protecting some other target, person, or property against crime—an example could be an audible alarm lanyard that is triggered if the bag is snatched. Securing products, by contrast, have a subsidiary security purpose additional to their principal purpose (for example, Stop Thief chairs[5] are primarily for sitting on, but a pair of notches cut in the front of the seat enables a bag to be securely hitched beneath the owner's knees, in a café or pub).
- The above approaches make for a secured product, protected by external means. But the product itself could be designed to be secure, one that protects itself:
  ○ Through inherent security—e.g., a TV set that is too large/heavy to be removed by opportunist burglars.

○ By the incorporation of security or securing components. These may either be retrofitted or factory-fitted, where product and component are designed or selected to fit one another well, such as the tamper-evident lid on food containers. In the case of the bag, an RFID (wireless) chip could be inserted to protect against shoplifting; since this could also help with stock control and supply chain monitoring, the RFID would be a securing product.

○ By deliberate security adaptations (Ekblom and Sidebottom 2007) to its inherent causal properties, features, and materials. These adaptations either work by themselves (such as anti-slash textile incorporated within the Karrysafe bags), or in conjunction with human action such as guardianship (for example, where the opening flap of a handbag is fastened by Velcro, as described).

There is one final ecological issue to cover, captured in a distinction noted in Ekblom (2009), between a product as object of crime—an asset—and the same product in function. A laptop bag can be stolen for its own value, as well as for the objects it contains and perhaps protects (as a securing product itself) or fails to protect.

C. Mechanisms

Purpose must ultimately link to more practical aspects of design. But it's best not to leap straight from high-level purpose to technology. To achieve smarter understanding of risks and interventions, better design proposals, and better feedback in trials and sharper evaluation (Pawson and Tilley 1997) requires an intermediate consideration of the immediate causal mechanisms—how the design intervention works by interrupting, diverting, or weakening the proximal causes of criminal events. An understanding of causal mechanisms of crime and its prevention is also key to more efficient knowledge transfer to other design tasks replicating the core principles of successful crime prevention in ways that are intelligently and perhaps innovatively customized to new contexts (Ekblom 2005a).

Usually, one can identify several parallel mechanisms that may underlie a preventive effect. For example, physical blocking of crime (e.g., by an electronic password on a mobile phone) operates alternatively or in parallel to subjective discouragement of offenders from anticipated effort. (Whitehead et al. [2008] emphasize the importance of semiotics in signaling to the potential offender that "here's a robust-looking and well-protected phone, so don't consider it worth attempting to steal.") Intervention can be direct, as in these examples, or indirect, involving the participation of someone such as the user acting in a crime-preventer role (Ekblom 2011). For example, a security product such as an anti-shoplifting wireless tag hidden in an expensive coat is ultimately only effective to the extent that the detector device at the shop exit picks up the signal, sounds the alarm, and brings a security guard running.

Offenders are obviously central to causal mechanisms. They can be seen as both "caused" in their motivation, emotion, and perception by influences they encounter in the proximal situation (e.g., prompts or provocations) or earlier (recent family stress, tiring commuter journey, ingestion of alcohol); and as active, goal-directed, planning and decision-making agents (Ekblom 2007, 2009, 2012b)—"caused agents," for short. Given this, a useful parallel discourse to straight causal mechanisms is that of scripts (Cornish 1994) and perpetrator techniques (or modus operandi). For example, the offender must seek a crime target (say, a handbag), see and select the target, approach without arousing suspicion, steal the bag, and escape preferably unnoticed before converting and/or enjoying the value of the loot and perhaps covering his or her tracks. The task of preventers (including designers) is to disrupt these offender scripts and frustrate plans and goals.

Ekblom (2009) extends the script concept in design terms to cover script clashes—where the offender's script engages with the user or preventer's script in such issues as surveil versus conceal, challenge versus excuse, pursue versus escape. These are, as it were, the pivots upon which designers and other professional crime preventers tip the design of products, environments, and procedures to favor the good party.

D. Technology

Technical descriptions state how the causal properties of the product, which contribute to the mechanisms of prevention described above, are realized through construction, manufacture, and operation. Construction is about materials and distinguishable structural features of the design. Manufacture is about how it's made. Operation is about how it acts in tangible terms with human action (or under control of artificial intelligence), such as keys turned, faces recognized, cards swiped, or actuators releasing locks.

In sum, an abbreviated security function statement could say something like this, using the Stop Thief chair as example:

1. (purpose) The Stop Thief chair is designed with principal purpose to serve as a fully functional and appropriately styled chair, and subsidiary purpose to reduce the risk of theft of customers' bags in places like bars and restaurants.
2. (security niche) It is thus a securing product.
3. (mechanism) It works by supplying physical anchorage of the target bag, which is differentially easier to release by the bag owner; by mobilizing usage of the security function of the chair, and the surveillance and reaction that it favors by the user/owner and others acting as preventers; and by deterrence through increasing the offender's perception of risk of being detected and caught in the act.
4. (technology) All these mechanisms are supported by the incorporation of a twin-notch feature cut or molded in the leading edge of the seat part of the chair, over which the bag handle is placed by the user/owner, the bag then being anchored due to its handle being enclosed between the seat and the back of the user/owner's knees.

IV. Issues in the Secure Design
of Products

Design raises several issues whose implications extend to crime prevention as a whole. They include contradictions, trade-offs, and how these are resolved; reactions and countermoves of offenders to preventive interventions; anticipation of new crime problems; and "arms races" between offenders and preventers.

A. Contradictions and Troublesome Trade-offs

An awkward-to-use pin code, intended to prevent theft of a particular type of video recorder, in fact discouraged legitimate buyers and the model was withdrawn (Design Council 2000). Always-on alarm functions may significantly boost a product's lifetime carbon footprint, as well as generating nuisance false alarms. Cages for valuables (like computer projectors in schools) are often hideous, and a constant reminder of the risk of crime and the existence of "fortress" conditions.

These are instances of bad design, where crime was considered only as a last-minute or retrospective technofix poorly integrated into the rest of the product's design; and/or solutions devised by engineers failing to consider desire and hygiene requirements. Where crime was considered, the priority may have been excessive. In some cases, as Gamman and Thorpe (2007) put it, "paranoid products"[6] invade the market and serve as much to increase fear as to prevent crime (while lining manufacturers' pockets). Gamman and Thorpe further attack "vulnerability-led" design, arguing that user-centered approaches should always predominate: user-friendly while being abuser-unfriendly (Ekblom 1997). This is particularly so with securing products, whose main purpose is unconnected with crime.

Good design, addressing security requirements from an early stage in the design process, according it appropriate priority, and applying focused creativity, ingenuity, and well-researched understanding (Gamman and Thorpe 2009) can avoid these problems. It can resolve these troublesome trade-offs with other commercial or social values such as aesthetics, cost, safety, sustainability, inclusion, or reassurance. The Stop Thief chair range favors bag owner over bag thief, and it is designed to fit both technically and aesthetically with several classical chair styles. Security can be designed to piggyback on other functions such as safety so as to minimize cost and complex operating menus. Paint manufacturers, coping with frauds where shoppers bought expensive paint, replaced it with water, and returned the can for cash, approached designers. These decided to shave a thin layer off one part of the mold for making the lid, which left a membrane of plastic where one inserts the screwdriver to prize off the lid. In the course of this action, the membrane is split, indicating that the can has been opened.[7] The enormous three-D letters spelling ARSENAL at that soccer team's stadium in London are designed to block a truck laden with explosives crashing through into the arena—but don't show it. Safer beer glasses,[8] whose material composition is designed to break into relatively harmless chips (like tempered car windscreens) rather than create a deadly weapon, are not detectable as such.

Designers work best when the requirements for the product to be developed clearly express the relevant trade-offs and contradictions. This is not exclusive to crime. What is particular, though, is the contradiction at the heart of the definition of the crimes to be prevented themselves. With theft, for example, the issue is one of supporting legitimate possession and stopping illegitimate possession acquired through stealthy transfer. What appeals to the legitimate owner also appeals to the offender (value, enjoyability, etc.); what helps the owner also helps the offender (concealability, removability, etc., as with hot products). The designer, thus, must make a fine discrimination between the two elements. This could be by lock and key, password, fingerprint, place of use (plugged into a particular network), or configuration. The Grippa clip, a table-mounted fixture designed to reduce theft of customers' bags in bars,[9] uses positioning (at the corner of the table, where leg meets table top) and orientation (facing the customer), making it hard for the offender to release the hanging bag, but easy for the customer to do so.

B. Offenders Fight Back

Displacement of crime is a familiar concern in situational prevention, but one where evidence suggests that the problem is not pervasive (see Johnson, Guerette, and Bowers this volume). With secure, securing, or security products, problems emerge over various timescales (Ekblom 2005a): from immediate countermoves like deadening the loudspeaker of a car alarm with quick-setting cavity-filling foam, to deliberate reverse engineering and counter-design (Ekblom 1997)—dismantling locking mechanisms, say, by discovering weak points and designing tools to overcome them. More broadly, Felson (1997) identified a particular "criminal career" of products that parallels their legitimate phases of novelty, "must have" and saturation. Pease (2001) introduced the concept of "crime harvests," whereby products like mobile phones are first designed naïve to crime risk; they engender a wave of offending triggering panic governmental responses; and finally they have retrofit modifications imposed that may be costly, awkward, and limited in scope compared to those which could have been incorporated had designers considered crime from the start.

C. Anticipation

Rather than reacting to emergent crime risks associated with particular products, is it possible to anticipate at the design stage, with sufficient reliability to inform manufacture? And to justify government intrusion in the form of standards and guidelines like the European Directive on compulsory vehicle immobilizers of 1995? Certainly the crime-proofing exercise of Project MARC (described earlier) indicated that this was not a straightforward task, for a number of reasons. Horizon-scanning and foresight approaches (Department of Trade and Industry 2000;

Rogerson, Ekblom, and Pease 2000) generally acknowledge that diverse possibilities must be considered when making policies or products robust to the future: specific predictions will probably be wrong. An example was the TV set-top box, designed to enable analogue TV sets to receive digital broadcasts. This seemed a probable hot product, until the marketing strategies of service providers changed from selling the boxes at cost to providing them virtually free and collecting revenue from the additional service. In the face of such changes, designers should cope by incorporating into their products the flexibility and upgradeability of the security function.

D. Co-evolution and Arms Races

As offenders and preventers get to know and anticipate one another's scripts and mutual script clashes, the scripts may co-evolve toward greater elaboration of security countermoves and crime counter-countermoves. This process is described further in the design sphere, as well as in conventional crime prevention, in accounts of "arms races" between preventers and offenders (Ekblom 1997, 1999, 2005a). This obviously renders useless many once-effective interventions (as with security codes, which offenders have discovered how to bypass). From a strategic perspective, it requires that designers are given both the capacity and the motivation to continually outinnovate adaptive offenders and adapt their own products to changing social and technological contexts.

Knowing what the product and its owner or guardian is up against is important for design. Understanding the resources offenders may deploy (Ekblom and Tilley 2000; Gill 2005), now and over the lifetime of the product, is helpful. These resources may be tools, as with a bolt-cutter for defeating a bike chain; skills, such as deft movements for pickpocketing a music player; or more cognitive and social ones, such as intimidation or distraction techniques.

V. Responsibility for Secure
Product Design

Following the threads of causation back in time from the criminal event, the pathways to crime on the offender side are familiar and well addressed in this handbook. But upstream causes exist on the situational side, too (Clarke's concept of opportunity structure, for example (e.g., Clarke and Newman 2006)). Focusing on product design, we see a complex implementation chain of agents emerging. Take the Grippa clip as example: the agents are the customers who operate the security clips to protect their bags; the bar staff who maintain them and who encourage the customers to use them; the bar managers who install them and monitor their use; and the regional and central management of the bar company that issues instructions to the bar managers. Behind this operational chain is another, evolutionary chain of agents, one involving the marketers, manufacturers, designers, and ultimately the design decision makers who determine bag theft is a problem and set the designers working. All these agents carry some measure of responsibility for preventing the crime of bag theft—but it's generally of a civil, not criminal, kind. In the design-against-crime field, this responsibility extends to some combination of business and government.

A. The Roles of Business

Businesses relate to crime, and to the civil responsibility for prevention, in various ways.

- Businesses can be the corporate victims of crime, losing revenue—for example, through shoplifting of their merchandise, losing assets to damage or theft (such as computers); or losing customers because of the crime reputation of their premises or location. Businesses can suffer both individually, disadvantaging their competitive position, and collectively, affecting the profitability of a whole trade, such as the music industry, which suffers from illegal downloads.
- Their staff can be individual victims—for example, when a security officer is assaulted while challenging a shoplifter.
- They can generate crime, as with companies designing insecure vehicles, or expensive music players whose distinctive earphones betray their presence. This has been likened to an economic externality, where the company gets the profit, individual victims and taxpayers (funding police and criminal justice) suffer the costs, and young offenders are perhaps drawn into criminal careers— hence, an interest in "polluter pays" policies (Roman and Farrell 2002).
- They can profit from crime, replacing all those (easily) stolen items, or selling security/securing products (which may or may not be necessary or effective, and which may or may not boost fear of crime); or they can provide a service to mitigate crime, as with insurance companies.
- They can gain positive image from corporate social responsibility (Hardie and Hobbs 2005)—for example, sponsoring summer play schemes for young people, one aim of which may be crime prevention. This sanitized activity rarely touches on crime externalities from their mainstream business products, however.

Unless companies have something directly to lose, as with revenue or reputation, and without external pressure, they rarely assume responsibility for the prevention of crime associated with their products. "Naming and shaming" has been used, for example, to get unwilling mobile phone service providers to tighten security (the former Metropolitan Police Commissioner Sir John Stevens, and crime broadcaster Nick Ross, once publicly indicted the companies as "pimping for crime"). So has consumer pressure (Design Council 2000; Learmont 2005). The UK government publishes a car theft index that, since 1992 (Houghton 1992), has enabled purchasers to identify vehicle makes and models at particular risk. Combined with immobilizer legislation already described, and with pressure from insurance companies (which collectively attack-test new models and assign them a security rating that influences the insurance premium costs), this has succeeded in raising the priority manufacturers accord security, and nowadays they proclaim their security credentials in advertisements.

B. The Roles of Government

Government action has been implied in much of the above. Where the market fails to deliver secure products, governments wishing to reduce crime and considering that product design can contribute, must step in (Home Office, 2007a, pp. 33–37). Clarke and Newman (2005b) list diverse roles government can play, including direct procurement of secure products for their own use, incentivization, and establishing a research and development capacity. Government interest in product design in the UK has frustratingly waxed and waned over the last two decades (while police, courts, and corrections are ever in favor). A recent positive manifestation has, however, been the emergence of the Home Office–sponsored, and Design Council–serviced, Design and Technology Alliance against crime. This initiative, involving designers, industrialists, and academics, has generated prototypes for various products, including the safer beer glasses mentioned above and various mobile phone security initiatives. Governments have also indirectly fostered the field through public funding of research centers, including the Design Against Crime Research Centre (London); the Design Against Crime Solution Centre (Salford); and the Designing Out Crime Research Centre (Sydney).

Encouraging manufacturers and their designers to make products more secure is not straightforward, since business motivation is confined to self-interest (Clarke and Newman 2005b). Government has been reluctant, save in extreme circumstances (as with vehicle immobilizers and mobile phones), to make legal requirements to encourage crime prevention on a "polluter pays" basis. But it has shown interest in developing wider policy levers with which to influence business (Home Office 2006), including positive incentives, negative naming and shaming, and awakening consumer pressure as described. A framework—CLAIMED—to mobilize designers, and indeed all other potential crime preventers, is in Ekblom (2011) and at www.designagainstcrime.com/methodology-resources/crime-frameworks.

VI. Evaluation

Iterative assessment and feedback from workshop tests, field trials, user and service engineer experience, and ultimately sales, profitability, and market leadership are inherent to the iterative process of directed improvement that is product design

(Thorpe et al. 2009). These can be made more systematic in criminological terms through use of the Security Function framework to develop performance measures for purpose, niche, mechanism, and technology. In the impact evaluation and cost-effectiveness terms normally applied to crime prevention, however, there is unfortunately little hard evidence to report that relates to product design as opposed to target hardening and other situational approaches in general (see Eck and Guerette this volume). Such evidence as exists is often characterized by weak research designs; formally evaluated products were summarized in Clarke and Newman (2005b, table 4).

Circumstantial, correlational evidence points to the contribution of vehicle security technology toward the substantial and sustained reduction of theft of cars in the UK in recent years (Sallybanks and Brown 1999; Webb 2005). British Crime Survey figures (Home Office 2007b, table 2.01) show theft of vehicles reduced by 65 percent from 1995 to 2006–7 following the incorporation of improved security design into the vehicle. None of the case studies commissioned by the Design Council for the Home Office[10] has been formally evaluated. This contrasts with evaluation of built environment interventions (e.g., Armitage 2000).

Other evidence is more anecdotal in conventional terms but (as Clarke and Newman 2005b note) almost entirely self-evident. An example already mentioned is the plastic housing on the ends of train carriages to stop boys riding there. The most superficial glance reveals that there is now simply nowhere for them to stand. Self-evidence cannot be taken for granted, however (the ingenuity of adolescent males knows no bounds), and besides, this yields no information on comparative cost-effectiveness.

A recent study (Sidebottom, Johnson, and Thorpe 2009) of attempts to reduce bike theft by installing advisory stickers on the bike stands[11] has yielded reliable intermediate outcome evidence—important where behavioral change of people acting as crime preventers or promoters (Ekblom 2011) is sought. The stickers were designed following systematic observation of bike-locking behavior and analysis of perpetrator techniques. Their simple advice—lock both wheels and frame to the stand—led to a significant and substantial reduction (from 62 to 48 percent of observations) in the proportion of bikes locked in ways judged insecure.

Another recently completed project[12] sought to mount a rigorous field evaluation of second-generation antitheft clips to secure customers' bags to bar tables—the Grippas already mentioned. Despite intensive design effort and contextual research (e.g., Sidebottom and Bowers 2010), "involvement failures" (Ekblom, forthcoming) occurred at every stage of the implementation chain. The customers, though liking the clips and approving the concept, didn't use them; the bar staff, weakly motivated and directed by their immediate managers in turn, didn't encourage customers to use them; bar managers and regional managers frequently moved on; the original, supportive, senior management team of the company was removed. Following a trial in two pilot bars prior to a full 13-site action bar, 14-site control bar quasi-experimental impact evaluation, the bar company (probably due to the 2008 financial crisis and relaxation of police pressure to reduce thefts), unilaterally pulled out of the project.

Although disappointing, this experience yielded valuable lessons for the impact evaluation of product design. A major issue in designing the evaluation itself was in deciding on statistical power. The production cost for prototype hardware is high— the final Grippas cost almost $14 each, and coverage of all seats at all tables could be over a hundred per bar, so in order to remain in budget while maximizing power, a spreadsheet program[13] was developed to enable the team to consider alternative practical combinations of cost, effort (number of bars to be fitted), and an indicator of power. This was later modified to take account of the J-curve (Eck, Clarke, and Guerette 2007) that was found in the bar crime counts (a few bars accounted for most of the crime), leading to economies in the planned action bars. The work, summarized as CRITIC,[14] is further described in Bowers, Sidebottom, and Ekblom (2009).

But the effort to find hard evidence must continue; only then will design against crime fare better in securing sustained funding and attention from government. The evidence may also help convince consumers to prefer products so designed and manufacturers to include security in their requirements capture.

VII. Discussion and Conclusions

Design against crime as a whole is simultaneously a narrow domain of intervention within situational crime prevention and a broad approach that can contribute to every kind of preventive intervention and, indeed, to every stage of the preventive process. Bringing together innovation, technology, business, and government, it faces as many practical and policy challenges as the rest of crime prevention, plus some uniquely its own. To surmount these challenges and realize the promise, the narrower domain requires consistent (rather than blow-with-the-wind) government support, pressure from police, and an awakened consumer interest to overcome market failure and establish a climate where products (and places, systems, and services) are simply expected to be fit and proportionately adapted for all purposes, including safety and security.

It is also necessary to accumulate a substantial body of reliable evidence showing cost-effectiveness and benefit to diverse stakeholders in public and private domains; and to identify contextual factors and mechanisms that determine success or failure. This, too, cannot seriously be attempted without sufficient funding and sustained commitment and effort. Moreover, this task must continually be repeated because social, commercial, and technological change means that what works, where, and now cannot be guaranteed to work in the indefinite future. Designers, too, must be trained and inspired to address safety and security issues. Beyond this, understanding and influencing the psychological, socio-cultural, and organizational context of alerting, informing, motivating, empowering, and perhaps directing people to design, manufacture, purchase, install, and use products with an enhanced security function is as much a challenge as undertaking the central design task, and a potentially major constraint. This involvement domain (Ekblom 2011, forthcoming) requires an action-research–based understanding of incentives, markets, social marketing, and social (rather than purely technological) innovation; and a capacity to handle complex adaptive systems (Chapman 2004).

The broader approach requires injecting a certain mindset and approach—the design way of thinking—into the practice of crime prevention of all kinds and at all levels. To make this happen necessitates training, the creation of a body of rich and inspiring exemplars; knowledge capture of the processes of design and those of the transfer of design knowledge; and the willingness of designers to share their expertise and open up their professional defensible space to others. However, the benefit from such an investment and a lowering of barriers should itself not be assumed, but assessed.

NOTES

1. www.index2005.dk/Members/mefebo/NEW_workObject#.
2. www.designagainstcrime.com/index.php?q=dacimages.
3. www.designagainstcrime.com/index.php?q=dacimages.
4. www.grippaclip.com.
5. www.designagainstcrime.com/index.php?q=dacimages.
6. Such as the Anti Terror Bag and Tag, which normalizes emergency conditions. This is a see-through duffle style bag that the manufacturers argue is "perfect for use under the current climate of terror threats at airports and many other commuter areas."
7. This and other case studies obtained for the UK Home Office are described in depth at http://extra.shu.ac.uk/dac/casdown.html and www.designcouncil.org.uk/Case-studies/Design-Out-Crime/.
8. www.designcouncil.org.uk/about-us/Media-centre/World-first-prototype-pint-glasses-developed/and see research on safer beer glasses reviewed by Shepherd (1994).
9. www.grippaclip.com.
10. See note 6.
11. www.bikeoff.org/2007/03/12/lock-the-frame-and-both-wheels-to-the-stand-sticker/.
12. Mainly funded by UK Arts and Humanities Research Council.
13. www.grippaclip.com/publications/academic-papers/critics-link-to-spreadsheet-calculator.
14. CRITIC is a systematic prospective planning tool intended to raise awareness and discuss the effect, on the likelihood of statistically significant outcome analyses and cost-effective results, of the following: crime history (how crime-prone the action and control sites are), reduction (proportional reduction in the crime problem anticipated in the action sites compared to controls), intensity (number and/or strength of interventions per target exposed to crime risk), time period (over which action and control sites are tracked before and after implementation), immensity (number of units of analysis at risk of crime to be tracked), and cost (unit cost per intervention).

REFERENCES

Armitage, Rachel. 2000. *An Evaluation of Secured by Design Housing, in West York-shire.* Policing and Reducing Crime Unit Briefing Note 7/00. London: Home Office.

Armitage, Rachel, and Ken Pease. 2007. "Predicting and Preventing the Theft of Electronic Products." *European Journal on Criminal Policy and Research* 14:11–17.

Booch, Grady. 1993. *Object-Oriented Analysis and Design with Applications,* 2nd ed. Boston: Addison-Wesley.

Bowers, Kate, Aiden Sidebottom, and Paul Ekblom. 2009. "CRITIC: A Prospective Planning Tool for Crime Prevention Evaluation Designs." *Crime Prevention and Community Safety* 11:48–70.

Chapman, Jake. 2004. *System Failure: Why Governments Must Learn to Think Differently.* London: Demos.

Clarke, Ronald. 1999. *Hot Products: Understanding, Anticipating and Reducing Demand for Stolen Goods.* Police Research Series Papers 112. London: Home Office.

Clarke, Ronald, and John Eck. 2003. *Become a Problem Solving Crime Analyst in 55 Small Steps.* London: Jill Dando Institute, University College London. Available from www. jdi.ucl.ac.uk/publications/manual/crime_manual_content.php.

Clarke, Ronald, and Graeme Newman. 2005a. "Secured by Design. A Plan for Security Coding of Electronic Products." In *Designing out Crime from Products and Systems.* Vol. 18 of *Crime Prevention Studies,* edited by Ronald Clarke and Graeme Newman. Monsey, NY: Criminal Justice Press and Cullompton, UK: Willan.

Clarke, Ronald, and Graeme Newman. 2005b. "Modifying Criminogenic Products—What Role for Government?" In *Designing out Crime from Products and Systems.* Vol. 18 of *Crime Prevention Studies,* edited by Ronald Clarke and Graeme Newman. Cullompton, UK: Willan.

Clarke, Ronald, and Graeme Newman. 2006. *Outsmarting the Terrorists.* London: Praeger Security International.

Cohen, Lawrence, and Marcus Felson. 1979. "Social Change and Crime Rate Changes: A Routine Activities Approach." *American Sociological Review* 44:588–608.

Cornish, Derek. 1994. "The Procedural Analysis of Offending and its Relevance for Situational Prevention." In *Crime Prevention Studies,* vol. 3, edited by Ronald Clarke. Monsey, NY: Criminal Justice Press.

Cornish, Derek, and Ronald Clarke. 1986. *The Reasoning Criminal.* New York: Springer-Verlag.

Cozens, Paul, Greg Saville, and David Hillier. 2005. "Crime Prevention Through Environmental Design (CPTED): A Review and Modern Bibliography." *Property Management* 23:328–56.

Cropley, David. 2010. "The Dark Side of Creativity—A Differentiated Model." In *Creativity: The Dark Side,* edited by David Cropley, J. Kaufman, A. Cropley, and M. Runco. Cambridge, UK: Cambridge University Press.

Department of Trade and Industry. 2000. *Turning the Corner. Report of Foresight Pro-gramme's Crime Prevention Panel.* London: Department of Trade and Industry.

Design Council. 2000. *Design Against Crime. A Report to the Design Council, The Home Office and the Department of Trade and Industry.* Cambridge, Salford, and Sheffield Hallam Universities. Available online at www.shu.ac.uk/schools/cs/cri/adrc/dac/designagainstcrimereport.pdf.

Eck, John, Ronald Clarke, and Rob Guerette. 2007. "Risky Facilities: Crime Concentration in Homogeneous Sets of Establishments and Facilities." In *Imagination for Crime Prevention: Essays in Honor of Ken Pease.* Vol. 21 of *Crime Prevention Studies,* edited by Graham Farrell, Kate Bowers, Shane Johnson, and Mike Townsley. Monsey, NY: Criminal Justice Press.

Ekblom, Paul. 1997. "Gearing up against Crime: A Dynamic Framework to Help Designers Keep up with the Adaptive Criminal in a Changing World." *International Journal of Risk, Security and Crime Prevention* 2:249–65.

Ekblom, Paul. 1999. "Can we Make Crime Prevention Adaptive by Learning from other Evolutionary Struggles?" *Studies on Crime and Crime Prevention* 8(1): 2–51.

Ekblom, Paul. 2005a. "Designing Products against Crime." In *Handbook of Crime Prevention and Community Safety,* edited by Nick Tilley. Cullompton, UK: Willan.

Ekblom, Paul. 2005b. "How to Police the Future: Scanning for Scientific and Technological Innovations which Generate Potential Threats and Opportunities in Crime, Policing and Crime Reduction." In *Crime Science: New Approaches to Preventing and Detecting Crime,* edited by Melissa Smith, and Nick Tilley. Cullompton, UK: Willan.

Ekblom, Paul. 2007. "Making Offenders Richer." In *Imagination for Crime Prevention: Essays in Honor of Ken Pease.* Vol. 21 of *Crime Prevention Studies,* edited by Graham Farrell, Kate Bowers, Shane Johnson, and Mike Townsley. Cullompton, UK: Willan.

Ekblom, Paul. 2008. "Designing Products against Crime." In *Environmental Criminology and Crime Analysis,* edited by Richard Wortley and Lorraine Mazerolle. Cullompton, UK: Willan.

Ekblom, Paul. 2009. "Standard Generation through Application of CCO Framework." Final report WPA2 of "Bike Off 2—Catalysing Anti Theft Bike, Bike Parking and Information Design for the 21st Century." At www.bikeoff.org/2009/01/05/final-report-wpa2-of-bike-off-2/.

Ekblom, Paul. 2011. *Crime Prevention, Security and Community Safety using the 5Is Framework.* Basingstoke, UK: Palgrave Macmillan.

Ekblom, Paul. 2012a. "The Security Function Framework." In *Design Against Crime: Crime Proofing Everyday Objects.* Vol. 27 of *Crime Prevention Studies,* edited by Paul Ekblom. Boulder, CO: Lynne Rienner.

Ekblom, Paul. 2012b. "Happy Returns: Ideas Brought Back from Situational Crime Prevention's Exploration of Design Against Crime." In *The Reasoning Criminologist: Essays in Honour of Ronald V. Clarke,* edited by Graham Farrell and Nick Tilley. Crime Science series. Cullompton, UK: Willan.

Ekblom, Paul. Forthcoming. "Citizen Participation in Crime Prevention—Capturing Practice Knowledge Through the 5Is Framework." In *International Perspectives of Crime Prevention: Contributions from the 4th Annual International Forum,* edited by Marc Coester and Erich Marks. Forum Verlag: Mönchengladbach.

Ekblom, Paul, Kate Bowers, Lorraine Gamman, Aiden Sidebottom, Chris Thomas, Adam Thorpe, and Marcus Willcocks. 2012. "Reducing Bag Theft in Bars." In *Design Against Crime: Crime Proofing Everyday Objects.* Vol. 27 of *Crime Prevention Studies,* edited by Paul Ekblom. Boulder, CO: Lynne Rienner.

Ekblom, Paul, and Nick Tilley. 2000. "Going Equipped: Criminology, Situational Crime Prevention and the Resourceful Offender." *British Journal of Criminology* 40:376–98.

Ekblom, Paul, and Aiden Sidebottom. 2007. "What Do You Mean, 'Is it secure?' Redesigning Language to be Fit for the Task of Assessing the Security of Domestic and Personal Electronic Goods." *European Journal on Criminal Policy and Research* 14:61–87.

Felson, Marcus. 1997 "Technology, Business, and Crime." In *Business and Crime Prevention*, edited by Marcus Felson, and Ronald Clarke. Monsey, NY: Criminal Justice Press.

Gamman, Lorraine, and Adam Thorpe. 2007. "Profit from Paranoia—Design Against 'Paranoid' Products." European Academy of Design conference 07: Dancing with Disorder: Design, Discourse, Disaster, Izmir, Turkey. Available at www.bikeoff.org/2007/04/30/profit-from-paranoia-design-against-paranoid-products/.

Gamman, Lorraine, and Adam Thorpe. 2009. "The Design Against Crime Evolved Twin Track Model of the Iterative Design Process." Available at www.designagainstcrime.com/index.php?q=designmethodology.

Gill, Martin. 2005. "Reducing the Capacity to Offend: Restricting Resources for Offending." In *Handbook of Crime Prevention and Community Safety*, edited by Nick Tilley. Cullompton, UK: Willan.

Hardie, Jeremy, and Ben Hobbs. 2005. "Partners against Crime—the Role of the Corporate Sector in Tackling Crime." *Designing out Crime from Products and Systems*. Vol. 18 of *Crime Prevention Studies*, edited by Ronald Clarke and Graeme Newman. Monsey, NY: Criminal Justice Press and Cullompton, UK: Willan.

HM Treasury. 2005. *The Cox Review of Creativity in Business*. London: HM Treasury.

Home Office. 2006. "Changing Behaviour to Prevent Crime: an Incentives-Based Approach." Online report 05/06. London: Home Office. www.homeoffice.gov.uk/rds/pdfs06/rdsolr0506.pdf.

Home Office. 2007a. Cutting Crime. *A new Partnership 2008–2011*. London: Home Office. http://webarchive.nationalarchives.gov.uk/20100413151441/homeoffice.gov.uk/documents/crime-strategy-07/.

Home Office. 2007b. *Crime in England and Wales 2006/2007*. Statistical Bulletin 11/07. London: Home Office.

Home Office/Office of the Deputy Prime Minister. 2004. *Safer Places: The Planning System and Crime Prevention*. London: Department for Communities and Local Government.

Houghton, George. 1992. *Car Theft in England & Wales. The Home Office Car Theft Index*. CPU Paper 33. London: Home Office.

Learmont, Simon. 2005. "Design Against Crime." In *Designing out Crime from Products and Systems*. Vol. 18 of *Crime Prevention Studies*, edited by Ronald Clarke, and Graeme Newman. Monsey, NY: Criminal Justice Press and Cullompton, UK: Willan.

Meyer, Sunniva, and Paul Ekblom. Forthcoming. "Specifying the Explosion-Resistant Railway Carriage—A 'Bench' Test of the Security Function Framework." *Journal of Transportation Security*. Published 'online first' 2011 at http://www.springerlink.com/content/qj3541v703765145/

Norman, Donald. 2004. *Emotional Design: Why We Love (or Hate) Everyday Things*. New York: Basic Books.

Pawson, Ray, and Nick Tilley. 1997. *Realistic Evaluation*. London: Sage.

Pease, Ken. 2001. *Cracking Crime through Design*. London: Design Council Publications.

Rogerson, Michelle, Paul Ekblom, and Ken Pease. 2000. "Crime Reduction and the Benefit of Foresight" In *Secure Foundations: Key Issues in Crime Prevention, Crime Reduction and Community Safety*, edited by Stuart Ballintyne, Ken Pease, and Vic McLaren. London: Institute for Public Policy Research.

Roman, John, and Graham Farrell. 2002. "Cost-benefit Analysis for Crime Prevention: Opportunity Costs, Routine Savings and Crime Externalities." In *Evaluation for Crime Prevention*. Vol.14 of *Crime Prevention Studies*, edited by Nick Tilley. Cullompton, UK: Willan.

Sallybanks, Jo-Anne, and Rick Brown. 1999. *Vehicle Crime Reduction: Turning the Corner*. Police Research Series Paper 119. London: Home Office.

Shepherd, Jonathan. 1994. "Preventing Injuries from Bar Glasses." *British Medical Journal* 308:932–33.

Sidebottom, Aiden, and Kate Bowers. 2010. "Bag Theft in Bars: An Analysis of Relative Risk, Perceived Risk and Modus Operandi." *Security Journal* 23:206–24.

Sidebottom, Aiden, Shane Johnson, and Adam Thorpe. 2009. "Using Targeted Publicity to Reduce Opportunities for Bicycle Theft: A Demonstration and Replication." *European Journal of Criminology* 6:267–86.

Thorpe, Adam, Lorraine Gamman, Paul Ekblom, Shane Johnson, and Aiden Sidebottom. 2009. "Bike Off 2—Catalysing Anti-Theft Bike, Bike Parking and Information Design for the 21st Century: an Open Innovation Research Approach." In *Designing for the 21st Century: Volume 2. Interdisciplinary Methods and Findings*, edited by Tom Inns. Farnham, UK: Gower.

Webb, Barry. 2005. "Preventing Vehicle Crime." In *Handbook of Crime Prevention and Community Safety*, edited by Nick Tilley. Cullompton, UK: Willan.

Whitehead, Shaun, Jen Mailley, Ian Storer, John McCardle, George Torrens, and Graham Farrell. 2008. "IN SAFE HANDS: A Review of Mobile Phone Anti-theft Designs." *European Journal on Criminal Policy and Research* 14(1): 39–60.

Wortley, Richard. 2008. "Situational Precipitators of Crime." In *Environmental Criminology and Crime Analysis*, edited by Richard Wortley and Lorraine Mazerolle. Cullompton, UK: Willan.

CHAPTER 20

ONCE BITTEN, TWICE SHY: REPEAT VICTIMIZATION AND ITS PREVENTION

LOUISE GROVE AND GRAHAM FARRELL

THE subject of this essay is the prevention of repeat victimization. Repeat victimization is the repeated criminal victimization of a person, household, business, place, vehicle, or other target, however defined. Around 40 years of research show that crime is not randomly distributed and that this is largely because targets already victimized are at much greater risk than others. In fact, most crimes are repeats of some sort. One classic study found that 1 percent of people experience 59 percent of personal crime, including violence, and that 2 percent of households experience 41 percent of property crime (Pease 1998). The most chronically victimized people and places are known as supertargets (Farrell et al. 2005).

The same perpetrators often commit repeats. This is because they have learned how to successfully victimize a target and know it will be easier next time around. Crimes are often repeated quickly, minimizing the likelihood that anything has changed. For example, burglars return quickly if they know what they left behind and know the household layout - though some may wait a few weeks for insurance payments to replace stolen goods, as found by Clarke, Perkins and Smith (2001). Even relatively rare crimes such as street robbery are experienced disproportionately by the same victims, perhaps because they cannot change their travel route or because they know the offender—as with much school bullying robbery and assaults. And success breeds repeats: bank robbers return more often to the same branch when they escape with significant amounts of money (Matthews, Pease, and Pease 2001).

Different offenders may also victimize the same target. A store that is a lucrative target because it handles a lot of cash but has little security, or a row-end house that other houses do not overlook (so it has less guardianship), or a car frequently parked in the same risky spot, may attract different offenders who may also return.

Repeat victimization can involve different crime types. Some schools are frequent targets of vandalism as well as break-ins (Lindstrom 1997). Within any particular group of targets, some of them are more prone to repeats than others, so there are some risky professions, risky facilities, risky vehicles, risky places, and risky lifestyles. For example, nurses, firefighters, police officers, and other service or caring professions are more likely to experience crime, and within those groups, certain individuals are far more frequently victimized than others (Clare, Kingsley, and Morgan 2009). Lifestyle plays a role more generally (Hindelang, Gottfredson, and Garafalo 1978). A person who goes out often, say to bars and clubs, may experience assault and theft while out and also a break-in if his or her property is left unguarded. Offenders also become victims, as when drug dealers and customers rob each other because they have money and drugs and are unlikely to call the police.

Not only are the same targets prone to further crime but so, too, are similar targets. Following a successful burglary, a neighboring household may be targeted in anticipation of similar success (Townsley, Homel, and Chaseling 2003; Bowers and Johnson 2004; Bernasco 2008; Short et al. 2009). This is known as near repeat victimization or near repeats. In addition to the spatial nearness of neighbors, the concept of nearness can apply to other characteristics of a crime. The theft of frequently stolen hot products such as smartphones and laptops is a form of near repeat because of the repetition of the characteristics of the target. Repeat victimization often causes geographical concentrations of crime known as hot spots (Levy and Tarturo 2010). The result is that the study of repeats is beginning to merge with other areas of crime concentration. The key issue is that of the similarity of crimes. Very similar crimes afford greater potential for prediction and prevention than those that are dissimilar. We are, however, yet to develop practical indices of similarity to improve efforts to address concentrations of crime.

There are now dozens of studies of different crime types across a wide range of countries that find similar patterns of repeat victimization. An annotated online bibliography by the present authors (Grove and Farrell 2011) lists studies relating to Australia, Canada, Denmark, Germany, Hungary, the Netherlands, New Zealand, Poland, Spain, Sweden, the United Kingdom, and the United States, plus comparative analysis of repeat victimization in 17 industrialized countries.

The importance of repeat victimization for crime prevention is that it means we should know where and when to go, and what to do, to prevent crime. This is because crime occurs against the same people and at the same places, and because if we know how the crime occurred previously, then we are more informed about how to go about preventing its recurrence. Hence, the essence of this crime-prevention theory is that *targeting repeats and near repeats provides a means of allocating crime-prevention resources in an efficient and informed manner.*

This essay explains how the evidence strongly suggests that preventing repeat victimization can be an effective crime-prevention strategy. However, it also shows that there has been variation in the successes, and that reducing crime it is not necessarily easy. Even if we know where and when crime will occur, it is not always clear what to do to prevent it. Crimes vary greatly by place, time, and type of crime, which means the same prevention tactics do not necessarily transfer. It is also not always easy to introduce crime-prevention tactics in the manner that we might want. Public funds for crime prevention are rarely available, and some victimized householders and business owners are unwilling or unable to spend money on prevention even though it could be cost-effective in the long run. Hence, the design of tactics and their implementation are important issues that we will also discuss.

The main points of this essay are that:

- Most crime occurs as a form of repeat victimization.
- The chronically victimized supertargets are typically 1 or 2 percent of potential targets but experience half or more of crime.
- A comprehensive review of the evidence suggests repeat victimization can be prevented and overall crime thereby reduced.
- The impact of prevention efforts varies, with reduced success due to failure to develop or implement appropriate crime prevention tactics.
- This significant potential suggests there is a dire need for further efforts to prevent different types of repeats.

Here is how this essay is structured. Section I summarizes key issues in research, policy, and practice that have emerged from repeat victimization research to date. Section II examines the effectiveness of previous efforts to prevent repeat victimization, and section III looks at how prevention efforts were developed and implemented. Section IV is a short conclusion with a discussion of future research.

I. Joined-Up Research, Policy, and Practice

A range of research has identified different characteristics of repeat and near repeat victimization. Many of them are summarized in table 20.1, which indicates the relevance to crime prevention of each research finding. The strong relationship among research, policy, and practice is a key characteristic of this area of crime prevention. Gloria Laycock, formerly head of the UK government unit that oversaw development of much of the research, has documented the story of how it evolved (Laycock 2001). Laycock notes that the Kirkholt burglary-prevention project was a landmark. It used a crime analysis problem-solving approach to identify multiple tactics focused on preventing repeat residential burglary, successfully implemented to dramatic effect. The Kirkholt project served as a catalyst for much of the research that followed. We will not describe table 20.1 in detail here because it should be self-explanatory, but it requires close scrutiny by the reader.

Table 20.1 Key research findings and their strategic implications

Research Finding	Implication
1. Most crime is repeat victimization of the same targets.	Preventing repeats would prevent most crime.
2. Repeat victimization occurs for all crime types except murder (which can be a repeat assault)	Preventing repeats can be a general crime prevention strategy.
3. Two+ percent of potential targets are usually the supertargets that experience half or so of all crime.	Focus more resources on supertargets.
4. High-crime areas have high levels of repeats.	Focusing on repeats naturally allocates resources to high-crime areas and hot spots.
5. Repeats and near repeats show as hot spots on maps.	Analysts should be aware that hot spots are repeat victimization locations.
6. Repeats occur after a previous crime, not all at once.	The gradual drip-feeding of crime prevention reduces strain on resources and personnel.
7. There is a broad spectrum of near repeats to targets with similar characteristics and situations.	Be aware of risk at nearby and similar targets and situations.
8. Spatially near repeats–e.g., of neighboring households–have increased risk.	Cocoon watch and similar local measures may be appropriate.
9. Frequent theft of hot products is a form of near repeat (often a tactical repeat).	Beware crimes against the same product types (esp. using same modus operandi).
10. Risky facilities identifies repeat victimization of schools, businesses, etc.	Focus on repeats to target risky facilities.
11. Repeats are committed disproportionately by same offenders returning.	Focus on repeats to detect repeat and prolific offenders.
12. Other offenders also repeat at attractive vulnerable targets.	Focus on repeats to detect repeat and prolific offenders.
13. Risk increases with each repeat—e.g., a 3rd more likely than 2nd, and so on.	Allocate more crime-prevention resources to risky targets.
14. Repeats more likely when crime is a success (e.g., successful bank robbers return).	Prioritize crimes where offender succeeded.
15. Repeats occur quickly—risk is highest soon after crime.	Put crime-prevention resources in place quickly (temporarily if necessary).
16. Risk of displacement is less when repeats prevented.	Lower displacement risk means prevention is more efficient.
17. Repeats often use the same tactics or modus operandi.	Prevent repeats by that modus operandi; tactics should be locally and individually appropriate.
18. Known tactics can be focused on repeats.	New crime-prevention tactics are not necessarily needed.

continued

Table 20.1 (continued)

Research Finding	Implication
19. The focus on repeats can generate new tactical insight.	New crime-prevention tactics may be suggested by the nature of repeats.
20. Strong preventive mechanism work best to prevent crime.	Appropriate situational measures often effective where appropriate.
21. Victims may fail to implement prevention (due to lack of money or motivation).	Practical assistance (e.g., free security and installation), follow-ups, and other nudges are better than advice alone.
22. Victim support services may assist.	Victim services adopt a prevention focus to empower victims.
23. Police are empowered to assist victims.	Victim-oriented policing and good police-community relations can result.

II. The Success of Prevention Efforts

The majority of evaluated prevention efforts to date relate to burglary. The types of prevention tactics varied by crime type and place. Interventions for residential burglary and commercial burglary often included an initial security survey followed by securitization of properties. This usually involved improving locks on vulnerable doors and windows, but also other techniques such as reinforcing doors. Alarms were occasionally given or loaned to victims, including repeat victims of domestic violence. Property marking for burglary victims was often facilitated by the provision of either SmartWater (a microdot solution that can be uniquely identified) or access to a property register, usually with decals (stickers) to promote deterrence. Neighborhood Watch, or the smaller Cocoon Watch among nearby neighbors, programs were established within some repeat burglary or domestic violence projects. Less common measures included offender-focused interventions, blocking off access to rear alleys used by burglars, and media publicity to promote deterrence.

The impact on crime varied a lot across projects and is only summarized here, drawing on the review by Grove et al. forthcoming; see also Grove 2010; Farrell and Pease 2006). A summary of key indicators is shown in table 20.2. The table lists studies chronologically by crime type. Residential burglary is first because it accounts for 22 of the 31 studies that have been evaluated, then domestic violence, commercial burglary, and sexual victimization. Study identifiers (often the location name), date of the evaluation's publication, and the crime type to be prevented are shown in the first three columns. The two main outcome indicators are the change in repeats and the change in the overall level of crime. There had been evaluations conducted where preventing repeats was part of a broader crime-prevention effort, but these are not included if the repeat victimization component could not be distinguished.[1]

Table 20.2 Summary of outcomes for repeat victimization prevention studies

Evaluation	Author and Year	Crime type	Change in repeats	Change in overall crime count (incidence)	Summary as +ve or -ve (u= uncertain)[1]
Kirkholt	Forrester et al. 1988, 1990	Residential burglary	-100%	-62.8%	+
St. Anns	Gregson 1992	Residential burglary	NA	-9.2%	+
The Meadows	Gregson and Hocking, 1993	Residential burglary	-40.4%	-57.5%	+
Eyres Monsell	Matthews and Trickey, 1994a	Residential burglary	Yes	-6%	+
New Parks	Matthews and Trickey, 1994b	Residential burglary	-50%	+17.5%	u[A]
Huddersfield	Anderson et al. 1995	Residential burglary	Equivocal	-30%	+
Blackburn	Webb 1996	Residential burglary	-68.8%	-62%	+
Burnley	Webb 1996	Residential burglary	-33.3%	-27.2%	+
Lambeth	Webb 1996	Residential burglary	NA	-80%	+
Merthyr Tydfil	Webb 1996	Residential burglary	-92%	-26%	+
Cambridge	Bennett and Durie 1999	Residential burglary	No	+13.8%	-
Baltimore	Weisel et al. 1999	Residential burglary	No	-23.7%	u[B]
Dallas	Weisel et al. 1999	Residential burglary	No	+16%	-
San Diego	Weisel et al. 1999	Residential burglary	No	-24.7%	u[B]
Beenleigh	Budz et al. 2001	Residential burglary	>-15%	+9.9%	u[A]
Ashfield	Taplin and Falherty 2001	Residential burglary	Equivocal	+1.8%	-
Tea Tree Gully	Morgan and Walter 2002	Residential burglary	Equivocal	+7.5%	-
Liverpool	Bowers et al., 2003	Residential burglary	-70.5%	-39.2%	+

continued

Table 20.1 (continued)

Evaluation	Author and Year	Crime type	Change in repeats	Change in overall crime count (incidence)	Summary as +ve or -ve (u= uncertain)[1]
Hartlepool	Sturgeon-Adams et al. 2005	Residential burglary	Yes	-18.3%	+
Bentley	Cummings 2005	Residential burglary	Yes	-26.2%	+
Morley	Cummings 2005	Residential burglary	Yes	+2%	u[A]
NDV[2]	Morgan 2004	Domestic violence	Yes	-8.2%	+
Multnomah	Pearson 1980	Commercial	Yes	-14.9%	+
Leicester	Taylor 1999; Tilley and Hopkins 1998	Commercial	Yes	-19.7%	+
Merseyside	Bowers 2001	Commercial	Yes	-39.2%	+
		Note that the five sexual victimization projects below refer to crime prevalence not incidence.			
Sexual Assault Prevention	Hanson and Gidycz 1993	Sexual	NA	-17.8%	+
Reduce multiple sexual victimization	Breitenbecher and Gidycz 1998	Sexual	NA	-2%[3]	+
Sexual Victimization Prevention	Marx et al. 2001	Sexual	NA	-36%	+
Acquaintance rape prevention	Gidycz et al. 2001	Sexual	NA	12.1%	-
New York and Seattle Field Test	Davis et al. 2006	Sexual	NA	-10.3%	+

[1] u = uncertain where the superscript A denotes three sites where repeats fell but incidence increased, and superscript B denotes two sites where repeats did not decrease but incidence did. See text for further details.
[2] Outcomes measured as domestic violence calls to the police.
[3] Note that the five sexual victimization projects show change in crime prevalence not incidence in the fifth column.

Whether a reduction in repeat victimization was found among those receiving the crime-prevention effort (the intervention group) is shown in the fourth column of table 20.2. By this indicator, repeats fell in over 80 percent—that is, in 17 out of 21 studies. In the other 10 studies, the extent of change in repeats was unknown. On average, repeats were reduced by more than half (mean = 56 percent, median = 54 percent) across the 14 studies where it was measured. However, there was wide variation, from one project where repeats were eliminated to one where the best estimate was that repeats fell 10 percent. Readers interested in evaluation method should note that repeat victimization was typically not measured in comparison groups.

For each study, overall crime—not just repeats—in the intervention group was compared to a similar group. The aim of such comparison is to try to rule out the possibility that any change in crime was due to factors other than the intervention. This process of counterfactual inference is possible when both groups have all factors in common other than the intervention. For example, a national fall in crime would be experienced in both an intervention and the comparison area, and so it could be distinguished from the effect of the intervention: only the remainder of any fall in crime can be reasonably attributed to the intervention in such an instance. There was some variation in the extent to which comparison groups were comparable to their intervention groups.

The fifth column of table 20.2 shows the percentage change in the overall crime count in the intervention group relative to the comparison group. The sixth column shows whether the project had a positive outcome of reduced overall crime, denoted by + (plus), or a negative outcome of increased crime, denoted by – (minus). Five studies are categorized as uncertain, or u, due to apparently conflicting indicators. With those five excluded, 73 percent, or 19 of 26 studies, reduced both repeats and crime incidence. Crime was reduced on average across the studies by a fifth (mean = 21.4 percent, median = 19.7 percent).[2]

Another way to examine this data is represented in figure 20.1, which shows impact as an effect size (the point) with confidence intervals around it (the lines) for each study. Many but not all of the studies listed in table 20.2 could be included in this analysis. This more conservative analysis suggests 13 of 21 studies (62 percent) reduced crime, but only five studies showed that with greater statistical certainty (where the confidence interval does not cross the value of 1, which would indicate no effect). The overall key indicator here is the weighted mean effect size of 1.22 (CIs: 1.06–1.40), shown at the base of the chart. This indicator supports the previous ones and strongly suggests that crime can be prevented.[3]

The conclusion of this fairly conservative assessment is that it is possible to prevent repeat victimization and that this can reduce crime overall. However, there can be quite some variation in impact across time and place. Consequently, the next section looks at why some efforts succeed more than others.

III. Development and Implementation of Prevention Tactics

A key problem is that it is often difficult to get prevention measures put in place, or implemented, for various reasons. It was possible to gauge the extent of implementation and figure 20.2 shows the relationship between implementation rate and

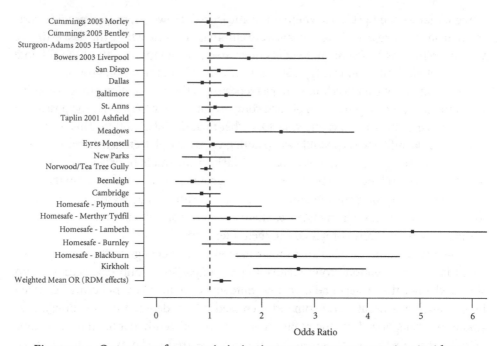

Figure 20.1 Outcomes of repeat victimization programmes upon crime incidence (odds ratios with confidence intervals)

impact on crime for the 19 studies where both measures were available. The implementation rate is the percentage of those eligible who received the prevention measure. The impact on crime is the percentage change in crime relative to the comparison group. Where the intervention was given to victims as "advice," the implementation rate was measured as the percent of those eligible who followed the advice by implementing the prevention tactics.[4]

Figure 20.2 shows a generally positive relationship between implementation and impact. Were the data of better quality, or implementation easier to gauge, then perhaps the relationship would be stronger. The linear best fit line does not fit the data well ($R^2 = 0.413$), but if taken literally it suggests that a project must implement measures at a minimum of more than a fifth of targets (22.5 percent) before any impact is achieved, that every 0.6 percent additional increase in the implementation rate brings a further 1 percent reduction in crime, and that crime is eliminated when implementation exceeds 80 percent (81.5 percent). Clearly, the best fit line cannot be interpreted so literally, but it may be indicative of the overall nature of the relationship between implementation and impact.

The three overarching determinants of success in efforts to prevent repeat victimization were:

1. Successful conception and development of a functioning project.
2. Identification of locally appropriate and effective preventive tactics.
3. Thorough implementation of those tactics.

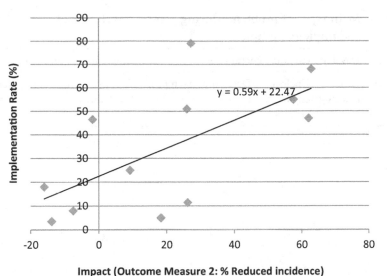

Figure 20.2 Relationship between implementation rate and impact on crime

In some instances the crime-prevention tactic was inappropriate as it was not tailored to the crime problem. For some of the burglary projects in particular, it seemed that 'the usual' target-hardening security measures were introduced without checking whether or not they were appropriate to the type of burglary problem or whether other tactics were also needed. The type of measures needed varies by time and place. For example, prevention measures appropriate to prevent burglary of inner-city apartments are not necessarily the same as those for suburban burglary.

Sexual victimization prevention schemes emphasized the education of repeat victims, with the provision of general advice on how to avoid or manage risky situations. The specific nature of this advice was not necessarily clear in all of the evaluation reports. However, a key problem with education is that it may change attitudes without necessarily changing behavior or situations, or if behavior and situations are changed, it is not necessarily in a way that prevents crime. Such problems with the identification of effective prevention measures are categorized in table 20.3 as "lack of tailoring."

Some burglary prevention projects compromised their focus. In some instances they were required to provide security to other sections of the population deemed vulnerable by local agencies, such as elderly people and single mothers. This meant that it was not only the prevention of repeat victimization being evaluated. For present purposes, this is categorized as "unclear eligibility criteria."

Four types of implementation problems appeared to arise. "Staff problems" relate to the staff employed to implement the project: it is often difficult to recruit staff, to train staff, to retain staff, and to ensure that staff are undertaking work in the desired manner. "Communications breakdown" could be detrimental and are quite common in multi-agency projects where different agencies and parties are involved with different goals and different means of achieving them. Projects with "inflexibility"

Table 20.3 **Main types of problems during project development and implementation**

Evaluation study	Development and General Issues				Implementation Issues		
	Lack of tailoring	Unclear eligibility criteria	Data problems	Staff probs	Comms break down	Inflexibility	Resistance to measures
Kirkholt							
Blackburn	X	X					
Meadows		X	X				X
Liverpool		X					X
Burnley					X		
Merthyr Tydfil		X					
Bentley				X			X
Baltimore			X	X	X	X	
Hartlepool			X	X	X		X
San Diego	X		X	X	X	X	X
St Anns				X			
Eyres Monsell	X				X	X	X
Ashfield	X		X	X			X
Morley				X			X
Norwood/ TTG	X			X	X		
Dallas			X			X	X
Cambridge							X
New Parks	X			X	X	X	
Beenleigh	X		X	X			X
Never Again						X	
Lambeth		X	X	X	X		
Huddersfield			X				
NDV		X	X				X
Leicester			X		X		
Merseyside							X

Notes to *table
[1] Implementation data not available for the five sexual victimization studies.
[2] X indicates this type of problem was identified in the study's report.

did not tend to learn from their mistakes and failed to accommodate changing demands within the project. In some projects, there was "resistance to tactics" that were to be implemented, either from potential recipients who did not want them or from those tasked with implementation.

"Data problems" were a more general issue. Particularly with respect to the collation or analysis of police data sets, data problems led to difficulties identifying how many households or persons had been victimized, and in determining whether crime had been prevented.

An example will emphasize the importance of implementation. One project evaluation report was sufficiently dispirited at the failure of police officers to conduct security surveys at victimized households that it noted "If we take the results at face value, those officers who declined to carry out the survey thereby facilitated the revictimisation of many of those they were charged to help." (Thompson, Townsley, and Pease 2008, p. 132). The types of problems encountered, as identified in the main reports of each project included in the previous section, are summarized in table 20.3.[5]

Those projects that were most effective were those with both high implementation rates and strong preventive mechanisms. Typically, a range of situational security measures targeted at preventing repeats by the same modus operandi were most effective. Thus, stronger doors and window locks plus other measures can prevent crime when appropriately targeted. In contrast, education and advice do not necessarily trigger a strong preventive mechanism either if nothing substantive is implemented or if the measures conceived are weak and unlikely to have much effect. However, it is important to note that, where there was no reduction in repeats, this does not represent falsification of the theory of preventing repeat victimization. Even where a project does not reduce crime, this does not invalidate the theory if the project had poor tactics or implementation.

IV. Discussion and Conclusions

There has been significant success to date in preventing repeat victimization. Generally, the most successful efforts used appropriate situational crime-prevention measures that were comprehensively implemented. When little or no crime was prevented, this was for two reasons. First, some prevention tactics were weak or inappropriate. Well-meaning advice and education will not prevent crime—unless it results in implementation of a strong prevention tactic—any more than sticky tape around a damaged door will prevent repeat burglary. Second, a failure to adequately implement preventive tactics means nothing is in place to prevent further crime.

In light of the evidence, it is most unfortunate that there appears to have been a steep decline in the number of evaluated efforts to prevent repeat victimization, as

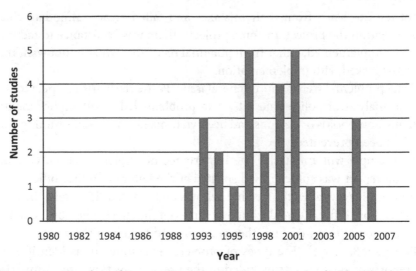

Figure 20.3 Number of Repeat Victimization Prevention Studies by Year (n=31)

shown in figure 20.3. While repeat victimization can be prevented, for the full potential of this crime-prevention strategy to be achieved, there needs to be significant additional investment in research and development. Problem-solving and action-research approaches that develop strong prevention tactics based on analysis of the crime problem should be developed. These should cover a broader range of crime types than have been addressed to date. Figure 20.3 suggests that policymakers and crime-prevention research in general may be missing significant opportunities, at a cost to victims of crime. It could be argued that policy is causing crime by failing to develop this area of crime-prevention strategy.

Research on preventing repeat victimization should include greater efforts to prevent near repeats of various sorts. This is because there is an increasingly clear conceptual overlap around the repetitive nature of crime and its tendency to cluster along whatever dimension it is measured. The similarity of further crimes is the common factor among these repeat crime clusters, and the more similar the crimes, the greater the potential to develop an informed and efficient response. Hence, we conclude that further development of research and policy in this area would be to the significant benefit of society.

NOTES

We thank Shane Johnson, Ken Pease, Nick Tilley, Melanie Wellsmith, and the editors for comments on earlier drafts.

1. In addition, Wellsmith and Birks (2008) is the only study, to our knowledge, evaluating the prevention of near-repeat burglary, and they tentatively indicated some success. Related areas of crime concentration from hot products to hot spots are not included, though we suspect the time will come when such areas are more integrated.

2. The inter-quartile range is 33.2 percent. When the "ambiguous" projects were included, the mean fall in crime incidence is 17.8 percent and the median 19.0 percent with an inter-quartile range of 31.3 percent.

3. Using a random effects model (Q = 284.2861), the weighted mean effect size (WMES) is 1.22 with confidence intervals (CIs) of 1.06 and 1.40. The WMES gives greater weight to studies with a smaller standard error (s.e.). The CIs shown for each study in figure 20.1 were computed using 1.96 standard errors, but as the s.e. is likely to be underestimated using the standard formula, they were multiplied by 2. Without doubling each s.e., the WMES would be 1.25 with CIs: 1.10–1.44.

Additional studies evaluating advice to victims of family violence and elder abuse have been conducted by Robert Davis and colleagues (e.g., Davis and Medina-Ariza, 2001; Davis et al. 2006). There is much in common with work reviewed here, but the studies were not part of the Grove et al. (forthcoming) review on which this section is based. And while more work is needed to integrate that body of work, if its results seem less promising, we suspect this may be a result of what is assessed here as low implementation rates and weak crime-prevention mechanisms, particularly when prevention relies on education and advice rather than tactics with stronger situational mechanisms.

4. The chart excludes the five studies of sexual victimization.

5. We recognize the need for further work and inter-rater reliability tests to confirm this preliminary typology of problems.

REFERENCES

Anderson, David, Sylvia Chenery, and Ken Pease. 1995. *Biting Back: Tackling Repeat Burglary and Car Crime.* Crime Detection and Prevention Series Paper 58. London: Police Research Group, UK Home Office.

Bennett, Trevor, and Linda Durie. 1999. *Preventing Residential Burglary in Cambridge: From Crime Audits to Targeted Strategies.* Police Research Series, Paper 108. London: Home Office, Police and Reducing Crime Unit.

Bernasco, Wim. 2008. "Them Again?: Same-Offender Involvement in Repeat and Near Repeat Burglaries." *European Journal of Criminology* 5(4): 411–31.

Bowers, Kate. 2001. "Small Business Crime: The Evaluation of a Crime Prevention Initiative." *Crime Prevention and Community Safety: An International Journal* 3(1):23–42.

Bowers, Kate J., and Shane D. Johnson. 2004. "Who Commits Near Repeats? A Test of the Boost Explanation." *Western Criminology Review* 5:12–24.

Bowers, Kate, Shane Johnson, and Alex Hirschfield. 2003. *Pushing Back the Boundaries: New Techniques for Assessing the Impact of Burglary Schemes.* London: Home Office.

Breitenbecher, Kimberley Hanson, and Christine Gidycz. 1998. "An Empirical Evaluation of a Program Designed to Reduce the Risk of Multiple Sexual Victimization." *Journal of Interpersonal Violence* 13(4): 472–88.

Budz, Dennis, Neil Pegnall, and Michael Townsley. 2001. *Lightning Strikes Twice: Preventing Repeat Home Burglary.* Queensland: Criminal Justice Commission.

Clare, Joe, Jenny Kingsley, and Frank Morgan. 2009. *Assault Public Officer Trends in Western Australia.* Report to the Western Australian Office of Crime Prevention. University of Western Australia: Crime Research Centre.

Clarke, Ronald V., Elizabeth Perkins, and Donald J Smith Jr. 2001. *Explaining Repeat Residential Burglaries: An Analysis of Property Stolen.* In *Repeat Victimization.* Vol. 12 of *Crime Prevention Studies,* edited by Graham Farrell and Ken Pease. Monsey, NY: Criminal Justice Press.

Cummings, Rick. 2005. *Operation Burglary Countdown: Evaluation Study Final Report.* Perth, Western Australia: Estill & Associates.

Davis, Robert. C., and Juanjo Medina-Ariza. 2001. *Results from an Elder Abuse Prevention Experiment in New York City.* National Institute of Justice, Research in Brief. Washington, DC: United States Department of Justice.

Davis, Robert, Pamela Guthrie, Timothy Ross, and Chris O'Sullivan. 2006. *Reducing Sexual Revictimization: A Field Test with an Urban Sample.* Unpublished report to the US Department of Justice. Available at https://www.ncjrs.gov/pdffiles1/nij/grants/216002.pdf.

Farrell, Graham, Ken Clark, Dan Ellingworth, and Ken Pease. 2005. "Of Targets and Supertargets: A Routine Activities Theory of High Crime Rates." *Internet Journal of Criminology,* www.internetjournalofcriminology.com.

Farrell, Graham, and Ken Pease. 2006. "Preventing Repeat Residential Burglary." In *Preventing Crime: What Works for Children, Offenders, Victims, and Places,* edited by Brandon C. Welsh and David P. Farrington. Dordrecht: Springer Press.

Forrester, David, Mike Chatterton, and Ken Pease. 1988. *The Kirkholt Burglary Prevention Project, Rochdale.* Crime Prevention Unit Paper 13. London: Crime Prevention Unit, UK Home Office.

Forrester, David, Samantha Frenzz, Martin O'Connell, and Ken Pease. 1990. *The Kirkholt Burglary Prevention Project: Phase II.* Crime Prevention Unit Paper 23. London: Her Majesty's Stationery Office.

Gidycz, Christine A., Steven Jay Lynn, Cindy L. Rich, Nichole L. Marioni, Catherine Loh, Lisa Marmelstein Blackwell, Jane Stafford, Rachel Fite, and Joanna Pashdag, 2001. "The Evaluation of a Sexual Assault Risk Reduction Program: A Multisite Investigation." *Journal of Consulting and Clinical Psychology* 69(6): 1073–78.

Gregson, Mick. 1992. *The St Ann's Burglary Reduction Project.* Crime Reduction Research Unit: Nottingham Trent University. Nottingham, UK: York House Publications

Gregson, Mick, and Allison Hocking. 1993. *The Meadows Household Security Project.* Crime Reduction Research Unit: Nottingham Trent University. Nottingham, UK: York House.

Grove, Louise E. 2010. "Synergies of Syntheses: A Comparison of Systematic Review and Scientific Realist Evaluation Methods for Crime Prevention." Ph.D dissertation, Loughborough University, Department of Social Sciences.

Grove, Louise E., and Graham Farrell. 2011. "Repeat victimization." In *Oxford Bibliographies Online* (Criminology), http://www.oxfordbibliographiesonline.com/view/document/obo-9780195396607/obo-9780195396607-0119.xml.

Grove, Louise E., Graham Farrell, David P. Farrington, and Shane Johnson. Forthcoming. *Systematic Review of Preventing Repeat Victimization.* Stockholm: Swedish National Council for Crime Prevention.

Hanson, Kimberley, and Christine Gidycz. 1993. "An Evaluation of a Sexual Assault Prevention Program." *Journal of Consulting and Clinical Psychology* 61:1046–52.

Hindelang, Michael J., Michael R. Gottfredson, and James Garafalo. 1978. *Victims of Personal Crime: An Empirical Foundation for a Theory of Personal Victimization.* Cambridge, MA: Ballinger.

Laycock, Gloria. 2001. "Hypothesis-Based Research: The Repeat Victimization Story." *Criminology and Criminal Justice* 1:59–82.

Levy, Marissa P., and Christine Tartaro. 2010. "Repeat Victimization: A Study of Auto Theft in Atlantic City Using the WALLS Variables to Measure Environmental Indicators." *Criminal Justice Policy Review* 21(3): 296–318.

Lindstrom, Peter. 1997. "Patterns of School Crime: A Replication and Empirical Extension." *British Journal of Criminology* 37:121–30.

Marx, Brian P., Karen S. Calhoun, Amy E. Wilson, and Lori A. Meyerson. 2001. "Sexual Revictimization Prevention: An Outcome Evaluation." *Journal of Consulting and Clinical Psychology* 69(1): 25–32.

Matthews, Roger, Catherine Pease, and Ken Pease 2001. "Repeated Bank Robbery: Theme and Variations." In *Repeat Victimization*, edited by Graham Farrell and Ken Pease. New York: Criminal Justice Press.

Matthews, Roger, and Julie Trickey. 1994a. *The Eyres Monsell Crime Reduction Project*. Leicester, UK: Centre for the Study of Public Order, University of Leicester.

Matthews, Roger, and Julie Trickey. 1994b. *The New Parks Crime Reduction Project*. Leicester, UK: Centre for the Study of Public Order, University of Leicester.

Morgan, Frank. 2004. *The NDV Project Final Evaluation*. Perth: Crime Research Centre, University of Western Australia.

Morgan, Frank, and C. Walter. 2002. *The South Australian Residential Break and Enter Pilot Project Evaluation Report*. Canberra: Commonwealth Attorney General's Office.

Pearson, D. 1980. *Evaluation of Multnomah Countys Commercial Burglary Prevention Program*. Salem, OR: Oregon Law Enforcement Council, Evaluation and Research Unit.

Pease, Ken. 1998. *Repeat Victimisation: Taking Stock*. Crime Prevention and Detection Series Paper 90. London: Home Office.

Short, M. B., M. R. D'Orsogna, P. J. Brantingham, and G. E. Tita. 2009. "Measuring and Modelling Repeat and Near Repeat Burglary Effects." *Journal of Quantitative Criminology* 25:325–39.

Sturgeon-Adams, Louise, Sue Adamson, and Norman Davidson. 2005. *Hartlepool: A Case Study in Burglary Reduction*. Centre for Criminology and Criminal Justice, University of Hull.

Taplin, Stephanie, and Bruce Flaherty. 2001. *Safer Towns and Cities Housebreaking Reduction Report*. New South Wales: NSW Attorney-General's Department.

Taylor, Geoff. 1999. Using Repeat Victimisation to Counter Commercial Burglary: The Leicester Experience. *Security Journal* 12(1): 41–52.

Thompson, Simon, Michael Townsley, and Ken Pease. 2008. "Repeat Burglary Victimisation: Analysis of a Partial Failure." *Irish Journal of Psychology* 29(1): 129–37.

Tilley, Nick, and Matt Hopkins. 1998. *Business as Usual: An Evaluation of the Small Business and Crime Initiative*. Police Research Series; Paper 95. London: Home Office, Policing and Reducing Crime Unit.

Townsley, Michael, Ross Homel, and Janet Chaseling. 2003. "Infectious Burglaries: A Test of the Near Repeat Hypothesis." *British Journal of Criminology* 43:615–33.

Webb, Janice. 1996. *Direct Line Homesafe*. Lincolnshire, UK: Janice Webb Research.

Weisel, Deborah L., Ron V. Clarke, and Jon R. Stedman. 1999. *Hot Dots in Hot Spots: Examining Repeat Victimization for Residential Burglary in Three Cities*. Final Report to the National Institute of Justice. Washington DC: Police Executive Research Forum.

Wellsmith, Melanie, and Daniel J. Birks. 2008. "Research on Target: A Collaboration Between Researchers and Practitioners for a Target Hardening Scheme." *International Review of Law Computers and Technology* 22(1–2): 181–89.

PART IV

ADVANCING KNOWLEDGE AND BUILDING A SAFER SOCIETY

CHAPTER 21

IMPLEMENTING CRIME PREVENTION: GOOD GOVERNANCE AND A SCIENCE OF IMPLEMENTATION

ROSS HOMEL AND PETER HOMEL

EARLY in 1999, the UK Home Office started implementing what it described as "the biggest single investment in an evidence-based approach to crime reduction which has ever taken place in any country" (Home Office 1999, p. 3). While certainly true at the time, the Crime Reduction Programme (CRP) also came to represent the single best example of a major crime-prevention initiative that had its overall effectiveness systematically undermined by a failure to pay adequate attention to principles of good governance in the design and management of its implementation processes (P. Homel et al. 2004).

The failure of the Crime Reduction Programme to institutionalize evidence-based prevention is by no means unique, or even unusual. Sutton and his colleagues (2008), writing about the Australian experience, focus explicitly on the political dimension, observing that while Australian crime policy over the past four decades has been characterized by periods of renewed interest in large-scale crime prevention, "prevention and community safety remain background tasks, as far as the mass-media and government crime policy are concerned" (p. 3). Little in the way of a systematic body of knowledge has been created through a series of federal funding programs over some years sponsored by both major parties. Politics has trumped science, with evidence-based crime prevention being largely abandoned for projects proposed by community groups that often are not built on sound scientific foundations. The problem in Australia, it seems, is primarily a lack of political vision concerning science-based prevention, and a consequent failure to articulate and agree on goals.

The Australian experience is, sadly, consistent with the global picture. In their 2010 International Report on Crime Prevention and Community Safety, the International Centre for the Prevention of Crime (ICPC) conclude that "although there has been considerable progress in the development of prevention policies, they are still marginalized within the broader scope of public safety policies" (Idriss et al. 2010, p. vii). The ICPC documents a wide range of apparently successful and innovative initiatives, so the problem is not so much a lack of evidence (although one could wish for much more rigorous standards of evaluation) as a failure to move to national or mainstream practice from "success in miniature," to use Lisbeth Schorr's (1998) evocative phrase.

This essay is about the process of moving from small-scale or one-off demonstration projects that have been carefully evaluated and shown to be successful to implementation or dissemination on larger scales while preserving at least some of the effectiveness of the original demonstration model. We take as a starting point Schorr's statement that "the attributes of effectiveness are consistently undermined by the institutions and systems on which they depend for funding and legitimation" (p. 19). The UK Crime Reduction Programme well illustrates this phenomenon, the barriers to implementation including (among many others) inappropriate program design and management, which resulted in unfeasible timescales, slow-moving bureaucratic procedures, and capacity shortages (Maguire 2004), as well as the inability of the Home Office as a government agency to both sponsor and appropriately respond to the sort of evidence that can emerge from the evaluation of such a high-profile and politically contentious initiative (Hope 2004).

What the CRP story points to is an overall failure to effectively manage program implementation in a coherent, cohesive, and productive manner. It also points to the need to build comprehensive governance systems designed to support effective implementation. *Governance* refers to the processes and systems by which societies or organizations make their important decisions, determine who has a voice and who will be engaged in the process, and how account is to be rendered (Edgar, Marshall, and Bassett 2006). The word relates to older English and French notions of "steering," and can be contrasted with the traditional top-down approach of governments driving or controlling society. Good governance combined with strong and consistent leadership provides the framework within which evidence-based crime-prevention policies and programs can flourish.

The failure to make the design of good governance systems central to the prevention enterprise is, in turn, one manifestation of the larger failure to recognize the processes of implementation and dissemination as major scientific problems in their own right. Researchers in many disciplines have long assumed that rigorous experimentation and publication of findings in peer-reviewed journals, perhaps followed by some media releases and television appearances, would lead automatically to the diffusion of knowledge and the adoption of innovative new approaches by practitioners and the organizations that employ them. This passive, one-directional model of "science to service" (Fixsen et al. 2009, p. 532) is now widely recognized as a failure (Schorr 1998; Knutsson and Clarke 2006; Nutley, Walter, and Davies 2007; Whittaker 2009). In practice this means that we need to develop a science of implementation that incorporates the emerging sciences around the domains of knowledge and practice dissemination (e.g., Rogers 1995; Bammer, Michaux, and Sanson 2010) and that systematically and rigorously addresses the cultural, structural, and organizational contexts of implementation that we have adumbrated.

In this essay we outline what a science of implementation means in the context of prevention science and crime prevention. We make a number of assumptions and observations and come to several conclusions:

- In prevention science terms, we identify implementation with prevention initiatives that have moved beyond efficacy trials in controlled settings; that is, we define as implementation both the process of testing effectiveness in organizational or other real-world settings and the process of dissemination of an effective approach on a large scale.
- Two sets of concepts developed within implementation science from research on human services organizations are the six stages of implementation and the core components of successful implementations. Both the stages and the core components can be applied fruitfully to crime-prevention implementations.
- Researchers do not possess all the critical knowledge for effective implementation. Practitioners and policy experts also possess important knowledge about what makes programs work, or not work, in complex settings; and successful innovations will incorporate governance arrangements that facilitate the free and open flow of different kinds of knowledge across all stages of implementation.
- There are many valuable lessons to be learned about implementation from the UK Crime Reduction Programme and other case studies. These include, for example, the importance of linkages between local activities and partnerships and central resources and policy units; the centrality of strong leadership and shared goals; and the necessity of adequate resources and support systems provided for a sufficiently long period to achieve sustainable change.
- We view the elements of successful implementation through the lens of good governance, arguing that adherence to five governance principles is essential for successful crime-prevention partnerships. In the context of the exercise of power, these principles relate to legitimacy and voice; direction/strategic vision; performance (including monitoring and reporting); accountability; and fairness.

- At an organizational level, good governance for effective implementation of evidence-based programs revolves around structures and arrangements that support staff recruitment, training, coaching, and performance evaluation. Essential elements of such arrangements include decision support data systems, facilitative administrative supports, and external system settings that support the work of practitioners (such as enlightened policies and adequate funding).

By using examples of crime-prevention initiatives that have been both more and less successfully implemented throughout the world, with a particular focus on the CRP, we demonstrate how one might go about identifying good governance systems and build and apply a science of implementation. We begin in section I with a brief discussion of the nature of contemporary crime prevention, moving to an exploration of prevention science, including the key concepts of efficacy, effectiveness, and dissemination. This section also includes an examination of the stages of implementation. In section II we analyze the CRP in some detail, and in section III expand the analysis to contrast experience with the CRP with other crime-prevention implementations. In section IV we summarize the lessons from the implementation case studies, placing them into two complementary frameworks for good governance derived from studies of multi-agency collaborations and human service organizations.

We should emphasize that implementation research is a large and rapidly growing field, and it is not possible in one chapter to present a comprehensive review. Important recent work in criminology that has yet to be fully incorporated in our framework includes, for example, Ekblom's (2010) 5Is model of knowledge transfer, as well the ongoing work of Clarke, Goldstein, Knutsson, Scott, Laycock, and others on situational prevention and problem-oriented policing (Knutsson 2003; Knutsson and Clarke 2006). In the developmental prevention field, two excellent resources for future analyses (among many others) are the large-scale implementation and dissemination of the Triple P-Positive Parenting Program (Sanders et al. 2008; Sanders 2010) and the New Zealand Government's *Inter-Agency Plan for Conduct Disorder/Severe Antisocial Behaviour* (Ministry of Social Development 2007; Advisory Group for Conduct Problems 2009). We aim in this essay to point in promising directions rather than to arrive at definitive conclusions based on an exhaustive search of the literature.

I. Implementation and Prevention Science

Many serious crime problems just won't go away. A good example is alcohol-related violence and crime, which seems to be getting worse in many (but not all) countries (Hadfield 2009). In the past, initiatives to address this problem were frequently framed in terms of short-term projects directed at specific one-off local issues, but increasingly attempts are being made to design and implement more systematic and comprehensive solutions that address some of the deeply embedded social, economic, and cultural factors that foster the conditions under which crime and violence flourish. For alcohol-related crime, effective strategies include measures to control the affordability of alcohol, regulate its physical availability, or modify drinking contexts (Babor et al. 2010). These measures can in turn be broken into components, such as staff training and police enforcement, to improve venue management and hence create safer drinking contexts, which in turn are generally these days incorporated into collaborative multi-agency partnership arrangements.

However, even well-executed and sophisticated crime-prevention endeavors frequently fail because the problem is poorly or narrowly defined and understood, including by those working to achieve crime-prevention goals (Anderson and Homel 2006; P. Homel et al. 2004). The alcohol and crime problem, for example, is frequently conceived wrongly in terms of individual patron responsibility (identifying and cracking down on the "bad apples") rather than in terms of the easy availability of alcohol and criminogenic nightlife environments (Graham and Homel 2008). This illustrates Eck's (2003) point, which is that getting the theory right really does matter. Relevant crime data on their own will not reveal the most appropriate interventions, while using sound theory will.

Thus, in the crime-prevention field we observe a tendency to want to attempt too much too soon: to address entrenched problems with complex strategies (that usually revolve around multi-agency collaborations) on the basis of poorly understood theories and program components that have not been tested sufficiently rigorously. At this point we believe we can learn from our colleagues in allied fields who have been thinking about prevention for somewhat longer.

In the health sciences and many other fields that aspire to practice prevention science, a clear distinction is made between efficacy, effectiveness, and dissemination. These distinctions have been helpfully elaborated by the Society for Prevention Research in their *Standards of Evidence* document (Society for Prevention Research n.d.). It will be useful for our purposes to explore these concepts given their wide use in the health and behavioral sciences, and therefore their relevance to much work in crime prevention. In particular, closer attention is warranted because, as we have already noted, in this essay we pragmatically identify implementation with both the processes of testing effectiveness and broader dissemination—in other words, with interventions that have moved beyond the starting point of efficacy trials.

Efficacy is defined in the SPR document as the extent to which an intervention (technology, treatment, procedure, service, or program) does more harm than good when delivered under optimal conditions. To reach the standard of evidence required, interventions must be sufficiently well described to permit replication; outcome measures must be psychometrically sound with pre, post, and follow-up measures over time if appropriate; and there must be at least one comparison condition with assignment to treatment and comparison conditions preferably at random to ensure internal validity. An example of an efficacious intervention is the

Elmira Prenatal/Early Infancy Project in which community nurses conducted structured visits to pregnant socially disadvantaged single teenagers or single mothers with young babies (Olds et al. 1998; Eckenrode et al. 2010). Evaluation of this randomized trial showed a decrease in recorded child physical abuse and neglect during the first two years of life; in a 15-year follow-up, both mothers and the children had fewer arrests than control groups where the mothers were not visited; and at a 19-year follow-up, intervention girls (but not boys) were much less likely to have entered the criminal justice system.

Effectiveness trials test whether efficacious interventions produce benefits under real-world conditions or in "natural" settings. Often this means testing the impact of promising strategies in organizational settings such as schools or human service agencies where staff are typically not as highly trained as in the efficacy trials and where organizational culture and work practices may not provide an ideal environment for effective prevention. In other cases, demonstrating effectiveness might mean extending the implementation of a program to a larger number of settings of the same type in which it was developed. In either case, success will depend on the development of resources such as manuals, training programs, and technical supports such as Web sites, with efforts being made to ensure that the intervention is delivered in a manner that is as faithful as possible to the original model (preserving program fidelity).

For example, the Communities That Care (CTC) model of community capacity building for the prevention of youth crime and substance abuse has been developed and found to be very promising in a number of relatively small-scale implementations over the years (Hawkins, Catalano, and Associates 1992). Recently, a large randomized effectiveness trial of CTC has been completed in the United States (Hawkins et al. 2008). Twenty-four communities were selected and 12 pairs similar on youth characteristics were matched, with one community in each pair randomized to receive the CTC process over five years. A cohort of over 4,000 students has been followed up. Those exposed to the 12 CTC intervention communities had, by age 12, fewer risk and more protective factors and lower rates of externalizing behaviors than control community children; and by age 13, they showed greater reductions in substance use (Hawkins et al. 2009).

Finally, *broad dissemination* moves beyond effectiveness trials to large-scale use nationally or internationally. Ideally, all the criteria for effectiveness will be met, with the addition of clear cost information, monitoring and evaluation tools, and resources to sustain the strategy. The Triple P parenting program is an example of a prevention program that has been proven to be effective in large-scale trials and it is currently being disseminated in a wide range of countries, using not only Level 1 or universal Triple P (a media-based parenting information campaign) but the other levels as well (Sanders et al. 2008; Prinz et al. 2009; Sanders 2010).

The Society for Prevention Research (SPR; 2008) has advanced the discussion of how scientific findings can more effectively influence policy and practice by publishing a working paper on Type 2 Translational Research, borrowing the term from the health professions. *Type 1 translation* refers to the application of basic discoveries to the development and preliminary testing of preventive interventions—that is, the process up to efficacy trials. *Type 2 translation* investigates factors, models, and processes associated with the adoption, implementation, and sustainability of effective prevention strategies in communities, service settings, and populations (Greenberg 2010). The SPR proposes a framework with the acronym TIES for Type 2 translation based on Diffusion of Innovations theory (Rogers 1995): Translation stage-setting during pre-adoption phases; Institutional adoption of evidence-based interventions; Effective implementation; and Sustainability.

All commentators are agreed that Type 2 translation research is much less well developed than Type 1 translation research. In Greenberg's (2009) words, "In the real world, translation of science-based practices stumble, largely unguided, toward uneven, incomplete and socially disappointing outcomes." Others are equally forthright: Fixsen and colleagues (p. 531), for example, describe the outcomes of the evidence-based movement within human services over the past few decades as "not encouraging," while within criminology, Scott (2003, p. 10) states that "the implementation phase of problem-oriented policing initiatives may well be the most crucial yet least well-understood phase."

Systematic reviews of implementation processes in the human services suggest that implementation is a recursive process with six functional stages: exploration, installation, initial implementation, full implementation, innovation, and sustainability (Fixsen et al. 2009). These stages fill in some of the details that are missing in the TIES framework, and they help begin the systematic analyses required to develop implementation science. Later in this essay we examine the core components of successful implementations as part of an analysis of implementation governance systems.

The six implementation stages are recursive since they are not necessarily achieved sequentially, like walking up a staircase; it is possible, for example, to move from full implementation back to initial implementation in the context of rapid staff turnover, or to be involved in several stages simultaneously, such as working on sustainability issues from the outset. The six stages, and the complex interplay between them over time, are evident in most crime-prevention implementations, although when implementation is dominated by a command-and-control agency like police, the dynamics may differ somewhat from those in the child welfare, education, mental health, or substance-abuse services that have supplied most of the raw material from which the stages have been derived (Fixsen et al. 2009). Since the stages are a useful tool for thinking about crime-prevention implementation, we outline each one, drawing on materials from the US National Implementation Research Network (NIRN) (http://www.fpg.unc.edu/~nirn/), with illustrations from crime prevention and related implementations.

A. Exploration

Exploration is concerned with assessing needs and readiness for intervention. This might involve, for example, assessing the match between community needs, evidence-based practice, and program needs, and the community resources to help make a decision about whether to proceed. Much of the research on knowledge diffusion and knowledge brokering is useful at this point, since there are many ways that research evidence can be acquired as a foundation for exploration and action (Nutley, Walter and Davies 2007; Bammer, Michaux and Sanson 2010). As an illustration of exploration, Welsh and Hoshi (2002) have summarized levels of community readiness to implement different crime-prevention measures, depending on the theoretical and empirical analysis of what is causing local crime problems. A community disorganization diagnosis, for example, in which offending behavior is the result of the breakdown in community social order related to low socioeconomic status, multiple ethnic groups, and residential mobility, suggests as preventive strategies physical community renewal or community mobilization. On the other hand, a community empowerment analysis, which diagnoses a need for the sharing of power with residents in decision-making processes that affect the social conditions that sustain crime, suggests community development interventions that enable residents to form new organizations, influence municipal decisions, and have appropriate local services introduced.

B. Installation

Installation refers to all the activities after the decision has been made to adopt a program up to the point of opening one's doors for business. These include finding funding streams, putting in place human resource strategies, hiring or retraining staff, setting expectations, developing reporting frameworks, and creating referral mechanisms or methods for reaching the target population. In practice, much of this work is ongoing, since in our experience it is extremely difficult to accomplish all these tasks in final form at the outset. In the case of major crime-prevention initiatives, a critical part of the installation process is frequently the establishment of functional partnerships at the organizational and local levels. The crime-prevention task, in other words, involves an installation process in several organizations simultaneously, based on shared goals that must be negotiated, operationalized, and harmonized across often diverse organizational cultures. This model of collaborative multi-agency action operating through partnership arrangements to implement evidence-based programs to achieve shared outcomes makes crime-prevention implementation more challenging than most initiatives in the human services (P. Homel 2009).

C. Initial Implementation

This phase encompasses at least the early stages of the major change processes entailed in implementation. Key challenges include changes in skill levels, organizational capacity and culture, and often "diamond-hard inertia" (National Implementation Research Network, http://www.fpg.unc.edu/~nirn/implementation/06/06c_initimpl.cfm). The introduction of mass random breath testing (RBT) by police in Australia in the 1980s is an excellent example of how the challenges of organizational inertia and an entrenched culture were overcome (R. Homel 1988, 1993). Police are wedded to a "catch the crook" model of law enforcement that seldom achieves substantial general deterrent effects, and so they had to be persuaded that an approach to law enforcement that was based on highly visible, random testing of large numbers of motorists who had committed no offence and that yielded very few arrests would be a general deterrent that reduced accidents. One key strategy was sustained advocacy by researchers interacting face to face with politicians and senior police, resulting in knowledge transfer and a willingness by police managers to try the new approach. The second key strategy was to use accident data to show the immediate success of mass random testing.

D. Full Implementation

Full implementation of an innovation can occur once new learning about evidence-based practice becomes integrated into practitioner, organizational, and community policies and practices. Ideally, over time the innovation becomes accepted practice, and crime should be going down if evidence-based programs have in fact been effectively embedded. The illustrations and quotes from earlier in this essay reflect the fact that we are far from this happy state in most parts of the world, although one can argue that the continuing declines in crime in most developed countries are partly an outcome of effective prevention strategies (P. Homel 2009). The initial and full implementation stages are currently the focus of much active research and experimentation, particularly with regard to practical ways of facilitating knowledge integration through such techniques as co-locations of expert researchers in service delivery organizations, or (equally effectively) embedding practitioners in research settings for a period (Michaux 2010).

E. Innovation

Innovation can occur when enough has been learned from the full implementation of evidence-based programs to introduce improvements that might become part of the standard model of practice. The flip side of innovation is program drift, when old and ineffective habits come to the fore. An example of innovation is the way in which Australian police were able to increase the visibility and reach of RBT by making random enforcement a part of every traffic patrol's shift, rather than concentrating the program in especially equipped and very expensive vans (R. Homel 1988).

F. Sustainability

Sustainability is concerned with the long-term survival of effective preventive practices in the context of a rapidly changing world. Threats to sustained effectiveness include the loss of skilled staff and knowledgeable leaders, loss of funding perhaps due to changes in political priorities, changes in the larger system within which the organization hosting the innovation is situated, and changes in the nature of social problems that can make a once effective program increasingly irrelevant. An example of a structural and political change that may have helped to preserve the effective early prevention program Sure Start in the UK was the decision in 2005 to transform Sure Start programs into Children's Centres, ensuring "that Sure Start Children's Centres became embedded within the welfare state by statute, making it difficult for any future government to eradicate" (Melhuish, Belsky, and Barnes 2010, p. 160). Another example of how an innovation has been sustained is again provided by RBT. Once police had fully implemented the new enforcement strategy, it became part of the DNA of Australian police services—that is, it became business as usual. Being command-and-control organizations, police departments were able to ensure that officers all over the state performed what is often a boring task, and gave them all the necessary resources. The continued commitment of the police has been underpinned by reliable accident data and evaluations that show the large and continued impact of RBT (Henstridge, Homel, and Mackay 1997).

II. The UK Crime Reduction Programme

The UK's Crime Reduction Programme (CRP) from the late 1990s, which we referred to at the beginning of this essay, is one of the most closely studied crime-prevention implementation experiences internationally. Given its scope, ambition, and complexity, much can be learned from the CRP, justifying its place in this essay as our central case study. In this section, we draw heavily on the review of the implementation of the CRP prepared for the Home Office by Peter Homel and his colleagues (2004), and in the next section widen our survey to include selected implementation experiences in other parts of the world.

The CRP was an ambitious and comprehensive program based on 25 years of accumulated research and experience and a commitment to turning research findings into mainstream practice that would achieve sustained reductions in crime and in the UK's £50 billion crime bill (Nutley and Homel 2006). Research and evaluation personnel were to work hand-in-glove with policy and resource managers to ensure that successful initiatives flourished, that necessary changes were made to those strategies that were shown to be less effective, and that resources were allocated to where they would achieve greatest impact. Thus, a considerable effort was made to lay strong foundations through the implementation stage of exploration of needs and adoption of evidence-based strategies, but in hindsight it is clear that despite good intentions and a thorough implementation plan, the installation stage was not well executed, largely it seems because the skills and organizational capacities a collaborative multi-agency strategy required simply could not be delivered.

The program was developed as 20 specific but linked initiatives of varying scale organized around five broad themes:

1. Working with families, children, and schools to prevent young people becoming offenders of the future
2. Tackling crime in communities, particularly high-volume crime such as domestic burglary
3. Developing products and systems that are resistant to crime
4. Promoting more effective sentencing practices
5. Working with offenders to ensure that they do not re-offend

These themes involved innovative action by all parts of the criminal justice system, as well as the development of new modes of operation within a multi-agency, mixed service sector framework across every level of government in England and Wales. This meant encompassing action at national, regional, and local levels. The initiatives that made up the program addressed broad-based issues of community concern (e.g., violence against women, youth inclusion), specific types of crime (e.g., domestic burglary), and special and difficult populations (e.g., offenders). A great variety of strategies were employed, ranging from situational measures to reduce burglary and develop crime-resistant products, to developmental and early intervention measures to reduce youth crime as part of the first theme.

There were very clear ideas from the outset about how the CRP should work. It was to accumulate the best available research-based evidence for approaches to "what works" from any area that might contribute to the achievement of crime-reduction outcomes. This knowledge was to be organized in terms of whether the initiatives were: (a) promising but so far unproven; (b) based on stronger evidence, but confined to limited research settings or derived from noncriminal justice areas (e.g., health or education); or (c) proven in terms of small-scale initiatives and, therefore, ready for larger scale implementation. On the basis of this knowledge, a portfolio of viable evidence-based initiatives was to be developed, with sufficient resources budgeted for the effective implementation and evaluation of these. Thus, in prevention science terms, the assumption was that many of the foundations had been laid through various kinds of efficacy trials, and the next step was to move on to large-scale effectiveness trials followed by national dissemination of good policy and practice.

Apart from the Home Office, a wide range of other government agencies was to be engaged in the delivery of these viable evidence-based initiatives. Additionally, much of the delivery of local level CRP subprograms was to be undertaken by other agencies by way of a competitive grants program. Alongside the bidding process, a comprehensive evaluation and assessment strategy was to be developed.

It was intended that the implementation of initiatives would occur progressively through a series of funding rounds, consistent with a stages model of implementation. The initiatives would be reviewed, refined, and further developed during implementation using program evaluation feedback. The overall learning from the initial (three-year) implementation phase would be accumulated and disseminated, with successful initiatives moved into mainstream funding while unsupported or cost-ineffective strategies would be withdrawn. By the end of its three-year cycle in 2002, the CRP had implemented more than 1,500 separate initiatives that were managed by a variety of agencies at all levels of government, from the center to local government and community-level partnerships.

As can be seen from this program logic, the CRP was attempting simultaneously to implement and review a complex array of initiatives with varying levels of evidence to support them. Further, it was seeking to determine which initiatives were individually strong and cost-effective, as well as assessing the best mix of strategies for maximizing crime-reduction impacts. It was also aiming to learn about sustainability, in terms of both the impact of initiatives and how they might be transferred to mainstream programs and continued over time. Most important, the CRP was designed to operate in a joined-up way across government agencies at the central and regional level and in partnership with local government and community groups at the local level. In other words, it was attempting to manage the implementation of a complex innovative program with multiple interventions and outcomes simultaneously in a vertical direction (i.e., from a central policy level through a regional structure to local delivery) and horizontally (i.e., across diverse central agencies).

Given these ambitious aims and the need to implement new forms of governance, it is not surprising that from the beginning the CRP encountered numerous problems that ultimately frustrated its ability to achieve its goals. The initial implementation stage did not go at all well, with only 13 percent of the program's allocated budget spent at the end of the first year. Even three-quarters of the way through the time available for implementing the entire program (four years) significant delays, funding underspends, and other frustrations were still occurring, with 17 percent of the allocated budget unspent and some program areas not started. Within one program area it was found that nearly half of the projects had experienced some significant implementation problems. Of these, a third could be said to have experienced very serious problems—to the point that the money had been spent but the programs had not occurred. Full implementation was therefore not achieved, building on the failure in the initial stages.

Some of the most important reasons for widespread implementation failure revolved around staff skills, poor support systems from the center, and a lack of facilitative administrative support. In more specific terms, the major implementation problems involved:

- Difficulties in finding, recruiting, and retaining suitably qualified and skilled staff
- Generally inadequate technical and strategic advice and guidance from the center (i.e., the Home Office) and the regions
- Inadequate levels of project management competence and skill, particularly in financial and resource management

The outcome was that even with a significant financial and political commitment, in combination with a relatively well developed evidence base about what works best for crime reduction, only modest levels of innovation and system change were achieved.

The good news is that all these barriers to effective implementation have been encountered elsewhere, and so the CRP experience can be located in the larger body of literature devoted to the development of implementation science (Fixsen et al. 2009). However, before turning again to that literature to assist in the formulation of general lessons, it will be instructive to expand our survey to include experiences with crime-prevention implementation in some other countries, including some examples where things have generally gone right.

III. Implementation Case Studies: Examples of Challenges and Achievements

While the reviewers of the CRP implementation argue that it may have been possible to anticipate many of the difficulties identified and plan to overcome them within the British context, a bigger question is whether these experiences and problems are echoed in equivalent programs around the world. The short answer is, yes, they are—but that there are also some success stories, albeit with implementations of programs to help prevent specific crime problems rather than crime in general.

A. The New Zealand Crime Prevention Program

In a comprehensive review of a key component of the New Zealand crime-prevention program, the Safer Community Council (SCC) Network (NZ Ministry of Justice 2003) reported that, in spite of a 10-year implementation experience, "there is no discernible evidence that the SCCs are making a strong contribution to reducing crime in local communities" (p. 4). The explanation for this apparent failure, echoing the UK experience, was a lack of specific crime-prevention expertise at the local level, inappropriate local coordination, and a breakdown of the relationship between central government and local stakeholders.

The report's recommendations for how the New Zealand Crime Prevention Unit (NZ CPU) should refocus its approach to working with communities to improve the effectiveness of crime-prevention delivery at the local level also has many parallels with the findings from the CRP implementation review. Specifically, the report by the NZ Ministry of Justice (2003, p. 7) recommended that the NZ CPU should be able to offer communities the following services:

- Leadership—by setting the national crime-prevention policy direction and effectively managing partnerships
- Operational support—including facilitating access to appropriate crime-prevention training, coaching, and contract management

- Resources—funding, expertise, knowledge transfer, and capacity building in the areas of crime-prevention program management and governance
- Information—provision of timely, accurate, and relevant information on policy [through the Crime Reduction Strategy], crime data analysis, problem identification, program planning, and best practices
- Marketing—advocacy to [Government] Ministers on behalf of SCCs.

B. Sustaining a Reduction in Alcohol-Related Violence: The Queensland and Stockholm Projects

Both of these projects, which are discussed in more detail in Graham and Homel (2008), revolved around multi-agency partnerships, but the ways in which they operationalized those partnerships and linked the local with the national or central government levels and with police and liquor-licensing regulators are completely different. While both were very successful in reducing violence in and around licensed premises, the Queensland safety action projects by and large failed to sustain these benefits (R. Homel et al. 2004). By contrast, the Stockholm Prevents Alcohol and Drug Problems Project (STAD) has maintained a reduction of around one-third in levels of violence on an ongoing basis (Wallin, Lindewald, and Andréasson 2004). A brief comparison of the methods used in these two projects throws considerable light on what it takes to achieve long-term, sustainable reductions in crime.

In the Queensland projects, the exploration, installation, and initial and full implementation stages were thoroughly executed, including the formation of an effective partnership among the university, the health department, local councils and community groups, and residents and businesses in the four coastal cities in which it was implemented. However, the two agencies that were never effectively engaged (despite strenuous efforts) were the police and the state liquor licensing authority. The police focused on periodic blitzes on the streets to round up drunken troublemakers, failing to appreciate the preventive philosophy involved in persuading the owners of bars and clubs to change the way they managed their premises and served alcohol. Similarly, the liquor-licensing authorities at the time had little interest in systemic reform supported by innovative regulatory action. Since the implementation failed from the outset to imbue the two relevant law enforcement agencies with the preventive philosophy that made the project so successful, the appropriate types of formal enforcement that were required to maintain compliance with the improved code of practice that was readily adopted for the first two years by most licensees were not implemented after initial project funding ceased.

The STAD Project was launched by the Stockholm County Council in 1995, inspired by experiences elsewhere with multicomponent interventions based on local mobilization, training in responsible beverage service (RBS), and stricter enforcement of licensing laws regulating the service of alcohol to minors and intoxicated persons. The project coordinator was very successful in creating an effective working relationship among the many groups involved in STAD, beginning with an action group consisting of "representatives from the county council, the licensing board, police officers from the task force for restaurant-related crimes, local police officers, the county administration, the National Institute of Public Health (NIPH), the Organization for Restaurant Owners (ORW), the union of restaurant employees, and the specially selected owners of popular nightclubs/restaurants" (Wallin, Lindewald, and Andréasson 2004, p. 398). This comprehensive action group, which brought together around the one table local, city, and national stakeholders, including representatives of the retail liquor industry and regulators, became the "engine room" for mobilizing political, public, and financial support and for facilitating training and enforcement activity.

Why was STAD so successful, in both the short term and long term? A key feature was the 10-year period allowed for the full implementation process, from exploration and adoption to institutionalization. It is noteworthy that this long period of time was essential, even in a country with highly developed public services and a long history of strong government controls on access to alcohol. This realistic time period is perhaps one of the major lessons that can be learned from STAD, since one of the chief enemies of the good leadership and effective governance that underpin successful crime prevention is the tendency for governments to expect results too quickly or constantly reorganize the manner in which crime prevention is delivered. Many crime prevention implementations in other countries attempt much more complex tasks than STAD in a much shorter time, and—like the CRP—fail.

Another key success factor was the head of the licensing board who served as chair of the action/steering group and provided strong, credible, and consistent leadership from the beginning. In contrast to the Queensland experience, this leadership, in the context of the distinctive features of Swedish society that we have noted, facilitated an action approach that created a powerful partnership between formal regulatory systems and informal regulatory processes at the local level and at the level of industry associations. Thus, police, restaurant owners, and employees appeared to take a strongly cooperative approach that increased over time. A further critical strategy to achieve sustainability was the signing halfway through the project of a written agreement making explicit that the cooperating organizations, independent of specific persons within those organizations, would take responsibility for the continuing work (Wallin, Lindewald, and Andréasson 2004).

C. Implementing a Drug Law Enforcement Performance Measurement Framework

Over a five-year period commencing in 2005, the Australian Institute of Criminology (AIC) undertook the development and trial implementation of an innovative performance measurement system for assessing the value of drug law enforcement (DLE) in achieving the goals of Australia's National Drug Strategy—namely, demand control, supply reduction, and harm minimization (P. Homel and Willis 2007; National Drug Strategy Consultation 2009). There was particular interest in assessing the effects of DLE on public health and community safety and well-being. What this case study demonstrates is the complexity associated even with the apparently simple task of introducing new operational systems into existing organizations. However, the more important lesson is the need to give careful consideration to the process of implementation, a process that in this case was very successful.

One of the key outputs of the project was a comprehensive implementation plan, including the resources needed for the national rollout of the framework. This plan is a model of how to conduct the exploration/adoption and installation stages, while simultaneously planning for sustainability. A series of key challenges were identified relevant to all six implementation stages. In addition, important lessons were learned from the conduct of the project about what is needed for national implementation. These challenges and lessons have relevance more broadly, especially for policing organizations, so are summarized in table 21.1.

IV. DISCUSSION AND CONCLUSIONS: EFFECTIVE IMPLEMENTATION AND GOOD GOVERNANCE

Throughout this essay, and particularly in the last two sections, we have illustrated the six implementation stages and identified a wide range of factors related to the success or failure of crime-prevention implementations. While each example and case study provided some unique lessons, some common features could also be discerned. One recurring issue is the relationship between local activities and the central level of government. Often, top-down plans fail to be operationalized adequately at the local level, as in the CRP and New Zealand examples. However, the reverse can also happen: the Queensland safety action projects were developed locally to great effect by university researchers working in partnership with communities and the human service agencies, but the central regulatory agencies failed to take up the preventive model, undermining its sustainability.

Other key themes included the importance of a clear sense of direction through strong leadership and agreed goals, as in the STAD project; acceptance of an intervention as legitimate and of value to staff at all levels (as in the DLE performance management project) or to local communities as well as the authorities (which did occur in the Queensland interventions); the necessity of adequate resources and support systems from the center over a sufficiently long period to allow full implementation and sustainability (as in STAD and DLE but not in the CRP and NZ examples); the crucial role of information systems and outcomes data in reinforcing initial implementation and promoting sustainability (as in the RBT, STAD, and DLE

Table 21.1 Implementing a drug law enforcement (DLE) performance measurement framework: Challenges identified and lessons learned

Challenges identified in planning	Lessons learned about national implementation
• Persuading practitioners to really accept the need for a new DLE performance measurement framework • Determining who is responsible for the DLE performance measurement • Identifying the major steps needed for the development of a sound measurement framework • Determining a realistic timeframe for national implementation of the framework • Identifying and recognizing data limitations • Resourcing the framework • Anticipating key change management issues • Considering a future evaluation of the framework	• The measurement system will not be accepted in hierarchical police organizations unless it focuses on performance improvements rather than on identification and correction of failures • Performance measurement must support management decisions and not be a counting exercise • The system must accurately reflect organizational culture and practices and not be expressed in jargon • Staff from bottom to top must be involved from the start in defining operational goals and measurement systems and must participate in analysis and reporting • The measurement system must be able to adapt to changing goals • A communication strategy is essential for dissemination of results within and across agencies and to demonstrate openness and accountability

examples); the fundamental importance of having staff with the skills to implement innovative programs (all examples); the importance of openness and accountability through clear communication (STAD, DLE, Queensland); and the need for clear and harmonious staff roles within organizations or partnerships (CRP, STAD, DLE).

In concluding this essay, we aim to make these and other critical features of successful implementation more digestible by viewing them through the lens of good governance, as part of our contribution to the development of the science of crime-prevention implementation. We draw on two governance frameworks, one focused on the kinds of collaborative partnerships that are so much a feature of contemporary crime prevention, and one developed in an analysis of core components of successful implementations of evidence-based programs in service delivery organizations (Fixsen et al. 2009).

Crime prevention requires the exercise of power in the form of legitimate authority and the application of knowledge and resources to achieve goals that are often contested. Achieving good governance is about how well power is exercised, but it is important to recognize that power in society is distributed in complex ways that can give rise to unintended consequences. As described in figure 21.1, three sectors of society participate in the governance process, all of them situated among the citizens at large: the private sector, the institutions of civil society (including the NGO sector), and government. Media, a fourth player, can be an intermediary but

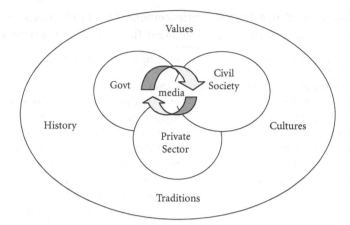

Figure 21.1 Societal context and participants in governance
Source: Adapted from Edgar, Marshall, and Bassett 2006, p. 3.

is not itself a separate player, as it is essentially part of one or more of the other sectors. The relative size and strength of the players varies according to the history, culture, and politics of the country. There are no firm boundaries between these players and the boundaries between them are quite permeable.

Partnerships represent a sustained commitment to cooperative action to achieve a common objective. The exact nature of what a sustained commitment represents in a partnership will vary depending upon the complexity of issues, the players involved, the political and cultural backdrop, the resources available, and so on. Bearing this in mind, there are five core principles described in table 21.2 that have been identified by Edgar, Marshall, and Bassett (2006) as being central to creating good governance arrangements that foster successful partnerships, particularly those between civil society and government. It is essential to recognize that all five principles must be present to some degree to ensure good governance. Since addressing all five principles will inevitably generate some friction or tension, it should be recognized in planning and implementation that it will be necessary to expend effort on balancing the inherent conflicts.

The governance principles and conditions for success shown in table 21.2 address the essential requirements for the effective implementation of collaborative partnerships, but do not speak to all of the critical organizational challenges that must be overcome if practitioners are to be enabled to use innovations effectively. Dean Fixsen and his colleagues (2009) have used systematic reviews of studies of human service implementations, including preventive initiatives, to develop a powerful framework for identifying the core components for successful implementation. We have reproduced their schematic representation of these core components in figure 21.2. As indicated in the figure, these components are integrated and compensatory: each component depends on the operations of the other components; all work together to achieve the maximum impact on staff behaviors and organizational culture; and weaknesses in one component can be overcome by strengths in others. We consider this model to be an excellent depiction of good governance arrangements for service

Table 21.2 Five principles of good governance for crime-prevention
          partnerships

Governance principle	Conditions for success
Legitimacy and Voice Those in positions of power are perceived to have acquired their power legitimately and there is an appropriate voice accorded to those whose interests are affected by decisions	• Everyone who needs to be is at the table • There are forums for bringing the partners together • The forums are managed so that the various voices are listened to and the dialogue is genuine and respectful • There is a consensus orientation among all those at the table
Direction/Strategic Vision The exercise of power results in a sense of overall direction that serves as a guide to action	• All parties share a joint and clearly articulated vision of their goal • Each party to the partnership sees how his/her organization can contribute to the vision • Roles and responsibilities are clearly defined • The parties have adequately adjusted to any changes to the vision that have occurred over time
Performance Institutions and processes are responsive to the interests of participants, citizens, or stakeholders	• There is a clear idea among participants as to what constitutes success • Performance is monitored and reported • The framework for performance measurement and reporting is developed jointly • There are sufficient resources to build and maintain the partnership • The different contexts in which the parties work are understood and accepted
Accountability There is accountability between those in positions of power and those whose interests they serve, and transparency and openness in the conduct of the work	• The accountabilities of all of the parties are clear • There are open, transparent, and accountable relationships between the parties • The accountability relationships of the parties to their respective organizations is recognized and respected • The effectiveness of the partnership is reported publicly
Fairness There is conformity with the rule of law and the principle of equity	• All parties believe they receive sufficient value from the partnership • The clients of the parties and the public benefit from the partnership • The laws that govern each party are recognized and respected

Source: Adapted from Edgar, Marshall, and Bassett 2006.

Core Implementation Components

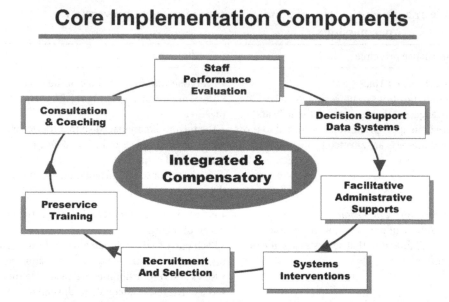

Figure 21.2 Core components that work together to implement and sustain the effective
use of human service innovations such as evidence-based programs
Source: Adapted from Fixsen et al. 2009, p. 534.

delivery organizations, and a useful way of summarizing many of the lessons that that
have been learned from crime-prevention implementations.

Staff recruitment, training, coaching, and performance evaluation are at the
heart of the model and are also at the heart of many of the challenges facing those
involved in crime-prevention implementations, as the CRP, NZ, and other case
studies illustrate. A particularly important feature of successful implementations
that has implications for how crime prevention is currently delivered is the use of
ongoing coaching and consultation to ensure that practitioners gain essential skills
from experts who are embedded in organizational settings. Organizational supports through data systems and a facilitative administration are also vital (e.g., DLE,
STAD), with staff issues and organizational support being influenced in turn by
larger system variables. It is difficult, for example, to select qualified staff for relatively low paid but demanding community-based interventions in an environment
where graduates can attract higher salaries in other, less stressful fields. Similarly,
we have noted the vulnerability of prevention programs to changing political whims;
crime prevention is nothing if not political. Table 21.2 links directly to the Fixsen
model in that it highlights the fact that implementation for sustainability depends
on a stable political and organizational environment, long-term funding, and external system settings that support the work of practitioners.

Implementation science is in its infancy, but in this essay we have attempted to
describe some of its elements and suggest, through a series of examples and case
studies, how Type 2 prevention science, applied particularly to crime problems,
could be developed. We have argued that any science of implementation will have
as a core component the study of governance arrangements for effective large-scale

crime prevention, and have presented two complementary models that address the challenges of organizational change and collaborative partnerships. The need for this development is urgent if the promise of the evidence-based movement is to be fully realized.

REFERENCES

Advisory Group on Conduct Problems. 2009. *Conduct Problems: Effective Programs for 3-7 Year-olds 2009.* Wellington: Ministry of Social Development.

Anderson, J., and Peter Homel. 2006. *Western Australian Office of Crime Prevention Community Safety and Crime Prevention Evaluation Survey one report.* Canberra: Australian Institute of Criminology.

Babor, Thomas, Raul Caetano, Sally Casswell, Griffith Edwards, Norman Giesbrecht, Kathryn Graham, Joel Grube, Linda Hill, Harold Holder, Ross Homel, Michael Livingston, Esa Österberg, Jürgen Rehm, Robin Room, and Ingeborg Rossow. 2010. *Alcohol: No Ordinary Commodity. Research and Public Policy,* 2nd ed. Oxford, UK: Oxford University Press.

Bammer, Gabriele, Annette Michaux, and Ann Sanson, eds. 2010. *Bridging the "Know-Do" Gap: Knowledge Brokering to Improve Child Well-Being.* Canberra: ANU E Press.

Eck, John. 2003. "Police Problems: The Complexity of Problem Theory, Research and Evaluation." In *Problem Oriented Policing: From Innovation to Mainstream,* edited by Johannes Knutsson. Vol. 15 of *Crime Prevention Studies,* edited by Ronald V. Clarke. Monsey, NY: Criminal Justice Press.

Eckenrode, John, Mary Campa, Dennis Luckey, Charles Henderson, Robert Cole, Harriet Kitzman, Elizabeth Anson, Kimberly Sidora-Arcoleo, Jane Powers, and David Olds. 2010. "Long-Term Effects of Prenatal and Infancy Nurse Home Visitation on the Life Course of Youths: 19-Year Follow-up of a Randomized Trial." *Archives of Pediatric and Adolescent Medicine* 164(1): 9–15.

Edgar Laura, Claire Marshall, and Michael Bassett. (2006). *Partnerships: Putting Good Governance Principles in Practice.* Ottawa: Institute of Governance.

Ekblom, Paul. 2010. *Crime Prevention Security and Community Safety Using the 51s Framework.* Melbourne: Palgrave Macmillan.

Fixsen, Dean L., Karen A. Blase, Sandra F. Naoom, and Frances Wallace. 2009. "Core Implementation Components." *Research on Social Work Practice* 16(5): 531–40.

Graham, Kathryn, and Ross Homel. 2008. *Raising the Bar: Preventing Aggression in and Around Bars, Pubs and Clubs.* Cullompton, UK: Willan.

Greenberg, Mark. T. 2009. Presentation to the Prevention Science Network, ARACY ARC/ NHMRC Research Network, June 28, Melbourne.

Greenberg, Mark T. 2010. "School-based Prevention: Current Status and Future Challenges." *Effective Education* 2(1): 27–52.

Hadfield, Phil. 2009. *Nightlife and Crime.* Oxford, UK: Oxford University Press.

Hawkins, David J., Sabrina Oesterle, Eric C. Brown, Michael W. Arthur, Robert D. Abbott, Abigail A. Fagan, and Richard F. Catalano. 2009. "Results of a Type 2 Translational Research Trial to Prevent Adolescent Drug Use and Delinquency: A Test of Communities that Care." *Archives of Pediatric and Adolescent Medicine* 163(9): 789–98.

Hawkins, David J., Eric C. Brown, Sabrina Oesterle, Michael W. Arthur, Robert D. Abbott, and Richard F. Catalano. 2008. "Early Effects of Communities that Care on Targeted Risks and Initiation of Delinquent Behavior and Substance Use." *Journal of Adolescent Health* 43(1): 15–22.

Hawkins, David J., Richard F. Catalano, Jr., and Associates. 1992. *Communities that Care: Action for Drug Abuse Prevention*. San Francisco: Jossey-Bass.

Henstridge, John, Ross Homel, and Peta Mackay. 1997. *The Long-Term Effects of Random Breath Testing in Four Australian States: A Time Series Analysis*. Canberra: Federal Office of Road Safety.

Home Office. 1999. *The Government's Crime Reduction Strategy*. London: Home Office.

Homel, Peter. 2006. "Joining up the Pieces: What Central Agencies Need to Do to Support Effective Local Crime Prevention." In *Putting Theory To Work: Implementing Situational Prevention and Problem-Oriented Policing*, edited by J. Knutsson and R. V. Clarke. Vol. 20 of *Crime Prevention Studies*, edited by Ronald V. Clarke. Monsey, NY: Criminal Justice Press.

Homel, Peter. 2009. "Lessons for Canadian Crime Prevention from Recent International Experience." *Institute for the Prevention of Crime Review* 3:13–39.

Homel, Peter, and Katie Willis. 2007. "A Framework for Measuring the Performance of Drug Law Enforcement." *Trends and Issues in Crime and Criminal Justice* 332:1–6.

Homel, Peter, Sandra Nutley, Barry Webb, and Nick Tilley. 2004. *Investing to Deliver. Reviewing the Implementation of the UK Crime Reduction Program*. Home Office Research Study no. 281. London: Home Office.

Homel, Ross. 1988. *Policing and Punishing the Drinking Driver: A Study of General and Specific Deterrence*. New York: Springer-Verlag.

Homel, Ross. 1993. "Random Breath Testing in Australia: Getting it to Work According to Specifications." *Addiction* 88(Suppl.): S27–33.

Homel, Ross, R. Carvolth, M. Hauritz, G. McIlwain, and R. Teague. 2004. "Making Licensed Venues Safer for Patrons: What Environmental Factors Should Be the Focus of Interventions?" *Drug and Alcohol Review* 23:19–29.

Hope, Tim. 2004. "Pretend it Works: Evidence and Governance in the Evaluation of the Reducing Burglary Initiative." *Criminal Justice* 4(3): 287–308.

Idriss, Manar, Manon Jendly, Jacqui Karn, and Massimiliano Mulone. 2010. *International Report Crime Prevention and Community Safety: Trends and Perspectives*. Quebec: International Centre for the Prevention of Crime.

Knutsson, Johannes, ed. 2003. *Problem Oriented Policing: From Innovation to Mainstream*. Vol. 15 of *Crime Prevention Studies*, edited Ronald V. Clarke. Monsey, NY: Criminal Justice Press.

Knutsson, Johannes, and Ronald V. Clarke, eds. 2006. *Putting Theory to Work: Implementing Situational Prevention and Problem-Oriented Policing*. Vol. 20 of *Crime Prevention Studies*, edited by Ronald V. Clarke. Monsey, NY: Criminal Justice Press.

Maguire, Mike. 2004. "The Crime Reduction Program in England and Wales: Reflections on the Vision and the Reality." *Criminal Justice* 4(3): 213–36.

Melhuish, Edward, Jay Belsky, and Jacqueline Barnes. 2010. "Evaluation and Value of Sure Start." *Archives of Diseases in Childhood* 95:159–61.

Michaux, Annette. 2010. "Integrating Knowledge in Service Delivery-Land: A View from The Benevolent Society." In *Bridging the "Know-Do" Gap: Knowledge Brokering to Improve Child Well-Being*, edited by Gabriele Bammer, Annette Michaux, and Ann Sanson. Canberra: ANU E Press.

Ministry of Social Development. 2007. *Inter-Agency Plan for Conduct Disorder/Severe Antisocial Behaviour 2007–2012.* Wellington: Ministry of Social Development.

National Drug Strategy Consultation. 2009. *Australia's National Drug Strategy Beyond 2009: Consultation Paper.* Canberra: National Drug Strategy Consultation.

Nutley, Sandra M., Isabel Walter, and Huw T. O. Davies. 2007. *Using Evidence: How Research Can Inform Public Services.* Bristol: The Policy Press.

Nutley, Sandra, and Peter Homel. 2006. "Delivering Evidence-Based Policy and Practice: Lessons from the Implementation of the UK Crime Reduction Program." *Evidence and Policy: A Journal of Research, Debate and Practice* 2(1): 5–26.

NZ Ministry of Justice. 2003. *Review of the Safer Community Council Network: Future Directions.* Wellington: NZ Ministry of Justice.

Olds, David, Charles Henderson, Robert Cole, John Eckenrode, Harriet Kitzman, Dennis Luckey, Lisa Pettitt, Kimberly Sidora, Pamela Morris, and Jane Powers. 1998. "Long-Term Effects of Nurse Home Visitation on Children's Criminal and Anti-Social Behavior: 15-Year Follow-up of a Randomized Controlled Trial." *Journal of the American Medical Association* 280(14): 1238–44.

Prinz, Ronald J., Matthew R. Sanders, Cheri J. Shaprio, Daniel J. Whitaker, and John R. Lutzker. 2009. "Population-Based Prevention of Child Maltreatment: The U.S. Triple P System Population Trial." *Prevention Science* 10(1): 1–12.

Rogers, E. M. 1995. *Diffusion of Innovations,* 4th ed. New York: Free Press.

Sanders, Matthew R. 2010. "Adopting a Public Health Approach to the Delivery of Evidence-Based Parenting Interventions." *Canadian Psychology* 51(1): 17–23.

Sanders, Matthew R., Alan Ralph, Kate Sofronoff, Paul Gardiner, Rachel Thompson, Sarah Dwyer, and Kerry Bidwell. 2008. "Every Family: A Population Approach to Reducing Behavioral and Emotional Problems in Children Making the Transition to School." *Journal of Primary Prevention* 29(3): 197–222.

Schorr, Lisbeth B. 1998. *Common Purpose: Strengthening Families and Neighborhoods to Rebuild America.* New York: Anchor Books.

Scott, Michael S. 2003. "Getting Police to Take Problem-Oriented Policing Seriously." In *Problem Oriented Policing: From Innovation to Mainstream,* edited by Johannes Knutsson. Vol. 15 of *Crime Prevention Studies,* edited by Ronald V. Clarke. Monsey, NY: Criminal Justice Press.

Society for Prevention Research. n.d. *Standards of Evidence: Criteria for Efficacy, Effectiveness and Dissemination.* Monsey, NY: Society for Prevention Research.

Society for Prevention Research. 2008. *Type 2 Translational Research: Overview and Definitions, May 19 2008.* Retrieved from http://www.preventionscience.org/commlmon.php#maps.

Sutton, Adam, Adrian Cherney, and Rob White. 2008. *Crime Prevention: Principles, Perspectives and Practices.* New York: Cambridge University Press.

Wallin, Eva, Birgitta Lindewald, and Sven Andréasson. 2004. "Institutionalization of a Community Action Program Targeting Licensed Premises in Stockholm, Sweden." *Evaluation Review* 28:396–419.

Welsh, Brandon C., and Akemi Hoshi. 2002. "Communities and Crime Prevention." In *Evidence-Based Crime Prevention,* edited by Lawrence W. Sherman, David P. Farrington, Brandon C. Welsh, and Doris Layton MacKenzie. London: Routledge.

Whittaker, James K. 2009. "Evidence-Based Intervention and Services for High-Risk Youth: A North American Perspective on the Challenges of Integration for Policy, Practice and Research." *Child and Family Social Work* 14:166–77.

CHAPTER 22

THE IMPORTANCE OF RANDOMIZED EXPERIMENTS IN EVALUATING CRIME PREVENTION

DAVID WEISBURD AND JOSHUA C. HINKLE

PROGRAM evaluation is one of the most important tasks social scientists can undertake. Evaluation researchers answer key questions about what works in targeting various social problems, and as such can have a large impact on public policy. Only through rigorous evaluation research can we know whether programs and policies are reducing the social problems they are designed to alleviate, whether the benefits gained are worth the cost of delivering the program, and whether the program has any unintended "backfire" effects. In terms of crime-prevention research, the key questions are whether social programs reduce crime and delinquency, whether these efforts are cost-effective, and whether they have any harmful effects—be it for communities (such as increased crime) or unintended harm to program participants.

Given the importance of answering such questions, the key issue facing evaluation research today is ensuring that the most rigorous methods are used to evaluate programs. In this essay we illustrate that randomized experiments offer the most persuasive evaluations of the effects of crime-prevention efforts (see Boruch 1975; Boruch, Victor, and Cecil 2000; Weisburd 2000; McCord 2003; Weisburd 2003). This is because randomized experiments offer the most "believable" method for identifying program effects in social contexts where treatments or interventions are likely to be confounded with other factors. Given the importance of allocating limited crime-prevention resources efficiently and effectively, as well as the risk of social programs themselves potentially causing harm (see McCord 2003), it is imperative that randomized trials be used as often as possible when evaluating crime prevention.

In this essay we outline why randomized experiments offer the most persuasive evidence on the true impacts of crime-prevention policies and interventions. Some key points raised include:

- Given the importance of crime-prevention evaluation research in enhancing public safety and informing decisions about how to best use limited crime-prevention resources, evaluators have an obligation to use the most rigorous methodology possible.
- The gravest threat to the believability of evaluation research is confounding factors that may bias the findings of outcome evaluations. The social world is very complex, and it is seldom reasonable to assume that all relevant confounders are known and measured, and thus can be controlled for in a multivariate statistical design or used to identify or create truly equivalent groups in quasi-experimental evaluations.
- Randomized experiments solve this problem of confounding through randomly allocating treatment. As such, with experiments we can assume that no omitted variables are systematically related to both the treatment and the outcome. Thus, experiments offer the strongest methodology for producing unbiased estimates of treatment effect.
- Despite these strengths, experiments are not widely used in research evaluating crime prevention. We note that a number of "folklores" are used to justify nonexperimental evaluations and discourage experimental studies. Such folklores are not persuasive and should not be key factors in hindering the development of experimental evaluation in crime prevention.
- While experiments offer the most persuasive evidence on program effectiveness, they are not a panacea and may not be feasible in every instance. Experiments are most likely to succeed in circumstances detailed in this essay, including when the program is well developed and is based on theory and/or has received prior research attention. Additionally, it is crucial that treatment dosage and integrity be maintained throughout the study period as experiments are limited in their ability to account for such confounders introduced after the study is under way.

The organization of this essay is as follows. Section I outlines the limitations of nonexperimental methods in reaching conclusions about the effectiveness of crime-prevention interventions. Section II turns to the specific statistical advantage of randomized experiments. Section III illustrates the risk we run by not using the most rigorous methodology to evaluate crime prevention. In particular we discuss the importance of identifying "cures that harm" (McCord 2003). Section IV presents a discussion of why crime-prevention researchers have often neglected to use experimental methods. We note that many of these reasons can be classified as folklore and are based on very weak assumptions. Section V examines the conditions under which randomized experiments are likely to be most successful, and suggests ways for maximizing the appropriateness of experiments for dealing with the complexities of crime-prevention research. Section VI discusses arguments raised by critics of experiments who suggest the method may be too simple and naïve for the complexities of evaluating crime prevention. Section VII summarizes our essay's main themes and overall contribution.

I. THE LIMITATIONS OF NONEXPERIMENTAL METHODS

The central challenge to evaluating crime prevention is getting unbiased estimates of treatment effects. Even if crime drops after a hot-spots policing program, or recidivism among drug users is reduced after a rehabilitation program, how can we be sure the reduction was due to the treatment? The social world and human behavior are very complex, with an uncountable number of factors that can lead to change. For example, suppose that addicts who had volunteered for participation in a drug rehabilitation program had lower rates of drug use after the program, as compared with addicts who did not participate in the program. In this case, the fact that those in the treatment group were volunteers already alerts us to a possible confounding of the program effect. Volunteers have been found to be much more likely to be highly motivated to succeed in programs than individuals who are not volunteers (Taxman 1998; De Leon et al. 2000; see also Rosenthal 1965). Accordingly, in this case, treatment is confounded with "motivation" to be rehabilitated. Perhaps the observed program effect was due not to the treatment but simply to the fact that the program participants were more motivated to succeed at the outset.

All evaluation methods must deal with this problem of confounding, and it stands as the major barrier to drawing believable conclusions in evaluation studies. Nonexperimental methods, such as regression techniques using observational data, and quasi-experiments using approaches such as matching of subjects, rely on a similar logic to solve the problem of confounding. The logic is easily stated: if we know what the factors are that confound treatment, we can take them into account.[1] In other words, nonexperimental methods rely on a "knowledge solution" to the problem of confounding. This solution fits very well into the academic milieu, which itself is about the search for knowledge. What is more natural than to have a solution to a statistical problem that states that knowledge is the key?

The problem with these approaches is that they demand a level of knowledge about the processes that underlie treatment that is lacking in criminology, and perhaps in all fields of social evaluation. If we know what the confounders are, we can take them into account or "control" for them in statistical terms (Weisburd and Britt 2007). For example, if we know that volunteers are likely to be highly motivated, we can measure motivation at the outset of the study and control for this variable in our analysis. The problem is that in theory we would have to know about all potential confounders at the outset so that we could measure them and then take them into account in our modeling of treatment. The question is whether this is a realistic expectation. A review of all empirical tests of theory published in *Criminology* suggests that it is not.

Weisburd and Piquero (2008) found that empirical attempts to test criminological theory in *Criminology* were likely to explain only about 40 percent of the variance in the dependent measures examined. About a quarter of the studies reviewed explained less than 20 percent of the variance in crime and over 70 percent of theory tests explained less than half of the variance in crime. Variance explained is one measure of how well criminologists are doing in understanding the complex world of crime and justice. These findings from *Criminology,* the most elite journal in our field, raise important concerns regarding whether we are likely to be able to identify all relevant confounders in evaluating the effects of a program on a crime and justice outcome.

In short, to get a truly unbiased estimate of program effects using nonexperimental methods, one must identify every variable that has an impact on the outcome and is related to treatment, and then use those variables either in creating matched groups that are truly equivalent (e.g., in a quasi-experiment) on all relevant factors or including all of those variables in a multivariate model. If any of these variables are omitted, then the estimate of treatment effect will be biased.

Figure 22.1 illustrates how positive and negative biases are gained. Positive bias, meaning that the variable of interest is inflated when the confounder is excluded, is illustrated in figure 22.1A. Here, the relationship between the confounder (V_2) and the treatment (V_1), and the confounder and the outcome (Y), are both in the same direction (which can either be positive or negative). This is the kind of bias that is ordinarily seen as a concern in evaluation research. That is, that the effect of treatment is overestimated when the confounder is not taken into account. But the effect of treatment can also be underestimated. This would happen if the relationship between the confounder and the treatment, and the confounder and the outcome, are in opposite directions (see figure 22.1B).

The threat of excluding relevant confounding factors is clear. Not only can we under- or overestimate the impacts of interventions, we can also draw mistaken conclusions. What if the impact of the intervention without the confounder in the example in figure 22.1B were a standardized coefficient of 0.25 instead of 0.75? A coefficient of 0.25 represents a small but meaningful effect according to Cohen (1988). The standardized coefficient in this case would have declined from 0.25 to 0, leading us to conclude that there was no effect of the intervention.

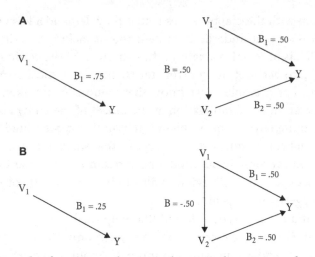

Figure 22.1 Example of positive and negative biases in the estimate of a treatment effect
using standardized coefficients
A. Example of positive biases (inflating the variable of interest) when the relationship
between confounder and outcome and confounder and treatment
are in the same direction
If V_2 is excluded, the bias = B * B_2 = .50 * .50 = .25
B. Example of negative biases (underestimating the variable of interest) when the
relationship between confounder and outcome and confounder and treatment
are in the opposite direction
If V_2 is excluded, the bias = B * B_2 = -.50 * .50 = -.25

The examples we have given are cases in which only one confounder has been excluded. We would expect in the real world that many more factors would likely fail to be measured by the investigators. In such situations, the extent of bias is of course unknown. But it is reasonable to conclude that biases may be meaningful and might at times lead us to erroneous conclusions regarding the effects of interventions.

II. THE STATISTICAL ADVANTAGE OF RANDOMIZED STUDIES

Randomized experiments offer a way to get unbiased estimates of treatment impact without requiring knowledge of every possible confounding factor. This is not to say that experimental research is infallible and always leads to valid conclusions. As will be discussed later, experiments have their own host of challenges like any research design, but when implemented properly they offer a more valid test of program effectiveness than a nonexperimental research design with the same quality of implementation.

Randomized experiments start with a different logic from nonexperimental solutions to confounding: if we cannot control out for confounding, we can make it irrelevant for the problem at hand. This is done through the process of randomizing treatment. If treatment is randomized, then there is no reason to suspect systematic biases. It does not rely on knowledge; it relies on the opposite of systematic knowledge—random relationships. In a randomized experiment, a group of subjects is first identified and then randomly assigned to the treatment or intervention condition and a control or comparison condition. There is no reason to suspect that men or women in the sample, or more motivated or less motivated subjects, or indeed subjects with any specific traits, are more likely to end up in the treatment group than the control group. Random assignment allows us to minimize the possibility that the groups created are different on traits we measure, as well as traits that we do not measure.

This fact allows us to make a very important assumption about the relationships between all possible confounders and the treatment. We can assume that they are not systematically related and this assumption allows us to "believe" that the observed effect of treatment is indeed unbiased. This can be illustrated by returning to the simple diagrams we used earlier to illustrate the dangers of confounding. In figure 22.2, we show the simple relationship between a treatment and outcome, as in figure 22.1 above, but this time use the example of a randomized study. We also include a confounder, as in the earlier example. But in this example, unlike that in figure 22.1 above, the confounder does not affect the estimate of the treatment effect. That is because the bias, which can be calculated as the simple multiplication of the relationship between the treatment and confounder, and the confounder and outcome, is 0. If we can assume that the treatment and confounder correlation is 0, then there is under this assumption no bias. Randomization makes this assumption possible for the reasons outlined above.

Experiments in this context offer a simple method for ruling out known and unknown sources of bias to our estimates of a program or treatment effect. It demands that we make an assumption based on randomization, and not one based on our willingness to say that we have identified and measured all possible

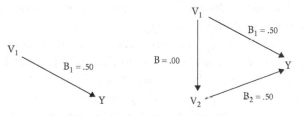

Figure 22.2 Example of the lack of confounding in the treatment effect when the treatment and potential confounder are assumed to have no relationship because of randomization.
If V_2 is excluded, the bias = B * B_2 = .00 *.50 = .00

confounding variables. In this sense, experiments provide a much more "believable" solution to the problem of confounding. This is the reason most evaluation researchers recognize that randomized experiments provide the most persuasive evidence about the effects of crime-prevention efforts (see Campbell and Boruch 1975; Cook and Campbell 1979; Flay and Best 1982; Farrington 1983; Wilkinson and Taskforce on Statistical Inference 1999; Boruch, Victor, and Cecil 2000; Feder, Jolin, and Feyerherm 2000; Weisburd 2000; Weisburd, Lum, and Petrosino 2001; Shadish, Cook, and Campbell 2002).

III. Is There a Cost to Using Nonexperimental Evaluation Methods?

While our discussion so far illustrates the statistical advantage of randomized experiments over other methods of program evaluation, we might question whether the use of nonexperimental methods is likely to lead in the long run to our coming to "wrong" conclusions in crime-prevention evaluations. To examine this question, Weisburd, Lum, and Petrosino (2001) compared experimental and nonexperimental studies from the comprehensive Maryland Report that had identified program evaluations relevant to crime and justice (Sherman et al. 1997).

The authors coded every study in the review as either working (had intended effect), having no effect, or having a backfire effect. Their findings showed that nonexperimental research was more likely to conclude programs worked and less likely to find backfire effects. Their statistical tests found a significant inverse relationship between type of research design and outcomes. Nonexperimental designs were more likely to find a positive outcome (and larger effect sizes), while experimental designs were the least likely to find a positive outcome (and the smallest effect sizes) and the most likely to detect harmful backfire effects. The key implication of their finding is that there is a positive bias in nonexperimental evaluation of crime-prevention programs. A recent study of research design in the specific area of public surveillance replicates Weisburd et al.'s conclusions (see Welsh et al. 2011).

The finding that nonrandomized studies are less likely to find harmful backfire effects is particularly troubling. This suggests that not only are nonexperimental tests more likely to produce Type 1 errors and conclude that programs work when they had no effect, they are also less likely to detect "cures that harm" (McCord 2003). As McCord (2003) argued, it is crucial not only to identify whether prevention programs reduce crime, recidivism, drug use, and other outcomes as intended, but also whether the programs lead to any harm. For instance, policies can backfire and lead to increases in recidivism.

Given the benefits of conducting randomized experiments and the possible costs of relying on nonexperimental evaluations, it is in some sense surprising

that experiments are the least common evaluation design used in crime prevention. While it is difficult to estimate the extent of prevalence of nonexperimental
research designs in evaluating crime prevention, the Maryland Report (Sherman
et al. 1997), found that only about 15 percent of evaluation studies used randomized experimental methods (Weisburd, Lum, and Petrosino 2001). MacKenzie
(2006) identified a similar proportion of randomized designs in a review of correctional evaluations.

IV. WHY ARE EXPERIMENTS SO "UNCOMMON" IN CRIME PREVENTION?: THE ROLE OF FOLKLORE

It is very difficult to explain why experiments are not more commonly used in
evaluating crime-prevention programs and practices. But we suspect that the reason may lie in part in folklores that have developed that both justify the use of
nonexperimental methods and suggest that there are difficult to overcome barriers
to experimental studies. We call these folklores because, as we argue below, we do
not think that they are based on solid evidence.

For example, it is sometimes argued that nonexperimental methods are generally
okay because overall we identify "the most important causes of crime," and any
omitted variables are thus unlikely to be major threats to the validity of our estimates
of program impacts. However, as outlined earlier in this essay, this is an untenable
assumption given the current state of criminological theory. If theory tests only
explain 38.9 percent of the variance in crime on average (Weisburd and Piquero 2008),
how can we safely assume we know all the major causes of crime and can thus control
for all major confounders in nonrandomized evaluations of crime-prevention programs? Even if we had fuller knowledge of possible confounders, often times there are
not reliable data for every relevant variable in a particular study.

A second common folklore justifying the use of nonexperimental methods is
the belief that if treatment effects are large, we can assume that excluded causes of
the outcome would not change the estimate of the treatment effect in a meaningful way. This is a very tenuous assumption to make, as there is no way to know
with certainty how important a confounder may be in the system of effects that
are studied.

As an illustration of this possibility, take the example of a study examining the
impact of race on death penalty sentences in New Jersey (Weisburd and Naus
2001). This study found initially that the race of the victim was significantly related
to the likelihood of a death penalty eligible case advancing to a penalty trial (in
which a death sentence would be considered). Specifically, in logistic regression
models it was found that cases involving white victims were more likely to advance

to the penalty stage. However, a state prosecutor challenged these findings, suggesting that the effect was confounded. In particular, the prosecutor noted that cases with white victims were more likely to go to trial not because the victims were white but, rather, because such cases were likely to be found in nonurban areas with fewer death penalty eligible cases. The state prosecutor argued that in these areas prosecutors were more likely to treat such cases very aggressively either because they had more resources to do so or because that they simply viewed such cases more seriously as there were so few of them compared with the more urban areas. Weisburd and Naus (2001) were skeptical of this claim, as the race impact appeared to be a strong and robust effect that remained significant across a number of different model specifications and samples. However, they nevertheless tested the prosecutor's theory by controlling for the rate of death penalty cases in each county.

Their findings supported the prosecutor's theory. In nearly every model specification, adding a control for the rate of death penalty eligible cases rendered the impact of victim's race on death penalty decisions nonsignificant. This example shows the risk one runs when assuming that effects are large enough to not be meaningfully altered by confounders. Absent full knowledge of all causes of an outcome, it is never possible to be sure there are no major confounders omitted that could fundamentally alter the conclusions drawn from nonexperimental research.

Additionally, crime-prevention researchers will sometimes argue that any biases from omitted variables (after the known confounders are identified) are likely to balance out in the long run. This logic is based on the assumption that we can presume that some omitted variables inflate the estimate of treatment effect while others deflate the effect size. Thus, at the end of the day, it is argued that these omitted variables have no meaningful impact on the estimate of program effect since they balance each other out. This is a tenuous assumption, as it relies on a model where the omitted variables were excluded randomly. However, this is not likely to be the case. Variables are often systematically excluded for various reasons. Research may, for example, include only variables related to certain theories of interest while omitting others, or variables may be excluded as agencies like police or courts systematically collect data to fit their needs rather than those of researchers. The likelihood that variables are often systematically omitted thus challenges the notion that bias will balance out and thus not impact treatment estimates.

Even when researchers have accepted that experiments offer a more powerful statistical method for dealing with the critical problem of confounding, they have often raised other folklores that justify not using randomized experiments. One is the common claim that randomized experiments are not ethical, particularly in crime-prevention settings. For instance, it is argued that it is unethical to withhold treatment from the control group for research purposes when they could also benefit from receiving the program in question. Or that it is unethical to randomly impose criminal sanctions or other punishments. However, a number of scholars in recent years have argued that exactly the opposite is true—that it is unethical *not* to use randomized experimental methods to answer key policy questions (for example, see Boruch 1975; Boruch, Victor, and Cecil 2000; Weisburd 2000; McCord 2003; Weisburd 2003). In this case, scholars claim that harm can be caused by using less rigorous methods that are more likely to lead to false conclusions about the impact of programs or policies, be it falsely finding that a program worked or not being able to identify programs with harmful effects (Weisburd, Lum, and Petrosino 2001; McCord 2003).

Moreover, a recent study suggests that ethical concerns may not be a major barrier keeping researchers from conducting randomized experiments. Lum and Yang (2005) surveyed a sample of evaluators of studies included in the Maryland Report (Sherman et al. 1997) who had used experimental or nonexperimental methods in their evaluations. The survey gathered information about why they chose their method, as well as assessing their views on experimental and nonexperimental research. The survey found that both experimenters and researchers who used nonexperimental methods agreed that experiments were the best method for linking cause and effect. More relevant to the current discussion, the survey found that both types of researchers generally disagreed with a statement suggesting that randomized experiments could not be carried out ethically in crime-prevention evaluation research.

This is not to say that ethical concerns should not be examined when considering the use of randomized experiments in evaluation research. These findings simply suggest that ethical concerns are often exaggerated. The ethical implications of experiments (or any research design) should be considered specific to the context of each program being evaluated. In certain circumstances, it will not be ethical to conduct randomized experiments and there is long-running debate over what those circumstances should be (Farrington 1983; Boruch, Victor, and Cecil 2000; Asscher et al. 2007; Solomon, Cavanaugh, and Draine 2009). Nevertheless, Lum and Yang's (2005) findings suggest that evaluation researchers who evaluate crime prevention generally do not consider ethical concerns as a major barrier to conducting experimental studies.

A second folklore justifying not using randomized experiments comes in the form of practical concerns that experiments simply cannot be implemented in the real world of crime-prevention research. These concerns suggest that, irrespective of ethical concerns, it is simply not feasible to carry out randomized experiments in most crime-prevention contexts. The body of evaluation research in crime prevention simply does not support this claim. While experimental research is less common than nonexperimental studies, there is nonetheless a growing body of experimental research covering a wide variety of programs, policies, and tactics in various areas such as policing, corrections, courts, drug prevention, and more.

Telep (2009), for example, identified 185 experiments in a study of citation counts to randomized experiments in crime and justice. In a more comprehensive earlier review covering a wider literature, Petrosino and colleagues (2003) identified 267 experiments from 1945 to 1993. Moreover, recent reviews show an increase in experimentation in crime and justice in recent years. Farrington and Welsh (2005) identified 82 experiments involving at least 50 subjects in each group published between 1982 and 2004 compared to only 54 conducted between 1957 and 1981. While these numbers are small compared to fields like medicine (see Shepherd 2003), they nevertheless show that experimentation is clearly a feasible method for evaluating crime prevention and that practical barriers are not insurmountable. Again, this does not mean that experiments will be feasible in every circumstance, but simply that the method should be evaluated on a case-by-case basis rather than dismissed out of hand, based on folklore suggesting that experiments are not feasible in the real world of crime-prevention evaluation research.

Finally, scholars often justify not using randomized experiments because they are assumed to have lower external validity than nonexperimental studies. *External validity* refers to the ability of the results from a specific study to be generalized to other contexts or settings. For instance, does a finding of nurse home visits reducing child abuse and neglect in one large city mean that approach will also be effective in other cities? We argued above that experiments offer the strongest internal validity, which means that experiments are the strongest design for producing believable results about treatment impacts on subjects of the current study. However, this matters little if critics are correct that experiments have low external validity and we can thus not draw inferences to other populations of interests. While a key function of evaluation research is determining whether a specific intervention or policy is effective in a specific setting, the ultimate goal is to generate a body of evidence about treatments that can be effective in any relevant population.

In our view, there is little reason to believe that experiments are any less generalizable than nonexperimental research. In fact, all crime-prevention evaluation research is relatively limited in terms of the level of inferences that can be made. For instance, studies of police practices or prison programs are almost always conducted in a single site or jurisdiction. In such, cases the findings are really only generalizable in statistical terms to those populations—that is, all areas in that police jurisdiction or the population of prisoners from facilities involved in a given study of a prison rehabilitation program. However, this is true regardless of whether experimental or nonexperimental methods are used. The problem is having only a single site, not the particular research design that is adopted.

The critiques of the external validity of randomized experiments often suggest that the problem is more severe in experimental research based on a notion that there is something different about agencies willing to participate in randomized trials. Critics suggest that agencies willing to participate in randomized studies may be more innovative or different in other ways that make them not representative of the general population of criminal justice agencies. However, this is likely true of participation in research in general. More innovative agencies are more likely to agree to participate in research studies regardless of the methods used. To our knowledge there is no empirical evidence showing that agencies participating in randomized trials are any less representative of the universe of criminal justice agencies than are those participating in quasi-experiments, pre/post tests, or other nonexperimental forms of research. Moreover, the history of large randomized trials funded by the National Institute of Justice suggests that "ordinary" agencies can be drawn to participate in such studies if there is strong governmental encouragement and financial support to reward participation (Weisburd 2005).

V. When Can Experiments Be Most Successful?

While many of the barriers to experiments are largely folklores, this does not mean that the method is a panacea, without challenge, and sure to succeed in every context. Like any method, it has its challenges and there are a series of principles for when experiments are more likely to be able to be successfully implemented and carried out. In regard to ethical issues, experiments have been more feasible when either or both of two circumstances are met. First, experiments that add additional resources to criminal justice agencies or communities or provide additional treatments for subjects will encounter fewer ethical barriers than those that seek to randomly allocate existing resources. In such cases, the control group is not being deprived of resources they were receiving before. Second, in terms of testing sanctions, experiments are more likely to succeed if they are randomly allocating penalties that are more lenient than existing sanctions. While there are clear ethical dilemmas in randomly giving out harsher penalties, there are fewer objections to randomly assigning more lenient penalties and testing whether the reductions have any impact on recidivism. For instance, we are unaware of any major objections to the California Reduced Prison Experiment (Berecochea and Jaman 1981), in which thousands of prisoners were randomly released earlier than those in the control group.

In terms of political barriers, experiments are more likely to avoid pitfalls if three principles are met. First, experiments will be easier to implement if they have lower public visibility. As such, researchers should avoid publicizing their study in the media or other outlets until the conclusion of the experiment. If a study becomes public knowledge before or during its implementation, it is more likely that citizens, community groups, and others will raise objections about the program not being delivered in their area. Second, experimental studies will raise fewer political objections if the subjects of intervention are less serious threats to community safety. For instance, there will likely be fewer outcries over an experiment diverting nonviolent drug offenders from prison than a similar experiment focused on violent offenders— though as we argue later, it may be most important to bring treatment to more serious offenders. Finally, random allocation is less likely to be controversial if the program being tested could be implemented only in select locations rather than jurisdiction wide. In these cases communities or individuals are less likely to feel that they have been systematically excluded, since resources available make it impossible to deliver the program everywhere it may be needed.

Lastly, turning to practical barriers to experimentation, there are three principles related to getting agencies to buy in and successfully carry out experimental studies. First, experiments that reduce the discretion of crime-prevention practitioners or criminal justice agents who ordinarily operate with a great deal of autonomy and authority will be the most difficult to implement. For instance, judges are more likely to have objections to having their decisions made randomly than are patrolmen in a police agency who are used to following orders. Of course, this varies by the type of decisions involved, and criminal justice actors with a high level of autonomy will be more likely to comply when the treatment conditions are more similar to the control conditions. For instance, judges are more likely to accept randomization if the two conditions are similar in leniency than if one condition is much harsher than the other.

Building off this principle, it follows that experiments can be implemented more easily in agencies in which there is a high degree of hierarchical control, and this is true even if the actors usually have a great deal of autonomy. For instance, patrol officers in a police agency have a great deal of autonomy and discretion in their field work. However, they also follow orders regarding how and where to exercise their discretion, and this hierarchical system makes it easier to implement experimental studies.

Finally, arguably the most serious practical concern with experimental research is maintaining the integrity of the treatment. It is crucial that the treatment dosage is maintained through the study period and is confined to those in the treatment group. If the dosage fluctuates throughout the study period, or subjects/areas in the control groups accidentally receive treatment, the validity of the experiment is severely challenged. This is true of any research design, but it is a particularly important issue in randomized studies, as there are few options for taking these treatment failures into account once the experiment is under way. As such, treatments that are complex, involve multiple actions, or actions that are not part of the normal routine of the criminal justice agency raise difficulties for evaluation research. First, they are harder to implement successfully owing to their complexity and/or being a task that the agency does not usually perform. Second, they risk becoming prohibitively cumbersome and expensive to carry out as complex interventions require a higher level of monitoring by the research team to ensure the treatment was implemented properly and dosage was maintained throughout the study period.

A. The Power Few

Taking a different approach to the issue of when experiments are most likely to succeed, Lawrence Sherman (2007) attempted to tackle the issue of experiments' often finding small or null effects. Sherman examined three hypotheses about why experiments often fail to show large effect sizes. First, he noted (as did Weisburd,

Lum, and Petrosino 2001) that it may just be that experiments are more likely to detect weak programs—be these weaknesses owing to bad theory behind the program, poor implementation of the treatment, or insufficient dosage. Second, he suggests that it could be that many experiments have been focused on samples that were too heterogeneous. Sherman noted that Weisburd and colleagues (1993) found that, contrary to expectation, larger sample sizes were tied to studies being *less* likely to find significant treatment impacts. Sherman called this "Weisburd's paradox." The reason behind this paradox is as follows. All things being equal, larger samples should provide more statistical power and make studies more able to detect treatment effects; however, in practice all things are not equal, and larger samples often reduce statistical power of studies by increasing the heterogeneity of samples. This heterogeneity in turn increases variance, which reduces statistical power.

Sherman's third hypothesis for the reason behind null findings in many experiments is that many studies have focused primarily on "low-harm units" rather than on what he calls the "power few"—those small percentages of individuals, groups, or locations that account for a large proportion of crime. By focusing on more than just these "power few" cases, studies may find null results even if the treatment works on these serious cases as the low-harm cases may water down the study. As such, the main thrust of Sherman's essay is the need for experimental research to focus on the power few. Just as research has shown that police can be most effective when focusing on crime hot spots (or power few locations) of crime, Sherman suggests that experimental research more generally can be most effective if it focuses on evaluating programs that target the "power few."

VI. Are Experiments Too Naïve and Rigid for the Complexities of Evaluating Crime Prevention?

As outlined throughout this essay, randomized experiments offer the strongest method for linking cause and effect, and thus offer the most promise for believably evaluating crime-prevention programs. However, experiments can and do fail, and the experimental design is certainly not without its own set of challenges—just like any other evaluation methodology. While experiments excel at linking cause and effect, they have difficulty controlling for confounders introduced after implementation, such as lapses in dosage or contamination of treatment into the control group.

Along similar veins, many have argued that the rigid nature of the experimental design leaves the method too simple for the complexities of evaluating crime-prevention programs and policies (e.g., see Clarke and Cornish 1972; Heckman and Smith 1995; Pawson and Tilley 1997; Manski 2011). The thrust of these criticisms is that the experimental design usually examines treatments as a "black box" and only tests the mean impact of the treatment across all subjects. As such, these critics suggest that experiments do not provide answers to many questions asked by policymakers, such as why a treatment works, whether it works better for certain types of people or places, and so forth.

In our view, these criticisms point more to a central flaw in the field of criminology and criminal justice than to any objective shortcoming to applying the experimental method in this area. For any evaluation to examine specifics of why a program works, or to do a thorough examination of differential treatment impacts, it is required that the program be based on well-developed theory that lays out specific causal pathways to be targeted by crime-prevention programs. Lacking this information, it is unlikely that any evaluation study will be able to provide sufficient answers to such questions, regardless of whether an experimental or nonexperimental design is employed.

While it is true that many experimental evaluations of crime-prevention programs cannot answer these types of questions about specific causal mechanisms or differential treatment impacts, this is a result of the way these studies were designed rather than a shortcoming of the experimental method itself. There is no reason that randomized experiments must treat interventions as black boxes, and no reason that they can only examine mean treatment impacts for one treatment group relative to one control group. In fact, a recent report from the National Research Council suggested that experimental research should not treat interventions as black boxes but, rather, should collect detailed information about the intervention and dosage in an effort to be able to make stronger conclusions about why a program did or did not work (Lipsey et al. 2006). Further, Robert Boruch (2010), noting the tendency of experimental research to find null outcomes, has recently argued that experimenters need to spend more time examining why programs failed rather than simply reporting that the program did not work or failed to reach significance. The corollary of this is that experimenters should also examine why programs achieve positive results. There is no reason experimental studies cannot simultaneously collect qualitative and ethnographic data to help make sense of the findings from the experimental outcome evaluation.

Additionally, while the experimental design is rigid by nature, it is not impossible to account for differential treatment impacts. Experiments can be designed to explicitly test such impacts if prior research and/or theory on the intervention suggest the potential for differential treatment effects. For instance, if a past study found evidence that a school violence-prevention program had differential impacts across juveniles not at risk and at-risk juveniles, a future experiment could employee a block-randomized design where juveniles and at-risk juveniles are separately randomized into treatment and control groups. Examining the interaction between risk classification and treatment in subsequent analyses will provide policymakers with strong experimental evidence on whether their program is more effective for specific groups.

As such, the real key in examining the complexities of crime prevention has much less to do with the evaluation design chosen and much more to do with the state of theory and prior evidence on the program being tested. In short, as others have noted, programs and policies not grounded in strong theory are much more likely to fail (see Eck 2006). Not only are they more likely to fail, they are also more difficult to evaluate as researchers have little guidance on what causal mechanisms they should be examining or what possible differential treatment impacts they should be considering. Even strong advocates of experimental research have noted these issues, and have argued that experiments are not always appropriate and the choice of evaluation method should be based on the specific questions of interest and other factors on a case-by-case basis (see Lipsey et al. 2006).

Experiments are going to be most appropriate and offer the most bang for their buck when the program or policy is based on strong theory that can be used to guide the design of the evaluation, and initial basic research using observational methods shows that data support the theories. In short, experiments are most appropriate when the existing program is well established and there is theory and evidence from prior research that can be used to design block-randomized studies to test for differential treatment impacts across relevant factors. One mechanism for improving evaluation research on this front is to follow Lawrence Sherman's (2006) suggestion that researchers be involved in both the development and evaluation of crime-prevention programs (see also Weisburd 1996). Such a strategy maximizes the integration of theory and practice, and reviews (see Losel and Schmucker 2005) have found that some of the strongest positive evidence on crime prevention comes from programs where researchers were involved in both program design and testing. A notable example of this is the work of David Olds on nurse-home visitation programs (see Olds et al. 1986).

Finally, another central theme of these criticisms of experimental crime-prevention evaluations is their supposed low external validity. This was discussed in an earlier section of the essay, with our response being that there is no systematic evidence that agencies and subjects participating in randomized trials are any less representative than those participating in quasi-experiments or evaluations relying upon official data and statistics to control for confounding. Nevertheless, concerns over the generalizability of findings are a key issue in evaluation research regardless of the research design employed. As these critics note, it is often difficult to collect a sample that is truly representative of the entire population for whom the treatment or policy could potentially benefit. For instance, a program that works in one community may or may not be effective in another.

Such problems are typically addressed though replications and systematic reviews and meta-analyses. If a program is found to work in multiple locations and contexts, the generalizability is higher than that of a study conducted in only one site. Alternatively, it has been suggested that programs based on sound theories have higher levels of generalizability (Eck 2006). More recent developments in experimental research in crime prevention provide another avenue for improving generalizability—multisite randomized trials (see Weisburd and Taxman 2000; Weisburd 2003). This methodology involves implementing a specific intervention protocol with a randomized design simultaneously in multiple sites. For instance, a drug treatment program can be simultaneously tested in multiple locations, improving generalizability by producing results across different regions, facilities, and so on.

VII. Discussion and Conclusions

As noted at the outset of the essay, evaluation researchers have an important obligation to produce valid evidence of treatment impacts. Only through evaluation research can we identify programs that work and deserve to have precious crime-prevention resources devoted to them, as well as identifying treatments that may harm rather than cure (McCord 2003). Given the important role of evaluation research, it is crucial that evaluation researchers use the most rigorous methods available to isolate the effects of crime-prevention interventions. In this essay, we made the case for randomized experiments as offering the most persuasive evidence on intervention effects.

The randomized design allows for ruling out confounders and producing unbiased estimates of treatment impact. However, we also stress that randomized experiments should not be viewed as a panacea, and as such our essay should not be viewed as arguing that experimental research is the only relevant evaluation methodology. Experiments provide the most "believable" evidence on treatment or intervention impacts, but are not possible or appropriate in every case. As such, quasi-experiments, multivariate modeling, and even pre/post case studies (see Eck 2006) all play an important role in evaluating crime prevention—be it through contributing to the evidence base or providing important information on contextual variation in treatment impact that can be used to inform the design of future, more rigorous evaluations of the intervention or policy.

To conclude, we offer the following suggestions for the future of crime-prevention evaluation research. First, the field needs to improve theory about crime and better integrate theory into the design of anti-crime programs and policies. Second, new programs and policies based on sound theory should receive intensive study focused not only on testing whether the program worked but also on examining specifics about why the program did or did not work and whether it has differential impacts across demographics and other factors. Finally, programs that are grounded in theory and have received some research attention should then be subjected to randomized experimental research when circumstances permit, and employ multisite designs when possible to enhance the generalizability of findings.

NOTE

1. In the case of quasi-experiments, the argument often is that we know the factors that confound treatment, and on the basis of this knowledge we can identify comparable groups that are alike on these factors.

REFERENCES

Asscher, Jessica J., Maja Dekovic, Peter H. van der Laan, Pier J.M. Prins, and Sander van Arum. 2007. "Implementing Randomized Experiments in Criminal Justice Settings: An Evaluation of Multi-systemic therapy in the Netherlands." *Journal of Experimental Criminology* 3:113–29.

Berecochea J. E., and D. R. Jaman. 1981. *Time Served in Prison and Parole Outcome: An Experimental Study (Report No. 2)*. Sacremento: California Department of Corrections Research Division.

Boruch, Robert. 1975. "On Common Contentions About Randomized Field Experments." In *Experimental Testing of Public Policy: The Proceedings of the 1974 Social Sciences Research Council Conference on Social Experimentation*, edited by Robert Boruch and H. W. Reikens. Boulder, CO: Westview.

Boruch, Robert. 2010. "To Flop is Human: Can We (Should We) Invent Orderly/Disciplined/Scientific Approaches to Anticipating Failure to Meet Expectations in Testing Innovations and to Learn from Such Failure?" Paper presented at the Second Annual Symposium of the Center for Evidence-Based Crime Policy at George Mason University, Fairfax, VA, August 9–10.

Boruch, Robert, Timothy Victor, and Joe Cecil. 2000. "Resolving Ethical and Legal Problems in Randomized Experiments." *Crime & Delinquency* 46:300–53.

Campbell, Donald P., and Robert F. Boruch. 1975. "Making the Case for Randomized Assignment to Treatments by Considering the Alternatives: Six Ways in Which Quasi-Experimental Evaluations in Compensatory Education Tend to Underestimate Effects." In *Evaluation and Experiment: Some Critical Issues in Assessing Social Programs*, edited by Carl A. Bennet and Arthur A. Lumsdain. New York: Academic Press.

Clarke, Ronald V. G., and Derek B. Cornish. 1972. *The Controlled Trial in Institutional Research: Paradigm or Pitfall for Penal Evaluators?* London: HMSO.

Cohen, Jacob. 1988. *Statistical Power Analysis for the Behavioral Sciences*. Hillsdale, NJ: Lawrence Erlbaum.

Cook, Thomas D., and Donald P. Campbell. 1979. *Quasi-Experimentation: Design and Analysis Issues for Field Settings*. Chicago: Rand-McNally.

De Leon, George, Gerald Melnick, George Thomas, David Kressel, and Harry K. Wexler. 2000. "Motivation for Treatment in a Prison-Based Therapeutic Community." *American Journal of Drug and Alcohol Abuse* 26:33–46.

Eck, John E. 2006. "When Is a Bolgna Sandwhich Better than Sex? A Defense of Small-n Case Study Evaluations." *Journal of Experimental Criminology* 2:345–62.

Farrington, David P. 1983. "Randomized Experiments on Crime and Justice." In *Crime and Justice: A Review of Research*, vol. 4, edited by Michael Tonry. Chicago: University of Chicago Press.

Farrington, David P., and Brandon C. Welsh. 2005. "Randomized Experiments in Criminology: What Have We Learned in the Last Two Decades?" *Journal of Experimental
Criminology* 1:9–38.

Feder, Lynette, Annette Jolin, and William Feyerherm. 2000. "Lessons from Two
Randomized Experiments in Criminal Justice Settings." *Crime and Delinquency*
46:380–400.

Flay, Brian R., and J. Allen Best. 1982. "Overcoming Design Problems in Evaluation of
Health Behavior Programs." *Evaluation and the Health Professions* 5:43–69.

Heckman, James J., and Jeffrey A. Smith. 1995. "Assessing the Case for Social Experiments."
Journal of Economic Perspective 9:85–110.

Lipsey, Mark, Carol Petrie, David Weisburd, and Denise Gottfredson. 2006. "Improving
Evaluation of Anti-Crime Programs: Summary of a National Research Council
Report." *Journal of Experimental Criminology* 2:271–307.

Losel, Friedrich, and Marin Schmucker. 2005. "The Effectiveness of Treatment for Sexual
Offenders: A Comprehensive Metal-Analysis." *Journal of Experimental Criminology*
1:117–46.

Lum, Cynthia, and Sue-Ming Yang. 2005. "Why Do Evaluation Researchers in Crime and
Justice Choose Non-Experimental Methods?" *Journal of Experimental Criminology*
1:191–213.

MacKenzie, Doris L. 2006. *What Works in Corrections: Reducing the Criminal Activities of
Offenders and Delinquents.* New York: Cambridge University Press.

Manski, Charles F. 2011. "Policy Choice with Partial Knowledge of Policy Effectiveness."
Journal of Experimental Criminology 7:111–25.

McCord, Joan. 2003. "Cures That Harm: Unanticipated Outcomes of Crime Prevention
Programs." *Annals of the American Academy of Political and Social Science* 587:16–30.

Olds, David L., Charles R. Henderson, Robert Chamberlin, and Robert Tattlebaum. 1986.
"Preventing Child Abuse and Neglect: A Randomized Trial of Nurse Home Visitation."
Pediatrics 78:1436–45.

Pawson, Ray, and Nick Tilley. 1997. *Realistic Evaluation.* London: Sage.

Petrosino, Anthony J., Robert Boruch, David P. Farrington, Lawrence Sherman, and David
Weisburd. 2003. "Toward Evidence-Based Criminology and Criminal Justice: System-
atic Reviews, The Campbell Collaboration, and the Crime and Justice Group."
International Journal of Comparative Criminology 3:42–61.

Rosenthal, Robert. 1965. "The Volunteer Subject." *Human Relations* 18:389–406.

Shadish, William R., Thomas D. Cook, and Donald T. Campbell. 2002. *Experimental and
Quasi-Experimental Designs for Generalized Causal Inference.* Boston: Houghton Mifflin.

Shepherd, Jonathan P. 2003. "Explaining Feast or Famine in Randomized Field Trials:
Medicine and Criminology Compared." *Evaluation Review* 27:290–315.

Sherman, Lawrence W. 2006. "'To Develop and Test:' The Inventive Difference between
Evaluation and Experimentation." *Journal of Experimental Criminology* 2:393–406.

Sherman, Lawrence W. 2007. "The Power Few: Experimental Criminology and the
Reduction of Harm. The 2006 Joan McCord Prize Lecture." *Journal of Experimental
Criminology* 3:299–321.

Sherman, Lawrence W., Denise Gottfredson, Doris L. MacKenzie, John E. Eck, Peter
Reuter and, Shawn Bushway. 1997. *What Works, What Doesn't, What's Promising.*
Washington, DC: National Institute of Justice.

Solomon, Phyllis L., Mary M. Cavanaugh, and Jeffrey Draine. 2009. *Randomized Controlled
Trials: Design and Implementation for Community-Based Psychosocial Interventions.*
New York: Oxford University Press.

Taxman, Faye S. 1998. *Reducing Recidivism Through a Seamless System of Care: Components of Effective Treatment, Supervision, and Transition Services in the Community.* Washington, DC: Office of National Drug Control Policy.

Telep, Cody W. 2009. "Citation Analysis of Randomized Experiments in Criminology and Criminal Justice: A Research Note." *Journal of Experimental Criminology* 5:441–64.

Weisburd, David. 1996. Preface. In *Policing Places with Drug Problems* by Lorraine Green. Beverly Hills, CA: Sage.

Weisburd, David. 2000. "Randomized Experiments in Criminal Justice Policy: Prospects and Problems." *Crime & Delinquency* 46:181–93.

Weisburd, David. 2003. "Ethical Practice and Evaluation of Interventions in Crime and Justice: The Moral Imperative for Randomized Trials." *Evaluation Review* 27: 336–54.

Weisburd, David. 2005. "Hot Spots Experiments and Criminal Justice Research: Lessons From the Field." *Annals of the American Academy of Political and Social Science* 578:220–45.

Weisburd, David, and Chester Britt. 2007. *Statistics in Criminal Justice,* 3rd ed. New York: Springer-Verlag.

Weisburd, David, Cynthia Lum, and Anthony Petrosino. 2001. "Does Research Design Affect Study Outcomes in Criminal Justice." *Annals of the American Academy of Political and Social* 578:50–70.

Weisburd, David, and Joseph Naus. 2001. "Report to Special Master David Baime: Assessment of the Index of Outcomes Approach for Use in Proportionality Review." New Jersey Administrative Office of the Courts, Trenton.

Weisburd, David, Anthony Petrosino, and Gail Mason. 1993. "Design Sensitivity in Criminal Justice Experiments." In *Crime and Justice: A Review of Research,* vol. 17, edited by Michael Tonry. Chicago: University of Chicago Press.

Weisburd, David, and Alex R. Piquero. 2008. "Taking Stock of How Well Criminologists Explain Crime: A Review of Published Studies." In *Crime and Justice: A Review of Research,* vol. 37, edited by Michael Tonry. Chicago: University of Chicago Press.

Weisburd, David, and Faye S. Taxman. 2000. "Developing a Multicenter Randomized Trial in Criminology: The Case of HIDTA." *Journal of Quantitative Criminology* 16:315–40.

Welsh, Brandon C., Meghan E. Peel, David P. Farrington, Henk Elffers, and Anthony A. Braga. 2011. "Research Design Influence on Study Outcomes in Crime and Justice: A Partial Replication with Public Area Surveillance." *Journal of Experimental Criminology* 7: 183–198.

Wilkinson, Leland, and Taskforce on Statistical Inference. 1999. "Statistical Methods in Psychology Journals: Guidelines and Explanations." *American Psychologist* 54: 594–604.

....

CHAPTER 23

PREVENTING FUTURE CRIMINAL ACTIVITIES OF DELINQUENTS AND OFFENDERS

....

DORIS LAYTON MACKENZIE

SINCE past behavior is the best predictor of future behavior, it is reasonable to attempt to prevent crime by preventing known offenders from continuing their criminal behavior. Once they are convicted, these individuals come under the supervision of correctional systems, and this provides an ideal period of time to attempt to change them so they will not continue to commit crimes. The questions this essay addresses are, Can the future criminal activities of known delinquents and offenders be prevented and, if so, how?

Reducing the future criminal activities of delinquents and offenders is of concern because many of these individuals are rearrested or convicted of new crimes a relatively short time after they are released from correctional supervision. For example, according to a Bureau of Justice Statistics study of prison releasees, three years after release 67.5 percent had been rearrested, 49.9 percent had been reconvicted, and 25.4 percent had been returned to prison with a new sentence (Langan and Levin 2002). With nearly 700,000 state and federal prisoners returning to the community annually, methods for preventing their high recidivism rates appears imperative for crime-prevention efforts (Petersilia 2003).

Perspectives on what to do with people who break the law have varied greatly among people and over time. In part, differences in points of view depend on political ideologies regarding what should be done to those who disobey criminal statutes. Equally as important are more utilitarian considerations related to what is believed to be effective in reducing crime and making communities safer. Central to the utilitarian perspective is the new "evidence-based" paradigm.

The focus on evidence-based practices in criminal justice communities began with a provocative essay by Sherman (1998) asserting that law enforcement, like medicine, should adopt an evidence-based perspective to guide police practice. Approaches to crime prevention would be based on evaluation research demonstrating what is effective. In this paradigm, evaluation research should be used to construct guidelines for effective police practices. The approach stresses the need for accountability and continual improvement through the use of the most current research results. The continual feedback from research studies would improve the effectiveness of policing. According to Sherman, the basic premise of evidence-based practice "is that we are entitled to our own opinions but not to our own facts" (Sherman 1998, p. 4). Too frequently, practitioners come up with their own "facts" with little evidence to support their views.

Interest in the evidence-based paradigm quickly spread to corrections where concern focused on evidence-based correctional treatment interventions (Cullen and Gendreau 2000; MacKenzie 2000, 2001). Ideally, decisions about correctional interventions would be based on research evidence demonstrating their effectiveness in achieving desired outcomes. A wide range of potential outcomes exist for correctional interventions including system-level impacts such as reducing prison crowding or reducing costs and individual-level changes such as increasing employment skills or educational obtainment. However, the majority of people seem to expect corrections to have an impact on crime prevention by reducing the future criminal activities of known offenders and delinquents. Thus, those who champion utilitarian goals for corrections frequently view reducing recidivism as the major desired outcome, and this has been the focus of the evidence-based model in corrections.

Every day correctional authorities are required to make decisions directly affecting the lives of those who break the law. The decisions have a direct impact on the later behavior of these individuals and on public safety. Policymakers decide what should be done to those convicted of crimes, and this also affects public safety. Too often decisions by these people are made on the basis of simplistic ideas, customary practices, gut feelings, or common sense. The evidence-based paradigm argues in favor of using empirical knowledge gained through scientific research to help with such decision making.

Many correctional practitioners and decision makers have expressed interest in the evidence-based perspective and wish to implement programs with demonstrated success in reducing recidivism. At times, this is more rhetoric than action, but it does denote awareness of the importance of research and its application. The degree to which this will be accomplished is dependent, in part, on scholars bridging the gap between research and practice (Cullen and Gendreau 2000).

Using an evidence-based perspective, this essay examines management of and programming for offenders and delinquents and reviews research on the effectiveness of these strategies in reducing later criminal behavior. Different philosophical models of corrections are discussed, as well as the changes that have occurred in these philosophies over the past century and the impact of these changes on correctional management and treatment. My review of the evidence base in corrections leads to several conclusions:

- Correctional philosophy has changed dramatically over the past 40 years, and this has greatly impacted both the programs implemented and the research conducted.
- The move away from the rehabilitation model of corrections led to an emphasis on justice, incapacitation, and deterrence, and has resulted in programs such as intensive supervision, urine testing, boot camps, and Scared Straight.
- Criminologists have engaged in systematic research to examine the various strategies and programs implemented in corrections.
- New research techniques and theoretical understanding of offenders and their behaviors has provided a body of research evidence demonstrating what is effective in changing criminal behavior.
- The "law and order" and "get tough" strategies focusing on deterrence and incapacitation have not demonstrated these are effective methods of reducing delinquent and criminal activities. Similarly, programs providing opportunities for housing and employment such as those in many reentry programs have been unsuccessful in changing offenders, most likely because they fail to cognitively change them so they are prepared to take advantage of the opportunities.
- Despite the emphasis on deterrence and incapacitation, some researchers have continued to investigate rehabilitation and the principles of effective interventions.
- Theoretical research has demonstrated that effective programs are cognitive-behavioral or behavioral in nature, skill oriented, and multimodal. Effective programs create cognitive transformations.
- Education, cognitive skills, cognitive behavioral treatment for sex offenders, Multi-Systemic Therapy, drug treatment, and drug courts are examples of programs effective in reducing recidivism.
- Two problems with the research are weak research designs and implementation. Future research should use stronger research designs (e.g., randomized trials) and examine the quality of program implementation.

The organization of this essay is as follows. Section I reviews the changing correctional philosophy, the reasons for these changes, and the impacts. Sections II, III, and IV discuss how these philosophical changes have had a direct impact on the type of programs developed and studied. Using systematic reviews and meta-analyses, Section V examines the effectiveness of the different types of programs. Section VI offers a few concluding comments.

I. Changing Perspectives in Corrections

A. Rehabilitative Model

From the turn of the previous century during the early progressive era until about 1975, US corrections moved increasingly toward a rehabilitation model. By the 1950s, all states and the Federal Bureau of Prisons had indeterminate systems that sentenced offenders to minimum and maximum sentence lengths. Parole boards and department of corrections personnel had wide discretion in determining how long an offender would serve in prison. The major goal of corrections was to rehabilitate offenders so they would return to the community and live law-abiding lives. Ideally, correctional officials and parole board members would be able to tell when offenders had been rehabilitated and when they were ready to be returned to the community.

The strong focus on rehabilitation in the 1960s is obvious from the report produced by the President's Commission on Law Enforcement and Administration of Justice (1967). This commission was formed in response to President Lyndon Johnson's 1965 address to the US Congress, in which he called for the establishment of a blue ribbon panel to examine the problems of crime in the nation. Prominent among the panel's recommendations was an emphasis on rehabilitation. The panel recommended such things as small caseloads for probation and parole officers so releasees would have adequate supervision and treatment; development of new methods and skills to aid in reintegrating offenders; model, small-unit correctional institutions for flexible community-oriented treatment; and educational and vocation training for all inmates who could profit from such programs. According to their report, the goal of correctional industries should be the rehabilitation of offenders. Furthermore, graduated release and furlough programs should be expanded and coordinated with community treatment services.

The recommendations of the panel as well as the indeterminate sentencing structure clearly demonstrate the strong emphasis at the time on rehabilitation of offenders. The focus on community treatment, diversion, reintegration, and education and employment programs shows the prominence of the rehabilitation philosophy. However, shortly after the panel completed its work, dramatic changes occurred in correctional philosophy and these had a major impact on correctional management and treatment.

B. Changing Focus of Corrections

The changes in correctional philosophy have been attributed, in part, to historical events occurring during the 1960s (Cullen and Gilbert 1982). This was a time of great social upheaval and radical changes in the United States. Racial and gender inequalities were becoming recognized, and many took steps to change the existing laws, regulations, and traditions that led to discrimination. Disagreements over the war in Vietnam created more controversy. Traditional mores were challenged by changes in drug use and sexual behaviors. Prison riots occurred and led to questions about the capability of correctional authorities and the adequacy of established practices. This social disorder led people to search for new ways of doing things. In all, it was a time of questioning the status quo—people began to distrust social institutions.

One specific event that significantly impacted correctional philosophy was a report by Lipton, Martinson, and Wilks (1975) examining the effectiveness of correctional programs. The authors of the report were researchers who had been asked by the state of New York to examine research on correctional programming in order to identify programs capable of reducing the criminal activities of offenders. They reviewed 231 studies of correctional programs, published between 1945 and 1967; the studies compared a treated group and a comparison. Martinson reported the results in an essay "What Works? Questions and Answers About Prison Reform," and wrote "with few and isolated exceptions the rehabilitative efforts that have been reported so far have had no appreciable effect on recidivism" (Martinson 1974, p. 25). On the basis of this report it was widely concluded that there were no effective correctional programs and the mantra became "nothing works." This often repeated phrase had a major impact on corrections because, if nothing could reduce recidivism, then the whole indeterminate model of corrections was faulty. Rehabilitation was supposed to be the goal of corrections; offenders were supposed to be released when they were determined to be "reformed." If no one could tell whether they were rehabilitated or there were no programs that were effective in reducing recidivism, then why keep people in prison under the pretense of rehabilitating them?

It is important to understand that Martinson and his colleagues were not saying nothing could work. What they did say was that the programs that had been studied were implemented so poorly, and the research designs were so inadequate, that it was impossible to determine whether anything could work. Other researchers investigating the same data concluded that there were a number of effective programs (Palmer 1983, 1992). There was a great deal of controversy in the research community about the conclusions from the Martinson report (Cullen and Gendreau 2000; Cullen and Gilbert 1982; Sechrest, White, and Brown 1979).

Despite the controversy over the report by Martinson and his colleagues, the times were ripe for a change in U.S. corrections. The social turmoil combined with the results of the Martinson report and a rising crime rate led both liberals and conservatives to demand changes in corrections. Liberals argued sentencing as it existed was unfair—if corrections could neither rehabilitate nor recognize when a person had changed, then the system was neither fair nor effective. In addition, the system was discriminatory because two offenders often received very disparate sentences despite having similar past histories of crime and being convicted of similar crimes. In other instances, offenders with vastly different past histories and criminal convictions received similar sentences.

C. The Justice Model

The iustice model of sentencing was proposed as a solution to some of the problems of the rehabilitative perspective (American Friends Service Committee 1971). From this perspective, sentencing should be fair and just, and should not have utilitarian motives such as rehabilitation. Sentences should be based on the crime of conviction and past history of criminal behavior. The motive should be retribution for the crime committed. The model, it was asserted, would limit the ability of the state to cause harm to offenders. Offenders would be given an array of legal rights to protect them and ensure equal treatment. They would be treated as "citizens" and not "correctional clients." Rehabilitation would be voluntary and not coerced.

Using the justice perspective, Logan (1993) proposed a confinement model of imprisonment. According to him, correctional practitioners should not be held responsible for what happens after prison. Sentencing and corrections should be rights based and not utilitarian or consequentialist. That is, people should be treated based on their past behavior, not on what they might do in the future. In his opinion, justice is not served by having utilitarian goals such as controlling crime through incapacitation, deterrence, or rehabilitation. Expecting prisons to "correct the incorrigible, rehabilitate the wicked, deter the determined, restrain the dangerous and punish the wicked" (Logan 1993, p.3) dooms them to failure. Instead, prison should have goals based on a "just deserts" theory of criminal justice—a model that is punitive and retributive but nonutilitarian. Essentially, the major purpose of imprisonment is to punish offenders fairly in proportion to their crimes.

Under the confinement model, an ideal prison provides basic human services in a decent and healthy environment. "The mission of a prison is to keep prisoners—to keep them in, keep them safe, keep them in line, keep them healthy, and keep them busy—and to do it with fairness, without undue suffering, and efficiently as possible" (Logan 1993, p. 3). Prisons should be judged only on how competently, fairly, and efficiently they administer confinement as deserved punishment.

Logan developed performance criteria that could be used to evaluate how effective prisons are in following the mandates of the confinement model. He used eight distinct dimensions for performance that could be used to evaluate effectiveness: security, safety, order, care, activity, justice, conditions, and management. Under his model, inmate programs are important because they have benefits in keeping inmates healthy and active, not because they might result in a reduction in future criminal activity. Preventing future crime was not a goal of the confinement model of corrections.

D. Law and Order Perspective

Those with more conservative viewpoints had a different rationale for changing the sentencing system. They were worried about changes in traditional mores and the rising crime rate. From their perspective, the strong emphasis on rehabilitation meant the system was coddling criminals. They supported more severe sentences and ways to restrict the ability of judges and correctional officials to mitigate the harshness of punishment. "Get tough" proposals such as mandatory minimum sentences, lengthy determinate sentences, boot camps, and "three strikes and you're out" laws became popular. These, "law and order" initiatives served to increase the time offenders spent in prison and decreased the discretion of judges and correctional authorities.

Philosophically, the conservatives supported incapacitation and deterrence as methods of changing criminals. In their opinion, criminals should be locked up or controlled so they would not be able to commit crimes. Furthermore, harsh punishments were expected to deter the general public from committing crimes (general deterrence) and the criminal who was caught and punished would be deterred from continuing to recidivate (specific deterrence).

Not only were policymakers and the public supporting changes in corrections and a move away from the rehabilitation model, but also many US academic criminologists disputed the rehabilitation model. As noted by Cullen and Gendreau (2000), "Criminologists, a progressive bunch due to their self-selection into the field of criminology and disciplinary training, embraced an anti-rehabilitation position almost as a matter of professional ideology" (p. 124). According to Cullen and Gendreau, the criminologists studied social problems such as prison violence, and racial and class inequalities. They had little interest in intervening in the lives of offenders; they viewed social problems as the major contributor to and explanation for crime. Therefore, in their opinions, efforts to reduce crime should target the existing social problems and not individual-level problems or differences that could be changed through interventions.

II. IMPACT ON US CORRECTIONS

The changes in sentencing and corrections philosophy had a huge impact on corrections. The most apparent effect was the large increase in the incarceration rate. From 1930 until the mid-seventies, the incarceration rate had remained around 100 per 100,000 in the population. The rate was so stable that Blumstein and Cohen (1973) proposed a "stability of punishment" theory. According to them, societies incarcerate a certain proportion of the population, and this rate remains stable over time. However, in a few short years it was obvious that the incarceration rate was not a stable phenomenon in the United States. After 1970, incarceration rates grew significantly; by 1980, the rate had increased to 202 per 100,000 adults, and it continued to grow to reach 754 by 2008 (Sabol, West, and Cooper 2009). In 2008, the total number of people under correctional supervision, including incarceration in prisons and jails and on probation, parole, or supervised release, was over 7.3 million (Sabol and West 2009).

Observing the new control philosophy with its reliance on imprisonment, surveillance, and custody, Feeley and Simon (1992) proposed that we were moving toward a "new penology." In their opinion, this penology reflected a shift of interest away from the traditional interests in individuals to concern with actuarial considerations. The new focus directed attention to managing aggregates of dangerous groups, and discourses revolved around probability and risk assessment instead of clinical diagnosis and needs assessment. In 1992, when they published their proposal, US corrections appeared to no longer value rehabilitation and reintegration. Feeley and Simon feared that the United States was moving to a new conception of poverty in which a segment of society was viewed as the underclass whose members would be permanently excluded from social mobility and economic integration.

As a whole, these new philosophies diminished attention to reducing recidivism through rehabilitation programming. Retribution, incapacitation, and deterrence became the foremost goals of sentencing and corrections. Programs like boot camps, intensive supervision, and electronic monitoring and urine testing were designed to increase the harshness of punishments and the control and surveillance of offenders. In the same vein, sentence lengths were increased and mandatory minimums enacted. Three-strikes laws were designed to punish repeat offenders. In all, these management strategies were designed to increase punishments for those who broke the law in order to restrict their activities so they would not be able to continue with their criminal activities (e.g., incapacitate), as well as to make punishments so onerous that both offenders and the general public would hesitate to commit crimes.

III. CANADIAN SCHOOL OF RESEARCHERS

Support for rehabilitation declined in the United States, but this did not occur everywhere. For example, researchers in the Canadian correctional service and in Canadian universities continued to examine the effectiveness of rehabilitation programs and to conduct research from a psychological perspective. Instead of focusing on social problems, these researchers examined the factors that distinguished those who committed serious criminal acts from those who did not. Furthermore, the researchers conducted evaluations of correctional programs to determine what programs were effective in reducing recidivism.

Using the empirical research examining correctional programs, a group of Canadian psychologists developed "principles of effective correctional intervention." The principles were designed to distinguish between effective and ineffective programs (Gendreau 1996; Andrews and Bonta 2003). The first principle was that interventions must target known predictors of crime and these must be directly related to criminal behavior. Two types of predictors place offenders at risk of criminal activity: (1) static predictors such as criminal history; and (2) dynamic predictors such as antisocial attitudes. Static predictors cannot be changed; dynamic predictors can potentially be changed. Research indicates that many of the strongest predictors of criminal behavior are dynamic—antisocial/procriminal attitudes and beliefs, procriminal associates, and personality factors (e.g., impulsiveness, risk-taking) are examples of characteristics that can be changed (Gendreau, Little, and Goggen 1996). Many factors thought to cause crime, such as low self-esteem, are unrelated or only weakly related to recidivism. An intervention targeting such factors would not be expected to have an impact on changing offenders' criminal behavior. Therefore, the first principle asserts that the most effective interventions target dynamic (changeable), criminogenic (directly related to criminal behavior) characteristics.

A second principle is that treatment should be behavioral in nature. The most effective interventions use cognitive behavior and social learning techniques. According to this proposal, treatment that is less structured, self-reflective, verbally interactive, or punishment based will be less effective or ineffective.

Effective programs must also be responsive to the learning styles and abilities of offenders and delinquents. Thus, the third principle overlaps with the second by arguing that certain types of interventions are more sensitive to offenders' modes of learning, personalities, and characteristics, and these types of interventions are most effective. There has been some debate about how race/ethnicity and gender sensitivity relate to this principle and how to design programs so they are responsive to these issues.

Fourth, interventions should be used for higher risk offenders. Frequently, low-risk offenders will not reoffend and, therefore, they do not require intervention; it is an unnecessary use of resources. Furthermore, there is a danger that some programs actually have a negative impact on low-risk offenders (Andrews and Bonta 2003). On the other hand, effective interventions can reduce the recidivism of high-risk offenders. High-risk offenders are capable of changing, and since they are at higher risk for recidivism, there is room to reduce their recidivism. Thus, it is important that interventions be used for high-risk offenders.

The implementation of interventions is the topic of the fifth and final principle. Implementation issues relate to program integrity and dosage. *Integrity* refers to program management and operation. Effective programs need the following: appropriately trained and experienced staff; proper management, and oversight and quality control. Additionally, they should be theoretically based. Programs must be of sufficient duration so offenders spend a suitable amount of time in the program. The intensity and dosage of the program must be appropriate for the participants. For example, a few hours in a session on anger management will not be long enough to successfully change offenders at high risk for violence.

The principles developed by the Canadian researchers were designed to distinguish between interventions that successfully reduce recidivism and those that do not. The foundation of the principles is a psychological approach to changing offenders through rehabilitation.

IV. Treatment in Corrections

The term *treatment* is used in diverse ways in research on corrections. Frequently, it is used to refer to any method or strategy used for managing offenders; it is also used to refer to a variety of programs provided to them. It does not necessarily refer to rehabilitation programs. Programming and the accompanying research often reflected the correctional philosophy of the times. During the 1970s until the mid-1990s, many programs referred to as treatments were actually designed to deter offenders or to control them. For example, one popular program during this time period was intensive supervision. These programs were designed to increase the control over offenders by requiring them to meet more frequently with their supervising agents and submitting to regularly scheduled urine tests. This control was thought to be a type of incapacitation because it was assumed that offenders would not be able to comply with the requirements and still commit crimes; if they failed to comply and were involved in criminal activities, theoretically they would be detected and incapacitated in a prison or jail.

In fact, it is interesting to note that Lipton and his colleagues examined 11 different treatment methods, including probation, imprisonment (sentence length), parole, casework and individual counseling, skill development, individual psychotherapy, group methods, milieu therapy, partial physical custody (halfway houses, etc.), medical methods (plastic surgery, castration), and leisure-time activities. Treatments such as probation, imprisonment, and parole can hardly be considered rehabilitation, although they would be considered treatments in the sense of methods or strategies for managing offenders.

V. What Works in Corrections?

From the perspective of evidence-based corrections, the question is, What works in corrections? As noted earlier, policymakers must consider many factors in sentencing and correctional decision making. Many and varied outcomes are important in these decisions, including such things as public perceptions of safety, public acceptance of punishments, victim satisfaction, costs, and impacts on the offender like increased educational achievement and reduced substance abuse. These are all considered germane for policymakers to consider; however, the one factor that almost always is considered primary is the impact of decisions on preventing future criminal activity. That is, does the sentencing or correctional option have an impact on recidivism?

In 1975, when Martinson and his colleagues completed their assessment of correctional research, they used state-of-the-art methodology. However, since that time new techniques for assessing the effectiveness of correctional programs have been developed. One important technique, used increasingly in the physical and social sciences, is meta-analysis. Meta-analysis is used to quantitatively examine a group of studies to determine if they are effective in achieving an identified outcome or outcomes (Lipsey and Wilson 2001). It is a statistical technique requiring the calculation of "effect sizes" for each study. The effect size for a study reflects the difference in the outcome for the treated and nontreated group. It is a standardized measure of the difference between the treatment and comparison group. In most cases, meta-analytical studies of correctional programs have used recidivism as the outcome. The effect size may indicate lower recidivism for the treated group, lower recidivism for the comparison group, or no effect.

Some of the problems inherent in reviews of the literature such as the review done by Lipton and his colleagues are solved by meta-analysis. Like literature reviews, meta-analysis is a method of drawing conclusions about a group of studies. However, in contrast to literature reviews, meta-analysis uses a specific statistical methodology. Quantitative data from a group of studies is used in the analysis to draw conclusions about effectiveness. A major benefit is that the work can be replicated by other researchers.

Meta-analysis requires careful attention to the studies included in the analysis. The procedure begins with a clear definition of eligible studies. Once the eligibility criteria are established, an intensive search is made for all studies, both published and unpublished, that might fit the criteria. These studies are located and examined in depth to determine eligibility. The goal is to identify all research studies that fit the criteria for inclusion. For each independent sample an effect size is calculated. Eligible studies are carefully coded. Where possible, characteristics of the samples, the treatment, and the methodology of the study are coded and used in the analyses.

There are several advantages in using meta-analytical techniques to assess research findings. Meta-analysis is able to detect differences that would not be clear in traditional research reviews because the low sample sizes limit the statistical power in many evaluation studies and real effects may be missed. By combining results across studies, meta-analysis avoids this problem.

Second, meta-analytical techniques allow researchers to assess the influence of methodological factors on treatment efficacy by introducing controls into the analysis. Particularly, important in this regard are assessments of the impact of research design components. For example, a meta-analysis can assess whether the results of the study are robust to changes in research designs. The question here is, Do the results change when stronger research designs—as, for instance, randomized trials—are compared with weaker quasi-experimental designs? Thus, both the differences in effects across studies and the impact of changes in research design features can be examined.

Meta-analysis also permits an examination of the factors that may increase or decrease the effectiveness of a treatment. These variables can be added to the statistical models. An analysis might ask if the programs were equally as effective or ineffective for offenders with particular characteristics. For example, are the results for the program the same when it is delivered to men or to women, young people or older offenders, or African Americans or whites? Factors related to the programs can also be used in the analysis. Are programs with individual counseling as effective as those provided to groups? If authors of the reports provide the information, data on the characteristics of participants and/or programs can be coded and used in the meta-analysis. The problem is that many research reports do not include sufficient data on these characteristics, and therefore, the information cannot be used in the analyses.

A. Systematic Reviews and Meta-Analyses of Correctional Treatment

Systematic reviews and meta-analyses examining correctional programs have taken two different directions. Some have combined a large number of different correctional evaluations in the research. The goal of these analyses is to examine support for various theoretical perspectives and to identify underlying principles of treatment. The second group of reviews and meta-analyses have focused on examining specific types of correctional programs in order to determine if the programs are effective in achieving the desired outcome.

1. *Theoretical Meta-Analyses.* Several theoretical meta-analyses have examined whether the rehabilitation principles proposed by the Canadian researchers did indeed distinguish between effective and ineffective programs. In a series of meta-analyses, Andrews and his colleagues have compared interventions they judge as conforming to the principles of effective rehabilitation to those that do not (Andrews et al. 1990; Andrews and Bonta 2006; Gendreau, Smith, and French 2006). Almost consistently these analyses have demonstrated that "clinically relevant" interventions were more effective than other modes of treatment. Relevant interventions were skills oriented and based on a behavioral or cognitive-behavioral theoretical model. Cognitive-behavioral and behavioral treatment programs are based on social learning principles. The techniques use modeling, graduated practice, role-playing, reinforcement, extinction, resource provision, concrete verbal suggestions, and cognitive restructuring. Multimodal programs treat all deficits and problems simultaneously. Skill-based programs focus on teaching offenders skills they need to resist delinquent and criminal behavior. Self-reflective, verbally interactive, insight-oriented, and less structured approaches such as casework and individual and group counseling were not found to be effective.

These findings were supported by subsequent work by Lipsey and Lösel and their colleagues (Lipsey 1992). Lipsey and his group of researchers meta-analyzed 397 studies of juvenile delinquency interventions. Similar to the findings of Andrew and colleagues, they found treatment modality had the largest effect—the most effective were behavioral, skills oriented, or multimodal. In another study, Lösel (1995) reviewed 13 meta-analyses of correctional interventions. His results supported the work by Andrews and Lipsey. Across all the meta-analyses, the most effective programs were behavioral, skills oriented, and multimodal.

From the perspective of the Canadian School of researchers, risk is an important variable to consider in selecting offender participants. In their opinion, treatment should be reserved for those at highest risk for recidivism. One reason for this proposal is that low-risk offenders may not continue to commit crime even if they do not receive treatment; therefore, treating them is a waste of scarce resources. Furthermore, giving them intensive treatment may actually have a negative impact and increase their criminal activity (Andrews and Bonta 2006). The results from studies examining this principle have been mixed. Antonowicz and Ross (1994) did not find support for the risk principle; Lipsey (1995) found only weak support.

Results have also been mixed for the responsivity principle. The concept refers to rehabilitation program delivery in a style and mode consistent with the learning styles and abilities of offenders. There is a continuing debate about how to design effective rehabilitation programs responsive to the needs of women, ethnic minorities, psychopaths, and mentally disordered offenders.

Meta-analyses have continually found that effective programs are based on a rehabilitation perspective and not on increased control or a deterrence model of intervention. In a recent review of systematic reviews and meta-analyses, Lipsey and Cullen (2007) investigated punitive approaches compared to rehabilitation treatments. Punitive approaches included community supervision, intensive supervision, drug testing, electronic monitoring, Scared Straight, incarceration, and boot camps. They concluded that punitive approaches, as in the crime control and law-and-order perspectives, fail to show that the aversive experiences of correctional sanctions greatly inhibits recidivism. In fact, a significant proportion of the studies demonstrated the opposite effect—these sanctions may actually increase subsequent criminal behavior.

2. *Examining Programs, Interventions and Strategies.* The findings from theoretical meta-analyses are consistent with findings from meta-analyses of specific programs (MacKenzie 2006). Using both systematic reviews and meta-analyses, I examined 284 evaluations of correctional programs, strategies, and interventions. Each program was located and scored for the quality of the research methods and the directional and significance of results (MacKenzie 1997, 2001). I systematically reviewed program areas to determine what was effective in reducing recidivism. My reviews included various correctional program areas (e.g., cognitive skills, education) and strategies (e.g., drug courts), as well as programs for specific types of offenders (e.g., drug offenders).

My systematic reviews, as well as reviews of other meta-analyses, indicate that the following programs have not been found to be effective in reducing recidivism:

- Correctional boot camps for juveniles
- Correctional boot camps for adults
- Correctional industries
- Community supervision for juveniles
- Domestic-violence treatment with a feminist perspective
- Domestic-violence treatment using cognitive-behavior treatment

- Electronic monitoring
- Intensive supervision
- Life-skills education
- Multicomponent work programs
- Psychosocial sex offender treatment
- Residential treatment for juveniles

Neither residential treatment nor community supervision for juveniles was effective in reducing recidivism, nor was intensive supervision, electronic monitoring, or boot camps for either adults or juveniles. Thus, the recent strong attention to deterrence and incapacitation programs with the goal of reducing crime does not appear to be effective. As found in the theoretical review by Lipsey and Cullen, these programs do not reduce future criminal activities.

No single explanation seems adequate to explain why some programs are not effective in reducing recidivism. Some possible reasons programs are not effective appear to be are: (1) they have a poor or no theoretical basis; (2) they are poorly implemented; (3) they focus on punishment, deterrence, or control instead of providing human service or rehabilitation; and (4) they emphasize the formation of ties or bonds without first changing the individual's thought process. It is unclear why the treatment programs for batterers were not effective (see also Feder and Wilson 2005).

Programs such as psychosocial sex offender treatment and community supervision and residential placement for juveniles appear to have little theoretical basis for expecting to have an impact on recidivism. There was little consistent theoretical basis for either the supervision and incarceration or what was done during the time on supervision or in the facilities. The psychosocial sex offender treatment is based on a psychodynamic theoretical perspective. This model of counseling requires insight, self-reflection, and verbal abilities that are often beyond the skill level of the offenders and, therefore, not responsive to their particular learning styles.

None of the programs focusing on deterrence, punishment, or control were found to reduce future criminal activity. These were the major goals of many of the programs emphasized in the United States during the 1980s and 1990s. A sufficient body of research now exists demonstrating that programs such as boot camps, Scared Straight, arrests for domestic violence, intensive supervision, and electronic monitoring are not effective ways to reduce recidivism. While these goals may fulfill other correctional goals and make law-and-order advocates supportive of correctional agencies, we can't argue in favor of them if reducing recidivism is the desired outcome. In fact, some of these programs such as Scared Straight may be more harmful for juveniles than doing nothing (Petrosino et al. 2003).

3. *Formation of Ties without Cognitive Changes.* Research examining the effectiveness of work, multicomponent work programs, and prison industries does not show that these are effective in significantly reducing recidivism (MacKenzie 2006; see also Visher, Winterfield, and Coggeshall 2006). Nor are life skills programs

effective (MacKenzie 2006). Giving assistance in job searches or resume writing skills, as is done in many life skills programs, or providing offenders with work experiences and opportunities without taking into consideration the cognitions of the individuals may not be an effective way to reduce recidivism.

The theoretical importance of bonds and ties to social institutions such as marriage, work, or school and the impact of these ties and bonds on reducing involvement in crime has been the emphasis of many recent sociological theories (Sampson and Laub 1995). According to Sampson and Laub, as bonds strengthen, social capital rises. This capital supplies resources to solve problems. As bonds form and social capital increases, criminal activity becomes more costly. Meaningful social bonds established during adulthood function as critical life events when offenders begin to conform and turn away from criminal activity. Crime becomes too costly because of the threat of loss of family, work, or school.

Research demonstrates an association between criminal activities and work and marriage. Employed and married people commit fewer crimes than those who are unemployed and unmarried. Furthermore, there are within-individual differences; during periods when people are employed and married, they commit fewer crimes than they do when they are unemployed and unmarried (Horney, Osgood, and Marshall 1995; MacKenzie et al. 1999; MacKenzie and Li 2002). However, in these theories little is said about how these bonds or ties are formed. Bonds in adulthood appear to form fortuitously. The question is, What happens to the individuals to bring about these changes in attachments?

The issue for correctional treatment is how to facilitate the formation of the bonds that are related to a reduction in recidivism. If marriage is a good thing and reduces criminal activity, maybe correctional personnel should organize parties for exiting inmates so they can meet eligible potential mates who are not criminally involved. This seems silly because just putting the offenders in a situation to meet members of the opposite sex will not necessarily lead them to want to make a permanent commitment and get married. Yet, this may be what we are doing with correctional work and life skills programs.

Opportunities for work and assistance in job searches appear prominently in many of the new reentry programs designed to assist releasees in adjusting to the community after a period of incarceration and thereby reducing their recidivism. It is assumed that if offenders are assisted in obtaining a job, they will show up every day on time, they will be appreciative and get along with the supervisor, and they will do the other things that are required to keep the positions. This may be a faulty assumption and the reason the research on work, prison industries, and life skills training does not demonstrate an impact on future criminal activities. Despite the fact that current theories emphasize the importance of work in reducing criminal activity, there is little evidence that correctional work programs are effective in bringing about this change. Before delinquents and offenders are ready to find and keep employment, they may need to make a major change in their thinking. This cognitive change makes them ready to form ties or bonds to social institutions.

4. *Cognitive Transformations.* Studies of rehabilitation programs, on the other hand, do find that many are effective in reducing criminal activities. In my work, I found the following programs to be effective in reducing recidivism:

- Academic education
- Vocational education
- Cognitive skills programs (Moral Reconation, Reasoning and Rehabilitation, Cognitive Restructuring)
- Cognitive behavior and behavioral treatment for sex offenders
- MultiSystemic Therapy
- Drug courts
- Drug treatment in facilities
- Drug treatment in the community

A consistency among these programs is a focus on human service. I propose that an important aspect of this is programming, and the reason for the success is that they address cognitive processes. From this perspective, an individual-level change in cognition must occur before the person is prepared to form ties or bonds to social institutions. In order to be committed to family, keep a job, support children, or form strong, positive ties to other institutions, the person must change in cognitive reasoning and attitudes. A focus on this individual change is critical to our understanding of what works in corrections. This position is consistent with Giordano and her colleagues' call for a cognitive transformation that is necessary before a person makes initial moves toward a different life style (Giordano, Cernkovich, and Rudolph 2002). Only if this transformation occurs is the person prepared to take advantage of opportunities for marriage and family.

The reason work and life skills programs are not effective for correctional populations is that the programs focus on giving opportunities for employment but do not emphasize individual change. The person may not have the individual abilities and/or attitudes to take advantage of the environmental opportunities, and thus a bond with the world of work is not formed. If a cognitive transformation must occur within the individual before he or she can take advantage of environmental opportunities, then programs for correctional populations should begin with programming designed to change cognitions. Many of the programs and interventions effective in reducing recidivism focus on individual-level change.

B. Research Quality and Program Implementation

Martinson and his colleagues concluded that there were few programs that could be said to be effective based on the research at the time of the study (Martinson 1974; Lipton, Martinson, and Wilks 1975). While many people interpreted this to mean nothing works in correctional treatment, the researchers actually attributed the failure to find effective programs to two factors: (1) poor research design and methodology, and (2) insufficient intervention implementation. These two issues remain important in assessing the effectiveness of programs today. The first has to do with the quality of the research and the strength of the design. The second deals with the integrity of the program. The implementation or integrity relates to how the program is designed and operated, dosage issues, and training and oversight of staff.

In regard to the first issue, at the time of the Martinson study, the research studies they examined were often so poorly designed that it was impossible to tell whether the results could be interpreted to be a true test of the effectiveness or ineffectiveness of the intervention studied. Thus, this was a problem with the research design and methodology, and not a manifestation of the effectiveness of the programs. Today, with better methodology of individual studies, as well as improved statistical techniques like meta-analysis, we can be more confident that the results reveal the impact of the interventions. The good news is that there is evidence that some interventions do work and these interventions have specific characteristics consistent with certain principles that can be replicated in future program development. Scientific evidence exists that some correctional interventions are effective in reducing future criminal activity of delinquents and offenders.

Yet, problems still exist with study designs. The field of corrections is far from that of medicine in its use of randomized trials to examine effectiveness. In my study of correctional interventions, I found only 14.8 percent of the evaluations were successful randomized trials (MacKenzie 2006). In contrast, 23.2 percent were scored very low in the quality of the research methodology. The latter were considered to have very dissimilar comparison groups and, therefore, it was impossible to tell if results were due to differences between the groups being compared or to the intervention. Thus, in the future it will be critical to increase the rigor of the research designs if we are going to successfully employ an evidence-based corrections perspective.

The second issue in the work of Martinson and colleagues was related to intervention implementation. Implementation of the programs was often so poor that it was impossible to tell whether a well-implemented program would have had an impact. Implementation of programs remains an important element in the research today. Certainly, a program with well-trained staff, designed and operated according to plans in accordance with principles of effective programming, providing sufficient dosage appropriate for the risk level of participants, and having enough administrative oversight to afford quality control would be expected to be more effective than a program without such essentials. Some researchers are beginning to examine ways to study implementation by measuring the characteristics of programs, participants, and administration (Latessa and Holsinger 1998; Taxman and Friedmann 2009).

Our inability to say much about the implementation of treatment programs is a great limitation for the existing meta-analyses. Meta-analyses could control for implementation issues. For example, it would theoretically be possible to examine whether more effective programs were longer or shorter, were provided daily or once a week, had adequately trained staff and/or were given to offenders at high or low risk of recidivism. Yet sufficient information is seldom provided in research reports and, therefore, the meta-analyses provide only limited information on the characteristics of the interventions and the participants.

Even if the reports included information on the planned implementation, we might still be left with questions about whether the programs were implemented as intended (Latessa and Holsinger 1998; Taxman and Friedmann 2009). That is, do participants really attend for the planned time and are trained staff the ones who spend most of the time with the participants? This adherence, and protocol fidelity and implementation information, is not available in many of the reports. Some research studies do include a process or implementation study as well as outcome study. The difficulty is finding the two and being sure that the process study describes what was going on at the time of the outcome study.

VI. Discussion and Conclusions

A large number of delinquents and offenders who come under the supervision of correctional personnel continue to be involved in criminal activity while they are in the community or return to crime when they are released from a facility. How to change this behavior in order to prevent crimes is the critical question for correctional intervention. The good news is that corrections has developed effective interventions that can have an impact on preventing crime.

Current research examining correctional programming clearly points in the direction of the need to develop programs that will address dynamic criminogenic characteristics. Meta-analyses have demonstrated the type of programs that are effective in reducing criminal behavior. Programs that are based on cognitive-behavioral theoretical models, and are skill-based and multi-modal, are more effective than others. Interventions that were popular during the law-and-order stage of US correctional philosophy have not effectively reduced recidivism. Future research should examine the effectiveness of programs that bring about cognitive changes prior to providing employment opportunities, because such changes may be required before delinquents and offenders are prepared to take advantage of the environmental opportunities.

REFERENCES

American Friends Service Committee. 1971. Struggle for Justice: A Report on Crime and Punishment in America. New York: Hill and Wang.

Andrews, Donald A., and James Bonta. 2003. The Psychology of Criminal Conduct. Cincinnati, OH: Anderson Publishing.

Andrews, Donald A., and James Bonta. 2006. The Psychology of Criminal Conduct, 4th ed. Newark, NJ: Lexis/Nexis.

Andrews, Donald A., Ivan Zinger, Robert D. Hoge, James Bonta, Paul Gendreau, and Francis T. Cullen. 1990. "Does Correctional Treatment Work? A Clinically-Relevant and Psychologically-informed Meta-analysis." Criminology 28:369–404.

Antonowicz, Daniel, and Robert R. Ross. 1994. "Essential Components of Successful Rehabilitation Programs for Offenders." *International Journal of Offender Therapy and Comparative Criminology* 38:97–104.

Blumstein, Alfred, and Jacqueline Cohen. 1973. "A Theory of the Stability of Punishment." *Journal of Criminal Law and Criminology* 64:198–207.

Cullen, Francis T., and Paul Gendreau. 2000. "Assessing Correctional Rehabilitation: Policy, Practice, and Prospects." In *Criminal Justice 2000*, vol. 3, edited by Julie Horney. Washington, DC: National Institute of Justice.

Cullen, Francis T., and Karen E. Gilbert. 1982. *Reaffirming Rehabilitation*. Cincinnati, OH: Anderson Publishing.

Feder, Lynette, and David B. Wilson. 2005. "A Meta-analytic Review of Court-mandated Batterer Intervention Programs: Can Courts Affect Abusers' Behavior?" *Journal of Experimental Criminology* 1:239–62.

Feeley, Malcolm M., and Jonathan Simon. 1992. "The New Penology: Notes on the Emerging Strategy of Corrections and Its Implications." *Criminology* 30(4): 449–70.

Gendreau, Paul. 1996. "The Principles of Effective Intervention with Offenders." In *Choosing Correctional Interventions That Work: Defining the Demand and Evaluating the Supply*, edited by Alan T. Harland. Newbury Park, CA: Sage.

Gendreau, Paul, Tracy Little, and Claire E. Goggin. 1996. "A Meta-analysis of the Predictors of Adult Recidivism: What Works!" *Criminology* 34:575–607.

Gendreau, Paul, Paula Smith, and Sheila A. French. 2006. "The Theory of Effective Correctional Intervention: Empirical Status and Future Directions." In *Taking Stock: The Status of Criminological Theory—Advances in Criminological Theory*, vol. 15, edited by Francis T. Cullen, James P. Wright, and Kristie R. Blevins. New Brunswick, NJ: Transaction.

Giordano, Peggy C., Stephen A. Cernkovich, and Jennifer L. Rudolph. 2002. "Gender, Crime, and Desistance: Toward a Theory of Cognitive Transformation." *American Journal of Sociology* 107(4): 990–1064.

Horney, Julie, Wayne D. Osgood, and Ineke H. Marshall. 1995. "Criminal Careers in the Short-term: Intra-individual Variability in Crime and Its Relation to Local Life Circumstances." *American Sociological Review* 60:655–73.

Langan, Patrick A., and David J. Levin. 2002. *Recidivism of Prisoners Released in 1994*. Washington, DC: US Department of Justice, Bureau of Justice Statistics.

Latessa, Edward J., and Alexander M. Holsinger. 1998. "The Importance of Evaluating Correctional Programs: Assessing Outcome and Quality." *Corrections Management Quarterly* 2(4): 22–29.

Lipsey, Mark. 1992. "Juvenile Delinquency Treatment: A Meta-analytic Inquiry into the Variability of Effects." In *Meta-analysis for Explanation*, edited by Thomas D. Cook, Harris Cooper, David S. Cordray, Heidi Hartmann, Larry V. Hedges, Richard J. Light, Thomas A. Louis, and Fredrick Mosteller. New York: Russell Sage.

Lipsey, Mark. 1995. "What Do We Learn from 400 Research Studies on the Effectiveness of Treatment with Juvenile Delinquents?" In *What Works: Reducing Reoffending*, edited by James McGuire. Chichester, UK: Wiley.

Lipsey, Mark W., and Francis T. Cullen. 2007. "The Effectiveness of Correctional Rehabilitation: A Review of Systematic Reviews." *Annual Review of Law and Social Science* 3:297–320, http://lawsocsci.annualreviews.org.

Lipsey, Mark W., and David B. Wilson. 2001. *Practical Meta-analysis*. Thousand Oaks, CA: Sage.

Lipton, Douglas, Robert Martinson, and Judith Wilks. 1975. *The Effectiveness of Correctional Treatment: A Survey of Correctional Treatment Evaluations*. New York: Praeger.

Logan, Charles H. 1993. *Criminal Justice Performance Measures for Prisons*. Washington, DC: US Department of Justice, Bureau of Justice Statistics. http://www.ojp.usdoj.gov/ BJA/evaluation/guide/documents/documentI.html.

Losel, Frederich. 1995. "Increasing Consensus in the Evaluation of Offender Rehabilitation? Lessons from Recent Research Synthesis." *Psychology, Crime, and Law* 2:19–39.

MacKenzie, Doris L. 1997. "Criminal Justice and Crime Prevention." In *Preventing Crime: What Works, What Doesn't, What's Promising*, edited by Lawrence W. Sherman, Denise Gottfredson, Doris L. MacKenzie, John Eck, Peter Reuter and Shawn Bushway. A Report to the U.S. Congress. Washington, DC: US Department of Justice, National Institute of Justice.

Mackenzie, Doris L. 2000. "Evidence-Based Corrections: Identifying What Works." *Crime and Delinquency* 46(4): 457–71.

Mackenzie, Doris L. 2001. "Corrections and Sentencing in the 21st Century: Evidence-Based Corrections and Sentencing." *Prison Journal* 81(3): 299–312.

MacKenzie, Doris L. 2002. "Reducing the Criminal Activities of Known Offenders and Delinquents: Crime Prevention in the Courts and Corrections." In *Evidence-based Crime Prevention*, edited by Lawrence W. Sherman, David P. Farrington, Brandon C. Welsh, and Doris L. MacKenzie. London: Routledge.

MacKenzie, Doris L. 2006. *What Works in Corrections: Reducing the Criminal Activities of Offenders and Delinquents*. New York: Cambridge University Press.

MacKenzie, Doris L., Katharine Browning, Stacy Skroban, and Douglas Smith. 1999. "The Impact of Probation on the Criminal Activities of Offenders." *Journal of Research in Crime and Delinquency* 36:423–53.

MacKenzie, Doris L., and Spencer D. Li. 2002. "The Impact of Formal and Informal Social Controls on the Criminal Activities of Probationers." *Journal of Research in Crime and Delinquency* 39(3): 243–76.

Martinson, Robert. 1974. "What Works? Questions and Answers about Prison Reform." *Public Interest* 35:22–54.

Palmer, Ted. 1983. "The 'Effectiveness' Issue Today: An Overview." *Federal Probation* 47:3–10.

Palmer, Ted. 1992. *The Re-emergence of Correctional Intervention*. Newbury Park, CA: Sage.

Petersilia, Joan. 2003. *When Prisoners Come Home: Parole and Prisoner Reentry*. Oxford, UK: Oxford University Press.

Petrosino, Anthony, Robert F. Boruch, David P. Farrington, Lawrence W. Sherman, and David Weisburd. 2003. "Towards Evidence-based Criminology and Criminal Justice: Systematic Reviews and the Campbell Collaboration Crime and Justice Group." *International Journal of Comparative Criminology* 3:18–41.

President's Commission on Law Enforcement and Administration of Justice. 1967. *Task Force Report: Corrections*. Washington, DC: US Government Printing Office.

Sabol, William J., and Heather C. West. 2009. *Prison Inmates at Midyear 2008—Statistical Tables*. Washington, DC: US Department of Justice, Bureau of Justice Statistics, http:// bjs.ojp.usdoj.gov/index.cfm?ty=pbdetail&iid=839.

Sabol, William J., Heather C. West, and Matthew Cooper. 2008. *Prisoners in 2008. Bureau of Justice Statistics Bulletin*. Washington, DC: US Department of Justice.

Sampson, Robert J., and John H. Laub. 1995. *Crime in the Making: Pathways and Turning Points Through Life*. Cambridge, MA: Harvard University Press.

Sechrest, Lee, Susan O. White, and Elizabeth D. Brown. 1979. *The Rehabilitation of Criminal Offenders: Problems and Prospects*. Washington, DC: National Academy of Science.

Sherman, Lawrence W. 1998. *Evidence-based Policing*. Washington, DC: Police Foundation.

Taxman, Faye S., and Peter D. Friedmann. 2009. "Fidelity and Adherence at the Transition Point: Theoretically Driven Experiments." *Journal of Experimental Criminology* 5:219–26.

Visher, Christy A., Laura Winterfield, and Mark B. Coggeshall. 2006. "Systematic Review of Non-Custodial Employment Programs: Impact on Recidivism Rates of Ex-Offenders." *Campbell Systematic Reviews* 2006:1 DOI: 10.4073/csr.2006.1.

CHAPTER 24

PUBLIC OPINION AND CRIME PREVENTION: A REVIEW OF INTERNATIONAL TRENDS

JULIAN V. ROBERTS AND ROSS HASTINGS

EMPIRICAL research into the views of the public regarding crime and criminal justice has been conducted for over a century now. This scholarship has focused on public knowledge of and attitudes toward the criminal justice system as a whole, as well as toward its individual components (police, courts, prison, and parole; for reviews of the literature, see Roberts 1992; Cullen, Fisher, and Applegate 2000; Roberts and Hough 2005; Wood and Gannon 2008). In spite of the fact that the field of crime prevention has evolved considerably, and that a large volume of polling data on this topic has accumulated, relatively little attention has been focused on the questions of public knowledge of and attitudes toward crime prevention. To date, few reviews of the literature have been published (e.g., Roberts and Grossman 1990; Roberts and Hastings 2007; see also Cullen, Vose, and Jonson 2007). The purpose of the present essay is to review the accumulated research to date on this important issue.

Why should scholars or practitioners care about public opinion on crime prevention? There are several explanations for the interest and research in this area. First, crime-prevention programs depend in large measure on public participation for their effectiveness. Sometimes this participation is of a direct nature—for example, when the public participates in prevention programs such as Neighborhood Watch. Public surveys shed light on why people do or do not participate in local prevention schemes. But there is also an important indirect link between public attitudes and crime prevention. Many prevention initiatives and programs require public support for their funding. If the public feels that punishment is more effective than prevention, it will want its tax dollars diverted to the criminal justice system—particularly prisons—and away from prevention initiatives.

Second, our understanding of community responses to crime requires elucidation— we need to know where the public stands regarding the balance between punishment and prevention. Politicians seeking to ensure that the state response to crime aligns with community values obviously need a scientific evaluation of community opinion. Third, one of the justifications for some crime-prevention schemes—such as CCTV—is that they reassure the public and attract the strong support of the community. We conduct research into public opinion to demonstrate the validity of such claims.

Finally, we need to know about public knowledge in the area, with a view to educating the public about the most effective responses to crime. For example, many people tend to think that harsher sentencing—putting more people in prison for much longer periods of time—will reduce the crime rate. Criminologists have demonstrated that sentencing policies can have only a limited effect on the crime rates (see Ashworth 2010) —and this information needs to be communicated to the public—or we will continue to confront high crime rates and to invest in expensive, yet ineffective criminal justice policies. People need to have an appreciation for evidence-based approaches to preventing crime, and for this reason, researchers need to document the limits on public knowledge in the area. Research into public knowledge of and attitudes toward crime prevention is, therefore, an important priority.

Our essay addresses a number of important and related issues, including levels of general public support for crime prevention (compared to punishment); levels of public support for different crime-prevention strategies and programs; and public awareness of, and participation in, crime-prevention initiatives. Throughout the essay, we pay particular attention to findings that have been replicated over time and across different jurisdictions. We embrace a relatively broad definition of crime prevention, one that includes crime-prevention initiatives aimed at promoting social development and social capital, as well as more targeted situational crime prevention programs (see Hastings 1996; Welsh and Farrington 2006).

This essay provides an overview of the research on public attitudes toward crime prevention and discusses some of the implications of this work. In general, this research shows that the public has a complex view of crime and its causes. In spite of the focus of the media on punitive approaches, the public remains supportive of crime-prevention strategies and considers them to constitute a rigorous approach to addressing the crime problem. The following principal conclusions may be drawn from the review:

- The majority of the public in western nations believes that the primary causes of crime and the primary responsibility for prevention lie outside the realm of the criminal justice system.

- Across countries and over time, polls of the public consistently reveal more support for nonpunitive responses, such as child development programs, than for punitive interventions, such as harsher sentencing or stricter parole.
- When asked to allocate funding to various criminal justice priorities and initiatives, the public consistently favors prevention over punishment.
- The public wants value for its money and believes that crime prevention is a cost-effective way of reducing crime. The public also indicates that it would be willing to support politicians who move in this direction.
- The public is well aware of crime prevention in general, but less knowledge-able about specific types of prevention programs and initiatives. People also indicate a willingness to get involved, though actual participation seems linked to a number of other factors.
- Participation rates vary widely across jurisdictions, but are generally relatively modest; this suggests that public support for crime-prevention initiatives is often of a passive rather than an active nature.

The organization of this essay is as follows. Section I discusses the political and news media context in which public attitudes are considered. Section II discusses the public's view that both the primary causes of crime and the responsibility for prevention lie outside the criminal justice system. Section III describes public perceptions of the most effective responses to crime. Section IV directly compares public support for prevention and punishment and shows that the support for prevention remains steady even when the public is made aware of the financial costs associated with prevention programs. Section V reports on public awareness of prevention initiatives, and briefly addresses the gap between expressed intentions to participate and actual involvement in prevention initiatives. Section VI offers some conclusions and proposals for future research.

METHODOLOGICAL NOTE

First, it worth saying a little about the appropriate research methodology needed to explore these issues. The most critical issue here concerns public attitudes toward prevention versus punishment. Polls exploring public reaction to criminal justice generally demonstrate widespread dissatisfaction with the perceived leniency of the system. This finding emerges from every poll that has explored the issue, and this suggests that there is little public interest in preventing crime, but great public interest in punishing offenders (see Roberts and Hough 2005). In the course of this essay we will explore public reaction to prevention and punishment. To do so, we draw upon research that has adopted a variety of methods, although one element is common: all have employed representative samples of the general public.

Although both qualitative (e.g., in-depth interviews and focus groups) and quantitative methods have been used, we focus on the latter in this contribution, as the primary interest is in drawing inferences from population trends. Surveys that employ a representative sample of the public permit researchers to make accurate estimates of the attitudes of the population on the basis of a small sample of respondents—assuming the sample was appropriately constructed. Sometimes people are asked a general question about crime prevention; sometimes they are asked to rate some specific form of crime prevention. A number of studies have asked people to allocate funding to crime-prevention policies and programs. As we shall demonstrate, although methodological approaches vary, a common theme emerges: strong support for prevention.

I. Crime Prevention: Political and Media Context

A. News Media

It would be surprising if the public were very knowledgeable about crime-prevention policies and programs. After all, these initiatives lack the high visibility of punitive responses to crime. "Get tough" crime policies attract far more attention from the news media. For example, "three-strikes" mandatory sentencing laws have an eye-catching appeal, based in large measure on their simplicity. This explains, in part, the popularity and proliferation of such policies across western nations (see Roberts Stalans, Indermaur, and Hough 2003). As well, news stories about crime and punishment tend to focus on high-profile cases; usually this means the most serious crimes of violence. When was the last time you read a headline about crime prevention through social development?

Crime prevention has less relevance in this context since the crime has been committed and the focus has shifted from preventing crime to punishing or incapacitating the individuals responsible. Stories about prevention are unlikely to attract much attention from the media—or interest from the public. It is perhaps only natural for people to be more interested in how the system responds to an offender convicted of a serious crime than in programs designed to prevent the commission of the crime. Accordingly, crime prevention accounts for far fewer media stories about crime or criminal justice. One content analysis of news media stories about criminal justice found that less than 1 percent dealt with crime prevention (Roberts and Grossman 1990). The intense media focus on violent crime, and the allegedly punitive nature of public responses to offenders, might suggest little public interest in crime-prevention policies—unless like CCTV they are of intrinsic interest to the news media. However, a careful review of the research evidence reveals a very different picture. As will be seen in the course of this essay, the public around the world remains supportive of crime-prevention strategies—at least when these programs are brought to their attention.

B. The Politics of Punishment and Prevention

It has often been observed that getting tough with offenders carries political benefits. Politicians in a number of western jurisdictions have promoted punitive criminal justice policies such as mandatory sentencing in order to attract public support. There appears to be a widespread perception that the public sees crime prevention as representing a "soft" approach to crime and that tougher responses to crime—such as mandatory sentencing—are more popular. The former British Prime Minister Tony Blair was well known for using the slogan "Tough on crime, tough on the causes of crime." The first part of the phrase was clearly aimed at balancing what was seen as the "softer" philosophy behind the second phrase. In fact, the public do not see crime prevention as a soft response to crime, and appealing to a "get tough" approach to crime may backfire—politicians may not necessarily enhance their electoral prospects by advocating punitive rather than preventive strategies.

Punitive responses to offending—such as mandatory sentencing laws or more austere prison conditions—have the advantage of appearing to represent a rigorous response to crime. Politicians often use this perception to promote these policies. Indeed, one explanation for the slow uptake of restorative justice programs and policies in some jurisdictions has been that they have an unfounded reputation for representing a 'soft' response to crime (see Roberts and Hough 2005). But prevention and restoration do not necessarily represent a soft response to crime—and the public appear aware of this fact. For example, when Canadians were asked about this issue, they were significantly more likely to *disagree* that putting more emphasis on crime prevention means getting soft on crime[1] (Ekos Research 2004).

Data from the United States demonstrate that promoting prevention over punishment is likely to attract, not lose, votes. A poll conducted in the United States found that over four-fifths of respondents stated that they would be much more likely to vote for a political candidate who endorsed investing in crime-prevention programs (Cooper and Sechrest Associates 2008). In comparison, a much lower proportion of respondents said they would be more likely to support a candidate who endorsed tougher sentencing. This is an important finding, especially in light of all the attention that has recently been focused on the premise of a "punitive turn" on the part of both politicians and the public. Public views are clearly more complex than is generally assumed; policymakers can promote crime-prevention initiatives without fear of a strong public backlash that these programs represent a less rigorous approach to offending.

Research supports the idea that the public has a relatively complex view of the relation of crime and punishment. For example, recent polling in Canada, Great Britain, and the United States suggests that the public supports getting tough with offenders through the imposition of longer sentences, but is even more supportive of rehabilitation and crime prevention (Angus Reid Public Opinion 2010). The data are summarized

Table 24.1 Public support for various approaches (% of respondents who strongly agree/moderately agreed)

	Canada	Great Britain	United States
When lawmakers set mandatory minimum sentences, they are getting tough on crime and sending a message to criminals	65%	63%	67%
Long prison sentences are the most powerful way to reduce crime	62%	57%	74%
I think trying to rehabilitate people who have committed crimes is an important part of prevention crime	79%	78%	78%
I think our criminal justice system should focus, above all else, on preventing crime before it occurs	88%	91%	90%

Source: Angus Reid Public Opinion 2010.

in table 24.1. As can be seen, the highest level of agreement—across all three countries—is with the statement that the criminal justice system should focus on preventing crime before it occurs. Thus, in the United States, 90 percent of the polled public agreed that the primary focus of the criminal justice system should be on prevention.

II. Causes of Crime and Perceptions of Who Is Responsible for Preventing Crime

As long ago as 1947, when Americans were asked to identify the causes of crime, "lack of parental control and supervision" headed the list (47 percent of the sample; see Erskine 1974). In other words, the responsibility for preventing crime was seen as lying somewhere other than in courts and prisons. People in other countries share this perception: When Canadian respondents were asked to identify the primary cause of crime, "Poor parenting" headed the list—it was identified by approximately two-thirds of respondents. Another poll conducted generated a similar result. Respondents were asked to identify the "most significant factor producing crime."

While "a lenient criminal justice system" was identified by approximately one-third of respondents, two-thirds of the sample was looking in another direction. Thus, 30 percent cited poverty, 21 percent difficult family situations, and 11 percent inadequate social programs or services (Ekos Research 1999).

Populist politicians often propose harsh crime-control policies such as longer terms of imprisonment and justify this by claiming that they are simply responding to a punitive public. If the public is punitively oriented, people would cite the criminal courts, and particularly sentencing and corrections, as the solution to preventing crime. In fact, public responses to the challenge of preventing crime are remarkably consistent and in the opposite direction.

The public in many countries sees the primary responsibility for preventing crime as lying outside the criminal justice system. This helps explain the strong public support for crime-prevention initiatives across a range of countries, as well as the widespread preference for prevention over punishment (see subsequent sections of this essay). In fact, the public has always seen the solutions to crime as lying outside criminal justice. The home has long been viewed by many as the principal location of crime prevention. When Canadians were asked to identify who was responsible for controlling crime, almost half the sample identified "society in general" and only 24 percent cited "the courts" (Roberts and Grossman 1990).

III. Perceptions of the Most Effective Ways of Reducing Crime

If people see the responsibility for preventing crime as lying outside the justice system, they are also likely to believe that the most effective responses to crime are preventive rather than punitive—and this is exactly what many polls reveal. For example, when asked to identify the most effective ways of preventing crime, two-thirds of a sample of Americans identified "teaching young people responsibility and having after school programs to keep children off the streets" (Peter D. Hart Research Associates 2002). This finding is echoed in polls conducted in many other countries. A survey conducted across 15 European countries found that four out of five respondents agreed with the statement that: "Young people would commit less crime if they were taught better discipline by their parents" (European Opinion Research Group 2003). Similarly, when respondents in a British survey were asked to choose two or three measures that would be most effective in preventing crime, 60 percent of the sample cited "better parenting" (Esmee Fairburn Foundation 2004).

The durability of public support for nonpunitive, preventive responses to crime[2] can be demonstrated by reviewing responses to a poll conducted a generation ago. Respondents were asked to identify "the most effective response to crime" and were given a list of possible options, some of which were punitive (e.g., make sentences harsher) and some of which involved prevention through social development (e.g., reduce the level of unemployment). The public in Canada clearly regarded the non-punitive options as being more effective: slightly over half the sample chose reducing the level of unemployment or increasing the number of social programs (Roberts 1988). Moreover, a survey conducted in 1997 described two approaches (crime prevention through social development; and crime prevention through community crime-prevention programs). Respondents were then asked whether these forms of crime prevention should be assigned a higher, lower, or the same level of priority. It is important to note that Canadians assigned a higher priority to both approaches; only 16 percent assigned the same or a lower priority. Crime prevention through social development attracted more support: 51 percent of the sample assigned a much higher priority to this approach, compared to 36 percent who adopted this response with respect to community crime-prevention programs (Angus Reid Group 1997).[3]

This general finding that prevention is perceived to be more effective than punishment at reducing crime also emerges from public opinion surveys in other countries. Amelin, Blair, and Donnelly (2000) found that when residents of Northern Ireland were asked to identify effective ways of reducing crime, there was more support for prevention programs such as Neighborhood Watch than for policies such as making sentencing tougher. A study in England conducted for the Esmee Fairburn Foundation found that prevention-orientated responses such as "creating more constructive activities for young people" were seen by the public as being more effective in reducing crime than enhancing levels of punishment. Thus, over 40 percent of the sample endorsed creating activities for youth, while only 10 percent perceived putting more offenders in prison as an effective way of reducing crime. Finally, confidence in the effectiveness of crime prevention—relative to punishment as a crime control strategy—is not restricted to western industrialized societies. Nuttall et al. (2000) explored these issues with a sample of residents of the Caribbean. These researchers found that respondents in that part of the world also regarded crime-prevention initiatives such as better parenting as more effective than tougher sentencing as a means of reducing crime.

Table 24.2 summarizes public reaction to crime-prevention, as measured by a poll conducted across 15 European jurisdictions (European Opinion Research Group 2003). Respondents were asked to agree or disagree with a number of statements pertaining to crime prevention. As can be seen, there was strong public support for crime prevention. The statement attracting the highest level of agreement across all countries affirmed the importance of crime prevention targeting the young. In addition, the survey revealed considerable public faith in the efficacy of specific prevention programs—across all jurisdictions, approximately two-thirds of the public agreed that Neighborhood Watch was an effective way to reduce crime (see table 24.2).

A. Cross-Jurisdictional Variation

Although exploring the inter-jurisdictional variation is beyond the scope of this essay, it is important to note that the responses summarized in table 24.2 mask a great deal of variation. For example, the percentage of the public agreeing that

Table 24.2 Attitudes toward crime prevention in 15 European nations

	% Agree (all countries combined)	% Disagree (all countries combined)
Measures such as burglar alarms and locks can reduce crime	75%	19%
Neighborhood Watch can reduce crime	65%	27%
Police should share the responsibility for crime prevention with local and national government	76%	12%
Police should share responsibility for crime prevention with private individuals	60%	28%
There should be more crime-prevention programs targeted at young people	85%	8%

Source: Adapted from European Opinion Research Group 2003; "don't know" responses have been excluded.

Neighborhood Watch can reduce crime ranged from a low of 44 percent in Austria to 90 percent in Sweden. Similarly, 35 percent in Austria but 80 percent of respondents in Sweden agreed that "private individuals should share responsibility for crime prevention" (European Opinion Research Group 2003).

Attitudes to specific crime-prevention schemes also vary greatly. Hempel and Hopfer (2004) report findings from surveys of the public in five European countries that explored attitudes toward CCTV. The results revealed very discrepant reactions to the use of cameras in public locations. For example, almost three-quarters of respondents in London but only 3 percent of Viennese respondents agreed with the statement that CCTV would be welcome in their streets. The variation may be explained by differing perceptions of the effectiveness of CCTV in terms of crime prevention. Thus, approximately half of the London sample agreed that "CCTV protects against crime," compared to only 4 percent of Viennese residents who held this view.

IV. PUBLIC SUPPORT FOR PREVENTION
VERSUS PUNISHMENT

At this point, we turn to an important question addressed in a number of polls: how does public support for prevention compare to levels of support for punishment? Although respondents are often asked to make a simple choice between punishment and prevention, this is a rather false dichotomy: the criminal justice system attempts both to prevent crime *and* to hold offenders accountable through the imposition of legal punishments. Nevertheless, responses provide important insight into public reaction to crime prevention. The results are consistent whenever and wherever respondents have been asked to make a choice between punishment and prevention.

There are two general approaches to measuring public support for crime-prevention programs and policies. One consists of asking the public to express its level of support for prevention strategies when these are set against other responses to crime—punitive or deterrent crime-control policies, for example. An alternative, more concrete approach is to ask respondents to allocate funds to preventive or punitive responses. As will be seen, regardless of the approach used, public support for prevention emerges repeatedly, across jurisdictions and over time.

An important survey was conducted in the United States that reveals a clear public preference for prevention over punishment. On several occasions Americans have been asked to choose their preferred approach to crime: one approach involved introducing tougher sentencing and parole arrangements, the other approach favored crime-prevention alternatives such as increasing the number of neighborhood facilities for young people and improving job training. Crime prevention has often emerged as the public's preferred option, with greater support for prevention emerging in the more recent administration. Thus, in 1994, the American public was divided in its response to a choice between prevention and deterrence; approximately equal proportions of respondents supported these two options. However, the 2001 poll found that the public in the United States favors dealing with the roots of crime (rather than stricter sentencing) by a margin of two to one (65 percent compared to 32 percent; see Peter D. Hart Research Associates 2002). The same survey asked Americans to identify the top priority for dealing with crime. Respondents were twice as likely to support crime prevention as punishment (Peter D. Hart Research Associates 2002).

Whether this change in public opinion reflects a decline in faith in the ability of punishment to deter or an increase in the visibility of prevention initiatives is unclear. In recent years, several researchers (e.g., Peter D. Hart Research Associates 2002; Roberts and Hough 2002) have documented declining public support for punitive responses to crime (such as mandatory sentencing) and a rise in support for preventive options. This is true in a number of jurisdictions, including the United States. Finally, it is worth noting that this preference was shared by Democrats and Republicans, suggesting that crime prevention appeals to all respondents of contrasting political affiliations.

Canadians also share this preference for prevention over punishment. In fact, the views of the public in the United States and Canada with respect to this question are remarkably similar. For example, when Canadians were asked to identify the main goal of the criminal justice system, there was significantly more support for prevention than for punishment (41 percent and 23 percent, respectively; Ekos Research 2004). This pattern of findings is consistent with findings from earlier surveys in that country—in 2000, 44 percent of the sample supported prevention, 19 percent punishment (Ekos Research 2001). Finally, the primacy of prevention over punishment emerges from surveys in other countries as well (e.g., the Czech Republic; see Bures 2005) suggesting that crime prevention carries a fundamental appeal to the public.

A. Criminal Justice Spending Priorities

Another way of exploring public reaction to the prevention-punishment dichotomy is to measure support for preventive and punitive responses to crime by asking respondents to consider both within a funding framework. A number of polls over the past decade have posed the following question to respondents: "Which of the following approaches to lowering the crime rate comes closer to your own view—do you believe that more money and effort should go to attacking social and economic problems through better education and job training or should more money and effort go to deterring crime by improving law enforcement with more prisons, police and judges?" This question requires respondents to choose between a preventive approach and a punitive response that relies on punishment and deterrence. Table 24.3 summarizes responses to this question from several surveys conducted over the period 1989–2007. As can be seen, Americans see more promise in prevention than punishment, and this has been true throughout the 1990s (see table 24.3). In 1989, addressing social problems attracted almost twice as much support as 'more law enforcement' (61 percent vs. 32 percent). The percentages of respondents favoring these two alternatives were approximately the same in 2006 (65 percent vs. 31 percent, excluding "don't know" respondents; see table 24.3).

Table 24.3 **Public attitudes toward approaches to lowering the crime rate (US, 1989–2006)**

	Address social and economic problems through better education and job training	Improving law enforcement with more prisons, police, and judges
1989	61%	32%
1990	57%	36%
1992	67%	25%
1994	57%	39%
2000	68%	27%
2003	69%	29%
2006	65%	31%
Seven-year average	63%	31%

Source: Adapted from US Sourcebook of Criminal Justice Statistics 2010; excludes "don't know" responses.

The degree of public support for preventive rather than punitive responses to crime also emerges in a poll in the United States, which asked the following question: "Which of the following options would you most want your tax dollars spent on: building more prisons so that more criminals can be locked up for longer periods of time, or programs that try to prevent crime through early intervention in the lives of youth?" In response, 81 percent of the sample chose the crime-prevention option, 11 percent chose prisons (Sims and Johnston 2004).

Cullen et al. (1998) asked respondents to state the extent to which they supported or opposed eight statements describing early intervention programs.[4] High levels of support emerged for all programs; the average level of support across the programs was 86 percent (Cullen et al. 1998). The research by Cullen and his associates makes it clear that the US public strongly supports investing in crime prevention—even when the costs of this investment are salient. Thus, respondents in one study were asked to state whether they supported a number of early intervention programs "even if it might mean raising taxes." Cullen, Vose, and Jonson (2007) found "near universal support" for seven intervention programs (see Cullen, Vose, and Jonson 2007; Moon, Cullen, and Wright 2003).

B. Willingness to Pay for Prevention

Earlier polls found the same result: over 30 years ago, respondents were asked: "Do you think more money should be spent on strengthening police forces to crack down on crime, or should more money be spent on trying to improve the economic and social conditions underlying social problems?" Less than one-quarter of the sample favored strengthening police forces; over half of the sample supported what may be termed the "crime prevention through social development" response to crime (21 percent endorsed both options; Moore 1980).

Polls sometimes sensitize their respondents to the cost implications of crime-prevention programs and then ask how much emphasis governments should place on crime prevention initiatives. One specific example is the following: "Bearing in mind that most crime prevention programs are funded by tax dollars, what emphasis should governments place on crime prevention?" Over half the sample held the view that more emphasis should be placed on crime prevention; only 6 percent believed that less emphasis would be appropriate (Ekos Research 2004). The second cost-related question was the following: "Currently the Government spends about $2 per Canadian per year on crime prevention (or $64 million per year). Do you think the government should invest more, less, or about the same?" In response, approximately two-thirds favored spending more; only 4 percent favored spending less, 31 percent responded "about the same," and 1 percent said "don't know" (Ekos Research 2004).

When members of the Canadian public were asked to imagine that they had to choose how to invest $10 million to reduce crime, there was very little enthusiasm for trying to reduce crime by harsher sentencing: increasing the use of imprisonment to allow for longer sentences attracted the support of less than one respondent in five. In contrast, two-thirds of the sample favored crime-preventive strategies such as expanding youth literacy and training programs (Ekos Research 2004). Increasing early childhood intervention programs and parenting programs attracted almost as much support from the public. Surveys conducted in other countries tell the same story. An Irish poll found that when people were asked to spend a 10 million euro budget for tackling crime, prevention programs such as drug treatment and child intervention were significantly more popular than increasing the use of imprisonment (Irish Prison Reform Trust 2007).

A consequence of the economic crisis that confronted the world's economies in 2008–9 is that members of the public have become increasingly concerned about getting value for money spent for public services. One of the most robust findings in the research literature is the strength of public support for spending money on crime-prevention initiatives. This has been demonstrated in a number of ways. Let's begin by noting an important finding from over 30 years ago. In 1980, Canadians were asked how much effort the government should put into a number of public policy initiatives. Respondents were additionally told that: "Remember that putting more effort into one of these areas would require a shift of money from other areas or an increase in taxes."

Table 24.4 lists the options in the ranking that emerged from the responses. As can be seen, crime prevention emerged as the second most important priority, even ahead of addressing the unemployment problem. This pattern of findings demonstrates the longstanding support for crime prevention in Canada. Priorities were ranked almost a quarter of a century later, and as can be seen, crime prevention continued to attract strong support, notwithstanding the changes in other priorities (see table 24.4).

Cohen et al. (2006) explored public spending priorities by asking US respondents to allocate specific dollar amounts to various programs and initiatives. Results

Table 24.4 Rankings of public spending priorities, Canada in 2003 and 1980

Issue	2003	1980
Health care	1	10
Crime prevention	2	2
Environment	3	—
Reduce poverty	4	7
Reduce national debt	5	1
Lower unemployment	6	3
Tax cuts	7	—
National unity	8	—
Aboriginal issues	9	—

Source: Ekos Research 2004; Moore 1980.

indicated that the highest spending priority was crime prevention targeting at-risk youth. These researchers found overwhelming support among US residents for preventive initiatives such as drug treatment programs, but little support for building more prisons.

Finally, clear evidence of the public's preferences for spending money on prevention rather than punishment emerges from research reported by Doob et al. (1998). Survey respondents were asked whether the government should "build more prisons or invest in crime prevention." Half the sample was asked about adult offenders, the other about juveniles, but the pattern of responses was the same: almost nine respondents out of ten (89 percent of the juvenile group, 86 percent of those asked about adults) preferred the government to spend money on crime prevention than on prison construction.

One potential weakness of surveys that ask the public general funding questions is that people may agree that funding is a good idea in part because this may seem the appropriate response to make. A more sophisticated approach involves deriving the public's opinion quantitatively. Nagin et al. (2006) offer an example of this more innovative methodology for exploring public opinion. Their survey employed a technique known as "contingent valuation," which gauges the level of public support for different approaches to crime by quantifying respondents' willingness to pay for programs through taxation. These researchers found clear evidence of a public preference for crime-prevention programs over longer terms of imprisonment. Once again, this willingness to pay for prevention programs emerged even from respondents who self-identified themselves as conservative—suggesting cross-political support for crime prevention.

Taken together, these findings demonstrate that public support for crime prevention remains high, even when respondents are sensitized to the costs of prevention initiatives.

V. Crime-Prevention Programs: Public Awareness Levels and Participation Rates

A. Awareness

As noted earlier, crime-prevention initiatives and programs do not attract the same degree of media attention as do punitive responses to crime, such as mandatory sentences of imprisonment. For this reason, one impediment to the successful implementation of crime-prevention initiatives has been limited public awareness. This problem was noted by Roberts and Grossman (1990) and matters appear to have deteriorated since that review was published.

As with public attitudes, public awareness of crime-prevention programs and strategies can also be measured in different ways. If the public is asked whether it is aware of crime-prevention strategies—a rather general question—the results suggest high levels of awareness. For example, one survey asked respondents in the United States to agree or disagree with the following statement: "I am aware of crime prevention strategies and apply them in my home." Fewer than 10 percent disagreed; 60 percent of the sample was in agreement (Anderson-Draper Consulting 2004). Questions of this nature may reveal more about attitudes than actual awareness, as respondents were not asked to identify the specific strategies of which they were aware, nor about which of these they applied. There may also be a tendency for respondents to represent themselves as being more aware of these programs than they in fact are.

When people are asked to identify specific crime-prevention schemes, the results are rather different. This point can be made by examining data from over 25 years ago. Respondents were asked to state whether they had heard of a series of crime-prevention programs, as well as whether they participated in these programs. Awareness of crime-prevention programs was widespread. For example, almost half the sample reported being aware of the Block Parents program (Brillon, Louis-Guerin, and Lamarche 1984).

Since then, awareness levels appear to have declined. Representative surveys conducted in Canada in 2000 and 2003 shed light on the levels of public awareness today (see Ekos Research 2001, 2004). Members of the public were asked first whether they were aware of any crime-prevention programs in their neighborhood. In response to this general awareness question, less than half the sample (43 percent) responded affirmatively. These respondents were then asked to name one of these programs. Less than one-fifth expressed awareness of Neighborhood Watch and approximately one-tenth was aware of Block Parent schemes (Ekos Research 2001, 2004).

Levels of awareness of crime prevention appear to be higher across the United States. A survey conducted in 1999 found that over half (53 percent) of respondents were able to name a crime-prevention program, and of these almost half (45 percent) identified Neighborhood Watch. Longevity may explain the higher level of awareness in the United States. The Neighborhood Watch program began in that country and is the nation's oldest national crime-prevention scheme. Similarly, almost one respondent in five (17 percent) was aware of Crimestoppers; this compares to less than 5 percent of Canadians who were aware of the program.

B. Participation Rates in Crime-Prevention Programs

An interesting finding emerges when people are asked about their level of interest in participating in crime-prevention programs. According to one Canadian study, interest in participation was high: almost half the sample stated that they were "very interested" in participating in crime-prevention programs. A further 30 percent were "somewhat interested," and less than one-quarter (24 percent) responded that they were "not very interested" (Ekos Research 2004). Of course, not all respondents who state that they are very interested in participating are actually going to participate. Nevertheless, this pattern of findings is encouraging for crime-prevention initiatives that rely on the active participation of the community. This outcome establishes the clear bedrock of support on which crime-prevention initiatives may draw.

The difficulty is that the research on public participation in prevention, and on the sustainability of these initiatives, indicates that support is generalized but that participation is primarily linked to neighborhood homogeneity, stable patterns of residency, home ownership, and high levels of education and income (e.g., Rosenbaum 1987; Rosenbaum, Lurigio, and Davis 1998). It appears that public support is a necessary precondition for action, but it is only a building block—public support is not sufficient in itself to ensure local mobilization (see Roberts and Hastings 2007). The point is that the public must be both willing and able to participate. It may be, at least in part, that politicians and policymakers prefer to believe that there is little public support for prevention and little willingness to actually get involved because this justifies the failure to invest significant levels of energy and resources in the task of building local capacity for action.

C. Participation Rates in Other Jurisdictions

Research in the United States, the United Kingdom, and other western nations has consistently found the same relatively modest rates of participation in community-based prevention programs (see Knowles 1979; and discussion in Roberts 1992). For example, a survey conducted in the United States measured the extent to which Americans participate in crime-prevention activities. Overall, fewer than one resident in five reported participating in a crime-prevention program (Wirthlin Report 2001). This level of participation marked a decline from the previous administration of the survey. In 1999, almost one-quarter of the sample reported participating (Wirthlin Report 2001). Neighborhood Watch was the program that generated the highest rate of participation: 40 percent of respondents reported participating; crime-prevention programs based in schools attracted the lowest participation rates (9 percent; Wirthlin Report 2001). A similar pattern emerges from polls conducted in South Africa. Although Neighborhood Watch and similar programs exist in that country, only 15 percent of respondents knew of any crime-prevention initiative operating in their area. Only 9 percent of the sampled population stated that they participated actively in community prevention programs (Masuku and Maepa 2004).

Finally, the British Crime Survey (BCS) has repeatedly measured levels of participation in Neighbourhood Watch—perhaps the best-known and most widespread crime-prevention program in Britain. The BCS has been conducted for several years now, and can therefore provide insight into trends in participation rates. The most recent data from the British Crime Survey confirm a decline in participation rates. Thus, in 2007, 16 percent of British households belonged to a Neighborhood Watch scheme—down from 27 percent in 2000 (Nicholas et al.

Table 24.5 Percentage of UK households reporting participating in
Neighborhood Watch

Year of Survey	% of Sample Reporting Belonging to Neighborhood Watch Scheme
2007	16%
2006	16%
2005	17%
2000	27%
1996	24%
1994	23%
1992	23%

Source: British Crime Survey (Nicholas et al. 2008).

2008). Table 24.5 provides participation rates for the period 1992–2007. As can be seen, less than one respondent in five reported participating in this crime-prevention scheme in the latest administration (2007). Moreover, rates appear to have declined somewhat, from almost one-quarter in the early 1990s to 16 percent in 2007 (see table 24.5). It seems clear that the high levels of public interest in crime prevention do not always translate into equally high levels of active participation in prevention schemes.

VI. DISCUSSION AND CONCLUSIONS

The question that remains is what to make of these findings. The good news is that the levels of support for prevention are strong and consistent over time and across jurisdictions. That said, this has not translated into the development of the type of constituency or political pressure groups similar to those that can be marshaled in support of repressive strategies and more punitive responses to crime and criminals. Nor has it resulted in high or consistent participation rates for local crime-prevention initiatives. The strong public support for crime prevention also carries lessons for policymakers and politicians. It is wrong for them to assume—as they appear to do so on a regular basis—that the public endorses harsh responses to crime and has little interest in preventive approaches.

This review of public attitudes to crime prevention has demonstrated the abiding public support for prevention—often in preference to punitive responses to crime. Even during the 1990s—an era in which criminal policies were heavily influenced by populist punitiveness—the public still saw the merit of attempting to prevent rather than simply punish crime. Moreover, the public across different countries regard crime-prevention programs as representing a cost-effective response to offending. In this sense, their intuitions are consistent with the evidence base. Most criminal justice scholars agree that significant reductions in crime or criminal recidivism cannot be achieved by relying solely on punitive policies such as making sentencing harsher[5] (e.g., Ashworth 2010). The public clearly supports the notion that prevention is an efficient and effective strategic response to crime and victimization.

We need to know more about how perceptions of crime and attitudes toward prevention translate into action in the context of specific decisions about the merits of different types of approaches or investments. People clearly support crime prevention, but it would be useful to know more about the saliency of crime and the priority of prevention, and about how these influence decisions in the electoral booth or elsewhere. It would also be interesting to know more about whether there are systematic patterns hidden within the larger results of opinion polling, such as whether direct or indirect victims of crime are as supportive of prevention (since they are more likely to mobilize to pursue their own interests, and may well be more newsworthy and attractive to the media). The key for proponents of prevention will be to build on the base of support by becoming more effective at getting their messages to key audiences and at mobilizing political and administrative support for moving to a greater priority for and investments in crime prevention.

The polls conducted in various countries demonstrate that the public supports crime prevention as a general response to crime, and also favors specific schemes such as CCTV and Neighborhood Watch. It is important, however, to ensure that people have a realistic appreciation of the magnitude of preventive effects. For example, many members of the public believe that CCTV has a powerful crime-reduction effect. Systematic reviews of the evaluation literature, however, suggest that the preventive impact of surveillance cameras is more modest. For example, Welsh and Farrington (2006) concluded that CCTV had a "small but significant effect on crime" (p. 204; see also Ratcliffe, Taniguchi, and Taylor 2009; Welsh and Farrington 2009). Researchers, therefore, need to document the extent to which public support for CCTV and other schemes is founded upon a realistic appreciation their benefits (and potential costs).

Researchers also need to explore to a greater extent why the public enthusiasm for crime prevention does not convert into a more active citizenry with respect to participating in crime-prevention programs. An analogy may be made to the issue of crime reporting. We now know a great deal about the reasons victims report, or decline to report, crimes to the police. A similar comprehensive analysis is needed to determine why some individuals and communities are actively engaged in crime-prevention programs at the local level and why others are not.

Finally, researchers need to explore the limits—and also the consequences—of public support for crime-prevention programs and policies. For example, one consequence of the strong interest in crime prevention has been a proliferation of closed-circuit surveillance cameras (CCTV). The use of CCTV is often justified by its potential to prevent crime, and also to assist the prosecution of perpetrators when crime does occur. Advocates of CCTV also note the high level of public support for crime prevention in general and CCTV in particular. What is missing, however, is a careful examination of whether public support can justify greater or more intrusive state interventions in pursuit of a crime-prevention agenda (see von Hirsch 2000).

NOTES

1. Fully 50 percent disagreed with the statement, 29 percent agreed, and 19 percent neither agreed nor disagreed.

2. Except, that is, for serious crimes of violence, which have always elicited a more punitive reaction from members of the public, both in Canada and elsewhere (see Roberts and Stalans 2000, for a review).

3. When asked to identify the best example of crime prevention, members of the public were clearly influenced by their intuitions that crime often originates in poor parenting or misspent childhoods. Thus, 60 percent identified programs that support parents and programs that provide recreational activities for children as the best examples of crime prevention that they could think of (Ekos Research 1999).

4. The options included programs addressing pre-schoolers; parental training; and services to adolescents experiencing difficulties.

5. The principal reason for this is that case attrition from the original crime to the number of cases actually sentenced means that a sentence is imposed in only approximately 2–3 percent of all crimes. Thus, only a minority of crimes are reported to the police, only some of these reports result in a criminal charge being laid, and only a fraction of these result in a conviction and sentencing of an offender. With such a small percentage of all offenders being sentenced, even a highly punitive sentencing policy will have only a limited impact on the overall crime rate (for further information, see Ashworth, 2010).

REFERENCES

Amelin, K., M. Willis, C. Blair, and D. Donnelly. 2000. *Attitudes to Crime, Crime Reduction and Community Safety in Northern Ireland*. Belfast: Northern Ireland Office, Statistics and Research Branch.

Anderson-Draper Consulting. 2004. *Alberta Community Crime Prevention Association. 2004 Survey Results*. Edmonton: Anderson-Draper Consulting.

Angus Reid Group. 1997. Crime and the Justice System. *National Angus Reid/CTV News Poll*. Ottawa: Angus Reid Group.

Angus Reid Public Opinion. 2010. *Americans, Britons and Canadians take Harsh Stance on Crime*. Toronto: Vision Critical. Available at http://www.visioncritical.com/2010/01/americans-britons-and-canadians-take-harsh-stance-on-crime/.

Ashworth, A. 2010. *Sentencing and Criminal Justice*, 5th ed. Cambridge, UK: Cambridge University Press.

Brillon, Y., C. Louis-Guerin, and M.-C. Lamarche. 1984. *Attitudes of the Canadian Public Toward Crime Policies*. Montreal: International Centre for Comparative Criminology.

Bures, R. 2005. *Findings on Alcohol and Drug-related Violence. A Public Opinion Survey*. Prague: Czech Ministry of the Interior.

Cohen, M., R. Rust, S. Steen, and S. Tidd. 2004. "Willingness-to-pay for Crime Control Programs." *Criminology* 42:89–109.

Cooper and Sechrest Associates. 2008. *Third Way Crime Poll Highlights*. Washington, DC: Cooper and Sechrest Associates.

Cullen, F., B. Fisher, and B. Applegate. 2000. "Public Opinion about Punishment and Corrections." In: *Crime and Justice. A Review of Research*, edited by M. Tonry. Chicago: University of Chicago Press.

Cullen, F., J. Wright, S. Brown, M. Moon, M. Blankenship, and B. Applegate. 1998. "Public Support for Early Intervention Programs: Implications for a Progressive Policy Agenda." *Crime and Delinquency* 44:187–204.

Cullen, F., B. Vose, and C. Jonson. 2007 "Public Support for Early Intervention: Is Child Saving a "Habit of the heart"?" *Victims and Offenders* 2:109–24.

Doob, A. N., J. Sprott, V. Marinos, and K. Varma. 1998. *An Exploration of Ontario Residents' Views of Crime and the Criminal Justice System*. Toronto: University of Toronto: Centre of Criminology.

Ekos Research. 1999. *Rethinking Government*. Ottawa: National Crime Prevention Centre.

Ekos Research. 2001. *Rethinking Government 2001*. Ottawa: Ekos Research Associates.

Ekos Research. 2004. *Canadian Attitudes Towards Crime Prevention. Final Integrated Report*. Ottawa: Ekos Research Associates.

Environics Research. 1998. *Canadian Public Attitudes toward Crime and Crime Prevention*. Ottawa: Environics Research Group.

Erskine, H. 1974. "The Polls: Causes of Crime." *Public Opinion Quarterly* 50:288–98.

Esmee Fairburn Foundation. 2004. *Rethinking Crime and Punishment: The Report*. London: Esmee Fairburn Foundation.

European Opinion Research Group. 2003. *Public Safety, Exposure to Drug-related problems and crime. Public Opinion Survey*. Report for the European Commission. Brussels: European Commission.

Hastings, R. 1996. "Crime Prevention and Criminal Justice." In *Post-Critical Criminology*, edited by T.O'Reilly Fleming. Scarborough, ON: Prentice-Hall.

Hempel, L., and E. Hopfer. 2004. *CCTV in Europe*. Working Paper No. 15. Available at: www.urbaneye.net.

Irish Penal Reform Trust. 2007. *Public Attitudes to Prison*. Dublin: Irish Penal Reform Trust.

Knowles, J. 1979. *Ohio Citizen Attitudes: A Survey of Public Opinion on Crime and Criminal Justice*. Columbus, OH: Office of Criminal Justice Services.

Masuku, S., and T. Maepa. 2004. "Public Response to Crime." Chapter 6 in *City Safety*. Monograph No. 103. Available at: www.iss.co.za/pubs.

Moon, M., F. Cullen, and J. Wright. 2003. "It Takes a Village: Public Willingness to Help Wayward Youths." *Youth Violence and Juvenile Justice* 1:32–45.

Moore, R. 1980. "Reflections of Canadians on the Law and the Legal System: Legal Research Institute Survey of Respondents in Montreal, Toronto and Winnipeg." In *Law in a Cynical Society? Opinion and Law in the 1980s*, edited by D. Gibson and J. Baldwin. Calgary: Carswell.

Nagin, D., A. Piquero, E. Scott, and L. Steinberg. 2006. "Public Preferences for Rehabilitation versus Incarceration of Juvenile Offenders: Evidence from a Contingent Evaluation Survey." *Criminology and Public Policy* 5:627–52.

Nicholas, S., J. Flatley, J. Hoare, A. Patterson, C. Southcott, S. Moley, and K. Jansson. 2008. *Circumstances of Crime, Neighbourhood Watch Membership and Perceptions of Policing.* London: Home Office, Research, Development and Statistics Directorate.

Nuttall, C., E. DeCourcey, I. Rudder, and J. Ramsay. 2000. *Views and Beliefs about Crime and Criminal Justice.* Bridgetown: Attorney General of Barbados.

Peter D. Hart Research Associates. 2002. *Changing Public Attitudes toward the Criminal Justice System.* Washington, DC: Open Society Institute.

Ratcliffe, J., T. Taniguchi, and R. Taylor. 2009. "The Crime Prevention Effects of Public CCTV Cameras: A Multimethod Approach." *Justice Quarterly* 26:746–70.

Roberts, J. V. 1988. *Public Opinion and Sentencing.* Ottawa: Department of Justice Canada.

Roberts, J. V. 1992. "Public Opinion, Crime and Criminal Justice." In *Crime and Justice, vol. 16*, edited by Michael Tonry. Chicago: University of Chicago Press.

Roberts, J. V., and M. Grossman. 1990. "Crime Prevention and Public Opinion." *Canadian Journal of Criminology* 32:75–90.

Roberts, J. V., and R. Hastings. 2007. "Public Opinion and Crime Prevention: A Review of the International Findings." *Institute for the Prevention of Crime Review* 1:193–218.

Roberts, J. V., and M. Hough. 2002. "Changing Attitudes to Punishment: The Context" In *Changing Attitudes to Punishment. Public Opinion, Crime and Justice*, edited by J. V. Roberts and M. Hough. Cullompton, UK: Willan.

Roberts, J. V., and M. Hough. 2005. *Understanding Public Attitudes to Criminal Justice.* Maidenhead: Open University Press.

Roberts, J. V., and L. Stalans. 2000. *Public Opinion, Crime, and Criminal Justice.* Boulder, CO: Westview

Roberts, J. V., L. Stalans, D. Indermaur, and M. Hough. 2003. *Penal Populism and Public Opinion. Lessons from Five Countries.* Oxford, UK: Oxford University Press.

Rosenbaum, D. 1987. "The Theory and Research behind Neighborhood Watch: Is It a Sound Fear and Crime Reduction Strategy?" *Crime and Delinquency* 33:103–34.

Rosenbaum, D., A. Lurigio, and R. Davis. 1998. *The Prevention of Crime: Social and Situational Strategies.* Toronto: West/Wadsworth.

Sims, B., and E. Johnston. 2004. "Examining Public Opinion about Crime and Justice: A Statewide Study." *Criminal Justice Policy Review* 15:270–93.

US Sourcebook of Criminal Justice Statistics. 2010. *Tables 2.00013.2006 and 2.28.2006.* Available at: www.albany.edu/sourcebook/.

von Hirsch, A. 2000. "The Ethics of Public Television Surveillance." In *Ethical and Social Perspectives on Situational Crime Prevention*, edited by A. von Hirsch, D. Garland, and A. Wakefield. Oxford, UK: Hart Publishing.

Welsh, Brandon C., and David P. Farrington, eds. 2006. *Preventing Crime.* New York: Springer-Verlag.

Welsh, Brandon C., and David P. Farrington. 2009. "Public Area CCTV and Crime Prevention: An Updated Systematic Review and Meta-Analysis." *Justice Quarterly* 26:716–45.

Wirthlin Report. 2001 *Special Report: Americans' Attitudes toward Crime and Prevention.* February Issue. Available at: www.wirthlin.com.

Wood, J., and T. Gannon. 2008. *Public Opinion and Criminal Justice.* Cullompton, UK: Willan.

CHAPTER 25

THE SCIENCE AND POLITICS OF CRIME PREVENTION: TOWARD A NEW CRIME POLICY

BRANDON C. WELSH AND DAVID P. FARRINGTON

THE first three parts of this volume establish that crime prevention is a theoretically sound, feasible, highly effective, and worthwhile approach to reducing crime. Operating outside of the confines of the formal justice system, it is in many respects a socially progressive approach. It is also considered the fourth pillar of crime reduction, alongside the institutions of police, courts, and corrections (Waller 2006). For sure, each of the major strategies of developmental, community, and situational crime prevention has its own strengths, and the evidence base is stronger in some areas than in others. Some of the essays in this fourth and final part of the volume rightly note that the work is by no means complete. More attention needs to be paid to how crime-prevention programs are implemented and disseminated for wider public use, even moving toward a science of implementation. There also needs to be greater efforts to ensure that these programs are evaluated with the most rigorous methods that are feasible.

It is also important to recognize that crime prevention does not exist in a vacuum. Our organization of crime prevention into the three distinct strategies of developmental, community, and situational by no means precludes their integration or combination as part of a package of measures. Indeed, this combination is at the heart of community crime prevention, and it is a core feature of comprehensive partnership models like Communities That Care (Hawkins et al. 2009). The integration of different prevention strategies has even been the focus of research (see Welsh and Farrington 1998, 2011b).

Crime prevention is also subject to the political realities and whims of the day. For example, there are many different government priorities, such as military defense spending, environmental protection, or healthcare reform, which are competing for scarce public resources. National polls may show that the public is more concerned about issues other than crime. Politicians may be worried about being perceived as soft on crime by supporting prevention instead of law-and-order measures (Gest 2001). Another factor is the short time horizons of politicians (Tonry and Farrington 1995), which makes programs that show results only in the longer term rather unappealing to those who come up for election every few years. All of these are important considerations that have a direct bearing on whether or not crime prevention will be given its deserved priority.

Within the context of these and other political considerations and the science of crime prevention, this essay argues for a new crime policy—one that strikes a greater balance between crime prevention and crime control. Several observations and conclusions emerge:

- Prevention science and evidence-based policy are two contemporary developments that have strengthened crime prevention. Each is concerned that the highest standards of science are used to advance knowledge and improve public policy.
- The linkages between research and policy are sometimes less than clear, with evaluation influence on policy taking a number of different routes. The imposed use of evaluation seems especially promising.
- Crime prevention faces a number of unique challenges, including concern by politicians that they will be labeled soft on crime for their support of prevention and the short time horizon of politicians. The good news is that these challenges can be overcome.
- Crime prevention is an important component of an overall strategy to reduce crime. Striking a greater balance between crime prevention and crime control will go a long way toward building a safer, more sustainable society.

The organization of this essay is as follows. Section I discusses key features and the importance of prevention science and evidence-based policy. Section II looks at some of the most pressing political challenges confronting crime prevention. It also explores some opportunities for overcoming these challenges and changing the status quo. Section III makes the case for a new crime policy.

I. PREVENTION SCIENCE AND EVIDENCE-BASED POLICY

Prevention science and evidence-based policy are two contemporary developments that have strengthened crime prevention. Both are best understood as frameworks that can be applied across a wide range of contexts, settings, and populations. At their core, each is concerned that the highest standards of science are used to advance knowledge and improve public policy.

Prevention science has its roots in public health and begins with a commitment to prevention that is grounded in the developmental epidemiology of specific health or social problems. In the case of youth violence prevention, for example, "prevention science has provided a bridge between an understanding of how chronic violence develops and how prevention programs can interrupt that development" (Dodge 2001, p. 63). Only the highest quality methods of scientific investigation are employed. Prospective longitudinal studies are used to identify the most important risk factors for offending. Randomized experimental designs are used to evaluate the efficacy and effectiveness of prevention programs designed to tackle these factors. Prevention science is also characterized by a number of "logically sequential stages in the general development of prevention programs" (Dodge 2001, p. 64).

Prevention science is by no means restricted to prevention in the first instance; it is equally applicable to interventions designed to reduce offending among high-risk populations or reoffending by adjudicated youth. The idea of an alternative, non–criminal justice response to the prevention of delinquency and offending is a crucial element in the mission of prevention science. Its influence on crime prevention can be found in its adherence to the highest scientific standards, its effort to base prevention on epidemiology, and its focus on the process of taking prevention programs to scale and studying how to mitigate the problem of attenuation of program effects (Welsh, Sullivan, and Olds 2010).

An evidence-based approach to crime policy embraces prevention science's commitment to the use of the most scientifically valid studies to evaluate programs. What it adds is the utilization of accumulated scientific research evidence on effectiveness. It seeks to increase the influence of research on policy.

At the heart of the evidence-based model is the notion that "we are all entitled to our own opinions, but not to our own facts" (Sherman 1998, p. 4). Use of opinions instead of facts to guide crime policy may cause iatrogenic effects (McCord 2003), may lead to the implementation of programs that do not work at all, may waste scarce public resources (Drake, Aos, and Miller 2009), and may divert policy attention from the most important crime priorities of the day (Mears 2010).

Support for an evidence-based approach to crime policy in the United States and elsewhere is growing (Welsh and Farrington 2011a). This growth has been fostered by a number of recent developments, including a movement toward an evidence-based approach in other disciplines such as medicine (Millenson 1997), education (Mosteller and Boruch 2002), and the social sciences more generally (Sherman 2003); large-scale reviews of "what works" in crime prevention and criminal justice (Sherman et al. 1997, 2006); and, most recently, the establishment of the Campbell Collaboration and its Crime and Justice Group, which aims to carry out and disseminate reviews of the effectiveness of criminological interventions (Farrington, Weisburd, and Gill 2011).

The US interest, as well as the interest of many other western countries, in an evidence-based approach to crime policy may be said to have begun with the release of *Preventing Crime: What Works, What Doesn't, What's Promising*, by Lawrence Sherman and his colleagues (1997). This report was commissioned by the US Congress as an independent, scientifically rigorous assessment of more than $4 billion worth of federally sponsored anti-crime programs. Using a scientific methods scale to rate program evaluations combined with a vote-counting review method, they drew conclusions about the effects of the full range of crime prevention and criminal justice measures.

The evidence-based approach has had some interesting influences thus far on how crime prevention is viewed in the United States. The *Preventing Crime* report and its subsequent public and scholarly attention served to (ever so slightly) shift the debate away from the perception that support for crime prevention is tantamount to being soft on crime, which was at the heart of the opposition to the prevention spending in the 1994 crime bill (see Welsh and Farrington this volume). The report put the focus squarely on what scientific evidence had to say about effectiveness. It left no room for moralizing about crime or politicizing what works or does not work; it sought to make the facts—arrived at by scrupulous evaluation—the centerpiece of the policymaking processes.

II. POLITICAL CHALLENGES AND SOME REMEDIES

Integral to the evidence-based paradigm, whether in the context of crime prevention, policing, sentencing, or correctional treatment, is the notion that decision makers are rational actors who will consider the best available information in making public policy. This is not to suggest that in the case of the release of new scientific evidence—showing that a crime-reduction policy works, does not work, or causes harm—government or political leaders will immediately embrace the evidence and change policies wholesale. It is, of course, wholly naïve to think that the evidence base on the effectiveness of a particular program or strategy will be the sole influence on policy. There are many considerations involved in the policymaking process. Some of these were touched upon above, and they range from more global ones about the relative importance of crime in society to particular views or biases held about one approach compared with another.

What is really at issue here is the need to increase the influence of research on policy or, in a manner of speaking, put systematic research evidence at center stage in the policymaking (and political) process. In addition to the above considerations, we must also be mindful that the linkages between research and policy are sometimes less than clear, with evaluation influence on policy taking a number of different routes. This is a central finding from the research utilization literature (Tonry and Green 2003).

As part of this literature, Carol Weiss and her colleagues (2005) have delineated a number of ways that evaluation research can exert influence on policy decisions. The one that is most applicable to evidence-based policy is what the authors refer to as "imposed use." In this case, state or federal government agencies mandate that for any local program to receive funding it first needs to be evidence-based. This usually comes in the form of a list of best practices that are put together and approved by the agency. One example is the "list of exemplary and promising prevention programs" of the US Department of Education's Safe and Drug-Free Schools program. Programs not on this list are not eligible for government funding. Research by Weiss and her colleagues (2008) on the application of this list with respect to DARE (Drug Abuse Resistance Education) and other school-based substance-abuse prevention programs showed some advantages and shortcomings. In concluding that the imposed use of evaluation is in need of some tinkering, the researchers were also clear in asserting that, "giving evaluation more clout is a worthwhile way to increase the rationality of decision making" (Weiss et al. 2008, p. 29).

This last point is further support for our contention that the movement toward rational and evidence-based crime policy is here to stay. It does not appear to be yet another fad or fleeting idea in the annals of crime policy. While there remains much to be done to move systematic evidence to center stage in the policymaking process, the good news is that this movement is well under way. In England and Wales, there is a correctional services accreditation panel that specifies accredited programs that can be used in prison and probation settings (see McGuire 2001).

Another challenge that confronts crime prevention is the worry by politicians that they may be perceived as soft on crime by supporting prevention instead of law-and-order measures. As Michael Tonry (2011, pp. 139–40) reminds us, this view has persisted despite two decades of declining crime rates and increasing imprisonment rates, and is shared by Republicans and Democrats alike. It is rooted in a number of belief systems. One of these involves entrenched, moralistic views about crime. Here, crime is seen as evil, with redemption only achievable through extreme state-sanctioned deprivations of liberty, sometimes including even the death penalty. There is no room for prevention. It is held that the general deterrent effect of harsh sanctions will be sufficient to persuade others from embarking on a life of crime. The moral reformers of the 17th and 18th centuries would surely be proud.

Another view equates crime prevention with social welfare. Like the dismantling of federal welfare in the 1990s, and the present concerns about President Obama's healthcare reform, crime prevention, particularly developmental and community measures, is seen as just another taxpayer-subsidized handout that is not deserved.

The most widespread justification for the concern about being seen as soft on crime is that politicians think that citizens are punishment oriented. Politicians who support get-tough responses to crime (and rebuke prevention) have long claimed to have the full backing of the general public, and that it is indeed the public that demands more punitive sanctions such as military-style boot camps, mandatory minimums, and three-strikes laws. To be sure, there is public support for get-tough responses to crime, especially violent acts. But this support does not reach the levels often claimed and, more important, is not as high when punishment is compared to alternatives such as rehabilitation or treatment for offenders or early childhood or youth prevention programs (Cullen et al. 2007). This exaggeration of the punitiveness of the general public on the part of politicians and others has become known as the "mythical punitive public" (Roberts 2004). Indeed, new research provides evidence to substantiate that the "punitive public" is mythical rather than actual— that is, citizens are highly supportive of crime prevention and are even willing to pay more in taxes to support these programs compared to other responses (Roberts and Hastings this volume).

Encouragingly, the evidence-based movement may go some way toward breaking down or tempering the soft-on-crime concern. Instead of emotions and opinions, facts and evidence are becoming the new currency in federal, state, and local debates about crime policy (Greenwood 2006). There is an emphasis on taking account of financial costs and benefits in formulating public policies. This is happening for many reasons, including a renewed commitment to science in the United States and the dedicated work of various international and national groups, such as the Campbell Collaboration, the Coalition for Evidence-Based Policy, and the Association for the Advancement of Evidence-Based Practice. It may take some time, but the slogan "get tough on crime" may one day be replaced with "get smart on crime" or "reduce crime in the most cost-effective way." The public should demand that its tax dollars are invested more efficiently.

Yet another challenge that confronts crime prevention, especially developmental and sometimes community approaches, is that the benefits from reduced crime will not be apparent for a number of years—at least until children reach adolescence. This can conflict with the short time horizons of politicians—that is, programs that show results only in the longer term can be unappealing to those who have to face reelection every few years. One potential remedy for this situation is to educate politicians about the many other desirable effects that these prevention programs can produce in the short-term. For example, preschool intellectual enrichment, child skills training, and parent training programs show improvements in school readiness and school performance on the part of the children, greater employment and educational opportunities for parents, and increased family stability (Lösel and Bender this volume; Piquero and Jennings this volume; Schindler and Yoshikawa this volume). These short-term benefits alone can translate into substantial cost savings for government (Farrington and Welsh 2007).

The problem of the short time horizons of politicians is not restricted to crime policy. Jens Ludwig (2012) suggests applying ideas from other policy areas to crime prevention. For example, in the area of government budgeting, this same problem has led to calls for "'intergenerational accounting'—the idea that we should think about government expenditure and revenues as flows over long periods of time, and make clear to the public the impact that different policy decisions will have on these long-term flows" (p. 37). Another suggestion is to expand the definition of gross domestic product (GDP) in order to account for nonmonetary considerations, such as the "value of a country's stock of environmental quality" (p. 37). When people invest, they are not necessarily looking for quick results but for long-term benefits. Government policymakers should also be able to defer gratification, plan for the future, and think about what legacy they are leaving the next generation.

III. A New Crime Policy

In a recent thought experiment, Steven Durlauf and Daniel Nagin (2011) argue that a reduction in the use of imprisonment can lead to a reduction in crime rates. This is possible, they contend, if the cost savings from this policy change are allocated to hot-spots policing and other effective policing strategies (see Skogan and Frydl 2004; Braga and Weisburd 2010). This is an important piece of scholarship and it has great relevance to US crime policy. For sure, policing and corrections are the two most dominant crime-reduction approaches in this country, accounting for $168 billion (in 2006 dollars), or almost four-fifths of annual criminal justice spending (Perry 2008). Completely absent, however, is any consideration of the benefit that crime prevention holds for lowering crime rates and reducing government spending on criminal justice.

To be fair, the authors make passing reference to the effectiveness of early childhood development programs in reducing criminality (e.g., Piquero et al. 2009). Nonetheless, what makes this a glaring omission from their study is that what is really needed is a crime policy that strikes a greater balance between prevention and control. Policing may indeed represent a better alternative to the present practice of mass incarceration in the United States, but it is often another form of crime control, dealing with offenders after the fact. In some respects, these arguments are analogous to shifting resources from increasing incarceration rates to correctional treatment without any plan to stop the very development of offenders and their subsequent flow into the system. There needs to be a focus on the front end, without which we surely are just playing at the margins.

Some studies have compared the effectiveness of crime-prevention and crime-control strategies. The most well known of these was conducted by the RAND Corporation (Greenwood et al. 1998). It assessed the cost-effectiveness (i.e., serious crimes prevented per $1 million spent, using 1993 dollars) of California's three-strikes law compared with four prevention and intervention strategies with demonstrated efficacy in reducing crime: a combination of home visiting and day care; parent training; graduation incentives; and monitoring and supervising delinquent youths. Each of these alternatives was based on well-known experiments with small to moderately large sample sizes.

The first step in the modeling process was the estimation of program costs and crime-reduction effectiveness of the four alternative interventions. In order to conduct fair comparisons among these interventions and with the three-strikes law, three main "penalties" were assigned to the former. These were: (a) targeting: the proportion of the population targeted by the program who are likely to become involved in criminal behavior (e.g., children of low-income, teenage mothers for the home visiting/day-care program); (b) decay: the loss of effectiveness after treatment ends; and (c) scale-up: the decrease in program effects from expanding the program statewide (Greenwood et al. 1998, p. 16).

The study found that parent training and graduation incentives were the most cost-effective of the five programs, while home visiting/day care was the least cost-effective. The number of serious crimes prevented per $1 million was estimated at 258 for graduation incentives, 157 for parent training, 72 for delinquent supervision, 60 for the three-strikes law, and 11 for home visiting/day-care.[1] It is important to comment briefly on the poor showing of the home visiting/day-care program. The small number of crimes prevented per $1 million is attributable to two key factors (a third factor is discussed below): first, the long-term delay in realizing an impact on crime; and second, the high cost of delivering the services, particularly the day-care component, which was estimated at $6,000 per child per year over a four-year period.

The other major study—a thought experiment like Durlauf and Nagin (2011)— was carried out by John Donohue and Peter Siegelman (1998). The authors set out to investigate if the "social resources that will be expended a decade or more from now on incarcerating today's youngsters could instead generate roughly comparable levels of crime *prevention* if they were spent today on the most promising social programs" (1998, p. 31, emphasis in original). These included a range of early prevention programs and the national Job Corps program; and most of the estimates were based on well-known experiments or quasi-experiments with small to large sample sizes.

The first step involved estimating the crime reduction and cost associated with a continuation of US prison policy of the day. On the basis of a 50 percent increase in the prison population over a 15-year period (assumed from the level in December 1993 and trends at the time), it was estimated that this policy would cost $5.6 to $8 billion (in 1993 dollars) and result in a 5 to 15 percent reduction in crime. The next steps involved estimating the percentage of the cohort of three-year-olds who could be served by allocating the saved prison costs (the $5.6 to $8 billion) to the different social programs and then estimating the crime-reduction benefits that could be achieved by selected programs under a range of targeting conditions (i.e., the worst 6 percent of delinquents, males only, and young black males only). Two early developmental prevention programs were selected: the Perry Preschool project (Schweinhart, Barnes, and Weikart 1993) and the Syracuse University Family Development Research program (Lally, Mangione, and Honig 1988). It is at this stage that the authors applied a scaling-up penalty of 50 percent to each program. This had the result of lowering Perry's crime-reduction effectiveness from 40 to 20 percent and Syracuse's effectiveness from 70 to 35 percent.

In the final analysis, it was found that both prevention programs could achieve reductions in crime that were within the range of what was expected from a continuation of the prison policy of the day (5 to 15 percent) even if they were allocated the lower bound amount that would have been spent on prisons ($5.6 billion). This was considered the worst-case scenario. In the best-case scenario, which did not include the scaling-up penalty and allocated the upper bound amount of prison spending ($8 billion), the Perry and Syracuse programs produced crime reductions of 21 and 26 percent, respectively—better than increasing the prison population.

Interestingly, Nagin (2001a, 2001b) reexamined these two studies. While he praised their innovative methods, one of his main concerns was that they failed to consider the full potential benefits of the early prevention programs. By its very nature, developmental crime prevention is designed to improve individual functioning across multiple domains. Indeed, this is precisely what extant evaluations of the included programs showed. But Greenwood et al. and Donohue and Siegelman only considered the benefits following from lower rates of delinquent and criminal activity. Educational, employment, family, health, and other important benefits were not taken into account, which had the effect of greatly reducing the true economic return to society of these programs. A more recent benefit-cost analysis by Donohue (2009) embraces this view; he concludes that "there is reason to believe that alternatives to incarceration might well be more socially attractive than our current reliance on incarceration as the predominant crime-fighting strategy"(p. 308).

These studies make a strong case for the need to strike a greater balance between crime prevention and crime control. But perhaps the strongest case for a balanced portfolio of prevention and control comes from the real-life policy experiment that is under way in Washington State. In 1997, the legislature commissioned the Washington State Institute for Public Policy to assess the effectiveness and economic efficiency of a range of crime prevention and criminal justice programs with the aim to "identify interventions that reduce crime and lower total costs to taxpayers and crime victims" (Aos, Barnoski, and Lieb 1998, p. 1). The researchers referred to their methodological approach as "bottom line" financial analysis, which they considered to parallel the approach used by investors who study rates of return on financial investments. The research began with a literature review of high-quality programs. A five-step analytical model was then used to estimate each program's economic contribution.[2]

What started out as a highly rigorous yet fairly modest policy research initiative soon turned into the most comprehensive approach to develop evidence-based crime policy in the United States and one revered by other states and other countries (Greenwood 2006; Aldhous 2007). Following the Institute's first set of reports, the legislature authorized a number of system-level randomized controlled trials of the most effective and cost-beneficial juvenile and adult intervention programs. The results of these trials helped to refine local practice and service delivery. By 2006, the Institute had systematically reviewed and analyzed 571 of the highest quality evaluations of crime-prevention and criminal justice programs, estimated the benefits and costs of effective programs, and "projected the degree to which alternative 'portfolios' of these programs could affect future prison construction needs, criminal justice costs, and crime rates in Washington" (Aos, Miller, and Drake 2006, p. 1). This most recent work was commissioned by the legislature to address the projected need for two new state prisons by 2020 and possibly a third by 2030. Based on a moderate-to-aggressive portfolio of evidence-based crime-prevention programs (i.e., $63–$171 million expenditure in the first year), it was found that a significant amount of future prison construction costs could be avoided, about $2 billion saved by taxpayers, and crime rates lowered slightly (Aos, Miller, and Drake 2006, p. 16).

In 2007, the Washington State legislature abandoned plans to build one of these two prisons and in its place approved a sizable spending package ($48 million) on evidence-based crime-prevention and intervention programs (Drake, Aos, and Miller 2009). What makes this initiative even more important is that it was a political decision that was made on the basis of scientific research. This research showed that other strategies were more effective than prison and would generate substantial financial savings to the Washington State government and taxpayers.

Building a safer, more sustainable society will require using the best available research evidence, overcoming political barriers, and striking a greater balance between crime prevention and crime control. This is within our reach and the work has already begun. In the most optimistic scenario, what Washington State is doing today the world will be doing tomorrow. But let's be clear: without a sound focus on crime prevention, any crime policy will not be worth the paper it is written on.

NOTES

1. Crimes prevented were not calculated on a per annum basis. Instead they represent the predicted total effect produced by each program on each California birth cohort (an estimated 150,000 at-risk children born in California every year).

2. The first step of the model involves estimating each program's "most likely practical application within the state's justice or early intervention systems" (Aos, Barnoski, and Lieb 1998, p. 8). Step two looks at whether previously measured program results can be replicated in the state. Step three involves an assessment of program costs, estimated on the basis of what it would cost the Washington State government to implement a similar program (if the program was not already operating in the state). Step four involves monetizing each program's effects on crime. Savings to the criminal justice system and

crime victims are estimated. The final step involves calculating the economic contribution of the program, expressed as a benefit-to-cost ratio. Based on this, programs can be judged on their independent and comparative monetary value.

REFERENCES

Aldhous, Peter. 2007. "Applying Science to Prison Overcrowding." *New Scientist*, February 10. Available at: http://www.newscientist.com.

Aos, Steve, Robert Barnoski, and Roxanne Lieb. 1998. "Preventive Programs for Young Offenders: Effective and Cost-Effective." *Overcrowded Times* 9(2): 1, 7–11.

Aos, Steve, Marna Miller, and Elizabeth Drake. 2006. *Evidence-Based Public Policy Options to Reduce Future Prison Construction, Criminal Justice Costs, and Crime Rates.* Olympia: Washington State Institute for Public Policy.

Braga, Anthony A., and David Weisburd. 2010. *Policing Problem Places: Crime Hot Spots and Effective Prevention.* New York: Oxford University Press.

Cullen, Francis T., Brenda A. Vose, Cheryl N. L. Jonson, and James D. Unnever. 2007. "Public Support for Early Intervention: Is Child Saving a 'Habit of the Heart'?" *Victims and Offenders* 2:109–24.

Dodge, Kenneth A. 2001. "The Science of Youth Violence Prevention: Progressing from Developmental Epidemiology to Efficacy to Effectiveness to Public Policy." *American Journal of Preventive Medicine* 20(1S): 63–70.

Donohue, John J. 2009. "Assessing the Relative Benefits of Incarceration: Overall Changes and the Benefits on the Margin." In *Do Prisons Make Us Safer? The Benefits and Costs of the Prison Boom*, edited by Steven Raphael and Michael A. Stoll. New York: Russell Sage.

Donohue, John J., and Peter Siegelman. 1998. "Allocating Resources among Prisons and Social Programs in the Battle against Crime." *Journal of Legal Studies* 27: 1–43.

Drake, Elizabeth K., Steve Aos, and Marna G. Miller. 2009. "Evidence-Based Public Policy Options to Reduce Crime and Criminal Justice Costs: Implications in Washington State." *Victims and Offenders* 4:170–96.

Durlauf, Steven N., and Daniel S. Nagin. 2011. "Imprisonment and Crime: Can both be Reduced?" *Criminology and Public Policy* 10:13–54.

Farrington, David P., David Weisburd, and Charlotte E. Gill. 2011. "The Campbell Collaboration Crime and Justice Group: A Decade of Progress." In *Handbook of International Criminology*, edited by C. J. Smith, S. Zhang, and Rosemary Barberet. New York: Routledge.

Farrington, David P., and Brandon C. Welsh. 2007. *Saving Children from a Life of Crime: Early Risk Factors and Effective Interventions.* New York: Oxford University Press.

Gest, Ted. 2001. *Crime and Politics: Big Government's Erratic Campaign for Law and Order.* New York: Oxford University Press.

Greenwood, Peter W. 2006. *Changing Lives: Delinquency Prevention as Crime-Control Policy.* Chicago: University of Chicago Press.

Greenwood, Peter W., Karyn E. Model, C. Peter Rydell, and James Chiesa. 1998. *Diverting Children from a Life of Crime: Measuring Costs and Benefits*, 2nd ed. Santa Monica, CA: RAND.

Hawkins, J. David, Sabrina Oesterle, Eric C. Brown, Michael W. Arthur, Robert D. Abbott, Abigail A. Fagan, and Richard F. Catalano. 2009. "Results of a Type 2 Translational Research Trial to Prevent Adolescent Drug Use and Delinquency: A Test of Communities That Care." *Archives of Pediatrics and Adolescent Medicine* 163:789–98.

Lally, J. Ronald, Peter L. Mangione, and Alice S. Honig. 1988. "The Syracuse University Family Development Research Program: Long-Range Impact of an Early Intervention with Low-Income Children and their Families." In *Parent Education as Early Childhood Intervention: Emerging Directions in Theory, Research and Practice*, edited by D. R. Powell. Norwood, NJ: Ablex.

Ludwig, Jens. 2012. "Cost-Effective Crime Prevention." In *Contemporary Issues in Criminological Theory and Research: The Role of Social Institutions*, edited by Richard Rosenfeld, Kenna Quinet, and Crystal Garcia. Belmont, CA: Wadsworth.

McCord, Joan. 2003. "Cures That Harm: Unanticipated Outcomes of Crime Prevention Programs." *Annals of the American Academy of Political and Social Science* 587: 16–30.

McGuire, James. 2001. "What Works in Correctional Intervention? Evidence and Practical Implications." In *Offender Rehabilitation in Practice: Implementing and Evaluating Effective Programs*, edited by Gary A. Bernfeld, David P. Farrington, and Alan Leschied. Chichester, UK: Wiley.

Mears, Daniel P. 2010. *American Criminal Justice Policy: An Evaluation Approach to Increasing Accountability and Effectiveness*. New York: Cambridge University Press.

Millenson, Michael L. 1997. *Demanding Medical Excellence: Doctors and Accountability in the Information Age*. Chicago: University of Chicago Press.

Mosteller, Frederick, and Robert F. Boruch, eds. 2002. *Evidence Matters: Randomized Trials in Education Research*. Washington, DC: Brookings Institution Press.

Nagin, Daniel S. 2001a. "Measuring Economic Benefits of Developmental Prevention Programs." In *Costs and Benefits of Preventing Crime*, edited by Brandon C. Welsh, David P. Farrington, and Lawrence W. Sherman. Boulder, CO: Westview.

Nagin, Daniel S. 2001b. "Measuring the Economic Benefits of Developmental Prevention Programs." In *Crime and Justice: A Review of Research*, vol. 28, edited by Michael Tonry. Chicago: University of Chicago Press.

Perry, Steve W. 2008. "Justice Expenditure and Employment Extracts, 2006." Available at: http://bjs.ojp.usdoj.gov/index.cfm?ty=pbdetail&iid=1022.

Piquero, Alex R., David P. Farrington, Brandon C. Welsh, Richard E. Tremblay, and Wesley G. Jennings. 2009. "Effects of Early/Family Parent Training Programs on Antisocial Behavior and Delinquency." *Journal of Experimental Criminology* 5:83–120.

Roberts, Julian V. 2004. "Public Opinion and Youth Justice." In *Youth Crime and Youth Justice: Comparative and Cross-National Perspectives. Crime and Justice: A Review of Research*, vol. 31, edited by Michael Tonry and Anthony N. Doob. Chicago: University of Chicago Press.

Schweinhart, Lawrence J., Helen V. Barnes, and David P. Weikart. 1993. *Significant Benefits: The High/Scope Perry Preschool Study Through Age 27*. Ypsilanti, MI: High/Scope Press.

Sherman, Lawrence W. 1998. *Evidence-Based Policing*. Washington, DC: Police Foundation.

Sherman, Lawrence W. 2003. "Misleading Evidence and Evidence-Led Policy: Making Social Science More Experimental." *Annals of the American Academy of Political and Social Science* 589:6–19.

Sherman, Lawrence W., David P. Farrington, Brandon C. Welsh, and Doris L. MacKenzie, eds. 2006. *Evidence-Based Crime Prevention*, rev. ed. New York: Routledge.

Sherman, Lawrence W., Denise C. Gottfredson, Doris L. MacKenzie, John E. Eck, Peter Reuter, and Shawn D. Bushway. 1997. *Preventing Crime: What Works, What Doesn't,*

What's Promising. Washington, DC: US Department of Justice, National Institute of Justice.

Skogan, Wesley G., and Kathleen Frydl, eds. 2004. *Fairness and Effectiveness in Policing: The Evidence.* Washington, DC: National Academies Press.

Tonry, Michael. 2011. "Less Imprisonment Is no Doubt a Good Thing: More Policing Is Not." *Criminology and Public Policy* 10:137–52.

Tonry, Michael, and David P. Farrington. 1995. "Strategic Approaches to Crime Prevention." In *Building a Safer Society: Strategic Approaches to Crime Prevention. Crime and Justice: A Review of Research*, vol. 19, edited by Michael Tonry and David P. Farrington. Chicago: University of Chicago Press.

Tonry, Michael, and David A. Green. 2003. "Criminology and Public Policy in the USA and UK." In *The Criminological Foundations of Penal Policy: Essays in Honour of Roger Hood*, edited by Lucia Zedner and Andrew Ashworth. New York: Oxford University Press.

Waller, Irvin. 2006. *Less Law, More Order: The Truth about Reducing Crime.* Westport, CT: Praeger.

Weiss, Carol H., Erin Murphy-Graham, and Sarah Birkeland. 2005. "An Alternative Route to Policy Influence: How Evaluations Affect D.A.R.E." *American Journal of Evaluation* 26:12–30.

Weiss, Carol H., Erin Murphy-Graham, Anthony Petrosino, and Allison G. Gandhi. 2008. "The Fairy Godmother—and Her Warts: Making the Dream of Evidence-Based Policy Come True." *American Journal of Evaluation* 29:29–47.

Welsh, Brandon C., and David P. Farrington. 2011a. "Evidence-Based Crime Policy." In *The Oxford Handbook of Crime and Criminal Justice*, edited by Michael Tonry. New York: Oxford University Press.

Welsh, Brandon C., and David P. Farrington. 2011b. *The Future of Crime Prevention: Developmental and Situational Strategies.* Washington, DC: U.S. Department of Justice, National Institute of Justice.

Welsh, Brandon C., and David P. Farrington. 1998. "Assessing the Effectiveness and Economic Benefits of an Integrated Developmental and Situational Crime Prevention Programme." *Psychology, Crime and Law* 4:281–308.

Welsh, Brandon C., Christopher J. Sullivan, and David L. Olds. 2010. "When Early Crime Prevention Goes to Scale: A New Look at the Evidence." *Prevention Science* 12:115–25.

INDEX